Theologies of Asian Americans and Pacific Peoples

A Reader, 1976

Theologies of Asian Americans and Pacific Peoples

A Reader, 1976

Complied by Roy I. Sano
Edited by Daniel D. Lee

Claremont Press
Claremont, CA

Contents

New Preface

Daniel Lee is to be thanked for republishing the PACTS *Reader*. He began his efforts in 2019, the year academicians recognized as the fiftieth anniversary of when Asian Americans began to reformulate their faith theologically with a distinct ethnic perspective.

PACTS, the Pacific and Asian American Center for Theology and Strategies, which originally published the *Reader*, developed from a gathering the Rev. Wilbur Choy convened in 1972 in Oakland, California. Later that year, Rev. Choy went on to become the first Asian American bishop of the United Methodist Church. The clergy that Rev. Choy convened came from Asian American caucuses of mainline denominations, including American Baptists and Episcopalians, as well as those from the United Church of Christ, the United Methodist and the United Presbyterian Church.

Although the clergy who participated in PACTS benefitted at many points from the Protestant theological renaissance of the mid-third of the twentieth century, at other points that training catapulted them out of their communities. Laity agreed, and therefore joined PACTS in its efforts to reformulate their faith and refocus their ministries.

The Asian American denominational caucuses the clergy and laity represented paralleled other racial ethnic minority caucuses in religious bodies. The caucuses reflected the resurgence of distinct ethnic identities in the larger society, and their efforts in seminaries were dramatized in the ethnic studies movement launched at San Francisco State University, 1968–1969, and spread rapidly across the nation to other colleges and universities.

Connections to these movements in ethnic studies are evident in four assumptions that pushed PACTS ahead. First, Asian American communities are not disappearing but growing rapidly with issues too easily overlooked; second, churches were the most pervasive and persistence organizations in these communities because of the range contributions they provided their people; third, training leaders for churches therefore became a high priority; and fourth, although seminaries are the gatekeepers to certify clergy, fundamental changes were required to do the job adequately. Changes were needed in the courses and faculty, student recruitment and scholarships, administrators and support staff, trustees and libraries.

Times have changed from the 1970s and 1980s, when PACTS worked in seminaries, the churches, and their communities domestically and internationally. While White racism in the post-WWII integrationist era and East-West Cold War rivalries set the agenda for PACTS, the items in the *Reader* may nevertheless provide insights to inform faith and action for Asians in North America and in their homeland under the domination of the American Empire and its challengers.

Roy I. Sano
November 24, 2019

Introduction

Daniel D. Lee

Academic Dean of the Center for Asian American Theology and Ministry and
Assistant Professor of Theology and Asian American Studies
Fuller Theological Seminary

The publishing of this Pacific and Asian American Center for Theology and Strategies (PACTS) *Reader*, compiled forty-five years ago by Rev. Roy Sano, represents an effort to recover a historical memory. PACTS, which first incorporated in 1974 as the Asian American Center for Theology and Strategies (ACTS) and later changed its name for greater inclusivity, was the first Asian American theological center. Fumitaka Matsuoka chronicles the important history of PACTS and the PANA Institute (the Institute for Leadership Development and Study of Pacific and Asian North American Religion) that became its direct heir in his essay "Inheritors of the America in the Heart: PACTS and Its History" in this volume. Matsuoka served as the Executive Director of the PANA Institute.

Drawing from mainline Protestant theologies, such as the social gospel and neo-orthodoxy of Reinhold Niebuhr and Karl Barth, and also burgeoning Black theology, PACTS was inspired and driven by the civil rights movement and the Third World Liberation Front protests of 1968, which led to the launch of ethnic studies at San Francisco State College and elsewhere and also introduced the pan-ethnic political label of "Asian American." Early Protestant pastors like Roy Sano, Paul Nagano, Lloyd Wake, and others formed Asian American caucuses within their respective denominations and sought to raise the racioethnic consciousness for theology and ministry. Chrissy Yee Lau's essay "The Asian American Christian Movement of the Sixties and Seventies," also in this volume, narrates the experience of Asian American Christians in the Asian American movement.

Through its conferences and events, PACTS produced other papers and historical documents, all stored in the Graduate Theological Union (GTU) library archives. Among them, the *Reader* is the most widely known and distributed work of PACTS. However, because it was compiled and literally photocopied and bound together, never formally published, only those in a small circle of Asian American religious studies scholars were aware of its existence — a problem we are seeking to rectify with this publication.

There are broader reasons why the *Reader* and the history of PACTS are important and particularly compelling today. PACTS and the Asian American movement that brought it about arose out of a particular historical context with a specific set of intersecting factors. Interestingly, these provocative factors are repeating themselves in new ways in our time, thus driving this generation's interest in recovering our history and affirming our racial and ethnic identities.

In this introduction, I will identify at least four sociological factors that fostered the revolutionary awakening of Asian Americans in the 1960s and how the recent similar manifestations of these factors are conscientizing the contemporary Asian American community. Reflecting on my perspective leading Fuller Theological Seminary's Center for Asian American Theology and Ministry, I will then offer some important lessons that the PACTS *Reader* provides for the future of Asian American theology.

Past and Present Asian Americans Coming of Age

There are a number of key factors that helped create a fertile ground in the late 1960s for Asian America to come of age politically and racially. What is fascinating is seeing similar factors repeat themselves in a new way in our time, awakening a new generation of Asian Americans. Because Asian American theology and ministry are a faith expression of living communities, recognizing these factors is the necessary groundwork to which we must attend. These factors might be summarized as the maturing of the second and third generation, anti-Asian racism at a national level, the catalytic role of Blackness, and the popular progressive movements.[1] These four factors should be thought of in an interactive and parallel manner and not in an ordered or sequential one. We can see how these factors were at work for the previous generation as well as among our own.

First, the maturation and the gathering of the native-born second and third generation of Asian immigrants at colleges set the stage for a growing Asian American consciousness and the beginning of the Asian American movement in the 1960s. They understood that although they were not immigrants, Asians living in the US were not treated like Americans either. The first generation to arrive in the US saw themselves as foreigners living in the US, hoping to become American, "American" here meaning white Americans. The problem is that, instead of a smooth and wholesale transition from "immigrant" to "American," there exists also the liminal state of racially minoritized Americans. Although it should not be used in a technical sense, "Hansen's Law" of a theorized third generation return, where the third generation seeks to recover what the second generation tried to forget, gives insight to the intergenerational reactive dynamic at play.[2]

---

[1] My outline summary of these key factors is indebted to Liu et al. See Michael Liu, Kim Geron, and Tracy Lai, *The Snake Dance of Asian American Activism: Community, Vision, and Power* (Lanham, MD: Lexington, 2008).

[2] Marcus Lee Hansen, *The Problem of the Third Generation Immigrant* (Rock Island, IL: Augustana Historical Society, 1938). While it was popular, the idea of "third-generation return" is a gloss generalization and rather more of a cultural and ideological trope. See Peter Kivisto and Dag Blanck, eds., *American Immigrants and Their Generations: Studies and Commentaries on the Hansen Thesis after Fifty Years* (Urbana: University of Illinois Press, 1990).

Roy Sano recalls that through the 1950s and '60s, Asian Americans "assumed that if we became like them, whites would like us."[3] Using a biblical metaphor, they sought to be like Ruth, making white Americans their people and the white American God their God, abandoning their ethnic and cultural identity in the process. However, ultimately disillusioned with the unattainable dream of the "melting pot," Asian Americans exchanged this Ruth mentality for an apocalyptic or revolutionary one of Daniel and Revelation. Instead of the US as the Christian promised land, it became the empire, requiring an exilic understanding of their existence.

In our contemporary Asian American context, a similar generational shift has been occurring, a maturing of the 1.5, second and third generation from the post-1965 immigration and post-1975 refugee waves. The Hart-Celler Immigration and Nationality Act of 1965 opened the door previously closed by a number of racist Asian exclusionary laws, starting with the Chinese Exclusion Act of 1882. The wave of post-1965 immigrants dramatically increased the Asian American population but, in a sense, they started as earlier Asian immigrants did, with a "Ruth" mentality, believing that by working hard to assimilate they could one day reach full (white) Americanness. Refugee communities from the Vietnam War and the greater Southeast Asian region from 1975, and later through the Refugee Act of 1980, grew up with the narrative of the US saving them from war-torn countries of origin with its material, moral, and spiritual wealth. This established an early promised land perspective and a conservative political alignment. As latter generations mature but find themselves to be still strangers confronted with the "bamboo ceiling" and everyday racism, the realization arises that there is no straight path from immigrant or refugee to American, but rather they are stuck as racially minorized Americans in a "liminal space," as Sang Hyun Lee proposed.[4]

Since their founding fifty years ago, Asian American studies has helped many Asian Americans see the reality of a racially minorized experience. But their influence has still remained marginal in the popular psyche and cultural literacy. However, with the present calls for Asian American representation and agency, this Asian American awakening is becoming more prevalent within the community thorough popular sources. This awakening is bringing a critical view of US imperial and racist history, again affirming that this nation is in many ways more a "Babylon" than the "Israel" it claims to be.[5]

Second, along with the maturing of later generations, the PACTS cohort acutely experienced anti-Asian racism. The history of anti-Asian racism in the US is storied

---

[3] Roy I. Sano, "Shifts in Reading the Bible: Hermeneutical Moves Among Asian Americans," *Semeia* 90/91 (Spring/Summer 2002): 109. Sano develops some of the hermeneutical possibilities in "The Bible and Pacific Basin Peoples" in this volume.

[4] Sang Hyun Lee, *From a Liminal Pace: An Asian American Theology* (Minneapolis: Fortress Press, 2010).

[5] See Yên Lê Espiritu, "Toward a Critical Refugee Study: The Vietnamese Refugee Subject in US Scholarship," *Journal of Vietnamese Studies* 1, no. 1–2 (February 2006): 410–433.

and deeply embedded within American psyche, continual and punctuated by particularly egregious low points like the Chinese Exclusion Act of 1882, Japanese American incarceration during WWII, and the surge of post-9/11 violence against South Asian Americans. However, because of white normative American education excluding Asian American history and the lack of a strong communal tradition of historical remembrance, each generation ends up having to discover and awaken to the long and heinous history of anti-Asian racism in the US during the 1960s and '70s; the prolonged Vietnam War traumatized the nation and firmly ingrained the Viet Cong's Asian face as that of the enemy. With memories of WWII and the Korean War in the back of American historical consciousness, the Vietnam War provoked the nation, which saw its ugliness televised in their living rooms.

Asian American soldiers, drafted and sent to fight an enemy who looked like them, experienced a pan-ethnic racializing experience as well as collective identification with the Vietnamese. Dealing with reality of anti-Asian racism and undoubtedly convinced of their Asian racial identity as well, "Asian America was born at the peak of the Vietnam War."[6] The Viet Cong defeating the US inspired early Asian American leaders to believe that they might be "capable of winning a victory for the control of [their] own lives."[7]

Reflecting upon our contemporary context, over the last decade, China has established itself as a global superpower, no longer only seen as the source of second-rate mass-manufactured products. In terms of soft power, the global success of the Korean Wave ("Hallyu") of K-drama shows, K-pop acts, and popularly acclaimed films have challenged the hegemony of US cultural imperialism and made being Asian "cool."[8] Inferiority about Asianness is fast becoming a thing of the past for Asian Americans. On the other hand, while China's rise has provoked a slow-burning concern and anxiety in the US, the rise of overt anti-Asian racism during the COVID-19 pandemic has jolted Asian Americans awake to the realities of racism and racialized identity. Through this wave of anti-Asian verbal and physical attacks, Asian Americans are realizing that "yellow peril and the model minority, although at apparent disjunction, form a seamless continuum."[9] The model minority myth is just a different manifestation of yellow peril concepts and can easily become dangerous. Provoked by this latest manifestation of widespread anti-Asian attacks, many Asian Americans, include Christians, are seeking and discovering the anti-Asian racism present throughout US history.

Third, the Black Power movement was critical for the development of the Asian American movement. As Asian American activists became aware of the racial

---

[6] Karen L. Ishizuka, *Serve the People: Making Asian America in the Long Sixties* (Brooklyn: Verso, 2016), 97.

[7] Ishizuka, *Serve the People,* 112.

[8] Euny Hong, *The Birth of Korean Cool: How One Nation Is Conquering the World Through Pop Culture* (New York: Picador, 2014).

[9] Gary Y. Okihiro, *Margins and Mainstreams: Asians in American History and Culture* (Seattle: University of Washington Press, 2014), 141.

structures of American society, they rejected their "honorary white" status and sought to rethink their racial identity through the lens and modeling of Black Americans. Through this way of "performing blackness" serving as a formative process, they learned to forge their own racialized identity as "Asian Americans."[10] Learning from and understanding the features of Black activist identity, the Asian American activist saw the need to develop a pan-ethnic identity for political power. Modeled after the Black liberation movement, slogans like "yellow power" and "yellow is beautiful" represented self-determination and self-pride against white supremacy and white norms.[11] Because of their particular history and influence upon other racial minorities, Black Americans might be seen racial ancestors in a sense.

Lessons from Black liberation theology directly influenced the contributors of the PACTS *Reader* as well. Roy Sano notes in his original Preface that "Appropriation of the contribution of Black theology" was among the many themes that the selections were ordered by Paul Nagano connects his ideas about Japanese American ministry to Black theology in "The Japanese Americans' Search for Identity, Ethnic Pluralism, and a Christian Basis of Permanent Identity." However, in his paper from 1970, entitled "An Overlay of So Called 'Yellow Theology' upon Black Theology," the genealogical dimension of Paul Nagano's theological development is displayed. Nagano proposes what he calls a "Yellow theology," by explicitly echoing insights from James Cone's *Black Theology and Black Power* and Joseph R. Washington Jr.'s *Black and White Power Subreption.*[12]

Whereas Black Power was the primary source of influence back then, in our contemporary context it is the Black Lives Matter movement and its provocative energy.[13] The Black Lives Matter movement was birthed in an awakening from the post-racial fantasy of the Obama presidency, akin to the changing of the guard and generational shift between civil rights and Black Power. While there are those who have been schooled in the Asian American activist movement, benefiting from hard-earned lessons of the past, many historically uninformed contemporary Asian Americans continue to reinvent the whole process over and over again by rejecting whiteness, performing blackness and then looking beyond to what an Asian American identity might be. Asian Americans could prevent this cyclical detour by coming to see the elders within their own community, realizing that they are far from the first ones to awaken but are rather quite late to the fifty-year-old Asian American movement.

---

[10] Daryl J. Maeda, *Chains of Babylon: The Rise of Asian America* (Minneapolis: University of Minnesota Press, 2009), 75.

[11] Michael Liu, Kim Geron, and Traci Lai, *The Snake Dance of Asian American Activism* (Lanham, MD: Lexington Books), 62–63.

[12] Paul M. Nagano, "An Overlay of So-Called 'Yellow Theology' upon Black Theology" (unpublished term paper, Spring 1970), typescript. James Cone, *Black Theology and Black Power* (Maryknoll, NY: Orbis Books, 1969). Joseph R. Washington Jr., *Black and White Power Subreption* (Boston: Beacon Press, 1969).

[13] Keeanga-Yamahtta Taylor, *From #BlackLivesMatter to Black Liberation* (Chicago: Haymarket, 2016).

Lastly, the PACTS generation lived with the counterculture and activism that became part of popular culture in the 1960s, with multiple protests and causes simultaneously occurring. The United Farm Workers Movement, which began with Larry Itliong and Filipino American workers, partnered with Cesar Chavez and Mexican American laborers to bring about the Delano grape strike of 1965–1970, garnering national attention and resulting in a collective bargaining agreement for the workers. Second-wave feminism, with an agenda that included birth control, sexism in cultural representation, physical violence, and sexual assault, excited protests and struggles for political action. This revolutionary era birthed a number of liberation theologies. The PACTS *Reader* represents the ethos of this time period.

In our day, a similar progressive activism has become a part of popular culture. The #MeToo movement decries sexual abuse and sexual harassment, especially that committed by powerful men. #OscarsSoWhite struggles for diverse representation in pop culture; Greta Thunberg and the Fridays for Future movement join with other diverse protests for environmental justice; and a long list of protests were mobilized against Trump administration policies, including the Muslim ban, family separation, and the detention of immigrant children. Asian Americans have participated in these protests while also having their social consciousness formed by them.

While history is even more complex, these four key factors, at least, give us an insight as to why and how the Asian American movement came about and why a similar kind of awakening is happening again in our time. Whereas the past generation's struggle was for the creation of an Asian American identity, our challenge is to recover, understand, and own this Asian American identity, reminding ourselves that the Asian American story, including Christian activism, stretches even further back than this 1970s generation and the pan-ethnic identity they developed.

Lessons for Asian American Christians Coming of Age

Jonathan Tan's helpful volume *Introducing Asian American Theologies* narrates the history of Asian American theology and helps to acquaint us with PACTS and other earlier theologians.[14] Actually reading and conversing with the PACTS *Reader* represents another level of historical awareness, finding siblings and cousins beyond our contemporary circles. Beyond the last fifty years of the Asian American movement, the over 170-year scope of Asian American history matters for all Asian American Christians.[15] This is the story of our community and our larger family, as the God revealed in Christ is the God of history and covenant in time and space.

---

[14] Jonathan Tan, *Introducing Asian American Theologies* (Maryknoll, NY: Orbis Books, 2008).

[15] This "170-year" timeline counts up from the large number of Chinese workers who arrived on the West Coast during the 1850s and 1860s. Counting Asian American history from this period is not without its limitations. For example, Filipino sailors were the first Asians to land on what would become the US back in 1587, and there was a Filipino settlement in Louisiana in the mid-1700s. However, there is an argument to be made about the critical mass of Asian population that

The Center for Asian American Theology and Ministry at Fuller Seminary was founded in 2016 after six years of development. The Center reflects an evangelical ethos that differs from the mainline perspective of PACTS—an ethos that has become prominent among Asian American Christians beyond even evangelical or Protestant boundaries.[16] While the evangelical-mainline rift has a long history with significant theological differences, the recent reckoning of white evangelicalism's complicity with white nationalism, bigotry, and xenophobia have problematized this confessional identity. Asian American evangelicals disillusioned with white evangelicalism are realizing that they have more in common with Asian American mainline Christians than white evangelicals.[17] In that mold, our center took up the work of editing and publishing this reader, which represents the importance of three themes for the future of Asian American theology: historical awareness, political engagement, and the ecclesial orientation.

Our Center, with its evangelical flavor, was preceded by the Asian American Center at the American Baptist Seminary of the West (ABSW), founded by Timothy Tseng in 2000, which was an evangelical response to PACTS and PANA. Unable to find a supportive institutional home for the Center, Tseng founded the nonprofit Institute for the Study of Asian American Christianity (ISAAC) in 2006, later publishing a reader of its own.[18] Beyond evangelical circles, the interreligious Asian Pacific American Religions Research Initiative (APARRI), ecumenical Asian Theological Summer Institute (ATSI), and Pacific, Asian, and North American Asian Women in Theology and Ministry (PANAAWTM) all have been and continue to do the important work of research, resourcing, and mentoring. Still more broadly, the Asian American theological task takes place among the scholar community that serve our community like the Association of Asian American Studies (AAAS) and the Asian American Psychological Association (AAPA), a community that the Asian American evangelical community is too often ignorant of.

Along with this historical awareness, the PACTS *Reader* points to the importance of political engagement. Some Asian American ministry resources focus exclusively on cultural concerns, such as Confucian values, shame, and intergenerational tension. However, the problem with this approach is that the Asian cultural dimension ultimately ends up being pathologized, a problem to be solved, never questioning the white norms governing the discussion. Cultural dimensions can only be properly theologically engaged by taking into consideration the deeply embedded Orientalism in the structures of our society, the white European normativity of our

---

begins with this Chinese migration in the mid-1800s and its impact on the US and the rise of anti-Asian reaction.

[16] Jane H. Hong, "In Search of a History of Asian American Evangelicals," *Religion Compass* 13, no. 11 (2019): 1–9.

[17] Tim Tseng problematizes the mainline-evangelical divide as something Asian American evangelicals inherited from white Christianity. Tim Tseng, note to the author, January 28, 2021.

[18] Timothy Tseng and Viji Nakka-Cammauf, eds., *Asian American Christianity: A Reader* (Castro Valley, CA: Institute for the Study of Asian American Christianity, 2009). ISAAC later changed its name to Innovative Space for Asian American Christianity.

education system and theological education, and the way the model minority myth urges Asian Americans toward political quietism.

The gospel calls all dimensions of our lives and our world to come under the gracious lordship of Jesus Christ. Our faith is thus as inherently political as it as sociological and cultural. Through the Trump years, we have come to see that while Christianity does not line up well with any political party and should generally be nonpartisan, there are real situations where the church can and must take sides on public issues of justice and peace. Whether it be for refugees and immigrants, Black lives, or religious or sexual minorities, the church has a divine call towards a faithful witness of God's Kingdom values.

Finally, the PACTS *Reader* is a work of church leaders, who read scripture, prayed, preached, and taught. They were not "ivory tower" theologians disconnected from the everyday lives of the people on the ground. This ecclesial orientation, for them, did not mean a myopic parochialism but a worldly Christianity that is actually *in* the world while not *of* it. Asian American theology must serve the Asian American church. Of course, these kinds of works should also contribute to the global church and even academic discourse as well, but there is an important role that it should play within the Asian American Christian community. While this statement seems like a truism, academia as an industry dominated by white male voices has a habit of forming and rewarding works that serve the guild.

The ecclesial orientation calls for a deeper understanding of God, discipleship, healing, transition, witness, and of service in the world. Decolonizing Christianity from white norms involves deconstruction and critique, but it cannot stop there. The gospel for Asian Americans and from Asian American Christians to the world must be *good* news, beyond the judgment upon oppressive powers and principalities.

There is comfort in knowing that you are not "the first," a lonely pioneer, but rather that a whole community of mothers and fathers have gone before us and that there are others in different confessional communities that you might not know about. Hoping that this knowledge encourages all of us towards more joy in our struggles, we have published this work for a wide readership and theological engagement.

Christmas 2020
Pasadena, CA

Coalitional Organizing

*The Origins of the Asian American Protestant Movement of the '60s and '70s**

CHRISSY YEE LAU

During the five-month strike where Black, Latinx, Indigenous, and Asian American-led student organizations demanded ethnic studies at San Francisco State University (SFSU) in 1968, Reverend Lloyd Wake, a pastor at Glide Memorial Church, marched daily to show his solidarity alongside students and faculty.[1] Some members of the Japanese American community expressed their disapproval of the student strikes and thought that Wake should stay in his lane solely as a pastor. Once when Wake entered into a Japanese American establishment, one of the owners angrily labeled him as a "n***** lover" and reprimanded him that he should stick to church work. Such an ethic reflected the Cold War integrationist model minority mentality that designated Wake's vocation, mainline Protestant work, as primarily a vehicle for assimilation into whiteness, not radical protest. But the Black Freedom movement had radically altered how Wake understood his vocation: as a vehicle for social change and racial justice. He believed that marching with student strikers was as much a part of his daily Christian practices as leading prayer, preaching sermons, or singing hymns. Moreover, Wake believed that cross-racial coalitional building was the only means to achieve social and spiritual justice.[2]

While historians typically understand the radical '60s as the birth of Asian American Christian organizing and theology, Wake's spiritual activism highlights the influential role of cross-racial coalition building with Black and Brown Protestants during the radical '60s. Historian Anne Michele Blankenship argues that the racial integration of ethnic churches into white churches during the 1950s and

---

* Thank you to Rudy Busto, Diane Fujino, Annie Betinol, Rowena Quinto, Leigh Saito, and Michael Ozamoto for their shaping of this research in its beginning stages. Thank you to my peer reviewers and Jane Hong for their incisive feedback in the final stages of this research.

[1] A word about terminology: In the 1960s/1970s, the PACTS authors and the groups themselves were thinking through and working out a variety of terminology, such as Negro and Black, Latino and Latin, and Asian American and Oriental. I use post-1960s/1970s terms to identify groups of people: Black, Latinx, Indigenous, and Asian American. These terms are used to honor the humanity and the gender fluidity of those of that group as well as acknowledge the historical and ongoing discussions and debates over terminology, decolonization, and inclusivity.

[2] Lloyd Wake, "Preaching into Practice," *Nikkei Heritage* 13, no. 2 (Spring 2001): 12.

1960s was a failed experiment that backfired and ultimately led to the fight for the reestablishment of a religious organization based on race or ethnicity.[3] Just how did Asian American Protestants fight for this reestablishment? Historian Helen Kim points out that although the Asian American intellectual tradition has largely omitted religion as a category of analysis, ironically, the tradition—the Asian American Movement—nevertheless provides the context from which Asian American Christian thought began.[4] Taking their cue, I argue that Wake's Christian activism reveals just how Asian American Protestants fought for the reestablishment and serves as the starting point for how Asian American Christian thought began: through cross-racial coalitional organizing with Black and Brown Protestants.

This essay explores how Asian American Protestants organized an Asian American theology movement in the radical '60s and '70s. It is a history of how Asian American Protestants moved away from the integrationist, model minority paradigm in the 1950s and '60s and towards a coalitional, self-determined spirituality in the 1970s. Utilizing oral histories, journals of Methodist conferences, and essays from the original Pacific and Asian Center for Theological Study (PACTS) *Reader*, this essay will focus on the case of Japanese American Methodists in California. First, this chapter will examine how the Methodist dissolution of the ethnic church left a Japanese American Christian community in desperate need of a new approach to racial integration. Second, I detail how Japanese American Methodists organized in coalition with Black and Brown Methodists to reshape church organization and structure. Third, I examine how Japanese American Methodists embraced a pan-ethnic approach to Asian American theology.

Racial Integration and the Disbandment of the Ethnic Church in the Cold War Era

Sociologists have defined the "ethnic church" as a religious organization that can play a conservative role in maintaining ethnic customs and/or an adaptive entity that transforms a group over several generations.[5] My research shows that between the 1890s and the 1950s, the ethnic church had become an important spiritual resource that catered to the specific evangelical needs of Japanese American communities over time. In the late nineteenth and early twentieth centuries, the ethnic church began as missions that provided an important gathering space and a network of resources to Japanese immigrants, such as providing language

---

[3] Anne Michele Blankenship, "Foundations for a New World Order: United Protestant Worship during the World War II Japanese American Incarceration," *Interpretation: A Journal of Bible and Theology* 72, no. 3 (July 2018): 304–316.

[4] Helen Jin Kim, "Reconstructing Asian America's Religious Past: A Historiography," in *Envisioning Religion, Race, and Asian Americans*, ed. David K. Yoo and Khyati Joshi (Honolulu: University of Hawaii Press, 2020), 13–40. See also, Helen Kim, "*Niseis* of the Faith: Theologizing Liberation in the Asian American Movement, 1950–80s" (bachelor's thesis, Stanford University, 2006).

[5] Mark Mullins, "The Life-Cycle of Ethnic Churches in Sociological Perspective." *Japanese Journal of Religious Studies* 14, no. 4 (1987): 321–334, http://www.jstor.org/stable/30233997.

accessibility and housing. By the 1920s and 1930s, the ethnic church remade itself through newly organized youth ministries, such as the Epworth League, and expanded facilities for young people's social gathering. By the 1940s, missions had developed into the Japanese Provisional Conferences. During World War II, when Japanese Americans were forcibly removed from the West Coast into incarceration camps, ethnic churches helped to store Japanese American belongings when they packed up and left. After incarceration, ethnic churches played a key role in resettling families back into society. Although in the first half of the twentieth century, ethnic churches had provided unique ministerial tools for a community that experienced tumultuous racism across the decades, by the 1950s, the Methodist Cold War agenda, whose new spiritual imperative was to lead by example their vision of a free and capitalist world, viewed the ethnic church as a blemish.

In the period of Japanese American resettlement, between 1948 and 1964, the United Methodist Church called for the integration of the Japanese Provisional Conferences into the General Conference and ultimately the dissolution of the ethnic church. At the General Conference of 1948, Methodist leaders embraced their new postwar mission: to defeat communism abroad by establishing democracy at home. Methodist leaders gave an impassioned speech that the church must prepare for a victory against communism by reexamining existing practices of segregation and economic injustice.[6] Methodist leaders adopted a policy of racial integration and led the way towards world peace. The General Conference of 1948 adopted an enabling act to "integrate the Pacific Japanese Provisional Annual Conference. . . . with the Annual Conferences which these groups are geographically distributed."[7] Integration meant conference integration or administrative integration of the annual conference. Leaders decided that 1964 would be the date of completion for integration.[8] Methodist ideologies of integration reflected the general shift of racializing Asian Americans from yellow peril to model minority during the Cold War period, highlighting their successful integration into US society under their new political imperatives to showcase the US as the leader of the free world and to highlight Asian Americans as a well-integrated minority who overcame histories of racism.[9]

Members of the Japanese Provisional Conferences discussed and debated over the new policy of integration. Some agreed and felt that the Provisional Conferences should just disband and become members of the regional conferences. Others, especially those whose primary language was Japanese, were reluctant to join a regional conference where their primary language would not be the language used

---

[6] *Journal of the 1948 General Conference of the Methodist Church,* 154–201, https://archive.org/details/journalboston00meth/page/n3/mode/2up.

[7] *Journal of the 1948 General Conference,* 585.

[8] *Twenty-Fourth Annual Session of the Pacific Japanese Provisional Annual Conference of the Methodist Church,* https://www.calpacumc.org/archiveshistory.

[9] See Ellen Wu, *The Color of Success: Asian Americans and the Origins of the Model Minority* (Princeton: Princeton University Press, 2015).

in worship. Still others were scared that a dissolution of a specialized ministry meant they might lose their Japanese American identity. However, others like Roy Sano felt mixed. He wondered if their specialties were going to be promoted, pursued or in partnerships, or if they were all going to be on their own, which would make them ineffective in their mission to spread Christ.[10]

In some instances, local congregations supported a merger precisely because of a lack of resources and to support the idea of a united Christian brotherhood. The Nisei Methodist Church in Oxnard, for instance, had to seriously consider the idea of a merger with St. Paul's Methodist Church in Oxnard because they were confronted with the need to provide additional church classroom space for an expanding congregation of adults and children. They considered and dismissed two other proposals, such as building additional classroom space upon their present location or moving and rebuilding the current property in a new area. They met with St. Paul's Methodist Church to discuss a merger, since that church was already about to embark on an expansion program. The members of the Nisei Methodist Church in Oxnard voted unanimously to merge with St. Paul's. One of their members had stated, "We live together on the same streets, we send our children to the same schools, we work side by side in our fields of employment, why should we not worship together?"[11] A merger became the solution to a growing ethnic church's needs while meeting the political imperatives of unity promoted by Methodist leadership.

On the other side of the merger, some white Methodists displayed paternalistic and racist concerns. Some wondered if integrating Japanese American members would become a "burden" and if they could stand on their own two feet. One white bishop expressed to Sano and other Japanese American Methodists, "I want you to be self-supporting and I want you to take part of the mission-giving of the church. People supported you and you are supposed to support them."[12] Such remarks prepped Japanese American Christians to embrace a model minority ethic, specifically to be self-sufficient in the face of unequal access to resources and not to rely on structural support. Sano believes that while on its face, Methodist leaders wanted to integrate because they must be one in Christ, they felt embarrassed that they had a racially defined structure in the church. In fact, the bishop mobilized guilt and shame of Japanese Americans, telling them that he didn't want them to embarrass him by not integrating.[13]

Before the Japanese Provisional Conferences were dissolved in 1964, Sano gave a speech about responsible integration. Sano argued that a "disbanding" of a racial conference and merging of several churches ought not to mean "abandoning the specialized but legitimate responsibilities, concerns, and aspirations." Sano envisioned that a responsible integration would provide adequate freedom for the

---

[10] Roy I. Sano, interview with the author, March 30, 2006.
[11] *Twenty-Fourth Annual Session*, 70.
[12] Roy I. Sano, interview with the author, March 30, 2006.
[13] Roy I. Sano, interview with the author, March 30, 2006.

specialized ministries while maintaining their goal of unity. He warned against the eagerness to appear unified without putting in the effort to work with the once segregated communities. Sano tried to distinguish between assimilation and collaboration, calling for adequate recruitment of "specialized ministers in ethnic work," the inclusion of lay voices in the establishment of leadership, and stewardship. He called for the promotion of "intercultural relations" between Asian American, Latinx, and Black populations. He believed the church needed to carry the responsibility in promoting fair housing and providing equal opportunity. He believed specialized ministries should have full participation in government and be able to seek justice in the courts. Ultimately, he believed that Methodist leadership needed to respect minorities as equal and embrace their full humanity, including the addition of Japanese and Black spiritual songs into the hymn books.[14]

Five years later, Methodist leaders did not heed Sano's call for responsible integration. Sano believed an ice age had set in for the appointment of minority ministers. Although the Methodist leadership had convinced Japanese American Methodists that they would have a place in an integrated church, they did not follow through. Instead, white bishops contemplated whether a Japanese American clergy would be able to fill the shoes of a white minister in a white church. Because Japanese American ministers were not assigned to positions within white churches and were, moreover, discouraged to continue their ministry in Japanese American congregations, Japanese American ministers sought other jobs outside of the church. Peter Chen, pastor of the Gardena Community Church in the Japanese Provisional Conference, reported, "Since 1960, twenty-three Japanese ethnic ministers have sought employment in non-church related positions. Five of the formerly ethnic churches are now led by Caucasian ministers."[15] Moreover, when Japanese American ministers were appointed, they were assigned to dying churches. Although Japanese American ministers held prestigious degrees, their education did not match their assignments.[16]

Historian Blankenship argues that racial integration was a failed experiment largely because white leaders never saw their Japanese American counterparts as their social equals. Leaders utilized the voices of the few that supported integration but ignored those that promoted the re-formation of the ethnic church and those like Sano who encouraged responsible integration. Church leaders never consulted the

[14] Roy I. Sano, "This Matter of Integration," in *The Theologies of Asian Americans and Pacific Peoples: A Reader*, comp. Roy I. Sano (Berkeley: PSR/PACTS/PANA, Graduate Theological Union, 1976), 262–264, previously published in the *Methodist Layman*, February 1963. It is reprinted in this volume on pp. 221–224.

[15] Paul Nagano, "An Overlay of So-Called 'Yellow Theology' upon Black Theology" (term project for the seminar History and Theology of the Black Church, Spring 1970), box 22, folder 13, Pacific and Asian American Center for Theology and Strategies Collection, Graduate Theological Union, Berkeley, CA.

[16] Roy I. Sano, "Yes, We'll Have No More Bananas in Church," in *The Theologies of Asian Americans and Pacific Peoples: A Reader*, comp. Roy I. Sano (Berkeley: PSR/PACTS/PANA, Graduate Theological Union, 1976), 51–54. See pp. 45–49 in this volume.

predominately white organizations that Japanese American Christians were going to join and, moreover, did not do the work to educate the several who did not want Japanese Americans to join. The integration of the church led to the vast majority of Japanese Americans no longer attending church. Ultimately, however, removing the ethnic churches had the opposite effect: It made Japanese Americans revalue segregated worship and fight for their reestablishment.[17]

Cross-Racial Coalitional Building or How the Black Christian Freedom Movement Shaped Asian American Christian Organizing in the Radical '60s

After the disbandment of the Japanese Provisional Conferences and failed integration, Japanese American Methodists turned to organizing in coalition with Black, Brown, and Indigenous members of the Methodist Church to address racial equity. The Black Christian Freedom movement—a Black-led movement for racial justice and a racially contextualized theology and worship—inspired and influenced the organizing of Asian American Protestants in multiple ways. First, a few Asian American Christians, like Wake, joined Black-led multiracial churches that centered cross-racial solidarity and coalitional organizing. Second, Asian American Methodists benefitted from coalitional organizing with Black and Brown Methodists through the establishment of the General Commission on Religion and Race, first temporarily in 1968 and permanently in 1973, as well as the creation of the Committee on Racism in 1970.

Reverend Wake is an example of a pastor from the Japanese Provisional Conference who did not experience integration as a failed experiment primarily because he served first in a historically Japanese-serving church in the 1950s and then moved to a Black-led multiracial congregation during the 1960s. Since he was young, Wake and his family had attended the Pine United Methodist Church in San Francisco, one of the oldest churches dedicated to the ministry of Japanese immigrants. When Executive Order 9066 forcibly relocated Wake and his family to Poston, Wake began to answer a call for ministry. Wake left Poston to attend Asbury College in Kentucky. After the incarceration camps closed, Wake returned to California and began his service. By 1950, Wake was appointed pastor of the Pine United Methodist Church, where he assisted Japanese American resettlement.[18]

In the 1960s, Wake felt called to serve in solidarity with Black activists of the civil rights movement. In 1963, Glide Church—a multiracial, urban, inner-city church—organized a march in response to the four Black children killed by a white terrorist bomb explosion at a church in Alabama. Wake felt compelled and invited the congregation of Pine Church to march with Glide Church on Market Street. Wake

---

[17] Anne Michele Blankenship, "Foundations for a New World Order: United Protestant Worship during the World War II Japanese American Incarceration," *Interpretation: A Journal of Bible and Theology* 72, no. 3 (2018): 304–316.

[18] Lloyd K. Wake, interview by Martha Nakagawa, Densho Digital Archive, April 7, 2011, https://ddr.densho.org/narrators/568.

was attracted to Glide Church's involvement with civil rights issues, disenfranchised communities of color, and the development of young people. A change in ministries was fast approaching. Pine Church wanted to maintain their focus on Japanese American resettlement, but Wake was motivated to join in cross-racial coalitional building to meet the pressing needs of differentially vulnerable communities. In 1967, Wake was appointed minister of community life at Glide Church. This transition allowed Wake the freedom to participate with a church that addressed and engaged his life in radical coalitional movements of justice and liberation.[19]

As a pastor of Glide Church, Wake felt that it was his responsibility to serve as a liaison between the Japanese American community and third-world social movements. He supported activists and explained their motives to the wider Japanese American community. Wake and others created a forum for the Japanese American community to come together at the United Presbyterian Church, in the heart of Japantown. They discussed the controversial leadership of S. I. Hayakawa, the SFSU president who became notorious for backing the university administration in silencing student protestors by pulling out the plugs of their speakers. Hayakawa promoted an assimilationist Americanism that directly contrasted from student strikers and members of the Third World Liberation Front, who refused assimilation and embraced agitation.[20] At the end of the forum, the Japanese American community decided to declare their opposition to S. I. Hayakawa's suppression of the student strikes.[21]

At the same time, Wake's service in the Pine Church and Glide Church was made possible because his wife, Marion, spent most of her time raising their four children at home. Marion was also an Asbury College graduate who had been working in Chicago when she moved to California to join Lloyd, where he finished seminary and became appointed to Pine. Lloyd had told Marion that pastor's wives do not usually work or they only work for the church, but Marion wanted to work in the community.[22] She became a teacher at a school for severely disturbed children in San Francisco. Later, as they had children, she became the primary caregiver. She recalled, "He was really married to the church. That's the common complaint of minister's wives. When I look back upon it, you know I realize he was a young minister trying to establish himself, trying to become self-confident, and he felt like he needed to put all this time relating to the young people."[23] Marion's reproductive labor in the home, as well as her mental health work among younger generations,

[19] Lloyd K. Wake, interview with the author, March 31, 2006.
[20] Karen Umemoto, "On Strike! San Francisco State College 1968–69: The Role of Asian American Students," *Amerasia Journal* 15, no. 1 (1989): 5.
[21] Lloyd K. Wake, "Reflections on the San Francisco Strike," *Amerasia Journal* 15, no. 1 (1985): 47.
[22] Marion Yamabe Wake, interview by Taeko Joanne Iritani, California State University, Sacramento, May 25, 2000, https://californiarevealed.org/islandora/object/cavpp%3A22608.
[23] Jun Stinson, "Marion Wake," *API Women, Faith & Action*, October 2009, http://apiwomenfaithaction.blogspot.com/2009/10/marion-wake.html.

allowed Lloyd to focus his energies on cross-racial coalition building with Black Protestants towards structural change in the church.

Wake worked in coalition with Black and white pastors to create a commission focused on race in the Methodist Church. In 1968, Wake was part of the delegation that proposed to establish a special study commission, the Commission on Religion and Race, at the annual conference. As a member of the regional California-Nevada Conference, Wake had been elected to the General Conference and was part of a team that prepared the legislation to form the General Commission on Religion and Race.[24] Wake and other writers purposefully wrote that Black Methodists and other Methodists of color would have some representation on the commission. At the general conference of one thousand members, Wake was one of two Japanese American Methodists present (the other, Wake recalls, was Paul Hagiya).

When reviewing the proposal for the Commission on Religion and Race, General Conference members debated on the constitutionality of a racially defined commission. Some argued that any organization that was racially defined violated the constitution and the original intentions of racial integration and the merging of conferences. Others argued for a more liberal interpretation and that a race-based organization was a necessary step towards establishing racial equality. After much debate, the general conference passed the legislation and temporarily established the Commission on Religion and Race.[25] This commission set a precedent for racially defined structures within the Methodist church with the purpose of moving towards racial equality at the national level.

While Wake worked at the national level, other Japanese American Methodists organized through coalition building at the regional level. For instance, in 1968, an ad-hoc group of former members of the Japanese Provisional Conference called for a jurisdictional consultation on Japanese work by the Board of Missions. At the same time, Black members of the Conference attended a special meeting to examine the status of Black men in the United Methodist Church. Simultaneously, Latinx Methodists in Los Angeles also voiced their concerns. This chorus of distinct voices called on their conference to make a more articulate strategy on the state of ethnic ministries. At their request, the Southern California-Arizona Methodist Conference created their own commission, the Ethnic Strategies Committee, which conducted research on issues of racism within the church with a specific focus on Black, Latinx, and Asian American ministries.[26]

Under the Ethnic Strategies Committee, both Latinx and Japanese American ministries made reports to the church. The Latinx ministries called for a new concept of integration, which had formerly been understood as "Angloization," or that ethnic peoples could be absorbed into the Anglo church, and moved towards "coalition"

[24] Lloyd Wake, interview with the author, March 31, 2006.

[25] *Journal of the 1968 General Conference of the United Methodist Church: Volume I*, https://archive.org/details/journalofgeneral01unit/mode/2up.

[26] *Journal of the Southern California-Arizona Conference of the United Methodist Church, 1968*, 172, http://www.calpacumc.org/archiveshistory/#1560029628489-899cd698-f59a.

and support programs that strengthened Mexican American identity. Japanese American ministries called for Japanese American work to be taken up by the Conference as a whole, more strategic focus on language ministries for new migrants in Los Angeles, and scholarship grants to provide cultural and educational training for those engaged in ethnic ministry.[27] Because of the work of the Ethnic Strategies Committee with the Western Jurisdiction of the United Methodist Church, the jurisdiction provided a staff member to work with Japanese and other ethnic and language minority groups on the West Coast. A similar advisory committee on Native American populations was created after a similar consultation.[28]

Just as regional conferences were beginning to develop an Ethnic Strategies Committee, in 1969, the Black Economic Development Conference published the Black Manifesto, which became a game changer for all Protestant denominations. The Black Manifesto demanded reparations from all Protestant churches by way of institutional support. Acknowledging that white America has exploited the resources, minds, bodies, and labor of Black people, the Black Manifesto pointed out that the church was part and parcel to capitalism and demanded reparations of $500,000 from white churches and Jewish synagogues. They called for the $500,000 to be spent on (1) a Southern land bank for Black farmers, (2) the building of major publishing and printing industries in majority-Black metropoles, (3) television networks that can provide alternative programming, and (4) a research center to focus on Black issues.[29]

A grassroots group called the Black Caucus of the United Methodist Church published a "Manifesto Statement" in response to the Black Manifesto and called for a comprehensive study in the Methodist Church, which led to several initiatives of accountability for Black, Latinx, and Asian American representation at all levels of the church. In 1970 and 1971, twenty-four members of the Methodist Church formed the Committee on Racism. Members of this committee included Black, Latinx, and Asian American Methodist leaders, including Peter Chen, a pastor who established the Gardena Community Methodist Church under the direction of the Japanese Provisional Conference. The Committee on Racism organized around four subcommittees and issues and conducted studies.

First, they called for ethnic representation on all boards and agencies—at every level of the conference, particularly on committees on finance, research and planning, and professional personnel. This entailed that efforts be made to change the nomination procedure to ensure greater grassroots involvement and a shorter tenure. Second, because racial minorities should have a say in where the money goes, they demanded ethnic representation on the program committee for World Service and Finance. While the committee found that Black-led missions, such as the

---

[27] *Journal of the Southern California-Arizona Conference*, 177–184.

[28] Sano, "Yes, We'll Have No More Bananas in Church."

[29] Black Economic Development Conference, "Black Manifesto," 26 April 1969, The Church Awakens: African Americans and the Struggle for Justice, Archives of the Episcopal Church, https://episcopalarchives.org/church-awakens/items/show/202.

Metropolitan Urban Mission, did incorporate the community in their decision making, it said that more needed to be done at the local and conference levels. Moreover, Indigenous participation was not happening in many of the local projects.

Third, the Committee on Racism critiqued the policy of "open itinerancy," which meant that appointments to ministry were made irrespective of the race or ethnicity of churches and pastors. In reality, they found that ethnic ministers who were highly qualified were letting their talents go to waste because they were not appointed. The committee reaffirmed that open itinerancy provided numerous benefits when assignments were made across racial lines. The committee called on all Bishops and cabinets to expand the process of appointing pastors along racial lines. Fourth, the Committee on Racism felt strongly that the properties belonging to racial minorities should remain within the jurisdiction of "Black, Latin American, and Oriental Churches." After conducting a study on financial accountability, they found that all property and funds had been handled with integrity.

At the conclusion of their study, the Committee on Racism made three recommendations to the annual conference. First, they recommended a conference-level commission to develop strategies and coordinate with ethnic ministries, with resources to adequately serve them. Second, they recommended that the bishop and his cabinet use their appointment powers to assign ministers across racial lines. Finally, they recommended greater support be given to training of pastors in service of different ethnic backgrounds.[30]

With these recommendations, by 1973, the Commission on Religion and Race became a permanent agency. Peter Chen, the vice-chairman of Ethnic Planning and Strategy, brought the resolution that there shall be in each annual conference a Conference Commission on Religion and Race, that it be created in 1973–1974, and that they work in consultation with the Ethnic and Planning Strategy Department.[31] The Commission on Religion and Race established a Minority Fund for Self-Determination, to which church and community groups alike could apply for funding.[32] The fund would provide the financial sustenance to implement innovative programs for community service and provide the financial backing for grassroots organizing, such as with the Asian American Caucus.

Towards a Pan-ethnic Asian American Christian Theology

Drawing lessons from coalitional organizing with Black and Brown Methodists at the conference level as well as the Black and Brown grassroots organizing through caucuses, Japanese, Chinese, Filipino, and Korean American Methodists organized across ethnic lines to form an Asian American Caucus. Black members of the Methodist Church had created a Black Caucus and provided a formal response to the

---

[30] *Journal of the Southern California-Arizona Annual Conference, 1970,* http://www.calpacumc.org/archiveshistory; *Journal of the Southern California-Arizona Annual Conference, 1971,* http://www.calpacumc.org/archiveshistory.

[31] *Journal of the Southern California-Arizona Annual Conference, 1973,* http://www.calpacumc.org/archiveshistory.

[32] Lloyd K. Wake, interview with the author, March 31, 2006.

Black Manifesto. Latinx members of the Methodist Church had created a Latinx Caucus (under various names including Latin American Caucus and Brown Caucus) and voiced their demands. For the first time, Asian American Methodists organized their own pan-ethnic caucus and used it as a political muscle for empowering Asian American leadership and theology.

By 1972, George Nishikawa argued that the church had learned from the Black experience, but that race tended to only be seen as a Black and white issue. He believed that Asian Americans had been racialized uniquely and differentially. An ad hoc group of people connected with the former Japanese Provisional Conference met with the board of missions to set up an advisory committee on Asian American ministries in 1969. The committee served as a channel between the board of missions, local pastors and churches, and the college of bishops for four main purposes: (1) to seek ethnic unity, consciousness, and self-identity; (2) to seek fellowship which will uplift morale and renew evangelistic zeal through methods indigenous to them; (3) to communicate the unique ministry and customs of Asian American Methodists; and (4) to affirm the concept of an inclusive church and critique assimilation. The committee addressed workplace discrimination by proposing Asian American appointments and held training seminars for Asian congregations. By 1971, over two hundred Asian American Methodists gathered for a convocation and created an Asian American Caucus to address their own issues as well as work with other ethnic groups in order to combat racism. Along with the Commission on Religion and Race, the committee initiated an Office of Research and Development for Asian Ministries.[33]

Asian American caucuses in other Protestant denominations followed suit. Asian American caucuses were created among the American Baptists (1971), the United Presbyterians (1972), the Episcopalians (1974), and the United Church of Christ (1974). According to Sano, these caucuses represented four aspirations. First, Asian Americans recognized the need to redefine their identity and particularly question the model minority. Second, Asian Americans sought to address neglected social issues, including education, employment, housing, and social welfare, among their own communities. Third, these social problems made Asian Americans aware for the need for political muscle to affect change. Fourth, amidst all the struggles of the first three aspirations, Asian Americans hoped the caucus would meet a need to sustain themselves.[34]

As their first step towards becoming a political muscle, Asian American caucuses organized for the election of the first Asian American bishop. Wake had recalled, "It

[33] Joint Strategy and Action Committee, Inc., "Asian Americans: A Forgotten Minority Comes of Age," *JSAC Grapevine* 4, no. 4, (October 1972). Also found in *The Theologies of Asian Americans and Pacific Peoples: A Reader*, comp. Roy I. Sano (Berkeley: PSR/PACTS/PANA, Graduate Theological Union, 1976), 437–439, and in pp. 389–393 of this volume.

[34] Roy I. Sano, "A Quest for Asian American Integrity," *Engage/Social Action* 2, no. 6 (June 1974): 7–10, https://archive.org/details/sim_esa-engage-social-action_1974-06_2_6/page/n3/mode/2up.

was somewhat outrageous for us to even think about an Asian American bishop."[35] No Asian American had served at the level of bishop, and it would be difficult to navigate white Methodist conceptions that devalued Asian American leadership. At first, the Asian Methodist Caucus supported the nomination of Wake. However, white Methodists viewed Wake as too radical since he performed gay marriages. Next, the caucus supported the nomination of Wilbur Choy, who had recognizable qualifications and an unassuming political record. Their strategic maneuvering worked. In 1972, Wilbur Choy was successfully elected as the first Chinese bishop in United Methodist history.

The grassroots organizing for ethnic representation in leadership empowered some Asian American women to step outside of expected gender roles. Violet Masuda, longtime member of the Livingston Elementary School Board of Education, discussed the significance of the Asian American caucus in her own spiritual and political awakening. She lived as a housewife for thirty-one years to farmer Mamoru James Masuda in Livingston after World War II. She had experienced the "oppressive psychological games" within the Japanese American community as well as the expected docility of Japanese American women at their church. During the radical '60s, she reclaimed her time and no longer allowed others to steal it. She took college courses, studied theology, read and meditated at around the same time as Asian American clergymen and lay leaders began questioning the racial discrepancies within the Methodist church. Masuda joined in the Asian American Protestant Movement. Once she was asked why the Asian Caucus was so strongly determined to have more Asian American leaders at all levels of the church and she believed strongly that Asian American youth should be given equal opportunity to pursue ministry vocations if they would like to. Masuda hoped to change the image of the Asian American woman and not be "quiet, unassuming, docile, and accepting" for the next generation.[36]

Pan-ethnic caucuses not only organized for representation and equal opportunity in governance and leadership, but also served as the political muscle for the curricular integrity of theological study. In stride with student strikers that fought for an Ethnic Studies program at San Francisco State University, Asian American caucuses created the Asian American Center for Theology and Strategies (ACTS), a center dedicated to the theological development of Asian Americans. Directed by Roy Sano, in 1972, ACTS began at Mills College and served as an interdenominational center that operated in two distinct directions. First, ACTS aimed to serve Asian American communities. Second, the center sought to influence institutions of higher education, with special attention to theological seminaries. ACTS promoted five major goals: (1) recruitment, support, and placement of Asian American students; (2) prioritization in hiring and retaining Asian American staff;

[35] Lloyd K. Wake, interview with the author, April 1, 2006.
[36] Violet Masuda, "Amazing Grace," in *The Theologies of Asian Americans and Pacific Peoples: A Reader*, comp. Roy I. Sano (Berkeley: PSR/PACTS/PANA, Graduate Theological Union, 1976), 2–3. See pp. 3–6 in this volume.

(3) enrichment of libraries and archives for Asian American interests; (4) curriculum changes; and (5) establishing new criteria with appropriate citations and contributions of Asian Americans to Christianity and the Asian American community.[37]

ACTS appealed to theological seminaries to meet the programmatic needs of Asian American students, staff and faculty; however, this was easier said than done. As Sano charged, theological seminaries were "bastions of special privilege."[38] Theological seminaries did not rethink their white colonial Christianity despite the fact that many claimed to be racially progressive. Although Sano showed up to endless meetings, he exclaimed, "After more than a dozen negotiating sessions for meaningful change with several seminaries on the Pacific Coast, no significant changes have been initiated to indicate sensitivities to Asian American needs." For instance, Asian American, Latinx, and Native American students, faculty and staff were invited to participate in a consultation on theological education for ethnic ministries at the School of Theology at Claremont, but there had been no response on the part of the denominational hierarchy. The theological seminaries showed no intention of changing their systems beyond the performance of listening to the concerns of seminary students of color.

ACTS also appealed to theological seminaries to prioritize the hiring of faculty of color. Few Asian American faculty had been placed on seminary faculty across the nation. Moreover, theological seminaries would not make new lines for Asian American seminary faculty. Although some fundraised for the expressed purpose of hiring faculty and staff of color, as Sano put it, the funds were "impounded" and utilized for "white luxuries." This was a most scandalous event: siphoning funds in the name of affirmative action to prop up a system that benefitted white theological studies.[39] By hiring nonwhite faculty, they could help theological seminaries steer away from the white-centric theologies. As it was, when theological classes attempted to incorporate Asian theology, more attention was given to the study of white Christianity in East Asia rather than Asian Christianity in Asia. But Sano felt that if ACTS continued on this road of appeals to indifferent seminaries, they would only undergo more indignities, stolen funding, and wasted time before they could see any changes.

Sano called for a ministry of resistance. Since current administrators of seminaries would not reevaluate their own programs, Sano called for Asian American Christians to develop their own criteria for evaluating seminary programs in recruiting and retaining Asian American seminary students. He urged for Asian American Christians to band together across ethnic lines and pursue action to initiate

---

[37] Roy I. Sano, "Toward a Liberating Ethnicity" (lecture, Earl Lectures and Pastoral Conference, First Congregational Church, Berkeley, CA, February 27–March 1, 1973), box 13, folder 114, Pacific and Asian American Center for Theology and Strategies Collection, Graduate Theological Union, Berkeley, CA.

[38] Roy I. Sano, "A Quest for Asian American Integrity," 11.

[39] Sano, "A Quest For Asian American Integrity," 12.

changes to those seminaries. Although this put the burden onto Asian American Christians to ensure their own equity, Sano believed theological seminaries were worth the effort since it was an institution that provided one's sustenance of faith. If such a powerful institution did not change its approach to theology, not only was faith at risk, but the questions of identity, social service, and political action that had profoundly been dependent on faith also became at risk. As Sano concluded, seminaries that maintained white-centric theologies and faculties severely dampened the Asian American quest for redefinition of faith.

Sano and other ministers gathered on September 20, 1973, for a consultation on ethnic minority ministries in preparation for a statement to the United Methodist Church on the state of ethnic minority ministries. Sano presented and argued that the primary goal of ministries should be to foster movements that would produce a "liberating ethnicity" to "mitigate racism in American society, including the church." Sano drew from ideologies of Black Power and Chicano Liberation to argue for the centrality of liberation. In the end, Sano recommended two important means for developing a ministry for a liberating ethnicity: evaluate the training of ministers by reforming theological education to take the study of ethnicity seriously and redirect church funds to support dying ethnic minority churches.[40]

Historian Helen Kim argues that liberation theologians were activist in nature, applying the same theological motivations for developing a caucus within their churches to their activism in the larger Asian American Movement.[41] While the Methodist Caucus served as the main vehicle to protest racial discrimination and transform the church, many members of the Methodist Caucus had joined other grassroots collectives in the Asian American Movement. Sano, for instance, worked with and supported students who pushed for ethnic studies at Mills College. He also supported students that occupied the office to support workers' rights to unionize on campus. Students also became involved with the struggles of the communities in housing and employment practices. Sano also opposed military intervention in Asia and attended peace rallies in the anti-Vietnam War movement. Later, he was part of a fact-finding delegation in the human rights struggle against dictators in Korea and the Philippines.[42]

Women like Marion Wake had long believed in the integration of theology and social work as she continued to pursue her own goals for the community while performing the reproductive labor at home. She eventually attended San Francisco State University to receive her master's in marriage and family counseling. As part of a federally funded program that was created to encourage ethnic minorities to

---

[40] Roy I. Sano, "Ministry for a Liberating Ethnicity: The Biblical and Theological Foundations for Ethnic Ministries," in *The Theologies of Asian Americans and Pacific Peoples: A Reader*, comp. Roy I. Sano (Berkeley: PSR/PACTS/PANA, Graduate Theological Union, 1976), 281–295. See pp. 241–255 in this volume.

[41] Helen Kim, "Niseis of the Faith: Theologizing Liberation in the Asian American Movement" (undergraduate thesis, Stanford University, 2006).

[42] Roy I. Sano, interview with the author, March 30, 2006.

enter into the field of counseling, Wake trained to work in communities with large populations of ethnic minorities. She studied and wrote a thesis on the needs for marriage and family counseling for the Japanese American family in the US.[43] Wake created counseling sessions for marriage partners within the church. She also fought against racism within the field of counseling. For instance, when a board of people refused to give funding to projects to help ethnic minorities, Wake organized a group to outvote the board and allow funding to go to projects serving ethnic minorities. By 1975, Wake helped build mental health services for the Asian American community by establishing the Richmond Area Multi-Service Center, which provided community-based, culturally-competent services.[44]

While Methodist individuals joined a number of different grassroots collectives, including the caucus, to achieve social change, other Asian American Protestants utilized the caucus as a vehicle to transform the church *and* serve the Asian American Movement. Some caucuses saw a need to provide ministries to new immigrant populations as well as young activists. One of the purposes of the United Presbyterian Caucus, for instance, was to "develop new ministries to Asians and Asian American movements." Other caucuses wanted to engage with people in the community. The American Baptists Caucus, for instance, aimed to "recapture the sense of power and identity lost by Asian Americans" by participating in projects "related to Asian American ministries and social action and cultural programs," including "support of Asian youth programs in communities and on campus," and "support of an Asian American social worker to do research in the way Asian Americans in certain localities are faring with regard to housing, childcare needs, drug abuse, mental health, and old age homes."[45] In both the Presbyterian and Baptist churches, the caucuses served as the political and spiritual nexus between theology and practice both in the church and the Asian American Movement.

Conclusion

Between the 1950s and the 1970s, the Asian American Protestant Movement emerged from the failure of racial integration into white churches, coalitional organizing with Black and Latinx Protestants, and the political strategizing of a pan-ethnic caucus. During the first half of the 1960s, the Methodist leadership aimed to bring global peace through Christian models of unity and adopted a policy of integrating the Japanese Provisional Conferences to regional conferences. The dissolution of the ethnic church and the paternalism of white Methodists resulted in unequal job placement for Asian American ministers, an abandonment of specialized ministry, and an exodus of Japanese American Methodists from the church. By the

---

[43] Marion Wake, "Counseling the Japanese Family in the United States," in *The Theologies of Asian Americans and Pacific Peoples: A Reader*, comp. Roy I. Sano (Berkeley: PSR/PACTS/PANA, Graduate Theological Union, 1976), 129–148. See pp. 99–118 in this volume.

[44] "Marion Wake," Interview by Jun Stinson, *API Women, Faith & Action*. http://apiwomenfaithaction.blogspot.com/2009/10/marion-wake.html.

[45] Joint Strategy and Action Committee, Inc., "Asian Americans: A Forgotten Minority Comes of Age," *JSAC Grapevine* 4, no. 4, (October 1972). See p. 392 in this volume.

late 1960s, Asian American Protestants began organizing alongside Black and Brown members of their church for racial justice and accountability. Enabled by the reproductive labor of women, pastors like Wake first assisted in Japanese American resettlement and then joined a Black-led multiracial church. He, along with Black and white members of the church, established the Commission on Religion and Race at the Annual Conference. At the regional level, Black, Latinx, and Asian American Methodists worked under the Ethnic Strategies Committee to argue for equitable representation in governance, financial decision-making, job placement, and financial ownership over church properties. By the 1970s, the Commission on Religion and Race funded the grassroots organizing of pan-ethnic caucuses like the Asian American Caucus. Caucuses organized as a political muscle to elect the first Asian American bishop and set out to decolonize theology through a reassessment of theological education curricula. Through the caucus, women felt empowered to step outside of their expected gender roles, and they and others could join in direct participation in the broader Asian American Movement. Out of this context, the caucuses created the Pacific and Asian American Center for Theology and Strategies (PACTS) and from it, emerged this reader.

Inheritors of the America in the Heart
PACTS and Its History

Fumitaka Matsuoka

The struggle for the recovery of the memory of buried anguish, of pain and promise as well as the epistemology of harmony of opposites in the quest for "realizing America in the heart," this struggle itself, is what PACTS was all about.

Passion for Memory: The Recovery of Humanity in Pathos

"A readiness to find in their faith hallowed," the Asian American Center for Theology and Strategies (ACTS) was first conceived in 1972 and officially incorporated in March 1974 in Oakland, California. The purpose of the center was to recover the buried and neglected hallowedness embedded in the unquenched anguish and pathos of Asian American communities amidst triumphalism and optimism that were prevalent in the dominant faith discourse of the day in North America. Its first annual report talks about a new vision of possibilities, developing new structures, and fostering a greater sense of spirit for Asian American Christian ministries. "The theme of liberation—political, economic, social, cultural, and spiritual—was the key" for the center in its initial stage. PACTS was "committed to conduct workshops and training which fostered theological reflection, negotiate with seminaries in ways their programs could be changed to include training in Asian American ministries, relate to churches through local and regional bodies and denominational caucuses, and produce publications for dissemination of news, new developments, and sharing concerns."[1] The director of ACTS was Prof. Roy I. Sano of the United Methodist Church, who was a chaplain and on the faculty of Mills College in Oakland, California, and later became a bishop in the UMC.

The genesis of PACTS goes back to a confluence of events stretching from the 1950s to early 1970s.[2] Noteworthy were several gatherings of Asian American religious leaders in the early 1970s, beginning with the meeting of Chinese, Filipino, and Japanese American Christian clergy convened by the first Asian American bishop, Wilbur Choy of the United Methodist Church, in the spring of 1972 in Oakland, California. The participants discussed the establishment of a center to address the needs of Asian American ministries. A subsequent retreat was held at

---

[1] PACTS, *PACTS First Annual Report, 1972–74*, box 5, folder 23, Pacific and Asian American Center for Theology and Strategies Collection, Graduate Theological Union, Berkeley, CA.

[2] Philip Kyung Sik Park, "Significant Dates in Asian American History," in *The Theologies of Asian Americans and Pacific Peoples: A Reader*, comp. Roy I. Sano (Berkeley: PSR/PACTS/PANA, Graduate Theological Union, 1976), 472. See pp. 427–428 in this volume.

Mills College in March of 1973, where a "Statement of Priorities and Programs" was adopted. It calls for "a center which would relate to programs of higher education with special attention to seminaries, and also relate to Asian American communities with special attention to churches."[3]

The following year, in July 1973, an Asian American liberation theology course, "Developing an Ethnic Theology of Liberation," was taught at the Pacific School of Religion by Dr. Roy Sano of the UMC and Dr. James Chuck of the American Baptist Churches. The course was followed by another course taught at Claremont School of Theology in southern California in August of 1973, "Developing an Asian American Theology." Dr. Sano and Dr. William Shinto were the instructors. The last two days of the course featured the first conference on "East Asian and Amerasian Theology." The resource persons for the conference included Prof. Robert Fukuda and Masao Takenaka of Doshisha University School of Theology in Kyoto and Prof. Yoshinobu Kumazawa and Kiyoshi Sakon of Tokyo Union Theological School. These events culminated in the founding of ACTS. In order to reflect the inclusiveness of constituencies, ACTS was later changed to Pacific and Asian American Center for Theology and Strategies (PACTS) and was housed in Pacific School of Religion in Berkeley, California, in 1977. Director Prof. Sano was also appointed to the faculty of PSR. In its inception, PACTS was a locus for an "action/reflection, resource and service center for faith and ministry."[4] A national board of directors was formed that reflected the several Protestant denominations as well as broad representations from Pacific and Asian ethnic groups. The center held various conferences, workshops, courses, and other events under the direction of Prof. Sano. A resource bank was built up that included articles, unpublished papers, reports, proceedings, dissertations, theses, periodicals, and other informational materials. The resources were made available for research for Pacific and Asian Americans and beyond.

It can be said that one of the foremost contributions of PACTS to the North American faith communities is the recovery and reclamation of the hallowedness and sacredness of anguish and pathos that are central in the lived faith of Pacific and Asian Americans. PACTS was founded out of distinct memories of Pacific and Asian Americans, memories of deep anguish stemming from the painful history of historical injuries inflicted upon their communities since their arrival in North America. A noteworthy memory of pathos that was still raw at the time of the founding of PACTS was the incarceration of Japanese Americans in concentration camps during World War II. A few months after the defeat of Japan in 1945, the concentration camps that housed Japanese Americans were all shut down. The dwellers of the camps returned to their homes to find nothing, not even a public acknowledgement of their incarcerations. Less than twenty years later, in 1960s, they

---

[3] PACTS, *Statement of Priorities and* Programs, box 5, folder 23, Pacific and Asian American Center for Theology and Strategies Collection, Graduate Theological Union, Berkeley, CA.

[4] PACTS, PACTS Catalogue, Publications, Services, and Resources 1979, box 22, folder 13, Pacific and Asian American Center for Theology and Strategies Collection, Graduate Theological Union, Berkeley, CA.

were still nobodies, the "forgotten people."[5] The invisibility of Japanese Americans is indicative of the forgotten sufferings of other Pacific and Asian Americans in North American society and its history. Pacific Asian Americans are people proud of their histories and memories no matter how painful they might have been. "Memory is a passion no less powerful or pervasive than love," says Elie Wiesel. "What does it mean to remember? It is to live in more than one world, to prevent the past from fading and to call upon the future to illuminate it."[6] How would Pacific and Asian Americans face the erasure of memory, the unresolved pain of betrayal, the eerie silence of people around them, the persistent echoes of lingering gestures of resentment that continue to come upon them, and the unfamiliar sense of disorientation of how to go on in the society that abandoned them in the name of democracy? Anguish is "the combination of pain and promise, anger and aspiration, the experience of 'being had' as being a 'have not,'" says Bishop Sano. The memory of anguish lingered on, often in stealth, among Asian Americans when the civil rights movement began to emerge among other people of color, particularly among African Americans, in late 1950s and into the 1960s. The issues that emerged in the civil rights movement were familiar and similar among Pacific and Asian Americans: racial segregation, disfranchisement, discrimination, and racism. All these issues were often taken for granted by the people of the majority race, but for Asian and Pacific Americans, their challenge was particularly focused. For Pacific and Asian Americans, their struggle was to rescue lost beings and to drive back the sands that cover the surface of their history, to combat oblivion and to reject death. The recovery of memory of anguish was driven by a dream, a dream to "realize the America in the heart" amidst the never-ending disappointments and betrayal that continued to come upon them.[7] The liberation for Pacific and Asian Americans did not end with overcoming oppression, racism, and inequality. The bitter memories of anguish they carried with them and continued to live in needed to be told publicly, the erasure of their history needed to be stopped and their history restored in order for their people to be whole and for their children and grandchildren to have their places in their world. They wanted to be remembered, not forgotten. They wanted to be visible in the world that reduced them to invisibility.

In order to pursue this struggle, the places to anchor a new vision was needed. One such avenue was a community of faith. Particularly, "the church is one of the community organizations in Amerasian communities which has been overlooked in historical studies, sociological analyses, psychological studies, and political actions."[8] As Pacific and Asian Americans struggled to be "liberated" from being less than

---

[5] Joint Strategy and Action Committee Inc., "Asian Americans: A Forgotten Minority Comes of Age," in *Amerasian Theology of Liberation: A Reader*, ed. Roy I. Sano (Oakland, CA: Asian Center for Theology and Strategies, 1973). See pp. 389–393 in this volume.

[6] Elie Wiesel, *All Rivers Run to the Sea: Memoirs* (New York: Random House, 2010), 150.

[7] Carlos Bulosan, *America in the Heart* (Seattle: University of Washington Press, 1973).

[8] Roy I. Sano, "Preface," in *Amerasian Theology of Liberation: A Reader*, comp. Roy I. Sano (Oakland: Asian Center for Theology and Strategies [ACTS], Mills College, 1973), 1.

human in the society that treated them as subhuman, their communities of faith became a powerful locus of their endeavors.[9] Being human needs a passion for memory that is equally as powerful and pervasive as love, particularly the passion for the memory of neglected pathos that is indispensable to being fully human. The establishment of PACTS came about amid the yearnings of Americans of Asian DNA, their passion for the "liberation" of memory.

Inheriting the Cultural and Spiritual DNA of Asian Interfaith Beings

The liberation of memory needs the understanding and appreciation of Pacific and Asian American ethnic, cultural, and spiritual distinctness and the affirmation of unique historical heritages. The quest for the communal identities of Pacific Asian Americans thus took on the question of what this distinctness is all about. The memories of the historical injuries that Pacific and Asian Americans endured alone cannot be what life, personal and communal, is all about. Equally significant is the sense of something full and hopeful. And yet, the fullness of life and hope are also entangled with the continuing experiences of pathos. Pacific and Asian Americans turned to their cultural and spiritual DNA to address this complex notion of reality. "We have been taught in recent decades to find the Christ-figure inside and under all kinds of ostensibly secular phenomena, quasi-religions, and 'non-Christian' religions."[10] PACTS served as a critical agent for "the *conscious* recovery of elements in our cultural heritage that" Asian and Pacific Americans previously rejected because of their fear of further rejection by society.[11] In the midst of the "officially optimistic" neo-orthodoxy that prevailed in Christian theological America (Douglas John Hall), for that matter, throughout the Western theological world, with its unquestioned primacy of the positivistic divine revelation, a profoundly prophetic statement came out of PACTS:

> We will increasingly find ourselves asking whether we can be Christians without being Buddhists . . . Confucians . . . Taoists . . . Shamanists . . . Animists . . . Muslims . . . or some combination of these and others. Some Christians are already asking whether they can be Christians without being Marxists, as early Christians asked how they can be Christians without being Jewish.[12]

Unlike the prevailing posture of interfaith relations where the focal point of theological discussions is often that of identity differences of faith traditions and practices, Pacific and Asian American scholars and practitioners of faith talked about their coexisting interfaith traditions in their own lives: "Can we be Christian without being Buddhists?" Their faith orientations did not begin with the Aristotelian *either/or* worldview that is often assumed uncritically in the world of faith

---

[9] Lloyd Wake, "Oppression—White Domination," in *The Theologies of Asian Americans and Pacific Peoples: A Reader*, comp. Roy I. Sano (Berkeley: PSR/PACTS/PANA, Graduate Theological Union, 1976), 352–353. See p. 315 in this volume.

[10] Roy I. Sano, "A Sword and a Cross: Japanese American Christians," *Pacific Theological Review* 15, no. 3 (Spring 1982): 28.

[11] Sano, "A Sword and a Cross," 23.

[12] Sano, "A Sword and a Cross," 28.

discourse. Prof. Sano's question came out of a different worldview and epistemology, the *yin and yang* harmony of opposites, not out of the epistemology of the incompatibility of opposites. This epistemological distinctness of Pacific and Asian Americans and their communities named in PACTS's scholarly contributions is still to be acknowledged today, some forty years later, let alone to be genuinely appreciated by a wider public and in scholarly discourse.

The Yearning to Realize the America in the Heart

James Baldwin talks about the heart of race relations in the US as being the incomprehensibility of the languages we speak across the race line, others speaking a language and of a reality alien to our own. They each had different "systems of reality."[13] For Pacific and Asian Americans, this different system of reality is exacerbated by the added stigma of European Americans' fascination with the exotic and esoteric. The quaint and mysterious Orientalized perceptions are further complicated by the prevailing racism. Even today, with the generational shifts and multiracial and multiethnic trends that affect Pacific and Asian American racial identities, Americans remain at odds in the reading of different and "alien systems of reality." PACTS was established to address these different systems we speak, to expose the different realities across the race lines. The challenge was daunting, perhaps an impossible task, a hope against hope, in order to establish a radical shift in the way we relate across racial divides. It was the challenge to be multilingual in communication across the lines of difference, a challenge for a multilingual society that is still fresh today.

This is to say that the passion for memory is simultaneously the humanization of all people. The recovery of the memories of Pacific and Asian Americans, in which PACTS played a critical role, was not only for the excavation of our own cultural, spiritual, and historical heritages. The loss of memories for Pacific and Asian Americans not only defies our own dignity but also diminishes the dignity of all people. The foremost objective of the establishment and endeavors of PACTS was to join other groups of people to search for the "America in the heart" for the whole society, as Carlos Bulosan puts it. The "humanization" of Pacific Asian Americans was not limited to their own people. The evil of racism, oppression, and neglect they experienced extended to the people of all races. The dominant group of Americans needs to acknowledge their complicity in the foundational inequalities that that structure society. But they also need to recognize that the mistreatment of other racial groups of people also diminishes their own lives. No one is an island entirely in themself. Any group's invisibility and neglect diminish everyone. Until North Americans summon the will to recognize this brutal fact and to address it, North American society and its fullness will not be realized. PACTS was the expression of the yearning for the fullness of society.

---

[13] James Baldwin in his debate with William Buckley at Cambridge University, 1965 (see "The American Dream and the American Negro," *New York Times*, March 7, 1965, https://www.nytimes.com/images/blogs/papercuts/baldwin-and-buckley.pdf).

The programs and activities undertaken by PACTS were extensive:

- Provided a "safe space" for students and Christian pastors to gather at PACTS office, and engaged with the faculty of Pacific School of Religion where the Center was housed, e.g., Professors Archie Smith, Durwood Foster, and David Stewart in particular;

- Resourced Asian American Protestant denominational caucuses in their formation, e.g., the United Methodist Church; American Baptist Convention, Episcopalians, and United Church of Christ;

- Offered courses for academic credit on Asian American liberation theology and ministries. This dual focus reflected the theology and strategies in PACTS. The course eventually branched out to cross-racial courses, with Prof. Archie Smith, and broader Asian American cultural heritage in history and the philosophy of religion, e.g., Polarities & Paradoxes; Christ, Krishna, and the Buddha;

- Collected theological statements from individuals and organizations, particularly as Asian American Christian denominational caucuses were being formed;

- Photocopied the statements of Pacific Asian Americans and bound them into readers, apparently in at least two editions;

- Collected worship resources, e.g., lyrics of songs, prayers, poems, etc., and bound them into worship resources with the title *Pacasiana*;

- Conducted national Asian American theological consultations. *Contours and Currents* was one of the photocopies of presentations. Publisher Orbis rejected publication;

- Staged consultation for Asian American women theologians, initially held at San Francisco Theological Seminary. The support continued from the Institute for Leadership Development and Study of Pacific and Asian North American Religion (PANA Institute), which existed from 2000 until its closure in 2009. It was the successor to PACTS in Berkeley, CA;

- Resourced denominational officials interested in the development of ethnic theologies. It was at a UCC consultation;

- Worked with other seminaries, particularly Princeton, Claremont, and Drew, on developing Asian American and ethnic theological education;

- Joined efforts with other North American liberation theologians at consultations, e.g., Detroit gathering;

- Organized documents for archiving at Graduate Theological Union, with much of it catalogued;

- Staged consultations on human rights struggles in South Korea and the Philippines. Supported demonstrations at the consulates of both nations in SF. Persons associated with PACTS served on fact-finding tours to South Korea and joined rallies at the SF South Korean consulate. Rev. Lloyd Wake and his son Steve Wake were arrested in one of those demonstrations in order to publicize the issues. Director Roy Sano joined another delegation at the same consulate, but the delegation got away before police arrested them;

- Conducted several training sessions for United Methodist Church Global Ministries mission interns before they went to Japan, South Korea, Hong Kong, etc. Focus was on ministries amidst neocolonialism. Students include Norman Fong in San Francisco, the Chinatown housing alliance, and a faculty member at Candler School of Theology;

- Trained US Navy chaplains to work in Asia and among Asians in what would be called, "cultural competence." PACTS Director Roy Sano went to Norfolk to video tape some training sessions used by Navy chaplains;

- Videoed *Faces of Faith* for Trinity Institute and also the Institute's consultation on theological developments at Hotel Fairmont in San Francisco. The manuscript was published in a book, *Truth in Myth*.

Planting an Apple Tree

PACTS became an informal affiliate of GTU in 1976 and an official affiliate in 1986. PACTS offices were moved to GTU in 1994. Its programs were expanded to include women in ministry, ministry with immigrants, refugees, and native people, and human rights. Following the election of Prof. Sano to the United Methodist episcopacy, Lloyd Wake served as director during 1983–85; Fumitaka Matsuoka, 1985–87; and Julia Estrella (or Matsui-Estrella), 1987–95. Active and long-serving staff members included Kathleen Thomas-Sano, Clifford Alika, and Yoichi Shimatsu. The 1991 mission statement described PACTS as "an ecumenical center for research, resourcing, recruiting, training, and consciousness-raising, with foci on the Pacific and Asian American constituencies, to promote the fulfillment of God's mission through the ministries of the churches and the service of community groups." Deborah Lee served as director during 1995–2000. The program emphases by then included ministry with gays and lesbians.

PACTS, throughout its history, was often in transition as it grappled with issues of mission, program, funding support, and staffing. Kyle Miura came to serve as director in 2000. Vital programs were still offered, but by 2002, it was not possible to continue. PACTS closed in May 2002 when GTU reduced the number of its centers and affiliates. The remnants of its members continue some inherited programs in Hawaii to this day. Many of these programs and activities of PACTS were later passed onto another Pacific and Asian American organization, the Institute for Leadership Development and Study of Pacific and Asian North American Religion (PANA Institute), founded in 2000, which was also housed at the Pacific School of Religion until the institute's closure in 2009. Numerous centers and institutes for Pacific Asian Americans have emerged in the recent past. Their historical DNA has been inherited by such groups as the Asian and Pacific Americans and Religion Research Initiative (APARRI) and Pacific Asian North American Asian Women in Theology and Ministry (PANAAWTM). While there is no guarantee for the accomplishment of the stated goals of PACTS, the work toward justice for the sake of the health of North American society, its efforts and struggles still continue in different ways. The efforts to achieve a just and healthy world is a communal and intergenerational act. They are an act of planting an apple tree even if the world would come to an end tomorrow, as reformer Martin Luther said. The solidarity of people for the continuing quest is the expression of the Pacific and Asian Americans in the history of PACTS. It can be said that the struggle for the recovery of buried anguish and the epistemology of the harmony of opposites in the quest for realizing America in the heart, this struggle itself, is what PACTS was all about.

Editor's Notes

In preparing the original 1976 compilation for publication, a number of edits were made. The reasons for the changes fall into six main categories:

1. **Format.** The original version was a compilation of papers in various formats photocopied together. Thus, each document — whether a dissertation chapter, a denominational record, an unpublished seminary paper, or a journal article — retained its particular formatting, which we made uniform for this version. Also, where previously underlining was used for emphasis, as was common during the use of typewriters, the words have been italicized.
2. **Grammar and punctuation.** Grammar and punctuation were corrected or updated to follow contemporary guidelines.
3. **Antiquated phrasing.** A number of antiquated phrasings that could obscure the meaning of the text were updated or simplified.
4. **Inclusive language.** Following common contemporary practice, incidents of masculine language for humanity and for God were replaced with gender inclusive language, in the spirit of the progressive orientation of this work.
5. **Dated racial language.** The accepted language around race and culture has changed significantly in the last forty-five years. During the time of the *Reader*'s writing, various labels were used for Asian Americans, such as "Amerasian" or "Yellows." While we sought to maintain the original wording where possible, we updated the dated racial language when it would distract from the message of the text.
6. **Citations and references.** Citations were edited to contemporary standards and, when possible, missing bibliographic data has been inserted.

Overall, the principles of readability and clarity guided decisions around textual changes.

We hope that these changes will ease the sense of distance that new contemporary readers might experience as they become acquainted with the context and concerns of the writers in this *Reader*.

Jane Iwamura   Jason Chu
Rudy Busto   Lilly Li
Tim Tseng   Sooho Lee

Our editors at Claremont Press,
Thomas Phillips, Andrew Schwartz, and James Rogers

Contributors

Roy I. Sano (complier) served as the Director of the Pacific and Asian American Center for Theology and Strategies in Berkeley, Professor of Theology and Pacific and Asian American Ministries at the Pacific School of Religion, and a bishop of the United Methodist Church.

Daniel D. Lee (editor), a Presbyterian minister, is the Academic Dean of the Center for Asian American Theology and Ministry and Assistant Professor of Theology and Asian American Studies at Fuller Theological Seminary. He is the author of *Doing Asian American Theology: A Contextual Framework for Faith and Practice*.

Chrissy Yee Lau is Assistant Professor of History at California State University, Monterey Bay, and the author of *New Women of Empire: Gendered Politics and Racial Uplift in Interwar Japanese America*.

Fumitaka Matsuoka served as the Robert Gordon Sproul Professor of Theology at the Pacific School of Religion and the Executive Director for the Institute for Leadership Development and Study of Pacific and Asian North American Religion (PANA Institute).

Original Contributors
[Ed. note: This list was compiled for this revised edition, not for the original compilation in 1976. Thus, the biographical information provided here is uneven, often including the contributors' later positions and accomplishments.]

Donna Dong served as the National Director for Multiethnic/Multicultural Ministry for the Inter-Varsity Christian Fellowship of Canada.

Toge Fujihara was a staff photographer for the United Methodist Board of Global Ministries.

David Junichi Harada was a Methodist pastor at Palolo Community Methodist Church, Honolulu, Hawaii.

David Y. Hirano was the Senior Minister of Nuuanu Congregational Church, Honolulu, Hawaii, and later served as the Executive Vice President at the United Church Board for World Ministries.

Frank Ichishita served as pastor of The Peoples' Presbyterian Church, Denver, Colorado, a historically African American congregation.

Lemuel Ignacio served on the Pilipino Organizing Committee, San Francisco, and was Chairman of the Asian Presbyterian Caucus.

Chan Hie Kim served as an ordained deacon in the United Methodist Church and later as Professor of New Testament and Christian Ministries at Claremont Graduate School.

Teruo Kawata was a member of the staff of the Council for Lay Life and Work and later served as Conference Minister of the Central Pacific Conference and also the Hawaii Conference of the United Church of Christ.

June I. Kimoto was an active organizer, volunteer, and philanthropist with Asian Presbyterian Women.

Kim, Hyung-Chan was Associate Professor at Western Washington State College and later Professor of Education and Asian American Studies at Western Washington University.

Eun Ja Kim Lee was a graduate of Union Presbyterian Seminary in Richmond, Virginia, and later worked at Union Theological Seminary Library in New York.

Warren Lee was an associate pastor of Westminster Presbyterian Church in Los Angeles, the oldest and largest African American Presbyterian church in the western US, Assistant Professor of Ministry at San Francisco Theological Seminary, and later a minister at Donaldina Cameron House.

Dennis Loo was Associate Director of the Office of Ethnic Affairs (OECA), Synod of the Golden Gate of the United Presbyterian Church, a member of the Asian Presbyterian Caucus, and on the Board of Governors for ACTS.

Leslie Loo studied sociology, working with Asian women at the University of California, Berkeley, and with Third World women in the San Francisco area.

Patricia Ling Magdamo was coauthor of *Christ in Philippine Context: A College Textbook of Theology and Religious Studies* and Vice President of the United Board for Higher Education in Asia.

Frank G. Mar was a pastor of Chinese Presbyterian Church in Oakland and one of the founders of the East Bay Asian Local Development Corporation.

Marilyn J. Mar was a student at the University of California, Berkeley.

Violet Masuda taught church school at the Livingston United Methodist Church and served three times over as President of its Women's Society. She was a member of the Asian caucus in the United Methodist Church.

Joann Miyamoto was a songwriter, dance and theater artist, author, and Artistic Director of Great Leap.

Jitsuo Morikawa served as the Associate Executive Secretary and later Vice President of the American Baptist Churches USA.

Paul M. Nagano was the founder of the Japanese Evangelical Missions Society, the Asian American Caucus of American Baptist Churches, and the Council for Pacific Asian Theology.

David Ng was a Presbyterian minister and Professor of Christian Education at Austin Theological Seminary, San Francisco Theological Seminary, and Graduate Theological Union.

Philip Kyung Sik Park was Associate for Asian Church Development with the Program Agency of the United Presbyterian Church in the USA.

William Mamoru Shinto worked for United Ministries in Education, an interdenominational ministry representing American Baptists.

Steve Sangkwon Shim was the first executive of the Hanmi Presbytery the nongeographical Korean Presbytery of the Presbyterian Church (USA) and later Executive Director of the AAPC-accredited Korea Christian Institute of Psychotherapy based in Seoul, South Korea.

A. C. Ubalde Jr. was the pastor of Bethany United Methodist, San Francisco.

Alan S. Wong was a community organizer and an elder at Cumberland Presbyterian Church in Chinatown, San Francisco, and later the Executive Director of the Chinatown YMCA.

Lloyd K. Wake was a community life minister at Glide Memorial United Methodist Church in San Francisco.

Marion Wake was a licensed marriage and family therapist who was instrumental in expanding mental health services to ethnic minorities in the United States. She was also married to the Reverend Lloyd K. Wake, a United Methodist minister and civil rights activist.

Franklin Woo was a chaplain and lecturer in religion at Chung Chi College, Chinese University of Hong Kong, and the Director of the China Program, the National Council of the Churches of Christ in the USA.

Wesley Woo was Associate for Racial Justice and Asian Mission Development, Presbyterian Church (USA).

THE THEOLOGIES OF ASIAN AMERICANS
AND PACIFIC PEOPLES

A Reader

Roy Sano

Compiler

Asian Center for Theology & Strategies
Pacific School of Religion
1976

Preface (1976)

ROY I. SANO

This book contains a sampling of theological reflections on the part of Asian Americans and Pacific Islanders. An earlier reader, *Amerasian Theology of Liberation*,[1] is no longer available. Since circulating the previous reader, the Asian Center for Theology and Strategies (ACTS) has continued to receive theological statements from individuals and groups. The manuscript files now contain an estimated 250 items. In addition, ten dissertations, scores of specialized books, tapes, pictures, etc., related to Pacific and Asian American ministries have been collected. Hence, the statements in this volume represent a very limited selection of resources.

At first, the present volume was envisioned as a workbook for persons engaged in theological reflection and development of ethnic ministries. It contains a survey of Pacific and Asian American history, summaries of reports on their social conditions, and representative voices from East Asia. All of these items have been deleted from this volume. We have been forced to restrict ourselves to theological statements because of the lack of space. The resulting volume represents those persons and groups who have felt the emergence of ethnic consciousness and address the issues of oppression.

The selections have been arranged in the following order:

- Autobiographical statements
- Theological analysis of historical developments
- Experiments in the indigenization of the Christian faith to East Asian cultural heritage
- Appropriation of the contribution of Black theology
- Theological statements on general topics
- Perspectives on the specific issue of women
- Theological statements related to the emergence of caucuses and the promotion of specialized ministries

We are indebted to the authors for providing us with statements. No one of us would claim to have uttered the definitive word. We would hope these expressions of our faith would inspire others to take pen, or brush, in hand. The "internal colony" which we have experienced has rendered far too many of us speechless, convinced that we have nothing to offer. If liberation means anything, it should release the

---

[1] Roy I. Sano, ed., *Amerasian Theology of Liberation: A Reader* (Oakland, CA: Asian Center for Theology and Strategies, 1973).

wealth of stories, insights, vision, and courage which God has given us. Where the Spirit of the Lord is, there is freedom (2 Cor. 3:17).

Finally, we acknowledge the contributions of Clifford Alika, Larry Hasegawa, and Kathleen A. Thomas-Sano, who assisted in the preparation of this volume. If the compiler had started earlier and given the assistants more time, we would have had a far more attractive volume to offer the reader.

Perhaps a third edition of such a reader will be sufficiently inclusive so that a publisher would consider printing and distributing the volume to a wider audience. Manuscripts for that project are welcomed.

Perspective[*]

Joann (Nobuko) Miyamoto

When I was young
kids used to ask me
what are you?
I'd tell them what my mom told me
I'm an American
chin Chinaman
you're a Jap!
Flashing hot inside
I'd go home
my mom would say
don't worry
he who walks alone
walks faster
but there was always
someone asking me
what are you?

Now I answer
I'm an Asian
and they say
why do you want to separate yourselves
now I say
I'm Japanese
and they say
don't you know this is the greatest country in the world

Now I say in America
I'm part of the third world people and they say
if you don't like it here
why don't you go back.

[*] Originally published in *Roots: An Asian American Reader*, ed. Amy Tachiki, Eddie Wong, Franklin Odo, and Buck Wong (Los Angeles: UCLA Asian American Studies Center, 1971), 98–99.

Amazing Grace[*]

Violet Masuda

I once was lost, but now am found, was blind, but now I see.

Is this a sign of the times? It is not my children who ask, but I, an Asian American woman who has lived in this country for over half a century and who has experienced an identity crisis. Now I see.

Without any warning, like a cancerous growth, my frustrations began to grow slowly but surely deep down inside, developing a vague, uneasy dissatisfaction, I was a supposedly happy housewife, mother, grandmother, busy all my life within the church. My life was organized, well-planned, and filled with all the daily comforts. But I felt something was wrong and I was being trapped. It puzzled me that I, who had attended church faithfully, sent the children to Sunday school and taught for seventeen years, presided over the Women's Society, and considered to be one of the more active members and one respected for a deep spiritual life, could lack peace of mind and satisfaction. I felt a disenchantment with life, self-hate (which I do not think is too rare among church members), and reacted with pretense and the falsehood that everything was okay. William James wrote that unhappiness and boredom are warnings to the spirit that something is wrong with us as we are. It is the starting point of religious experience.

In my alienation, I began a quest in search of myself and found that I had been denying my Lord. Today, instead of the question that had haunted me too long, "Why me Lord, why me?" I can now, with peace, truth, and meaning say, "I know now why, Lord, I know now." Since the realization that my life was not what it should be, I have come a long way. Today, at 54, I am truly doing what I believe my Lord intended me to do on earth, and no less; and since "my cup runneth over," I want to share my message of peace and love.

To understand the full meaning of my new life, I must go back to the early 1900s, to Tokyo, Japan. My grandfather, Aihara Ichigoro, the son of a samurai (warrior), harbored Christian missionaries when my mother was a child. Had her fascinating stories of those rock-throwing youngsters had any influence on my thinking? I wonder also about my Buddhist grandfather, Yoshida Hidezaburo, who came to

---

[*] Originally published in *Radical Religion: A Quarterly Journal of Critical Opinion* 1, no. 2 (Spring 1974): 45–47.

America and struggled with his commitment to his faith in this Christian country. How rich I am in my heritage to know of the struggles of those before me.

But I came from a culture which had always rejected the female as less than human and in typical, stereotype, Japanese fashion. I had lived my role. Once, the disadvantage became an advantage, for when my grandparents wanted to enjoy a grandchild in Japan, I was sent (my brother being the valuable, male child). I lived in Tokyo from the age of two until six. It was a time of love and unconditional security, and it gave me the great psychological strength to face my growing pains.

In 1925, after returning to this country, I attended an Oriental public school in the Sacramento Delta where white children were excluded but other minorities such as Mexicans and blacks were allowed to attend. We were taught in English. We were told to "speak English" when most of our parents could not. That is a very confusing position for a child and I now realize that it was then, in my confusion that I began to question the educational system for asking of us the impossible. The school did not create a learning atmosphere but complained of our ignorance.

Most of my life, I remember my mother's pride in playing the role of the charming, gracious, nonverbal, subservient, non-involved, polite, proper, decent, servile woman that she was in church and society. She only perpetrated what most people expect of the Japanese American woman.

When World War II brought the evacuation of 110,000 Japanese Americans to life in concentration camps, I felt the loss of dignity, the shame of my race, the guilt of being Japanese for "sins" I had not committed. I was married during that period of turmoil—living in the most remote parts of this land, behind barbed wire fences, under military guard (ironically, with our sons, husbands, and brothers in service to this country). The scar that I bury in my heart is Manzanar, a desolate area in southern California. This is one of the "whys" of my life. My husband spent four and a half years in the service, yet after he had returned from Europe, he was not allowed to attend his father's funeral in the concentration camp in Amanche, Colorado. At that time, we would not have dared to look at our true feelings, for that would have revealed a part of us that would not have been acceptable—it would not have been good Americanism.

At the end of the war, my husband and I returned to Livingston, California, a small, rural town. There I became aware of the oppressive psychological games the Japanese community plays to maintain its security in a racist society perpetrated by whites. Today I live on the soil where history was made by my father-in-law, Masuda, Yosuke. This once barren, sandy area was settled by a group of white people who were not able to survive the conditions. In 1909, the Japanese arrived and established it as one of the first Japanese colonies (Yamato Colony) in the country. They were the pioneer settlers of the community, weathering sand, wind, and drought.

These are the experiences that make it an imposition when white Americans expect me to feel as they do about life in this country. When one is asked to forget personal experiences and feel as another, how can I believe I am created in God's image? I cannot pretend; I cannot live in contradiction; I cannot play a dual role. This is the conflict of identity which plagues many minority people. Americans generalize the Japanese people, yet there is an amazing difference between the *nisei* (my generation) and those who were born and raised in Hawaii or who came from Japan. Hawaiian Japanese have been the majority and tend to be spontaneous, friendly, fun-loving and outgoing while my parents, who tended to be more quiet, inhibited, overly serious and hardworking were a minority, yet were *still* Japanese.

It has been a very difficult struggle for me as a Japanese American woman. I saw the oppression of my parents and their generation under racism, sexism, and exploitation. I experienced the segregation, discrimination, and injustice in the educational system, in society, and in our churches. And I am *not* willing to be quiet, unassuming, docile, and accepting for my children's generation or my grandchildren's.

During my years of growing discontent, I had also become disenchanted with my role as a housewife, my role in the family, my role as a church woman for it seemed we all came out of the same mold—looked alike, spoke alike, acted alike. I was fearful because of small-town pressures, but dauntless, I became determined to change the course of my life.

The past five years have given me new insights and the ability to decide, accept, love, and most of all, to grow. I have been a housewife for thirty-one years, but I no longer allow others to steal "my" time. It is mine and I use it for my priorities. I have bolstered my confidence with college classes, pampered my ego with God's love, nourished my mind with books and more books, spent time alone in meditation and reflection, evaluation and direction. The psychology of the Japanese is very difficult for most Westerners to understand. I believe this greatly inhibited my search for identity as a person, created in God's image. Spiritual life for the Asian American woman does not come easily, for it necessarily includes cultural "hang-ups" and the Americanization process.

During my parents' generation, the church had to provide the social satisfaction in their lives. But today, unless that church has a spiritual foundation, a sense of living life well, it will not grow. When churches are like other institutions, when it is people-controlled and not God-willed, we have then smothered spiritual life, and only encouraged organized social activities, gossip columns, etc. Because I feel it is less than human to place blame without responsibility, I have, in my own way, tried to instill Christian values in my life and church. Christ did not conform and was crucified. He lifted those who were oppressed so that they might have human dignity. I was terribly naive and ideological in thinking that the church would value what Christ valued in His life.

Measuring religious faith by attendance each Sunday, praying before meals, being active in church programs, reading the Bible is not faith nor religion. But I, too, was once participating in church because "everyone else did," because of "tradition," and out of "sheer habit." I was also there because I feared losing my position in the church hierarchy, the system where I was secure and "in" the group. I was not taught to question, to make decisions.

Was it only a coincidence that about this time a group of Asian American clergymen and lay leaders were beginning to question the validity of religion in America for Asians? They saw the lack of involvement of our people, the lack of ministry, the lack of potential leadership and the continual loss of that which we had. I too learned to question and to make decisions. Now that I am more aware of my own identity and even more involved in the hierarchy of the church, I am finding a true lack of understanding of how minority church members *feel*. It has not been dealt with at all, and now the church must listen.

When the former Japanese Provincial Conference was operating under Jurisdiction, we had opportunities for leadership development yet were treated merely as an appendage of the larger body. The parent-child relationship of control kept us immature, and was a handicap to our spiritual growth. Through the course of my traveling, I now experience more and more of these truths. A naive bishop asked me why the Asian Caucus was so strongly determined to have more Asian American leaders in all levels of church life! Very few white church members realize what it means to never have had the opportunity to tell one's children, "Christian vocations are equal opportunities," for there was virtually no visual aid to prove it.

The hope and destiny of the church lies in the potential of all of its people and in the church's nurturing of the liberation of personhood for all ethnic minorities. When we can accept ourselves as the God-created image, our full potential can be known. By ignoring the minority, by treating so many as if they did not exist, or by turning a deaf ear because of cultural differences or peculiar lifestyles, the church will never create the atmosphere of the spiritual life that it pretends to seek. The paternalistic WASP attitude will have to give way to a more deeply sensitive understanding of our diversified cultural backgrounds before the church can hope to understand and minister to the theology and spiritual life of ethnic minorities.

I hope I can be an agent in changing the image of the Asian American (especially the woman), both the image cast on us by others, and the image we hold of ourselves. This will mean changing fear into courage, inhibitions to assertions, silence to articulate speech, inactivity to involvement, a life of economic survival to one of spirituality. I have finally found a peace that many spend a lifetime searching for. For the Asian American the contradictions have been great and the price has been high. But I cannot but hope and believe that we, too, are God's children and that we will be a part of a new mainstream in the church. As it has been for me, I hope it will be for others, so that these words from Luke can come alive for them also: "Knock and it shall be opened, seek and ye shall find, ask and it shall be given unto you."

My Spiritual Pilgrimage

Jitsuo Morikawa

Few persons have been as close to the center of the development of American Baptist thought as Jitsuo Morikawa. Canadian-born and of Japanese ancestry, he has influenced thought patterns within the American Baptist Churches to an unparalleled degree. His contribution to our thinking and our evangelistic stance are directly related to the particular experiences which have influenced his life.

Jitsuo has walked a steady path from teenage conversion—through the comparative assurance of the Southern Baptist Theological Seminary, through the anxiety of dealing with the urban scene as pastor of a major church in Chicago—through the volatile office of Secretary of our Division of Evangelism—to his present position as Associate Executive Secretary of the Board of National Ministries.

He has been both acclaimed and defamed by his colleagues within the American Baptist Churches. His dedication to truth and the variety of personal experiences have allowed him to view both acclaim and defamation as stepping stones. Jitsuo Morikawa, through the ministry of his own life, has enabled many of us to engage in deeper pilgrimages into our own souls.

I

My own spiritual pilgrimage, spanning forty-five years, has meaning as a possible reflection of the pilgrimage of the church in history's stormiest period of collective upheaval, when the meaning of eternity and time, God and history, church and world, has come to cosmic conflict; and we are still in the maelstrom of that tortuous struggle.

We have been living through history's most revolutionary period, and the church as a piece of that history has been at the very center of the storm like the eye of a hurricane; and while the whole human enterprise has been up-rooted from its ancient moorings, the church, battered and dismantled, has tried to keep in touch with the disclosures of eternity in the midst of collapsing time, and with ultimate reality when history seemed to be crumbling all around about us.

One would hardly attribute significance to a simple event, the personal decision of an anonymous boy sixteen years of age to accept Jesus Christ as personal Savior, receive baptism, and join a Baptist church. But little events conceal enormous realities, for behind that event was a struggle of adolescence waging war with moral and psychic conflicts in that crucial frontier when a child ventures into the awesome, frightening world of what it means to be a man.

And in that life and death encounter, defeats and failures appeared beyond repair to the sensitive conscience for when in life does hopelessness appear as the only option, and self-liquidation become seductive as in those gentle years, before the moral tissues have become toughened by scars of adult cynicism? No one but God knew the burden I carried behind the mask of youthful indifference, no adult was aware, no adult seemed to care; and isn't this a universal phenomenon of historic proportions that is shaking our culture to its very foundations?

You can sense what conversion meant: to know my sins were forgiven and accepted by God, I accepted myself. The fierce storm of human existence rages precisely where vision is purest and hope is unsullied and faith so trusting, and where the greatest possibilities of human redemption and transformation reside, among the adolescent youth of a tortured and tormented generation. The awkward adolescent signals for help may be the last desperate signals the church receives; and left unheeded, the human spirit may lose its beautiful capacity to cry for help. "Whosoever shall receive this child, this youth, in my name," said Jesus, "receiveth me!"

But also behind this boy saying "Yes" to Jesus was the unsuspected birth of a revolutionary, the birth of a stubborn will which refused to acquiesce to a society which deprived me the elemental rights of citizenship. My acceptance of Christ was not only salvation from despair, but serving notice on institutions that the moral power of the universe would prevail and the awesome institutions will one day capitulate to the demands of divine justice.

For when I was told "The earth is the Lord's," that God "created the heavens and the earth," that God created me "in His own image," that in Christ I was "a new creation," I began to think big thoughts, dream dreams, and see visions that I amounted to something in the eyes of God and in the judgment of men, that I was called to a mission to serve God and humanity. How else can you explain the audacity of a sixteen-year-old boy testifying to the leading Buddhist leader of the community, winning seven young men to Christ in the first six months after his conversion, among them his school teacher twice his age and his brother five years older? How else can you explain the courage of a boy preaching from a crowded street corner at a sensitive age when peer reaction and peer acceptance means more than life itself, but chose to be a "fool for Christ" in the eyes of his peers?

My conversion also meant the death of a powerful center of meaning, the primitive instinct to hate with a noble passion, to crush for a righteous cause, to use the weapons of the enemy against them, and brutalize those who sought to brutalize us. I knew the seduction of primitive powers, primordial instincts, and primeval emotions, to be a noble savage in the jungle of human survival. I knew the enticing appeal of narrow loyalties and bitter biases, and enormous possibilities of using them to achieve my lust for power. But my conversion struck a fatal blow to that virile source of energy, the power that resides in smoldering hate against a cruel society. I was castrated, emasculated of the power to hate and destroy. I was left a psalm-singing eunuch for Christ, a harmless man of peace who lost the will to kill his fellow human, mouthing innocuous sentimentalities such as "The meek shall inherit the earth!"

During these forty-five tumultuous years we have seen the church sow seeds of rebirth and reap revolutions: racial, social, political revolutions at home and abroad. For when conversions occur in the human soul from apathy to purpose, from despair to hope, from death to life, from self-rejection to self-affirmation; revolutions for freedom, independence, equality and justice occur in the soul of society, among suppressed races, bandaged peoples, and colonial nations. This is the era in human history when the vision of the prophets no longer appeared to be totally remote: "Every valley . . . lifted up, and every mountain and hill . . . made low, the crooked made straight, and the rough way made smooth . . . and all flesh shall see the salvation of God."

So my conversion was a crisis of faith, the pivotal struggle in a human soul as to who prevails: Christ or culture, God or human, Jesus Christ as Sovereign Will or a people's will. Who is the ultimate reference point and the ground of our being? I experienced in my conversion the pain and loneliness and austerity of the gospel, the Sovereign Lord Who brooks no rivals, for He alone is God. My father was the first to sense this; he was losing his son to a higher loyalty and a deeper devotion beyond himself, and he couldn't tolerate that, and swords were drawn "father against son," a wedge was thrust in the form of a cross, and never again would I belong to him as I had, for I now belonged to the Ultimate Owner of my soul.

II

If my spiritual pilgrimage is a sign of the pilgrimage of the church, then the events of one congregation living in these apocalyptic times have some meaning for us all. The story of the First Baptist Church of Chicago is one of the most intriguing in the annals of American Baptist history. A historic church, facing possible demise, resorts to an act of madness, calling a Japanese American minister in wartime, when Pearl Harbor and Iwo Jima associated anything Japanese with infamy and treachery; and the church whose death knell seemed sounded by that act, had the brazen audacity to come to life, and a flourishing life at that.

Even those whose ultimate criterion was in "The Book of Numbers" were impressed. Pews filled, budget quadrupled, building renovated, multiple staff, high giver to the World Mission Campaign, and the church even developed a great choir. Dr. Samuel Kincheloe, the dean of church analysts, reported to the congregation: "Seven years ago I said this church would die. By every criterion of analysis this church should have died, unless a miracle of God occurred; and today I am happy to say that a miracle of God has actually occurred!" We received honors from the denomination, the City's Commission and the Governor's Commission on Human

Relations, and no church in Chicago received such a wide and regular press coverage as the First Baptist Church.

But just as the clown and comic are a disguise of human tragedy and triumph, bearing the weight of centuries and finding ways of turning tears into laughter, so the romantic story of this congregation concealed an agonizing struggle of historic proportions. For behind the lovely facade of a white church calling a non-white minister were centuries of human anguish telescoped into a moment of time. We knew white people could minister to non-white people as centuries of the missionary movement had proven, but we didn't know that non-whites, a non-white pastor, could minister to a white congregation. Preach perhaps, but could he perform the intimate pastoral ministries—visiting the sick, marrying the young and burying the dead, especially before a sensitive public. "We who know him are willing to accept his ministry," they said, "but how can we attract and convince new Caucasian prospects to join our church so that we can grow?" . . . even though the church had not grown in the past years even under white ministers. They said, "He speaks as well as an American, preaches like one, eats and dresses like one, but he doesn't look American—he looks Japanese!"

This was striking at a core of the human struggle in which Western civilization and its mythology of preeminence comes into collision with the values of the gospel in which the least may enter the Kingdom; and the first may be last and the last first. The issue was whether the church was to be shaped by the culture, or whether it would stand against the culture or above the culture, or stand at least in ambiguous paradox; or whether the church in its practice become a sign of the Kingdom and transform the culture toward the New Creation.

I bore the popular mythology of an "inscrutable Oriental" whose courtesy concealed hidden treachery, for General DeWitt of the Western Defense Command was saying "A Jap will always be a Jap—he can't be trusted!"; and acts of subversion and sabotage by Japanese Americans were being reported regularly through the press and radio, despite the fact that not a single case had been reported by the naval and military intelligence nor by the FBI. Yet, I was called to be pastor of the First Baptist Church of Chicago.

A gentle descendant of the Mayflower found it hard to accept her pastor and maintained her distance and refused to speak to him for the first six months. Twelve years later she found it hard to lose her pastor, and refused to speak to him because he had resigned. "When I first saw you in our pulpit," said an executive of the Crane Company, "the thought which went through my mind was, 'Every Japanese American should be lined up against the wall and shot by a firing squad.'" But over the succeeding years this same Japanese American and his family were frequent guests at his summer cottage located ironically in a racially pure summer community, whose purity was now permanently defiled!

A truck driver for the American Express Company couldn't quite bear the social anxiety of outside friends attending his daughter's wedding performed by their Japanese American pastor, so they invited a neighboring white clergyman to conduct the ceremony. But when the Donelleys of the Lakeside Press, one of Chicago's leading families, each time a member of their family died, and with the funeral attended by some of the city's leading citizens, without question had their Japanese American pastor conduct the service, never again was the question raised; the social umbilical cord of a thousand years was forever severed.

The casual observer saw a sanctuary full of nice people every Sunday. But who were these people? Caucasians, Japanese Americans, and Blacks, the most incredible mixture to comprise a congregation twenty-five years ago. The Japanese Americans had come through the trauma of collective indictment, treated as enemy aliens by their country, placed in public custody in concentration camps, and lost even their right to defend their nation against a common enemy. Yet these custodial inmates volunteered from behind barbed wire fences and organized themselves into the 442nd Infantry Battalion, and on the battlefields of Europe became the most decorated unit in American history.

Each Sunday, these Japanese Americans and these Black Americans who endured the stripes of humiliation for on hundred years and more, and these white Americans: three historically separated peoples risked physical proximity in the pews and spiritual affinity in their prayers and social community as they reached out to each other for forgiveness and love. Then on Wednesday nights as they broke bread together, it seemed like centuries of human hostilities dissolved in tears of common identity as a new race, a new priesthood, a new nation, God's own people.

We had Southern Baptists who survived the trauma of being greeted by Black ushers and remained and joined the church to become some of our finest members, and I valued them especially because they invariably tithed!

On his last day with us a young man from Louisiana, just graduated from medical school in Chicago, accompanied me as I made pastoral calls, some in Black homes on the South Side. And as we bade farewell, the young Southern doctor's eyes filled with tears as he said, "I wouldn't exchange all the gold in Fort Knox for the experience I had today."

Perhaps the most sacred experience revolved around our Black members, who constituted some of our leading professional and business people in the church. I will always cherish the kind of trust and confidence they placed in me, undeserved but as a gift of grace, to be willing and courageous to open up the dammed up inferno of centuries, and let it pour out like molten lava: fears and hates and hopes and dreams in one torrential outburst, searing and redeeming, burning and cleansing, torturing and healing. A brilliant Black scientist, a highly respected citizen in Chicago, who as a youth knew what it meant to hide from a lynch mob, whose anger at prejudice mounted as he rose in social mobility, spilled out like vomit in a moment of tortured and irrepressible anguish, "Pastor, today I almost killed my white colleague! I couldn't stand his white arrogance, his insulting affront to my dignity and worth!"

I shall always treasure the moments when human souls reached out to show their enormous capacity to embrace me in their confidence, to share so lavishly of their trust, to risk their innermost thoughts without fear, when they had every reason to mistrust. That's one of the incredible miracles of history, a mark of the divine nature of life, that a Black man in America can trust anybody.

These stormy years have shaken history to its foundations, but my faith in the church is undiminished. It's the one place I found to be "like the shade of a rock in a weary land." When historical events suddenly made us unwanted people to be avoided, it really wasn't the universities, the liberal press, the intellectuals, and the artists, not even the Supreme Court which came to our support: it was the church, and among the churches the American Baptists and the Quakers were the first to lay their commitment on the line without waiting to see what others would do; and when another historical crisis should arise and suddenly a people is left adrift, one group of Americans they can count on, that I will count on, is the church!

It would be inappropriate to mention names, for they are too numerous to risk omission; but they were magnificent in their courage, heroic in unlikely and unexpected places, and they came from the whole wide theological spectrum of fundamentalists, conservatives, and liberals. Courage has a way of crossing theological partisanships, and no brand of American Baptists seem to have a proprietary ownership on nobility and integrity. And my ecumenical colleagues have wondered why I have never apologized for being an American Baptist!

The church is a sign and witness in history of God's eschatological future, and the gates of Hell and death shall not prevail against it, because of the One to Whom it bears witness, in Whom alone is hope for the church and the world, for "There is none other name under heaven given among men whereby we must be saved."

III

If my spiritual pilgrimage has wrestled with the crisis of faith, as to who prevails as ultimate reality, and with the crisis of love, as to whether love can prevail against impossible odds; today I face the crisis of hope, whether there is an open future for the world. Personal destiny was the issue of my conversion; the meaning of church community was the issue of my incorporation into the Body of Christ; the meaning of history and the future of the world is an absorbing issue of my relation and mission to the world.

When in human history has apocalypse seemed so near, and when has finitude and limitation of the planet so troubled the human consciousness, or the issue of planetary survival entered the human agenda? And what does the gospel say to that, and how does theology of missionary strategy cope with this?

When has there been such an erosion of integrity, lawlessness in high places, the absence of greatness and the prevalence of mediocrity? Is the church to remain aloof, and is there no word of hope of a new future of greatness and nobility? Where are the heroic spirits, the Olympian characters, with majesty to embrace the world, and spiritual capacity for transcendence?

Is there no connection between the quality of life in the church and the quality of excellence in the world? Personal and private sins of lawless individuals are bad enough, but how about corporate evil, collective transgression, institutional sin against God and man of a lawless system? Is there no need for institutional confession and systemic repentance before God and the moral tribunal of the world, and before events have wrenched a reluctant confession?

Can the church live only for itself, its own salvation, its own survival, its own identity and rule, living in the shelter of its own parochial cave? We need our shelter and our cave, but we're also made for horizons and hopes to explore the whole world landscape; and the future and destiny of the whole world is the concern of the gospel and the purpose for which the church exists in mission.

The fate of my soul was the urgent, compelling issue of my life as a boy. The fate of the world and the fate of the planet confront us today with equal insistent spiritual urgency; and there must be and there is a word of hope from Jesus Christ. The realization of community in the life of the church was the compelling challenge we faced in Chicago. But the realization of community in the world, of Spaceship Earth and Global Village, is not only one moral option but the only moral option if the world is to survive. And what is true for the church is true for the world; unity and community, reconciliation and hope, come to congruent coherence only in Jesus Christ, for "In Him alone all things hold together."

This world I once feared, I love; which I once rejected, I affirm; from which I wished to be rescued, I want to be identified; for which I had no hope, I now live with expectant hope; which I regarded as hopelessly corrupt, I now regard as possible of transformation. This is our Father's world, the world He created and peopled and loved and died for and rose again; the world He is refashioning and renewing toward the New Creation. The gospel is the incredible Good News about God and the world, His vision and purpose, His plan and action, creation, redemption, and consummation. The parameters of His grace and judgment embrace not only the world but the whole cosmos' history and nature, so that the divine-human enterprise which began in the Garden will consummate in a New Heaven and a New Earth, and the final victorious outcome we have been assured by the resurrection of Jesus Christ from the dead. To a nation suffering erosion of hope, this is our vision of hope, that He Who has triumphed over the principalities and powers and put all things under His feet "in the fullness of time will unite all things in Him—things in heaven and things on earth, and every tongue confess that Jesus Christ is 'lord, to the glory of God the Father.'"

The preacher is a steward of that gospel, the teller of the Good News, the Christian philosophy of history, the eschatological message of hope, dealing with world destiny and cosmic consummation. Therefore, the preacher is the indispensable person in the human community. It's the preacher who has kept alive the central understanding of reality as a theological enterprise, that history is a divine human encounter, and the scene and arena in which God is working out His purpose, a purpose which has a Beginning and an End, in which the Exodus and the Christ Event loom as pivotal events, as signs of eternity in time. Whatever we say about the ministry of the clergy, this theological perception of reality would long ago have disappeared from human consciousness without the constant retelling of the story through word and sacrament, from the largest and tiniest little churches and pulpits in every land around the world. The ecclesiastical structures with the clergy as the prime actors keep alive that meaning, that memory and remembrance of the One "in Whom alone we live and move and have our being," "the One in Whom all things hold together," "that Name which is above every name."

No one is more essential than the minister, not only as preacher and theologian but as pastoral manager of the laity. Who has such access to the deepest levels of the human spirit as the pastor as spiritual counselor? Who has within their available pastoral management the rich resources, the enormous professional capabilities, the gifts and talents, commitments and dedication, of laity from every sector of the whole cultural spectrum, not legally coerced or financially bought, but voluntarily given by self-determining free spirits who choose to participate in the church?

Who but pastors deal with men and women in issues of ultimate meaning, personal and corporate accountability to God and neighbor, interpret time in the light of eternity, bring political and economic policies under the scrutiny of the gospel? And who but the preacher of the gospel would dare the prophetic word that corporations and governments are accountable to Almighty God, that they exist not for the sake of themselves but for the sake of the world, that the arrogance of power God will judge, that God has put down and will put down the mighty from their thrones and exalt those of low degree, that power is a trust and stewardship to be shared with equity and justice?

The pastor is not an expert in economics, politics, medicine, or the arts. They don't have to be. The mark of a good manager is to work with men and women more capable than them, better educated than them, more brilliant than them, who know far more than they do; rejoice and affirm and exploit and maximize their capabilities and weld their total powers, lured by a common vision into a singular purpose of God's mission of social change and reshaping of history toward the creation of a new social order under the governance of Jesus Christ.

We all have different hopes: self-fulfillment and success, to see our children make it, achieve security or power or position, to be affirmed and respected and loved, which are all legitimate hopes. But my overriding ambition and longing and hope is not for myself or my children or my family, but for my American Baptist ministerial colleagues to awaken to a new consciousness and a new sense of self-identity as preachers of the gospel, as theologians dealing with Ultimate Realities, and as pastoral managers forging lay people into teams of moral power and spiritual vision, and turning them loose in the world to become architects and builders of a New Age, as disciples and co-workers of the Lord of history, Jesus Christ!

"I Know Who I Am"*

FRANK ICHISHITA†

I learned about President Franklin Roosevelt's Executive Order No. 9066 of 1942 from a white playmate. He said that because I am a Japanese American, I would have to go away to a "relocation" camp. I said I wasn't going. But he was right. I had to go. But why?

Once, after I made a speech to a suburban white group, a lady commented, "You speak such good English!" Why was my diction so remarkable to her?

I am and have been the pastor of churches where most of the members are black. One of my fellow pastors once said that I had to make a choice between identifying myself as a white or a black person. He was afraid, given the congregation I was serving at the time, that I had made the wrong choice. Why did he feel I had to make this choice?

The answers to these questions may be found in one basic fact: the overriding ethnic concern in this country has always been between black and white. Anyone who does not fit neatly into one of these two fundamental American categories is automatically assigned to a third category of "foreigner."

As a Japanese American, I am neither black nor white. Thus, despite the fact that America is my native land, I am seen essentially as a foreigner. At best, I remain an honored guest. When I work hard, keep a low profile, and make myself useful to the larger society, I am accepted as a positive asset (a touch of the charming Orient in our midst). The role of honored guest, however, is not a secure one, as Japanese Americans found out during World War II. I am a foreigner in a land whose caste system is determined by whether one's skin is black or white. I am a member of an American ethnic anomaly that forms a third corner to the basic black/white gut issue at the very heart of this nation.

Do I, therefore, have an identity problem? No. I know who I am. I am, first, a child of God. Secondly, I am a native son of this land. Thirdly, I carry in my soul a measure of the heritage of Japan, and that is precious to me. And finally, I am not white and have no desire to be.

The last point is vitally important. In our society, anyone who is white or identifies with white, even though he is nonwhite, becomes captive to this nation's history. To that extent he is saddled with the burden of being white: the guilt over slavery and its aftermath of inherent racism. I, not being white, have not been the

---

* March/April 1973.
† Mr. lchishita was pastor of the Peoples United Presbyterian Church, Denver, Colorado.

oppressor, nor am I now the enemy. That makes me free, a truth that came to me as I chose to involve myself in the cause of human rights, especially with black people.

White people can be free and are free, to the extent that they acknowledge their guilt, repent of it, and become involved in the struggle for human rights. But I am already free, through choice and ethnic makeup. This is a source of great joy and liberation for me. There are those who assume that I would find my "Asian-ness" to be a problem to me in this land. But it isn't. I find it to be a great and wonderful feeling.

My entire ministry has been spent with black people. I got into the ministry because I, being a country kid, fell in love with the city when I attended the University of Chicago and McCormick Theological Seminary. I then determined to do social work in the city, which quite naturally put me into contact with black people. But to be honest, I also fell into this kind of ministry because there was no real market for Asians in white churches. In the black churches I have served, I have been received openly and honestly and with joy. Why? I think it is because I come without the burden of being the oppressor, and because I come as a nonwhite who has suffered because of his non-whiteness. I am therefore able to share in and empathize with the experience of human suffering in an atmosphere of commitment and trust. Of course, that's what an authentic ministry is all about anyway. White people, if they put their heart and soul into it, may do this just as well, for it is not basically a matter of color. It is a matter of empathy, sharing, commitment, and trust. And it is on this basis that my own ministry has been a joy beyond compare.

I would also like to make a few comments about American society based on my own life experience. It seems to me that the melting pot concept was valid only if one was white. Blacks were kept out entirely and other nonwhites were invited in gingerly so as not to disturb the basic mix. As long as this concept prevails, the society is in trouble. I would rather see our society as a tossed salad, where no one need lose his identity by blending into a mass. Rather, each keeps his own individuality, which becomes his specific contribution to the whole. And there is no order of importance for the ingredients of a salad! Nor is the size of the individual ingredients a problem, because a touch of this and a touch of that improves the taste of the whole.

Margaret Mead and others have described a global village in which every person on earth is a neighbor to every other. Our American society is already such a village, for what other nation can boast the racial mix that is ours? But it has not yet become a humane and just society, a "tossed salad." There is urgency in this. How this nation works out its present racial and ethnic tensions will determine not only its own health, but the health of the whole "global village."

As little children we used to sing,
Red and yellow, black, and white,
They are precious in his sight;
Jesus loves the little children of the world.

With apologies to the browns, for they belong in there too, is this not a living vision of what our land, and indeed the world, must be?

The Asian American
Bi-Cultural Experience*

Donna Dong

I was Chinese American, whatever that meant. That I was not an individual, not just a human being. Just a human being in this culture, in this society, is a white man, he can disappear. I couldn't disappear, no matter how enlightened I was, no matter how straight my English was. Someone, just because they saw my skin color, would detect an accent. Someone would always correct me. And well, then I began to look at my writing, what I'd been writing about in my letters and everything was just to this point. The Chinese American, well, schizophrenia. That I'd been playing a kind of ping-pong game, you know. Now I'm Chinese, now I'm American. But up against real Chinese . . . I saw that I had nothing in common with them. That they didn't understand me, and I didn't understand them. We both use chopsticks okay, that's recognizable. But that's mechanics, not culture.[1]

Last night Roy Sano directed us to the consideration of the reality of racism and the emergence of liberation theology. In considering Asian American Problems and Possibilities, especially from the viewpoint of Chinese Americans, I choose as my starting point a unique experience of Asian Americans: the attempt to integrate the lifestyles of two different cultures, the problems and possibilities connected with this attempt.

On paper this experience looks like this:

---

* April 20, 1974.

[1] Victor G. Nee and Brett DeBary Nee, *Longtime Californ': A Documentary Study of an American Chinatown* (New York: Pantheon Books, 1973), 383.

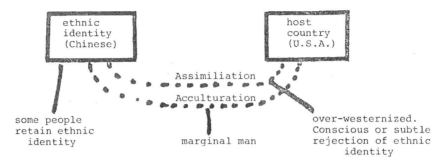

Bicultural individuals face the demands of two cultures; in the case of Chinese Americans the way of life of the host country, the United States, and the way of life of the ethnic identity, the traditional Chinese way of life. There is a whole spectrum of responses that individuals have made to this double demand. Some, by insulation from the culture of the host society, have managed to retain their ethnic identity. Others have so accommodated themselves to the culture of the host society that they have consciously or subtly rejected their Chinese identity, thereby becoming over-Westernized. They have undergone what we call "assimilation." Still others walk the precarious path of "acculturation," with one foot each in the two cultures, very much the marginal men and women who can no longer identify with any one culture.

This is what the bicultural experience looks like on paper. However, confrontations between two cultures do not happen on paper. Cultures are not abstract entities that stand eyeball to eyeball and slug it out. Concretely, only a person can be in conflict within himself over different cultural beliefs and behaviors; only people in society in conflict with one another, and only societies of people in conflict with one another.

Frank Chin, whom I quoted at the very beginning of this talk, illustrates what this cultural conflict is like on the blood and guts level. Let me quote him further:

> I identify with my father. My father tried, in his own way he tried as hard as I am to make it in his terms in this country. Yeah, I think he failed and I think he thinks he's failed. But in his eyes I'm irresponsible. I'm fooling around and I'm an insult to him. . . .
>
> We live in different worlds. And when my world comes in contact with his we just destroy each other. I look at the way he tunes the television set, it's all wrong. The people look like they're dead. They come on looking dingy, gray, the color of Roquefort cheese. But that's the way he sees the world. And he lives in Chinatown, so it's in Chinatown, his world. And he can't see that it's partly my world, too. So you know, I'll never have his respect. And I could win a Nobel Prize, you know, and prove that my writing's been worthwhile and he'll say, "You dress like a bum." And then I see that I've broken the guy's heart. So I feel bad about that.[2]

This internal struggle of being a Chinese American is a serious problem because it hits the closest to the person. It touches his or her identity, the self-image, the self-worth. Identity, then, is inseparably tied to culture, that is, to language and manner of thought and mode of behavior.

---

[2] Nee and Nee, *Longtime Californ'*, 388.

The Persistence of the Bicultural Experience

The bicultural problem will continue in the United States for Chinese Americans. On one hand, this is due to the high visibility of Asians in a predominantly white society. As Frank Chin described it, it is impossible to melt like a white man into the superculture. The interesting thing is that a book like Michael Novak's *The Rise of the Unmeltable Ethnics* describes the tenacity of such white ethnics like the Poles, Italians, Greeks, and Slavs to persist in the American society.

For the Chinese American community in the United States, the bicultural identity will persist because of a new major wave of Chinese immigration after 1956, when the immigration quota for Chinese was finally raised on par with other national quotas. In the ten-year period between 1960 and 1970, there were 126,437 Chinese immigrants, 77.5% of them emigrating after 1965. That has meant for my home community of San Francisco an increase of 61.1% in the Chinese population during the ten-year period and a revitalization of San Francisco's Chinatown, with urgent new needs in housing, employment, and bilingual education.

Challenge to the Chinese Churches

How can individual Christians, the local church, and the United Church of Christ as a whole respond to the problem of Asian American bicultural identity and offshoots of that problem? We know that our Lord Jesus Christ caught men and women alive when He went fishing. He restored identity to alienated people. The church that belongs to Christ must also participate in the task of giving life, restoring identity, affirming worth. What does this mean concretely?

We have already suggested that the identity problem will persist for Chinese Americans because of the high visibility of being Asians in the United States. We then need to ensure that the visibility is an accurate one. That is, we need to eliminate stereotypes of Chinese that are presented in media to the American public and to familiarize the public with the real situation. One member of my home church, the UCC Chinese Congregational Church in San Francisco is a member of the Chinese Media Committee and has participated with the Committee to remove objectionable TV ads from local network viewing. He has also been key to getting *Yut Yee Sahm, Here We Come*, a bilingual and bicultural TV project, produced for children. Our local congregation and the entire United Church of Christ should follow him into his work and support him there.

With the increased influx of Chinese immigrants, ethnic church ministry and bilingual worship services continue to be a necessity for Chinese American churches. As we have stated earlier, language is inseparably tied in with culture; erase the language, and you'll lose the culture and imperil the identity. Recently, the Supreme Court took action on the Lau versus Nichols case that will affect the Chinese in San Francisco. The Court ruled that a large number of Chinese children in San Francisco were not being granted an equal education because they were receiving instruction only in English when many were literate only in Chinese. The church needs to be actively aware and involved in situations such as the above.

Another challenge to the Chinese American church is pastoral counseling with sensitivity to Chinese American problems, problems like interracial dating and the conflicts involved in two sets of ideas about family structure and dynamics.

The Bicultural Experience: A Possibility

We have talked at great length about some Asian American problems, as highlighted from the Chinese American community. We also need to talk about a positive possibility. For example, we have talked about the possibility of an Asian American theology. I think there is a real contribution that the Asian American bicultural experience, with all of its tensions and identity stresses, can make to illuminate the Christian experience and lifestyle, to throw light on the life of our Lord Jesus Christ. Richard Wright, in his book *White Man, Listen!*, dedicates his book to bicultural people, whom he describes as

> The Westernized and Tragic Elite of Asia, Africa, and the West Indies—
> The lonely outsiders who exist precariously on the cliff-like margins of many cultures—men who are distrusted, misunderstood, maligned, criticized by Left and Right, Christian and pagan men who carry on their frail but indefatigable shoulders the best of two worlds—and who amidst confusion and stagnation, seek desperately for a home for their hearts; a home which, if found, could be a home for the hearts of all men.[3]

Chinese Americans are lonely outsiders who exist precariously on the cliff-like margins of two cultures. They cannot be identified with either culture and are extremely vulnerable to charges and self-doubts about having "sold out" or having become "bananas"—yellow on the outside, white on the inside. This sheds light on the Christian lifestyle, where Christians, like their Lord, have been misunderstood and maligned, not fitting into old packages, because they have given themselves to larger allegiances. Some would love to claim Jesus exclusively for the side of the oppressed, the poor, the ethnic minorities. But it is the same Jesus, who bigger than a possible identification with any one camp, invites himself home to dinner with Zacchaeus, the sellout who has become a tool for Roman imperialism—a tax collector—who uses his office to exploit his people. He has come to save Zacchaeus as well. Jesus could not be boxed in, and Chinese Americans, spilling out their identification with either of their two cultural heritages, cannot be boxed in either. This can be our contribution to an intimate understanding of the Christian lifestyle we are called to.

Summary

My time is up. What I have been trying to say is that there are problems in the Chinese American community that arises from our bicultural experience, that this problem will not disappear overnight, and that in fact, with the problem comes a possibility, a great promise. It's okay to be Chinese American.

---

[3] Paul Clasper, *The Yogi, the Commissar, and the Third-World Church* (Valley Forge, PA: Judson Press, 1972), 47.

The Role of Religion
in Asian American Communities

WILLIAM MAMORU SHINTO

In the early years of Asian American Studies at California State University at Long Beach, I taught classes in Asian religions in America. Although students had mixed motives for attending, the prevailing one was a spiritual quest rather than academic curiosity. Their search was taking place in the midst of a vast rejection of religious institutions; consequently, only a few were active in a church or temple.

The general attitude at the beginning of each course was a fascination for Asian faiths, particularly Buddhism. Some practiced meditation and even claimed to be converts of Asian religions. Most of the students began with a denial that they had a value system based on religious beliefs. Conversely, they insisted, though, that they believed in some "essence of religion" which would provide guidelines in a chaotic world, at that time fraught with racial strife, the Vietnam War, and vast generational gaps. There was also a student consensus of rejecting Christianity as irrelevant. However, by the end of the term most students admitted that American Protestantism had and continues to have an impact on their lives and that their understanding of Asian faiths was, indeed, superficial.

My teaching method was to help students bring to the surface their own feelings and to become conscious of their own value systems. Though none advanced much beyond a belief in some "essence of religion," they gained a sense of the complexities of theology. They left class with an uneasiness about the possibility of syncretizing religious faiths into some universal value system.

From these encounters with students, both Asian and non-Asian, and in long conversations with many, I am convinced that this college generation is as deeply interested in religion as any other generation in American history. Asian American students on the whole also share this concern for at least two reasons. First, their search for cultural roots leads them directly into the sphere of their heritage of Asian religions. Secondly, Asian American students by and large express their religious life through either a faith such as Buddhism, which is considered as alien by the larger society or a "borrowed" faith with Judeo-Christian roots.

Though generally unrecognized religion has played a large role in the shaping of most Asian American communities because the church and temple have been one of the key institutions in these communities. However, for this generation of Asian Americans, one of the unforeseen consequences of fighting for their legitimate rights as Asian Americans has been the breaking away from rather isolated but close-knit

Asian American communities and moving into the general "mainstream" of American society. Thus whatever earlier influence religion had on their lives while living in an Asian American community appears to have disappeared with their leaving that setting. The church and temple no longer play a key role in their lives.

Nonetheless, as one traces more deeply the impact of religion, it becomes apparent that it has played a large role in the shaping and conduct of most Asian American communities, but because of a peculiarly "Western" circumstance, it has not become a major concern either of the Asian American movement or ethnic studies. In the midst of intense concern about the problems of race and nation we are rapidly becoming more conscious of making distinctions between races and questioning the economic and political factors that make each group distinct. When meeting a person therefore we now make immediate observations of differences of language, race, and color. Surjit Singh notes however that, "These are the things that strike us first. We do not start by noticing that other people whom we happen to meet have another God."[1] The religious factor, which is largely ignored by the Western world in academic circles, cannot long go unrecognized if we want to understand ethnic communities.

Contributing to our ignorance of the impact of religion on our society are three major factors. First, the separation of church and state is a basic constitutional principle in the United States. The second factor is the rapid displacement of the church from a position of power in the American establishment. The immigrant nature of American society, the rapid growth of population, and high mobility in an industrialized society have contributed to this displacement. Up to this point in history, religious traditions have been family-centered and rooted in small rural communities. When immigrants leave this stable though at times static situation and find themselves in an extremely mobile, urban setting, they drop their earlier institutional ties rather easily. For the Asians, the fact that their religious roots may have been dramatically different from the Protestant base in America also added to their estrangement from earlier religious ties.

The third factor is the assumed irrelevancy of religion today. However, it is unnecessarily harsh to blame the religious congregations for not making religion relevant. The plain fact is that we all live in a new situation. Hendrik Kraemer stated this bluntly:

> All religions without exception are functioning in coalescence with forms of social structure which are frameworks of a society of the past, or at any rate of a type of society which is passing away. . . . Therefore all religions face the same huge proposition of achieving a break with their own social past . . . It is an emigration towards and immigration into a wholly different world.[2]

---

[1] Surjit Singh, "Nation and Race," in *Biblical Authority for Today: A World Council of Churches Symposium on "The Biblical Authority for the Churches' Social and Political Message Today,"* ed. Alan Richardson and W. Schweitzer (Philadelphia: Westminster Press, 1951), 311.

[2] Hendrik Kraemer, *World Cultures and World Religions* (Philadelphia: Westminster Press, 1960), 349.

In fact, the issue is not whether religion is relevant but rather is any present form of religion anything more than a relic of the past? Is it now divorced from any human activity?

How then do we begin to make sense out of the religious impact on Asian American communities? My analysis of the role of religion in these communities will be divided into three parts: first, the religious institutions—the expressions of churches and temples; second, the professionals—clergy and priests; third, the philosophical basis—the religious quest.

I. Institutional Religions

Religious organizations in the Asian American communities are basically groups composed of Asian Americans who are sponsored by larger outside organizations. For the Christians, their sponsors were predominately white American churches, while for the Buddhist, theirs were in Asia. The following examples are largely about the Japanese American, which is my own experience. However, much of what applied to one group is a key issue among another.

The influence of the larger Christian organizations on the Asian American communities began abroad with American overseas missionary activities that then continued in the United States. These missionaries, in setting up their missions overseas, focused much of their efforts on China, which resulted in the establishment of many churches and schools. To this day, older Chinese Americans are the descendants of these Christian missions. In the Japanese American communities, mission-sponsored ethnic churches were also established. However, in both the Chinese and Japanese communities in the United States, Christians remain a minority.

This, however, is not the case for the Koreans in America. The early Christian missions, especially the Presbyterian and the Methodist, have been so effective that the predominant groups in the Korean American community are mission products with strong Christian ties. In many ways, the Pacific Islanders also parallel the Korean situation. Exerting much effort, missionaries converted whole islands to Christianity so that today in the Fijian and Samoan communities, for example, the church is a key institution. The Pilipino situation is the most complex with successive cultural invasions of Islam, Roman Catholicism, and American Protestantism.

The Christian missionary efforts coupled with those of the Buddhist and other Asian faiths created a significant network of religious institutions in Asian American communities. These institutions became an integral part of Asian American life. Though little research has been done in this important area, the history of these religious institutions parallels the history of Asian Americans.

Just to mention briefly two examples. Among the Japanese the first Christian group to form was composed of eight young men who in 1877 organized *Fukuin Kai* (the Gospel Society) in San Francisco. Gradually, networks of Protestant churches were established throughout the United States by various denominational groups. And even as late as the 1960s and early '70s the church, though indirectly, was involved in the ethnic movements. Many of the *Sansei* who participated in the Asian

American movement attended Christian Sunday schools and conferences in their formative years.

As for the Buddhists, the Hompa Hongwanji of the Jodo Shinshu Sect of Kyoto, Japan, in 1898 sent two priests to America to investigate the possibility of establishing a mission. From this modest beginning, the Buddhist sect has now grown into the Buddhist Churches of America, a large and well-organized network of sixty temples and forty branches. And many of the activist *Sansei* have also participated in Buddhist activities.

The main reasons for establishing Christian churches in the early period still hold true today. The primary purpose was the *Issei* need for companionship and mutual support while living in a hostile and alien society. This need for a cultural haven was and continues to be a major, if not overriding, reason for the existence of churches. Here, they also could continue their cultural practices, such as celebrating their Japanese holidays. One major role in the early churches was providing English language classes.

A second purpose was to impart a "moral" influence on the lives of the *Issei* living in an unstable frontier society. Regrettably, the puritanical views of the conservative missionaries in the early period have left its mark on the churches. In fact, these views give many *Sansei* a negative image of the church, a point to which I will return later in this essay. Another reason was to find a way to be identified quickly as American rather than to bear the burden of continually being labeled as "alien." *Issei* assumed that one quick, acceptable way was to convert to Christianity, the principal faith of the new land. And though of least importance, another reason was the desire to promote Christianity.

The Christian churches, however, paradoxically became a place to acculturate the Japanese to American life. While a pastor in Los Angeles, I noticed that many children of Buddhist families enrolled in our church school. I believe that many did this so that their children could learn about Christianity, the religion of the West, in hope of mitigating White racism.

Buddhism, on the other hand, has had to fight the image of being a foreign faith. Although the hostility to the religion itself is now tempered, this was not always the case. For example, at the beginning of World War II, Buddhist priests in America were jailed as enemy agents. In fact, one of the key issues still to be resolved is the public recognition that Buddhists are indeed American and their faith is not alien.

In addition to the missionizing efforts of the religious groups, they also championed for the rights of Asians in America. In the early years of Chinese immigration the Christian missionaries fought many court battles and argued in many city halls for the rights of the Chinese. Also, immediately after Pearl Harbor white church organizations and their spokespersons were at the forefront opposing the forced evacuation of the Japanese Americans. Moreover, the churches provided educational opportunities for many Asian Americans and contributed to the high level of education among certain segments of these groups.

Notwithstanding the present struggle for community control and cultural pluralism, the history of the involvement of white churches in Asian American communities still needs to be told. Of course, this is not to gloss over the issues of white paternalism and the push for assimilation, but a wholesale rejection of white involvement in Asian American communities as negative seems to be both unwise and unfair.

What then is the future of the ethnic churches and temples? Among the older groups, principally the Japanese and the Chinese, there is growing anxiety for the future. In contrast, among groups with strong cultural ties and new immigration there is much optimism. For Asian Americans as a whole, the network of churches and temples cannot be ignored or overlooked. For good or ill, they persist in shaping Asian American life. My own pessimism in 1967 when I left the local congregation is now replaced by a firmer belief in the ethnic churches as vital and potentially positive centers of strength for the communities.

II. Religious Professionals

The role of the minister and priest in the Asian American communities has been and to some degree, continues to be an important one. Our communities are still largely interpersonal because of our small populations. When I first came to Southern California, after growing up in New Mexico and studying in the South, where few Asian Americans lived, I was literally dumbfounded by the relatively high status and degree of influence of ministers in the geographically dispersed Japanese American communities in such a large urban center as Los Angeles. Although the influence of the ministers is decreasing, it still continues to be significant.

Strangely, the activist ministers are accepted in both the "straight" as well as the "radical" communities. Moreover, they are able to move across class lines and to relate with their own ethnic communities as well as with the larger society with relative ease. In my own experience, I found that the ethnic congregations do not make the same heavy demands of their clergy to maintain a restricted ministry that white churches often do. This is probably because of the small size of most ethnic congregations and their assumption that the clergy has to operate on many levels, namely, with his/her own congregation, the surrounding community, other ethnic groups, and the larger white community. On the other hand, Asian American ministers at times seem to have more credibility in the Asian American community as a whole than with their own congregations.

One explanation for this peculiar situation is that the ministers and their congregations sometimes have different expectations of the ministry. The activist ministers view ministry beyond the bounds of the ethnic church, so that their community of trust is not limited to the gathered few but extends to those who espouse the same causes and concerns as they do.

Both Buddhism and Christianity are universal religions which seek the basic commonality of all humans. Asian American ministers as members of minority groups may seek their cultural heritage in the need for personal and group identity but at the same time critically view the parts of their respective cultures they consider not in harmony with their religion's commitment to the whole of humanity. Indeed, this humanistic worldview should take precedence over cultural differences.

Asian Americans come from different ethnic groups which should be seeking their specific cultural identity but without losing sight of the need for political unity among Asians in America. Yet it is precisely the conflict between cultural nationalism and Asian American unity which is the central issue in the Asian American movement. It is, for example, not realistic immediately to expect Koreans, who have suffered centuries of Japanese oppression, to easily "fit" into a single movement with the Japanese.

To continue, the clergy, at its best, sees the archaic sectarian fences erected by the churches as irrelevant and tries to persuade the churches to move to more deeply socially based ethics. In the church, a major dilemma is whether to maintain their sectarianism while emphasizing their otherworldliness, or to joint allies in the world to combat worldwide dehumanizing forces in order to conserve positive human values. This conflict in views on the role of the ministry and the church between some of the clergy and their congregations may largely explain the displeasure directed towards some of the activist ministers by some of the ethnic churches and the paradoxical acceptance of these ministers by the larger Asian American communities.

In fact, this fundamental difference of views has closed the doors of traditional church ministries to some of the clergy, and has opened other avenues for them to express their concern for the humanizing process of life. To this end, some of these ministers in order to better pursue their concern for social justice have left the institutional church and are now working outside the church in secular positions. Among my acquaintances are social workers, educators, and businessmen who are also ministers and priests but no longer work in the church.

But what of those who remain within the religious establishment? What are they doing? There is a new burst of activity and direction largely initiated by religions professionals who organized Asian American caucuses inside the major religious denominations. The "caucus" is a group of like-minded persons who bypass regular procedures to pressure the larger organizations to accept responsibility for caucus concerns. They claim the support of the local churches and their communities, but in fact the caucus acts *without* the consensus of the local congregations. It is an important breakthrough in asserting leadership on the basis of *values* rather than consensus. The initial impetus came from the organizing methods of the Asian American movement in its dealing with the educational and political establishments.

Within the Christian churches there are now firmly established caucuses among the United Methodist, United Presbyterian, American Baptist, Episcopal, and United Church of Christ (see Appendix I). One accomplishment of the Methodist caucus was the election of the first Asian American Bishop in The United Methodist Church, The Rev. Wilbur Choy, Seattle, Washington.

But the major impact is the renewed activity both within the congregations and the communities. Church funds have been granted to social activist groups and social service programs in the Asian American communities. Financial aid, new programs for recent immigrants and other projects are just beginning. Nonetheless, thorny questions are arising. Is the formation of the religious caucus within the church for the sake of survival or for a revitalized ministry? Will the layperson enthusiastically support the initiative of the clergy? Will the caucus movement with time become more establishment and "church-oriented" and not continue its outward stance towards the communities? The latter is already happening. Even in the changing of the names—almost all have dropped the word "caucus" (which in the eyes of white church administrators means "radical"). Furthermore, the white church leadership has insisted on a "consensus" presentation of the local congregational issues rather than an analysis of the total Asian American situation. The movement from "prophetic" to "domestication" is rapid.

Whether or not there will be a revitalized ministry mainly concerned with the question of social justice depends largely on another recent movement by some of the clergy within the church. The blacks, as in many other ethnic activities, began to redefine their theology by setting forth a "black theology of liberation." Similarly, a revolutionary theology is arising out of the Catholic churches in Latin America, while the Native Americans are championing their native religions. Among Asian Americans a similar move to redefine Christian theology is taking shape, especially on the part of The Rev. Dr. Roy Sano of the Pacific School of Religion and Director of the Asian Center for Theology and Strategies (ACTS) (see Appendix II).

In a capsule, although practitioners in any profession may daily function without a conscious philosophy of work, they gradually find themselves in deeper and deeper trouble because of a lack of clarity of purpose. The very existence of religious institutions, in this instance, the ethnic ministries, depends in the long run on a lucid theological foundation. The pessimism with the church and the uneasiness among the ethnic clergy is largely attributable to the lack of a real rationale for ministry.

For years ethnic churches have been viewed as appendages to the "real church" and ethnic ministers as "second rate." No organization or person can long function with creativity under that cloud. Only as a liberating process becomes effective will the clarity come for a positive and outreaching ministry.

The impact of the religious professionals, both inside the religious institutions and outside in the larger Asian American communities, has not been adequately noted or researched. With the rise of "secularized ministers" operating in situations outside the churches, the organized caucuses inside, and the growth of Asian American theologies, there is hope that the religious professionals in our midst will become more creative and relevant.

III. The Religious Quest

Although the manifestation of religious life through institutions and the professionals has a definite impact on Asian American communities, the major force is religion itself. The shape of Asian communities in America is rooted in both Asia, where religion, culture, and life cannot be easily separated, and America, where the society, including all levels of education, is permeated by Judeo-Christian concepts.

28 | WILLIAM MAMORU SHINTO

As for the latter, the persistence of influential groups demanding the restoration of prayer in public schools is but the tip of the iceberg. Much of law, psychology, medicine, economics, and politics continue to be shaped by Western Christian thought, and too often by a perversion of even that body of knowledge.

What is religion, then, and what is its future? One thing for certain, it is not simple. The persistence of seeking some uniform "essence of religion" is a true mark of ignorance and superficiality.

The more one penetrates different religions and understands them in the total, peculiar entity, the more one sees that they are worlds in themselves, with their own centres, axes and structures, not reducible to each other or to a common denominator, which expresses their inner core and makes them all translucent.[3]

One real consequence is the coming (actually already begun, but not consciously so) encounter among, at least, Buddhism, Maoism, and Judeo-Christian faiths. At base it is a religious encounter although it is discussed in economic, philosophical or technical terms. The Asian American stands in the peculiar position of being multicultural in the very middle of one of the most crucial religious dialogues in history.

The impact may not be immediately felt when one articulates this on such a world and universal scale. However, internally each Asian American, unless they have dogmatically asserted an identity from which they will not budge, will be affected. The religious factor has its deepest impact on the feelings and identity of persons. In the larger sense, the religious factors which influence and at times dictate the national values is one of the basic keys to how each nation will act out its economic and political life. Thus religion as an ideal/idea/faith/value commitment rather than in its purely institutional or professional form will be the real element which impacts all of our lives.

Religion performs both a practical and a theoretical function. It has a cosmology, an anthropology, and a view of the shape of the future; it answers the question about the origin of the world and of human society. From basic beliefs it derives humanity's duties and obligations, the personal and social ethics which pragmatically guide living. It is the substratum of ultimate concern out of which persons, groups, and whole nations work out of their destinies.

There are, for example, two very important ideas that may help clarify what religion and values are. Abraham Maslow, out of his psychological discipline, developed the idea of a "hierarchy of values" which ultimately finds the "basic values" (b-values) at the apex. [4] These are the absolutely final values that a human being affirms. One has reached his/her point of ultimate concern. Now the question is whether the specific cultural heritage contributes to such a b-value. In the case of Asia one of the persistent values in the interdependence of all living creatures and the natural world, in contradistinction to the prevailing Western concept of the

---

[3] Henrik Kraemer, *Religion and the Christian Faith* (Philadelphia: Westminster Press, 1956), 76.

[4] Abraham Maslow, *Motivation and Personality* (New York: Harper and Row, 1970).

independence of humans from nature and man's superiority over nature. In current ecological concerns, which "value" most clearly meets our needs? Which value most clearly is destructive? And, if the prevailing values are not positive ones, what is the educational process by which our society can move to a more humane and holistic life?

The other theoretical study which sheds much light for me are the works of Ernst Cassirer and Susane K. Langer, who surface the connection/framework underlying religion. They root their idea in the affirmation that humans are *animal symbolicum* rather than *animal rationale*.[5]

As compared with other animals, man lives not merely in a broader reality; he lives, so to speak, in a new dimension of reality . . .

No longer in a merely physical universe, man lives in a symbolic universe. Language, myth, art and religion are parts of this universe.[6]

Symbolic form and behavior are the most characteristic features of human life and the whole progress of human culture is based on these.

Furthermore, Susanne Langer is now articulating the basic idea that all symbol making is a result of "feeling" — which "includes the sensibility of very low animals and the whole realm of human awareness and thought, the sense of absurdity, the sense of justice, the perception of meaning, as well as emotion and sensation."[7] Upon this base she develops a philosophy of mind that has real ramifications for the understanding of religion as a human activity.

This line of investigation points to the need to rediscover the meaning of myth and symbol, language and intuitive thought. It is especially pertinent to undertake the study of the Asian religions, philosophy and life, specifically in China with the rise of Mao and the way in which the largest nation of the world underwent a complete revolution based upon both new ideas and directions and ancient cultural patterns and myth.

Needless to say the expansion of these ideas is both beyond the purpose of the article and my own competence, but the fact of religion as an integral part of human existence needs to become a major concern for us all.

For Asian Americans such robbing is especially important since the problem of self and cultural identity is on the forefront. To neglect religious roots and impact is to do irreparable damage to ourselves and our communities.

Epilogue

The illusiveness of the concept of religion and the difficulty in assessing its impact is apparent. The following Chinese verse from the eighth century may help us gain some insight:

---

[5] Ernst Cassirer, *An Essay on Man* (Garden City, NY: Doubleday, 1944), 44; cf. Susanne Langer, *Philosophy in a New Key* (New York: Pelican Books, 1948).

[6] Cassirer, *An Essay on Man*, 44. Cassirer's major work in this area is his three-volume *The Philosophy of Symbolic Form*.

[7] Susanne K. Langer, *Mind: An Essay on Human Feeling*, vol. 1 (Baltimore: John Hopkins University Press, 1967), 55.

The wild geese fly across the long sky above.
Their image is reflected upon the chilly water below.
The geese do not mean to cast their image on the water;
Nor does the water mean to hold the image of the geese.[8]

It is the unintentionality of mutual interaction which is the point. Yet, the flight of the geese and the image or the water is an existential moment of beauty and creation for one who reflects upon the whole scene. One major contribution of the Asian American is to discover anew the refreshing and renewing moments which emerge out of the interaction of nature, humanity, and the internal integration of the whole person.

Appendix I: Asian American Church Organizations (Protestant)
Asiamerica Ministry, Executive Council of the Episcopal Church
The Rev. Winston W. Ching, Director
815 Second Avenue
New York, New York 10017

Asian American Baptist Caucus
The Rev. Dr. Paul M. Nagano, Director
901 East Spruce Street
Seattle, Washington 98122

Asian Presbyterian Council, United Presbyterian Church, USA
The Rev. Dr. Lester Kim, Chairman
P. O. Box 2769
Rolling Hills Estate, California 90274

The Rev. Phil Park, National Staff
Room 1244, 475 Riverside Drive
New York, New York 10027

National Federation of Asian American United Methodists
The Rev. Jonah J. Chang, Director
330 Ellis Street
Room 508
San Francisco, California 94102

Pacific and Asian American Ministry (PAAM), United Church of Christ
The Rev. Harold Jow, Chairman
467 North Judd Street
Honolulu, Hawaii 96817

---

[8] Chang Chung-yuan, *Creativity and Taoism: A Study of Chinese Philosophy, Art, and Poetry* (New York: Harper Colophon Books, 1963), 57.

PAAM Newsletter
c/o Montebello Plymouth Congregational Church
144 South Greenwood Avenue
Montebello, California 90640

The organizations listed above are those of the "mainline denominations." They are also, in some cases, umbrella organizations for regional groups. All of them to some degree or other sponsor or are directly related to various other organizations.

There are other nondenominational Asian American groups, often missionary and evangelical. They are numerous and my only comment is that the mainline denominations for years resisted appointing Asian Americans to missionary service, thus encouraging the development of "faith" and "nondenominational" work.

Appendix II: Asian Center for Theology and Strategies (ACTS)
Director: The Rev. Dr. Roy I. Sano
(Director of ACTS and Professor of Theology, Pacific School of Religion, Berkeley)
1798 Scenic Avenue
Berkeley, California 94709
Telephone: 415-848-0173

ACTS is the Asian American church institute for research (theology and strategy) and educational concerns. It is the only ecumenical organization formally endorsed and supported by all of the Asian American denominational groups.

The base of operation is now at PSR. ACTS is *at* PSR and not *of* PSR. The distinction is important because ACTS works cooperatively with a number of seminaries, among them San Anselmo (UPC USA), Claremont, other members of the GTU, etc. Not only that but it is committed to research and education through a variety of means, not limited to seminaries. Because of the limitation of resources very little work has been done through higher education institutions, but ACTS is in dialogue with all of the Asian American studies centers. In some instances courses have been jointly sponsored on university campuses.

Although there is a central office, ACTS is many parts. There are groups meeting throughout the country sponsoring workshops and devising joint strategies. To date there are organized ACTS groups in Northern California, Southern California, Pacific Northwest, Hawaii, Great Lakes, Eastern Seaboard, and Southwest.

The major publications have been in conjunction with workshops sponsored by ACTS during the Earl Lectures in Berkeley. Other materials are also available through the ACTS main office in Berkeley.

The ecumenical nature of ACTS has also carried it into areas somewhat afield of its purely educational purpose. For instance, with the repression of civil rights in Korea, ACTS has sponsored study teams to go to Korea to continue to keep up with the developments there, giving aid and support to the Koreans in this time of oppression.

Furthermore because each denomination chose to develop their group on a denominational base, ACTS has been acting as a conduit and coordinating body for a number of common concerns.

ACTS, like many ethnic organizations, is operating on limited resources and is, in many ways, a very fragile institution. On the other hand, it has been instrumental in a variety of ways in instigating programs, encouraging and helping to develop denominational groups, and doing the first steps toward an "Amerasian theology."

Cultural Genocide and Cultural Liberation Through Amerasian Protestantism

Roy I. Sano

Introduction: Purpose, Scope, and Method

The ethnic studies strikes of the winter of 1968–69 set in motion the Asian American "Movement." The strikes and the movement represent a watershed in the histories of the Asian American communities. From that point in their history, Asian Americans have since redefined their identity, addressed neglected social issues, undertaken political action, and experimented with indigenous cultural expressions.

The time for reflection and analysis of these wide-ranging activities and varied experiences is now in order. Several purposes can be served thereby. Reflection and analysis can provide a more coherent and inclusive picture containing diverse groups and their approaches. The rivalries between contending community organizations might be diminished somewhat if they see the place differing approaches have within the total picture. Furthermore, a comprehensive vision might sustain the activists when the fanfare fades, the troops are depleted, and the supply lines are cut. Although the role of rhetoric remains, the enlistment of new recruits now requires appeals based on thorough analysis of issues and a convincing rationale for action. Finally, reflection and analysis may uncover fruitful avenues for action that the frenzy of work has forced us to overlook.

The Protestant churches in Asian American communities represent one such potential avenue worth considering. The reasons for this suggestion can be outlined at this point and developed later. The participants and the programs of these institutions have performed a list of useful services for generations of Asian Americans. They span the life of individuals from the cradle to the grave and cover a wide range of human concerns and aspirations, whether political, social, economic, cultural, or religious. Approximately five hundred churches with a constituency of five hundred thousand to seven hundred thousand have continued their work among Asian Americans through the vicissitudes of their life here. Thus, a recital of their deeds is to recall the total Asian American experience. If their records are ever collected and investigated, we will unearth a wealth of information unequalled for its comprehensiveness by any other organization in their communities. Although the future of Asian American Protestantism contains uncertain elements, the promise of humanizing influences remains.

Since the scope of the church's activities covers a plethora of human experiences, it requires an organizing principle to review them. I will employ the roles of four religious figures to classify the variety of church activities. These figures are the priest, pastor, prophet, and apocalypticist. Subsequent discussion will clarify the use of these terms.

Two cultural functions of the church's activities will be examined. I will ask whether the churches have acculturated the immigrants into the host culture, and, on the other hand, whether the churches have transmitted an alien culture to America. I will argue that the Christian churches in Asian American communities excelled in acculturating the immigrant but functioned less effectively in transmitting an alien culture or creating a distinctive subculture. Religious bodies originating in East Asia, such as the Buddhist churches, Shintoist groups, Confucianist temples, and Taoist organizations, surpass the Protestant churches in enriching American society with unique cultural contributions. However paradoxical it may seem, I will go on to argue that acculturation into a neglected part of the Judeo-Christian heritage may enable Asian American Protestant churches to reverse their historic function.

This article will not present fully developed arguments. What follows is a collection of hypotheses and "guesstimates" which should be tested with additional research. This article moves from observations of the past to proposals for the future.

In brief, the paper outlines the investigations necessary for a convincing case to enlist the participation that the ethnic Protestant churches deserve in order to fulfill its potentialities. Make no mistake. The article expects pragmatic uses of the data gathered, mythologies constructed, and theories developed from subsequent research and analysis.

However, the church itself is not the only institution that will benefit. Other persons and community organizations may find in this analysis rationale, strategies, and tactics that may prove fruitful for consideration.

Priestly Roles

The examination of the two cultural functions in the four religious figures begins with the priestly roles in the "rites of passage" and the meanings they inculcate in the immigrants. Whether at birth, the onset of puberty, the wedding ceremony, or the funeral rites, the converted immigrants were exposed to a distinct set of values, to say nothing about the different course of action. The churches announced that sanctity was present at critical junctures in the ordinary circle of life. The individual assumed worth primarily in the presence of their Maker. Their worth as persons or lack of it did not rest ultimately on the credit or discredit they may have brought to a group such as the family, the village, or the nation. Though many other meanings were conveyed in the "rites of passage," this will suffice to illustrate the kind of acculturation immigrants experienced through the priestly roles.

The Protestant churches among Asian Americans did very little to express the substance of their adopted religion through their cultural heritage. The symbols and rituals, the music and incantations, the vestments and the architecture came from Europe or New England. Only in the funeral rites do we find restrained vestiges of their cultural roots, and only in exceptional cases do we find a church building reminiscent of their homeland. The Makiki Christian Church in Honolulu, Hawaii, suggestive of a Japanese imperial castle, is a case in point, as is the St. Mary's Church in San Francisco Chinatown an attempt to evoke images of China.

The Asian American convert shied away from the annual festivals practiced in his or her homeland. For some, refusal to participate in New Year's celebrations, folk dances, and in a few cases, the martial arts, established the purity of their faith. Humorous samples are reported, such as the one in Loomis, California. To prove the sincerity of his conversion, a Christian testified that he quit eating rice, threw away his chopsticks, and stopped using the *o-furo*, a Japanese bathtub! The *senpai*, respected elders, of the Japanese Methodist Churches once cautioned us fledgling young ministers against members of our women's society who would offer flower arrangements for the altar. Japanese flower arrangements informed by Zen aesthetics would desecrate the sanctuaries of our churches.

Converts to new ideologies being what they are, one may condone these activities. However, the fact remains: The demand for pure faith and the aversion against religious syncretism prevented Asian American Christians from experimenting with new expressions of their faith through the use of their cultural heritage. The patterns may vary when we compare the unique practices of each of the national groups. However, as a whole the priestly roles in the Chinese, Japanese, Korean, and Filipino churches have led to the acculturation of these immigrant groups to the host culture. Little of their cultural heritage was transmitted to America.

Pastoral Roles

There is a second set of activities that we can call the pastoral services. Since the church related to all stages of life, it nurtured its own code of behavior in the interim between the critical transitions of life discussed in the priestly roles. This included childhood, youth, marriage, family life, and other aspects of adulthood such as employment, leisure, and citizenship.

The churches provided children and youth with religious instruction at Sunday School and character building through activities such as the Boy Scouts and Girl Scouts, YMCA and YWCA, athletic leagues, the martial arts, and camping programs. The churches conducted Chinese, Korean, and Japanese language schools so long as the foreign language speaking division was strong and the public schools failed to teach these languages.

For adults, the churches offered classes in sewing, cooking, childcare, and other elementary skills in preparation for family life and outside employment. In the meantime, men were trained to lead community groups, speak in public, handle finances, read, and write. Again, as in the priestly activities, the pastoral services indoctrinated the immigrant to Euro-American value systems, patterns of behavior, and social structures more than they transmitted Asian cultures to America.

Prophetic Roles

Third, the Protestant churches performed the prophetic tasks. The prophet can be distinguished from the priest and pastor. By means of rituals the priest inculcated various meanings into the regular cycle of life, with special focus on the critical junctures, be it in the pilgrimage of an individual or the history of a social unit. The pastor nurtured values and promoted action appropriate to people between the rites of passage celebrated by the priest. The prophet interpreted the emergence of unique events in their history and clarified the course of action peculiar to that moment. These two roles, the one of depicting the course of events and the other of calling people to action, require separate elaborations.

The task of interpreting history helps explain one of the most important historic functions of the Christian churches for all immigrant groups in America. The churches provided the history of the Hebrews and a mythic pattern for immigrants to make sense of their labors and hopes. They too left their homes as did Abraham, uncertain about his destination. They too would resist their oppressive Pharoah as did Moses who liberated his people from bondage. They too would endure the long trek through the barren wastelands as did the children of Israel. They too would toughen themselves for their conquests in the promised land as did Joshua. Secular models from their recent past, be they Abraham Lincoln or Horatio Alger, told of the journey from the log cabin to the White House, from rags to riches.

Although many early Asian immigrants only came in order to earn enough to return home as rich persons, unexpected circumstances prolonged their stay. They were forced to find a mythic framework that could make their toil bearable. The majority of immigrants, whether they were churched or unchurched incorporated the outlines of Hebrew history into their own lives. The practice pervades the history of waves of immigrants whether they came across the Atlantic, the Pacific, or the Rio Grande. The churchgoing sector of these immigrant groups were distinguished by their self-conscious use of the Hebrew mythos for their own lives.

Again, we have the question of the chicken and the egg. Which came first? Did the aspiration to succeed in American society lead selected immigrants to adopt the Judeo-Christian myths as a paradigm for their lives? Or did the outlines of Hebrew history convert the short-term sojourner into a homesteader who was determined to make it in America? No doubt both explanations are serviceable. And what is relevant for the development of the argument of this paper is that Asian American Christians were likely candidates for both. They came from that sector in their communities that wanted to be acculturated and, therefore, adopted the stories of the host culture. In turn, this adoption facilitated their acculturation even more.

A case in point is the World War II loyalty test of the Japanese Americans reported in *The Spoilage*.[1] There was a distinct correlation between being Christian

---

[1] Dorothy S. Thomas and Richard Nishimoto, *The Spoilage: Japanese American Evacuation and Resettlement During World War II* (Berkeley: University of California Press, 1946), 57–58,

and saying "yes, yes" to questions about serving in the armed services if ordered and defending the United States if invaded. Similarly, there was a correlation between being Buddhist and saying "no, no" to the same questions. Looking at the records today one gathers that a majority of Japanese American Christians in Tule Lake concentration camp had been acculturated to the point of accepting orders to serve in the armed forces and defending the country which had deprived them of their civil rights. That should not surprise us. They had a myth about a people who overcame the bondage of Egypt, endured setbacks in the wilderness, and eventually triumphed in the conquest of the promised land.

The schools and the mass media in American society have effectively written the Hebrew mythos into the psyche of great masses of people. More particularly, the Asian American Protestant churches effectively performed this function in their communities. It would require several elaborate studies to detail the contributions, hazards, and the problems that this observation suggests.

As indicated above, the prophetic tasks include another responsibility. The prophet not only outlines what has happened and can happen, but specifics in the present situation what issues call for action. Karl Marx illustrates the dual responsibilities. He is not so much a Judeo-Christian heretic because he proposed to substitute the Bible with his own Manifesto, a priesthood with his own vanguards of the revolution, the church with his cell, and the confessional with self-criticism. He may well be one of the most orthodox Hebrew prophets of the nineteenth century. The impact he has had on history follows the pattern set by the ancient Hebrew prophet. Like the prophets, he recited a history that includes a paradise of pre-capitalist society, a fall with the introduction of private property, an ensuing class conflict, the inevitable revolution, and the heavenly society without class conflicts or governmental tyranny. Marx was orthodox because his framework of history followed the ancient Hebrew prophets.

What is important for the moment is that the eventualities of history did not foster fatalistic acquiescence to the course of history. His interpretation of history liberated a most extraordinary exertion of human energies which sought to redress wrong. Human action in the present would facilitate the course of events which the myth predicted would happen.

On a much more minuscule level, one finds the same pattern among Asian American Protestant churches. The recital of history did not only promise human fulfillment but exposed the frustrations of legitimate human spirations. This meant that churches which lived up to their heritage would expose the contradictions in

---

105–106. While mentioning this series of studies and the uses immigrants made of the Hebrew history to understand their experience, one should note a serious error which appears in Jacobus tenBroek, Edward N. Barnhart, and Floyd W. Matson, *Prejudice, War, and the Constitution* (Berkeley: University of California Press, 1954), xv and 97, where the evacuation is called an "Exodus." The use of the word is inappropriate. "Exodus" recalls the deliverance from bondage experienced by the Hebrews, not an incarceration or captivity, the subject with which the book deals.

society. The criteria that determine what constitutes human need may have changed, but earlier generations had their list of issues. There were the Reverend Keiichiro Imais who "rescued" prostitutes in California and the followers of Donaldina Cameron who did likewise for the Chinese in San Francisco.[2] There were the Reverend Kosaburo Babas who staged strikes with Japanese sugar beet workers and then tried to protect them from pistol-wielding gamblers in Oxnard, California. The story of these and other leaders is yet to be written.[3]

Admittedly, there are plenty of cases where churches have neither recited a history that sustained immigrants in their difficulty nor offered leadership to alleviate the evils they suffered. However, there remain instances in Asian American churches that practiced their prophetic roles. Whenever they did, they reflect an acculturation to the host culture that has had many positive contributions. The problems attending this acculturation will be discussed later.

At the moment, however, more specific illustrations of the prophetic stance should be offered from recent years. The widespread development of denominational caucuses and the continuing strength of evangelical Protestants serve this purpose. As the recovery of ethnicity and the focus on liberation spread through various Protestant denominations, Asian Americans created caucuses to spell out their unique identity, tackle social ills, and redress racism in the church. The caucuses have sprung loose seed money for budding community organizations and have placed several Asians in conspicuous leadership positions such as the election of Wilbur W. Y. Choy to become the first Asian American bishop in the United Methodist Church in 1972.[4]

The mainline denominations now have caucuses. They include the United Methodists, organized in 1971;[5] the American Baptists, 1972;[6] the United Presbyterians, 1972;[7]

---

[2] See Carol Green Wilson, *Chinatown Quest* (San Francisco: Cameron House, 1974).

[3] Yuji Ichioka's study, "A Buried Past: Early Issei Socialists and the Japanese Community," *Amerasia* 1, no. 2 (July 1971): 1–25 cites the widespread participation of Christians in the early socialist movement in the Japanese community.

[4] Dr. Chan-Hie Kim reports what is probably the first election of an Asian born in Asia who was elected to the episcopacy in the United States. The Reverend Motozo Akazawa in 1930 was elected to the episcopacy in the Methodist Church, South. Bishop Akazawa was born in Japan and returned to serve there until his death in 1936.

[5] Convocation on Asian American Ministries, United Methodist Church, Santa Monica, CA, 12–14 March 1971. The caucus activities are reported in *Asianews*, George Nishikawa, ed., 1971–73 and *Asian American Newsletter*, Jonah Chang, ed., 1973–.

[6] The Asian Caucus of American Baptist Churches has also compiled a pamphlet of sermons, position papers, and studies.

[7] The Asian Presbyterian caucus has continued the tradition of its parent denomination. They have been among the most productive in written documents. Witness: Asian Presbyterian Caucus, The First National Meeting of the Asian Presbyterian Caucus, 16–19 March 1972, White Sulphur Springs, St. Helena, CA; Second Annual Assembly, Pacific Palisades, CA, 26–28 April 1973; and To Grow in Crisis, Third Annual Assembly, Mills College, Oakland, CA, 26–28 April 1974. In addition, special issues on Asian Americans appeared in *Trends* 1, no. 4 (March/April 1973) and *Church and Society* 64, no. 3 (January/February 1974). The United Presbyterian

the Episcopalians;[8] and the United Church of Christ, 1974.[9] The more recent immigrants from the South Pacific Islands have joined the Asian caucuses of the United Presbyterian Church and the United Church of Christ. A separate Samoan organization now exists in the Southern California Conference of the United Methodist Church.[10]

These caucuses represent united work among Asians within their respective denominations. However, the earlier national groups which crossed denominational lines have not been strengthened as much in recent years, at least not as much in the two older Asian immigrant groups, namely, the Chinese and Japanese. The Japanese church federation in Northern California and Southern California, which bridges denominations, and the National Council of the Christian Work Among Chinese in America continue to function but have not undergone the growth experienced by the caucuses.[11] Thus, the recently created caucuses promote pan-Asian consciousness but do so within denominational channels.

Institutional structures for work among Asians have gone through three phases in the Protestant denominations. First, these churches worked within a national group through their own denominational channels. Second, national groupings of Asians worked together but across denominational lines. Third, the caucuses promoted pan-Asian cooperation but concentrated on denominational units. Fourth, and most recently, The Asian Center for Theology and Strategies, with the acronym ACTS, was organized in 1972 to promote activities that are both pan-Asian and inter-denominational. On the one hand, ACTS relates to Asian American communities, with special attention to their churches as neglected community organizations, and, on the other hand, it relates to institutions of higher education with particular reference to seminaries which train leaders, whether clergy or laity. In relation to the communities, ACTS had conducted workshops, staged conferences, and distributed literature to strengthen the work of the churches.[12] ACTS has also supported

---

Church, Mission Service Unit on Church and Race, through Philip Park has distributed a *Study of Chinese, Filipino, Japanese and Korean Populations in the United States and Projection* (New York: UPC, Research Division of the Support Agency, 1974).

[8] Asiamerica Ministry, First National Conference, Asian American Episcopalians, Grace Cathedral, San Francisco, CA, 7–9 February 1974.

[9] United Church of Christ, National Conference on the Concerns of Asian Americans and Pacific Islands, San Francisco, CA, 19–21 April 1974.

[10] The United Methodist Church, *Journal of the Southern California-Arizona Annual Conference*, ed. James K. Sasaki (1974), 248–249.

[11] The National Conference of Christian Work Among the Chinese in America, *Proceedings of the Sixth Triennial Meeting, Confab '71*, ed., James Chuck, (Pacific Palisades Conference Grounds, 21–27 June 1971).

[12] The Asian Center for Theology and Strategies (ACTS) publishes an *Occasional Bulletin* and distributes a number of manuscripts. ACTS is negotiating for space in the archives of various seminary libraries that will become depositories of historical documents related to Asian Americans and Pacific Islanders. Sample copies of documents are welcomed for temporary holding until final arrangements are completed. Pictures, diaries, church minutes, and newsletters will also be included.

community organizations working for affirmative action in employment and the protection of Vietnamese students threatened with deportation. In relation to institutions of higher education, ACTS has been seeking at least one center among West Coast seminaries which will specialize in training church leaders as well as work with ethnic studies programs on college and university campuses.[13]

An additional word should be written about the evangelicals or the theologically conservative churches. They have retained their predominant national groupings in interchurch affairs, which was mentioned earlier in the second institutional arrangement. There are notable exceptions at the local level. The Japanese Evangelical Missionary Society (JEMS), for example, is not strictly Japanese. The Agape group in Southern California and the Pacific Area Chinese Evangelicals (PACE) are also inclusive, though predominantly Japanese and Chinese, respectively. My knowledge of Roman Catholic groups among Asian Americans is so sketchy I cannot hazard a guess about their work.[14]

A comparison between mainline denominational Asian Caucuses and the evangelicals can be ventured. Whereas the caucuses tend to specialize in political, economic, social, and cultural issues, the theologically conservative groups are more effective in evangelism, religious nurture, and overseas missions. In both groups, however, there are leaders who are seeking to bridge the gap between the social and personal, and the secular and sacred dimensions of their faith. As they do so, the social issues will come under more and more critical scrutiny. An intensified religious orientation could evoke a more radical social critique.[15] This leads to an exploration of the fourth set of roles as they appear in the apocalyptic figure.

Apocalyptic Roles

The apocalyptic figure supplements the prophets as the prophets supplement the inadequacies of the priestly and pastoral roles. The priest was likely to say that good existed in evil, just as their rituals celebrated the presence of extraordinary qualities in the ordinary experiences of life. When the priest announced good in evil, he was likely to prompt pious acquiescence to social ills. Thus, the pastor offered a corrective by nurturing those ideals that would inspire the convert to reshape various phases of life in conformity to desirable norms. In turn, although these ethical norms and customs had their contributions to offer, this wasn't enough. The prophet was

---

[13] Probably the first class to be offered on the Asian American churches and their communities as an independent study will be sponsored by Ling-Chi Wang at the University of California, Berkeley, in the spring of 1975.

[14] A study of local parishes and schools operated by dioceses or religious orders such as the Maryknoll Sisters would be productive. Mention should be made of the scholarly work of Fr. Matthias Lu, who is presently translating Aristotle and Thomas of Aquinas into Chinese while working with overseas Chinese in the Oakland Diocese.

[15] The schizophrenia within American Protestantism between the personal and the social orientation is evident in Asian American Protestant divisions. Only a few indigenous East Asian Christians have resisted the schismatic consequences. Korean Protestants whose religious foundations and active resistance to oppressive Japanese colonialism or their own repressive regimes offer a most notable exception to the widespread division.

necessary to storm the centers of power and to try to alter systems when the pastor only permitted the slightest cosmetic changes to society. The prophets in ancient Israel frequently contested political figures, such as Nathan before King David or Amos before King Jeroboam. Their reading of history forced prophets to do battle against abuses of power.

The limitations of the prophetic figure have become increasingly evident to ethnic minorities. First, they arc time bound. The prophets came into their own when Israel had acquired nationhood. No prophet of the classical sort (850–600 BCE) existed when the Hebrews were only a wandering nomadic tribe, or even a pastoral people (1800–1050 BCE). Only when they were sedentary enough to create political entities which federated constituent elements in their society do the prophets come into their own. This is worth noting since the prophets were speaking for people who had nationhood and exercised power. Second, the prophets proposed solutions limited to changes within existing systems.

The apocalypticists began to assume power just at the time Israel was losing her independence as a nation and continued their influence into a time when they were vassals of foreign powers (ca. 600 BCE and on). The apocalypticists said the body politic had become so sick it would die and that the end of nationhood was at hand. Foreign powers would reduce the children of Israel to a colony. The prophets may have argued for improvement of morality among leaders or changes within the system; the apocalypticists announced the system must come down, it was beyond repair.

Asian American churches and other ethnic minorities inside and outside the church will take the apocalyptic tradition more seriously in the days ahead. It is not enough to be priestly, pastoral, and prophetic. The insufficiency of the priest and pastors should be obvious. The inadequacy of the prophet requires elaboration.

As noted above, the prophetic use of Hebrew history as myth led the church to promise immigrant peoples a favorable outcome to their struggles. They too could come with uncertainty as did Abraham; they too could overcome oppression as did Hosea; and they too could make their conquests in the land of promise as did Joshua. The plot helped thousands and millions maintain their sanity. But we need to ask: Did the immigrants from Asia actually achieve what they set out to accomplish? Did they actually experience what had been promised? To some extent, yes. But we are corning to see increasingly that we continue to be "internal colonies" despite our advances.[16] If we follow the analytical model of the two category system outlined by Roger Daniels and Harry Kitano in *American Racism*,[17] we notice the two categories are shaped similarly in the diagram, both are squares. However, the lower category remains on the bottom. That is to say, minorities may have become like the majority,

---

[16] For a discussion on the concept of "internal colonies" as it relates to minority status in the United States, consult Robert Blauner, *Racial Oppression in America* (New York: Harper & Row, 1972), 54, 75n2 (a useful guide to literature), 82–104, 105–106.

[17] Roger Daniels and Harry H. L. Kitano, *American Racism: Exploration of the Nature of Prejudice* (Englewood Cliffs, NJ: Prentice-Hall, 1970).

in this case squares in the diagram, and in some cases minorities may even be liked by the majority. But the minority still occupies the lower position in terms of power and social status. We are acculturated, that is, we look and act alike, but we are not fully assimilated.[18]

The unfulfilled promise reminds us of a story of a scientist who graduated from college with honors. The research laboratory where he went to work did not seem to recognize his brilliance and talents. They assigned him to projects reserved for flunkies. To demonstrate his competence he proposed to produce a new species of animal. He would cross an abalone and a crocodile and produce an "abodile." Much to the surprise of his colleagues, after months of failures, he produced something. But the cross between a crocodile and an abalone was not an "abodile" but a "crock of baloney."

The "melting pot" ideology which prophetic religion came to serve has turned out to be a "crock of baloney." People were not as assimilated as had been promised. Even intermarriage among third-generation Japanese Americans so widely practiced will not contradict this fact.[19] In the crunch the children of Asian and white marriages will not have the same privileges as pure white children.

Even in the churches, the melting pot social theory is a crock of baloney. The now familiar analysis of Albert Hemmi in *The Colonizer and the Colonized*[20] holds true in the church, despite all advocacy for "brotherhood" to the contrary. The two categories persist. In the church, you are either a colonizer or colonized, white or Asian, but not both. "Marginal man" is a myth, if by marginal we have in mind someone who can operate at will between the two categories or within both categories. If an Asian American penetrates the system of colonizers, that person will serve the needs of whites who hand him or her their agendas, and only at great personal expense or hazard can that person expect to represent the needs and aspirations of their ethnic minority people. When the crisis comes the white-dominated system will find it easier to jettison Asian Americans and their interests in order to keep the church in orbit, far removed from the earthly minorities.

Thus, the promise of assimilation which prophets have offered minorities is at best only a half truth. It does not apply to the colorful people but only to the colorless European immigrants who may enter the true centers of power. No amount of changes within existing racist systems will alter that fact. The two categories remain, the one colorless and the other colorful, the one colonizer and the other colonized.

But that may not have to concern us very much. The apocalyptic vision may lead us to see that the very system we sought to penetrate is crumbling; the "sacred cow" we tried to milk may become dry shortly. Or, to change the figure of speech, the

---

[18] For a distinction between acculturation and assimilation, refer to Milton M. Gordo, *Assimilation in American Life: The Role of Race, Religion, and National Origins* (New York: Oxford University Press, 1964), 81.

[19] *The Journal of Social Issues* 29, no. 2 (1973) contains several articles concerning recent trends in intermarriage among Asians.

[20] Albert Memmi, *The Colonizer and the Colonized* (Boston: Beacon Press, 1967).

"treasure chests" we have tried to crack open may prove to be whited sepulchres containing decayed remains of past greatness. If that is not the case, we should make these events transpire. At least one interpreter of history sees the passing of the Euro-American phase of history. Stephen Neill, in his *Colonialism and Christian Mission*,[21] speaks of three successive centers of world history. Speaking as a Euro-American he says history was centered first in the Middle East, second in the Mediterranean Sea, and third in the Atlantic Ocean. "Today," he writes, "we seem to be seeing the beginnings of the fourth age, in which the Pacific Ocean will become the center of world history."[22]

This is a mild version of an apocalyptic vision that predicts the passing of Euro-American hegemony. There are political and cultural implications worth exploring. In political terms, if the American superpower is to diminish its stature, we immediately think of violent means whereby that would happen. At the moment the possibilities of a wholesale revolution catching hold of great masses of people seem unlikely. Further repression may produce it, but too many people are duped today to evoke a widespread movement. If there are any violent attempts to reduce America to her knees, it will come from insurrectionists who seek to accelerate the process of attrition now at work. A few may even work without pragmatic considerations but simply to cry "No!" as a faithful witness. More likely than not, the system will not go out with a "bang" but with a "whimper," to use the familiar phrase of T. S. Eliot.

If America becomes a colony of an East Asian superpower, it will probably occur gradually as Great Britain changed in stages from an empire to a commonwealth and eventually into a colony of the United States, as she is now to all intents and purposes. If the dislocation of power occurs abruptly, it will be the result of a coincidence of events that no one planned or predicted and was, therefore, unmanaged.

Besides the violent and abrupt reduction of American power, we also need to consider more modest means. We should be penetrating American society to take over pockets of that society for the benefit of ethnic minorities. All other penetrations produce sellout achievers. We should erode the hold this racist society has on the media, educational institutions, financial agencies, welfare programs, judicial systems, legislative bodies, and cultural strongholds such as art museums and libraries that articulate what is defined as beautiful and wise. These approaches may be piecemeal, but that may be all that is available to us at the moment.

The cultural implications of the demise of Euro-American hegemony concern us next. Some changes are occurring, others are required. Up to the present, the expanding white Christianity could practice cultural genocide with little threat of being challenged. To become a Christian meant an Asian American would commit virtual cultural suicide. Today, however, great numbers of peoples are already disenchanted with Euro-American expressions of their religious faith. The eighteenth

---

[21] Stephen Neill, *Colonialism and Christian Missions* (London: Lutterworth Press, 1966).
[22] Stephen Neill, *Colonialism and Christian Missions*, 16.

and nineteenth-century hymns from Europe and England, the architecture reminiscent of medieval Europe or colonial America, the Byzantine scent in the incense, the vestments with Roman senatorial origins, and the sermons with illustrations laced with Shakespeare all seem to be "whited sepulchres." It has come time for Asian American church persons to experiment and create new expressions for their religious aspirations, using wherever appropriate their own cultural heritage.

If there are to be changes in churches, however, it will require changes in seminaries that train the professional leaders of churches. The seminaries that presently train these leaders are among the most sophisticated practitioners of racism. They handpick those who have subjected themselves to thirteen bleaching vats called public education, and then four more vats of even more concentrated bleach called college education, to attend their seminaries. And for three to four additional years, they subject them to an additional bleach. The reason why the Asian Center for Theology and Strategies focuses on seminaries should be clear. If cultural liberation is fundamental, we need to change the churches that are one of the critical institutions which deal with basic values. If we are to change the churches, we will need to change the professional leadership who have on the whole served as functionaries of cultural genocide. Finally, if we are to raise a group of leaders who will reverse genocide and turn it into cultural liberation, we will need to change the institutions which train these leaders, namely, the seminaries. Once that happens we might begin seeing Asian American Protestant churches practice their priestly, pastoral, prophetic, and apocalyptic roles for the liberation and fulfillment of their peoples.

Conclusion

Amidst all of these requisite changes, an additional one should be mentioned. Most activists continue to be preoccupied with political, economic, and social liberation. This is understandable. Political frauds, economic deprivation, and social oppression are conspicuously present. The subtler cultural oppression, however, can be overlooked. Culture deals with fundamental commitments, value systems, and their attending visceral responses, and yet cultural liberation remains one of the neglected considerations of movement people.

If religious institutions deal with anything, they deal with cultural questions. Hence, the importance of ethnic churches. Although Asian American Protestantism has contributed towards the cultural suicide of Asian American peoples, it has the ideological and human resources to promote cultural liberation. Ironically, by acculturating themselves to such neglected religious figures as the apocalypticists, Asian American Protestants may be able to reverse the dehumanizing consequences of Christianity.

"Yes, We'll Have No More Bananas in Church!"*

ROY I. SANO†

A Japanese American churchman says the white man's idea of "integration" is to make all yellow-skinned people think white. He argues for an assertive Japanese American church that will capitalize on the desire of Japanese Americans not to be totally assimilated into American culture.

"O God, grant me the serenity to accept what cannot be changed, the courage to change what must be changed, and the wisdom to know the one from the other."

Reinhold Niebuhr's classic prayer strikes a balance between the pastoral and the prophetic, between Christian piety and social action, for which two very appropriate symbols might be the folded hands ("serenity to accept what cannot be changed") and the clenched fist ("courage to change what must be changed").

At the moment a relevant ministry for Asian Americans calls for a heightened emphasis upon the clenched fist; for too long have Asians serenely accepted what they thought could not be changed. Within the past year the Asian communities in Southern California have seen the development of organizations which express this self-awareness.

A host of Japanese American organizations reject the images of self-effacing humility and perseverance common to previous generations. Such groups as the Council of Oriental Organizations, Asian American Political Alliance, Oriental Concern, and the Yellow Brotherhood assert a strong desire for self-determination, even within a certain amount of racial separatism. This development has profound implications for the Asian American churches and their leaders.

The previous generation which promoted "integration" could think only of abolishing racially distinct communities and groups. In the church, this has resulted in the continuation of Anglo-Saxon domination as in the wider community. For instance, the last years of the Provisional Conferences saw the development of leadership on the part of ethnic minorities in their own affairs. This included Japanese, Chinese, Koreans, Filipinos, and Mexican Americans. With the abandonment of these Provisional Conferences this new leadership was directed to

---

* August 1969.

† Rev. Roy I. Sano, formerly the associate pastor of Centenary United Methodist Church in Los Angeles, is now chaplain and assistant professor of religion at Mills College, Oakland, CA.

other interests and frequently restricted to narrow spheres of influence. Meanwhile, existing Annual Conferences dominated by white leadership assumed the responsibilities for ethnic affairs. The way "integration" has worked out so far tends to confirm Pascal's observation that "Man is neither angel nor brute, and when he acts the angel he becomes the brute." When churchmen "angelically" attempt to extricate their churches from complicity in racially defined structures, they act "brutishly." The general loss of leadership in their own affairs constitutes, for Asians especially, the most pronounced instance of the brutishness of integration.

Subtler forms of brutishness exist. There are neglected ethnic minorities without ministers who specialize with them. Specialized ministries, such as work with the aging, the youth, the drug culture, etc., have suffered because Asians let the program of the total church divert their attention from the concerns for which they are peculiarly equipped. Youth especially respond more quickly to programs staffed by their own kind, as is evident in work with narcotic traffic. On some campuses with large concentrations of Asians those close to the drug traffic claim three-fourths of these youth have experimented. "Integration" has resulted in neglect of these specialized ministries.

Other factors corroborate the low opinion Asian churchmen have of the white man's idea of "integration."

- When ethnic minority ministers are appointed outside their own ethnic churches, they are all too often appointed to dying or undesirable situations.
- The minority person who is appointed to a white church is among the cream of their kind; the white who is appointed to leadership of ethnic minorities can merely be a cull of his kind. Furthermore, they are appointed to some of the most desirable and strategic pulpits for evangelization of ethnic minorities.
- When an ethnic minority person is placed in a conspicuous position, it is more often for decoration and "show" than anything else. Few acquire decision-making power. In one case, a person with an earned doctorate and an honorary degree was asked to assume a prestigious office, but the job description sounds like little more than "stoop labor." Their job is to keep things in order, but not to introduce changes.
- Ethnic ministers are frequently involved in a kind of horse swapping between bishops. The appointment of ministers across Conference lines is not as easy as we were led to believe before "integration." It turns out that very little action takes place since no bishop feels the others make offers that match theirs. Once the Provisional Conferences were disbanded, a sort of "ice age" set in for the appointment of minority ministers.

Only if the church adopts specialized structures and programs to enter into these communities can we expect the church to make progress in its evangelization of ethnic minorities. We need not sanction the chauvinism or the prejudices of these communities. But some forms of organization and programs need to be preserved.

The basic justification of specialized ethnic ministries is similar to that for the military chaplaincy, the campus ministry, the industrial chaplain, and the community organizer.

The National Division of the United Methodist Board of Missions recently authorized an advisory committee on ethnic and language ministries. Request for such a committee came from a Consultation on Japanese Work in San Francisco in February. Together with the Western Jurisdiction of the United Methodist Church, the Division will provide budget for a staff member, who will work with Japanese and other ethnic and language minority groups on the West Coast. An Advisory Committee on Indian Work was created after a similar consultation last year and both will be related to the unit on Special Ministries of the National Division.

In another development, the Southern California-Arizona Annual Conference has formed an Ethnic Strategies Committee, which will conduct research and formulate a new course of action. Other conferences have felt the impact of caucuses formed along racial lines.

Part of the social tension of our day comes from a serious shift in the approach of minorities. Doing what is "right" (as defined by the white majority) has given way to demanding "rights." Acceptance at any cost into the larger culture is no longer desired. In its place has arisen aspirations for the power of self-determination. Nietzsche accused Christianity of perpetuating a slave ethic that made virtue of subjecting oneself to circumstances. If a man cannot rise up to state his claim and rights, he has permitted his views, even his religion, to dehumanize him.

In the process of this shift in approach by minorities, many whites are asking if the old goal of integration is no longer acceptable to minority groups. Many WASP (white Anglo-Saxon Protestant) ministers, who have fought hard for integration and its acceptance by whites, find these developments an offense and a disappointment. They say different racial structures can only mean discrimination; to set up any separate structures entails segregation.

We need to expose the questionable foundations of this stance and to propose a rationale for an alternative course of action.

In part, the stance is based on an unquestioned acceptance and application of the Supreme Court decision that struck down the "separate but equal" doctrine and its abuses. Recent developments, particularly growing self-awareness of racial minorities, offer the church an opportunity for the moment to say "separate and more than equal" in order to recover from past losses.

In part the integrationist stance also rested upon a questionable reading of scripture. Paul said, "There is neither Jew nor Greek, bond nor free" (Gal. 3:28). We often turn this passage into a sociological observation of empirical facts, as if all distinctions had been abolished. But what then do we do with "there is neither male nor female"? We can only conclude that the passage is rhetorical and religious, and should not be read as sociological dogma. It certainly provides no basis for burial of the ethnic church.

The social ferment of our days has helped us question the easy assumptions of the past models for integration. The past assumptions have begun with the proposition that America is a vast "melting pot" which ostensibly welcomed the unique contributions of each immigrant group. Actually, the theory concealed the "Anglo-Saxon" domination in the process of Americanization. Besides this hypocrisy operating in the "melting pot" theory, social scientists have now shown the limited truth it involved. We have now come to see at least two major processes operating in Americanization.

The first process is *acculturation*, whereby the immigrant group adopts the behavior patterns of the host culture. The immigrant learns the ways of language, diet, attire, residence, vocation, entertainment of the host culture. Acculturation limits itself to secondary relations or segmented groups that are impersonal, formal, or casual and non-intimate. By contrast, the second process, called *assimilation*, has to do with relationships within primary groups that are personal, informal, and intimate. These groups involve the entire personality and not merely a segmented part of it, such as our working hours or specialized interests.

According to social scientists such as Milton Gordon, there has been an extensive amount of acculturation among ethnic minorities. However, there is a serious lag at the point of assimilation. The lag in assimilation, particularly in the case of non-Europeans, has discredited the proponents of the melting pot theory.

In the case of the Japanese American community, some social scientists feel the process of acculturation has been the most extensive and rapid of all non-European groups. These acculturated peoples, however, maintain their own institutions paralleling the white community, thus showing the failure of assimilation. There is a growing vernacular press. Social and recreational clubs are formed along racial lines, whether for children, youth, or adults. Service clubs, veterans' groups, and professional bodies draw up memberships from ethnic characteristics. Insurance salesmen, dentists, doctors, merchants, and funeral directors continue to operate along ethnic groupings. They are saying, "We may want to be like you (acculturation), but we want to set up our own time schedule when and how we will join you (assimilation)."

The new pattern of "integration" now proposed operates under an assumption other than the old "melting pot" theory. It is that to join the American people might mean forming power blocs of interest groups based largely on ethnic and color lines and having these power blocks participate in policy making decisions which affect them. Even within the church we need special interest groups to check and balance each other. This is a serious departure from the melting pot theory and its updated version in the *Flower Drum Song* that said "America is chop suey." It is also a departure from putting a premium on the minority being "accepted" into the larger majority, frequently at the expense of the minority's integrity. Those who resist the old "acceptance" theory call S. I. Hayakawa, the acting president at San Francisco State College, a banana. "He has yellow skin," they say, "but a white inside." They feel light-skinned minorities are used by the white establishment to hold the Blacks in their place.

For the church, racially distinct structures are only a tactical move with a larger end in view. By permitting these specialized groups the power to decide about their destiny in the context of the wider church's work, these groups will come to feel a part of the total church and community. This is the irony of history's logic. By heightening these particular groups, the universality of the church's outreach is strengthened. We thereby set the stage for a more comprehensive unity.

For Japanese Americans within the church it is a time to reassert the clenched fist as well as the folded hands. More appropriate symbols would be those of the chrysanthemum and the sword, which cultural anthropologist Ruth Benedict used to characterize the Japanese Americans. By the chrysanthemum she partly had in mind the quiet poise maintained in the face of indignities and adversities. By the sword she had in mind the assertiveness that could prove both devious and destructive. This was probably one of the most adequate and accurate portrayals the Japanese Americans have yet received. In asserting anew the values of the ethnic group, Japanese Americans hope the new balance between the chrysanthemum and the sword will lead to a constructive goal.

History and Role of the Church in the Korean American Community

Kim Hyung-Chan[*]

When the first large group of Korean immigrants arrived in Honolulu, Hawaii, on January 13, 1903, there were among them some people who had already embraced Christianity as their religion.[1] These Christians became active catalysts in the establishment of churches in the Korean American community in the Hawaiian Islands and the mainland of the United States. That there were people converted to Christianity among the first group of emigrants from Korea was certainly not an historical accident; it was closely related to the history of evangelism in Korea and the cause of Korean emigration to the Hawaiian Islands.

As early as 1784, Christianity came to Korea in the form of Catholicism, when Yi Sung-hun, the son of an ambassador to China, returned to Korea with books, crosses, and other Christian artifacts. He had gone to China to study and was baptized in Peking. In 1794 a Chinese priest came into Korea, crossing the Yalu River border in secrecy in response to Yi Sung-hun's plea for more priests.

Catholicism began to gain converts shortly after its arrival in Korea. Many persons dissatisfied with their lot in the present life tuned to the teachings of Catholicism, as it promised a better life in the next world, no matter how vaguely they understood the real meaning of life after death. Others embraced the religion, as it symbolized the Western scientific knowledge. At any rate, as many Koreans turned to Catholicism, the Yi court (1392–1910) became deeply concerned with the doctrine of the Catholic Church that preached human equality and the kinship of mankind. The doctrine was considered dangerous to the preservation of the Confucian system of loyalties and ancestor worship, which was the foundation of the kingdom. Therefore, the Yi court issued an edict in 1785 banning Christianity. Shortly after the ban, many Korean Christians along with the Chinese priests were put to death, and the persecution of Christians continued. In 1839 three French missionaries

---

[*] Kim Hyung-Chan is an associate professor at Western Washington State College.

[1] Bernice Bong Hee Kim, "The Koreans in Hawaii." *Social Science* 9, no. 4 (October 1934): 410. In her later work, "The Koreans in Hawaii," a master's thesis submitted to the University of Hawaii, she mentions that "the Koreans were told that they were going to America, a Christian country, and that it would be the proper and advantageous thing to become Christians. All the young Koreans were eager to succeed in their venture, so one and all professed to become Christians." See "The Koreans in Hawaii" (master's thesis, University of Hawaii, 1937), 209.

and their Korean followers were executed, and this incident angered the French government, which sent a ship to Korea in 1846 to demand an explanation. As late as 1866 three bishops, seventeen priests, and numerous Korean Christians suffered martyrdom.

The treaty of 1882 between Korea and the United States and other treaties the Yi court had been compelled to conclude with other Western nations brought more Western missionaries to Korea. Although most of them sought first the wealth of the earthly kingdom upon their arrival in Korea, a few were dedicated to the cause of the heavenly kingdom.[2] Among them was Horace N. Allen, who was sent to Korea in 1884 by the Presbyterian Board of Foreign Mission of the United States. Shortly after his arrival in Seoul, an incident occurred that helped him gain the confidence of the king of Korea. During a coup d'état involving the conservatives and progressives of the Yi court, the queen's nephew was seriously wounded and the missionary doctor was called upon to give him immediate medical attention.[3] His successful treatment of the queen's nephew won him the position of the king's personal physician and his approval of Christianity.

For a number of reasons more Koreans in the north accepted Christianity than their countrymen in the south. First of all, Koreans in the northern provinces had been discriminated against by the Yi court, which was constantly plagued by regional factionalism. The Yi court sent to the northern provinces government officials who were considered dangerous to the security of the court. It also denied the people from the northern provinces access to high positions in the central government. Such a policy of discrimination pursued by the Yi court eventually led the people to revolt against the central government in an insurrection of 1811 led by Hong Kyong-nae. The rebellion was strongly supported by the people in the north who were also suffering then from a severe famine. Secondly, the north Koreans developed less rigid and more mobile social structure during the Yi dynasty, due to the lack of arable land in north, than their countrymen in the south. The north Koreans were therefore exposed to more egalitarian values that made them more amenable to the acceptance of Christian doctrine.

Thirdly, several decisive battles were fought in the northwestern region of Korea, particularly in the vicinity of Pyongyang, during the Sino-Japanese War of 1894–95. Koreans became victims between the retreating Chinese soldiers and the advancing Japanese army, and much of their property was destroyed in the war, the outcome of which was to determine the political fate of the Korean people in the years to come. Several missionaries stationed in the vicinity of Pyongyang gave their time and effort to alleviate the sufferings of the people caught innocently in a war created by foreign powers. Such unselfish devotion of missionaries to the care and cure of Koreans afflicted by war gradually endeared them to the Korean people, who flocked to churches to learn a better world to live in both spiritually and materially.

---

[2] Fred Harvey Harrington, *God, Mammon, and the Japanese: Dr. Horace N. Allen and Korean-American Relations, 1884–1905* (Madison, WI: University of Wisconsin Press, 1944), 103–108.

[3] Harrington, *God, Mammon, and the Japanese*, 19–25.

American missionaries by deed or word encouraged Koreans to emigrate to the Hawaiian Islands, as they saw "an opportunity for Koreans to improve their condition and to acquire useful knowledge and to better themselves financially," as pointed out by David W. Deshler in his letter to Mr. Huntington Wilson, chargé d'affaires of the American Legation in Tokyo, who was asked by Deshler to intervene on his behalf after the Korean emigration had been terminated by the Korean government in 1905.[4]

Commenting on influence of American missionaries on Koreans who made the decision to emigrate to the Hawaiian Islands, Yi Tae-song, executive secretary for the Korean Student Christian Movement of Hawaii, once stated,

> It was at this critical stage in her history that the great and good missionary, Dr. and Mrs. H. G. Underwood, and Rev. and Mrs. Henry G. Appenzeller, appeared in Korea and began telling the wonderful story of the Cross and what it could do for those who will accept it and undertake to carry it through life. To the timid, stoical Korean the message was one of hope and life. Eagerly he asked of its power and a sample of its results. The one was told him by the missionaries, the other was pointed out to him in the advanced life of the United States. Soon the United States was the hope of Korea, for was it not there that the wondrous Cross had brought beneficent results? Was it not worth the while of any timid, downtrodden Korean laborer to make the attempt of reaching the haven of peace and plenty? As the Korean embraced Christianity he began to look for a place where it might be lived in peace.[5]

Missionaries were not the only reason for Korean emigration to the Hawaiian Islands. There was a widespread famine in the winter of 1901 in the northwestern region of Korea, and the government made efforts to relieve the people from starvation by allowing them to emigrate. Also, there were agents from several overseas development companies who were sent to Korea to recruit laborers to work in Hawaiian sugar plantations. One of them was David W. Deshler of the East-West Development Company, who was responsible for the emigration of the first group of Koreans to Koreans to Hawaii in 1903.[6]

Of all American missionaries, the Rev. George Heber Jones of the Methodist Mission was most influential on Korean emigrants. He came to Korea in 1887 and was later sent to Chemulpo in 1892 to succeed the Rev. Appenzeller. Chemulpo, now Incheon, was a port city where Deshler was stationed to recruit Korean laborers. Partly due to his geographical location and partly due to his compassion for Koreans leaving their homeland for a strange place, Jones felt the need to encourage them by telling them about life in Hawaii. He also gave some leaders among them letters of

---

[4] Archives of Hawaii, Governors' Files, Carter-US Depts (October 1905–June 1907).

[5] Yi Tae-song, "The Story of Korean Immigration," in *The Korean Students' of Hawaii Yearbook* (Honolulu: The Korean Students' Alliance of Hawaii, 1932), 47.

[6] The study on Deshler's biography is incomplete. According to Ch'oe Song-yon, the author of *Kaehang kwa Yanggwan Yokchong,* or *Opening of Korea and History of Western-style Buildings,* as reported by Yun Yo-jun, the author of *Miju Imin Ch'ilsimnyon,* or *Seventy Years of Immigration in America,* Deshler had joined the Orient Consolidated Mining Co. and lived in Chemulp'o, now Incheon, with a Japanese woman. See *Kyonghyang Sinmun* (Kyonghyang Daily), October 13, 1973.

introduction to the superintendent of Methodist Mission in Hawaii so that they would be greeted by someone upon their arrival in Honolulu. The Rev. John W. Wadman, Superintendent of the Hawaiian Mission of the Methodist Episcopal Church, in his report "Educational Work Among Koreans" described the role Jones had played in the immigration of Koreans in Hawaii.

> While encamped at the seaport of Chemulpo, awaiting the transport to bear them away into a strange land, Rev. Geo. Heber Jones, a Methodist Episcopal Missionary, became interested in their welfare, and held large tent meetings in order to inspire them with laudable ambitions and prepare them for the strange experiences so soon to overtake them. He also handed a few of the leaders among them letters of introduction to the Superintendent of Methodist Missions in Hawaii, and gave them in parting his heartfelt blessing.[7]

Later in 1906 when Jones published an article under the title "The Koreans in Hawaii" in the *Korea Review*, the missionary mentioned that he met a Korean and his family whom he had baptized in Korea.[8]

As has been pointed out, some Korean emigrants were converted to Christianity even prior to their departure for the Hawaiian Islands. Therefore, the history of the church in the Korean American community may be considered a continuing saga of Korean Christianity.

The history of the church in the Korean American community may be divided into four major periods: (1) the period of beginning and growth, 1903–1918; (2) the period of conflicts and divisions, 1919–1945; (3) the period of status quo, 1946–1967; and (4) the period of revival, 1968–1974.

The period between 1903 and 1918 saw a rapid growth in the number of Koreans professing Christianity as their religion. It was estimated that during the period approximately 2,800 Koreans were converted to Christianity and thirty-nine churches were established in the Hawaiian Islands alone. This numerical growth is a remarkable achievement in view of the fact that the total number of persons of Korean ancestry in the Islands during this period was less than eight thousand. A number of factors seemed to have contributed to such a phenomenal growth. First, Korean society in the Hawaiian Islands lacked in strong social groups established on the basis of traditional ties. Although there were social groups such as clan associations and organizations by sworn brotherhood,[9] they were proven ineffective

---

[7] Department of Public Instruction, *Report of the Superintendent of Public Instruction to the Governor of the Territory of Hawaii, From December 31st, 1910, to December 31st, 1912* (Honolulu: The Hawaiian Gazette Co., 1913), 146.

[8] George Heber Jones, "The Koreans in Hawaii," *Korea Review* 6, no. 11 (November 1906): 405.

[9] Linda Shin in her study, "Koreans in America, 1903–1945," originally published in *Roots: An Asian American Reader*, ed. Amy Tachiki, Eddie Wong, Franklin Odo, and Buck Wong (Los Angeles: UCLA Asian American Studies Center, 1971), stated that "most of the emigrants who came to Hawaii before 1906 were relatively unorganized in traditional social groups." This seems to be an overstatement in view of the fact that Korean immigrants had maintained their traditional social organizations in Hawaii for the first few years. For a discussion of Korean

in dealing with the white Americans. Second, Christianity may have been used as a means of gaining a sympathy from the white Americans. This particular point was alluded to by Jones when he stated: One third of all the Koreas in Hawaii are professing Christians. They dominate the life in the camps on the islands of Oahu, Kauai, and Maui, where they are stamping out gambling and intoxication. The Koreans have fallen into sympathetic hands in Hawaii.[10]

Third, to those who were not members of either clan association or sworn brotherhood organization, the church was the only social group that enabled them to engage in social intercourse outside their work camps. Fourth, there seemed to have been a certain degree of group pressure on non-Christians, particularly after a significant number of Koreans had become converts. Thus parents who were not Christians would send their children to church.

During this period several churches of different denominations were established in the island of the United States. The first group to establish a church was Korean Christians of Methodist persuasion. It was on November 3, 1903, that efforts were made to establish a congregation when a group of Koreans in Honolulu chose An Chung-su and U Pyong-gil as their representatives to negotiate for a place of worship with a superintendent of the Methodist Mission. As a result, the Korean Evangelical Society was organized a week later and church services were held at a rented house. The Society did not receive regular church status until April 1905, when John W. Wadman was appointed as superintendent of the Hawaiian Methodist Episcopal Church by Bishop John W. Hamilton.[11] Wadman contributed greatly to the growth of the Methodist church in the Korean community in the Hawaiian Islands from the time of his appointment until his resignation on January 1, 1914.[12] He was instrumental in purchasing a piece of property situated on the corner of Punchbowl and Beretania Streets, Honolulu, at a sum of $12,000 with the purpose of organizing a boarding school for Korean boys. While serving as superintendent of the Mission, he also supervised the boarding school which was then directed by his wife until June 1913, when Syngman Rhee, later first president of the Republic of Korea, was appointed as principal of the school.

---

social organizations in Hawaii during the first few years of their emigration, see Kingsley K. Lyu, "Korean Nationalist Activities in Hawaii and America, 1901–1945" (unpublished manuscript, 1950, in the possession of Professor Donald D. Johnson). The paper was submitted to Professor Johnson as a partial fulfillment of a research course in History 300. [*Ed. note: See* Kinglsey K. Lyu, "Korean Nationalist Activities in Hawaii and America, 1901–1945," in *Counterpoint*, ed. Emma Gee (Los Angeles: UCLA Asian American Studies Center, 1976), 106-133; Kinglsey K. Lyu, "Korean Nationalist Activities in Hawaii and the Continental United States, 1901–1945," pt. 1, *Amerasia* 4, no. 1 (1977): 23–85; pt. 2 *Amerasia* 4, no. 2 (1977): 53–100.]

[10] Jones, "The Koreans in Hawaii," 405.

[11] Won-yong Kim, *Chaemi Hanin Osimnyo n-sa* [A Fifty-Year History of Koreans in America], (Reedley, CA: Charles Ho Kim, 1959), 47.

[12] Won-yong Kim, whose American name is Warren Kim, claims that Wadman was relieved of his duty in June 1914. However, according to a letter written by William Henry Fry, Wadman's immediate successor to L. E. Pinkham, governor of the Territory of Hawaii, dated July 27, 1915, Wadman was relieved of his duty on January 1, 1914.

It is alleged by Warren Kim, the author of *Chaemi Hanin Osimnyon-sa* (A History of Fifty Years of Koreans in America), that Rhee was given this position by Wadman as an expression of his gratitude to Rhee, who had helped him settle a dispute between Wadman and the people of the Korean community in the islands. The dispute began with a local newspaper report on October 4, 1912. In the report it was said that Wadman had received a sum of $750 from a certain Japanese consul of Honolulu who had donated the money with the ostensible purpose of helping poor Koreans. When he was confronted by a group of angry Koreans who hated anything symbolic of Japanese, he acknowledged the receipt of money, although he presented a reason different from the one reported in the newspaper. He said that he had accepted money in order to use it as a part of maintenance expense for the boarding school.

Koreans felt it their moral duty to oppose the acceptance of such financial assistance from an official of the government that had deprived them of their nation in 1910. Wadman was cornered further into an embarrassing situation, as Korean students refused to attend school. At this time Syngman Rhee arrived in Honolulu under the invitation of the Korean National Association. When he was asked by Wadman to intervene in the dispute, he gladly accepted the request and worked toward a solution. With assistance from Rhee, Wadman managed to avoid a confrontation of a more serious nature, but he also sowed seeds conflict and dissension by appointing Rhee as principal of the boarding school.[13]

The second Methodist church grew out of the Korean Evangelical Society organized by a group of Korean residents in San Francisco on October 8, 1905. Mun Kyong-ho assumed the responsibility of conducting church services until July 15, 1906 when Pang Wha-jung succeeded him as evangelist for the group. The Society was expanded after Yang Chu-sam arrived in San Francisco on his way to Nashville, Tennessee, where he was to attend the Divinity School of Vanderbilt University. Upon his arrival he saw everywhere around him the life of adversity and poverty to which his countrymen were subjected. He was so moved emotionally by what he had seen that he decided to postpone his study in order to take on the work of helping his countrymen spiritually and materially. The Society rented a building on California Street and held a church service dedicating the house of worship. The building had three floors. The first floor was used as dining hall for Korean boarders, who were accommodated on the third floor. The second floor was used as a place of church services. The Society was granted its present church status after the Rev. Yi Tae-wi was appointed as its pastor on August 5, 1911. The congregation moved to the present church building located on Powell Street in June 1928. Today, the Korean Methodist Church of San Francisco as the oldest such church on the mainland of the United States has a membership of three hundred. Its annual budget as of April 1974 is approximately $21,000, and its total assets are estimated at half a million dollars.[14]

---

[13] Won-yong Kim, *Chaemi Hanin Osimnyo n-sa*, 47.
[14] *Miju Dong-a* [The Dong-a daily in America], April 18, 1974, 1.

During the first period an Episcopal church was organized in Honolulu by the efforts of Chong Hyong-gu and Kim Ik-song, who was also known as Isaiah Kim. On February 10, 1905, a church service dedicating the Korean Episcopal Church was held at the St. Andrew Episcopal Church in Honolulu, and the Church then rented a classroom at a local elementary school as a place of church services. On October 16 of the same year the church was permitted the use of a part of the St. Elizabeth Episcopal Church, a local Chinese church.

The first period also saw the establishment of a Presbyterian church in Los Angeles in 1906, the first Presbyterian church ever to be established in the United States by Korean Christians. A group of Korean residents in Los Angeles sent a representative to negotiate with the Presbyterian Missionary Extension Board for a place of worship. The Board responded by dispatching the Rev. Richard who became instrumental in establishing the Korean Presbyterian Mission. The group rented a house situated on Bunker Hill Street as a place of church services. The group did not receive church status until April 1921.

The second period in the history of the church in the Korean American community was marked with disputes over policy on church administration, church financial business, and operation of the Korean boarding school which was later known as the Chung'ang Hagwon, or the Central Institute. As has been noted already, Syngman Rhee was able to secure principalship of the Central Institute in 1913. No sooner had he become principal than he wanted to have a lot on the corner of Emma and Punchbowl Streets, which was purchased by the Korean National Association of Hawaii at $1,500. Rhee wanted to use it for a dormitory to accommodate students at the Central Institute. His request was, however, denied by the delegates to the Annual Convention of the Korean National Association in 1915. Rhee then decided to use a less legitimate but a more effective means of threat and coercion to take the property away from the Association. Rhee learned that there had been some irregularities in the business of running the Association. It had been said that Hong In-p'yo, treasurer of the Association, and Kim Chong-hak, its president, dipped into the till entrusted to them. Upon learning of the irregularities Rhee demanded that he be given the power to supervise the treasury of the Association and that the Controversial property be turned over to him for use of the Korean school. Rhee seemed to have orchestrated his demand with another high-handed method. A group of students from the Central Institute led by Yang Yu-ch'an came to the Annual Convention of the Korean National Association in May 1915 to beat up Yi Hong-gi, Kim Kyu-sop, Yi Chong-gun, and Kim Chong-hak for opposing Rhee's request.[15] The *Honolulu Advertiser* ran an article concerning this incident in July 1915 under the title "Korean Trouble Gets Into Court," as follows.

> An Hung Kyong, (An Hung-gyong) General Manager, charged Hong In Pio (Hong In-p'yo) for embezzling $120 from membership fees, and Kim Chong Hak (Kim Chong-hak)

---

[15] Lyu, "Korean Nationalist Activities in Hawaii and America," 52–53. It should be pointed out that Yang Yu-ch'an was later appointed by Syngman Rhee as Korean ambassador to the United States, when Rhee became the first president of the Republic of Korea.

for embezzling $1,300. Yi Hong Ki (Yi Hong-gi) who was maltreated a month ago by a mob at Korean National Association brought a trial of 19 men in court.[16]

The beating incident and the revelation of embezzlement of funds by officers of the Association changed the mood of most members of the Association. When the request was put again for reconsideration, the delegates reversed their previous decision and thirty-five out of thirty-eight voted for the free grant of the land.

Rhee was not only a catalyst to disputes among Koreans but also a sharp wedge between the Hawaiian Methodist Mission and some Korean Methodist Christians. When William H. Fry was appointed to succeed Wadman as superintendent on January 1, 1914, he learned that the church financial matters had been dealt with in a less than a businesslike manner. He wanted to correct past mistakes in the Mission administration by means of his close personal supervision of both the church and the school. Also, it was alleged that Fry was opposed to the use of the church and the school as training centers of political leaders and political activities for the Korean independence movement against the Japanese Empire. Rhee, on the other hand, wanted to use them to teach Korean nationalism and to train Korean political leaders. Furthermore, Rhee refused to take orders from Fry and challenged him to turn the governance of the school and the church over to Koreans. Rhee was of the opinion that Koreans should have a complete control over the church and the school, as they were fully supported by Koreans in the islands. Two such diametrically opposed positions were certainly destined to travel a separate course soon or later.[17]

The inevitable separation came in the fall of 1916, when a group of seventy or eighty people left their Methodist Church in order to follow Rhee's leadership for the autonomy and self-determination of the church in the Korean community. The first church service was held at the residence of Pak Nae-sun after their separation, and the separatists then decided to bold their church services at the Korean Girls' Seminary building. In 1918 the place of worship was moved to the school building located at Wailaie Street and 7th Avenue. At the beginning, the congregation was known simply as the *Sirip Kyohoe*, or the New Church, which was changed to the Korean Christian Church sometime in 1917. This was not the only New Church in the islands. There was a New Church established at Koloa, Kauai, as early as 1915, and there were as many as fifteen when the separatist movement reached its zenith.

An important event in the development of New Churches took place on December 13, 1918, when the first annual Delegates Conference of the Korean Christian Churches was held to establish an organization to coordinate various church activities and to discuss methods of combating the established Methodist Church. Out of this conference emerged the Korean Christian mission known as the Central Korean Christian Church. The delegates seemed to have agreed on a major weapon to be used in competing with the well-established Methodist Church supported by a strong missionary organization. The idea of independence and self-government was to be their effective weapon, which was also that of Rhee, who later

---

[16] *The Honolulu Advertiser*, July 3, 1915, 10.

[17] *The Honolulu Advertiser*, July 3, 1915, 64.

expressed his philosophy for founding the church in a letter dated December 12, 1944, to Kingsley K. Lyu:

> When I founded the Korean Christian Church with you people, I was sure I would lose my Korean and American friends in the Methodist Church. But I was resolved that we Koreans should control our own church administration without depending upon the foreign missions, that we should govern our own affairs. It was natural that the Methodists criticized our Christian people and were bitter to us.[18]

From the beginning of the separatist movement to August 1945, when Korea was freed from the Japanese colonialism, the members of the Korean Christian Church were an indispensable part of the Korean national independence movement abroad. Ideologically, they advocated as strongly as they could that Koreans were ready to exercise self-government and independence. As evidence, they pointed to their Korean Church as a symbol of independence from foreign domination and of self-government in administration on their own affairs. Financially, they sent in their contributions out of their meager earnings as workers on sugar plantations or as manual laborers.

The rapid growth of the Korean Christian churches in the islands seemed to have had an adverse effect on the quality of the spiritual care for members of the churches. There were in the Korean Christian churches no persons trained in the Christian ministry until 1919. Those who had taken on the responsibility of church pastorate were people acquainted with some Bible lessons and written Korean language, hardly an acceptable qualification for the difficult task of caring for man's spiritual needs. Sometime in 1919, Min Ch'an-ho arrived in Honolulu after he had been ordained and admitted into the California Synod of the Presbyterian Church. As an ordained man of God, however, Min did not live up to expectations commensurate with either the training that he had received or the ministerial ethics that he had pledged to uphold. According to Kingsley K. Lyu, Min began to perform the office of a bishop immediately after he had become pastor of the Korean Christian Church in Honolulu, and ordained men into the ministry of the Korean Christian churches. It is alleged by Lyu that Min had ordained more than ten of Rhee's supporters into Christian ministry by laying his hands on their heads. Therefore, when the Charter of the Central Korean Christian Church of Honolulu was obtained on December 9, 1924, the churches on the Islands of Oahu, Maui, and Hawaii had pastors ordained by Min.[19]

The "ordained pastors" handpicked for their political and personal loyalty to Rhee soon began to turn churches into clubhouses for political lectures. Church services officiated over by them usually began with a topic of a political nature and ended with announcement for political activities in connection with the *Tongji-hoe*, or the Comrade Society, a political organization established on July 7, 1921, by Rhee to support his Korean national independence movement. It is said that during church services the pastors seldom neglected to praise Rhee who was remembered by them

---

[18] *The Honolulu Advertiser*, July 3, 1915, 68.
[19] *The Honolulu Advertiser*, July 3, 1915, 71.

in their prayers. Those who neglected such decorum found themselves soon without a job. According to Lyu, a pastor, formerly of the Presbyterian faith, had accepted the pastorate at the Korean Christian Church, but he was soon relieved of his duty, as he had forgotten to repeat the name of Rhee in his prayers.[20]

It is not surprising, in retrospect, that the people ordained in such a hollow manner to the Christian ministry confused personal loyalty to a political leader with services to mankind and an ideological message for an earthly kingdom with the universal message for the heavenly Kingdom.

Conflicts and disputes did not end with the separation of Rhee's followers from the Methodist Church. The Korean Christian Church had a series of its own internal dissensions. The first occurred soon after Min's resignation in 1929. Min was forced to resign, as he had been accused of misappropriating a $15,000 church building fund. His successor, Yi Yong-jik, was anxious to enforce the church regulations originally written by Syngman Rhee in the hope that the church would become a house of worship rather than a place for supporting Rhee's political activities. Soon the congregation was divided into two groups: one group supporting Yi and the other determined to oust him. Charges and counter-charges were made by both groups against each other, and thousands of dollars were spent as legal fees paid to determine the legitimate owner of the Korean Christian Church of Honolulu. Almost every Sunday the local police were called in to protect the church service officiated over by Yi against the violence committed by the anti-Yi faction.

Another controversy occurred in the summer of 1946, when the pastor of the Korean Christian Church made an attempt to make the church a place for worship by separating politics from church affairs. With the approval of the church board, the pastor announced that the board and the pastor decided not to allow any person or group to use the church building for purposes other than church-related activities. This announcement touched off a series of verbal attacks against the pastor and members of the church board. A small number led by a former assistant treasurer began to accuse the pastor of being anti-Rhee, as he had failed to repeat the name of Rhee in his prayers. When the church board refused to recognize such a characterization of the pastor, the group made an attempt to take over the church administration by force on September 29, 1946. The controversy over which group was the real orthodox congregation of the Korean Christian Church was finally decided by the court, which ordered the two groups to be united in October 1948.[21]

Several churches of different denominations were established on the mainland of the United States during the second period. As many Koreans began to move from the Hawaiian Islands to such metropolitan areas on the mainland as Oakland, Los Angeles, Chicago, and New York, there was an increasing need to establish local churches. As early as June, 1914, a small group of Korean residents in Oakland met at the residence of Mun Won-ch'il to conduct church services officiated over by the Rev. Hwang Sa-yong, who then worked for the Methodist Episcopal Church, South.

---

[20] *The Honolulu Advertiser,* July 3, 1915, 75.
[21] *The Honolulu Advertiser,* July 3, 1915, 76.

On August 10, 1917 the group moved its place of worship to the residence of Cho Song-hak and invited Im Chong-gu, a student of Pacific School of Religion, Berkeley, California, to serve as evangelist for the group. After Im had become an ordained minister, the group negotiated with the Methodist Episcopal Mission for a place of worship. The Mission sent the Rev. David, who appointed Im Chong-gu and No Sin-t'ae as evangelists for the church, which was officially established on March 2, 1929. In 1938 the group purchased a building located on Webster Street and dedicated it as a place of worship on December 20. In July, 1940, the congregation was moved to another building located on Harrison Street in order to accommodate the increasing membership.

A group of Korean residents in New York negotiated with a Methodist Mission to establish a place worship in February, 1923. The Mission extended its helping hand by giving a large sum of money to purchase a building located on West 21st Street. The church building was dedicated on April 23. The congregation moved to a larger building located on West 115th Street in order to accommodate an expanding church membership in October, 1927. During the same year the Korean Methodist Church of Chicago, which had been established in July 1924, moved to a new building situated on Lake Park Avenue.

The Korean Presbyterian Church of Los Angeles developed a conflict soon after its establishment, and on October 14, 1924, a group of church members severed their relations with the church and established their own church known as the Free Church. The members of the Free Church later sent their representatives on July 10, 1930, to the Methodist Episcopal Mission to ask for assistance in establishing a church. The Mission sent the Rev. David, who officiated over the establishment of the Korean Methodist Church of Los Angeles on October 16, 1930. Today, the church building is located on West 29th Street, dedicated on October 7, 1945.[22] Besides these Methodist churches established in major metropolitan areas, there was a Presbyterian church in Reedley, California, which was organized in June, 1936. Also, a Christian church modelled after the Korean Christian Church of Honolulu was established by members of the *Tongji-hoe* in September 1936.

Compared with the second period in the history of the church in the Korean American community, which was replete with controversial disputes and conflicting interests, the third period between 1946 and 1967 was characterized by efforts on the part of the *Ilttae* (first generation) to maintain the status quo, and by an attitude of indifference and rebellion on the part of *Idae* (second generation; Koreans born in America of their immigrant parents) and *Samdae* (third generation; children of the second generation). A number of social, cultural, and political factors seemed to have contributed to these intergenerational conflicts. First, the *Ilttae* had seen their national sovereignty gradually eroded by the Japanese Empire prior to their departure for the Hawaiian Islands and the mainland of the United States. After their arrival in America, most of them kept a burning patriotism for Korea intact, and they

---

[22] Yi Kyong, "Settlement Patterns of Los Angeles Koreans" (master's thesis, University of California, Los Angeles, 1969), 35.

participated directly or indirectly in the effort to regain Korea's national independence. The *Ilttae* as a whole had a political cause to fight and to live for through their life.

However, to *Idae* and *Samdae* the political independence of Korea was more ideological rhetoric than a political imperative. After independence came to Korea in 1945, the issue of Korean national independence no longer served as a rallying point for Korean in America. Second, to *Ilttae* the church was both a place of social interaction and cultural identification. After all they spoke the same language and shared the same values and customs, so much of their unique cultural behavior was mutually reinforced in the social contacts provided by the church. Although the *Idae* had been under strong cultural influence from the *Ilttae*, they must have felt at times strange and somewhat alienated when they were taken to church by their parents, who spoke only Korean to their contemporaries. So far as the *Samdae* was concerned, they could hardly identify themselves with the *Ilttae* religiously, for they did not understand either their language or their culture. As pointed out by Cho Kyong-suk Gregor in her study, the *Idae* "show a complete lack of interest in the matter of politics and region."[23] Third, the Asian Exclusion Act and the quota system in the American immigration policy from 1924 to 1968[24] prevented more Koreans from coming to the United States. Had they been allowed to enter, they would have provided their ethnic church with more vitality and spiritual leadership.

The fourth period in the history of the church in the Korean American community has begun with the new influx of immigrants into the United States, particularly into its large metropolitan areas, from Korea which has sent more than eighty thousand of its nationals since 1968. It is estimated that there are now as many as fifty thousand Koreans in the Los Angeles area alone, and more new arrivals are expected to join their countrymen in this area. This new wave of immigrants promises potential resources and leadership long needed badly for a revival of the ethnic church in the Korean American community. However, it also portends potential problems for the church. There are already some signs of stress and strain to which the church in the Korean American community has long been subjected. One of such signs is to be seen in the proliferation of churches founded on the bedrock of denominationalism. A number of historical and social forces seems responsible for the emergence of the denominational church within the American community today. Due to an influx of new immigrants who arrive in the United States with their own religious preference, it is quite reasonable to expect them to look for the church of their choice or to establish their own denominational church. This seems to be a major cause for the proliferation of churches. For instances, there are today in the city of San Francisco a total of nine churches attended almost exclusively by Koreans. Of these nine churches, only two share the same

---

[23] Cho Kyong-suk Gregor, "Korean Immigrants in Gresham, Oregon: Community Life and Social Adjustment" (master's thesis, University of Oregon, 1963), 54.

[24] Although the act of October 3, 1965 (Pub. L. no. 89–236) repealed the national origin quota system established in 1924, the act included a three-year phase-out period.

denominational affiliation. These churches were originally established as denominational churches.[25]

Other churches professing different brands of Christianity seem to have less than a clear philosophy for their denominational affiliation. Whether or not these churches have been established separately because of fine differences in the theological interpretation of the Bible is yet to be clarified. What seems clear to those who have carefully watched the painful and long metamorphosis of the Korean ethnic church is that the disputes over petty individual interests and honors rather than theological concerns have been a predominant reason for divisions within the church ever since its inception in the Korean American community. The recent dispute between two pastors of the Korean Missionary Church located on 11th and New Hampshire Streets, Los Angeles, is a case in point.

Apparently, the church had been established under the leadership of the Rev. Ko Won-yong. Ko was elected chairman of the church board and the responsibility of running the church fell on his shoulder as chairman. Ko later invited one of his friends, the Rev. Chang Yun-song, to take care of his congregation while he was away for missionary duty. When he returned from his mission work to take up his position as pastor of the church he had helped to build, Chang refused to give in and claimed that the congregation had recognized him as legitimate chairman of the church board. Chang continued to conduct church services and even refused to call upon Ko to officiate over Sunday services. As Ko related in an interview with a newspaper reporter later, he felt that he was alienated from his own congregation.

One Sunday Ko decided to lock the door of the church building where Chang was to hold his church service. Then he led a group of his sympathizers to the residence of a church elder for their own church service. Angered by Ko's action that had left approximately one hundred people stranded on the street, a group of four or five representatives from among Chang's followers came to protest against Ko and disrupted the church service in progress. Irritated by their unexpected visitors, someone from Ko's group called local police in to intervene in the dispute. Today the congregation remains divided without a hope for reunification.[26]

As has been observed, the new influx of large numbers of Korean immigrants into the United States also promises a potential force for the growth and development of the Korean ethic church. The number of churches is increasing by leaps and bounds. There are more than twenty churches in the Los Angeles area alone. There are three Korean churches in the vicinity of Seattle, where there was not even a single church for Koreans prior to 1968.[27] The sermons delivered from pulpits have shown an improved quality, and they have demonstrated deliberate efforts of pastors to interpret and teach the Bible without influencing the laymen's secular interests, which had plagued the church in the Korean American community during the first and second periods of its history.

---

[25] *Miju Dong-a* [The Dong-A daily in America], April 4, 1974, 2
[26] *Miguk Sosik* [The American News], February 26, 1973, 1.
[27] *Miguk Sosik* [The American News], April 23, 1974, 1.

In spite of the conflicts and problems within the church already mentioned, it served the Korean American community in a number of important areas of need that would not otherwise have been met. It is unfortunate, retrospectively speaking, that the church had been swept into a vortex of political controversies over philosophical arguments and strategies for the Korean national independence movement during its embryonic stage. It is tragic, particularly in view of the fact that so much of the energy and resources of the church were diverted to an unrealistic and native notion, that the leaders and their followers of "Christian America," when sufficiently supplicated by their fellow Korean Christians, would assist them in their fight against the Imperial Japan. The leaders of the Korean national independence movement were men who were largely ignorant of American foreign policy toward Imperial Japan, particularly during the early period of their independence movement. They were also too ignorant of the dynamics of American domestic politics of accommodation to utilize it for their cause. Given the historical conditions under which the Korean independence movement was undertaken, however, the church played an active role in supporting propaganda and diplomatic efforts to restore Korea's independence.

The Korean independence movement was supported financially by a great number of small contributions made largely by Korean residents in the Hawaiian Islands,[28] most of whom were members of local churches, particularly the Korean Christian churches. When the Korean Commission, established sometime in the autumn of 1919 in Washington, DC, issued bonds during the same year to generate the first $250,000 of the five million dollars to be used in diplomatic and propaganda purposes, many Korean Christians purchased them.[29]

The church also played an active role in educational and journalistic efforts to maintain and perpetuate Korean culture. Most of the Korean immigrants seemed to have sent their children to Korean language schools for practical as well as patriotic reasons. First of all, they wanted to bring up their children as Koreans. In order to achieve this goal in an alien culture, they needed an educational institution devoted to the teaching of Korean history, language, and culture. The church was chosen primarily for three reasons. First, there were already churches established in various work camps, and therefore there was a basic organizational structure for the task. Second, most of the people qualified to teach children anything about Korea were pastors,[30] who were literate enough to instruct them. Third, due to lack of instructional materials, the Bible and Christian hymn books were used as textbooks.

---

[28] A careful count of the number of people who promised to make a contribution, as reported in the *Korean Pacific Weekly*, an official bulletin published by *Tongji-hoe*, indicates that a total of sixty-nine persons promised a sum of $1,026. This is less than $15 per person. See *Korean Pacific Weekly*, series 28, vol. 12, no. 482, June 14, 1941, 19.

[29] Kim, Won-yong, *Chaemi Hanin Osimnyo n-sa* [A fifty-year history of Koreans in America], (Reedley, CA: Charles Ho Kim, 1959), 47.

[30] Helen Lewis Givens, "The Korean Community in Los Angeles" (master's thesis, University of Southern California, 1939), 38.

Secondly, Korean immigrants established their language schools as a symbol of their national independence. There were already foreign language schools operated by Japanese and Chinese in the islands, and the Koreans were determined not to be surpassed in this crucial area of national culture. Thirdly, they saw an opportunity to put into practical use the Korean language to be learned by their children who were attending English-speaking schools. They hoped that their children would serve them as interpreters.[31] Various bulletins were also published by a number of churches, and they were used both as newspapers and instructional materials, as they carried Bible lessons in Korean. One of the more important ones was published by the Korean Methodist Church of Honolulu. The church began its bulletin, called the *Honolulu Korean Church Bulletin*, in November 1904. The church continued to publish its bulletin until it was discontinued in October 1940.

Available reports on the projects sponsored by the church in Korean American community today seem to indicate that more emphasis is being given to recreational and social activities for group cohesion than to educational and political programs, though there are on the mainland a few Korean language schools supported by the local churches. This is certainly in accord with the needs of the Korean ethnic community today, and it is highly desirable that the church detach itself from controversies over Korea's internal politics.

There is, however, a vital need waiting to be filled in the Korean American community by either the church or other grassroots social organizations. If Korean immigrants in America are to share fully with other Americans what their adopted country has to offer to its citizens, then they have to participate sooner or later in American domestic politics of accommodation, separatism, or radicalism. Whatever the choice of their political style may be, the Korean immigrants will soon be in need of an organizational base for their political participation in American politics. In the past, Irish and Italian Americans have used their ethnic affiliation with Catholicism rather effectively to gain political power.[32] Whether or not Korean Americans will use their church as a political weapon remains to be seen.

---

[31] Lyu, "Korean Nationalist Activities in Hawaii and America," 33.

[32] Edgar Litt, *Ethnic Politics in America* (Glenview, IL: Scott, Foresman and Company, 1970), 60–80.

An Approach to Moral Education in Philippine Secondary Schools[*]

PATRICIA LING MAGDAMO

Chapter III
Selected Philippine Traditional Values
Affecting Learning

Introduction

In this chapter the focus will be on the descriptive analysis of selected traditional values that are found in a cluster or pattern in a large portion of Filipino society. They are considered to be of primary influence upon behavior of both individuals and groups. Any effort to reorganize moral education in the schools ought to begin with the examination of the "life-ways which constitute the designs for living in this society."[1]

Selection of the values has been arbitrary, the most obvious reason being the availability of materials. The basic source is the research report of Frank Lynch, a Jesuit anthropologist whose personal and professional interest has led to a fifteen-year study of the value system in lowland Philippine culture. By means of observation, interviews, language analysis, and data from related studies, Lynch identified and categorized the values that most influence Filipino behavior.[2] With his associates he conducted the better part of these studies under the auspices of the Institute of Philippine Culture of the Ateneo de Manila, one of the finest private universities in the country.

---

[*] Submitted in partial fulfillment of the requirements for the degree of Doctor of Education at Teachers College, Columbia University, 1974. Dissertation Committee: Professor Maxine Greene, sponsor, and Professor C. Ellis Nelson. Approved by the Committee on the Degree of Doctor of Education.

[1] Clyde Kluckhohn, "Values and Value Orientation in the Theory of Action," in *Toward a General Theory of Action*, ed., Talcott Parsons and Edward A. Shils (Cambridge, MA: Harvard University Press, 1967), 410.

[2] Lynch makes this claim for the majority of lowland Filipinos who comprise the major dialects and main geographical regions. His studies exclude the urbanized Filipino, though he recognizes that traditional values still operate in urban centers. Also excluded are the minority cultural groups who are diverse in religion and culture, the largest of these being the Filipino Muslims.

The earlier studies were used extensively in acculturation workshops and orientation sessions for religious workers and Peace Corps volunteers. In addition the Institute shares research projects with Penn State University through its Basic Research Program. Philippine social studies is fairly new and as yet incomplete. Even at that there are some divergent viewpoints about theory and methodology, it should be mentioned that the Ateneo group represents a theoretical position different to that of the University of the Philippines under the leadership of Dr. F. Landa Jocano.[3] Criticism in a group of scholars can be disturbing but, on the whole, it has led to more rigorous field testing and careful methods which can only raise the level of social science research in the Philippines. For our purposes, the three primary values in the Lynch study data remain useful to any evaluation of moral education.

To have an acceptable definition of the term "value," the description offered by Clyde Kluckhohn is in order. A "value," Kluckhohn writes, is "a conception, explicit or implicit, distinctive of an individual or characteristic of a group, of the desirable which influences the selection from available modes, means and ends of action."[4] Technical meanings for the term are to be found in each discipline, including philosophy and economics, and the term itself connotes several meanings in ordinary speech. Kluckhohn's definition recognizes the *affective* ("desirable"), *cognitive* ("conception"), and *conative* ("selection") elements essential to the notion of value. Such a view takes the culture, the relation of individual and group to that culture, and the individual's place in the group as primary points of departure in analyzing a system of action.[5] The most crucial, to Kluckhohn and his associates, is the term "desirable," which accords with the core of the traditional meaning of value in almost all fields of study. It implies the normative factor which places value above existential propositions. It also influences the conative—evaluation and selection from various alternative actions—in producing a coherent system or predictable individual behavior.

Like culture, values are not always directly observable but may be inferred and abstracted from immediate sense data based upon what is said and done by individuals. Value as a conception identifies itself with a social structure. Kluckhohn clarifies his definition by distinguishing between cathexis and valuation, both in terms of experience and conceptually. A cathexis is an impulse and is relatively short ranged, while a value "restrains or canalizes impulses in terms of wider and more perduring goals."[6]

Such a traditionally authoritarian and tightly knit community as exists in many Filipino barrios and urban centers provides innumerable occasions where impulses

---

[3] Robert Lawless, *An Evaluation of Philippine Culture—Personality Research*, Monograph Series J, Asian Center (Quezon City, Philippines: University of the Philippines Press, 1969). Essentially a review of all the research in social science up to 1969 with an evaluation of the methods and theories of each.

[4] Kluckhohn, "Values and Value Orientation," 395.

[5] Kluckhohn, "Values and Value Orientation," 395.

[6] Kluckhohn, "Values and Value Orientation," 399.

have to be severely restrained to serve larger group goals. The values to be discussed are behaviors that maximize such restraint for the sake of social harmony. The hierarchy or continuum of values helps persons to integrate a total action system out of often incompatible individual and collective needs; it is this inner coherence that binds Filipino society, that has either helped or hindered adjustment to change for the average person, and has often been misunderstood by foreigners.

Frank Lynch defines "value" as a standard used in making a decision and selecting a course of action. He regards values as extremely basic in nature, whether declared or implied, controlling behavior and stimulating activity, and tacitly approved or openly promoted in a society.[7] The basis for his definition is Robin Williams' fourfold test for determining and isolating values for study. The criteria are

1. *Extensiveness* of the value in the total activity of the system. What proportion of a population and of its activities manifest the value?
2. *Duration* of the value. Has it been persistently important over a considerable period of time?
3. *Intensity* with which the value is sought or maintained, as shown by effort, crucial choices, verbal affirmation, and by reactions to threats to the value—e.g., promptness, certainty, and severity of sanctions.
4. *Prestige of value carriers*—i.e., of persons, objects, or organizations considered to be bearers of the value. Culture heroes, for example, are significant indexes of values of high generality and esteem.[8]

The procedure involved arguing back from observation of what people do and say, or do not do and do not say, the choices they make or refuse, the things they punish and reward, their reasons and motives for specific actions. Lynch posits a scheme in which the thematic values, the most basic ones, are buried below two levels of less fundamental values. These are termed instrumental values and intermediate values, the former important for what they can achieve and the latter of cathectic and esthetic purposes. The thematic value more often exists below the level of awareness yet operates widely among lowland Philippine groups.[9]

It is clear that none of the values is uniquely Filipino. What makes each so is the emphasis and rank each occupies in a particular culture. Kluckhohn has pointed out that value orientation is a distinct modal aspect of any total action complex and one would look for it in the culture.[10]

---

[7] Frank Lynch, *Social Acceptance Reconsidered* (Quezon City, Philippines: Ateneo de Manila Press, 1970), 7.

[8] Robin M. Williams Jr., *American Society: A Sociological Interpretation* (New York: Alfred A. Knopf, 1951), 382–383.

[9] Lynch, *Social Acceptance Reconsidered*, 7–8, 55. Social scientists are well aware of the mix in value orientation and the variables of social organization, education, and sex among other factors. Rural values have been perpetuated in strongly urban centers, such as Manila, transferred by servants employed there to raise children and who have just recently left the rural areas themselves.

[10] Clyde Kluckhohn, "Values and Value Orientation," 412.

What distinguishes the Filipino's value orientations are the degrees of emphasis in patterning expressional, cognitive, and moral values. Lynch's own study of Americans and Filipinos show similar value orientations but differing degrees of emphasis. The traditional value of "saving face," for instance, is not confined only to Asia but is universal, operating with varying degrees of emphasis in each land and sometimes between differing groups within one land.

The majority of lowland Filipinos studied by Lynch represents 86% of the population who live in barrios and settlements of one thousand persons or less. No adequate study has yet been compiled among the minority urban dwellers who hold the largest share of skills and power, and who will be directly responsible for changes in the society. The results of future research can contribute to further understanding of the process of change, particularly with traditional values. What are known of the more important social values are discussed below.

Social Acceptance

In his research Lynch has found that the basic value of Filipinos is social acceptance. It is part of the good life on this earth that one should be accepted by one's fellows for what one is, thinks himself to be, or would like to be treated. It doubtless stems from the familistic nature of Philippine society which social scientists have observed to be a primary characteristic. Society is built on the image of the family, and high value is attached to family loyalty and solidarity. To apply Florence Kluckhohn's descriptive phrase about cultures, Filipino society is less the "getting-things-done" developmental type more common to the West than it is the "being-in-becoming" orientation of the individual within the large group.[11]

The relationships are lineal, with age and generational differences counting for much as well as collateral, with the individual placed in a pattern of lateral extended relationships. In a sense, all other social institutions are extensions of kinship. In industry or business, family corporations are more the rule than the exception. In politics it is the family system—dynasties and *pariente*—which controls entire regions and also the national organizations.[12] In religion churches tend to be family-centered rather than organization-centered. Many Filipinos are aware of this phenomenon and the need for changing attitudes if one is to change the system of action.

Social acceptance becomes very important in a centripetal society such as that found in the family or a barrio. Put negatively, it is had when one is not rejected or improperly criticized by others. There is no element of liking as there is for social *approval*. The Tagalog proverb best expressing social acceptance is translated to mean, "It doesn't matter if you don't love me, just don't shame me." It appears to be

---

[11] Florence Kluckhohn, "Value Orientations," in *Toward a Unified Theory of Human Behavior*, ed., Roy R. Grinker (New York: Basic Books, 1959), 85–6.

[12] Lynch, *Social Acceptance Reconsidered*, 1–3, 428–430. "Ritual co-parenthood" implies the extending of families through sponsors in baptism and marriage, bound by sacramental ties and obliged to assume responsibility for those *compradazgo* members.

a status relationship, avidly sought and keenly cultivated and appreciated when granted.

The concept itself is not generally verbalized nor is it deliberately pursued as a conscious, well-defined goal. As Kluckhohn reminds us, an implicit value is potentially expressible in rational language by actor as well as observer.[13] Lynch found the value existing widely despite the often inchoate state and inadequate verbalization of it. His analysis of the Tagalog dialect conversations reinforces this claim. Nuances and indirect phrases difficult to translate into English imply careful attention to social accept-ance on the part of the speaker as well as the hearer.

If social acceptance is more of an implicit value, parts of the cluster are not and Filipinos are very conscious and outspoken about two intermediate overt values that are useful to the achievement of social acceptance. They are (1) *pakikisama*,[14] or smooth interpersonal relations, and (2) sensitivity to personal affront, whose two sanctions are *hiya* and *amor propio*. The first is essentially outgoing, while the latter is a defensive sanction.

1. Pakikisama, or Smooth Interpersonal Relations

The Tagalog term is derived from the root *sama* which means "to go along with or to accompany." It describes the procedure used to maintain harmonious relationships in spite of conflict and tension. *Pakikisama* enables the individual to go along with the group, to be sensitive to group demands, to concede where circumstances require, and avoid open conflict. It requires restraint of impulse and desire for the sake of order and agreement, and ultimately, for the coherence of the system.

There are several mechanisms by which smooth interpersonal relations may be acquired and preserved: by use of euphemism in speech where an unpleasant truth or opinion or a request is stated as pleasantly and politely as possible; by equivocation, circumlocution, and indirection in speech and behavior; by use of go-betweens rather than direct confrontation in delicate negotiations and social arrangements, such as marriages and business negotiations; and, in many smaller communities, by use of gossip to convey information and inner feelings to the right parties.

These mechanisms are bridges crossing the social distance that separates kinsmen from non-kinsmen and in-group members from out-group members. In all cases, avoidance of conflict and minimizing tension is the goal. A second aim is to reconcile those affronted or injured in any way. The individual who possesses tact, pleasant and soft speech, and skill in reconciling parties is highly valued and greatly respected in the community.

---

[13] Kluckhohn, "Values and Value Orientation," 397.

[14] All dialect terms are Tagalog words. Each of the major dialects, and some of the others, use different terms with essentially the same meanings. Since the original study was conducted with Tagalog-speaking groups, and that language is the basis of Filipino, it is used here.

The tradition-oriented Filipino will anticipate and give the expected answer rather than a negative (and possibly a more truthful) reply that he feels might embarrass or humiliate another. Such an attitude makes poll-taking a travesty. Foreigners have great difficulty coping with such behavior and often mistake the form for the action or purpose underlying it. The Spanish observer Pedro Chirino noted the extreme courtesy and sanctioned behavior of Filipinos toward one another in 1604. Jose Rizal at the end of the nineteenth century commented that the Filipino prefers a beating to a scolding or insult.[15]

Robert Fox traces present-day values and systems of action to earliest times, noting that these have persisted through more than one colonial regime.[16] Peace Corps workers have been frustrated by the same behavior and are given careful instruction about interpersonal behavior during their orientation periods. As an example, Lynch's study of euphemistic devices in the language shows the frequent answer *siguro nga*, translated "I guess so" or "it could be," used to avoid open disagreement wherever possible. Self-deprecatory phrases are also used frequently for similar common refuge from a potentially disruptive situation. Many a teacher has come up against this particularly where an unpleasant task such as having to correct someone is involved.

Because marriage is essentially the union of two families whose kinsmen are being wed, careful negotiations are in order. This is one of the earliest customs that persist today in all but the most non-traditional, highly urban centers. The involvement of kinsmen points up the obvious differences from American society, where independence and personal effort are necessary to the achievement of one's goals. Americans may depend upon kinsmen when absolutely necessary but are not generally oriented to do so. In an argument or conflict the issue is settled by the principal protagonists without kinsmen rallying round them. Nonintervention is the rule and. there is ordinarily little danger of tension spreading beyond the two individuals who began it.

The average Filipino, however, considers it good, right, and even just to appeal to his relatives for support against outsiders. Security is interdependence. It is, in turn, reciprocated by the group accepting responsibility for the action of its individual members. Numerous are the accounts of families closing ranks around a son or kinsman who is obviously a felon or violator of the law. So much is at stake in preserving the coherence of the group's action system that the cultivation of smooth interpersonal relations is highly valued in the Philippines.

2. Sensitivity to Personal Affront

Through *pakikisama* the Filipino achieves full standing as a good member of his group. Apart from enhancing his own status, his behavior grants a measure of social

---

[15] Cited in Lynch, *Social Acceptance Reconsidered*, 11–12.

[16] Robert B. Fox, "Prehistoric Foundations of Filipino Culture and Society," in *Readings on Philippine Culture and Social Life*, edited by A Lardizabal and F. Leogardo (Manila: Rex Books Store, 1970), 436.

acceptance to those he deals with on a day to day basis. Contrary behavior is sanctioned in two ways.

Hiya

Hiya is the first and universal social sanction that Filipinos understand. It is best defined as the fear of exposure that inhibits self-assertion in situations perceived to be dangerous to one's ego. It has also been generally described as shame, acute embarrassment, humiliation, and self-depreciation. The value lies not in the sense that shame is desirable but that the ability to avoid it is to be desired by each person and a quality to be approved in others. For all the group awareness, *hiya* is a personality element whose main purpose is the avoidance of "ego diminution" before others.[17] In those terms social acceptance could be considered "ego magnification" because it seeks well-being for oneself before others.

The person who anticipates unpleasant behavior, words or action may inhibit his own behavior from a sense of *hiya*. On the other hand, one who violates the socially approved norms of conduct causes *hiya*. He is said to be *walang hiya*, without shame. The effort to gain social acceptance is thus negated by the embarrassment and humiliation caused another, often producing a reaction far out of proportion to the insult or misdeed. Relationships with all the possibilities for personal affront cover the whole spectrum and have to be carefully tended. Some of these are the employee-employer relationship, also landlord-tenant, teacher-pupil, older and younger members in a family or organization, politician-constituent, master-servant, and in-groups and out-groups.

Hiya is one of the ways by which the traditional community prevents transgressions against its local customs and norms. One research report reveals the preservation of *hiya* and *pakikisama* as strongly operating values in the Manila slums among gang members. Their homes broken, fathers often in prison, the pressures of ghetto life upon them, they turn their loyalties to the gang (*kabarkada*, our group), against all outsiders, and behave according to this group's values. It is dependency that encourages *hiya*, and it is *hiya* that helps to perpetuate the closeness of the group by inhibiting self-assertion.

It is a socializing mechanism, used in-group situations to educate the young to accept and obey the norms of the group and to maintain form and order in an often crowded household or society. The most grievous punishment possible is not a physical one. It is to be called "shameless." The Tagalog *talaban ng mukha* ("the person's face can be cut") and *kapal-kapal ng mukha* ("the person's face is thick") are severe reproaches. They are akin to the Western phrase "thick-skinned." To be without *hiya* is to be asocial, vulgar, uncouth, insensitive to others, and unconcerned for order in the group. In an interview study of nearly three hundred mothers in the vicinity of Manila, George Guthrie and his associates found that certain interpersonal

---

[17] The terms are used in the Cornell Values Study Group research. The report suggests that one of two main operational tests for identifying the presence of value-phenomena be a personality one, evident in ego diminution.

skills were of crucial significance for the development of the child. A summary is given below:

1. Recognize subtle cues which reveal the unspoken feelings of others.
2. Cope with angry feelings without striking out at others.
3. Give and receive help; pool his well-being with that of his nuclear and extended family.
4. Ignore activities of others, which, although visible, are said to be none of his concern.
5. Tease and be teased without losing his self-control.
6. Recognize his obligations to others for favors received.[18]

At least three of the skills (#1, 2, and 5) are directly concerned with the assurance of smooth interpersonal dealings and imply the *hiya* value. Thus the child early learns his place and function in the larger family group.

Another interesting study was of mental patients in the Manila area. What psychoanalysts now know about mental stress when anger is suppressed corresponds to the findings of the study team. In most cases, stress arises from interpersonal relations where the necessity for smooth social conditions leads to verbal and physical suppression of hostility by the individual in the family or community group.[19]

Hiya makes no distinction between the individual and the position he occupies. Criticism of a man's work is taken as criticism of him as a person, reflecting upon his family as well.[20] Employers are loath to fire incompetent workers. Some observers find that there is little critical review of one another's work among Filipino scholars, although this is rapidly changing in urban areas and with exposure to graduate study abroad. The frankness and bluntness of Americans and other foreigners are tolerated because they are outside the system, and therefore, know no better. Politics is often less a matter of national issues than it is of a man's status, family ties, and influence in the community.[21] Democracy is interpreted in terms of the leader's ability to care for and to "deliver the goods" to his constituents who elected him rather than a grassroots movement in government.

The Roman Catholic Church introduced the notions of sin and guilt, the cleansing of which was achieved through the sacraments of baptism and penance. It is possible to regard *hiya* in similar ritualized terms, functioning as guilt in the minds of people. The work of Helen Lynd and Gerhart Piers enables us to make a distinction between the two. Piers regards guilt as the transgression of prohibitions and shame

---

[18] Kluckhohn, "Values and Value Orientations," 40. The Guthrie study was a part of the Pennsylvania State University Basic Research Program.

[19] Lee Sechrest, "Philippine Culture, Stress, and Psychopathology," in *Mental Health Research in Asia and the Pacific*, ed., W. Caudill and Tsung-Yi Lin (Honolulu: East-West Center Press, 1969), 306–334.

[20] Fred Eggan and Frank S. J. Lynch, eds, *Area Handbook on the Philippines*, Vol. 1 (New Haven: Human Relations Area Files, Inc., Yale University, 1956), 436.

[21] Frank Golay, "Some Costs of Philippine Politics," *Asia* 23 (Autumn 1971): 45–60.

as the failure to reach one's goals or ideals.[22] Guilt becomes conscious as anxiety. Shame arises from the tension between the ego and the ego-ideal. It is literally a "shortcoming," a goal not being reached. Shame brings a shattering of the sense of self that is so important in maintaining an authoritarian-oriented society. Unlike guilt, however, it cannot be removed or cleansed by punishment or expiation.

Hiya tends to be more deeply felt the less familiar the social group one is dealing with and where there is greater potential threat to individual self-esteem and status. The phenomenon of *amok*—the sudden, seemingly irrational outburst that usually ends in violence and tragedy—has been attributed to this sensitivity to affront. It is a deviant system of action but occurs often enough to be considered a pattern of behavior, albeit a demonic one. One observer remarks that Filipinos dread *hiya* more than guilt.[23]

Jaime Bulatao sees it as a mechanism that perpetuated the "colonial" or "servant" mentality of Filipinos, it has also contributed to the maintenance of an authoritarian structure in religion, education, and government, besides the family. In moving from servant to master in his attitude toward himself, the individual needs to confront, and to transcend, the dilemma of whether or not he is to be "inner directed" (guided by moral principles) or "other directed" (guided by public opinion).

Amor Propio

This second of two sanctions in maintaining smooth interpersonal relations is more limited in scope than *hiya*, dealing as it does with individual self-esteem and functioning as a defense against severe interpersonal stress. *Amor propio* is not aroused by every insult or offense but only when one's most valued attributes are questioned by others. Camilo Osias has explained how "the ordinary Filipino is willing to sacrifice anything at the altar of his dignity and honor. He is keenly sensitive and highly intolerant when his personal dignity is injured."[24] This explains how an ordinarily gentle and soft-spoken person can suddenly turn violent.

One illustration of sensitive behavior affecting working relationships is taken from the 1967 field study of the social organization of stevedore groups. *Pakikisama* was discovered to be a vital concept on the waterfront where the men worked each day. Of three kinds of stevedores—those who know their jobs but cannot get along with others, those who do not know their jobs but can get along with others, and those who know their jobs and can also get along with others—the last group was the most prized but had the fewest workers for hire.

Of the other two groups, the *cabos*, or gang bosses, preferred to work with those who do not know their jobs but who do get along with others. The first group listed

---

[22] Gerhart Piers and Milton B, Singer, *Shame and Guilt: A Psychoanalytic Study* (Springfield, IL: C.B. Thomas, 1953), 11ff.; Helen M. Lynd, *On Shame and the Search for Identity* (New York: Harcourt, Brace & Co., 1958).

[23] D. J. Elwood, "Filipino Family Values—*Hiya* and *Pakikisama*: Theological Implications" (unpublished manuscript, 1969), 23–24.

[24] Camilo Osias, *The Filipino Way of Life: The Pluralized Philosophy* (Boston: Ginn & Co, 1940), 133–136.

were considered not worth hiring in the groups. The cardinal rule for a *cabo* in his conduct toward a stevedore is to preserve his *amor propio*. "Never shout at an ignorant stevedore." It could be argued that this is prudent behavior, but the avoidance of *hiya* (either for one's self or for the other party) while working for the best and harmonious relationships was extremely important and verbalized by the dock workers, both for themselves and their bosses.[25]

3. Utang Na Loeb, *or Reciprocity*

This is the third value in the cluster around social acceptance that some observers consider to be even more basic than the previously discussed one.[26] Certainly it is found in all traditional societies. Reciprocity is also rooted in the family structure and is learned by the youngest member at an early age. The individual becomes aware of his built-in reciprocal rights and obligations, the complex kin lines, the relatives and extended family members who can be counted on for help in time of need and whom one treats with respect.

In addition to the formal indebtedness that Malinowski showed to be common in every society, the Filipino may incur an "internal debt" of gratitude to another person or family in exchange for a favor. A continuing relationship of indebtedness is built up through the years, sometimes being repaid in services or political support. Both within and without the extended family this value governs to a large extent what one may do or expect from another person.

Every child is expected to possess *utang na loob*, to be aware of his obligations to those from whom he receives favors and to repay them in an acceptable manner. On the other side, those in positions to show favor and supply needs ought to act on their responsibility towards other members of their family or in-group.

Mary Hollnsteiner uses a threefold classification of these values: contractual reciprocity, quasi contractual reciprocity, and *utang na loob* reciprocity. The first imposes a voluntary agreement between two or more persons who behave toward one another in a specified way for a specified time in the future (such as agreeing to plough one another's fields or move someone's house in a barrio). The amount of time and effort spent in each case is approximately equal. The obligation is settled when the work is complete. There is no compulsion to do more, everything is prearranged and no strong emotion is attached to the transaction.[27]

The second type regulates balanced exchanges where there are terms of repayment which are not explicitly stated before the contract is made; the terms are implicit in the particular situation. Failure to reciprocate brings censure, the accusation of being *walang hiya*, or without shame. Such transactions may extend to the borrowing of a cup of rice. It has to be returned in the same quantity and quality.

---

[25] Randolf S. David, "Human Relations on the Waterfront: The Cabo System," *Philippine Sociological Review* 15, no. 3–4 (1967): 133–40.

[26] Elwood, "Filipino Family Values," 23.

[27] Mary R. Hollnsteiner, "Reciprocity in the Lowland Philippines," in *Four Readings on Philippine Values*, ed., Frank Lynch, 23–24.

If the time interval lengthens, a greater amount should be returned, the added "interest" helping to maintain smooth relations between the parties. In a cooperative labor project, an entire barrio may turn out to build a house with the understanding that its new owner will do his share in later projects. No clear statement of obligation is made by either party yet the necessity to repay in kind when the opportunity arises is a mandatory one.[28]

Utang na loob is a debt of gratitude which highlights relations between members of two different groups. One does not ordinarily expect favors of anyone from outside his group. Such actions become literally a debt "inside oneself" and must be reciprocated with interest. Francisco Colin, writing in the seventeenth century, observed this standard operating in ancient Filipino society in ways that bound a *barangay* chief to his people.[29] Its modern counterpart has been described in a study of a southern city where rural values exist in the community. There the landlord is the patron whose gift of extended credit and other benefits binds the tenant and his family to years of grateful service.[30]

Some services can never be repaid, of course, and quantification is impossible. The Visayan proverb "A financial debt paid is paid, but a debt of gratitude paid remains a debt" is typical of this attitude. The worst excess is the custom of binding a child to years of service to someone to whom the family is obligated, often without salary or other benefits. A real danger is the thin line between reciprocal gift-giving and bribery or extortion in subtle forms. *Utang na loob* can be used to rationalize the custom of giving monetary gifts, which in turn can lead to graft and usury particularly in business and government.

Onofre Corpuz expresses considerable pessimism about changing the political scene when graft and corruption are so thoroughly rooted in the behavior of the Filipino, though generally in the form of reciprocity.[31] Unscrupulous politicians exploit the system by deliberately cultivating "debtors" who vote in blocs. Equally unscrupulous voters agree to the "gift" because they can, in their turn, make demands upon their elected officials. Nepotism is another result of reciprocity in the framework of the family, and its obligations. Businesses, schools, political positions are often extensions of the family where the "we-they" frame of reference is important.

Hiya regulates the give and take of reciprocity. In the family children are expected to be eternally grateful to their parents for giving them life and for nurturing them. The child's *utang* is thus immeasurable, and nothing he can do quite makes up for this debt. It places a heavy obligation upon him from the earliest stage.[32] In urban areas, where middle-class families dwell in houses suitable for a nuclear

---

28 Hollnsteiner, "Reciprocity in the Lowland Philippines," 27.
29 Emma Helen Blair and James Alexander Robertson, *The Philippine Islands, 1493–1898*, vol. 40, *1690–1691* (Cleveland: Arthur H. Clark Co., 1909), 96.
30 Mary R. Hollnsteiner, "Reciprocity in the Lowland Philippines," 29.
31 Onofre D. Corpuz, *The Philippines* (Englewood Cliffs, NJ: Prentice-Hall), 92.
32 Hollnsteiner, "Reciprocity in the Lowland Philippines," 32.

family, that obligation extends to care of kin who are visiting, waiting for jobs, or who remain for an extended period. The family can include affiliated kin into the second generation, and the burden is multiplied for the smaller family unit. However, the value remains an implied obligation.

Between close friends and family members, *utang na loob* is often not regarded as a burden. Hollnsteiner says that "affective sentiment is at a maximum" in such reciprocal situations. The spirit of self-effacement is extremely important in reciprocal relationships. The spirit in which the service is rendered and the giving of the self are emotional elements that enhance the relationship.[33] In a society where the gap between the social classes is marked, *utang na loob* reciprocity stabilizes the system by acting as a bridge between the separated groups. It particularizes the functional interrelationship of the upper and lower classes in a network of acceptable behavior.

The recent trend away from a redistribution dominated economy to a market-dominated one corresponds to a growing ambivalence toward this value on the part of many educated, middle-class Filipinos. Both redistribution of surplus goods and *utang na loob* were designed to achieve security through interdependence. Perhaps a cash economy is more compatible with contractual reciprocity which already has a precedent in rural life. Yet Hollnsteiner found considerable hesitance to refuse to comply with the traditional claims of the system though increase in resistance to the pattern of reciprocity was indicated in her studies. Further study is required to find the ways of avoiding and channeling reciprocal demands into other acceptable behavior. The value has long enabled Filipinos to avoid institutionalizing their aged, infirm, orphans, and other members in society in need of special assistance to live.

In the long years of Spanish colonial influence the values in the cluster were reinforced in the religious attitudes and perspectives of the people. Saints were mediators of the Almighty and understood the workings of *utang na loob*, offering a more personal relationship that was comfortable for the average believer. The attitude toward God was similar if one prayed, attended Mass regularly, practiced the required devotions and rituals, what one requested was usually granted to one.

Summary

Clyde Kluckhohn writes that "human life is a moral life precisely because it is a social life."[34] The norms and standards reflect the deepest values of the group and affect the system of action that characterizes it. The three traditional social values described in this chapter have remained part of the Filipino system of action throughout the long years of foreign domination. As more empirical data becomes available, the process of self-understanding is advanced. Value-choice and the consequences of particular courses of action—Kluckhohn's "judgments of practice"—become clearer in both the cognitive and affective areas and enable those concerned with moral education to better prepare themselves for classroom teaching.

[33] Hollnsteiner, "Reciprocity in the Lowland Philippines," 41.
[34] Kluckhohn "Values and Value Orientation," 388.

Indigenization—Liberation of the Chinese American Churches

ALAN S. WONG

Introduction

The 1970s reflect the beginning of a new era for Asian American churches in the United States. Our churches are much more articulate and are seeking adequate expression for a spiritual experience in a language that is inherited from Buddhist and Confucian literature. The gospel of Christ must be preached in our people's own language. I do not mean that our churches are not preaching in our native tongue. In fact, many are bilingual. My observation is that, in spite of the actual situation, the present type of teaching does not touch the heart of the vast majority of our people because it is interpreted from a language other than our own.

Many of our Asian American churches were caught in the assimilation bag in the hope of being accepted into the American mainstream of life. Many ministers and Christians felt it was their Christian responsibility to do away with the national churches because they perpetuated their identities as "unassimilable." Also, it was hoped to do away with the differences that made for segregation discrimination.

It is now recognized that forced segregation by design does not work. Integration at this juncture is a fantasy, for whenever we try to establish domestic tranquility without including in that tranquility persons adjudged as alien, alienation prevails. Whenever alienation prevails, reconciliation is impossible.[1] The assimilation stand has not only caused a loss of identity but has had a dehumanizing affect upon the Asian Americans. The process has created a critical situation for second and succeeding Asian American generations concerning their identity. They are asking, "Who am I? Am I white or Asian?"

Historical Perspective with the Chinese

According to Professor Latourette's encyclopedic work, it is recorded that before 1840 there were only twenty Protestant missionaries in China.[2]

---

[1] Anthony Towne, "Revolution and the Marks of Baptism," *Katallagete* (Summer 1967): 2–13.

[2] Kenneth S. Latourette, *A History of Christian Missions in China* (New York, 1929), 209–227.

79

Stuart Creighton Miller devoted an entire chapter to this in his recent book on "The Protestant Missionary Image, 1807–1870."[3]

Essentially, his writing is a vivid account of how the first American visitors to China failed to discover the fabled Cathay of hoary wisdom and social serenity. During the first half of the nineteenth century, the reports of traders, diplomats and missionaries were colored by allegations of Chinese deceit, heathenism, despotism, cruelty, filthiness, infanticide, cowardice, military and technological backwardness, intellectual inferiority and sexual licentiousness.

Countering the negative image being developed by the missionaries were people like Lin Shao-Yang whose book, *A Chinese Appeal to Christendom*, appeared in print in 1911.[4] In his writing, Mr. Yang skillfully treats the irony of the efforts of the missionaries in light of the West's decline in Christianity during this period.

An additional good source for studying the missionary movement and the growth of Chinese anti-foreignism from 1860 to 1870 is Paul A. Cohen's book entitled *China and Christianity*.[5]

In the nineteenth century, the vast majority of the educated classes of China either passively or actively rejected Christianity. Passively, they did so by remaining coldly indifferent to Christianity's message. Actively, they expressed their hostility by writing and disseminating inflammatory anti-Christian literature.

In part, the account explained the intense hostility towards Christianity due to peculiarly nineteenth-century circumstances—Christian influence on the ideology of the Taiping rebellion, Christianity's identification with the use of foreign force and gunboat diplomacy after 1840, the interference by some missionaries in Chinese administrative affairs.

More specifically, in the transmission of Christianity to China, the environment has not been largely disregarded, with the result that Christianity has taken on a threatening character. The most glaring instance was the Rite Controversy, when the Vatican issued orders forbidding the Chinese to use the terms *Tien* (Heaven) and *Shang-ti* for God.[6]

This gave the impression that God was the God of the Westerners and that the Pope had the authority to bestow God's grace on the Chinese and therefore also to withdraw it.

Gems from the Year 1958

Then why a Chinese church? As long as the difficulty of language exists, we have the need of a Chinese church. When this difficulty disappears, all Christian Chinese

---

[3] Stuart Creighton Miller, *The Unwelcome Immigrant: The American Image of the Chinese, 1785–1882* (Los Angeles: University of California Press), 57–80.

[4] Lin Shao-Yang, *A Chinese Appeal to Christendom Concerning Christian Missions* (New York: G. P. Putnam's Sons, 1911).

[5] Paul A. Cohen, *China and Christianity* (Cambridge, MA: Harvard University Press, 1963).

[6] Feng Shang-li, "The Chinese Church and Chinese Culture," *Ching Feng* 11, no. 2, (1968): 6.

should be privileged to take part in the larger fellowship. Besides language, there are needs to be met that are unique only in the Chinese church.[7]

A theological issue is at stake. At stake in this whole issue of stewardship and leadership in the Chinese churches is a theological issue, no less. A clear distinction must be made between the church of Jesus Christ and the Chinese churches.[8]

The key to this whole problem of integration is summed up so well in Mr. Jow's final paragraph: "The Chinese churches in America ought to be willing to sacrifice themselves that they may find their lives given back to them again." And, I might add, given back exceedingly more abundantly.[9]

"The Home Mission Board — Pater or Partner?" The relationship of the Home Mission Boards to the Chinese churches in America has unfortunately been largely paternalistic. Historically speaking, the Chinese churches owe a great debt to these same boards that started work among the Chinese on the West Coast and founded the original missions over a hundred years ago.[10]

Notwithstanding the desire for a non-segregated church in a non-segregated society, I believe that there is a place for the exclusively Chinese churches in the US. I, personally, do not believe that a minority group necessarily contributed best to the sum total value of American life or to Christianity by losing its own cultural characteristics. Educated and thoughtful Chinese want to retain their identity. They see too clearly that assimilation and integration usually mean wiping out a distinctive culture. The desire to stay Chinese does not mean to eschew our newfound faith, but to contribute our share to Christianity, universal religion. The Christian church demands that people of every race, in mutuality, give to and receive from the church and thereby make it a truly church universal. Above all we ought to encourage these now exclusively Chinese churches and their gifted people in making contributions to add to the luster of the universal church.[11]

The statement "Christianity as practiced here is too often a brand of American Christianity which is mainly to preserve the 'American way of life'" rings a true critical note of warning to the twentieth-century American church. The equation of Christianity equaling the "American way of life" is too often made, but worse, it is too often taken to be simply so.[12]

---

[7] A. Lau, "Evangelism in the Chinese Churches" (paper, Second National Conference of Christian Work Among the Chinese in America, San Francisco, CA, September 17–19, 1958).

[8] Harold Jow, "Stewardship and Leadership in the Chinese Churches" (paper, Second National Conference of Christian Work Among the Chinese in America, San Francisco, CA, September 17–19, 1958).

[9] Donald E. Keuper, "Comments" (paper, Second National Conference of Christian Work Among the Chinese in America, San Francisco, CA, September 17–19, 1958).

[10] Keuper, "Comments."

[11] Edwar Lee, "The Future of the Exclusively Chinese Churches in America" (paper, Second National Conference of Christian Work Among the Chinese in America, San Francisco, CA, September 17–19, 1958).

[12] Gilbert Lura, "Comments" (paper, Second National Conference of Christian Work Among the Chinese in America, San Francisco, CA, September 17–19, 1958).

Coming of Age

I strongly believe that the Asian American community must shoulder the leadership to ascertain the direction, strategy, and action to take during this historical pivot of confusion and generational ambivalence.

In the past we Christians have often failed to recognize in our own rendering of Christianity the considerable admixture of cultural elements from our own national heritage and to appreciate sufficiently the cultures hitherto associated with other religions.

One of the most profound changes of the church took place when Christianity moved out of the world of Jewish thought and understanding into the wider world of Greek language, thought, and life. Greek thought forms, language, and modes of understanding were taken over and have since become part of the very life of the church. Early Christianity took over many elements from ancient metaphysics and ethics, the Asian-Hellenistic mystery religions, and the hermetic neoplatonic mysticism, and even from popular pagan piety and legal wisdom.

Almost till our present time, Christian doctrinal thinking has moved within the limits of the traditional questions and categories derived from the inquiring minds of the Greeks.

The church tends to identify itself with that culture and with the nations in the lives of which it finds expression.

It is vain to imagine that religion can be kept uncontaminated by the process of cultural development. It cannot be kept separate from culture, and it ought not to be kept separate from culture.

The Task—Indigenization

"Indigenization," according to the dictionary, means "to make native," "to adapt to a given area," or "to acclimatize or to habituate to a new climate."

A more precise description of what the process of indigenization involves is given by Vern Rossman. "Indigenization," he says, "is the attempt to locate, in the country being evangelized, words, concepts, art forms, social groupings or psychological characteristics which can (1) become communicative links from the gospel to the people; (2) enable the church and its life to appropriate those cultural elements compatible with the gospel, to minimize the shock of transition from the old to the new community; (3) help to determine what a new and genuinely Christian church would be in the country. In other words, it involves communication, adaptation and cultural synthesis."[13]

Effective communication of the gospel to the Asian people is dependent on the effective use of the religious vocabulary with which they are familiar and the cultural pattern of life in which they find self-expression and community being. The dominant philosophical and religious concepts of the people must be made into the instruments of interpreting the gospel.

---

[13] Sverre Holth, "Towards an Indigenous Theology," *Ching Feng* 11, no. 4 (1968): 6.

In the adaptation of language, there are a few considerations. One way is to take a word related to the old culture and to attempt to give it new meaning. St. Paul used the terms of Stoic modality, as, for instance, (*arete*), the "excellence" of the well-rounded Greek gentleman. Putting them into the context of the revelation of Christ, he sought to empty them and to refill them with new meaning, using the original connotations as a bridge to the new meaning. The alternative is to take a previously colorless word, or even to invent a new word, and then fill it with the meaning to be conveyed. The outstanding example in the New Testament is, of course, the word (*agape*) for God's love, a word seldom used in the classical (Koine) Greek. A word in common use is likely to lead to a misunderstanding of Christianity in terms of its former connotations, as, for example, the word *zui* (sin) in Chinese that conveys the idea of transgression but not of estrangement or other aspects of the New Testament terminology.[14]

There are certain failures of traditional Western theology that many Asians find objectionable. Generally speaking, Asians do not attach the same importance to formulated doctrines. Our keenness for analysis and systems is something they find incomprehensible. It has been said that "the East has a civilization which tends to develop the emotions; the Western way of life tends to develop reason." With Europeans, many Asians would say, logically constructed statements of doctrine assume an undue importance. Our demand for definite and precise formulations of faith is a source of irritation.

The rigidity of much of Western theological dogmatism leaves the Asian man of religion cold. As a rule, many Asians prefer to state and describe even important matters in a vague and imprecise way. Examples of the difficulties and need for sharper clarification are reflected in such terms like Nirvana, T'ien, and Tao.[15]

Most Asians are undogmatic and many Chinese will only tolerate a Christianity free from rigid dogmas and confined to ethics. Many Asians have therefore advocated that the Christian religion's truths should be translated into the form of Indian, Chinese, and Japanese wisdom, for the real Christian faith is not Western, but universal.

In Asia, ideas and words often have an uncertain, vague, and fluctuating meaning, which allows Asians to form associations of the mind of vast multiplicity and variety.

Confucius said, "We know nothing about life, how, then, can we know about death?" "He who knows the Tao," says the *Tao Te Ching*, "needs no words; whoever needs words does not know."[16]

Any theology that claims to be relevant must start with the fundamental facts of the Asian interpretation of existence and the universe; Christ must be presented in terms that are relevant and essential to Asian existence.

---

[14] Holth, "Towards an Indigenous Theology," 15.
[15] Holth, "Towards an Indigenous Theology," 18.
[16] Holth, "Towards an Indigenous Theology," 19–20.

Urgent Task

The working out of an indigenous Chinese Christian theology is a matter of pressing necessity.

Whatever the process of indigenization is going to be, whether by adaptation, assimilation, interpenetration, or reconception, or by a combination of all these, it must lead to a theology that is related to, and involved in, the religious, cultural, and social life of the people among whom the church is planted.

The *Bible* must be our standard of faith and practice, but we must seek to discover what is essential rather than adhere strictly to the letter. We should trace the sources of God's general and special revelation and go back directly to the gospel of Jesus, our Lord. From this stance, we should make a reasonable assimilation of thought forms in the Chinese cultural tradition and blend it all into a theological system of our own.

Adaptation

The metaphysics of Chinese philosophy and Christian theology provide ample scope for adaptation. What is metaphysics? (a) It has to do with origins. (b) It certainly concerns the intuitive knowledge of the *tao-hsin* (one's spiritual nature). Origins have to do with the transcendental, the *tao-hsin* with the immanent.

Speaking practically, God's "Word" is a "principle" (*li*), for the law of the universe is God's "principle" and the order of the world a manifestation of God's will and power. Hence, to help the Chinese to understand the "in the beginning was the Word" of St. John's Gospel, it should be linked with the "reason" (or "principle") which of necessity the world must possess — that is, the Lord of Creation and God's unceasing activity. Thus we may make use of metaphysics as a servant of theology in order that Chinese intellectuals may more readily understand and become engaged.

The possibility of integration in the sphere of practical ethics is another area for adaptation.

(a) The chief principle of Chinese ethics is *jen* (human-heartedness, benevolence). Jen embraces all virtues and signifies a plurality of men, not a single individual as in Western individualism. Tsu Kung says, "Within the four seas, all people are brothers." And Cheng-Ch'u says, "The people are my brothers, things my companions." Chu Tzu amplifies this by saying, "To wish to make all under Heaven one family, and the nation as one man." This idea of universal harmony can be merged with the second half of the agape of Christian ethics, which has to do with loving one's neighbor as one's self, and by doing so one can build up a powerful system of ethics.

(b) *Chih*, which is wisdom to understand *jen*. In Western culture, wisdom is primarily directed towards the knowledge of things. For this reason it has resulted in the development of the natural sciences, industry, and skills. On the other hand, it has also expressed itself in a desire to probe man's mind and soul and things spiritual. This explains why in the West they have developed such things as psychology, psychiatry, and theology.

Professor Ch'ien Hu observes that "the history of Eastern philosophy may in the main be said to be a history of the study of the human soul, or at least that it has developed from such a study." He also states that, "when Westerners seek release from their inner tension in religion, it results in an antithesis of God and the Devil; when they apply it to the political structure of society, it creates class distinctions; when they apply it to life, it results in power struggle and progress; and when they apply it to the intellect, it shows itself in many-sided research and concentration."[17]

(c) *Yung,* which is courage to practice *jen.* What does it mean to have courage to practice *jen?* "To cultivate oneself in order to pacify all the people."[18]

(d) *Sheng* (sageness), which is the utmost perfection in human relationships. What is the substance of sagehood? What kind of man is the sage, and what kind of cultivation pertains to sagehood?[19]

Summary: In Chinese culture, *jen* (human-heartedness), *chih* (wisdom), and *yung* (courage) are certainly the comprehension of all virtues. Similarly is *sheng* (sagehood) the highest degree in the cultivation of character, the utmost in beauty as well as in goodness. *Jen* is the substance (*t'i*), *yung* (courage) its implementation.

Christ, the Eternal Tao, is the author of all beauty and all truth. What are some additional cultural factors to be considered for adaptation?

(a) Art — attunement to Heaven

A Chinese artist is devoted to nature because to them the beauty and splendor of the world, the trees and valleys, the distant view of a mountain, are all visible manifestations of the working of the universal mind. There is a distinct feeling of oneness with nature, and this is transferred especially to landscape paintings.

In Chinese thought, there is, however, not only beauty in the world around us, but the order of the universe is essentially moral. It is man's duty to be conformed with that order. If a human's life is attuned to Heaven, they can find that Heaven is trustworthy. Christians, too, believe that we must be reconciled to God, that we are working in harmony with Reality, which, at its deepest level, is *jen* or love.

(b) Family — Piety

There are four traditional Chinese family rites:

1. celebration of birth
2. wedding
3. funeral
4. ancestor worship

---

[17] Chi Pe-ssu, "Essential Points of Chinese Culture," *Ching Feng* 10, no. 4 (1967): 9–10.
[18] Chi "Essential Points of Chinese Culture," 12.
[19] Chi, "Essential Points of Chinese Culture," 16.

"The way of men is to love one's relatives. Because of love for relatives, the ancestors are honored, and honor for ancestors brings respect for the distant relatives, for distant relatives bring a sense of kinship."[20]

The Chinese family is democratic in function. There is subordination among members of the family, but each has his place and each has his dignity. "A young man should be treated with the utmost respect. How do you know he will not, one day, be fully equal to what you are now?" If the father has the supreme authority in the household, he must also shoulder the supreme responsibility.

Christian doctrine forbids doing obeisance to ancestors. Filial sons and virtuous grandchildren regard the observation of the Ch'ing Ming Festival and the Autumn Sacrifice at the Double Ninth Festival to be very important.

There are homes where disharmony often rises over funeral rites and ancestral sacrifices.

Ancestral practices may go with the march of time. What will remain will probably be the tradition of family piety.

From the adoration of one's ancestors it is only a step to the veneration of the saints and sages.

Dr. S. C. Carpenter realized the importance of family piety to the communication of the Christian message. "[The Chinese people] had been groping after the truth, if haply they might find it. The family piety, even the ancestral cult of China, would itself help them to understand better the Christian teaching about the communion of saints."[21]

Within the context of Chinese culture, one ought to make use of the aids provided by history, language, etymology, and concepts in order to preach the gospel in such a way that the Chinese may more easily understand and accept it.

In outward things, such as forms of worship, one ought to select usages that carry a Chinese flavor.

In church worship, Chinese musical instruments ought to have a place.

Chinese scrolls are a literary form that is appreciated by Chinese people. Therefore, it is most appropriate that the church should make use of it.

Conclusion

Effective communication of the gospel to the Chinese people depends on effective use of the religious vocabulary with which they are familiar, and the cultural pattern of life in which they find self-expression and the community being. The dominant philosophical and religious concepts of the people must be made into instruments of interpreting the gospel.

---

[20] Cheng Che-Yu, *Oriental and Occidental Cultures Contrasted* (Berkeley, CA: Gillick Press, 1943), 91.

[21] S. C. Carpenter, *Church and People, 1789–1889: A History of the Church of England from William Wilberforce to "Lux Mundi"* (New York: Macmillan, 1933), 462

Our task of theological work must be to salvage what is distinctly Christian from what may be an American expression of it.

> There is much justification in saying that one of the frustrating features in the life of the "younger churches" is that they are, in spite of all self-determination and independent or autonomy, still to a large extent, in their structure and style of expression, spiritual colonies of the West, copies of something, but not grown up.[22]

There must be a relevant, creative, and redeeming relationship between Christian theology and Asian community and culture. And this must make for a crucial contribution of the church to Asian society in all its ramifications — cultural, social, ethical, and political. In this process, we may arrive at a new insight, which may make a valuable contribution to the church universal as well.

Indigenization must not be confused with preoccupation with the antique and archaic. Indigenization must be forward-looking. Our church must not remain under the spell of the religious and cultural dimension of the past.

We have for a number of generations past been living on spiritual capitol. I mean clinging to Christian practice without possessing the Christian belief and practice unsupported by belief is a wasting asset, as we have suddenly discovered to our dismay in this generation.[23] A resurgence of Confucian ideals may very well be an antidote to our merely materialistic and technological culture. We must declare that our Christianity is an incomplete one and that we may try to extend it into Christian completion.

This does not mean a disregard for the Christian heritage of the West. It does mean taking it seriously in an Asian setting. It will result in an enriching, not an impoverishing, of the whole church.

Our task is a march to the future and not a return to the past or a mere adaptation to the present. God is moving and we must discern the signs of the time and move with Him.

---

[22] Holth, "Towards an Indigenous Theology," 14.
[23] Arthur J. Toynbee, *Civilization on Trial* (New York: Oxford University Press, 1948), 237.

Religious Values Among Japanese Americans and Their Relationship to Counseling[*]

David Y. Hirano

Chapter V
Pastoral Counseling with the *Nisei*

Religious values are ultimate values that stand at the center of personality and culture.[1] If this is so then there can be no contradiction in ultimate values because with the ultimate there is only wholeness. It is in the human perceptions of the ultimate that conflicts occur. When the perceptions of ultimate values cause conflict, the role of pastoral counseling becomes very important.

Counseling deals with values. The counselor has their values and the counselee theirs.[2] The pastor as counselor is no different. They will counsel with their set of values. It is essential that the pastoral counselor knows what values they bring to counseling. It is also necessary to know what internal value conflicts they face and have faced.

In cross-cultural counseling, it is well for the counselor to share their values with the counselee but not to impose them on the counselee. This is a difficult task. It is one of the functions of counseling to teach "values," but the counselor must be aware of the risk of imposing values upon the counselee. The counselor needs to enable the counselee to develop tools to find their own values. The counselor must not deprive the counselee of their right to and responsibility for self-determination.[3]

One of the tasks of pastoral counseling is education. A psychologist has said that "the purpose of education in Western society is to actualize the good and to minimize the evils in man's potentiality . . . Indeed in all human societies, education is a necessary means to helping him actualize himself fully."[4] It is the same in pastoral counseling. Put theologically it is to educate people to know what it means to be

---

[*] A dissertation presented to the faculty of the School of Theology at Claremont, in partial fulfillment of the requirements of the degree Doctor of Ministry (June 1974).

[1] John A. Hutchinson, "American Values in the Perspective of Faith," in *Values in America*, ed., Donald R. Barrett (South Bend: University of Notre Dame Press, 1961), 126.

[2] C. H. Patterson, *Theories of Counseling and Psychotherapy* (New York: Harper & Row, 1973), 73.

[3] Patterson, *Theories of Counseling and Psychotherapy*, 18.

[4] Patterson, *Theories of Counseling and Psychotherapy*, 12.

children of God and to live in the image of God. In the words of the Apostle Paul the task of education is to learn to "fulfill the glory of God."[5]

When counseling the *Nisei*, the Christian pastoral counselor will need to take a look at the exclusiveness and judgmental stance of Christianity. Exclusiveness of Christianity often excludes other religions and their practices and, therefore, may be a hindrance to the pastoral care of the *Nisei*. What should be developed is an open and accepting stance toward other religions. The pastoral counselor will need an understanding of and appreciation for the values that come from Japanese religion.

In an article called "A Cosmological Christology," Organ encourages Christians to get rid of exclusivist Christology and to accept a cosmological Christology that would affirm that to be acceptable to God everyone does not have to be Christian. He argues that Christianity does not have a monopoly on messiahs, bodhisattvas, and avataras. Furthermore, he maintains, redemption has always been a fact about the total environment. Jesus Christ is for all Christians the celebration of God's continuing saving love. Organ says that God does not leave Godself without witness in other lands.[6]

It is important that the pastoral counselor with *Nisei* realize that God is God, beyond us and beyond our conceptualization. God is God by whatever name he or she is called. The word is not important. He or she is beyond words. John McQuarrie says,

> To put it bluntly, it is idolatry to think that we have ever grasped God, that we have comprehended him either as an objective fact "out there" or as an exalted ideal "in here." In all such cases, we are trying to make God into our possession. But this is just impossible (as well as being blasphemous). God transcends anything we can grasp or contain, and when we think we have him the truth is that he has slipped through our grasp and we are left clinging to some pitiable idol of our own making. We can never know God by seeking to grasp and manipulate him, but only by letting him grasp us. We know him not by taking him into our possession (which is absurd) but by letting ourselves be possessed by him, by becoming open to his infinite being which is within us and above us and around us.[7]

In counseling the Japanese American, it is important to discover this cosmological Christ and to educate people to this view that is inclusive and accepting.

The argument often heard in response to the idea of the cosmological Christ is that this is universalism. Perhaps so, depending on the way one defines the term. For the author, it is a profession of a personal faith in the God revealed in Jesus Christ, who is the means to salvation (wholeness), and to whom one witnesses by word and

---

[5] A free interpretation of Romans 3:21–26.

[6] Troy Organ, "A Cosmological Christology," *The Christian Century* 87, no. 42 (November 3, 1971): 1293–1295.

[7] John McQuarrie, as quoted in *Input* 3, no. 13 (April 19, 1973). [*Ed. note: See also* John McQuarrie, "Subjectivity and Objectivity in Theology and Worship," *Theology* 72, no. 593 (November 1969): 500.]

deed. It is *witnessing* to the love of God in Jesus Christ and *not imposing* the love of God on others.

It follows then that another task of the pastoral counselor with the *Nisei* is to affirm the culture of the *Issei* as valuable. The task is to highlight the values in Japanese culture and thus to reinforce the dignity of all persons.

Paul Nagano writes,

> Man created in God's image was meant to be a son, not a bondservant under the law or under another man. It claims nothing more than the elemental biological identity of all human beings. Paul declares the elemental physical kinship of all men has to do with the unity and solidarity of all mankind biologically and religiously.
>
> ... In Japanese ethnic theology it means, first of all appreciation and respect of his God given heritage and being thankful to God for his Japanese ancestry. Secondly, it means seeking the humanness of all people. This naturally leads to the Christians' duty to destroy any attempt at dehumanization, whether it be racism or technology.[8]

For example, many Christians would consider some of the funeral practices in the Japanese Christian church to be pagan. There is the open casket, the bowing before the remains, a floral tribute, the black armband. To highlight the culture is not to erase or to condemn these practices but to see the value that is in them. For the bereaved these practices are ways in which to work through their grief. Likewise the memorials held on the forty-ninth day, one year, and three years after the death of a loved one are important in grief work. These periods are crucial in the lives of the bereaved. The value of these practices is to be preserved rather than to be condemned as heathen.

Japanese festivals are another example. It is important not to condemn these occasions, but to make use of them and to transform them. The Japanese festivals celebrated significant days in the year. They were based on the seasons and on agricultural calendar. But more so they were times when the family gathered to celebrate. In times when the family is being splintered in American society, it is well to preserve the Japanese festivals.

Filial piety was taken to an extreme in Japanese culture. The pastoral counselor needs to preserve what is good in that value. They ought to work to transform it into something that has meaning for contemporary times. For instance, they may teach the parents how to use authority so that it is respected.

Additionally, the pastoral counselor will educate their people to the values that are beneficial in American society. The ideals of freedom, justice, love, and individuality are to be preserved rather than belittled. They are to be learned rather than to be swept under the rug.

What the counselor with the Japanese American needs to remember is that the Japanese American is not Japanese and that they are not American. They are a hybrid: a Japanese American.

---

8 Paul M. Nagano, "Japanese Americans' Search for Identity, Ethnic Pluralism, and a Christian Basis of Permanent Identity" (DRel diss., School of Theology at Claremont, 1970), 140–141.

The task of education as prevention of mental illness is to select the best from two worlds and to fit them together into an authentic Japanese American value system. It can be said presently that the Japanese American has adopted wholesale white middle class values. But this has reaped a harvest of unhappiness. If the Japanese American is to be healthy and to contribute to a pluralistic society that is America, the Japanese American must find an authentic value system. This is difficult but nevertheless important.

The Pastoral Counselor

The pastoral counselor with *Nisei* will need to model effective ways of relating. In many cases the *Nisei* have only their parents to use as models for effective communication. More often than not these models have been less than desirable. Therefore the pastor will need to model ways of relating and communicating.

Because the *Nisei* are persons who are affected by *amae*, and because they have been taught to respect and follow the *sensei* (teacher, the title for a pastor), it will be a temptation for the pastor to be authoritarian and to be a benevolent dictator. It will be a temptation to be the one upon whom the people depend for benevolence. However, it would be counterproductive for the pastor to do either. Instead, they ought to model what it means to be a person who accepts responsibility for themselves and for no one else. In other words, to model what it means to be a person.

The pastor is to be a person who feels, who tires, who cries, who loves, who cares. This means that the pastor will need to shed some of the *bushido* with which they may have been conditioned, and to recondition themselves to express feelings. But it is not to shirk all of *bushido*; it is to take what is valuable and leave what is not. For instance, it is to take the quality of sincerity that is communicated through the demeanor of the samurai and to preserve it while shucking away the idea that the mind must always control the expression of feeling. It would be valuable to keep the *bushido* quality of honesty but to throw aside the lack of spontaneity. Likewise, to demonstrate tact rather than the crassness of Americans or to temper aggressiveness with politeness and courtesy.

It is important for the pastor to be a model of acceptance rather than judgment. To say in word and deed, "I love you. I may not like what you do or what you say, or even what you believe, but I love you."

The style of leadership that the pastor develops will do much to educate the people. If they strike an authoritarian pose, the parishioners will follow along because they are primed by Japanese values to respect authority and to follow it without question. But this will keep the church from realizing that they are the people of God, responsible for the life and ministry of the church, and put that responsibility upon the pastor.

An alternative style is to become a facilitator and enabler. Instead of conjuring up needs and developing programs around them, it is to be sensitive to needs as they arise and to enable the church to develop its own program. It is allowing the church leaders to use their judgment and to make decisions rather than for the pastor to make unilateral decisions. This style of leadership is fraught with frustration. It takes patience, but the laity will learn the value of individuality and responsibility rather than to continually be entrapped in dependency.

Because Japanese Americans have a tendency toward face-to-face or primary-group type of intimacy,[9] the use of groups to teach ways of communicating is excellent. Through the Evergreen Baptist Church in Los Angeles, the author has conducted several marriage enrichment groups. The response has been positive and he has noticed significant behavioral changes in many of the couples. The relationship that the pastor has with their family is important. It lets the church see that their family is important to them, to model living and accepting behavior with their own family. These are goals toward which the pastor ought to be working. It is important for the pastoral counselor to find most of their needs for intimacy satisfied in the home rather than to seek intimacy primarily in the church.

Kosaki, in her research on *Nisei* adolescents, discovered that they wanted their teachers to show sensitivity to their worries, dreams, and plans; warmth and affection for them based on friendliness that is wise and objective, not sentimental and uncritical; a respect for personality which fosters feelings of security and worth; a willingness to become interested in them as individuals and a desire to work with them; and an enthusiasm for teaching and faith in its value.[10] These are similar for the pastor. They ought to model sensitivity, warmth and affection, respect for people, and an enthusiasm about their work and faith.

It is well for the pastoral counselor to remember that in the prevention of mental illness as well as in treatment, the relationship that they have with the people is of primary importance. That relationship is characterized by caring, loving, and accepting.

The Treatment of the *Nisei*

Studies of mental illness in America point to the fact that persons who are mentally ill first turn to the clergy for advice and counsel.[11] It could be safely assumed that the *Nisei* are like the rest of the American population. Yet in studies of Japanese American mental illness the church is overlooked as a mental health agency.

In 1969 Kitano studied Japanese American mental illness. His survey indicated that Japanese Americans seldom use therapeutic resources of the larger community. They underutilized the services of psychiatry. Only the most severely disturbed

---

[9] Ruth Benedict, *The Chrysanthemum and the Sword* (Boston: Houghton Mifflin, 1946), 43–55.

[10] Mildred Doi Kosaki, "The Culture Conflicts and Guidance Needs of Nisei Adolescents" (MEd thesis, University of Hawaii, August 1949), 99.

[11] Derald W. Sue and Austin C. Frank, "A Typological Approach to the Psychological Study of Chinese and Japanese American College Males," *Journal of Social Issues* 29, no. 2, (1973): 145.

sought help, and a large number of less troubled were not seen by any mental health services.[12]

For the most part, Japanese Americans treated mental illness through the family, extended family, and the community. Additionally they had *gaman*, the handling of pain and frustration without any outward signs. They were skilled in internalizing problems and therefore in hiding them.

Churches were not part of Kitano's study. However, it would be safe to assume that more people turned to their clergymen than to the professionals in mental health. Kitano observes that as more experts in the field of mental health are produced, more Japanese Americans will seek professional services. He also indicates that because of acculturation, the rate of mental illness among Japanese Americans will become equal to that of the majority group in the United States.[13]

It is therefore important that the church become recognized as a mental health service and that the church become involved in community mental health. It would be well for the pastor with *Nisei* to be skilled in counseling. They ought to be a professional pastoral counselor. Because the Japanese Americans are influenced by education and title, it would be helpful, but not necessary, for the pastoral counselor to obtain a license in marriage, family, and child counseling.

Sue notes that counseling and psychotherapy are essentially white middle class activities geared to the highly verbal and emotionally expressive persons. This form of treatment may be inappropriate to many Japanese Americans who are in need of help.[14] Japanese Americans are not expressive and are reserved. Therefore other modes of counseling ought to be used. Alternative modes are discussed later in this chapter.

The pastoral counselor ought to remember their goals in counseling. It is not to make the counselee a Christian or to impose upon them Christian values. A goal of counseling is to enable the person to function creatively in society and to utilize and develop their human potential. When counseling with a *Nisei*, it is well to remember "that which the people who called themselves Christians claimed to have the only true religion, and pretended to be better than all other men; they did not, in that particular, differ from the Chinese or Japanese, who made the same claims for their religions."[15]

Kosaki's advice is worth noting:

---

[12] Harry H. L. Kitano, "Japanese American Mental Illness," *Changing Perspective in Mental Illness*, ed. Stanley C. Plog and Robert B. Edgerton (New York: Holt, Rinehart and Winston, 1969), 220.

[13] Kitano, "Japanese American Mental Illness," 283.

[14] Sue and Frank, "A Typological Approach," 145.

[15] Mori Arinori, "Life and Resources in America," in *Leaders of the Meiji Restoration in America*, ed., Charles Lanman (Tokyo: Hokuseido Press, 1931), 241.

Cultural differences among ethnic groups should be preserved as long as these differences help individuals to make their personal and social adjustments and that no individual should be forced to follow a cultural pattern which he continually repudiates.[16]

Dr. Frank Kimper, professor of pastoral care at the School of Theology at Claremont, California, and director of the Pastoral Counseling Center at Claremont, writes a goal that is a viable one for counseling the *Nisei*:

My concern that others also learn to love is the essence of my identity as a *pastor*. The methods I use to facilitate such learning of others identify me as a *counselor*. With persons oriented within the Christian faith, and concerned with spiritual growth as a Christian, all of my counseling is done in a "theological context." With persons who have no orientation as a Christian my counseling is done initially in a purely humanistic context, using exactly the same terminology, but without reference to God. This means that at any seemingly appropriate point I can interpret the inter-personal in terms of relationship with God, and give it immediately a theological perspective.

I am concerned in my counseling with helping people to experience what it means to be loved (i.e., what it means to experience "salvation" in the person-God relationship); and to learn the discipline of loving others (i.e., what it means to be a disciple in the person-God relationship). My basic assumption in this is that love is the missing ingredient in all destructive human experiences—intrapsychic and interpersonal.[17]

In his paper Kimper explains the word loving as seeing a "neighbor as precious simply because and only because he is a human being." Loving is not approval of behavior or agreeing with ideas or responding to an attractive personality or having sexual intercourse.[18]

Learning to love one's neighbor as oneself is a goal toward which to strive in pastoral counseling. However, with the *Nisei* it may be difficult because they have a low concept of the self. The *Nisei* has a conflict in achieving self-differentiation rather than accepting the personal submergence emphasized by Japanese ideals.[19] They have a weak ego integration.[20] Thus, to love neighbor as *self* is foreign. For the *Nisei* Christian, the concept of self is further distorted by the mistaken interpretation of "losing one's self," which leads to self-deprecation.

In counseling the troubled *Nisei* it would be worth trying a way of psychotherapy called psychosynthesis. Psychosynthesis helps one to discover the self and to realize its preciousness, and to live out of that center. Through psychosynthesis the counselor enables the counselee to make some important perceptual changes that affect their behavior:

First, the "self" one must gradually be "disidentified" from the equipment one has (body, mind, talents) and his performance (the way the self uses his equipment). Otherwise, the

---

[16] Kosaki, "The Culture Conflicts and Guidance Needs," 52.

[17] Frank Kimper, "My Pastoral Identity as a Counselor" (paper delivered to the staff of the Pastoral Counseling Center, Claremont, CA, December 1973), 1.

[18] Kimper, "My Pastoral Identity as a Counselor," 1.

[19] George DeVos, "Acculturation and Personality Structure: A Rorschach Study of Japanese Americans" (PhD diss., University of Chicago, 1959), 220.

[20] Marvin K. Opler, *Culture and Social Psychiatry* (New York: Atherton Press, 1967), 300.

immeasurable value of the self is always confused with the variable quality of both equipment and performance. But as one is "disidentifying" self from equipment and performance, one is simultaneously "identifying" with those polar thrusts of *individuality-intimacy*, *freedom-destiny*, and *dynamics-form* which are experienced as both dynamic and precious. Yet it is as the *Center of Awareness*, able to transcend itself—to "stand apart," so to speak, and evaluate its own activity that one recognizes the self as self . . .

> This makes possible a second perceptual change: namely owning responsibility for one's own thoughts, words, actions, attitudes, feelings; and disowning responsibility for one's neighbor's thoughts, words, actions, attitudes, feelings.[21]

Through the discovery of the self, the *Nisei* will be able to sort out the influences in their life and not become captive to either custom or tradition. They will be enabled to utilize the capacity to choose the direction of living that they want. Thus, they may choose what is of value for themselves from both the American and Japanese heritages.

Another approach to working with the Japanese American, which the author has found successful, is transactional analysis. Because the Japanese American has a strong superego, this technique is useful. To draw graphically the PAC chart and to let the counselee analyze themselves brings many helpful insights. The reading of the book *I'm Okay, You're Okay* during counseling has been beneficial. Through the analyzing of transactions, they are helped to find solutions to their problems.

Since *Nisei* appear to be more structure-oriented and nonverbal than middle class white Americans, it would seem as though the psychoanalytic methods of therapy would not be productive. These methods are long and non-directive. It is well to remember that the *Nisei* looks for direction and is not one who takes well to ambiguity.

Gestalt therapy with the *Nisei* may be indicated in treatment.

> The implicit message of Gestalt theory as translated into treatment is that there are values in living that persons know from their own experiences or from their observations of others to be valuable and enhancing: spontaneity, sensory awareness, freedom of movement, emotional responsiveness and expressiveness, enjoyment, ease, flexibility in relating, direct contact and emotional closeness with others, intimacy, competency, immediacy and presence, self-support, and creativity. The patient who comes for help, seeking to relate more adequately with other people and to be able to express his feelings more directly is instructed to express what he is feeling at that moment to another person. The ways in which he stops, blocks, and frustrates himself quickly become apparent, and he can then be assisted in exploring and experiencing the blockings and encouraged to attempt other ways of expressing himself and of relating.
>
> Thus the general approach of Gestalt theory and theory requires the patient to specify the changes in himself that he desires, assists him in increasing his awareness of how he defeats himself, and aids him in experimenting and changing.[22]

---

[21] Kimper, "My Pastoral Identity as a Counselor," 2.

[22] Joen Fagan and Irma Lee Shepherd, *Gestalt Therapy Now* (New York: Harper & Row, 1970), 1–2.

For the *Nisei* who has "gotten out of touch" with their feelings and wants to be able to express them, gestalt therapy seems to be a good methodology. It also appeals to the rational and encourages the person to set their own goals.

Reality therapy may be used effectively with the *Nisei*. William Glasser describes reality therapy as a therapy that leads all patients toward reality, toward grappling successfully with the tangible and intangible aspects of the real world.[23]

In enabling the *Nisei* to take responsibility to fulfill "one's needs and to do so in a way that does not deprive others of the ability to fulfill their needs,"[24] reality therapy is a good methodology. It would seem that this would be a way in which to get persons in touch with their feelings of wanting to *amaeru* and to receive *amae*.

It must be said that no particular methodology can be prescribed for all persons. Therefore with each person and with each circumstance the, methodology and approach will differ. The goal of enabling the person to choose their own values and to find their own way of living satisfactorily in society is to be sought.

Conclusion

The *Nisei* are a group of persons in American society who have struggled and are still struggling to find a place. Outwardly they have made a place in middle class American values. But inwardly they still face the tension of finding meaningful values to live by. They are caught in the tension of having to choose from two diverse cultures.

The pastor has a key role to play in the resolution of the tension. By word and deed, they can educate and counsel their parishioners, that they will learn to choose from both cultures, that they will experience the love, freedom, joy, and peace which are rightfully theirs.

---

[23] William Glasser, *Reality Therapy* (New York: Harper & Row, 1970), 6.
[24] Glasser, *Reality Therapy*, 13.

Counseling the Japanese Family in the United States[*]

MARION WAKE

Table of Contents

---

[*] Distributed by the Asian Center for Theology and Strategies (ACTS). [*Ed. note: As compiled in the original 1976 ACTS Reader, the citations in this piece were truncated and presented in the main text. For this edition, these citations have been converted to footnotes and supplied with additional bibliographic information.*]

Counseling the Japanese Family
in the United States

Introduction

The Japanese in the United States make up a rather small minority of the population. Of the one million Asians tabulated in the 1970 Bureau of Census statistics, 591,290 were Japanese. They are primarily located in the states of Hawaii, California, Washington, and Oregon. There are also concentrations of Japanese living in the metropolitan areas of New York, Chicago, and Boston. Because they are in these concentrated areas, there they do compose a significant percentage of the population.

The Japanese who immigrated to the United States from approximately 1870 through 1920 are called *Issei* (first generation), their children are *Nisei* (second generation), their grandchildren are *Sansei* (third generation), and their great grandchildren are *Yonsei* (fourth generation). The *Nisei* who were sent by their parents to live in and be educated in Japan and then returned here are called *Kibei-Nisei*. As a result of the presence of American soldiers in Japan during and following World War II, there was a sizable number of Japanese wives of these servicemen who came here with their husbands, usually referred to as "war brides." Japanese women who have married Americans more recently prefer to be called international brides. The more recent arrivals from Japan are often referred to as the Japanese nationals. They are *Kaisha* people (employees of Japanese firms), Japanese consulate employees, students, and relatives of resident families or Japanese wives of Americans.

The need for marriage and family counseling for the Japanese family in the United States has become increasingly evident. The cases that emerge are often difficult because of the reluctance of Japanese people to seek help until the situation has reached crisis proportions. In order to effectively counsel a given Japanese family in the United States, the counselor needs to fully understand the distinct differences between the generations and groups. Let us here consider the various types of Japanese families presently residing in the United States.

Part I: Stereotypes of the Japanese Family in the United States

Some people refer to the Japanese as the "model minority" in the United States, the ethnic group after which other ethnic groups should pattern themselves. There was a time when the Japanese were stereotyped as being exceptionally well behaved. These comments were from schoolteachers, the police, social workers, and other community people. Students were bright, worked hard and were never disciplinary problems. There were no "juvenile delinquents." It is significant that these observations are diminishing.

Since World War II, the problems of *Nisei, Sansei,* and *Yonsei* closely resemble the rest of middle-class America.

Ironically, a great controversy in the early 1900s was whether or not Japanese were "assimilable." Boddy[1] predicted that "the Americanization of the Japanese will take time." Iyenaga[2] summarizes, "In the question of assimilation, we find the heart of the Japanese problem in California." The problem now seems rather that the Japanese have assimilated too well and rapidly. "Juvenile delinquency," particularly in connection with drug abuse and runaways, increases among the *Sansei* and *Yonsei.* Marriage and family problems increase particularly among those people from Japan, whether married to Japanese nationals or to non-Japanese.

> Nonetheless, like many stereotypes, this one about the "goodness" of the Japanese probably contains a grain of truth. It is widely believed that this "good" behavior is due in large part to the Japanese family—its structure, its techniques of socialization and social control, and to its role in mediating the congruent and conflicting demands of the Japanese and American styles of life.[3]

Part II: The Family System in Japan When the *Issei* Emigrated (Tokugawa–Early Meiji Period)

The "family" in the Japanese Civil Code denoted something to which we have nothing analogous in the United States. It meant "a grouping of persons bearing the same surname and subject to the authority of one who is the head of the family and who may or may not be the common parent or ancestor." The Japanese family system was thus a combination of relatives into two groups. First, they were a member of the smaller family group subject to the authority of its head; and secondly, they were a member of the wider group of kindred, with whom they were closely connected by rights and duties. But their position as a member of both the smaller and larger family groups had little of the permanency and stability that are found in the American family. It was liable to constant change by separation from the family through the frequency of adoption, through abdication, and by the liberty given to a person to change their family allegiance. In 1922, Gubbins[4] included as some of the main features of the Japanese family system:

---

[1] Elias Manchester Boddy, *Japanese in America* (Los Angeles: E. Manchester Boddy, 1921), 32.

[2] T. Iyenaga and Kenoske Sato, *Japan and the California Problem* (New York: G. P. Putnam's Sons, 1921), 148.

[3] Harry H. L. Kitano, *Japanese Americans: The Evolution of a Subculture* (Englewood Cliffs, NJ: Prentice-Hall, 1969), 60.

[4] John Harington Gubbins, *The Making of Modern Japan: An Account of the Progress of Japan from Pre-feudal Days to Constitutional Government & the Position of a Great Power, with Chapters on Religion, the Complex Family System, Education, Etc.* (London: Seeley, Service & Co., 1922), 283–291.

A. Parental Authority

Prior to 1898, parental authority closely approached the rigor of the Roman *patria potestas*. Offenses were punished more severely when committed by children against parents than when the reverse was true. The doctrine of *oya-kooko* or filial piety since 1898 never in practice excluded the duties of parents to children. Parental authority was exercised over children during their minority or as long as they did not earn an independent living. Japanese law spoke of a person as a child, irrespective of age, as long as either of the parents was alive, and a parent's right to maintenance by a son or daughter had precedence over the rights in that respect of the latter's children and spouse.

B. Adoption Practices

The desire to preserve the continuity of a family was usually the motive of adoption. In countries like Japan where ancestor worship has survived in the practice of family rites, the anxiety to make due provisions for the performance of these rites has acted as an additional incentive. But nowhere else has adoption been conducted on so large a scale or played so important a part in the social life of its people. It is not limited, as with us, to the adoption of minors, for the adoption of adults is as common as that of children. Nor is it confined to the adoption of a single individual, the adoption of a married couple being a recognized custom. Nor is the procedure irrevocable, for a person may adopt or be adopted more than once, and adoption may be dissolved or annulled. The elaborate treatment given to the custom in the Civil Code testifies to its importance in Japanese social life, and at the same time shows the extent to which the *interests of the individual are subordinated to those of the family.*

C. Headship of the Family

The parental authority and the authority exercised by the head of a family were quite distinct, but the two may be vested in the same individual. The head of a family exercised authority over all its lawfully recognized members. It was not necessary that they be part of his or her household, for the family could embrace several households. Nor need they be relatives, though usually some tie of kinship existed. This authority included the right or consent to the marriage and divorce, the adoption and the dissolution of adoption of each member of the family; the right of determining his or her place of residence; and the right of expelling such persons from the family and of forbidding his or her return to it.

D. Family Registration (Koseki)

If proof were needed that society in Japan centered on the family, and not the individual, it would be supplied by the institution known as the family registration. In every district, a separate register was kept for each house in which the head of a household was also the head of a family. The names were those of all persons who, regardless of their place of residence, were members of the head's family at the time when the family register was prepared. The family, therefore, and not the household, is the basis of this registration.

> Marriage was effected by family action for purposes of familial continuity. Through the oldest son, family continuity would be achieved, parents would be protected in their old age, and obligations to the ancestors discharged. Marriage was usually arranged by a *baishakunin* or *nakoodo*, a "go-between," and there was small space for independent mate choice. In order to ensure continuity, families without sons commonly practiced adoption. If there was a daughter, the adoptee might be the daughter's husband (*yooshi*), thus assuming both ancestor worship and retention of property by the in-group. The adoption practices were capable of convenient variations such as the adoption of one's younger brother (*juyooshi*). Because the family's stake was so great, a careful scrutiny was made of the lineage of "blood" of the prospective in-laws. Tuberculosis, leprosy, inferior social status, or a prison record were liabilities.[5]

There were additional fairly constant patterns in the traditional family in Japan. It was characterized by strong solidarity, mutual helpfulness, and of course a patriarchal structure. In addition to filial piety, family themes included respect for age and seniority and a preference for male children. There were clear-cut patterns of deference, including the use of special words for addressing elders. Cohesion and harmony were valued above individual desires or achievement. Hard work, duty, obligation, and responsibility were strongly emphasized.[6]

Part III: The Japanese Family in the United States with Issei Parents
A. The Early Years

The earliest immigrants from Japan were young men, many still in their teens. When they later thought about marriage, the idea of marrying a non-Japanese woman must have occurred to some. However, this was made virtually impossible by such factors as language, culture, race, and lack of social contact with eligible women. Many *Issei* men had also emigrated with the idea of eventual return to Japan, and antimiscegenation feelings would have made his marriage to a non-Japanese unacceptable. Accustomed to arranged marriages, it was quite natural to have relatives and friends at home select a wife. The *baishakunin* or "go-between" set about matchmaking in a manner similar to the computerized dating services of this country. Couples were matched in as many ways as possible—origin in the same prefecture, often the same village, and similarity and suitability of family background. Women who were healthy and could bear children were given high priority. The reputation of the matchmaker depended on the success of his efforts. Literally thousands of young Japanese women were betrothed in this manner and sent off to America to join unknown bridegrooms. These imported brides must have been extraordinarily adaptable or extraordinarily dutiful—probably both. They were also not accustomed to intimate interpersonal relationships with men. Most received the news that they were being sent to a bridegroom in America with very little notice.

---

[5] Leonard Broom and John I. Kitsuse, *The Managed Casualty: The Japanese-American Family in World War II* (Berkeley: University of California Press, 1956), 2.

[6] Kitano, *Japanese Americans*, 61.

Both bride and groom often knew little more about each other than a photograph could provide.[7]

These *Issei* couples applied the principles of the late Tokugawa-Early Meiji child rearing to their *Nisei* offspring (briefly described in preceding section). In certain respects child rearing was harsher than in Japan. *Issei* parents rarely resorted to physical punishment, however. Rather the use of ridicule and teasing was much more likely. A common theme was that boys that were noisy, emotionally upset, or otherwise obstreperous, were teased for "behaving like a girl." In addition, they were reminded that they were Japanese and therefore obligated to avoid being crude, to speak good Japanese, and to avoid any association with the *Eta*, Japan's pariah caste.[8]

The early Japanese families were interdependent, with larger Japanese neighborhood and community units. Japanese community solidarity was quickly established, and the natural group cohesion was strengthened by hostility from the outside, non-Japanese community. There was one important exception to the traditional Japanese pattern of the family life. There were almost always no grandparents, no older generation to fulfill its traditional responsibility in teaching the young the roles and rituals of Japanese life. Japanese family patterns in rural America were probably the most traditional since contact with the outside community was even more limited and since the *Issei* father farmer role was quite similar to that in Japan.[9]

B. The Family Structure
i. Intact

The early Japanese family in the United States had many apparently unfavorable aspects: the arranged marriage, the requisite adaptation both to a new spouse and to a new land, the crowded and inferior housing, poverty, continuous deprivation, and little expectation of immediate social change. Under these circumstances, it might be logical to predict early disillusionment and a high rate of divorce, desertion, or separation. The disillusionment was there, but not the divorce. This was partly due to the lack of alternatives to staying together, but more importantly because of their Japanese values and expectations. Much emphasis was placed upon *gaman* (sticking things out) and upon the importance of "properly" rearing their children. Expectations of marriage lay not in the American reverence for love and romance, but in a conception of *giri* (duty and obligation).[10] The concept of *enryo* (modesty in the presence of one's superior), *on* (ascribed obligation), *chu* (loyalty to one's superior), and *ninjo* (humane sensibility) also contributed to the permanency of the marriages, though the advantages seemed to be heavily in favor of the husband!

---

[7] Kitano, *Japanese Americans*, 62–63.

[8] Hilary Conroy and T. Scott Miyakawa, eds., *East Across the Pacific: Historical and Sociological Studies of Japanese Immigration and Assimilation* (Santa Barbara, CA: American Bibliographical Center, Clio Press, 1972), 294.

[9] Kitano, *Japanese Americans*, 63–64.

[10] Kitano, *Japanese Americans*, 64–65.

ii. Vertical

This model of family interaction places the father in a position of indisputable leadership, with other positions in the family deriving from this authority and clearly prescribed. Everybody knows his place. A pure vertical structure is of course only hypothetical, and it is probable that few families ever functioned fully in this manner.

There were several factors that modified the father's authoritarian role. The most important one was the *Issei* father was at a cultural disadvantage—his *Nisei* children understood the American culture and spoke English better than him. The children were citizens, while he was an alien, and he could not become a citizen by law. The children could therefore own land and were better educated. However, the father made major family decisions. His wife probably exerted more influence on those decisions here than she would have in Japan, particularly if she played a significant role in the family's business.

Male dominance was reinforced by the Japanese community's expectations that a man, never a woman, would represent the family in any external relations, unless the husband was no longer living. Other circumstances also contributed to male dominance. *Issei* women rarely spoke English as most of the men did, though how crudely, and the women rarely learned to drive a car. The wife's role in the family was subordinate and submissive, and it often called for a stoical endurance of hardships. *Nisei* children may not have understood the system of authority in which they were involved, but they recognized the father's authority and the mother's role as a surrogate of the father. It was a code that parents had the right to control children's behavior and that children should yield to parental demands.[11]

iii. Traditional

Family interaction was based on clearly prescribed roles, duties, and responsibilities rather than on personal affection. Love, although undoubtedly present in many families, was not the prime leverage for gaining social control. Rather, rules and tradition had a higher value. It is likely that this early training, emphasizing the more impersonal types of interaction, made it relatively easy for the Japanese to fit into such structures as bureaucracies with little difficulty as compared to other immigrant Americans.

One of the most emphasized facets of family interaction retained from the family system in Japan was that of *oya-kooko*, or filial piety. The reciprocal obligation of parent to child and child to parent could be observed in everyday decisions, such as the parent buying less expensive clothes for himself in order to better clothe his children. A major decision might include the parents sacrificing anything outside of basic necessities in order to send the sons to college. Stories of aging parents living on practically nothing in order that their sons could gain a college education are not unusual. The idea of almost total parental responsibility for one's own children remains a strong one among the *Issei*, and many of them complain that the reciprocal obligation—that of the child to the parent—has been rapidly forgotten in the process

---

[11] Kitano, *Japanese Americans*, 65.

of acculturation of the *Nisei* to American life. The ungratefulness of their children is a common topic among *Issei*.[12] However, as LaViolette points out,

> The concern that Issei parents had for their children was a constant fear that the child may ruin the family name, may not be a "good Japanese," or may not acquire the proper manners and emotional control. It was not so much a concern for the individual happiness of the child as an anxiety that it fit into the prescribed ways of thinking and acting.[13]

These traditional patterns of family interaction were reconstructed in the immigrant community because they fulfilled a number of functions highly valued in Japanese society. Male primogeniture, apart from its economic function, assures continuity of the family name and status. The hierarchy of authority through the male head, and the interdependence of family members, assure control over the members. Representation in important community activities by the male head of the family assures its involvement in community affairs and reinforces its community standing.

The transmission of these family values to *Nisei* children was seriously hampered by linguistic barriers but nevertheless was accomplished effectively. Few *Issei* acquired a comfortable fluency in English, and the characteristic language of parent-child communication was Japanese. On the other hand, few *Nisei* ever learned to speak Japanese well, and parent-child conversations therefore tended to be confined to a crude basic Japanese interspersed with English. Nevertheless, the paratactic mode sufficed to transmit many parental attitudes, sentiments, and values.[14]

iv. Methods of Problem Solving

Nisei children were permitted to participate in family discussions when their age and achievement demonstrated their worth. They were treated until then as immature but developing children. Lyman states:

> Manhood was not merely coming of age; it was, more importantly, demonstrated by independent status achieved through steadfastness, determination, and single minded purposefulness. Self-control was central to the demonstration of maturity among growing *Nisei*. Although interdependence and real achievement could not be actually demonstrated until adulthood, emotional management was always worthy of exhibition and often tested for its own sake.[15]

And from LaViolette:

---

[12] Kitano, *Japanese Americans*, 66.

[13] Forrest Emmanuel LaViolette, *Americans of Japanese Ancestry* (Toronto: Canadian Institute of International Affairs, 1945), 20–21.

[14] S. Frank Miyamoto, "An Immigrant Community in America," in *East Across the Pacific: Historical and Sociological Studies of Japanese Immigration and Assimilation*, ed., Hilary Conroy and T. Scott Miyakawa (Santa Barbara, CA: American Bibliographical Center, Clio Press, 1972), 228–229.

[15] Stanford M. Lyman "Generation and Character: The Case of the Japanese Americans," in *East Across the Pacific: Historical and Sociological Studies of Japanese Immigration and Assimilation*, ed., Hilary Conroy and T. Scott Miyakawa (Santa Barbara, CA: American Bibliographical Center, Clio Press, 1972), 295.

There is very little reasoning with a child, even after he is fifteen or sixteen years of age. The technique of parental control is essentially that of ordering and forbidding . . . To fail to encourage the child to think for himself indicated, of course, that the child is to be completely dominated by the parents, that his sole duty is to obey their wishes . . . It stems from a wish to make the child conform to rigid norms, rather than to help him to develop his own individuality. As between old and young, the older person, having greater prestige, is invariably the superior, and the child is taught uncritical acceptance of things defined as "superior" by custom.[16]

The *Issei* were oriented toward their children in terms of their position in their birth order and their sex. A line of direct authority extended down from the father through the mother to the firstborn son and so on. A line of obligation extended upward from the youngest to the eldest. The authority system was frequently tested by elder brothers who harshly rebuked younger brothers, sometimes for no apparent reason. Younger brothers learned that if they could take these rebukes with outwardly calm detachment, they would ultimately be rewarded with recognition of their maturity. Firstborn sons received similar treatment from their fathers, and daughters sometimes found they had to live up to both the precepts of manhood, maturity, and womanliness. Boys who threw tantrums or gave way to violent emotional expression were regarded as immature and were teased and advised until they became conformative and quiescent. The stoic, mysterious, inscrutable Japanese is not just a stereotype. They were trained to be that way!

The most distinctive characteristic of Japanese family interaction was the absence of prolonged verbal exchange. Although some of the common strategies to gain support through manipulation or cajoling were present, very few problems were resolved through open discussion between parents and children. Rather, arguments were one-sided, and most *Nisei* can remember the phrase *damatte-ore!* or "keep quiet!" that concluded the arguments. Verbalization of feelings, disagreement, mutual discussion were actively discouraged. The most serious family problems of illness, delinquency, etc. often required help from sources outside the family but almost always within the ethnic community. The *Issei* family rarely used outside specialists, and when obligated, preferred a Japanese to a *hakujin*, a "white man." In general, the community was adequate to deal with most problems. Kitano tells of a Nisei who remembers how an instance of delinquency was handled in the '30s:

> I knew these two brothers who were pretty wild. They would get drunk . . . were always fighting, always in trouble and uncontrollable. Finally, their father came to talk to my father and other Japanese families in the neighborhood . . . all agreed that these boys would hurt the reputation of the other Japanese and provide poor models for the younger boys . . . so even though the brothers were already young adults and out of high school, they were sent to Japan.[17]

---

[16] LaViolette, *Americans of Japanese Ancestry*, 22.

[17] Kitano, *Japanese Americans*, 73.

Obviously, this method of handing deviance helps to account for the reported low official rates of delinquency and other problem behavior among the Japanese. The threat of being sent to Japan was another source of family control.

v. Sex

One of the functions of the family is to provide approved sexual outlets. Before the picture brides arrived, prostitution provided these outlets for the *Issei* man. With the arrival of the brides and the establishment of family life, prostitution almost disappeared. Gulick stated that by 1914, the number of Japanese brothels in San Francisco had been reduced from twelve to three, and in Oakland from eight to one.[18] The ability of the *Issei* male to repudiate completely his former hedonistic bachelor life is rather remarkable. Even more remarkable is the puritanical orthodoxy, after marriage, of their sexual attitudes that contrasted sharply with those of the married man in Japan, where bars, baths, and geishas were the time-honored province of the husband as well as the bachelor. Communication between the *Issei* and *Nisei* was difficult on any subject, and the discussion of sex was nearly impossible. Many *Nisei* therefore were thoroughly misinformed on the subject. Some thought of sex in terms of the delicate, self-conscious lectures provided by physical education teachers, and others picked up what they could from street and gang groups. Older brothers and sisters probably provided the most balanced information. *Nisei* boys, in general, tended to feel there were two kinds of girls. The kind they would marry was usually a *Nisei* of long acquaintance—either personal or through family contacts—and was "pure." She was not thought of as a sex object. Then there was "that kind of girl," who might be non-Japanese. This way of looking at sex almost ensured that there were few "shotgun" marriages among the *Nisei*, despite the fact that many did not marry until their late twenties.[19]

Techniques of Social Control

It is not surprising that a social system advocating an intact family, prescribed roles, and a high degree of family and community reinforcement was successful in controlling the behavior of its members, who in turn were characterized by conformity and little social deviance. Desired behavior was, of course, not accomplished merely by exposing children to correct models. Behavior was constantly rewarded, punished, reinforced, and reshaped by such parental techniques as emphasis on dependency, appeals to obligation, duty, and responsibility, the use of shame, guilt, and gossip, and, finally, an emphasis on ethnic identity. *Giri* connotes a moral obligation toward others and is related to role position, involving an individual through his family with the ethnic community as well. He therefore has a responsibility to his family and to his community, both of which exert much inhibiting pressure on deviant behavior.[20]

---

[18] Sidney Lewis Gulick, *The American Japanese Problem: A Study of the Racial Relations of the East and the West* (New York: Charles Scribner's Sons, 1914), 57.

[19] Kitano, *Japanese Americans*, 69–70.

[20] Kitano, *Japanese Americans*, 67.

Nevertheless, the assimilative influences of American society were at work in all families. From the *Issei* point of view, the *Nisei*, by their constant exposure to American influences and their lack of regard for Japanese traditions, were losing the values offered by their heritage. The *Nisei*, in turn, considered their *Issei* fathers to be unduly authoritarian, distant, and conservative. Mothers were thought to be overly anxious about their children and given to endless preaching. And the Japanese community was viewed as parochial in its concerns. Despite these potentially disorganizing influences, the social controls were extremely effective. A number of factors functioned to sustain effective controls. First, the values emphasized in the Japanese family were generally consistent with those of middle-class American society. Success at school, work, or play was doubly reinforced by both the Japanese community and American society. Second, despite the *Issei*'s apparent slowness of assimilation into American life, they eventually absorbed many American tastes and attitudes. Third, following Japanese principles, the *Issei* devoted a great deal of attention to their children, to the point of overprotection by Western standards. The effect on the parents' assimilation was twofold: to absorb them in their children's interests and attitudes and to increase their willingness to strike compromises with their children, if for no other reason than to preserve the solidarity of the family.[21]

Part IV: Effects of the World War II Concentration Camps on the Japanese Family in the United States

With the issuance of Executive Order 9066 on March 18, 1942, and the subsequent incarceration of the 110,000 Japanese Americans into concentration camps, the influence of the *Issei* rapidly declined. Though the official policy of the evacuation was to not split family units or communities, the sociological and humanitarian considerations underlying these decisions were not implemented. The evacuation of the family as a unit did not ensure its maintenance as an institution. Even less did the evacuation of fragments of neighborhoods ensure the transfer to the centers of cohesive communities. Indeed, the immediate impact of barracks housing with its fragmenting consequences for family organization would have suggested the need for important compensatory family activities if the group was to be sustained. Some families were physically broken up, and individual adjustment became determined in large part by associations outside the family.

Families were housed in one-room units (average size: twenty-five by twenty-five feet). The units in assembly centers were even smaller, some of the units were actually horse stables vacated by the racehorses in Santa Anita and Tanforan racetracks. In some cases two families, strangers to each other, shared a unit in these modified military barracks. The thin partitions that separated the units were meager protection of privacy. Family quarrels and celebrations alike were never free from the intrusions of visitors or neighbors, and the family was always constrained by the thought that the community was just outside the room. In the horse stable units there

---

[21] Lyman, "Generation and Character," 230–231.

were only thin partitions with the area above the partitions open. Privacy was a forgotten luxury.

A community mess hall, lavatories, showers, and washroom served more than fifty families. The organization of the mess hall did not provide for family dining, and the important mealtime socialization of children was hampered. The children often ate with their friends and rushed in and out of the barracks units on their separate ways. The limitation of space and the elimination of routine activities restricted opportunities for interaction. If all members were in the barracks unit at the same time, it was more by accident than plan, and there was little occasion for the repair of deteriorating group morale. In this setting, the barracks served only as a place to rest and sleep. It was housing in the most physical sense of the word and through the months and years of occupancy, few residents could think of the barracks as home.

The concern of the War Relocation Authority Administration for the "normal economic support of the family" was not manifest in its employment policy. The standard pay rate of $9.00 to $15.00 per month in the assembly centers and $12.00 to $19.00 per month in the relocation centers hardly retarded the dissipation of meager economic resources. Most families had to maintain payments on fixed obligations, such as insurance. Many felt the necessity of masking the starkness of the barracks and spent their own money on improvements. The monotonous and unappetizing mess hall fare "costing no more than 45 cents per person per day" was usually supplemented by purchases at the canteen. The clothing allowance was a mere token considering the extreme climatic conditions of the center locations. Families with young children were particularly affected since they received the earnings of only the father.

More mature families with older *Nisei* children were able to draw upon the earning power of several members and thus partly alleviate the drain upon family resources. However, in contrast to the prewar pattern, the economic activity of the family in the center was not an integrated enterprise. The Administration employed workers as individuals and did not treat the family as a unit. Nevertheless, the *Nisei* were experiencing a degree of economic independence relatively rare in prewar families. This independence undermined one of the supports for the family organization. In effect, the center attenuated the *Issei*'s control over both the economic and social bases of his authority.

The maintenance of family solidarity and integration in the center increasingly depended upon the family's ability to draw upon the affectional resources of the group. The family's use of affection as a defense against deteriorative center influences was limited by its prewar character. In rigidly authoritarian families, the formal parent-child relationships were not conclusive to the development of affectional bonds. Before the war, institutional supports for the traditional Japanese family against the impact of the dominant society were imperfectly integrated and weak. In such families, the socialization of the *Nisei* to their family roles was not clearly defined nor institutionally controlled. The arbitrary authority pattern imposed by the *Issei* lacked the compensation of reciprocal rights of the *Nisei*. For example, the eldest son may have carried major economic responsibilities for his family, but his parents withheld from him the authority to make independent decisions. The major source of strength of formal authority lay in the economic dependency of the *Nisei*, and the ambiguities of such family structures induced serious strains and instabilities. The acculturation of the *Nisei* and their increasing participation in peer groups introduced alternative definitions of family roles and reduced the *Nisei*'s emotional dependency.[22]

The center environment then encouraged the *Nisei*'s emancipation from the family in two ways: by granting economic independence and by strengthening peer groups against family groups. One of the first administrative policies was to assign preferential status to the *Nisei*. Special recognition was accorded to the leadership of the Japanese American Citizens League, which was committed to cooperation with the Administration. The preferential treatment toward the *Nisei* extended into all aspects of center life: community organization, employment, leisure, and relocation out of the concentration camps. Given the high value of family unity in the Japanese culture, the conditions of community disorganization, the destruction of the family's economic base, and the acute uncertainty of the future, it is understandable that the maintenance of family unity should become a major concern of the *Issei* whose orientation toward the future was bound to their children. For them, only the family could provide security against the future.

A major crisis encountered by the family in the center was relocation out of the camps and the registration program which preceded that. Theoretically, the registration was a means of expediting the relocation of the internees to areas of the Midwest and East. The criteria that separated the eligible from the ineligible were the infamous "loyalty" questions. There was tremendous confusion and concern about the implications that the answers would have for the conscription of the *Nisei* men and for the relocation of the family out of the camps. The coordination of the Army and the WRA registration programs inextricably linked the two issues. The people inferred that positive responses to the loyalty questions implied both a willingness to serve in the armed forces and a willingness to be relocated. This interpretation, which was in fact correct, aroused immediate and anxious concern in the family. A "loyal" response might make possible the drafting of the adult *Nisei* male and at the same time force the relocation of the rest of the family during his absence. This is precisely what happened in many families. If the drafted sons were the only employable persons in the family because the parents were too aged and the other children too young, the family would have one or more sons fighting on the battlefields while their family was in a concentration camp! The end result: Many Gold Star mothers in the barbwire-surrounded centers guarded by armed sentries in watchtowers.

---

[22] Broom and Kitsuse, *The Managed Casualty*, 39.

Part V: The Japanese Family in the United States With *Nisei* Parents

Relocation was primarily to metropolitan areas such as New York, Chicago, Boston, Cleveland, Cincinnati, Minneapolis, and St. Paul. Many remained in those areas, particularly the first three areas. Most others returned to the Pacific Coast when the ban was lifted. The *Nisei* continued their newfound roles of community and family leadership in their places of relocation and/or upon return "home."

Despite the general respect and personal deference paid to their parents by *Nisei*, they tended to see their parents as negative role models when it came to rearing their own children. The isolation, harshness, and communication difficulties of their own childhood were vividly recalled, and a great many *Nisei* parents vowed that their children would not experience any of that. As a result, *Nisei* parents rarely emphasized the ethics of samurai stoicism and endurance and the discipline associated with them. Rather they chose to follow the white middle-class ethos of love, equality, and companionship. As Lyman states,

> The principles of *bushido* have given way to those of Dr. Spock; the idea of age-graded obligation is supplanted by Gesell's age-cohort theory; and the social distance that separated parent and child is replaced by the idea that parents and children grow together. However, as a model, the Japanese American family with *Nisei* parents is more vertically structured and male-dominated than other comparable middle-class American families. Many *Nisei* women resent this position and marital conflicts arise from the differences in expectations.
>
> The children brought up by *Nisei* are quite different from their parents, and from the point of view of most *Nisei*, the result is disappointing. *Nisei* complain that *Sansei* seem to lack the drive and the initiative which once was a hallmark of the Japanese; that they have no interest in the characterological elements of the Japanese culture; that they are prone to more "delinquency" and less respect for authority than were the *Nisei*; that they lack psychological self-sufficiency and independent capacity for decision making.[23]

The *Sansei* offspring indicate an ambivalence and mild anxiety over their own situation. They exhibit a certain *hansen* effect, that is, a desire to recover selected and specific elements of the culture of old Japan.[24] In this endeavor itself they discover that their own Americanization limits the possibility of effective recovery. If juvenile delinquency among them is on the rise, they attribute it in small part to parental misunderstanding and in greater part to the effects of great social changes taking place in all of America. Their *Nisei* parents often appear old-fashioned to them, unprepared to understand them, and unwilling to offer them sufficient love and understanding. Finally, they seem "ready to claim the right to dissolve their geogenerational identity and that of their successor generations in favor of deeper intimate associations below the level of the generational group and interracial

---

[23] Lyman, "Generation and Character," 305.

[24] George Kagiwada, "The Third Generation Hypotheses: Structural Assimilation Among Japanese-Americans" (paper, Pacific Sociological Association annual meeting, San Francisco, CA, March 1968). [*Ed note: See also* Eugene I. Bender and George Kagiwada, "Hansen's Law of 'Third-Generation Return' and the Study of American Religio-Ethnic Groups," *Phylon* 29, no. 4 (1968): 360–370.]

intimacies transcending it."[25] Yet, they also wonder how and in what manner they can or should retain their Japanese identity.

The *Nisei* are beginning to sense their decline and eventual disappearance as the *Sansei* generation approaches maturity and establishes an independent existence and special group identity in America. "The inevitable end of the *Nisei* group has provoked a mild crisis in the *Lebensweld* (life-world) of the *Nisei*." *Nisei* are realizing with a mixture of anxiety and discomfort, but primarily with a sense of *shikata-ga-nai* (fatalistic resignation), that the way of life which they have been used to, and the arts of self-preservation and impression management which they so assiduously cultivated, will soon no longer be regular features of existence among the Japanese in America. The *Sansei*, and for that matter the other successor generations, will be different from the *Nisei* in certain fundamental respects, of course.

Nisei have always recognized the sociocultural and psychic differences between themselves and the *Sansei*. Some of these differences are based on clearly distinguishable generational experiences. Few of the *Sansei* experienced or remember the terrible effects of imprisonment during World War II. Some of them have identified with the experience and have strongly criticized the *Nisei* for allowing the imprisonment or at least not without more resistance. The *Sansei* seem not to realize that the average age of the *Nisei* was about sixteen and major decisions were being made by the *Issei* parents who by law were aliens. *Nisei* may seem to have been very weak in the eyes of the now liberated *Sansei*, but *Sansei* also do not bear the deep scars of this cruelty which many *Nisei* often are unwilling to discuss. Of course there are some *Nisei* who considered the incarceration as their patriotic duty and the dead of the 442nd Regiment (the all-Japanese American Combat Team which was the most decorated in World War II) as a necessary sacrifice to prove the loyalty of the Japanese in America!

Most *Sansei* have grown up in homes unmarked by noticeable cultural division between America and Japan, and most of them have benefited from the relative material success of their parents and have received parental support for their educational pursuits without difficulty. Finally, very few *Sansei* have felt the demoralizing agony of anti-Japanese prejudice. In all these respects *Nisei* recognize that the *Sansei* are beneficiaries of *Issei* and *Nisei* struggles and perseverance, and therefore, if the *Sansei* behave differently than an immigrant or oppressed people, it is only right and proper for them to do so. Some *Sansei* would retort, though the racism is now much more subtle, they are still an oppressed people.

The *Nisei* are really the last of the Japanese Americans. The *Sansei* are American Japanese. As Jitsuichi Masuoka observed three decades ago, "It is the members of the *Sansei*, who having been fully acculturated but having been excluded by the dominant group because of their racial difference, really succeed in presenting a

---

[25] Lyman, "Generation and Character," 305.

united front against exclusion by the dominant group. A genuine race problem arises at this point in the history of race relations."[26]

In the last decade there have been a number of *Sansei*, primarily in colleges and universities of San Francisco, Berkeley, Los Angeles, and Seattle, who have become concerned about their ethnic identity and felt a need to relate more significantly to their Japanese heritage. Playing a very active part in the San Francisco State College student uprisings of 1968 were *Sansei* students (as well as *Nisei* professors) demanding expansion of the Asian studies department among other needs. There are Japanese studies courses in most major colleges and universities and some high schools on the West Coast.

The motivation that partially drives the *Sansei* toward returning to their Japanese heritage is that they feel their *Nisei* parents have not only become middle-class in their value systems, they have also become "white." During and after World War II, in order to avoid further harassment, many of the *Nisei* refrained from using the Japanese language or in any way overtly broadcasting their cultural heritage. They also overcompensated with their Puritan work ethic and in doing so many "out-whited the whites."[27] Some *Sansei* are in a way trying to become more Japanese than their *Nisei* parents, and their associations are primarily with other *Sansei*s. They identify with the *Issei*. Groups of *Sansei* in San Francisco, Oakland, Los Angeles, and Sacramento have initiated special programs for the benefit of the recreational, educational, and social service needs of the *Issei*.

Twenty years ago, some had predicted that because of the seeming rapid assimilation of the *Nisei*, there would be a great deal of intermarriage with non-Japanese by the third and fourth generations. Intermarriage is common among the *Sansei*. Some estimates are as high as 50% of *Sansei* marry non-Japanese—this probably occurring more often in areas where there are not concentrated groups of Japanese living. To what degree will *Sansei* couples continue the family structure of the Japanese family? To what degree will *Sansei* who marry non-Japanese, consciously or subconsciously, have expectations of their spouses and children that are part of their Japanese family upbringing?

Part VI: The Japanese Family in the United States with Parents More Recently Arrived

Since World War II, changes in the social organization in Japan have been rapid. The change was accelerated by the impact of social and political developments in the rest of the world. Industrialization, urbanization, and population increase were the other major factors precipitating the change. Japan's defeat in World War II shattered temporarily the national pride and confidence of the Japanese in their traditional institutions, including the time-honored family system. One notable result was the promulgation of a new constitution, which was immediately followed by the partial

---

[26] Jitsuishi Masuoka, "Race Relations and Nisei Problems," *Sociology and Social Research* 30 (July, 1946), 459.
[27] "Success Story: Outwhiting the Whites," *Newsweek*, June 21, 1971, 24–25.

revision of the Civil Code, effective as of January 1, 1948. Although not all of the principles and ideas underlying the Code revisions were entirely novel to the postwar Japanese, many restrictions on individual activities found in the family-centered prewar Code were in obvious contradiction with the new principles of democracy, as they are summarily called. Ultimately, only two of the major concepts of democracy came to be recognized as legal principles: (1) dignity of the individual and (2) equality between the sexes before the law.

The *Issei* migration came to an abrupt end with the Asian Exclusion Act of 1924. The largest group of Japanese coming to the United States since then was the war brides of World War II. Many of their children have experienced an identity crisis. As they have grown older they have felt unwanted both among the Japanese and the cultural group from which their father comes. The *Issei* and *Nisei* have been particularly hostile to the families with black fathers.

The offspring usually feels most comfortable among blacks. The basic problem in the "war bride" marriages following World War II seemed to be the expectations the Japanese wife and the American husband had of each other. The G.I. thought he was getting the stereotyped sweet, subservient, uncomplaining Japanese wife; the wife thought she would have the freedom and equality and the material affluence she had heard American wives had. Though the shift in family patterns was slow in Japan, there had come to be more acceptance for the rights of the individual members of the family, including a more egalitarian marriage.

Berrien compared Japanese Americans in Hawaii, Japanese nationals, and Caucasian Americans on the mainland of the United States through the use of the Edwards Personal Preference Scale.[28] On some scales (e.g., deference, nurturance, order, and heterosexuality), the Japanese in Japan were more similar to mainland Caucasians than were the young people of Japanese ancestry in Hawaii. One possibility is that *Issei* raised their children maintaining the values as they were held in the homeland when they left it in the late 1800s and early 1900s. In Kimura's study of war brides in Hawaii, the least happy brides seemed to be those married to Japanese American personnel, while those married to Caucasian personnel appeared to fare better. Interviews indicated the major cause to be that the parents of the Japanese American soldier expected their daughter-in-law to conform to the traditional Japanese role of serving the husband's parents. On the other hand, the Japanese bride of Japanese American servicemen expected to enter the egalitarian marriage she had heard so much about as existing in the United States and bitterly opposed her in-laws' attempts to return her to the traditional Japanese daughter-in-law role of subservience. It seems probable that the woman would have found greater sympathy for emancipation from in-laws had she married a Japanese national![29]

---

[28] F. Kenneth Berrien, *Values of Japanese and American Students*, Office of Naval Research Technical Report No. 14 (New Brunswick, NJ: Rutgers University), 10.

[29] Yukiko Kimura, "War Brides in Hawaii and Their In-Laws." *American Journal of Sociology* 63, no. 1 (July 1957): 74.

There is a continuous flow of Japanese nationals coming to the United States, usually as employees of Japanese firms (*Kaisha*) or the Japanese consulate, as students or are relatives of people who already live here or who marry Americans and come to live here. They are the *Shin-Issei* or the "new *Issei*." The difference between the original *Issei* and these new *Issei* reflect seventy years of drastic sociological change in Japan. Each of these subgroups among the *Shin-Issei* has its unique problems and needs. Slowly various groups within the Japanese community are reaching out to help meet those needs. A group of *Nisei* wives may provide recreational and educational activities for the wives of the Japanese businessmen. The recent incident of one of these *Kaisha* wives killing her young son was a pathetic instance of how she reacted to the extreme feelings of isolation and loneliness. Her husband was the only employee of his firm assigned to San Francisco. Host *Kaisha* wives at least have the companionship of the wives of the other men working for the same company. The men are under tremendous pressure to succeed in their business ventures. The children are burdened with not only being expected to do well in their "English-speaking" school here, but must keep up their Japanese language studies so when their fathers return after an average stay of five years, they will be able to compete with their peers in Japan.

The International Institute has traditionally met the needs of many students from Japan as well as the Japanese wives of Americans and other Japanese nationals. Some of the original "war brides" participate in the activities of the "newcomers" groups, though they may be older than the recent arrivals. They sometimes feel uncomfortable with the *Issei*, *Nisei*, and *Sansei*, who invariably discuss the wartime concentration camp experience that of course they cannot identify with at all. Other *Nisei* and *Sansei* groups have tried to help meet the needs of the *Shin-Issei* international brides and their families and of students. The most pointed disadvantage many *Nisei* and almost all *Sansei* have for effectively assisting the *Shin-Issei* is their inability to communicate in the Japanese language.

Part VII: Implications for Counseling the Japanese Family in the United States

Behind the composed face of a Japanese client of any generation, his entire heritage as here outlined must be considered. And if it is a married couple or family that is in pain, the counselor should become familiar with the particular family structure, birth order of each of the marital partners in their original families, generation from which each comes, the social class from which each comes, and the amount of acculturation that has occurred for each family member. The problems are complex and the prognosis grim, mainly because of the reluctance to seek help outside of the family until the situations have reached crisis proportions. The *Nisei* are slightly more apt to consult "experts" than are the *Issei*, but the pattern of in-group dependence is changing only slowly. Community agencies and family service facilities of the larger community still report almost no Japanese clientele, unless operated by a Japanese staff. Self-disclosure is often not within the experience of these people, and it is a very difficult process for the Japanese. They are highly skeptical of the value of counseling, eager not to waste time, and ashamed in the first place that they haven't been able to work out their own solutions. There is also a strong stigma attached to mental illness or even emotional instability among the Japanese, and there is great shame involved in being seen at a mental health facility. There is a great need for a change in the practice of almost always insisting on having clients come into an office for counseling. Home visits would be much preferred.

Because Japanese people often expect to get "expert advice" from specialists, care must be taken not to allow the clients to become dependent on the counselor. However because of family practices that are quite authoritarian and directive, they often respond more quickly to such an approach at first rather than to approaches that would require more subjective self-disclosure and self-analysis. As discussed earlier, verbal exchange was discouraged by the *Issei*. Problem solving for *Nisei* does not come easily or naturally, particularly in the area of sexual problems. A common problem with *Nisei* couples is when the husband is a "Japanese" authoritarian person and the wife wishes to function as a liberated women. If one or both parents are as unwilling as their own *Issei* parents for open discussion with their *Sansei* children, conflict too is inevitable because *Sansei* are usually more openly rebellious.

There is an acute need for more Japanese marriage and family counselors, preferably bilingual for those Japanese-speaking. The "war brides" made a breakthrough, possibly in their desperation. As a group they are making the greatest use of community counseling resources such as at the International Institute, the Community Mental Health Centers, Japanese-operated social service agencies, and the Japanese churches. But they too ask for and rarely find Japanese staff persons at the larger community agencies. Until community agencies are willing to hire Japanese counselors on their staff, the non-Japanese workers must first become more knowledgeable and hopefully then better understand and be more effective in counseling the Japanese family in the United States.

All counselors of the Japanese must understand that in addition to the normal tensions of marriage and family life, the Japanese family here has "the need for making compromises and reservations in a bicultural milieu" and we have a particular responsibility to "those who become psychologically marginal because they are unable to accept them."[30] The drives of such people are to be mainly either American or Japanese. Because of race and living in America, such a Japanese American may become hostile toward Japanese symbols, indicating that there is a fundamental wish to escape racial as well as the Japanese component of cultural heritage. Hopefully our message to them will be, "It is okay to *be* what you *are*!"

---

[30] LaViolette, *Americans of Japanese Ancestry*, 178.

Three Articles by Chinese Americans

The following three articles were all written by theologically trained Chinese Americans now serving the church in the United States and Hong Kong. Two of them have recently visited China. Judging by the outpouring of material by Chinese Americans being published in *Bridge* magazine, *East-West*, and other journals of the Chinese and Asian community here, the reflections of these men on the new consciousness of a Chinese American identity accurately represent the mind and experience of their generation.

Another China Visit

*Religion, the Religious Dimension, and Religious Surrogates**

FRANKLIN J. WOO

In the early summer of 1973 my family and I spent three memorable weeks in China. We concentrated on two cities, Guangdong and Beijing, where many of our relatives and friends live. Through them we were able to see a very small part of a vast country and to gain somewhat of an understanding of what is happening there. In this short article I am writing a few of my impressions while they are still fresh in my mind. I will confine my words to the areas of *religion*, the *religious dimension* of life, and *religious surrogates*.

No Organized Religion

Anyone, especially a churchman, visiting China today would be struck by the obvious lack of any organized religion (in the traditional sense) there.[1] The church buildings that we saw both in Guangdong and Beijing were run down and badly in need of repair. Many had broken windows or showed other signs of neglect. Some were converted into schools, places of public meetings, storehouses, or simply left abandoned. On the three Sundays that we spent in China we asked our relatives and friends whether there was any service of Christian worship that we could attend. For most people this inquiry must have seemed an unusual one. On the Sunday morning that we arrived in Beijing one person, as if not to show her own embarrassment over our request, politely made a halfhearted attempt at asking the clerk at our hotel whether there were any Christian services or worship in the city.[2]

---

* Dr. Woo, a member of the theology faculty at Chung Chi College, the Chinese University in Hong Kong, visited China with his family in the summer of 1973.

[1] See Donald E. MacInnis, *Religious Policy and Practice in Communist China* (New York: Macmillan, 1972), especially xix–xxiv. The same observation seems to be true with regards to the Buddhist religion. See Holmes Welch, "Buddhism since the Cultural Revolution" in *China Quarterly*, No. 40 (Oct–Dec 1969): 127–136. The Muslims in China seem to have their dietary practices respected (we saw many and ate in a few Muslim restaurants). But this privilege is apparently part of the political rather than religious policy of the government towards China's minority nationalities.

[2] John Fleming reported that he attended one such service of worship in Peking on September 10, 1972. See John Fleming, "Religion and the Churches in China Today," *China Notes* (Winter 1972–73): 5.

"Religion" is a term not used frequently in communist vocabulary, except negatively in referring to something undesirable and belonging to the superstition of the "old society." The communists see religion as an effective tool in the hands of the ruling classes to exploit and to keep down the poor. In the name of peace and harmony religion has been used, they say, in both feudal and modern societies to suppress conflict and struggle between the classes. The Buddhist temples we visited in China were exhibited to the public as relics of an ignominious past with all its old ideas, habits, customs, and culture. Christianity is seen as an instrument of Western expansionism and imperialism, especially since the early part of the nineteenth century.

The ideology of the communists has no places for the eternal, the abstract, or the metaphysical. The proper focus of dialectical materialism is social practice, the actual economic and political situation, in short, man's "concrete history." As Mao Zedong himself said almost half a century ago, "Everywhere religious authority totters as the peasant movement develops. In many places the peasant associations have taken over the temples of the gods as their offices."[3] Organized religion has no place in the new China today.

At first it seemed to me rather strange to experience a society where there is apparently virtually no public practice of religion. In Hong Kong it is still not uncommon, and even expected, that Christians do go to church on Sundays. For many Christians here this custom has become so much a part of life that they feel uncomfortable if they happen to miss church on a Sunday. In China, where there are no services of worship to be had, one quite naturally begins to ask anew the question (as I was asked by a one-time leading philosopher-theologian of China), "What is the use of religion in the world today?"

In our modern secular culture, even for many who frequent the churches and other places of worship, religion has somehow become less and less a determining factor in their lives. Unconsciously or otherwise, they seem to gear their lives to science and technology much more than we do to a supreme being. While many, like people in China today, may not openly profess atheism, their secular world outlook is perhaps not altogether different from people in other modern secular societies. If God exists, God is hidden, or very far away. For many, God is someone convenient to have around, especially in times of emergency. The rest of the time, God is available, somewhere, and ready to answer humanity's beckoning.

China today is under a regime that openly claims to be atheistic. Many Christians in Hong Kong, as elsewhere, believe that this atheism must be opposed by some sort of theism. With this belief, I do not agree. To me God transcends both theism and atheism. He is above all ideologies, religious as well as political. What sort of a God would God be if God exists only because humans say that God does? Or does not

---

[3] Mao Zedong, "Report on an Investigation of the Peasant Movement in Hunan," in *Selected Works*, vol. 1 (Elmsford, NY: Pergamon Press, 1965), 45.

exist because men say so? God's presence is not determined by humans, neither the theist nor the atheist.

The Religious Dimension of Life

In a more secular culture, where is God to be found? To this question religion must suggest the answers. In Hong Kong, where the Christian religion is still very popular, many people do find meaning and reality in a personal relationship to God in Christianity. For others, God is simply not a point of reference in their lives. For that matter, any allusion to a deity that is to make any sense at all would have to be made in terms of some common venture of life, such as birth, marriage, sickness, or death where the element of mystery is hinted at. This element is what I would call the *religious dimension* of life.

It is in the midst of life with all its ups and downs, its joys and sorrows, its surprises and disappointments, and its hopes and fears, that God is to be found. In a modern society we are living in a situation of unprecedented and accelerated changes where any hint of transcendence has been indeed "reduced to a rumor."[4] In China today there is no organized religion to speak of, and the country claims to be atheistic. Does this, however, mean that as a nation China is "godless," as so many god-fearing people not living in that situation and unsympathetic to it would say? It is true that China today is religionless. But it does not necessarily follow that therefore it is a godless society. No society on earth can really be godless, if by definition, God is the creator and sustainer of the whole universe. To paraphrase the experience of the ancient psalmist we can say of God, "If I go to a place where religion flourishes, you are there; and if I go to a place where religion is dead or where there is no religion, you are still there!"[5]

With the eyes and ears of faith, travelers in China today can see the "signals of transcendence" and hear the "rumor of angels."[6] The religious dimension of life is there, just as it is in any human society. It can be seen in the quality of life, because life in its deepest sense is religious. Despite the fact that life is highly and most effectively organized down to the very last detail, and thought is controlled by and follows a general party line, in China there are still genuine courtesy and warmth between people; happy children with parents who love them; humor and play; great willingness to sacrifice self for the good of society; and an unremitting desire to do what is right.

On the crowded public buses in the two cities we visited, many times we have seen people offering their seats to an elderly person or to a young mother with little children. It is a common and beautiful sight to see a little boy on his way to school

---

[4] Peter L. Berger, *A Rumour of Angels* (London: Allen Lane, The Penguin Press, 1970).

[5] Neale Hunter has made this point emphatically clear in his "Religion and the Chinese Revolution," in *China the Peasant Revolution*, ed., Ray Wylie (Geneva: World Student Christian Federation, 1972), 81–97.

[6] Berger, *A Rumour of Angels*, 118–121.

hand in hand with his grandfather. There are many such little heartwarming incidents that for us pointed beyond the fact that China is only a nation in a hurry.

The common people seem to be getting a fairer share of the material resources in what is still a very poor and overpopulated country. Whereas in the old society mere physical survival was a major preoccupation of life for millions of people, now there is relative security in livelihood, health, shelter, and the future. There is a rediscovered dignity in human labor and production and the common purpose—of taking part in the life and destiny of one's own nation. As one uncle said to me, "What Christianity could not achieve in China, the communists are achieving!"

In the hospital where another uncle is surgeon, we saw him operate on a young farmwoman to reduce a broken neck suffered in an accident in a commune in Honan province a few days earlier. At the commune clinic she was given emergency treatment and was brought five hundred miles by fast train to Beijing, where she received the best specialized medical treatment that modern science could provide—all within five days of her accident and for the nominal fee of less than two *yuan*. In a private room next to her ward, we saw a factory worker who had been operated on the previous day to remove a tumor in his spine. During the course of a fifteen-hour long operation where there was profuse bleeding, the patient was given a transfusion of a total of 12,000 cc (three gallons) of blood. After the operation he was assigned to the private room with special nursing care, not because he could afford to pay, but because he needed it.

I thought about America, where doctors reign supreme in a medical hierarchical system, and how they acquire great wealth, prestige, and position. But in Peking, one cannot even tell by outward appearance that his uncle is a medical man: His clothing is no different from that of any other man in the street. He lives in a simple one-bedroom house. Each day he rides for about an hour in a crowded public bus to his work at the hospital. Once a year he goes with a team to one of the outlying provinces of China taking medical services to poor peasant farmers. To me, he embodies the very meaning of the phrase "serve the people." As the philosopher-theologian friend said to me, "Religion has no name in China today; it is not based on doctrines, dogmas, or hypotheses, but practice." Should religion ever be restored in China, if it is to have any contact with the new social order, it will have to point out and support this practice of the new order's religious dimension.

Religion Surrogates

Thus far we have said that even though there is no institutionalized religion in China today, there is still the religious dimension of life which points to the mystery and profound depth of human existence and experience. This dimension is present in any society either with or without organized religion. It is part of the givens of life simply because it is human life.

Now we will talk about what the sociologist of religion would call religion surrogates, or the substitutes that have taken the place that was once occupied by organized religion. It is in this functional sense that we can call these other phenomena "religion surrogates."[7] They are the modern viable alternatives to religious practices in the traditional sense. Whether they truly satisfy the religious needs of man is an open question.

Chinese communist society is without religion today, yet it is a most *religious* society, if we grant the broad definition of religion as Tillich's *ultimate concern*. The ideology of Marxism-Leninism and Mao's thought demands a total commitment on the part of all its adherents that is not unlike that of the Judeo-Christian faith. Its exclusiveness and doctrinaire approach to truth can be seen to be much akin to those of evangelical fundamentalism. It sees the struggle between orthodoxy and heresy as clearly as it sees the difference between white and black, good and evil, right and wrong. There is the unrelenting fight with all forms of revisionism, in both its capitalistic and its soviet forms. In China today life and the passage of time are marked by such salvation events in their history as the *long march*, the *liberation*, and the *cultural revolution*. Even though the communists reject metaphysics, the Marxist view of history and the process of dialectical materialism are in fact no less metaphysical than many of the doctrines of traditional religions.

Every public gathering can (and does) serve as a celebration, a quasi-sacred activity where ballet, drama, songs, and music extol the glories of the revolutionary past. The holy history of the nation under the leadership of the Communist party is retold over and over again as a form of spiritual exercise. The two evening events that we attended in Guangdong and Beijing were to us very similar to services of worship, or perhaps evangelistic rally. One of our distant cousins and her husband are both itinerant actors whose team goes from village to village within Kwantung Province to "educate" the masses and to raise their level of political consciousness. They are the new evangelists of the new secular gospel to the poor, the exploited, and the oppressed. The net result of these meetings seems to serve as a means of unifying the people and inspiring them to continual par-ticipation in the building of the nation. The new saints are the host of glamorized national heroes of model soldiers, workers, or farmers, who willingly sacrifice themselves for the progress of the new China; children are taught in schools to learn from and to emulate them.

Chairman Mao himself comes very close to being deified. His statues near the entrance of Peking University (and many other places) stands about thirty feet high. During our stay in China we visited close to a dozen homes; everyone, barring none, had at least one portrait of the chairman hung in a conspicuous place, as if to remind all those within under whose bounty life in China is enjoyed today. The chairman's writings too adorn the walls of such public places as museums, parks, train stations, restaurants, and hotels, and are quoted as if they were sacred scriptures or golden texts.

---

[7] Indeed, much has been written of the religious aspects of Marxism. See, for example, a standard text such as J. Milton Yinger, *The Scientific Study of Religion* (New York: Macmillan, 1970), 196–200 or Thomas F. O'Dea, *The Sociology of Religion* (Englewood Cliffs, NJ: Prentice-Hall, 1966).

And there is the firm conviction that the new man with a new spirit of altruism and self-sacrifice will come about with the building of the new social order. For this to happen man must first learn to rely on himself and himself alone. At Peking University the revolutionary committee decided that they needed a competition-size swimming pool; so students and faculty members got together and built one all by themselves in eighty-five days! More recently the committee felt that the university needed a larger library, so again students and teachers were mobilized to build it by themselves.

That there is a new spirit in China today is an undeniable fact. One colleague in the Chinese University of Hong Kong, upon his return from a visit to the mainland, suggests that the experiment there is even more profound than the Reformation in Europe in the sixteenth century. After having been there, one cannot help being caught in the excitement of nation-building and the almost I enthusiasm that seem to permeate the whole country.

In contrast to the vitality of the new China, our basely materialistic city of Hong Kong does seem rather exsanguine. Our visit to the mainland left me with as many questions about this place as it did about China. I kept asking myself what had Christianity sought to achieve in China, but failed, while the communists apparently are succeeding? Indeed, what is it that Christianity is trying to achieve in any place?

In China we had our many moments of elation. On the other hand there was that sustained and continuous pressing feeling (besides that caused by the weather) of being hemmed in, as if one had difficulty in breathing. Our son, who plays the violin, felt that there was no variety of music in China. Our daughter, who reads avidly, complained that there was no literature besides the stories of revolutionary heroes.

I remember one long conversation I had with a cadre at the Peking Hotel for Overseas Chinese where we were staying. I had asked him what one does in China when one held ideas that were contrary to that of the system. Without any hesitation he blurted out to me, "You keep them to yourself!" I was both glad that there is a self to keep one's own ideas and sad that one had to do so. Here I am not even quarreling with the content of Maoist ideology but only with the methods used. The human spirit seems to cry out for more options than one. Seen in this light, Calvin's Geneva was equally as spiritually limiting as Mao's China. Suppose that by some sort of miracle all the portraits and statues of Mao Zedong could be suddenly transformed into those of Jesus Christ, and suppose that all the people began to study and quote only the Christian Bible instead of the thoughts of the chairman. From my own point of view, such a development would not be desirable.

China and Chinese American Identity*

WESLEY S. WOO

Early this summer l was asked by the editor of this quarterly to write an article attempting to blend my perceptions as a Chinese American (born and raised here) of the new China and of the Chinese American identity issues. Here was a fascinating topic, one to which I had not given much thought. Yet it was one that was enticing, especially as a vehicle for carrying a series of heretofore random thoughts within the realm of the topic matter suggested.

It seems to me that the two perceptual themes (Chinese and Chinese American identity) are linked reciprocally as they pertain to the social and psychological dimensions of Chinese Americans. Thus it is that, as I reflect on one issue, it perforce has direct impact on my feelings about the other. Permit me to elaborate, and in so doing, presume that some of what I have to say can be generalized to some other Chinese Americans.

First, the impact of the Chinese American identity issue on my perceptions and feelings about China. My personal history has always include an "awareness" of China, albeit filtered through the phenomena of Chinatown, San Francisco. At one time his "awareness" was quite high; this during my grammar school days when I attended Chinese language school. One must realize that the China I learned about then was a China or the past, a China taught by highly patriotic nationalist teachers, and a China to which all *Hua Qiao* (overseas Chinese) looked longingly back and dreamt forever of returning. (In many ways this attitude is comparable to the attitude of dispersed Jews toward Israel.) At another time in my life his "awareness" was quite low; this during my high school and early college days when anything Chinese took a back seat to other problems of growing up and establishing identity in American society. Then in recent days this "awareness" has been raised again, to the point where I would prefer to call it "consciousness." This semantic play is meant only to convey the idea that only in the last few years has the issue of China become a deliberate and conscious concern of mine. Although "awareness" had been quite high in my Chinese school days, it was not something I gave much voluntary attention to. It was curriculum matter I was required to study.

Why the change? The major reason seems to be the rise of ethnic concerns and issues in this country, specifically those of Chinese Americans in the last five years.

---

* Born in America of Chinese ancestry and a graduate in theological studies, Mr. Woo visited China in 1972. He is a member of the pastoral team at St. John's Presbyterian Church, San Francisco.

Without delving into that specific topic, suffice it to say that it brought a new light onto the ethnic side of a hyphenated being, i.e., the "Chinese" dimension of "Chinese American." To diverge a moment, lest you think by "hyphenated" being I mean schizoid being—I don't. The hyphen I find symbolic of an enriching and multifaceted dimension of being, in spite of the negative feelings bred by racism in this country. At any rate, the point is that the rise of ethnic consciousness among Chinese Americans has generated new or renewed consciousness of China.

This differs, however, from past awareness on two levels. First, as already mentioned, this is voluntary and deliberate attentiveness to China. Witness the rising number of courses on China and anything Chinese on college campuses and their enjoyment by Chinese who heretofore kept distance from such curricula. Second, this consciousness focuses on the present reality of China. Now the romance of "China" and the dispersion mentality are still alive, even in some like myself, who was born and raised here (and who thus, when talking about my time in Hong Kong and China, speaks unconsciously of having *gone back* or *returned* there, even though for the first time). But the difference is that this is now focused on present-day Mainland China (People's Republic of China), and not on the pre-Liberation China, nor on Nationalist China. This change of focus is due, first of all, to the changing political scene. Nationalist China is steadily losing political credibility throughout the international scene while Mainland China is gaining it. Nationalist China has nothing, while Mainland China has much to command the attention and loyalty of Chinese Americans seeking to identify with a prestigious and powerful China; one with prestige and power enough to lend to their own ethnic identities.

A second reason for the shift is that for many generations of Chinese Americans, Mainland China is the only China we can come to know. It is the only China existent (e.g., in size, power, and location) if we demand proof of existence. (It is the only China with content.) It is China in reality, not reification. Now this is not to deny that Nationalist China exists. But of issue here is the political weakness of that "reality," as already mentioned, and the pragmatic issue that Nationalist China seems to have done little for the people of China. Also critical here, though seldom mentioned, is the fact that everything pro-Nationalist tends to converge with everything "conservative." Thus whenever someone is enjoined to be more "Chinese" (à la Nationalist), he is usually told to be quiet, humble, respectful, and subservient to his elders, diligent in work and study, abstaining of play, nonconfrontational in conflict, etc. So this notion of "China" and "Chinese" becomes for young people symbolic of a traditional and unacceptable lifestyle. This, of course, is a generalization. Yet one would be hard put to find an exception to this. Then also, there is the phenomenon that pro-Nationalist elements in all Chinatowns tend to be involved in maintaining and sustaining oppressive ghetto conditions therein. Chinese American identity concerns are playing a role in pointing out this sin. Merge all the factors mentioned so far and you can see Chinese American ethnic concerns as one major vector in the propensity towards identification with Mainland China.

Turning to the impact of China on the Chinese American identity issue, it is obvious that the rise of China and the opening up of relationships between the US and China has allowed for a resurgence of positive attention towards China. As alluded to earlier, this in turn has increased the prestige of Chinese Americans. It has also helped to effect a shift in the internal political situation in Chinese communities. The point is that Chinese have a new reference point, one that people take pride in; and one that can amass political power enough to influence the shape of Chinatowns. Witness the wide age range and sizeable number of people who took part in the October 1st celebrations in San Francisco this month. Such celebration and participation would have been impossible just a couple of years ago.

At this point let me diverge once more, long enough to say that none of my comments should be construed to mean that I find China the epitome of good government any more than I feel the same for the US. Both government styles impress me, and disturb me. The point is that a tangible present-day China is being treated to long overdue praise and respect, and I am Chinese. Having grown up in the twenty years of isolation and ill feeling between China and the US, and having heard too many negative things said about China, and thus about me, I now relish the change. Whereas being Chinese was once problematic in American society, now being American for Chinese Americans can be problematic. One only needs to look at the vast number of Chinese Americans coming back into Chinatown and trying to be very "Chinese" to understand the latter "problem." An overreaction? Perhaps, though perhaps not. It certainly is an aspect of identity long suppressed. It was the ethnic identity moment that pointed out the former problem as a legacy or racism and that helped create the circumstances for the latter in its insistence that being Chinese is positive, an affirmation to which China's rising power and presence gives credence and respect. The convergence of the rise of China and the rise of the Chinese American identity movement certainly helps make for the development of healthy Chinese Americans, willing to affirm their identity, at least on the ethnic level.

But where do we go from here? It seems that more dialogue needs to be generated from the interplay of the two themes. Perhaps there is more that our ethnic identity concerns might draw from China. For example, though perhaps sounding redundant, we might ask what it means to be "Chinese"? That is answered on one level genetically. Yet what of the socio-psychological dimensions! Much of our understanding of what it means to be Chinese is shaped by history, albeit unconsciously. Yet this is contingent on what part of and time in history we give credence and emphasis. Once upon a time the answer to this question might have been shaped by Confucian standards. Is it today to be shaped by communistic standards? Or once this may have been given form according to what class of Chinese society one was in. What is begotten of a classless society? Are there other possibilities? Then also, so much of our "Chineseness" is shaped by regional origins (e.g., district and province); are our models or prototypes to be found there? What will be the impact on ethnic identity if there is a generation of Cantonese who speak only Mandarin?

Another question that might be raised is how this new consciousness of China will affect attitudes and feelings about the "American" side of the hyphen? Just how much weight should be given to that dimension? Some might prefer to be called "Chinese in the US." Others might prefer to delete the Chinese part and be called "American" (I hope, though, not in the sense of "white"). China has said before that she is opposed to the concept of dual citizenship. Yet her concern seems more legal than cultural, for she still uses the category of "overseas Chinese." While I was in Hong Kong I had occasion to talk with different people about the problem of Chinese Americans in the United States. One repeated response was the query why don't we leave and return to Hong Kong? I must confess that that sounds logical at times. Yet I think I find that solution too easy and too escapist. It would also satisfy a few too many other people. The point is that the "American" dimension is mine by right. Yet at the moment I am not sure what that entails, nor what I want it to entail.

Lastly, there may perhaps be more ways in which our perceptions and feelings about China can and will be shaped by Chinese American concerns. No matter how I judge my experience of having been born and raised as a Chinese in this country, the fact is that it has influenced my lifestyle. Any feelings I have are filtered through that experience and lifestyle. Thus on one level my attitudes and feelings about China most certainly will be shaped by the way Chinese in this country are treated racially and politically. On another level it will be affected by what I deem unique and important to the Chinese American scene. As said initially, there is a reciprocal relationship between perceptions of China and the Chinese American identity issue. This holds true even for the rest of America, whose attitudes towards Chinese Americans reflect and shape their attitudes toward China and vice versa.

The Chinaman's Chances Are Improving

David Ng[*]

While you are awaiting your visa to visit Mainland China, consider these true/false questions about Chinese Americans living among you:

1. (True/false) Asian Americans, especially the Chinese, have no family welfare or juvenile delinquency problems.
2. (True/false) Chinese Americans see themselves as a fully accepted part of the American social and economic scene.
3. (True/false) Chinese Americans are well-educated and have joined the middle economic class.
4. (True/false) Asian American ethnic churches are decreasing in number because Asian Americans are joining majority culture (Caucasian) churches.
5. (True/false) Chinese Americans choose not to become involved in political and social activism, not even on their own behalf.

If you answered each question false, apparently you are aware of some of the problems faced by what was once a "silent minority." Asian Americans, including the Chinese, have suffered many years under stifling stereotypes held by the majority of Americans. An occasional sensational occurrence, such as the attempted shooting of a radio talk show host by a deranged Chinese American, gains national news coverage. Such reports surprise the majority of Americans, who maintain the notion that the Chinese Americans are quiet, law-abiding, family-centered, respectful citizens. The myth is too good to be true. Closer to reality is the realization that while there is a cultural foundation of respect for elders and for law, the edifice is eroding. Citizens in San Francisco's Chinatown think twice before stepping out at night for *sui yeh*, the erstwhile traditional midnight snack. The late night restaurants are now havens for gangs of youths. Similar problems exist in Manhattan's Chinatown.

Special pressures have always been present in the lives of the Chinese living in America, whether in the urban centers (ghettoes, really) of San Francisco, Seattle, Chicago, and New York, or in the smaller towns, such as Fresno, Salinas, and Reno. Difficulties with languages, differences in culture, the prevalence of poverty, the isolation of ghetto living, and age differences put pressure not only on the Chinese

---

[*] Born in America of Cantonese ancestry. David Ng was secretary for youth resources of the United Presbyterian Church, USA, and a leader in the Asian Presbyterian Caucus. He was a graduate in theological studies, and lived in Swarthmore, Pennsylvania, with his wife and two sons.

131

in relation to the majority culture but also among themselves. Fathers and sons found themselves unable to communicate with each other, unable to understand or appreciate each other's feelings and vision. Much of this tension went unnoticed by the majority culture, leading "only" to neuroses, broken hearts, and families held together by form but not by love or understanding. And once in a while, a deranged Chinese shoots at a radio announcer, or a gang terrorizes a tourist. The once-in-a-while are now statistically significant, as any policeman can tell you.

Attention must be paid. And fortunately, there is a growing awareness of the plight of Chinese Americans on the part of social institutions, city governments, churches, and other serving agencies. For example, what a glorious day it was in a West Coast city several years ago when one of the social agencies hired a Cantonese-speaking psychologist. (But consider also how many children in the past received good counseling from English-speaking counselors, only to have the gains wiped out at home. No one could explain to their parents in Cantonese how they were to work on the problem with their children.)

Gains have been made, often through the persistence and insistence of Chinese Americans themselves. But it is still common for a Chinese American, born and raised in the United States, to have to endure the question "How long have *you* been in this country?" Worse yet, to endure the epithet "Chink!" In one otherwise sophisticated college town in the East, a second generation American who happens to be Chinese responds to patronizing questions with a disarming "Got gum, GI Joe?" or with a counter question, "How long have *you* been in this country?" Some Chinese Americans are rich, others are poor. Some are well-educated, others illiterate; some skilled, others clumsy; some successful, others not. But one thing they all share in common: They do not look like the average American middle-class citizen—they are not white. And like it or not, even the most "successful" Chinese American living in the nicest suburb and claiming the longest string of graduate degrees and thickest telephone book of fiends' numbers will be able to cite examples of gross and glaring acts of prejudice directed at them. Total acceptance of Chinese Americans by the majority is an event for the future.

Significant numbers of Chinese Americans have entered the middle economic class. Perhaps these are the Chinese Americans the other Americans have come to know and to use as a gauge for the assimilation of an ethnic-racial group into the mainstream. But there are many, many more Chinese Americans whom the majority culture has not met, except impersonally while walking through Chinatown in New York or San Francisco—waiters, grocery clerks, seamstresses, and laundry workers. The fact is that the majority of Chinese Americans are poor. They work long hours under poor conditions for low wages. Others are unemployed or unemployable. Many are in poor health. Their tenement apartments are crowded and dirty. And their outlook is as closed off as their community. But when an American tourist walks the streets of Chinatown, he may see the glitter and not the gloom; he may smell the fragrance and not the filth. Chinatown is America's only slum that is a tourist attraction.

Even the most blasé of tourists should not have difficulty imagining the psychic scars that many Chinese Americans develop, living as they do in their fishbowl existence—they are so poor, so trapped, and yet these crazy tourists pay good money to come and see them. But the good news is that such passive thoughts are giving way to a new ethnic awareness and sense of pride. There is a surge in positive ethnic identity consciousness among Chinese Americans and other Asian Americans. And the churches can rightfully claim some credit for this raising or pride and power.

The Asian Presbyterian Caucus is one of several pride and power organizations. In its second year of existence and steady growth, it states its purpose in this way:

a. To coalesce isolated Asian Presbyterians to give effective voice and advocacy to their problems, concerns, and insights
b. To facilitate the Asian presence and representation in all judicatory levels and boards and agencies
c. To provide mission strategy to Asian American churches and the wider community
d. To cooperate and join in the struggle against racism, repression, and exploitation in the United States of America and throughout the world
e. To explore, study, and appreciate the values of our Asian heritage and develop new ministries to Asians and Asian American movements
f. To maintain communications with Asian Caucuses of other denominations
g. To provide in-service training and continuing education for Asian ministers and laymen

How effective the Asian Presbyterian Caucus is in effecting political change within the church remains to be seen. But there is no doubting the results of heightened pride in one's own racial and ethnic background on the part of APC members. With the gains in numerical strength and mutual support, there will also be movement from a mere sense of ethnic identity into the practical areas of influence, persuasion, power, and social change.

Even more dramatic changes and results can be seen in secular arenas of life. In San Francisco and New York, battles over adequate housing, literacy programs, representation in city government, employment, and aid to youths have been fought and won! Significantly, young persons have been in the forefront in most of these battles. Young leaders have gained knowledge and skills through schools and organizations while also cultivating and collecting the respect and cooperation of their elders. In San Francisco a young Presbyterian pastor fought city hall and won—with the help of several score *ah moes*, "old ladies," who invaded a city supervisors' meeting to demonstrate their concerns in what must have been to the supervisors an uncharacteristically loud and aggressive manner.

No unanimity of opinion and action exists, however. Vested interests are still strong and vocal in both Chinatowns, New York and San Francisco. The famous Six Companies in San Francisco still claims to speak for all Chinese Americans and still manages to gain the ear of the white business and political establishment and the press. For as many years as it has existed this confederation of business and social interests has been Chinatown's voice. In earlier days it spoke with confidence because there was no vocal dissent even if there was no unity. Those days are long past, never to return. A full-page advertisement in the San Francisco newspapers, signed by the Six Companies but generally recognized to have been paid for by money from Taiwan, proclaimed the support of the Chinese American community for the Republic of China and for Chiang Kai-shek. However, every lamp post and public wall in Chinatown was decorated by a contrary broadside published by the Committee of Chinese Americans for Normalization of United States and China Relations. In other words, more and more Chinese Americans want mainland China to be fully included in the community of nations.

The generation gap is most obvious for Chinese Americans when dealing with the issue of the People's Republic of China. The establishment, the older ones, the ones who lost their land and perhaps even their families when the Communists took over—they find it all but impossible to forget and to forgive. The younger ones find it necessary to accept the reality of a new China, and in fact find a source of pride in the advances in social and economic conditions in modern China. Dialogues and debates between old and young generally become stuck on "improvements" versus "lack of trust." But, to fall back on a caricature of the Chinese way: Time will take away the old people and the old ideas; the young people will see their visions become fact; time is on the side of the People's Republic.

Asian Americans and Blacks

Unable to relate either to Blacks or whites,
Asian Americans are facing an identity crunch

TOGE FUJIHIRA

When Toge Fujihira suddenly died of a heart attack while on a photographic assignment in Vancouver, British Columbia, last November, he had, at 58, scaled heights reached only by a few of the best of his profession. As a photographer he was, as others have so often described him, "an artist with a camera." A staff photographer of the United Methodist Board of Global Ministries for over thirty years, Toge had been to nearly every area of the world, photographing people, churches, community projects, raging floods, and devastating droughts.

There was, however, more to Toge than his expertise with a camera; he was a man of compassion and feeling for the plight of others. The issues of our time affected him deeply.

It was while we were on a thirty-three-day junket through the Caribbean nearly two years ago that we came to really know each other. The late night rap sessions in our hotel rooms in Guyana, the treks into the countryside in Antigua and Grenada, the exploration of the urban slums of Trinidad and Jamaica gave each of us ample opportunity to learn more about the other's particular problems. One of them, of course, was the relationship of Asian Americans and blacks. We talked about it throughout the Caribbean, and our conversations continued in St. Louis, MO, over a fried chicken, baked macaroni, and corn bread dinner at my mother's home.

This exclusive article is an outgrowth of those discussions and a friendship, though all too brief, that indelibly added another dimension to my own perspective on life.
—G. M. D.

"Niga-ho, Niga-ho, Niga-ho" (meaning n*****-whore)[1], we four, five, six-year-old kids shouted in "pidgin" English as we tapped on the dirt encrusted windows and rapped on the rickety door of a ramshackle, wooden frame shanty and aroused

---

[1] *[Ed. note: The asterisks do not appear in the original; they have been added in this edition.]*

the ire of an elderly Black man who would come out shaking his fist or waving his cane at us.

Retreating to a safe distance down the garbage-strewn alley on the edge of the Asian community, we gleefully continued to heckle the crippled old man, knowing that he could never chase nor catch us. When he disappeared behind his closed doors muttering under his breath, we kids, tired of harassing the Black man, would leave, looking for other excitement.

In those days I never knew that "n*****" was a derogatory word, nor did I know the meaning of a "whore." All we knew was that the combination of those two words always touched off the spark that angered the elderly man, and we kids got our kicks for the day by tormenting him.

Our parents, too, not knowing the meaning of the words were guilty of racist attitudes, as they put the fear of the Black man upon us by saying, "Niga-ho will catch you if you're not good."

My first encounter with a Black was at a summer Christian Youth Conference camp. During a recreational period, a game was played requiring all those in a circle to join hands. On one side of me was a white girl, and on the other a Black girl. I firmly gripped the white girl's hand, but hesitated upon reaching for the Black's until slowly contact was made. Certainly some of the blackness would rub off on my hands, I felt, but to my surprise, when I looked at my hand, there was no evidence showing. My childish, preconceived image of Black people vanished from that period, for I soon discovered that the Black campers were real people.

Other Asians timorously approach the same dilemma when they meet a Black face-to-face for the first time.

Vee Hernandez, a comely twenty-four-year-old girl, born in the Philippines, arrived in San Francisco six years ago. In her position, as a secretary to the Rev. Lloyd Wake (a Japanese American minister to community life at the Glide Urban Center), she deals with all kinds of people—drifters, panhandlers, prostitutes, pimps, drug addicts, homosexuals, hippies, ethnic minorities, and other Third World people. Vee felt that by working with people usually not accepted by the established society, she was without prejudice.

But she tells a story about her prejudice.

During a rap session with students from the University of Puget Sound a simulation game of interpersonal communications was played. "As the group formed partners," Vee relates, "my first companion was a handsome, tall, white man. He was my type—clean, neatly dressed, and hair not too long. I welcomed him with a big embrace and he really turned me on.

"Next, was a woman, and I hugged her like my sister or my mother with no uptight feeling.

"When I turned around to meet my third partner, he was Black—very, very Black. I was shocked and my mind went completely blank, I closed my eyes so that I couldn't see him when he grasped me. I stood rigid without any response because I wanted it to be over as soon as possible."

Vee was frightened by her reaction, as she realized that it was a deeply ingrained fear of the Black man that surfaced at the time. She thought she was not prejudiced, but after that experience, she knew she was just as biased as a white person. Having a guilt complex, Vee talked about her confrontation with a counselor until she was able to become more open to Blacks. She realized that she had to adjust herself to accepting them as fellow human beings.

In the "white social totem pole" structure, Asians believe that Caucasians are at the top, Asians in the middle, and Blacks the low man. Most Asian Americans have basic prejudices towards Blacks either because they feel superior to them or because they fear them.

Asians, being very white conscious, try to assimilate into the Caucasian culture. And, they have accepted and perpetuated the white man's stereotyped image of the Black man—a lazy, shiftless, immoral, loudmouthed, welfare seeking, criminally inclined, drug-addicted person.

Most of the twenty-five million Blacks in the United States probably haven't associated with Asians. Most Blacks' racist attitude towards Asian Americans have been influenced by the whites' stereotyped image perpetuated through newspapers, books, movies, television, radio, and military and educational establishments.

For example, the Rev. Cecil Williams, the charismatic, controversial Black pastor at Glide Memorial United Methodist Church in San Francisco, said that he had not seen an Asian until he was a student at Sam Houston College in Austin, Texas. The Asian images mirrored in his mind, he said, were little yellow people who were sneaky, sly, very passive, docile, and subservient. He also thought that they all lived in Asia and every one of them carried a hatchet.

"As middlemen minorities, Asian Americans know that they have to live in a racist country."

Another Black, Louis Sawyers, from Chicago, got the usual stereotyped picture of Japanese during World War II by reading the cartoon strip *Terry and the Pirates*. He assumed that all Asians wore glasses, had buck teeth, bowlegs, and were forever shouting "*banzai*."

At the outbreak of World War II and Japan's attack on Pearl Harbor, I can remember trying to get on a subway train in New York. A big, burly Black man brushed by me, saying, "Out of my way, you dirty Jap!" Such encounters were part of the war hysteria maintained by white Americans to stir up hate for the enemy. Although I was an American of Japanese ancestry, whites and Blacks could not nor would not distinguish me from the enemy.

Generally, Asian Americans do not seek to get involved with Blacks, and their attitude towards them is a polite indifference. However, there have been moments of tension.

During World War II, when Japanese Americans on the West Coast were sent to concentration camps, Blacks from the South seeking employment in the wartime industries moved into their vacated houses. After the war, not too many Japanese Americans were able to reclaim their homes.

Centenary United Methodist Church in Los Angeles is now completely surrounded by Blacks in a community that was well integrated with Japanese and whites some seventy years ago. Rev. Peter Chen, minister of the church, said when the Japanese congregation returned from the concentration camps and resumed their church activities, "Blacks started to break into the building, stealing what they could sell, and vandalizing property. The elderly Japanese were robbed, mugged, and physically assaulted on their way to church. Now they are afraid to venture out and no evening programs are held.

"The Japanese congregation has been eager to relocate to another area, so that more family type programs can be planned without harassment. It is not so much a matter of hatred for the Blacks as a fear of what might happen," continued Rev. Chen.

"Black men always terrify me," a twenty-seven-year-old Taiwan-born new immigrant Chinese woman wrote when asked in a questionnaire to list the six most important points that she did not like about America. Her candid remark showing real fear of Black people might well express the general feelings of most Asian women.

Some Asian American families are living in completely Black communities. For the children there is a sense of insecurity. At school, an Asian child may be the only non-Black in the class. There is a difference in lifestyle and language that the bewildered child does not understand. The behavior pattern is a real concern. Although Asian pupils may get along well with their Black classmates, they establish no close relationships. Some Asian children may play with their neighboring black friends, but usually their parents do not encourage it.

A Chinese American in relating his early school experiences in which there were only a few non-Blacks and he was the only Asian said, "Blacks were always picking on me because I was Chinese and not Black. Shouting in unison at me, they would yell, 'Ching, Ching, Chinaman / sitting on a fence / trying to make a dollar / out of fifteen cents!' I would get mad and some Black kid would beat me. Even Black girls would pick on me. I was hurt, confused, and didn't know what to do."

In a Seattle High School, a conflict developed a few years ago between Blacks and the newly arrived immigrants, mostly Chinese from Hong Kong and Taiwan. Unable to speak English well, the newcomers were the targets of ridicule by Blacks. A physical confrontation erupted and several Blacks and Chinese were beaten. The issue was resolved by the kids getting together and talking over their problems. They reached an understanding and the explosive situation was defused.

Frank Hom is a Chinese American graduate of Cal Poly Technical Institute at San Luis Obispo, California. Having grown up with African Americans, he was interested in studying Black history, race relations, the urban scene, and contemporary issues and took a minor in Black studies. Upon graduation, he wanted to teach a Black studies class in a junior high school, but the principal rejected him because he was not Black.

When Phil Hayasaka, a Japanese American, was appointed director of the Human Rights Department of the City of Seattle, there was an outcry from the Black community that an African American should have been named the administrator. Hayasaka said, "Blacks thought that only they had problems, not realizing that Asians had difficulties just as deep as African Americans. I am concerned with racial equality for all ethnic and minority groups."

Most Blacks consider Asian Americans as "whites." When I was with an all-Black motion picture crew in a small rural Black church in Mississippi, the pastor introduced me to his congregation as a "white" brother, although he announced that he couldn't pronounce my Japanese name.

Some Asians have tried relating to Blacks. One Asian recently said, "There are only two groups of people in America—Blacks and whites. I hated being Chinese and because I grew up in a Black neighborhood with mostly Black buddies, I chose to become a member of the Black group.

"I soon found out that fitting into the group was to feel and act Black. I was accepted by being a tough bastard with a profane, vulgar mouth that could spew out the vilest jokes. I was not the image of the quiet, enigmatic Chinaman.

"My whole junior high career could be summed up in, 'Happiness was being cool and Black.' Blacks were saying, 'Man! Ron is cool, he talks like a Black brother, dresses like one, dances like one, and even makes love like one.'"

On the other hand, Robert Moses Hopkins is a Filipino-Black. He was born in San Francisco from a Filipino mother and a Black father. Not being able to relate either to Blacks or Filipinos, Moses, as he is called, has mostly white friends. He grew up in a predominately Caucasian district. He finds that he is not "n*****" enough for Blacks, and Filipinos call him a "*mestizo*," a person of mixed blood.

His mixed blood has not been without its problems. The confusion of not knowing where he belonged created some mental problems for him, and he needed psychiatric help. Since he has not totally been received by Blacks or Filipinos, in his search for identity, he has turned to whites.

Currently, Asian Americans, unable to relate either to Blacks or whites, are facing an identity crunch. Asian Americans who thought they could assimilate into the American mainstream through education and acculturation discovered that their physical features were always a detriment to being completely accepted as white. No matter how many generations Asian Americans may have lived in the United States, there will always be some white who will ask, "How long have you been in this country?"

Other Asians, in trying to relate to Blacks by adopting their talk, dress, and manner, eventually find that their skin color is cause enough for rejection.

The rise of the Black power movement gave impetus to Asians seeking their identity, as it made them aware of their "yellowness," just as African Americans sought "blackness." At one time, Asians rejected their ancestral language, customs, history, and culture by trying to be good, white Americans. Now Asians are crying, "Yellow is beautiful," as they proudly proclaim their heritage. Filipinos, Koreans, Chinese, and Japanese in the United States are uniting as Asian Americans in the common struggle for identity.

The Rev. Philip Kyung Sik Park, a Korean American, who was at one time pastor of the Friendship Community Church, composed mostly of a Black congregation in Pittsburg, stated that "When the Black Power Movement started, I could no longer help them, as they sought their own identity. It was a useful experience for me to have served a Black church when I looked for my own identity and became involved in the Asian cause."

Many young Asian American activists believe that they should join the Third World movement in their struggle for liberation. David Bayle, a Filipino staff member of the United Methodist Council on Youth Ministry, recently remarked, "I myself became more aware of being a part of the Third World by working with Blacks."

Young Asian American activists and their counterparts in the Black movement relate well with each other as they work towards a common goal to protest against prejudice and discrimination or to stand up together for equality in employment, housing, and other areas where injustices occur.

However, Asian Americans are people caught in the middle of the Black-white struggle in the United States. Blacks consider Asians as "whites." White America will not accept Asians as their equals. As middlemen minorities, Asian Americans know that they have to live in a racist country. If Blacks were to become powerful enough to be at the top of the racial conflict and whites were relegated to the bottom, the Asian American would still be in the middle. Perhaps Asian Americans would then try to become more of a part of Black America, just as they have tried to assimilate into white America. But Asians in America know that they would not be treated any different than they are now, regardless of who's at the top or bottom of the totem pole.

Martin Luther King, Theologian

Warren Lee[*]

I agree with Herbert Richardson's view that Martin Luther King's primary theological genius was "his creative proposals for dealing with the structure of evil" based on his ability to discern the significant in the factual, but I do not believe that Dr. King understood the structure of evil to be "generated by modern relativism, vis., ideological conflict."[1] King's ideas at this point on the nature of human sin and evil were vitally shaped by the thought of Reinhold Niebuhr. He accepted the basic thesis of Niebuhr as first articulated in *Moral Man and Immoral Society*, namely that the root of evil in the modern world resides not so much in individuals as in the immoral social structures of society. King coupled this understanding of evil with a social and political strategy based on the tactics of Mahatma Gandhi and his theory of nonviolent passive resistance.

King's theological genius consisted in his ability, in the midst of incredibly complex and monumentally important social crises, to see the significant in the factual.[2] He possessed that almost uncanny ability, all the way from Montgomery to Memphis, to pick only those situations for nonviolent direct action that exposed the true depth and breadth of the nation's sin. Only insofar as this was accomplished could authentic redemption—significant social change in terms of racial justice—become a possibility.

Of course, the structure and institution of racism is so tenacious that Dr. King's efforts did not always meet with success. He also made mistakes both of diagnosis and strategy. But in the process of picking what battles to fight, the foremost question he kept in mind was not, as Bonhoeffer puts it, so much "How can I be good?" or "How can I do good?" but rather "What is the will of God?" Only when we appreciate the priority of that question can we come to understand why Martin Luther King never renounced his belief in nonviolence.

Until the day he died, he refused, despite the tremendous pressure to do otherwise, to begin down the path of racial separatism, black supremacy, the rejection of Christian faith as the white man's religion, and retaliatory violence. So it is that King, notwithstanding the widespread unpopularity of his stand and vociferous opposition to his position from black and white alike, spoke out against

---

[*] Assistant professor of ministry, SFTS.

[1] Herbert Richardson, "Martin Luther King—Unsung Theologian," in *New Theology*, no. 6, ed. Martin E. Marty and Dean G. Peerman (New York: Macmillan, 1969).

[2] I am here applying to King, Benjamin Reist's judgment made of Bonhoeffer in *The Promise of Bonhoeffer* (New York: Lippincott, 1969), 68.

the war in Vietnam long before it was fashionable and safe. The pressures on both King and Bonhoeffer to act contrary to the way they did were similar in intensity and character. In the final analysis, to pose the ethical question in terms of "How can I be good?" or "How can I do good?" would have raised the wrong set of issues. Obedience to the will of God alone was the ultimate test of faithfulness for both King and Bonhoeffer.

King did not actually conceptualize the theological problem in the same way as Bonhoeffer in terms of the Christological question; judging from his writing and actions, we can say that the question of obedience to God's will became his overriding consideration. King's stance is in accord with the following from Bonhoeffer's *Ethics*: "What is of ultimate importance is now no longer that I should become good, or that the condition of the world should be made better by my action, but that the reality of God should show itself everywhere to be the ultimate reality."[3]

I do not mean to claim that Dr. King was the most original or creative theological thinker of the twentieth century. Others, including Bonhoeffer, were and are better at that aspect of theology than he was. As a matter of fact, in reading the four books he published in his lifetime (*Strength to Love, Stride Toward Freedom, Why We Can't Wait,* and *Where Do We Go From Here: Chaos or Community?*) and judging from his articles and what he said in public, it is not difficult to see that he was a rather traditional Christian thinker and held orthodox theological views. His central and abiding theological conviction, for example, with respect to the doctrine of God, was his belief that "God is both infinite and personal—a loving Father who strives for good against the evil that exists in the universe." His position on the doctrine of eschatology was quite traditional, namely, God will triumph in the end. Think how many times he quoted the phrase, "Truth crushed to earth will rise again." Another favorite of his was James Russell Lowell's "Truth forever on the scaffold, Wrong forever on the throne,— / Yet that scaffold sways the future, and, behind the dim unknown, / Standeth God within the shadow, keeping watch above his own." King sang and believed these words; that is why he could say with such power, "We shall overcome," "I have a dream," and finally, "I've been to the mountaintop and seen the promised land."

Wherein, therefore, does this rather simple-minded, traditional-thinking, orthodoxy-holding, Baptist-preaching, and unselfconscious theologian's theological greatness reside, such that he should be called *the* theologian for our time? King combined all the best insights of history, sociology, psychology, and theology and reinterpreted them into a strategy for social change that was profoundly Christian in nature and in scope. He created something new, unique, and all his own in the process.

I believe that the only way to understand the effect of the life and thought of Martin Luther King is to look at him the same way Troeltsch analyzed the giants of Christian history, like Thomas Aquinas, Martin Luther, and John Calvin. It is not

---

[3] Cited in Reist, *The Promise of Bonhoeffer*, 69.

enough, for example, to see that Aquinas was a product of his time, that he merely "Christianized" Aristotle on the basis of medieval Catholic theology. It is not enough to recognize, articulated and mobilized the extant widespread discontent towards the Roman Church, nor to see Calvin as one who merely went a little further and in a different direction than Luther. True, these three men were products of their time and environment. But through "compromise," "accident," and their own novel genius, they added something unique to the ongoing Christian enterprise and to the whole of Western history that can only be described in terms of "greatness."

Their contributions cannot be explained away historically, sociologically, psychologically, or theologically. Part of the criteria for any good, much less great, theology, has to take this factor of novelty and uniqueness into consideration. A theology which does not shape, mold, and change history and speak to people where they are is not really theology at all. Influence, impact, and significance must be part of the measuring stick of theological excellence. So it is that as a pure academic scholar, Erasmus may have had the edge on Luther; Tillich was probably "smarter" than King. And just as surely as Luther and not Erasmus was *the* theologian for *his* time, so his twentieth-century counterpart is not any one of a number of his brilliant German theological descendants, but rather an American Black Baptist preacher whose theological reflection took shape in the midst of the people at the frontiers of social change in the greatest human crisis of our time.

When the history of our century is written, Martin Luther King will stand out as an outstanding and pivotal figure. He had a profound understanding of the nature of evil in modern day American society—and because of a number of strategically crucial historical "accidents," he found himself at *the* cutting edge of the most important human crisis of the day: race. With the development of modern mass media, the whole world was watching America as the most powerful and influential nation on the earth. In this context, Martin Luther King became *the* symbol of nonviolence as a means of effecting social change, especially for the poor and oppressed peoples of the world.

With this awesome responsibility, he forged a theology that was utterly realistic with respect to dealing with racism, materialism, and militarism—yet it was completely universalistic and encompassing in its scope and breadth. Over and over he insisted that all humanity is one. His battle was never a question of black against white. Racism, he claimed, is as damaging and dehumanizing in the final analysis to the oppressor as to its victim. He was fighting as much for white people to rid them of the cancer of racism as he was for black people to rid them of its effects. Because humanity is one, no one is free until all men are free.

He was one man fighting in behalf of all men against the forces of evil—nonviolently. He is the theologian for our time because he was the one universally acclaimed human symbol that empowered this Christian understanding of reality with meaning and viability. That is what theology is all about: translating abstract concepts into intelligible human language such that it has power to move men and change lives. If the result of "faith in search of understanding" fails to yield this, if it has no power, it is merely an intellectual game. I think this is why the theologies of academic professionals are subject to the phenomenon of faddism. They are simply not in touch with where people are, where they laugh and cry, smile and weep, hurt and bleed, where they experience the reality of the living God. These theologies are impotent. Theology, for Martin Luther King, as for Dietrich Bonhoeffer, could never be just a fad. It was a matter of life and death. It cost both of them their lives.

My lasting impression of Martin Luther King stems from a college lecture I heard given by James Baldwin when I was a student at UCLA. In the question and answer period following his formal presentation, he was asked to comment on his thoughts and feelings toward Dr. King. He smiled and said, "Well, whenever you talk about Martin, you've always got to remember one thing. He's a Christian. I mean, he really is."

Church and Society*

A. C. UBALDE JR.

America has often inhibited the possibilities of self-determination of the Filipino people; and today these people are strongly seeking self-determination on personal, community, national and international levels. They are seeking liberation— liberation of the total life of man from the non-participatory style that so often has been imposed on them.

To help the Filipino people, and society in general, a complete overhaul of the American social structures, cultural values, and attitudes must take place. There is a growing consensus that the acts of God are at work in the life of Filipinos, calling them to liberation. The signs are hopeful, but there must be a change in the social structure to fundamentally alter the present situations. The issue for the church and society is whether the church will encourage or nullify the search for liberation.

As the author elaborated earlier, this search for liberation is concentrated in *community identity* in order to effect a visible responsive thrust, in *organizing* for purposeful self-determination, in *political participation* in the arena where the shape of society is determined. Finally, the search for liberation is furthered in the maintenance of the *dialogical style of life* within and outside the broader society of human interactions.

The church must fully understand and listen to the Filipino community. Even though many of the problems and struggles of the Filipino community are to a great extent similar to most Third World communities, the feelings, attitudes and especially their cultural traits need to be understood. Human struggle for identity, integrity, responsibility and achievement is basic to all human beings, but the Filipino experience, context and history are different. Thus sensitivity to this back-ground is of utmost importance.

The task for the church today as she participates in the life of the Filipino community is to witness and act responsibly toward the new self-affirmation and search by the Filipinos for a new people and a new community. During the transition of the Filipino community toward becoming a visible and participatory member of society, the community must raise the questions that are real to it, even when they be painful and or confronting. For the harder the conflict, the more glorious the triumph toward becoming a genuine community. During this transition, the church must

---

* This is an excerpt from a dissertation entitled *The Impact of the Black Power on the Filipino Community and the Implications for the Church*, prepared by the Rev. Dr. A. C. Ubalde Jr. in completion of a Doctor of Religion degree.

learn how to relate herself to this new and emerging community. A new attitude that implies a new social structure with new leadership and new approaches is imperative.

Even though some changes are occurring within the institutional church through structure, leadership, and approaches, many are signs of tokenism. In other words, the changes that are occurring are not enough. Priorities within the church are still oriented toward the preservation of property and structural and hierarchical glorification. This is emphasized instead of support for innovative programs to remove racism in the church and support for various ethnic caucus groups emerging within the church such as the Asian, Black and the Hispanic groups attempting to determine their own directions in the church and in their communities. There may be a great acceptance among the general church toward the emergence of ethnic caucuses through proclamations and resolutions of establishment, but when financial resources are requested for the ethnic caucuses to function, token assistance is granted. This lack of commitment of the church toward these ethnic caucuses is simply a sign that the church is not interested in the ethnic churches.

Another implication of the changes occurring in the Filipino community is the emergence of demands on the local Filipino churches. The pressures of responsibility and accountability must not only be put on the larger institution of the church but also locally where the activities toward change are fully felt.

The author would like to think that this pain and growth toward change is first felt in the local churches, but in reality, this is not the case. Most local Filipino churches or ethnic churches are the last to take an active and militant part in the revolution that is happening in the Third World communities. Leadership in the church is one of the weakest links in change efforts in the Filipino community. With the recent developments in the life of the Filipinos in America, especially the community of consciousness, the threat and criticism of the position of the leader in the church, the pastor, is one of the most dramatic pressures moving some of the ministers out of their comfortable pulpits and away from the serenity of their altars. Of course, the problems do not solely lie with the pastor. Rather, a broader understanding of the general local Filipino church is needed for a full understanding of the problems.

The Filipino Church

The author finds most Filipino *ministers* possess an oppressive and conservative theology. Many were edu-cated in the "old schools" for training clergymen and most of the schools they attended were conservative or fundamentalist. It is not common to find many Filipino United Methodist churches in America today whose pastors were formerly from the conservative Baptist denominations and were trained theologically in a conservative Baptist seminary. Part of this problem is that the United Methodist Church did not have the foresight to prepare young Filipino people from their own denomination for the ministry.

Closely related to the theological conservatism is the oppressive theology that is common not only in the Filipino churches but throughout many Third World churches especially the Hispanic churches. The promise of "pie in the sky bye and bye" is still being preached in the Filipino churches. The tremendous absence of the theology of liberation or the theology of the oppressed, as the author shared earlier in chapter 3, is felt, especially among the young who are in constant touch with the revolutionary changes in the broader community.

In addition to the conservative style of ministry, the impact of the old Roman Catholic experiences among the Filipinos must not be overlooked, because the strict and oppressive Catholic church has certainly made an impact on the total life of the Filipino churches, both Catholic and Protestant.

The role of many ministers in the Filipino churches is rigid and authoritarian. One United Methodist pastor whose background was conservative Baptist, refused to baptize an infant unless the child was immersed under water even though most of the children of the United Methodist denomination are baptized by sprinkling. Members in another church who did not pay what they had pledged were threatened with loss of their membership in the church. Fortunately, these particular problems have been solved by the assistance of the District Superintendent of the United Methodist Church.

Many ministers have a narrow understanding of their role. Many believe that any services given outside of the ritual functions are the role of the social workers.

The other important problem facing the ministers in the Filipino church today is that many are removed from the movement of liberation among the young and progressive Filipinos in the community. Due to this lack of understanding, many make narrow and over-generalized views of what is going on outside the four walls of the church. Thus, many lose opportunities to take stands and risks in the liberation that is being demanded in the community. Because of this we find today many of these ministers supporting the status quo. Those in the greater community, especially the politicians, see these Filipino leaders in the church opposed to many of the changes demanded by the few young militants and progressive adults in the community. They can then "divide and conquer."

Another crucial problem that many Filipino ministers are facing is their lack of skill in facing the urgent crisis in the Filipino community. Creating political organizations and nonprofit community organizations to solve the urgent problems are needed. Bureaucratic expertise in understanding the dynamics and games played within the governmental agencies, gathering information beneficial for the survival of the community, coalition building, gamesmanship in fund raising in the private and public arena and understanding the public media and how to use it effectively, are just some of the crucial skills which many Filipino ministers today need, but do not have. Many Filipino ministers are threatened when these problems are presented to them.

One outstanding and commendable characteristic of Filipino ministers is their commitment to their pastoral work. Here, pastoral work means the practice of visitation among the families at home and hospitals and the spiritual counseling most members of the church receive. This is needed, but it is not sufficient alone.

Many Filipino *laymen* suffer from a conservative and oppressive theology because of the same influences as those on Filipino ministers. The impact of the Catholic church and the basically fundamentalist theological style of the protestant missionaries sent to the Philippines at the turn of the century are two of the major reasons for the Filipino laymen suffering from the culture of silence. Their understanding of their role as laymen comes from the oppressive teachings of the paternal-racist missionaries and ministers and deacons who are products of these missionaries through their theological and missionary schools.

Submissiveness to the authoritarian style of the Filipino ministers probably is one of the characteristics of many laymen today in the Filipino church. Whatever the minister in the church says usually prevails. In most cases, therefore, whatever understanding the minister has of the roles of laymen and the functions of the church dominates the view of the congregation. The messages heard by laymen from the pulpit are still fundamentally guilt-centered. Usually, the god heard about from the pulpit is an oppressive god and a god who perpetuates suffering and deprivation. It has been only recently that words of liberation may be heard from outsiders who are invited to be guest preachers for special occasions.

Looking at the leadership and the laymen in the Filipino church we witness a dehumanized and oppressive context. The urgency that faces the church today, then, is to lift the Filipino churches from this dilemma and to enable them to face a new environment—a New Order of liberation.

One dramatic step for the total church to take at this point is to provide the opportunity for the Filipino churches to participate fully in the total life of the church. Participation in the key positions where key decisions are made is one step the church can take to make life more meaningful for those facing the mundane cycle of depravity. Commissions or committees designed by the ethnic minorities within the church and with new leadership who have the mentality or consciousness toward liberating all people, to assist them in self-determination of their direction in the life of the church, need to be supported fully. Compensatory assistance is not a crime if the long term goal is to benefit those who have been deprived and thrust them in positions where they can humanly direct their lives and help them relate to others as equals.

Renewed theological and sociological education for many Filipino ministers through seminars and workshops would be a tremendous help for the church as a whole. Encouraging many of the ministers to participate in the secular enterprise of community development would enlighten them as to the realities and struggles of the Filipino community to survive in many areas of endeavor.

One of the greatest concerns that the church must attend to is the distorted *view of God* that is being taught not only in the Filipino churches but in many of our Christian churches. As the author indicated earlier, the god that is being spoken of in the churches is the oppressive god who is the originator of suffering, suppression, and degradation. To express the messianic God in our time, a new stance toward a God of liberation and away from the negative and pessimistic crisis theology of the past, must be discovered. The God, which the author suggests, needs no longer to be the God seen as "need fulfiller" the "problem solver." The author suggests a messianic God who experiences with his people the explosive happenings in human life which 1) empower men for responsible action, 2) open up new possibilities for self-actualization of human nature, 3) enable all men to participate in the shaping of their own lives and the life of the world, 4) and lastly address men at the point of their strength.

Closely related to this view of a messianic God is a theological thrust which 1) expresses the reality of God within the context of the Third World struggle in our time, 2) seeks to serve and facilitate human efforts to change the world—thus a God of change, 3) identifies and describes the kinds of situations and experiences that most appropriately give rise to the notion of a messianic God, and 4) connects God with contingent events, especially those which constitute new thrusts and new directions in human development.

Messianic View of God

If the church accepts the theological view of a messianic God, realistic application of *political power, responsibility,* and *economics* can have a tremendous impli-cation for our society.

Problems relating to *political power,* of course, are not new, nor is the theological analysis of these problems. All we need to remind ourselves is Richard Niebuhr's commentary that

> responsible ethical reflection requires us to take account of the role of power [in determining the] conflicting interests of human society . . . [But] the theological significance of power has . . . been reopened . . . [today by those] persons previously excluded from the decision making processes of society [such as the Third World community, the aged, the women, the youth, and the homosexuals, just to name a few] who are now showing determination to seize and exercise power in their own right.[1]

Considering the turmoil of the '60s and all the ramifications of its experiences, we know that power is not simply a political or social issue, though it is surely both of these. It is also a fundamental human matter. Being named and defined, having identity handed to Filipinos is basically a sin, a denial of one's basic humanity.

> Being a man means that you do not permit others . . . to decide who you are or what your place in society shall be or what you can appropriately expect from society. You must decide these things for yourself, and begin to behave in ways that can give actuality to what you have decided. . . . [The] conditions of the poor and the exploited . . . should . . . be equipped to participate in the process of determining their own goals and shaping their own future.[2]

---

[1] Thomas W. Ogletree, "From Anxiety to Responsibility: The Shifting Focus of Theological Reflection," in *New Theology,* no. 6, ed. Martin E. Marty and Dean G. Peerman (New York: Macmillan, 1969), 52. [*Ed. note: This quotation is from Ogletree's paraphrase of Niebuhr, not Niebuhr himself.*]

[2] Ogletree, "From Anxiety to Responsibility," 53.

By assuming responsibility for your own life and the life of the world, one becomes a mature man with power.

> If the human meaning of power is to be realized, it must be directed toward the emergence of an interdependent human community that has regard for the legitimate interests and aspirations of all men. It must, like the power of God, be used not to dominate or exploit others, but to empower them to participate in the direction of human life.[3]

And in order to participate effectively, they must discover and learn to utilize the levels of power in a way that will enable them to use the process of defining goals of human society.

The *economic* arena, obviously, may look fundamentally different if full participation is anticipated in the workings of the messianic God who employs changes and enables those who are deprived to realize a new hope and new purpose in their total life. In the economic experiences of those who have been deprived, their role and participation in this area has been limited and, in most cases, there has been no participation at all.

Between the fifteenth and the twentieth centuries, capitalism created a new type of human relationship. The economic thrust was toward the exchange of a commodity, including human labor. This phenomenon created the opposition of two differing classes — those possessing the means of production and those lacking such means, thus, subjected to the first. The worker became alienated because he was deprived of the human feature of his labor, i.e., free choice of its purpose as a *producer*, and he was also deprived as a *consumer* because the system conditioned him to need only goods that were deemed profitable.

> In short, he was exploited, and the exploitation took away not only what was due to him in the way of money, but what he needed in terms of life. . . . Turning money into the basic commodity entailed certain consequences. First, wealth and power were concentrated in fewer hands; [In the Philippines alone, ninety percent of its economic commodity is placed in the hands of less than one percent of its population.] Then, there was the struggle for profit for the sake of profit and expansion for the sake of expansion. [And finally] there was the supremacy of money over community. With such a system, human values became economic values in the crude stock exchange sense of words. . . . By turning the earth itself into a commodity and nature into an object of speculation, man's natural environment was surrendered to the blind laws of the market. [The result is urbanism that now makes so many cities uninhabitable,] the destruction of forests and parks, the pollution of air and water, (thus) the degrading of existence itself.[4]

After the Depression of the late 1920s and to overcome the economic confusion of the time due to the destruction of economic commodities, massive armaments were produced.

> This led to a policy of expansionism which would justify the arms race and to the creation of the nationalist and racist myth, which were required to legitimize this policy. . . . [In

---

[3] Ogletree, "From Anxiety to Responsibility," 54.
[4] Roger Garaudy, "New Goals for Socialism," *Center Magazine* 5, no. 5 (September–October 1972): 34.

this respect] capitalism ceased to be a mere economic system. Now it had become a political structure which reflected in various forms, the economic and social dependency on war and nationalism . . . It was also transformed into a culture in which men are molded by the demands of the market and are manipulated by those who hold not only the capital but the overwhelming means of communication [the media]. . . . In [this capitalistic] society, then, the laws of competition govern everyone while profits are shared by a few. [The] investment is not a social function but depends exclusively on private initiative. Society, thus, loses all conscious control of its aims and purposes. Hence, in a capitalist [economy], investments in . . . liquor and tobacco, [for example], exceed those assigned to public health . . . Such a system can solve none of its problems by self-reform. Its lack of goals can be solved only by questioning the basic principles of the system.[5]

The author is opting for dramatic change to overhaul the present inadequacy of participation. The direction is somewhat fuzzy because the direction suggests a democratic principle of government and socialistic economy, but not necessarily an absolute government and economy of such being. What is clear is that the change in structure needs to go hand in hand with the change in the way of thinking of the people today in America and in the World. Hopefully the direction, if it be socialism

should not be thought of as merely another way to satisfy the needs capitalism has created. A socialism truly responding to the demands of our time cannot, then, be built along the lines of the present Soviet model. It must be built on an entirely new concept of civilization . . . Socialism today cannot copy the models of the past. Its model is yet to be created. Such a socialism will be unable to answer the demands of our time unless at the same time it actualizes the self-determination of its purposes and the self-management of all social activities by the citizens . . . That every citizen should learn to think and act like a statesman, feeling personally responsible for the fate of all. [This] implies a change which no moral preachment could obtain. It is only within the frame-work of every basic unit . . . that direct democracy can begin to establish itself. Only when everyone shares . . . in the decision-making . . . [can] this basic change take place.[6]

Toward whatever economic direction it directs itself, the theological implications are evident, and the messianic spirit in the new explosive thoughts and creative happenings, are being felt throughout the Americas and the world, especially toward the thrust of self-determination and the freedom of responsibility.

The author suggests that the messianic theology implies the category of *responsibility*.[7] For the Filipino community and other Third World communities, responsibility has been only an academic jargon expounded by the master, who basically interpreted responsibility as submissiveness and loyalty in reciprocity for the payment earned through the hard labor of the workers. It also means a "readiness to behave in conventional ways . . . or in ways that are compatible with the smooth functioning of the established institutions of society."[8] But looking at it carefully,

---

[5] Garaudy, "New Goals for Socialism," 34–35.
[6] Garaudy, "New Goals for Socialism," 35.
[7] Ogletree, "From Anxiety to Responsibility," 60.
[8] Ogletree, "From Anxiety to Responsibility," 60.

responsibility has a richness compatible with the changes we are pursuing today in our time. First, responsibility suggests the freedom to deal with new situations in life. It suggests significantly,

> man's ability to transcend his own past [if it be a past of degradation and enslavement], in order that he might meet the problems and opportunities emerging in the forward movement of history . . . [This would also indicate the possibility of moving from the successes and failures of the past into an open future. It also means, as long as possibilities are alive, that the direction of] the past is continually being relativized, and maintaining its power only as it proves itself anew. . . . [Therefore] responsibility [offers us] the stimulus to creativity provided by the pressure of new possibilities.[9]

Responsibility also suggests, secondly, the *power* man has to shape his life and the life of the world. It emphasizes that man is not necessarily an end result of forces he cannot control and that man is able to participate in determining the future character of human life and to bring new possibilities or dimensions not already present in his time.

Finally, responsibility suggests accountability. Man must answer for what he does. This is an important social dimension to accountability. It points out a social process by which each man answers to the other who questions him about what he is doing. He must answer the other, both because his own selfhood is bound up with the other's reality, and because what he does invariably affects the other. Thomas Ogletree puts it this way:

> The other has an indispensable role to play in my determination of the fitting way to exercise my power in any particular situation. He enables me to test my understandings by setting them alongside or even against his own. He is the occasion of insight and encouragement for me in my confusion and uncertainty. He is the one who breaks open the self-enclosed circle . . . of reasoning by which I justify the evil I would do.[10]

Multi-Service Center Model

The Filipino church today needs to look at itself and the total Filipino community to survive. It must first understand the needs of its local parish and at the same time know what is going on in the community, and hopefully, penetrate through its protective shell of anguish. In order to maintain and accomplish this stance, the author would like to suggest a *multi-service center model* for the church to consider. If this model is not followed, at least at this time in the history of the Filipino community, the Filipino church will maintain the stance of a culture of silence.

The multi-service center should represent the multi-faceted needs of the community and the parish. Speaking from the extensive involvement of the author in the life of the Filipino community, the author would like to suggest a survival program for the church to consider. This survival program would consist of the *working* program and the *spiritual-reflective* program. Without these programs, the holistic view of the activities would not be experienced by those involved or

---

[9] Ogletree, "From Anxiety to Responsibility," 60.
[10] Ogletree, "From Anxiety to Responsibility," 60.

participating. The working program emphasizes the weekly community oriented programs such as social service, education, organization, plus the necessary programs that need to exist in the parish to maintain its visibility. The emphasis is on the community programs.

The reflective program emphasizes the time of "putting this together" or "putting our heads together." This is the moment for reflection on the activities of the past week and, hopefully, would enable the participants of labor to see the activities and programs as one whole program to benefit the community. Within this context of spiritual reflection, the individual's search for whole-ness or salvation must be considered as a high priority. The time for spiritual reflection is during the Sunday worship celebration of life.

Working Program

The working program must concern itself with the needs of the community. This is not negating the members of the parish. The community and the church must start looking at themselves as one. This would mean that those taking an active part could transcend both sides and even possibly at other times maintain duplicate roles in each other's areas of programs, but with separate accountability administratively. (The author will discuss the administrative accountability later,) The working program must in the beginning set priorities it wants to tackle and must choose its top priorities. In most basic community development, priorities such as social services, education, community forum, and labor are crucial. The *social service* activities can concentrate on programs such as mental health, housing, immigration and advocacy.

The *education* might focus on a bilingual program for children, hopefully, in relationship with the public school system; a skill center for the adults so that they can be assisted in the areas of language-speech training, new vocation programs, and retraining programs in various trades and; an educational forum to discuss the wide and varied needs of the community including the reentry of the educational, medical, legal, and other professionals in their respective fields in their new environment. *Advocacy* of any interest group is very important in order to be able to support and motivate the community to take further actions to right the plights of others who have not gained respectability.

And finally, the *labor* force must be recognized in the community as the means of energy and resources to finally sustain the community in the long run. Thus a focus on work placement and retainment are necessary. Advocacy must be available also in placing and retaining a labor force in the market. This is not necessarily the traditional sense of an advocacy role. It may focus also on the area of defining the roles of services in or inno-vating new roles for the labor force to fill.

Another very important function for the working program is to consider a *community forum*. The author sees the community forum as a means of organizing the community and moving the community toward coalition building among those who share issues with them in the larger community, especially the other ethnic-racial groups. The community forum may also be an arena for members of the community to deal with the affairs that affect them as consumers in the greater community.

The community needs to be mindful that community organizing is a very taxing endeavor. It takes time, energy, and experience to accomplish many objectives. For those who are inexperienced in community organizing, there is a need to solicit assistance and they must be prepared for failures and disappointments in the first rounds of organizing. The dialogical methodology that was expressed in the earlier part of this chapter is an excellent tool to master for community organizing. Various case studies in the experiences of many organizations are important resources of which organizers need to be aware. Groups that Saul Alinsky has trained would be excellent to begin raising questions about organizing. Understanding how various public and private interest groups maintain their visibility and influences, especially in the public arena where decisions are made, is imperative. The most important thing any organizer needs to know is the mastery of accomplishing a semblance of cohesiveness among the members of the organization. In other words, the degree of cohesiveness and intensity of the group's interest toward solving an issue or problem will determine their success or failure in the political arena. (Many political scientists concur in this analysis. The works of Robert A. Dahl, *A Preface to Democratic Theory*,[11] and David B. Truman, *The Governmental Process*[12] are especially helpful readings.)

The suggestions the author is giving are simply programs that the community may direct itself. They may not be able to attend to them all at once due to their limitations or circumstances, but, on the other hand, it also suggests a beginning point where they may start and go beyond. The importance of these suggestions is that the author sees these various activities as a basic necessity for the community's survival.

Within the working program, church activities are not neglected. The pastoral care of the parish must not be disregarded by the minister and its laity. Continued programs must be planned for the religious educational component, especially for the children and youth, and for adults through seminars and workshops. Finances and membership canvassing and other administrative functions must and can be maintained.

The most obvious problem one can encounter through this model of the working program is accountability, for both the secular programs and the church programs as well as the personnel to maintain the total working program.

The author alluded earlier to the importance of setting priorities. Included in this function is recognizing sources, such as talents, funds, manpower, and time. Therefore it would behoove the church to search within their church family and outside the community for the resources needed. Whatever findings they discover,

---

[11] Robert A. Dahl, *A Preface to Democratic Theory* (Chicago: University of Chicago Press, 1963), 90.
[12] David B. Truman, *The Governmental Process* (New York: Alfred A. Knopf, 1951), 213.

that is where they begin. This would entail also the degree, level, and the numbers of programs they can initiate.

Another important problem the church must be alert to is the legal provision for the separation of the church and state. If the church wants to be fully involved in the total life of the working programs suggested, it will face this issue immediately. Legal entanglement can cause a lot of headaches that are not necessary. Therefore, legal counsel is imperative. Various nonprofit articles of incorporation have been attempted by groups who want to make sure issues such as the separation of church and state do not become a problem. The other possibility, and probably the most convenient one, is inviting various special program groups, such as social service, educational, etc., to use church facilities for their activities. Therefore, these special groups could use the resources that are available within the church family. In this respect, the accountability of this program may be separated from the church accountability.

Whichever program is accepted, the advantages it would offer are enormous. It would mean that the activities of the church would not only occur on Sunday during the worship celebration, but that the church and the community would visibly function as one whether or not they be separate in legal and financial accountability and various networks of relationships would be built through the various activities developed.

Finally, the important element of roles must be distinguished in the working program between the minister and the laity. Hopefully, the role of the minister in the working program should be the role of an enabler or a midwife. The minister, if at all possible, must try to avoid the visibility of leadership, such as in taking an official position like the chairman of a committee. The working program is centered in the laity through the involvement of community people. Part of the reason for this is that many people in the community must feel and experience leadership and responsibility. The visibility of the minister as leader in this area may do more harm than help. The minister's role needs a low visibility in this area outside of his role suggested above as a midwife or as an enabler. The author feels that the minister can maintain his role more effectively, especially as a mediator and reconciler. This function as a mediator and a reconciler is a very important function in any community development program.

In respect to the overall direction in unifying the program, both the working and spiritual reflection, the author suggests a small group or council who are directly involved within the programs of the community and the church. A collective effort and direction is probably the most feasible and democratic device for the multi-service center model.

Spiritual-Reflective Program

The key position where the minister can fully use the leadership role is in the area of the *spiritual-reflective* program. Society has given the minister his specific role and has publicly ordained him through the institution solely given this responsibility — the church. The minister in the church is the sole individual in society who has the responsibilities of officiating in family rituals such as the performance of marriage, baptism, funeral, and the eucharist. The justice of the peace can only officiate in marriage. These ritualistic roles of the minister have been a historical tradition that needs to be preserved. The functions themselves are important but the expressions need to be flexible in their ways of fitting themselves to the occasions or context of the situations. Many young and old ministers today are using innovative expressions of their functions in society. The key point obviously is to be flexible or contextual in their approach.

The important emphasis in the spiritual-reflective program is its concern about the *salvation or wholeness* of the entire community. The activities of the week can certainly overwhelm many in that they forget the directions, goals, and objectives that they have set out to do in their earlier planning. Other individuals become fragmented psychologically, emotionally and spiritually because they too need the experience of spiritual reflection to help them to be whole again. The exercise of spiritual reflection also provides for individuals the opportunity to take time for evaluating programs and individual goals that they set for themselves at the beginning of their programs. In addition, spiritual reflection may also offer new directions and objectives. This is why the author suggested earlier that the minister's role is not in the area of key leadership but rather as an enabler or a midwife.

In addition, the minister's message to his community must embody prophecy, dialogue, and hope. And in so doing, hopefully, he attempts to fulfill the ministry of Jesus Christ in making his people whole through the spirit of salvation.

The *prophetic aspect* of the minister's message is necessary to education especially if the method of *conscientization* is applied. Special attention must be developed to call out the evils and injustices in society especially to those who are in power and who oppress the disenfranchised and the unfortunate. Also prophetic stands on issues which help liberate all people must be risked at all times to be consistent with the cry for self-determination and liberation in all human aspects. The prophetic aspect calls for a break with the present model of development, in favor of the awareness that man has the power to transcend his history. No education or politics is liberating unless the people question institutions and the results obtained in the construction of a responsible community. Thus, in prophetic ministry, the need to express and communicate a radical assessment of the very meaning on earth is urgent.

To be consistent with the theology of the oppressed, especially its emphasis on participation, it would be helpful for the prophetic minister to recall in his message to the community the importance of such liberating subjects as Freire's principles of self-determination and liberation.[13] The first principle, again, is the reflection on man himself by an analysis of the concrete environment of the individual. The second principle lies in man transforming the world after developing man's faculty of

---

[13] Thomas G. Sanders, "*Paulo Freire,*" *Terre Sauterre* (March-April 1969): 3. For the Spanish article see Convergence III, no. 3 (1970): 3.

awareness and a critical mind by means of which he makes choices and decisions and which, in turn, can liberate man instead of domesticating and adjusting him.

The third principle is that "man is able to lift himself to a higher level of awareness and become a subject in proportion to the extent to which he intervenes in his society, reflects on its context, and commits himself to it."[14] Thus, in relationships with man and nature, he becomes what he is. Freire's fourth principle is that "man creates culture to the extent to which he integrates his social and cultural environment, reflects on it, and responds to its challenges."[15] Freire uses the word culture as the total result of human activity, "of man's attempt to create and re-create, of his efforts to transform and to establish dialogues with other men."[16]

Finally, the fifth principle suggests that

> man is not only the creator of his culture by his relationships and his response to nature's challenges, but that he also makes history by this response and his relationships with others. It must be clearly understood that man can only make history if he is able to grasp the trends of his time. If he is incapable of doing this he will be carried along by the events of history rather than making history himself.[17]

In summary, then, the prophetic aspect confronts and supports those who break with evils and injustices and creates the context which enables an individual to become a Subject, to transform the world, to relate to other human beings, to mold his culture, and to make history.

Earlier in the chapter, the author suggested dialogical thrust as a methodological possibility toward community development. The minister must master this art of dialogue as he relates in the sphere of spiritual reflection. Reuel Howe spoke of this *dialogical* relationship through his *ministry* of mutuality.[18] The mutual ministry consists of mutual expectancy, mutual attention, mutual respect and mutual trust.

Dialogue in the spiritual reflection takes place in a relationship of *mutual expectancy*. It produces a personal encounter in which one addresses and the other responds, thus, leading to a real meeting. When we practice expectancy, according to Howe, we are

> preparing ourselves for possible depth meetings that may take place between others and ourselves. Preparation in this sense means ridding ourselves of prejudices and preconceptions, fears and anxieties, ulterior motives and purposes, in order that we may speak the word of love and truth to others, and to really hear the word of love and truth . . . that they speak to us. . . . Because we have prepared ourselves for a real meeting between people, we will not so easily seek to manipulate and exploit them.[19]

The dialogue of mutuality calls for mutual *attention*. This mutual attention is achieved through the attentiveness of both beings interested in each other. Thus,

---

[14] Sanders, "*Paulo Freire,*" 3.

[15] Sanders, "*Paulo Freire,*" 3.

[16] Sanders, "*Paulo Freire,*" 3.

[17] Sanders, "*Paulo Freire,*" 3.

[18] Reuel L. Howe, *Herein is Love* (Valley Forge, PA: Judson Press, 1961), 91.

[19] Howe, *Herein is Love*, 91–92.

listening and hearing are of prime importance. The reward for attentiveness is that others will respond with clues in the form of questions or comments that will enable us to meet them at the point of meaning of their life. "Attentiveness is . . . alertness to the lonely cry of man, and respects rather than violates the individual's separateness and sanctity."[20]

Mutual respect is another quality necessary for a meaningful dialogue of mutuality. "Respect for oneself and others is not as common as one might expect. We find self-concern and concern for others, but not respect."[21] Without respect for oneself, respect for others is hard to maintain. Further, mutual respect has some basic characteristics. First, there is respect for one another as *autonomous* deciding persons.

> We cannot make . . . others do what we may think they ought to do. We can only meet them with whatever resources we have, and out of respect for their own power of decision and action, leave them free to make their response.[22]

This is not saying that we would not be involved in their decisions. We can be involved through our presence, concern, and respect for the decisions as they make them. The danger of making decisions for others is the fact that our decisions and way of life may not work for them. Closely related to one's autonomous being is the respect for another's dependence. This is not saying that we need to increase their dependency by respecting them or exploit-ing their dependency, but we need to meet them in their needs.

> Mutual respect also calls for respect of others who must answer for their own lives. . . . Therefore we respect ourselves as having within ourselves the power to answer for our own lives. Mutual respect for one another, as responsible beings, increases our self-respect, and conversely our growing self-respect increases the respect we have for others.[23]

The third and last quality necessary for the dialogue of mutuality is *mutual trust*. This implies confidence that others will make the right decisions for themselves and that they will have regard for others as they make their decisions. The crucial point in trusting others through dialogue does not mean that we shall be successful in all our endeavors. People's response to being trusted is not dependable or consistent. "Trust, if it is to do its full work, must include mistrust, just as faith must include doubt."[24] Even with all of these obvious realities, trust still gives quality to life through trusting in what God is trying to accomplish in us and, thus we ought to trust one another.

The *message of hope* is one of the central messages of spiritual-reflection. If the theology of the oppressed is to speak realistically and cogently to a people whose lives have been worn down, whose best hopes have so often been frustrated, and

---

[20] Howe, *Herein is Love*, 94.
[21] Howe, *Herein is Love*, 94.
[22] Howe, *Herein is Love*, 96.
[23] Howe, *Herein is Love*, 96.
[24] Howe, *Herein is Love*, 98.

who have been reminded at every turn by human word and action that they are less worthy than other ordinary humans, it must have a new and fresh message of hope for the future.

The theology of the oppressed must be a theology of hope; it must hold within its content a promise to be redeemed within the earthly life span of those who possess such a hope and who discern such a promise. Under God, it must be clear gospel message of new light and new self-understanding of what it means to live, even in a world of despair, which can provide a sufficient reason and right for the Filipinos to hope within the American context.

If the gospel message is to be real for the Filipino community, the theology of the oppressed must concur with Moltmann that "those who hope in Christ can no longer put up with reality as it is, but begin to . . . contradict it. Peace with God means conflict with the world."[25] Further, to be adequate for the Filipino community, the theology of the oppressed must speak of a new vision, if there is no clear vision of the future, the Filipino people might easily adjust themselves to the present. The theology of the oppressed must provide them with some new words of hope; it must provide them with the will to break away from the present toward the future.

To be consistent with the messianic God mentioned earlier in the chapter, the new meaning of God is made important only as a new type of Filipino takes shape. An adequate hope for the Filipino community must rest upon a God concept that will embrace the aspirations of Filipinos for the future.

Within the aspirations of hope, the ultimate concern is for a community wherein all can share as equals. There will be a pluralism of ideologies, interests; aims, aspirations, and personhood, and no one will, for any purpose, be denied opportunity to achieve or be excluded from community. Such a climate, however, will not exclude the emergence of new concerns, new struggles, new aspirations, and a yearning for even newer levels of maturity for the individual and community.

---

[25] Jurgen Moltmann, *Theology of Hope*, trans. J. W. Leitch (New York: Harper & Row, 1967), 21.

An Ecology of Church Life
*Changing Patterns in a Multi-Ethnic Community**

DAVID JUNICHI HARADA

Hawaiian church life constitutes a unique phenomenon. No ethnic group in Hawaii forms a majority, but most minorities are large enough so as to maintain a certain degree of self-identity and community support without being absorbed into a dominant culture. What is emerging in Hawaiian communities is not the assimilation of minority groups into a dominant culture, but the development of a unique culture and lifestyle. It is basically "American" without being a direct transplantation of Orange County, California. It is a cosmopolitan community with a quality all our own.[1]

My assignment is to describe how this kind of community has affected one denomination, The United Methodist Church. It is not a complete or exhaustive description of all of our churches. Neither does it deal with the problem of Christ and Culture in the early years of the American Missionary movement and the Hawaiian people, since our denomination did not begin to work in Hawaii until almost two generations later.

The psalmist has a beautiful image of the man of faith:

> Blessed is the man
>> who walks not in the counsel of the wicked,
> Nor stands in the way of sinners,
>> Nor sits in the seat of scoffers;
> but his delight is in the law of the Lord . . .
>
> He is like a tree
>> planted by streams of water
> that yields its fruit in its season,
>> and its leaf does not wither.
> In all that he does, he prospers.
> (Psalm 1:1–3)

---

* Search for the Sandalwood Mountains, Education for Mission Conference, Hawaii Council of Churches and Asian Center for Theology and Strategies, Honolulu, HI, July 17–19, 1975.

[1] Shortly after being away on the "mainland" for five years, the writer was called to officiate at a wedding. The *Nisei* Japanese couple was dressed in traditional American garb. The service of worship was taken from an adaptation of the English *Book of Common Prayer* service. After the ceremony, we went to the wedding banquet, a Chinese nine-course dinner. Speeches were made in English and Japanese, the couple being toasted with *banzais*. After-dinner entertainment was provided by a Hawaiian musical group.

I am taking the liberty of appropriating this imagery to describe our churches. It is particularly apt, I think, because Hawaii's beauty is partly in our forests and valleys. Moreover, the particular nature of our biological and natural community reminds us somewhat of the way in which our churches have grown and shaped their lives in response to this peculiar environment.

We are becoming more and more aware of the special place that is Hawaii. Because of our isolation from other large land masses by at least two thousand miles, and because of our peculiar geology, plant, and animal life evolved here as nowhere else. It has been marked by a very closely developed system of interdependent adaptation. It is a fragile ecology in which some of our major groups of bird and animal life have become extinct within the last three generations. Today more bird species and plants are on the endangered list than any other area of the world.

I suggest this not to point to the imminent danger of our churches that we are describing, but to indicate the social context and milieu in which churches have been placed. It may also serve as a warning that thoughtless non-concern for the living context in which communities find their meanings may mean also the impoverishment and destruction of lifegiving forms of church life, which ought to be given the best opportunity to develop and flourish.

We are reminded by scientists that the depredation of our biota occurred not primarily through willful destruction but through introduction, deliberately or inadvertently, of hardier plant life that won the competition to grow in our fertile hills and valleys.

The theme of our conference *Search for the Sandalwood Mountains* indicates the value placed upon the fragrant heartwood of the Iliahi valued in China and by native Hawaiians. Even economic greed that took out thousands of tons of the wood for trade in the Orient did not cause the demise of luxuriant stands of the trees. The peculiar lifestyle and ecology of the forest made regeneration difficult. Today there are fewer and fewer sandalwoods in our forests.

E. C. Manunike, an African Christian, perhaps had Psalms in mind as he addressed a World Council of Churches conference with these words:

> Culture is like the leaves of a tree. They give the tree its shape and beauty while giving shade to people and animals. Remove the leaves and the tree loses a vital part of itself. But when the leaves have done their job and cease to add anything valuable to the tree, they wither, dry, and fall, thereby preparing room for new leaves. . . . Likewise culture should be allowed to do the job for which it was intended. Its premature destruc-tion might make the people whom it was meant to clothe suffer cultural and genuine spiritual and emotional "statelessness" . . . We must transform it into a dynamic and saving way of life whose seeds germinate in African soils and whose roots can hold firmly, anchoring the Church as it seeks to play its part in making God's will be done on earth as it is done in Heaven.[2]

---

[2] E. C. Makunike, "Evangelism in the Cultural Context of Africa," *International Review of Missions* 63, no. 249 (January 1974): 63

Hawaiian churches like the tree described have had a variety of foliages and forms. We turn now to their description in one branch of Christendom.

I. The "First" Immigration (1850–1910)

When ancient Marquesans first came to Hawaii around AD 500, they sailed 2,000 miles across open ocean to seek a new land. It must have been a deliberate voyage made possible by a fantastic ability in seamanship, endurance and faith. They were probably led by the kolea bird (Pacific golden-plover) that came each year from the north and returned north. (Thank God the Marquesans did not know that the small birds came from and returned to Alaska each year!) The first voyagers brought with them the major food plants (taro, sweet potato, *kukui*, *ti*, breadfruit, etc.). Without them, they might not have survived because this land did not have many edible food plants.

In similar manner, the first immigration that came from Asia brought with the pioneers not necessarily plants but the cultural meanings and values and practices so necessary for survival in this strange new land. Like the earlier pioneers which preceded them by 1,300 years, they too came looking for a better life in the sugar and pineapple plantations. Other immigrants came from the West to seek their fortunes.

All transplanted, in this new land, their own culture and values and language and styles of life. The church came too originally from Boston, began work among the Native Hawaiians and later with non-Christian cultures from Asia.

A. The Beginnings of the Issei Churches[3]

Our origins as a denomination involved in church life in Hawaii starts around the year 1855 when a group of "*haole*" immigrants was given a charter by King Kamehameha IV to hold property and hold services of worship. This group eventually became the First United Methodist Church. At about the same time a Japanese congregation in San Francisco heard of the plight of Japanese laborers in Hawaii and sent Kanichi Miyama to work among the Japanese. Eventually this became Harris United Methodist Church (1887).

Methodist work developed in subsequent years among the Haoles, Japanese, Koreans, and Filipinos. It had been decided by denominational leaders that since work already existed in other denominations among the Hawaiians and Chinese, the Methodist would not develop work specifically among them.

Whether it be a *Haole* or Japanese *Issei* church, work is done almost completely in the culture and language of the group. Essentially this means "transplanting" the church to meet the needs of the people. Of course, most immigrants were non-Christian among the Japanese, so the evangelism had to proceed as a new experience but was accomplished and shaped in the culture of the immigrant. *Issei* churches were necessary and important support systems. Like the tree described by

---

[3] *Issei* = Japanese term for "first generation," which we will use to refer to all immigrant groups.

Manunike, these churches provided useful shade and shelter for the sojourner in a strange land.

Today all of our churches are cosmopolitan to a certain degree, but First United Methodist Church still offers an identifiable structure and style in its ministry which welcomes warmly the "new immigrants" from the mainland US while reaching into the community itself. It also has a Tongan congregation that is a genuine part of the total life of the church.

Harris UMC too has persisted through the years with a self-identity with the Japanese community, although it too has "sent out new foliage." It is still considered a "central" Japanese church by members and children of members who live some distance from it but still consider it their church home. Harris has the only full-time Japanese language minister in our denomination, who works with a vigorous congregation composed both of *Isseis* of the first and the new recent immigration.

B. Generational Succession: Churches of the Nisei and Sansei [4]

After the turn of the century immigration from Asian countries ended almost abruptly for several reasons. Some laborers returned to their homeland. Many remained to make Hawaii their home. Since no new immigration came to reinforce the culture and social milieu from their lands of origin, ethnic communities began their process of adaptation for new times. Shifts began to occur in church life too, from a completely "language" orientation to more and more American-English ministries. As the *Issei* group grew older leadership in churches moved toward the *Niseis* and *Sanseis*. Most of the work became part of the ongoing American life of the community, and as the numbers of *Isseis* began to thin, language work began to diminish into part-time ministries served by one minister serving several congregations.[5]

---

[4] Here again, *Nisei*, or "second generation," and *Sansei*, "third generation," will be used for all the different groups as a convenience.

[5] The writer's experience in living through this changeover period may be typical. I grew up in Lahaina, a predominantly Japanese sugar and pineapple plantation community. My father came from Japan as a contract laborer in his earlier teens. My mother was born of Japanese parents. We were involved in the Japanese Methodist Church. There was also a Filipino Methodist Church in Lahaina. My earliest recollections in church have to do with going to Japanese language school after "English" school each day. Worship services were conducted in Japanese and so was Sunday school, although English was also used in youth groups and an English service of worship. When the war came, everything Japanese was suppressed. The language school closed down; we had no Japanese-language pastor, but the *Isseis* met in homes for cottage meetings. After the war, Japanese-language work was begun again, but the basic program of the church was in English. The Filipino Methodist Church, in the meanwhile, began to suffer attrition in membership and was soon merged with the Japanese Methodist Church. Today, there is a Japanese-language minister who pastors the United Methodist congregation in Lahaina as well as another congregation of another denomination in Central Maui. Since around the time of WWII till now, the pastor in charge did all the English-language work.

II. Cosmopolitanism: New Churches between Immigrations

Botanists remind us that plants have a way of developing and changing so as to adapt more effectively to new conditions. In Hawaii, original seeds arriving by drifting on the ocean, borne by winds or birds took root in these islands and in relative isolation developed into new species. In other areas access to larger genetic pools from neighboring areas tended to stabilize species, but in Hawaii the specific conditions and isolation created new kinds of plant life.

A similar process developed as far as churches are concerned. With the end of significant migration in the first decades of the twentieth century (as far as Asia was concerned), the culture of the immigrants tended to be shaped more and more by local conditions. The *Niseis* and *Sanseis* growing up in Hawaii began to be related more and more to the community at large. The exclusive ethnocentric life began to become more inclusive. The *Haole* dominance in most areas began to give way to leadership derived from non-Caucasian stock. This was true in business, government, and in professional life. Communities began to develop in new areas. The original ethnic "camps" on plantations began to give way to mixed communities of homeowners.

After World War II, and the general upswing in church attendance, resourcing, and programs on the mainland had an effect in Hawaii, as the appeal of our "Mission" generated substantial sums for "church extension." Coupled with the development of new housing areas, the United Methodist Church entered a period of expansion and extension. Several new churches were organized in new communities. Kilohana (Niu Valley), Keolumana (Kai lua), Ala Lani (Central Maui), Trinity (Pearl City) began in new communities. Waimanalo and East Kauai (Lihue) were organized in older communities at about the same time.

All of these churches differed from their predecessors in that each drew from the community around them that tended to be heterogeneous rather than single ethnic groups. Kilohana is typical. It was organized in 1958 as an outreach project of First UMC. Members living in this area began work that developed into a church. Mission funds made physical development possible relatively early in the process. Membership now is approximately one-third Japanese, one-third *Haole*, and one-third of other ethnic groups. The makeup roughly approximates the community.

Church life and style also reflect this engagement with the basic constituency of these new churches. Cosmopolitanism concerns the genuine additive process of multiethnic factors rather than assimilation, that is, the absorption of different peoples into a dominant pattern. Mainland guests comment (usually positively) on how "different" our churches are, although the continuity of English, use of common hymnology, etc., provide a basic "at-homeness."

Ethnicity in our cosmopolitan communities is partially made possible without loss of common life because each ethnic group appears to have sufficient community "back-up" systems of cultural reinforcement. The churches do not have to be primary foci of cultural reinforcement, as is the case in many mainland situations, where ethnic churches appear to be the primary agencies for ethnic celebration and identity.

In Hawaii it appears that many persons who are *Niseis* and *Sanseis* are becoming more and more cosmopolitan in outlook and have not deliberately pursued the "ethnic identity" route. But there is a difference from mainland situations, in that a person in Hawaii who does not consciously seek to be "Japanesy" is not necessarily becoming (what has been often unkindly characterized as) a "banana."[6] He may indeed be involved in the peculiar meaning-structure which is Hawaii, which is unique and a direct function of the peculiar mix of factors and ethnic makeup which is Hawaii.

We need to explore the meaning of these dynamics for church life as well as to develop programs that affirm our Cosmopolitan common life together. Perhaps a genuine Cosmopolitanism means that people have access to ethnic roots and meanings that they can bring to the common life of the churches. Unless people have genuine options in searching out and becoming identified with specific cultural streams and affirm their life in them, the resultant conglomeration may end up into some kind of "bland" homogenized culture that has little character.

III. The New Immigration: 1965 to the Present

While in-migration from the mainland US was never curtailed, foreign immigration ceased after the turn of the century and did not resume as a major force until after 1964, when congressional action relaxed restrictive regulations for permit Asians and Pacific Basin peoples to immigrate to the US. The dramatic increase in the coming of these "new *Isseis*" has created an exciting new time for the United Methodist churches in Hawaii as well as for other denominations.

A. *Impact of Asian Immigration on Our Churches*

Among the historically Japanese churches, there has been a revitalization, particularly in the city of Honolulu, where more new immigrants make their homes. Harris UMC has an enthusiastic and growing congregation of "old timers" as well as "newcomers." Aldersgate UMC has developed human services programs to meet the practical needs of the fastest growing group of immigrants—the Filipinos. (In another context we will describe the work done at Aldersgate with Samoan ministries.)

The most dramatic change in response to the new immigration has been at Christ UMC, originally organized as an *Issei* Korean church in the early 1900s. In 1955 strong administrative recommendations resulted in the change of the name from First Korean Methodist Church to Christ United Methodist Church to symbolize what was thought to be a changing mood in the communities to become more "integrative." (In our terminology, I suppose "cosmopolitan" would be

---

[6] In the politics of "ethnic empowerment" a "banana" is one who is yellow outside but white inside, just as an "apple" is a native American Indian who is red outside but has sold out his ethnic heritage to become assimilated into the white structure. One church leader who is sensitive and thoughtful was described as a "melon" because, although he is "white," inside he is a "yellow."

appropriate.)[7] This move was only minimally successful and had the negative effect that some *Nisei* and *Sansei* Koreans who had sentimental attachments to the Korean church decided they would join other churches. The loyal *Isseis* hung on but gradually English work began to suffer attrition. The *Haole* pastor in charge brought into effect this new philosophy, while worked in English and the Korean language pastors did work with the *Iseis*. Later a decision was made at the request of the church to have a bilingual pastor in charge. At about the same time increasing activity in new immigration tended to accelerate a move toward intensifying Korean language work. Today the congregation has become, in many ways, a classic *Issei* church. Most of the work is done in Korean, including worship, church board and committee meetings, and Sunday school from intermediate grades upward. English Sunday school is carried on in the earlier grades, and a bilingual preschool has been in operation. Because of specific requests for an English service of worship, a trial period of three months was attempted with guest preachers. This proved to be of only minor impact and has at present been discontinued. The church is one of our strongest congregations in the district and has a vitality and vigor that is exciting.

It will be interesting to watch its growth and history to see whether this *Issei* church will recapitulate the history of other *Issei* churches with the coming of *Niseis* and *Sanseis*. One difference to note is that whereas the first *Issei* churches were started almost exclusively with adults who started families here in Hawaii, most of the new immigrants come with families. Their children had part of their education in Korea. Implications of this factor may need to be studied further and appropriate assistance and services developed.

A brief survey of our original *Issei* churches may be helpful here:

- *Japanese work*: We have mentioned Harris UMC previously. At present Wesley, Wahiawa, Kai lua, Parker (Kaneohe) and Kahaluu churches continue Japanese language work with their smaller "language" groups by sharing one full-time minister who serves all of these congregations. In addition, on Maui, a pastor serves part-time in Lahaina and with another denomination in Central Maui. Harris UMC has the only full-time language pastor.[8]
- *Korean work*: At present we have work at Christ UMC, described in some detail above.[9] In addition there is a vigorous though smaller congregation at Olive in Wahiawa served by a part-time lay preacher. Olive is basically a cosmopolitan church now with not only a Korean congregation but also an active Samoan group.
- *Filipino work*: Aldersgate UMC is the only church in which Filipino work as such is being done. It is also a Samoan church. It is said that Aldersgate

---

[7] Likewise, the Filipino United Methodist Church changed its name to Aldersgate UMC for the same reason.

[8] Private communication by a church worker.

[9] Christ UMC may also be the largest Korean congregation among Methodists in our country.

is the largest Filipino congregation among Methodists in the US. While there are significant Filipino constituencies on the other islands, within recent years, we have not had bilingual pastors who could be deployed to serve this important area of smaller churches which cannot afford two workers. Kauai has developed an excellent agency to work with Filipino immigrants through joint state-county-church sponsorship.

In the United Methodist Church, across the country there appears to be a need: to recruit and train more bilingual ministers for most ethnic minority groups serving Asian and Pacific Basin peoples. The one exception seems to be Korean ministerial leadership that is available in significant numbers, most of them from Korea.

B. The New Immigrants: Pacific Basin Peoples

Among the new immigrants are groups that have entered the mainstream of United Methodist Church life who were not represented in the "first immigration." Those include the Samoans, Tokelauans, and the Tongans. (American Samoa, being part of our national concern and supervision, had no immigrant restrictions, although persons from Western Samoa come under our immigration laws.)

There is a very active and enthusiastic Tongan congregation at First UMC. The Tokelauans are worshiping at Palolo United Methodist Church. Samoan work has been done or is actively pursued at Olive (Wahiawa), Waimanalo, Parker, Aldersgate, Palolo, and Trinity (Pearl City).

Most recently, our Annual Conference (Southern California-Arizona) has created the Samoan Commission, duly authorized to plan, coordinate, and seek resources to aid the ministry of Samoan concerns both here and on the mainland. By tacit agreement they will also work with other Pacific Basin peoples.

With the coming of these "new" immigrants, certain factors are now at work that were not present when the first immigrants came. In terms of church life in Hawaii, we have now thirty organized churches within the Hawaii District. We are no longer recipients of massive financial and personnel support which makeup the heyday of "missions" two decades ago. The present economic situation has impressed on us also the need for more dedicated and selective stewardship in terms of expansion of work and a greater reliance on local resources.

On the part of the incoming islanders, there is also a difference. While Protestant or other Christianity was not the general background of many Asian immigrants, the situation is quite different among the Pacific Basin peoples who come with well-developed and intensely loyal church affiliations. Moreover, entry into a church is not a matter of individual decision but a clan affiliation so that Samoans become part of churches in whole social units. Sometimes they move their affiliation from one congregation to another, depending on where adequate housing can be found for the group. They often have within their number well-defined leadership roles and often lay religious leadership.

In an attempt to understand the dynamics of church affiliation we have tried below to describe different styles of relationships developed among our churches with regard to Samoan congregations. The stages represent "moments" within a continuous pattern but do not pretend to be anything but descriptive of some relationships. Certainly they are not prescriptive for any group. We draw upon analogies drawn from our rich ecology of plant life.

Stages in the Evolution of Relationships between Host and Guest Congregation

Since resources are scarce for the organizing of separate churches, recent patterns have involved a host-guest relationship which matures into something new and exciting in the way of cooperative ministries.

Stage One: Benevolent Hosts and New Congregations — The Kaumahana Church

In the hills and valleys there grows an interesting plant called *hulumoa* (chicken feathers) after a fancied resemblance, or more often *kaumahana* (to perch in a warm place) that is descriptive of its existence. This plant is a Hawaiian mistletoe and is a "young" plant in an evolutionary sense. It is dependent on a host *koa* or other tree, into whose branches it sends root-like structures to gather nourishment. It cannot derive sustenance like other plants and does not have true leaves or flowers or seeds. This mode of existence does not harm the host tree, but the host tree is needed if the *kaumahana* is to live.

Samoan groups often start like the *kaumahana* — a group is welcomed as guests by a local congregation, and while they become established in the community the host church provides various kinds of support, including helping with administrative costs and the support of a language minister who may start out as a part-time minister.

State Two: The Epiphyte Church — Ekaha

Ekaha is a bird's nest fern that grows in cool places. It is a crown-like arrangement of sword-shaped leaves. It signified life-giving powers to ancient Hawaiians, who often placed an *ekaha* fern on the stumps of newly felled trees needed for canoe building or house building. Normally *ekaha* makes a home in a convenient tree branch. Unlike the *kaumahana* it needs only a physical resting place since it is a self-sufficient plant in itself.

Samoan congregations become like *ekaha* plants in relatively short order, needing only a place for meetings and worship. Their stewardship is so dedicated and responsive that soon they become completely self-supporting and, indeed, astonish host churches with their insistence to participate in helping with their needs. At this stage programs, administration and other relationships are usually parallel though separate.

Stage Three: The Symbiotic Church — *Limu Wahine Maikai*

Limu wahine maikai (the good-woman plant) is a lichen. They are grayish-colored growths sometimes found even in barren lava fields where little else grows. The lichen is really a colony of two different plants. The fungus part breaks down mineral matter to make it available for nourishment to the algae. In return the algae synthesize food out of this and water and elements from the air that provide nourishment for the fungus. Thus a mutually dependent relationship is established. This symbiosis (which literally means "having life together") makes possible plant life even in the most inhospitable landscape.

We have found host and guest congregations to become more and more interdependent and symbiotic. Our peculiar church polity encourages a normal course of development along these lines. The new symbiotic church has a common life together, sharing common worship at times, a common administrative order, stewardship, and membership. Programmatically separate activities are developed to meet the peculiar needs of each part of the symbiosis. This stage seems to be where we are as United Methodists in relation to Samoan and Pacific Island congregations.

It is interesting to speculate as to where this type of church will go in the next *Nisei* and *Sansei* generations. Will Samoan congregations "spin off" and start new churches, or will they maintain this relationship over a period of time? Will there be a gradual Interpenetration of life and culture into a new kind of bicultural church? These and perhaps other options are open to these enthusiastic congregations. For the time being the vitality and lively expression of faith in these churches represent exuberant foliage in a new kind of "tree."

IV. The Churches of the Future: The Sandalwood Church (Iliahi)

The theme of our conference points to the symbol of the sandalwood tree, valued by Chinese merchants for the fragrant heartwood, and used also by the ancient Hawaiians to give fragrance to their *kapas* and as an ingredient in medicines they made. In Hawaii there are seven or more separate species of the sandalwood tree, all endemic and found nowhere else in the world. They all share a peculiar life-history. It appears that as seedlings they must send their roots in the root systems of other trees to derive nourishment. At a later time as they mature it appears they become self-sufficient to a large degree. Because of the early exploitation of the forests for the fragrant species, and because of the specialized mode of existence, *iliahi* are becoming scarce in our hills and forests.

This rugged cross which is used at Palolo United Methodist Church was made from a log of sandalwood in the early '50s. We share it with you as part of the symbol of this conference.

Hawaii is a socially rich and stimulating place. It has diversity and a kind of social ecology that is found nowhere else in the world. Perhaps in a place like ours we are given to develop a unique kind of church life like the sandalwood tree, developing into special creations that are responsive to the unique social climate of our island communities. Like the sandalwood, we may need to offer opportunities so that new seedlings can reach into the rootage of older "trees" of older cultures and find strength and help. Like the 40% of our native plant life now endangered, we may need to pay heed to what is happening here, among our churches. It is not that the church needs to be protected like a hothouse plant; far from it. But we need to exercise some care and stewardship so that the good seed of the Lord is not snatched away near the busy uncaring roadways or be found in rocky ground or be choked by thorns. Perhaps the symbol for the emerging church in Hawaii should be the *iliahi* used as incense and medicine and as a fragrance to make glad the lives of all. Blessed is the church which is like a tree planted by streams of living water, fed by the life of the people, that yields its fruit in its season and its leaf does not wither, and in all that it does it prospers.

Why an Asian American Theology of Liberation?

Dennis Loo[*]

Some important assumptions have been made in the previous presentations by the Black, Latino, Native American, and Appalachian brothers. One assumption is that, in understanding the church's ability to deal with ethnic people in this country and in the world, we must recognize that Christianity can never be completely separated from culture. The second assumption is that Western Christians, when they have related to other peoples, have imposed economic, political, and cultural dominance, and that many times there has been a confusion about what the core of the gospel is and the idiosyncrasies of Western culture. Now, this does not mean that everything that was done by the Western church was wrong. What we are expressing here today is that Christ and culture cannot be completely separated because of our human finiteness. Therefore we have to deal honestly with this, especially if we are talking about a universal church with a kind of plurality that takes into account the integrity of the cultural and racial backgrounds represented in America and throughout the world.

The third assumption is that the type of dominance which has continued historically until the present cannot continue any longer if we claim to be the church, the body of Christ which includes all the different peoples of the world. The fourth assumption is that theologies for ethnic self-development are not simply fads of the time that some people are wishing would go away so that they could go back to business as usual. Rather, there is a deep conviction that theologies of self-development are crucial for the future development of the church.

Having given that preamble, I would like to make a case for a theology of Asian American liberation. I specify the term "Asian American" since I am an Asian American. There are some distinctions between Asians in America and Asians in

---

[*] Rev. Loo was born and raised in Chinatown, San Francisco. During the last ten years, he has worked in racial minority communities throughout the country, including Wilmington, Delaware; Philadelphia, Pennsylvania; Lima, Ohio; and recently back in his native San Francisco Bay Area. He is a member of the Asian Presbyterian Caucus and on the Board of Governors for ACTS.

The following article was one presentation in a series of five lectures at the 185th General Assembly (UPCUSA) in Omaha, Nebraska, on May 18, 1973. It was part of a workshop on theologies on self-development from the perspectives of Black, Latino, Native American, Appalachian White, and Asian American peoples. The Asian American presentation was the final one in the series.

Asia; however, there are also close connecting links that we are beginning to recognize and develop as we move along toward a meaningful concept of self-development and liberation.

Myth of Ethnocentrism

There are a number of myths that have mitigated against the self-development of Asian Americans and against the need for even thinking about a theology of Asian American liberation. The first myth is the prevalent belief that Asians have a strong national pride, that we have a great cultural and historical past, and that our ethnocentrism in this country is even excessive. Therefore, we have nothing to self-develop since we already "have our own thing." The usual accusation is that Asians are too clannish and don't care about anybody else. There is some truth to that because when I was a child, I can remember my relatives and friends always referring to other racial groups in Chinese phrases which meant "white devil" or "black devil," etc. Everybody else was a devil, but we were "people of the central kingdom." We were the civilized ones and everyone else was considered barbarian. It is true that ethnocentrism among Asians is very strong. But that is only half the picture. In terms of the history of Asians in America, there were two parallel tendencies: On the one hand, our parents constantly reiterated the superiority of our Asian culture; on the other hand, we gradually but surely accepted and appropriated the dominant values of America. Even though Asian ethnocentrism was constantly verbalized, what had developed (especially among second and third-generation Asians) was an unconscious but real group self-hatred.

Our parents made sure that after American school we went to Chinese school for three hours, five days a week. I remember once in Chinese school doing my Latin homework. The Chinese school teacher caught me and, pulling my ear, said: "What are you doing this for? Don't you know that you are Chinese and that you will always be seen as a Chinese?" At that time, I didn't realize the truth of that statement. I look back and realize how strong my tendencies were toward total assimilation. I was denying my Chinese heritage, and not taking Chinese seriously. Neither did any of my peers. Attending Chinese school did not change the basic development and tendency for all of us to see American middle-class values as the superior values to which we should aspire.

Another consideration in understanding this myth of ethnocentrism is to recognize that the majority of Asians had come from countries in which passiveness and submissiveness to the dominant authority pervaded national behavior patterns. American racism added to this factor and encouraged an easy transition to submissive obedience to the various institutions in this country. There was little possibility of utilizing this ethnocentrism (as white ethnics have done) into a meaningful force that would make its own impact and contribution in American society.

The Myth of Success

The second myth is that Asian Americans have "made it." We are the model minority that all other minority groups should follow because we have made it into the professions as doctors, teachers, and scholars. We are the people who have not had to riot or to do any of the disruptive things that create problems for the majority. We have been featured in various magazines which highlight the success story of how well Asians have become assimilated and adjusted in American society.

The truth of the matter is that Asians have not made it in many ways (as documented in other articles in this issue). If you look at the job market and economic levels in this country, if you look at the ways in which Asians are allowed into certain lower management positions but never into the decision-making process of corporations, government, and the church, you will find that Asians have reached a certain level, but have never really participated fully as equals in this country or in the church. Also, there has been the problem that Asians can always be used as scapegoats. This was true during the anti-Chinese crusades in the 1870s, '80s, and '90s, when one of the most blatant and racist anti-Asian campaigns developed in the state of California and spread throughout the country. It culminated in exclusionary federal immigration laws and the World War II Japanese internment camps. This indicates how Asians could be used at any time as scapegoats for economic problems or employment problems in this country. It still arouses deep fear among Asians today. In any case, the exclusionary laws which developed earlier have something to do with why there is such a small Asian racial population in this country and why it is difficult to accept the idea that Asians have "made it" when the fickle winds of international policy can blow against Asians in America at any time.

Myth of the Problem-Free Community

A third myth is that Asians have few problems as a group today. "They have problems as individuals, but as a racial group they have few or none." When the average Americans see Asians, they usually see professional types, students, or superficial stereotypes portrayed by the media. So most Americans have the impression that Asians have no serious problems economically, educationally, socially, or otherwise. Another reason is that by cultural upbringing, Asians are not willing to throw "dirty laundry" out in public and, therefore, many community problems are concealed by those who say they are community representatives. That is very true in Chinatowns in San Francisco, New York, etc. Only a few years ago were Chinese representatives finally able to admit that Chinatown was a ghetto; that the average income was less than $4,000 among the majority; that the suicide rate was one of the highest in the country; and that, indeed, there were serious social and economic problems. There is also little political power. Those in Chinatown or any Asian American community have very little say in what goes on regarding their own community. Also, in reference to the Asian farm labor problem, many people do not realize that the Farm Workers Union, which has been raised to a high level of visibility by Cesar Chavez, was originally organized by some of the oppressed Filipino laborers. Many people are not aware of the present problems of Korean immigrants in this country. Overt and subtle harassment by US immigration authorities is common. It starts at the initial entrance process and often ends with the threat of deportation or restrictions on travel. Unemployment and underemployment are critical problems, especially for non-English-speaking Asian immigrants. These problems have not been highly visible, yet they are very real.

Oppression

All these myths and stereotypes reinforce oppression among Asians in America. Oppression works best when you get the subjective group to accept the dominant group's definition of them. It is said that the worst oppression operates among those who are not aware of their own oppression. Among Asians, one of the problems is that we have assimilated too well the values of the dominant society, to the point where we believe these dominant group myths ourselves—that we are the model minority, that we have no problems, and therefore, "Why should we worry?"

Oppression has many facets. (1) We are aware of economic oppression when some group or system oppresses another group with economic controls. (2) We know about political oppression when one small group has the political force to keep others out of the mainstream of decision-making, even when it affects the lives and destinies of those "others." (3) We know about social oppression when alienation and ostracism keep people from interacting with one another as equals.

The first three are aspects of oppression familiar to all groups, including the Asians. But there are two other aspects of oppression. (4) There is the psychological aspect of oppression when a person does not have the freedom, the capability, or the opportunity to define who he is and to define relationships with others. (5) There is the spiritual aspect of oppression when a person has lost the will to resist and fight against what he believes to be wrong, when he has become paralyzed so that he is unable to take any kind of action.

Psychological and spiritual oppression are the most subtle and yet the most devastating forms of oppression which victimize us all, but particularly Asian Americans. For Asians in America there is a definite need to rethink, to articulate, and to appropriate an interpretation of the Christian faith which combats rather than perpetuates oppressive thought patterns that say dogmatically, "Asian American self-development is unchristian," or "advocacy for Asian American self-determination is anti-Christian" or "the right and responsibility of Asian Americans to challenge present oppressive structures violates the principles of Christian love and reconciliation." Asian Americans need to begin the process of developing an interpretation of the Christian faith that encourages self-affirmation and indigenous self-development in Asian churches and communities. It must encourage a critical analysis of ideas, values, customs, and structures in America that oppress not only Asians but others as well. It must encourage collective action for changing that oppression. It must also encourage the development of an Asian American frame of reference that can make its own unique contribution to the developing Third World theological dialogue, to the global theological task, and to liberation movements in the United States and in the world.

The necessity for an Asian American theology of self-development and liberation is rooted not only in the growing awareness of oppression among Asians in America. It is also rooted in the growing awareness that the church must be more responsive to often-ignored groups if it is to relate meaningfully and effectively in a fast-changing world. There is a new challenge to the church's ability to relate meaningfully to Third World people. Since the Christian church has never really been indigenous to Asian or Asian American culture and development, the question is whether it will be able to respond adequately to the growing aspirations for self-development and liberation, especially among Asians in America. The old forms of paternalism cannot be perpetuated without violation of human integrity and the gospel itself. New and creative interpretations of the Christian imperative from the perspectives of non-Anglo-European peoples are as essential for the future growth of the church as any high-powered stewardship campaign.

The Right to Struggle for Ourselves[*]

Marilyn J. Mar[†]

Asian Americans — the Chinese, Japanese, Pilipinos, and Koreans — as an ethnic group in America are a unique and diverse minority. To begin to understand who they have been and are in the American society, it is necessary to recognize the importance of the different factors within the various Asian American communities. This must be done within the context of history.

There are many myths that must be erased before one can understand the problems Asian Americans face today. One misconception is that the Asians in America are, relatively speaking, a rather successful minority who have merely suffered inevitable and inconsequential oppression throughout history. This article will attempt to point out the fallacies of this belief by giving an overview of the historical injustice, racism, and oppression that Asian Americans have faced in America in the past. Secondly, it will bring to attention the roots of this oppression and the resultant sociological and psychological problems. Lastly, it will try to promote a clearer understanding of the struggle that the Asian American must presently continue to pursue in order to survive.

America Greets the First Asian Immigrants

The arrival of large numbers of Chinese in the late 1800s marked America's first major encounter with Asian immigrants. At that time the overwhelming majority were single males, who came with dreams of streets paved with gold, numerous jobs, and a new prosperous life. In the United States they hoped to make enough money to be able to return to China and live easy lives with their families. They were "sojourners" who did not plan to make the American "mountain of gold" their home.

They had left China, a country full of political turmoil, but in America they found a country where white racist forces already operated against nonwhites. American Indians and Mexicans on the West Coast were socially and economically persecuted in much the same way the Chinese were to be. Also, white Americans already had preconceived attitudes concerning the Asiatic immigrant. The Chinese — along with their customs, religion, clothes, and lifestyle — were looked upon with the Western elite ethnocentrism that is still typical of Westerners today when viewing Asian countries. Because the Eastern way of life presented such a different philosophy and lifestyle in comparison to the American way of life, the Chinese were looked upon as untrustworthy heathen: nefarious, evil, and perverted, a viewpoint often enhanced

---

[*] March/April 1973.

[†] Ms. Mar was a student at the University of California, Berkeley.

by tales of filth and depravity brought back from China by American missionaries and traders. It was widely believed that they could never hope to fit in or be accepted in America. These attitudes were also supported by the nationalism of the Americans and the belief of American political superiority. During the 1800s the weakness of China's international status was as apparent as was the assurance that America was to become a major political influence in international affairs.

The disillusionment of the sojourners was as great as the vast and hopeful dreams they had built about life in America. Their dreams were destroyed in the face of discrimination, menial labor opportunities, harassment, lack of jobs, little hope of returning to China, and finally, exclusion. These elements were all contributing factors toward the complete breakdown of family life. The myth that the Chinese "take care of their own" came about when they were forced to organize their community for friendship, protection, and survival. The psychosociological need for family life was replaced by community and mutual aid associations. The overabundance of Chinese males in relation to the small number of Chinese female immigrants, plus the illegality of sexual relationships between Chinese men and white women, led to the establishment of prostitution through the importation of young girls from China. Thus the Chinese immigrant came to rely on tong-controlled brothels for sex and gambling and opium for recreation. He also turned toward his fellow sojourners for mutual aid, protection, and companionship.

A Cyclical History of Oppression

It was inevitable that the Asian immigrants be exploited. Along with the growth of capitalism in the United States came the continual need for cheap labor. Racism flourished and was institutionalized by importing cheap labor. The Chinese, being the first Asian immigrant group, were initially welcomed, but exploited at the same time. As the Chinese were forced to accept cheaper wages for survival, they became a threat to the white laborers in California. Visions of the Chinese taking over the labor market increased as more capitalists employed the Chinese in order to compete with other capitalists. The attitudes at this time are reflected by excerpts from an article that appeared in the Nevada City transcript entitled "Speech of Mr. Mooney, at the Anti-Chinese Meeting at the American Theatre, Wednesday, March 6, 1867."

> As the Chinaman progresses, the white man will retire before him. One by one, three by three, men from each of the living branches of California employment will go; for although they may excel the Chinaman in finish, they cannot undersell him in the labor market . . .
>
> Let us make a vow against buying vegetables, fish, or anything else from Chinamen; a vow against giving them any clothes to wash; a vow against employing them in any shape or way; a vow against giving our vote to any public officer, from Governor to Constable, who refuses to join in our opposition to Chinamen; a vow to adopt every possible means to discourage Chinese employment; and a vow that every white man on the Pacific coast shall enroll in this grand organization, and resist with all his might any public or private officer who shall endeavor, openly or covertly, to surrender this vast,

fertile land — the richest prize of the Caucasian family — to a race of serfs whose presence is a nuisance, a pestilence, a calamity, and a curse.[1]

It was largely white labor leaders who instigated anti-Chinese sentiment. The workingmen used the Chinese as scapegoats in their own struggle to have their unions recognized and to receive higher standard wages. But while they wanted economic democracy, they did all they could to prevent racial democracy. Consequently, as the Chinese became an economic threat, anti-Chinese feelings began to sprout all over California. The Chinese were met with physical harassment as well as continuous exploitation in the labor market.

In 1877, riots occurred in San Francisco in which twenty-five Chinese laundries were destroyed. Other anti-Chinese riots took place in Colorado, Wyoming, Oregon, and Alaska — wherever there were concentrations of Chinese laborers. In some instances, many Chinese workers were run out of town, tortured, or killed. As these anti-Chinese attitudes grew, political pressure was also growing. Laws were passed to exclude additional Chinese immigrants. The first Chinese Exclusion Act, passed in 1882, suspended immigration of Chinese for ten years and also prohibited naturalization of the Chinese already in the United States. This new act smashed all hopes the Chinese immigrants might have had of bringing their families to America.

The history of other Asian immigrants who came after the Chinese followed the same cycle: disillusionment, exploitation, threat, harassment, and exclusion. While the Chinese Exclusion Act was being renewed every ten years, new laws (Gentleman's Agreement of 1907, Exclusion Act of 1924, Philippine Independence Act in 1934, etc.) were passed, supporting the segregation and suppression of the Japanese, then the Pilipinos, and finally the Korean immigrants.

Each group was excluded only to see another Asian group replacing it as the next solution to the capitalists' need for cheap labor. This replacement led to the absence of any positive relationships between Asians. Instead of developing unity under common oppression, there was disunity and competitiveness that, of course, was to the advantage of their oppressors and was heightened by the economic depression of the 1930s.

How to Stay Yellow Yet Be Accepted As White

In order to understand the Asian American of today, it is not enough just to know his history in this country. It is also important to understand the forces that have perpetuated and continue to perpetuate the oppressed minority status of each group — Chinese, Korean, Japanese, and Pilipino.

One of these forces is the melting pot theory. America, according to this theory, is the country where all men of all races can come together to form one "American way of life." Through the years there has been a trend among Asian Americans toward assimilation and acceptance, even if it means total rejection of their original Asian cultures. For example, consider the experiences of the Japanese Americans.

---

[1] David L. Weitzman, ed., *China and the United States* (Menlo Park, CA: Asian Studies Inquiry Program/Field Studies, 1969).

In contrast to the Chinese, many Japanese came to America intending to settle permanently and start families. Many of them bought property, often marginal land with which they accomplished agricultural miracles. But the California Alien Land Law of 1913 made it illegal for aliens ineligible for citizenship to own land or to lease it for three years. The Japanese farmers then had to resort to putting their land in the name of their native-born children or in the names of Caucasian friends if they were to hold onto it. In spite of this and other discriminatory laws—for example, they could not legally engage in any occupation requiring a license—the Japanese felt that they must continue to work for acceptance by the white majority if they were to survive. Consequently, many of them denounced Japan and swore their loyalty to America even *after* they were incarcerated in concentration camps for four years during World War II.

This effort of Asian Americans to prove they were more "American" than Americans led to a new type of problem—a psychological oppression. For although there were cultural influences that every Asian group felt must be preserved, they nevertheless felt the need to change toward Western ways of thinking and living. As a result, they developed psychological burdens arising from self-hatred and confusion.

These feelings were fostered even more when the Asian American was confronted with rejection by whites, with discrimination, emasculation, and an identity crisis. Thus he was faced with a major contradiction. He wanted to succeed in America, but to be successful he felt he must be completely accepted by the majority, which meant accepting white values and ways. But he could not do this, for in doing so he would have to denounce himself. Thus, many Asian Americans came to learn that justice and equality did not prevail among and between the majority and minority groups. Instead they faced the dominance, racism, political power, exploitation, and class control that are so much a part of the industrialized, capitalistic society of today.

The Asian American in That Mind-Blowing Tube

Another factor that the Asian Americans had not anticipated in their struggle for acceptance was the way the stereotypes, which were (and are) perpetuated by the mass media and the educational institutions, increased prejudice. How does the average American see the Asian American? Does he still see him as a threat, as cheap labor, as the inscrutable laundryman or the nefarious hatchet man? Sadly enough, many times the answer is yes. Why do teachers in the schools continue to stereotype Asian students as quiet, submissive, and studious? Why are Asian Americans who were born in the United States and show only physical signs of being Asian frequently asked, "How long have you been in this country?" The obvious answer in the minds of many Asians lies in the attitudes that are perpetuated by the illustrations

There are many lonely old men in Asian communities, without homes or families. The following data indicates the reason.

Male/female ratio for peak year of immigration:

Chinese	1875	20:1
Japanese	1900	25:1
Pilipino	1920	143:1

Year in which male/female ratio reached 2:1

Japanese	1920
Chinese	1950
Pilipino	1960

of Asians in the media and in history books. The perpetuation of these Western ethnocentric (racist) conceptions has two major consequences that affect the Asian American's life.

The first is the effect that these stereotypes have on the way non-Asians view Asians in America. Asian Americans as an ethnic group are a very small minority. To a large degree they are concentrated on the East and West Coasts. Their communities tend to be self-inclusive, with the result that most white Americans seldom have contact with Asian Americans.

The primary source of knowledge of the Asian American is, therefore, what can be read in books or magazines, watched on the news, or seen on television shows, commercials, and movies. What real knowledge does this give about the Asian American?

Take a look at the Asian on television. The Asian male is portrayed as the weak, docile laundryman or cook who stutters his gratitude in broken English to the white leading actor. Or he is shown as the evil Fu Manchu, the inscrutable Charlie Chan, or the immoral and brutal Japanese in World War II. On the other hand, his counterpart, the Asian female, is characterized as the sexy Suzy Wong who satisfies the desires of the brave and honorable soldiers who fight overseas. These stereotypes fit in nicely with international attitudes and United States relationships with Asian countries. Consider the portrayal of the Japanese during World War II. If Japan was looked upon as the enemy of democracy and the threat to freedom and justice, what distinction were Caucasian Americans allowed to make between the Japanese they were fighting and those who lived in America? No doubt it was easier for the American conscience to accept the fact that the Japanese had been put in concentration camps because they were convinced that the Japanese Americans were as dangerous as the Japanese Army they saw on the movie screen fighting John Wayne's men.

Moving closer to the present, there is the question of communism and the Vietnam War. Communism, the American people have been told, is the epitome of evil: a threat to democracy and the freedom of America, while spy movies portray the "bad guy" as a Chinese communist, Americans are told that if they don't fight Asiatic communism in Vietnam, they will have to fight the communist "yellow peril" in their own backyards. When the late J. Edgar Hoover spoke of the possibility of subversive Chinese in America sympathetic to the People's Republic of China (as reported in the *New York Times*, November 22, 1969), he was, in fact, telling the people of the United States not to trust any Chinese Americans.

The roots of prejudice go deep. There have been incidents where Asian Americans have been beaten up by soldiers returning home from Vietnam. A Marine, for example, attempted to justify beating up two Asian Americans by saying, "I've just returned from Vietnam. I've gotten medals for killing 'gooks'!"

This brings us to the second effect that results from these stereotypes: the feeling that Asian Americans develop about themselves.

What happens to the Asian American who goes to school and learns nothing other than distortions about his people in America? Usually he will begin to reject his Asianness. He learns early in school that it doesn't mean much to be an Asian. What he does learn about Asians—that they were all cooks or farmers or laundrymen—will probably make him ashamed of his race. When he is stereotyped by other classmates and by his teacher, when he reads about the stereotyped Chinamen in his history book, and when he sees them on television, he begins to believe that his race is inferior to the white man's. He is thus confronted with an identity crisis. Initially he may feel he can resolve this crisis by striving harder and harder to become more "white-oriented." But he will eventually find that his Asian face and yellow skin will always betray his utmost desires to be Caucasian. He can never be accepted as anything other than what his looks represent to non-Asians.

The Struggle for Self-Determination

So the Asian American is met with a dilemma in which he must resolve his own feelings about himself. Many times he will find that, in order to be accepted by those forces external to him, he must first accept himself for whatever he is—as a person and as an Asian American.

In the last decade Asian Americans have begun to realize the effects that subtle and institutionalized racism have had on them. They see themselves and their Asian friends going through identity crisis, and they feel the tensions growing between their parents and themselves as they attempt to move away from their culture to become more "American." They also feel the emptiness of not really knowing anything about their own history and a great sadness when they see other Asians in America living in ghettos and doing menial jobs. The result of this awareness was the organization of Asian American youth on college campuses in the '60s.

Stimulated by the Black Power movements, they began to work for Asian studies programs and also toward bringing about an Asian awareness and identification.

The implementation of Asian studies on the college campuses represented an institutionalized effort toward creating an awareness of what it means to be an Asian in America. As the Asian student groups grew, many young Asian Americans came out of their isolated worlds in which they had found difficulty in expressing themselves and began to identify with other Asian Americans or foreign-born Asians. They found that they could solve their own problems by working collectively toward common goals, a common understanding and analysis of their problems, and a common struggle to educate other Asian American sisters and brothers.

As the students became more conscious of the problems of Asian Americans, they realized that a simple move for Asian identity and unity was not really enough. They began to see the problems within their own Asian communities: the atrocious housing conditions, the high unemployment rates, the bad health conditions, and the rising problems of the growing number of Asian immigrants coming into the United States every year. As they learned more about the oppression and exploitation earlier generations had experienced, they began to realize that the Asian American's position in America really had not changed since the early period of immigration.

The new age of ethnic emphasis that brought about the call for a "return to the community" had begun. College students began to fill the Chinatowns, Manilatowns, Little Tokyos, and other Asian ghettos with "community organizations" devoted to bettering the living, working, and educational conditions. But now they were met with a situation they had not anticipated in their eagerness to become good missionaries, compassionate social workers, or even revolutionary organizers within the community. Their looks, mannerisms, clothes, and language quickly proved to be foreign to that community. A large number of the students, being American-born, did not even know the language of the new immigrants and therefore could not relate to their needs.

Many of these students were from middle-class families, second- or third-generation Asians who grew up thinking that Chinatown or Little Tokyo or Manilatown were just "good places to eat dinner." How could they grasp the complexities of the problems of the foreign-born immigrant families? How could a college student who has been education-oriented all his life understand why a young immigrant cannot see the importance of going to school? Such questions could be resolved only through changes within their own firmly set thinking and had to be dealt with before they could attempt to communicate with the people they were so eager to help. The students soon began to realize that working in the community was not a matter of changing it according to an intellectual concept that had been formed through historical and analytical study. Instead it required change within themselves, new attitudes and approaches.

Such a change required a practical, grass-roots knowledge and understanding of that community. The Asian Americans are a diverse minority and therefore their problems are complex and numerous. Within the present trend of the new Asian

American movement, there is still a great amount of factionalism and dissonance. Different Asian student and community groups are approaching the problems in many divergent ways. Some are placing the emphasis on Asian American studies, others on studies of Asia, and still others on a cultural identification. Some groups are diligently working in the Asian ghettos, implementing social-service-type programs that leave the communities with nothing concrete when their programs end. There are, of course, other approaches by the intellectually elite, the revolutionaries, the social change organizations, and, of course, the conservative "don't-rock-the-boaters" and the "we-have-made-it" believers. But many Asian Americans remain disassociated from one another, and in their own separate struggles do not see the importance of the need for mass unity and strength in the realization of their common goals.

The real plight of the Asian American community can be solved only through the attainment of genuine and unified self-determination. The Asian Americans must be able to determine the future of their own communities. Only the Asian Americans themselves can ascertain correctly what they need, want, and will get for their communities. This can be accomplished only through the Asian Americans' struggle to seek answers to questions they have been asking for decades. They must learn for themselves the real nature of their problems. As in other colonized societies, frustrations caused by the system's oppression are manifested in violence within the community. This energy must be redirected toward an understanding of the external forces that oppress their communities, and toward the determination to change those external institutions to meet the needs of the Asian Americans.

Identity, Identification, and Initiative (Hebrews 11:23-28)

Paul M. Nagano

Introduction

Moses stood at the crossroads. He had to make a decision. Either he could continue to be called the "son of Pharoah's daughter" or identify himself with the oppressed minority—the Hebrew people.

All people are faced with this choice—with their quest for identity. Who am I? Where do I belong? Where am I going?

This quest is compounded as far as the Japanese American is concerned. The Japanese American has his historic roots in Japan; his facial appearance is different; he belongs to a very small and negligible minority in the United States— approximately half a million. Besides, he is inevitably identified with the nation of Japan in spite of his citizenship and cultural training, and the relationship between the United States and Japan is in a constant flux. If you do not believe this, one needs but reflect on the corralling of 117,000 Japanese aliens and citizens during World War II in concentration camps because of the overall sentiment that "a Jap's a Jap!"

So we ask, who are we (the Japanese Americans), and what is our role in American culture?

I. Moses Refused to Forfeit His Identity (v. 24)

Moses stood at the crossroads. He had to make a choice: to forget his Hebrew heritage and be absorbed into the Egyptian mainstream, or to affirm his identity as a Hebrew and be identified with the oppressed people. It was a very crucial and historic decision. It was not easy. It meant for him either wealth and fame as an Egyptian, or poverty and ill-treatment with the Hebrews. For the Japanese American it means to be absorbed into the mainstream of American life or to affirm one's identity as a Japanese American with its accompanying discriminations.

For Moses to be identified with the Egyptians and the Japanese American, to lose himself in the mainstream of American society. it means many things. It may possibly mean affluence—the mobility to rise upward in the economic and social world, but always according to the terms and dictates of the dominant majority. He can never be "top man." It means the loss of identity, i.e., absorption by the majority. It means manipulation (emasculation), complying to the terms of the dominant group, and assuming a subservient posture. In this connection the Japanese Americans have been labeled the "silent minority," or, according to Hosokawa, "the quiet Americans," with the posture of being docile, acquiescing to the dictates of the power structure. It means perpetuating the superior-inferior dichotomy with no leverage to change it and finding advancement only as the result of the kind graces of the majority. It means, on the whole, a poor image of oneself—inhibited, lacking confidence, and with an inferiority complex. Socio-psychologists are unanimous in declaring that persecuted people have a poor image of themselves—confirming the posture projected upon them by the majority. Lastly, it means a dehumanizing of the person, making it difficult for the Japanese American to realize the full potential as a person with all its strength and dignity as intended by God. Too often the Japanese American acts according to the expectations of others rather than act according to his own convictions and personhood.

On the other hand, what does it mean for Moses to identify himself with the oppressed Hebrews or the Japanese Americans to affirm his identity as a Japanese American? It means, first of all, discrimination. It means you are different from the majority—a unique minority. It probably means persecution, used by the dominant majority for their advantages. It means to "rock the boat" or to assert oneself is to invite the wrath of the majority, or in the case of Moses, the anger of pharaoh. But it does mean self-determination and self-esteem. It means a wholesome self-image and confidence. It means the dignity to be a real person, the fulfillment of his God-given rights.

Moses refused to forfeit his Hebrew identity—"choosing rather to suffer affliction with the people of God." I believe this gives us a Biblical basis for seeking one's identity in the racial or cultural family to which one is born. It means the biblical endorsement for the existence of the Japanese Baptist Church and the Asian American Baptist Caucus.

Directly after World War II, when the interned Japanese Americans were resettling, well-meaning sociologists and denominational leadership were advocating the doing away with the ethnic Japanese church and the assimilation of the Japanese into the existing non-Asian churches. They sincerely felt that the perpetuation of the ethnic church would hinder the integration of the Japanese into the mainstream of American life. As the result of this policy, Japanese Americans discontinued to attend the Protestant churches, while those who attended were lost or absorbed. No meaningful Japanese American leadership developed; the Buddhist churches experienced a resurgence (although they were forbidden to meet during the war); and the work among the Japanese Christians in America experienced a setback.

Two of our strongest American Baptist leaders, Dr. Jitsuo Morikawa and Dr. William Shinto, both advocated the dissolution of the ethnic Japanese church, have long since made a complete turnabout, and are now the strongest proponents of the ethnic Japanese church and the Asian American Baptist Caucus. They refuse to forfeit their identity as Japanese Americans and feel that this is the only viable strategy to bring about genuine personhood and mutuality among the Japanese minority and in American society.

The recently organized Asian American Baptist Caucus is the affirmation of the Japanese Americans of their identity as a unique people. If you please, "the people of God," or people accepting their full dignity as children of God. The Caucus is the affirmation of the Asians in America in being proud of their identity, unashamed of their heritage and physical identifications.

The Japanese Americans have a very meaningful identity. We have learned to endure suffering without retaliation. We have demonstrated the Japanese cultural virtue of *gaman* (enduring suffering without complaint). Our *Issei* parents quietly accepted the Japanese Exclusion Act of 1924, denying immigration into the US, the denial of citizenship to Japanese immigrants, the denial of the right to own land in the United States, and the denial of civil liberties by accepting indiscriminate and mass evacuation and internment without trial and due process of law. In response to these successive waves of injustice, we volunteered to fight for the country that placed us in concentration camps. The Pentagon records revealed that the 442nd was the most decorated unit in the United States Army in all US history.

Something of the pangs of discrimination got the best of me back in February 1943 when my brother was being sent overseas to be involved in the invasion within the Pacific arena, and he was not permitted to visit his mother or father in the Poston Relocation Center. There was the apparent possibility that he may not return, but army regulations would not permit him to enter into the restricted zone where the camp was located. But we were forced to "take it." Something of the Japanese culture of *shikataganai* (can't be helped, just accept it) helped us to accept the injustices and discriminations without bitterness and retaliation.

How well I remember working in the fruit stands and seeing college graduates, some with the master's degree, others with PhDs, accepting their inevitable lot of menial employment. I recently officiated at a funeral service of a graduate of the University of Washington who spent all his life as a gardener. He had no other alternative.

The Japanese American has a rich and noble heritage of which he can be proud. In our ecological concern today, we could learn much from the Japanese who have a distinct reverence for nature. In our culture of activity and verbosity, we can appreciate the strength in the quiet serenity of the Japanese. We can take pride in the beauty of humility and quiet modesty in contrast to the forward, self-assertive posture of Western civilization. There is much in the culture of our parents that can contribute to the enrichment of our comparative infant American culture.

In affirming our identity, we affirm that we are basically a child of God, and, in our Christian concept, "made in the image and likeness of God." We affirm that we have the right to be human, with all the prerogatives of fulfilling what it means to be human. We affirm as citizens of the United States with all the rights and privileges of citizenship, unhindered from the pursuit of life, liberty and happiness as prescribed by our Constitution.

As I seek my identity, as I ask, "Who am I?" I cast my lot with the Japanese Americans, as Moses did with the children of Israel, grateful to God for my rich and noble heritage, the ability to suffer without self-pity or complaint, acknowledging that I am a child of God, and rejoicing in the dignity that is mine as a person.

II. Moses Identified with the Oppressed (v. 25)

Moses stood at the crossroads: the path of the affluent majority or the oppressed minority. Moses chose to identify with the underdogs. Not only his identity as a part of the oppressed minority but identification with the experience and lot of this group.

Many Japanese Americans disassociate themselves with anything Japanese or the Japanese ethnic community because they feel that to identify with the Japanese is to hinder their upward mobility—socially and economically.

I want to pay tribute to the non-Japanese, particularly the Caucasians, who cast their lot with the oppressed minority. The beautiful biblical illustration of their witness is found in the story of Ruth and Naomi. Ruth was a Moabite married to one who came from Bethlehem. Her husband died and she was given the option to return to Moab, where there was food, or cast her lot with her husband's people, who were experiencing a famine. Ruth chose to identify with her husband's people and said to her mother-in-law, Naomi, "Entreat me not to leave you or to return from following you; for where you go I will go, and where you lodge I will lodge; your people shall be my people, and your God my God; where you die I will die, and there will I be buried" (Ruth 1:16–17). It is a tremendous witness and responsibility to cast your lot with the minority, and for the White it means to say in all sincerity, "White is beautiful, and Yellow is equally beautiful, and I cast my lot with the Yellow to make this equality a reality."

To identify with the underdog, I believe is the Christian stance. This is confirmed in the initiative of Yahweh (God) in identifying Himself with the people in bondage as He appeared unto Moses and said, "I have observed you and what has been done to you in Egypt; and I promise that I will bring you up out of the affliction of Egypt, to the land of the Canaanites," etc. (Exodus 3:16–17). The Bible affirms that God has observed what has been done through prejudice and discrimination by the dominant group; that God identifies with them and promises to bring them out of their affliction—the affliction of inhuman treatment.

The Bible affirms that Jesus's work is essentially one of liberation. Becoming a slave himself, he opens realities of human existence formerly closed to humanity. Through encounter with Jesus, humankind now knows the full meaning of God's action in history of liberation and justice. In Christ, God enters human affairs and takes sides with the oppressed. Their suffering becomes his; their despair, divine despair, God's word of righteousness to the oppressed is, "I know the meaning of rejection because in Christ I was rejected; I know the meaning of physical pain because I was crucified; I know the meaning of death because I died; I know the meaning of loneliness because I was despised and rejected of humans, but my resurrection in Christ means I am present with you and that alien powers cannot keep from you the full meaning of life."

This then means identification with all oppressed people—all who are hurting because of the injustices and inequalities of life, be it Black, Chicano, Native American, or the poor.

The Asian Caucus provides the rallying point with which we can identify with the oppressed minority and create a vehicle to identify with all other oppressed people.

III. Moses Took the Initiative to Oppose the Power Structure (vv. 26–27)

Moses stood at the crossroads. He had to decide whether he should identify with God's purpose in opposition to the world standards or comply with the power structure. Moses dared to take the initiative to oppose the power structure. Here is where real faith is manifested. Real faith has the courage to oppose any structure that destroys love and justice. It was Luther who said, "The stronger work of love is to destroy what is against love." And more recently, the late Paul Tillich wrote, "Love wants to destroy what is against love." In order to do this, there is need for power. This is the rationale for the initiation and organization of the Caucus. Love, Christian love, insists the power be established to bring about love, justice, and equality to all people. Without the Caucus, there is no leverage, no voice that can be heard, no strategy for self-affirmation and equitable balance of power. Because of the nature of man, two kinds of power structures are necessary for any viable human social organization, a central organizing power and some institutional form of the balance of power.

The Caucus makes possible representation on the various decision-making bodies of our denomination, the determination of our own ministries and strategies of service, and the dignity of being treated as mature intelligent persons. It is not social expediency but the Christian faith that is the basis for the Caucus.

Moses was motivated by faith to identify with the oppressed Hebrews—the people of God; it was by faith he opposed the power structure—the Egyptians; it was by faith he led the people across the Red Sea.

Someone asked what's the difference between the Asian American Baptist Caucus and any other secular caucus. The basic difference is that the Asian Baptist Caucus is motivated by faith—by God and his purpose for the liberation of man.

Conclusion

A group of slaves were chained together and marched off to be transported by a slave ship. They were all depressed and resigned except for one slave. He was erect, dignified, and defiant. One slave master asked, "Why is he so different?" Then the answer came. "Don't you know, he's the child of the king, and he can't forget it!"

No matter how oppressed and discriminated we are, we need not resign to the status quo. We cannot be manipulated, emasculated, dehumanized by the power structure—the dominant majority. We are children of the King of kings; we have a heritage of which we can be very proud; we are human beings, and don't you forget it!

The Japanese Americans' Search for Identity, Ethnic Pluralism, and a Christian Basis of Permanent Identity*

Paul M. Nagano

Chapter V
The Ministry of the Japanese American Protestant Church in the Pluralistic Strategy

At the close of World War II, after the internment of over 117,000 Japanese Americans in concentration camps, it was the policy of almost every major Protestant denomination that there should be no more segregated Japanese ethnic congregations. Every effort was made to assimilate the Japanese Americans into the churches of their choice. But due to the unpreparedness of the established churches and the insecure hesitation of the Japanese Americans, the prewar pattern of small denominational ethnic churches was developed again.

Since then, several denominations have gradually closed their ethnic churches or merged them with neighboring churches of the same denomination. Others were encouraged to integrate In the churches of their residence. The Japanese Methodist Provisional Conference was dissolved and amalgamated into the regular larger Methodist Conference. Several churches have merged, with the consequences unfavorable for the ethnic members and ministers. Roy Sano, one of the Japanese American Methodist ministers, wrote,

> When two Japanese churches were merged in Northern California, the Japanese ministers understood both of them must move, and they did. When a Japanese and a Caucasian church merged in the same conference, the Caucasian man stayed and the Japanese was appointed elsewhere. What explains the disparity, especially when the Japanese ministers involved in the mergers were told that it was an unwritten policy to move both men in such cases? The explanation ought to be given in public, even in print, since it is a matter which has been discussed in the Japanese community. The explanation will receive careful scrutiny, since the explanation offered informally has not proved convincing.[1]

---

* A dissertation presented to the faculty of the School of Theology at Claremont, in partial fulfillment of the requirements for the degree Doctor of Religion, June 1970.

[1] Roy I. Sano, "The Church: One, Holy, Catholic, and Apostolic" (paper, National Consultation of Japanese Work of the United Methodist Church, San Francisco, CA, February 3–4, 1969), 14. [*Ed. note: See p. 233 in this volume.*]

Since the dissolution of the Methodist Provisional Conference, conversations have opened again, initiated by the ethnic group to reconsider the establishment of a structure similar to the Provisional Conference. Sano suggests an Ethnic Ministries Committee on the level of the Division of National Missions with specific assignment to churches in the Western Jurisdiction that were members of the Provisional or Mission Conferences.[2] Since 1960, twenty-three Japanese ethnic ministers have sought employment in non-church vocations or have left the ethnic church, while five of the Japanese ethnic churches in California are led by Caucasian ministers.

The American Baptist Convention also has closed several of the ethnic Japanese churches, while in cases of merger, the Japanese ministers have quietly left the ethnic churches to seek employment elsewhere.

Only the indigenous Japanese conferences, such as the Japanese Free Methodist Conference and the OMS Holiness Conference of America, have evidenced a somewhat healthy continuity and clear direction.

On the whole, there has been a decided ambivalence as to the future of the Japanese Protestant church in America, and as a result, the churches have been experiencing little or no growth, and the *Sansei* are not considering any church-related vocations. With the general disinterest In institutional religion throughout the country, the ambiguity about the future of the ethnic church has undoubtedly discouraged the *Sansei* in terms of the Christian ministry.

The position of this study stresses the need that the Japanese ethnic church be no longer ambiguous about its future by affirming itself in the pluralistic strategy. Instead of listening and obeying their "white fathers," this investigation will attempt to give an articulate rationale for the pluralistic approach for the Japanese American Protestant church in America.

Indigenous Initiative

Following the theses of ethnic identity and ethnic pluralism, we now see this strategy in terms of the Japanese Protestant church. The Japanese Americans have now come of age and must begin to make their own decisions. The "silent minority" posture of patiently acquiescing to authority, in this case, to the dictates of the denominational policies must be supplanted by indigenous initiative and courage, As Roy Sano pointed out,

> A minority appointed to prestigious positions should be given power to participate in the decision-making processes. Otherwise, he only becomes a decoration or *kazari-mono*. Certainly, the next district superintendent in Hawaii should be an ethnic minority.
>
> Our cultural heritage has told us that the eyes of the world are upon us and that we should therefore keep our best foot forward. Those who expressed them to the proper authority were reprimanded by their own kind. It was a kind of vigilante committee which saw to it that shame was not brought upon our name. That kind of stance won

---

[2] Sano, "The Church: One, Holy, Catholic, and Apostolic," 11. [*Ed. note: See p. 231–232 in this volume.*]

acceptance, at the expense of integrity. The time has come to deepen the acceptance and to authenticate the depth of our commitment to each other.[3]

As repeated once too often, the "don't rock the boat" posture gave the institutional security and created the "organizational man."

It is refreshing to know that all denominational leadership was not insensitive to the pluralistic strategy, although their voices were muffled in the postwar assimilation enthusiasm. The former executive secretary of the Los Angeles Baptist City Mission Society, Dr. Ralph L. Mayberry, in speaking of "The Future of the Ethnic Church," stated,

> Today, one idealism and ideology has its followers, who pose as the standard makers supreme in contemporary life. They are willing to kill the patient to try out a theory. They are propagandists. While the church loses her life, they would kill the so-called ethnic church to create something that is just as ethnic as anything that they think is ethnic. And so the church loses its life, loses its identity, becomes unnecessary, and becoming nothing, disappears in weakness.
>
> This idea is not new. At the time of the evacuation in 1942, the prominent Christian leaders in America were saying of one ethnic group, the Japanese Church, "Never again." "It must be assimilated," Now, what does that mean? That means it must be a part of something else. It must lose its identity to help the others. Now I want to say to you that anyone who tries to assimilate me is going to have the worst case of indigestion of which I've ever heard. I am not assimilable. I am an individual by the grace of God. And back in those days when the leaders (prominent denominational leaders) were saying, "Never again, never again shall we have a Japanese church," there was a man by the name of Mayberry, not even 80 years old then, who fought for the principles that the Japanese, or any other group, must have the right of self-determination. They must have the privilege to determine for themselves as to what they were, and what they wanted to be, and what they would be. And so I say, with some emotion, I have too large an investment in this whole ethnic idea to be a theorist of the popular type and surrender my friends or any group to the gas chamber of anonymity and oblivion.[4]

Most clergymen and even Christian social scientists and ethicists have been looking so intensely at the evils of segregation that they overlooked the deeper level of self-affirmation and the dignity of personhood, A good example of this is found in Kyle Haselden's *The Racial Problem in Christian Perspective.*[5] Perhaps it had an important role at the time it was published, in 1959 during the heat of the battle for civil rights.

Indigenous initiative calls for some serious research within the ethnic group for the development of a solid strategy for the pluralistic stance and the courage of decision. For the ethnic church it means the development of an indigenous theology.

---

[3] Sano, "The Church: One, Holy, Catholic, and Apostolic," 13. [*Ed. note: See p. 233 in this volume.*]

[4] Ralph L. Mayberry, "The Future of the Ethnic Church" (lecture, Evergreen Baptist Church, Los Angeles, CA, March 3, 1968), 5.

[5] Kyle Haselden, *The Racial Problem in Christian Perspective* (New York: Harper & Row, 1959).

Indigenous Theology

Indigenous theology, strictly speaking, has to do with the nature of God and his will in terms of a certain region or country. Here, we believe it is proper in thinking of "region" as one's position of existence. Hence, it could be anywhere, and every theology can be indigenous. But the other question is it legitimate to do this? Is not theology universal, and is not cultural isolation a thing of the past? My argument is that theology to be real has to be indigenous, for it cannot operate in a vacuum and must develop experiences. We cannot help but reflect upon God from our own setting. In this sense, theology cannot be left to professional theologians isolated in seminaries and corners of the universities; it must be hammered out in the encounters of life.

A good example of indigenous theology is seen in "Black Theology," Black Christian theologians are relating Christianity to the pain of being black in a white racist society. According to Cone,

> The task of Black Theology is to analyze the black man's condition in the light of God's revelation in Jesus Christ with the purpose of creating a new understanding of black dignity among black people, and providing the necessary soul in that people, to destroy white racism.[6]

Indigenous theology for the Japanese Americans is a theology that must speak to and for the Japanese Americans in their situation.

The authority of indigenous theology is the authority of one's experience in relation to the nature of God. An indigenous theology for the Japanese Americans is based on the authority of the Japanese American experience, it is adequate and practical as it is adequate, and meaningful for the Japanese American where he is. It is authentic in whatever way it is true to biblical primitive Christianity and not necessarily Western Christianity. To evaluate its authenticity, we can adopt Whitehead's three tools for evaluation in his *Religion in the Making*: 1) a logical coherence, 2) adequacy, and 3) exemplification.[7] The adequacy and exemplification of the Japanese American indigenous theology can be validated by its universal application—from the particular to the universal. An illustration of this can be the experience of Israel in the Old Testament and its universal application.

One more thought to legitimize indigenous theology is the understanding that theology is hermeneutic, for it consists of translating the Bible into the word for today. The new hermeneutic deals not only with the interpretation of biblical documents but also, as a theological position, with the reinterpretation of prior theological formulation, invoking the same principle applied in biblical interpretation, namely, that it is not the text itself which is to be interpreted but the intention or experience which gave rise to the text. The emphasis of the new hermeneutic is on meaning rather than on interpretation, although it includes the whole task of exegesis, interpretation, and reinterpretation of the historic documents

---

[6] James H. Cone, *Black Theology and Black Power* (New York: Seabury Press, 1969), 117.

[7] Alfred North Whitehead, *Religion in the Making* (New York: Macmillan, 1926), 88–89.

of the church, particularly the Bible. When we direct our energies to interpreting the biblical text, the text comes to interpret us in our situation. The text becomes the subject of interpretation rather than simply remaining an object to be interpreted. "The text is there not for its own sake but for the sake of the word-event that is both the origin and the future of the text. Word-event includes interpretation which takes place through the word; the text is there for the sake of the event of interpretation, The Word that once occurred, and in occurring became the text, must become interpreting word with the help of the text."[8]

Tillich, in his book *Biblical Religion and the Search for Ultimate Reality,* reinforces the legitimacy for indigenous theology in terms of the reception of revelation:

> Revelation is never revelation in general, however universal its claim may be. It is always revelation for someone and for a group in a definite environment, under unique circumstances. Therefore, he who receives revelation witnesses to it in terms of his individuality and in terms of the social and spiritual conditions in which the revelation has been manifested to him. In other words, he does it in terms of his religion.[9]

One major criticism of such a theology of hermeneutics is that this existentialist position is essentially subjective and is prone to take on various shades of interpretation depending on one's cultural situation. However, this is just the point, the real significance of interpretation emphasizes the ultimate and decisive existence of the hearer of the proclamation—calling him to an existential faith. Historical research, employing all the tools of biblical research, understands itself as serving the final task of proclamation and existential faith.

The need for an indigenous theology among the Japanese American Protestants is for a solid united base from which they can develop a meaningful direction and destiny. It is the responsibility of the Christian leadership to develop this theology and lead their people and the total ethnic community to the promised land. Without this, we can only expect confusion, fragmentation, loss of identity, and eventual dehumanization. This is the prophetic task for the ethnic leadership of the Protestant churches. The destiny and humanness of the Japanese American community seeks for such leadership at this crucial juncture in history.

The indigenous theologian will be faced with the task of what it means to be an ethnic man—the problem of identity and being a person. He will have to discover what God is doing in the world and to rally around to further his intentions. His task will include the demythologizing of Christ from America to make him truly universal—Christ must be freed from the "system," including religious institutions and what might be called the "Protestant ethic." This could mean, in God's providence, a corrective instrument to bring about repentance, purity, and humanness to a myopic Christianity.

---

[8] Edward W. Uthe, *Theology: An Assessment of Current Trends* (Philadelphia: Fortress, 1968), 59.

[9] Paul Tillich, *Biblical Religion and the Search for Ultimate Reality* (Chicago: University of Chicago Press, 1955), 3–4.

Primarily, the responsibility of indigenous theology is to bring the ethnic man to find his essential identity in relation to his Creator, to clarify the meaning of persons, of community, of love, and of history for the ethnic community and through it to all humans.

Content of Indigenous Theology

It is difficult for Western theology to take seriously the experience of the oppressed. The experiences of the oppression, and the subsequent exodus, and the hope of the promised land has existential meaning for oppressed people.

Indigenous Japanese American theology takes seriously the experience of the oppressed, since it is so close to their own experience of prejudice and evacuation into the wilderness. It is characterized by the belief that God identifies with people that are oppressed, even as Yahweh appeared to Moses.

> God said to Moses, "Say this to the people of Israel, 'The LORD, the God of your fathers, the God of Abraham, the God of Isaac, and the God of Jacob, has sent me to you:' this is my name for ever, and thus I am to be remembered throughout all generations, God and gather the elders of Israel together, and say to them, 'The LORD, the God of your fathers, the God of Abraham, of Isaac, and of Jacob, has appeared to me, saying, I have observed you and what has been done to you in Egypt; and I promise that I will bring you up out of the affliction of Egypt, and to the land of the Canaanites, the Hittites, the Amorites, the Perizzites, the Hivites, and the Jebusites, a land flowing with milk and honey" (Exod. 3:15–17).

Japanese American theology affirms that God has observed what has been done to them through prejudice and discrimination by the dominant group; that God has promised to bring them out of their affliction—the affliction of inhuman treatment. It means for them that God was with them during the exodus in the wilderness, the captivity, and is responsible for the "milk and honey" they are experiencing now.

It affirms, with Black theology, that Jesus' work is essentially one of liberation. Becoming a slave himself, he opens realities of human existence formerly closed to man. Through encounter with Jesus, man now knows the full meaning of God's action in history and man's place within it. Jesus uses the prophetic words of Isaiah to outline his own style of action:

> The Spirit of the Lord is upon me,
> because he has anointed me to preach the good news to the poor. He has sent
>   me to proclaim release to the captives
> and recovering of sight to the blind,
> To set at liberty those who are oppressed,
> To proclaim the acceptable year of the Lord (Luke 4:18).

It means identification with the oppressed wherever they are, and whoever they are. It means setting the racist captives free also.

Joseph Washington writes:

> It is my thesis, however, that Black Power, even in its most radical expression, is not an antithesis of Christianity, nor is it a heretical idea to be tolerated with painful forbearance.

It is rather Christ's central message to twentieth-century America. And unless the empirical denominational Church makes a determined effort to recapture the Man Jesus through a total identification with the suffering poor as expressed in Black Power, that Church will become exactly what Christ is not.[10]

James Cone asserts that nothing less than the church's faithfulness to its Lord is at stake, stating that "obedience to Christ is always costly."

> The time has come for the Church to challenge the power-structure with the power of the *Gospel* knowing that nothing less than *immediate* and *total* emancipation of all people is consistent with the message and style of Jesus Christ. The Church cannot afford to deplore the means which oppressed people use to break the chains of slavery because such language not only clouds the issue but also gives comfort and assistance to the oppressor.[11]

Oppression theology of the Japanese American calls for involvement with all oppressed people in their struggle against the oppressor. It means social concern, politics, confrontation, and the cross.

Indigenous theology means the dignity of all human creatures made in the likeness of God (Genesis 1–2). Man created in God's image was meant to be a son, not a bondservant under a law or under another man. It claims nothing more than the elemental biological identity of all human beings. Paul declares the elemental physical kinship of all men has to do with the unity and solidarity of all mankind biologically and religiously.

> And he made from one every nation of men to live on the face of the earth, having determined allotted periods and the boundaries of their habitation (Acts 17:26).

In the Japanese ethnic theology it means, first of all, an appreciation and respect of his God-given heritage and being thankful to God for his Japanese ancestry. Secondly, it means seeking the humanness of all people. This naturally leads to the Christian's duty to destroy any attempt at dehumanization, whether it be racism or technology.

As Morikawa states in addressing the Seattle Japanese Baptist Church,

> The Japanese Americans were bowing their heads to the majority and being grateful to the establishment, instead of being grateful to their Creator, God, in whose image they were created. The Japanese Americans were destroying the image of God by making themselves subservient beings and inviting their share of psychosocial "hang-ups."[12]

This leads to a theological implication of God's sovereignty. To maintain the superior-inferior posture is to deny the sovereignty of God, for it assumes bowing to man and destroying the beauty and dignity of manhood in oneself; of failing to love one's neighbor as oneself (Luke 10:26–27).

---

[10] Joseph R. Washington Jr., *Black and White Power Subreption* (Boston: Beacon Press, 1969), 144.

[11] James H. Cone, "Christianity and Black Power," in *Is Anybody Listening to Black America?*, ed. C. Eric Linchon (New York: Seabury Press, 1968), 4.

[12] Jitsuo Morikawa, "Freedom Under God," *JEMS Journal* (June 1969): 2.

The content of Japanese American theology is a theology of love that must seek to deal realistically with the evil and injustice in the world, and not merely to compromise with them. Thomas Merton understands this struggle as he proposes,

> Such a theology will have to take note of the ambiguous realities of politics, without embracing the specious myth of a "realism" that merely justifies force in the service of established power. Theology does not exist merely to appease the already too untroubled conscience of the power and the established. A theology of love may also conceivably turn out to be a theology of revolution. In any case, it is a theology of resistance, a refusal of the evil that reduces a brother to homicidal desperation.[13]

There is a danger in America today to lose one's "cool" in the midst of the revolution. The theology of revolution calls for the Christian leadership to be the prophetic community to warn against the overt demands of revolutionaries. It calls for the church to be the "suffering servants" as the agents of reconciliation.

It is difficult to agree with Washington when he says, "in a society in which hatred of Negroes is the dominant ethos, the most healthy response is hatred of whites by Negroes."[14] One can understand that to "keep turning one's cheek" is unhealthy for both the hater and the one hated. But to return hate for hate is to perpetuate hate. Although I do not wholly agree with Merton, there is a great deal of insight in his reasoning:

> The reason for emphasizing non-violent resistance is this: he who resists force with force in order to seize power may become contaminated by the evil which he is resisting and, when he gains power, may be just as ruthless and unjust a tyrant as the one he has dethroned. A non-violent victory, while far more difficult to achieve, stands a better chance of curing the illness instead of contracting it.[15]

I return again to my jiu-jitsu strategy suggested previously. The ethnic theology of love means to be trained in the art of political jiu-jitsu to infiltrate the racist society with a positive footing in one's own identity and using the strength and weight of the stronger opponent to bring about change. Instead of hatred and power, the theology of love calls for a strategy of love and power that brings about justice.

Tillich wrote, "love must destroy what is against love, but not him who is the bearer of that which is against love."[16] And with Luther, "Sweetness, self-surrender, and mercy are the proper work of love, bitterness, killing, and condemnation are its strong work, but both are works of love."[17] What Luther means is that it is the stronger works of love to destroy what is against love. This, however, presupposes the unity of love and power. "In order to destroy what is against love, love must be united with power, and not only with power, but also with compulsory power.... The criterion is: Everything that makes reunion impossible is against

---

[13] Thomas Merton, *Faith and Violence* (South Bend, IN: University of Notre Dame Press, 1968), 9.

[14] Joseph R. Washington Jr., *The Politics of God* (Boston: Beacon Press, 1967), 28.

[15] Merton, *Faith and* Violence, 12.

[16] Tillich, *Biblical Religion*, 114.

[17] Tillich, *Biblical Religion*, 20.

love."[18] Thus, it tries to save and fulfill the person that destroys by destroying in him what is against love. The theology of love that seeks to have all people come together as equals and therefore refuses to speak of love without justice and power is the meaning of love in indigenous theology.

Christian hope is also an affirmation of indigenous theology, and is not merely an eschatological longing for escape to a transcendent reality, but it is to be realized here and now for the Japanese Americans as it is for the Blacks. It is a theology of hope that believes that God uses history to make his eternal and holy purpose of redemption actual. That history is real, and this hope is for this life. It means it refuses to embrace any concept of God that makes the suffering of the oppressed as the will of God and hope in the hereafter as the reward for the suffering. It means that God is interested and involved in history. Ethnic theology relates eschatology to history, that is, to what God has done, is doing, and will do for his people. It is only because of what God is now doing in history that we can speak meaningfully of the future.

As Moltmann in his *Theology of Hope* argues,

> Eschatology does not mean merely salvation of the soul, individual rescue from the evil world, comfort for the troubled conscience, but also the realization of the eschatological hope of justice, the humanizing of man, the socializing of humanity, peace for all creation.[19]

Indigenous theology hopes for a new day to dawn for the Japanese Americans and for all people—a day when there will be no need for false identities and dehumanizing existence; a society in which people can affirm their true personhood and live together in solidarity in spite of plurality. But, I might add, not without tension and the tragedy of life and history.

Theological Perspective for Pluralism

The story of the tower of Babel in Genesis 11 presents a good perspective for an interpretation of pluralism. Arend van Leeuwen explains,

> This story may be characterized as a repetition of Paradise story in the setting of world history. Unity and plurality are the ends of the axis on which the story turns. The whole earth was one people, and they united their efforts in building the temple tower, the religious center of Babylonic society and a universal symbol of what I have called elsewhere the "ontocratic pattern" which underlies the great civilizations of Asia. This united human attempt to link heaven and earth is revealed as original sins and is judged by the Lord. Mankind is scattered over the face of the earth; and the city, with its tower, is left deserted, a symbol of frustration and disorder.[20]

Prior to this account, we find in Genesis 10 the so-called "table of nations." It related the proliferation of people under the providence of God. It results in the

---

[18] Tillich, *Biblical Religion*, 50.

[19] Jurgen Moltmann, *Theology of Hope*, trans. J. W. Leitch (New York: Harper & Row, 1967), 21.

[20] Arend Theodore van Leeuwen, *Christianity in World History: The Meeting of the Faiths of East and West* (London: S.M.C. Press, 1964), 165.

nations, tongues, and peoples. One point is clear: There is a diversity or plurality with God's providence.

Paul Verghese of India tells us that the concept of "pluralism" comes, for the Christian, not from social experience, but rather from the doctrine of the Holy Spirit and the Incarnation. He states,

> It is methodologically important to start our Christian social thinking from these two fundamental realities of the Christian faith (Holy Spirit and Incarnation) rather than from the Old Testament doctrines of the call of Abraham or the "history of salvation." Underlying these twin doctrines of the Incarnation and the Holy Spirit is the fundamental concept of "freedom in love."[21]

He argues "in a genuinely pluralistic human society there can be no imposition of religious or political views by fiat, instead of loving persuasion."[22] As an Easterner, he states, "The tragedy of eastern theology is precisely its development in an essentially homogeneous society. It is to be hoped that as pluralism develops in the West and the Western church is thrown into a pluralistic world community, it will clarify its wisdom thus to the benefit of the whole world."[23] From this argument, the conclusion is that there is meaning in variety and pluralism, that the highest expression of maturity, mutuality, and humanization is the recognition of the unique distinctions among people and yet to experience a solidarity within these distinctions. It means also that the church needs opposition and external criticism in order to be faithful to its calling, and God sees, therefore, to have decreed that the church can find true wisdom only in a pluralistic society.

Professor Hough, in summary, justifies pluralism as necessary for a more equitable balance of power in the political arena. He argues from Niebuhr's Christian understanding of man as sinner—man's pride and desire for power that leads man to believe that he is the master of his own faith, and the pride of power that manifests itself as the lust for power based on insecurity—that two kinds of power structures are necessary for any viable human social organization, a central organizing power and some institutional form of the balance of power.

In speaking of the Black-White power struggle, Hough writes:

> The white Christian, then, more than any other white man, should understand the attempt on the part of Negro leaders to achieve a better balance of power. Knowing that men are sinners, the Christian also knows that sin must be restrained. And knowing that sin must be restrained, he should also support attempts to make that restraint possible.[24]

Another reason, simply presented here, for the support of pluralism, and in the case of Professor Hough, the Negro pluralism, is that, "It reaches into the whole claim the Negroes are making for the right to live a life that is more fully human than the

---

[21] Paul Verghese, "Secular Society or Pluralistic Community?" in *Man in Community*, ed. Egbert de Vries (New York: Association Press, 1966), 364–365.

[22] Verghese, "Secular Society or Pluralistic Community?" 366.

[23] Verghese, "Secular Society or Pluralistic Community?" 366.

[24] Joseph C. Hough Jr., *Black Power and White Protestants* (London: Oxford University Press, 1968), 135.

caste system will allow."[25] In spite of Paul Lehmann's excellent *koinonia* ethics that support desegregation in order that men can be together, Hough states this answer does not take seriously the need for Negro pluralism for their own identity, humanization, and dignity.[26]

There is a need for more study by the indigenous theologian in this whole area, but this will suffice to show that pluralism is consonant with Christianity.

We now deal with the more practical aspects of the Japanese American Protestant church's ministry in the pluralistic strategy.

Leadership in Ethnic Community

Significantly, the Black Power movement—the pluralistic strategy of the Negroes in America—is dominated by the Protestant ministers of the Black church. One can confidently say, the main thrust of the movement is inspired by Protestant leadership.

In the Japanese American community, that numbers less than half a million in the United States; the Japanese American Protestant church can and should assume the prophetic leadership for the total community. Thus far, there has been no meaningful crusade in which the total Japanese community has been involved. In the Los Angeles area, the Noguchi fight against the Los Angeles County Administration, was the first indication of community cooperation. However, there has been no nationwide strategy or united ethnic concern.

The ethnic Protestant community has many charismatic leaders, although Burma and Meredith indicated a lack of such leadership.[27] These gifted leaders have been scattered in isolated places throughout the country, and out of touch with the ethnic community and their problems. Because of their talents and leadership, they have found their places in the dominant organizations and are in favored positions. There are many who like the "Black bourgeoisie" of which Frazier speaks have become isolated from their own cultural traditions.[28]

Adding to the atomization of leadership, the ethnic community is divided into many camps with their own generals. It is difficult to develop a united ethnic strategy. The summary given by Kitano regarding the Japanese ethnic community, and its development and structure, is applicable to the Protestant scene:

> Long-range goals were not formulated with much clarity, but the hostility, discrimination, and prejudice with which the Japanese were faced did much to foster internal cohesion. Group structure was usually simple, role positions were explicit, and the community groups had considerable meaning for the members. The cohesion of the whole community was reinforced by the fact that most individuals belonged to several of the

---

[25] Hough, *Black Power and White Protestants*, 136.

[26] Hough, *Black Power and White Protestants*, 144.

[27] John Burma, "Current Leadership Problems among Japanese Americans," *Sociological and Social Research* 37 (1953): 157–163; Gerald M. Meredith and Connie G. W. Meredith, "Acculturation and Personality among Japanese American College Students in Hawaii," *Journal of Social Psychology* 68 (1966): 175–182.

[28] E. Franklin Frazier, *Black Bourgeoisie* (New York: Collier, 1957), 141.

organizations within it. The primary leadership skill was therefore an ability to approach and handle different groups correctly.[29]

Articulating the Pluralistic Strategy

As the prophetic community, the Japanese ethnic church has the responsibility to make clear the pluralistic strategy to the whole ethnic community. The Christian leadership has the task of articulating to their people this strategy for their positive identity and the context for their moral, cultural, political, and human advancement within the limits set by the American scene.

The ethnic church is called to help its community become consciously aware of its identity as a group in America—their common situation as a people. The church should lead its people to strive together to redeem their community in order to insure their human dignity.

All movements need an identifying symbol around which they can rally. I am suggesting this strategy be called the "AI power" strategy, the initials "AI" for "Asian identity." Even more significant for the Christians is the word *ai* which means "love" in the Japanese language. The large Asian umbrella is used to widen the power structure to include all Asians, each with their unique identification references. In the *Pacific Citizen*, weekly organ of the JACL (Japanese American Citizens League), the March 20, 1970, editorial read,

> JACL may well be the Asian American organization of tomorrow—if it so chooses, JACL may have to change its name to make that leap—if it is required. Or it may be instrumental in establishing an all-embracing federation of Asian American groups, enabling each entity to retain its original identity.[30]

The Japanese ethnic church presents itself ideally for leadership in the AI power strategy for several reasons. First, it is an indigenous organization with indigenous leadership and has a positive concern for the humanness of its people. Its high calling under God is to minister for the highest welfare of their community.

Second, the Japanese ethnic church provides the most viable corps of dedicated leadership for participation and belonging, the clergy representing, on the whole, a well-educated and recognized leadership in the community.

Third, the ethnic churches are now independent and are mature enough to break away from Caucasian denominational dominance. This will take courage on the part of both the ethnic church and the mother denominations, but it will be for the health of the whole.

As mentioned before, the plurality of denominations is not to be condemned. The constant image of white leadership and control has impeded the initiative of the ethnic church. Independence from the denomination, except for fraternal ties, will increase the leadership initiative and authority for the group. Denominational assimilation and organizational ambition has hindered the growth of ethnic

---

[29] Harry H. L. Kitano, *Japanese Americans: The Evolution of a Subculture* (Englewood Cliffs, NJ: Prentice-Hall, 1969), 96.

[30] Harry K. Honda, "Ye Editor's Desk," *Pacific Citizen*, March 20, 1970, 6.

leadership due to misdirection from local ethnic needs. The Protestant clergy can become the spokesmen for the AI power strategy in this period of identity crisis.

Last, the ethnic church has had the longest continuity of any organization in the Japanese community. The Buddhist churches did not organize until the turn of the century, while the Japanese Protestant churches in America date back to 1877. From the earliest years, the ethnic church was the helper of the needy and the unfortunate and the interpreter of the signs of the times.

With clarity of strategy and destiny, the ethnic church is in position to lead the Japanese community as they are confronted with their survival in terms of identity and dignity or with their decision to plunge into the "melting pot" of anonymity within the stream of American society.

Role of Change Agent

The heart of theology has always been conversion—the changing of individuals, society, and culture from man's deification of himself to the Kingdom of God. As long as things are not right, there needs to be a revolution. Jesus came proclaiming "the Kingdom of God is at hand," Jesus knew God as the present active reality, and he lived and spoke out of the immediacy of this reality. The presence of Jesus and the presence of the Kingdom of God meant revolution and repentance, and the church as an agent of change is called to lead this revolution.

Revolution means change. It means repentance and conversion, and the Christians, in whom the Holy Spirit is operative, are part of the revolutionary force. It is important to understand the church as a revolutionary force responsible for the changing of society instead of the private stance of the church that is so prevalent today. The church is called to translate the gospel to the political arena—called to change individuals, institutions, and culture. As described in Paul Lehmann's *Ethics In a Christian Context*, if a man is a Christian, he is somehow already part of God's political activity in the world, consisting of doing all those things for making life more human. If a man is a Christian, he is already part of this ethical reality, and he is free to do what he ought to do in participating in God's activity in the world, in the creation of the conditions of human life by which human fulfillment is really possible.[31] It does not merely mean a change of heart in the sense of religious conversion; it means a change of racism and anything in our culture that reinforces this dehumanization.

Changes occur as the result of social processes that are constantly taking place. "Sociologists usually identify four or five separate processes—cooperation, competition, conflict, accommodation, and assimilation—"[32] to bring about social change.

In the struggle for true humanness in society, the first logical step is the formulation of a power structure as political leverage to change the superior-inferior

---

[31] Paul Lehmann, *Ethics in a Christian Context* (New York: Harper & Row, 1963), 45.

[32] Lyle E. Schaller, *Community Organization: Conflict and Reconciliation* (Nashville: Abingdon, 1966), 36.

system in American life—the task that Lewis M. Killian describes as *The Impossible Revolution*?

> After years of racial crisis we are brought to a grim realization of how deeply the roots of racism have extended into American society. The racial problem grows not out of the soil of individual prejudice, but out of the very social structure itself. No matter how much White Americans may deplore the cruder forms of discrimination and the more obvious consequences of prejudice, they are not likely to make the sacrifices needed to change the fact that America is still a white man's society.[33]

Four areas of influence are strategic in applying this power leverage for social change: 1) politics, 2) education, 3) economics, and 4) communications.

Politically, clear-thinking Christian leadership is needed for research and direction, implementing the power leverage for change. Where, when, and how pressure is to be applied should be clearly defined. Dialogue, legislation, and political penetration will have to be properly carried out. Political leadership among the minorities will have to be encouraged and groomed as a part of the overall strategy.

Educationally, the administration, faculty, and curriculum planning can be well represented by knowledgeable minorities to give an honest and clear picture of the world and national history as well as other subjects of image-making. Cultural pride of all ethnic groups can flood the curriculum to enhance a pluralistic society of equal appreciation and respect. The images developed in the student generation are of crucial consequence. As mentioned before, Asian studies can become a regular part of the college curriculum.

Economic opportunity should be provided for all the minorities, with special emphasis on executive positions. The development of the Negro executive under whom white Americans are willing to work can be a strong boost toward Negro pride and democratic loyalty. It is significant, in this connection, that the Negro bishops and denominational officers are being appointed and elected throughout the country within various major denominations. The change is gradually coming about.

Communications has seen a tremendous advancement recently, especially in the field of television. Through television commercials and regular series, the Negro, Mexican, and the Asian have been portrayed in a very wholesome light. Improvement can yet be made in terms of the Native American, who is often viewed as inferior to the white Americans.

Great strides have been made since the end of World War II, and patience is proposed in working out a strategy for the overall, long-range goals. The adult generation cannot be greatly changed. The student generation is developing a much healthier image of other minorities in America. With controlled and mature pressure upon the various institutions, social change and the process of humanization can be better realized.

The role of the ethnic church in prophetic fulfillment is to be the "suffering servant" as the agent of reconciliation. To this end, the Christian must be willing to

---

[33] Lewis M. Killian, *The Impossible Revolution? Black Power and the American Dream* (New York: Random House, 1968), xv.

sacrifice the security of minorities within the minority group for the health of the whole minority and consequently the majority. The ethnic church, aware of its role in the process of fundamental social change, can bring to bear upon white "preconsciousness" its contradiction of the biblical faith through relentless effort in dialogue and infiltration of churches and communities.

Although the ethnic church is small in number, it represents a viable voice as a third party. They can fulfill the role of a catalyst in the Black-White confrontation, the role of a second minority, hitherto known for their silence and good behavior, to reinforce the position of the oppressed and cause the dominant majority to take a second look.

Making Human Life More Human

The purpose of the ethnic church as a change agent in society is to make human life more human. What does it mean to fulfill one's humanity in America?

Professor Hough suggests Barth's description of human relationship as one of the finest statements in the humanization process:

> Barth says that there are four levels of humanity on an ascending scale. These are (1) the "eye to eye" relationships; (2) mutual speech and hearing; (3) mutual assistance; and (4) all of the other three levels together with a spirit of joy.[34]

To fulfill this description of humanness it is necessary for any persecuted ethnic group to separate from the outgroup in order to seek its own identity as described previously. Hough emphasizes that this segregation "is not necessarily reverse racism, but it may be an effort to solve the difficult problem of . . . identity."[35]

An "eye to eye" relationship, mutual speech and hearing, mutual assistance cannot be fully realized in a superior-inferior relationship of our present society. To force such a relationship would only perpetuate the status quo. The strategy calls for an indirect, "atmospheric," overall education and preparatory influence. The area of emphasis for the present is the development of wholesome humanness within the ethnic community, the development of the art of political jiu-jitsu, the sending forth of the missionaries and catalysts from this strategic base, and the conviction that one's own humanness is necessary for the humanness of others including that larger majority.

Within the pluralistic situation, the ethnic church can proclaim and demonstrate this "eye-to-eye" relationship. Our mutual dependence requires mutual concern in every phase of life. The human situation is that man finds it difficult if not impossible to help each other in sincere mutuality in the spirit of loving concern. Genuine loving concern out of which true humanity is created is the result of gratitude. The Christian response to the love of God is the necessary ingredient to release man from his selfishness and pride.

---

[34] Hough, *Black Power and White Protestants*, 139. See also Karl Barth, *Church Dogmatics III/3: The Doctrine of Creation*, ed. G. W. Bromiley and T. F. Torrance, trans. H. Knight, G. W. Bromiley, J. K. S. Reid, and R. H. Fuller (Edinburgh: T&T Clark, 1960), 111–112, 250.

[35] Hough, *Black Power and White Protestants*, 138–146.

The Japanese Protestant community has the potentiality as well as responsibility to exemplify the redemptive power of God's love, whereby men are made truly human. This should be an admonition for the whole Japanese Protestant community to demonstrate their ecumenical mutuality and humanness in Christ.

To begin with, the contemporary church, both ethnic and the majority group, will need to restructure their church pattern to permit a greater interpersonal "eye-to-eye," mutual speaking and hearing, and mutual assistance opportunities. The institutional church as structured today gives very few opportunities for deep relationships. The impersonality of the present-day church, rather than enhancing humanization, becomes a deterrent to what the church professes to fulfill. Opportunities must be provided in the modern church for small groups to meet in real human relations. Within this pluralistic posture, intimate human groups can be created to bring about a sense of identity and humanness.

People cannot truly become human except in the context of helping each other and being helped by each other. What the Christian experiences in the fellowship of the Holy Spirit is the redemptive power of agape — love whereby human beings are made truly human.

Asian Identity and Interracial Marriage

PHILIP KYUNG SIK PARK

Without trying to be funny, every marriage that involves a man and a woman is mixed. Obviously that is not a problem. Perhaps there is no real problem with racially mixed marriages either. I know about some which have been "successful" in the sense that they've withstood the test of a great many years. The real question is what about ethnic identity and racially mixed marriages? Can one really be Asian in the best sense of what that term has come to mean and yet have a marital partner who is not Asian?

For me, this question is no rhetorical exercise. On one side of the coin, even though there's a Korean name connected with that title, I'm the product of a mixed marriage. And I'm involved with another. On the flip side, as I have come to grips with my own Asian identity, I have tried to be involved in and sensitive to the struggle of the Asian community. During the last couple of years, I have served on the national steering council of the Asian Presbyterian Caucus. My current job is trying to deal with Asian issues and the development of ethnic churches from the perspective of the United Presbyterian Church.

So much for credentials, or the lack of them. What can be said about the question of racially mixed marriages and Asian identity? The first thing that can't be ignored is that interracial relationships and marriages are happening. A leisurely stroll down Broadway indicates that a lot of people are exploring the possibilities. A continuing phenomenon is what might be called "war brides," Asian wives of American soldiers who met in Vietnam or Korea or elsewhere. Even Syngman Rhee, the late president of Korea, married a white woman. Let me hasten to add that this comment is not meant to be a justification of Mr. Rhee's politics or marital practices, but simply the recital of a fact.

A lot of theories have been advanced as to why interracial marriages happen. One holds that it may be the result of an unconscious desire to assimilate into the American scene. A popular theory among Asians in the movements says that IRM (interracial marriage) is the result of the general mind developed through the American culture. Asian women are seen generally as more sexy or mysterious than American women. Perhaps too, according to this theory, white men are seen as more "manly" than Asian men. One problem with this is that it may deal with the general, but it doesn't cover the specific. My father, part of a pioneer Korean family in this country and one of the first Koreans born in America, married a white woman because he did not have much choice. I do not mean that this was his only reason, but it was certainly one.

So interracial marriage and relationships do occur because of mistaken theories or due to an idea that opposites attract, who knows why. The point is that they do happen.

Perhaps the more serious question is this. Should interracial marriage happen? Arguments exist on both sides and I can cite a lot of them from personal experience. But I believe the time has come to deal with this question on a different level. Questions like cultural differences or "what will the children look like?" come in here. These questions are important but for me the overriding concern is identity. How does one, an Asian, deal with his personal identity and his identity in relation to a community that is perhaps increasingly taking its identity seriously. Or perhaps it can be put another way. Can one deal with his personal identity and the identity of his ethnic community in a mixed marriage?

My own answer to this question is built around certain premises which I believe in strongly but which the shortness of this article prevents me from defending to any great extent. To begin with, let's talk about being a human being. My belief is that the positive social influences in society all have a similar goal, the humanization of society. By being human I mean a number of things.

One is to be concerned about a common good and not merely personal aims. Another is to work against oppression. My point is this: To be human is to take one's identity seriously. A person has to take himself seriously before he can take any good cause seriously.

Being Asian in America is time-consuming. Those of us of Asian heritage have to take our identity seriously, precisely because no one else has. And if we take this Asian identity as a major concern, it means working at it, to shape and mold it on our terms. We cannot be the white person's yellow person. We have to uphold our ethnic pride so that all of us can avoid the previous condition which Asians faced here—a lack of identity at all.

But once we have found ourselves, there is an additional response. Finding our identity is part of becoming human. As Asians our humanity is rooted in the Asian community. The total community. We have to be involved in youth issues and overbearing poverty in Chinatown. The Korean confronted with sweeping floors when he is a pharmacist at home needs to be an object of our concern. We have to be aware of, and participate in, the struggle for the kind of societal changes that permit immigrants to come here and not force them into real trauma and difficulty. And increasingly we need to be aware of a growing generation in the United States who does not understand Hong Kong or Japan or Korea or Formosa. We have to provide an atmosphere where racial identity can be strengthened and involvement in the Asian movement in America can be nurtured.

To be Asian and not deal with Asian issues and concerns in some way is a cop-out. We cannot afford the luxury of dealing with those who still want to play the role of assimilating to the extent that our heritage is denied and our community suffers because their skills and abilities have not been added to the struggle.

In the light of the above, there is another premise on which this article is based. Being Asian and marrying other than an Asian person has serious consequences. To begin with, it is hard to live in two worlds — one Asian and the other something else. Then, too, to marry someone who is not Asian may not be doing him or her a favor. For example, most whites in America, male and female, have not really come to grips with their identity. In some respects, there may be a parasitic quality in the white partner who ignores his or her identity, to participate as much as possible in the spouse's Asian identity. Some aspects of this, of course, are legitimate since children should perhaps be raised with a positive experience of their own Asianness. The Asian partner in such a marriage is not exempt from this kind of problem. An oppressive quality may exist in a relationship which demands too much of a partner who is not Asian.

I don't want to be boxed in, having said all of this. I refuse to say that interracial marriage is wrong. Homogeneity is not to be treasured above all else. But dealing with the realities of the Asian community, or of your particular ethnic group within this community should raise serious questions as to whether an interracial marriage is the way to go.

One more point. We haven't dealt with the matter of individual choice. One Korean friend who has married a white woman says simply that white girls are more fun. But those free to make a choice should ideally try to take these issues I have tried to raise in this article seriously. We cannot afford to play games with either our identity or our humanity.

Whom Does S. I. Hayakawa Speak For?[*]

PHILIP KYUNG SIK PARK[†]

"Mostly, I hope, S. I. Hayakawa speaks for himself. But the situation unfortunately is not quite this simple." That was Phil Park's initial answer to this question. Hayakawa, you may recall, is president of San Francisco State University. Born in Canada, he was a noted semanticist before moving into college administration. Several years ago he attracted a great deal of national publicity when student demonstrations closed his school. On that occasion Hayakawa voiced strong opposition to the stands on issues which his students were taking.

S. I. Hayakawa is a dapper individual with a neat moustache who sports a Scotch plaid beret (a reminder of his Canadian roots, at least). He became a public figure as a result of playing "Horatio at the bridge" at San Francisco State. The media coverage of that event alone stamped him indelibly in the minds of many Americans as one man who was not afraid to stand up to those "hippie radicals." He was seen as a strong exponent of order—even of "law and order." As a result of these events, Hayakawa also became one of the few Asians, perhaps the only one, whose public statements have been noted by the national media. The situation placed him in a rather unique position, particularly with regard to white Americans.

Whites turn readily to someone like Hayakawa. He has spoken forthrightly on an issue that most whites are concerned about—order in our society. S. I. Hayakawa has also reinforced what most whites believe—Asians are the model minority. For white society, then, Hayakawa has become the believable Asian. If he speaks for anyone, it is for whites—and to whites—about the Asian in American society.

The critical matter is how this happens and the effect it has. Because the Asian American community has generally been quiet about itself, it is an unknown entity to white Americans, even more so than other minority groups. Whites therefore tend to pay little attention to what's going on in the yellow world and probably couldn't care less. They believe what they hear from public figures like Hayakawa or what they read in badly written, stereotyped magazine articles, such as "Success Story of

---

[*] March/April 1973.

[†] Mr. Park was associate executive director of United Presbyterian Health, Education, and Welfare Association (UPHEWA).

213

One Minority Group in the U.S." in *U.S. News & World Report* or "Success Story: Out-Whiting the Whites" in *Newsweek*.

Hayakawa would have everyone believe that success is the epitome of the process as far as Asian Americans are concerned. On at least one occasion he has advised blacks to imitate the *Nisei*, "Go to school and get good grades, save one dollar out of every ten you earn to capitalize your business." And if we would believe this "believable Asian," at least one minority group has no difficulties. Whites would like to believe that Asians are the most "successful minority."

So what's wrong with success? The problem is not success itself, obviously. The difficulty is that whites generally have only dealt with Asians by stereotyping them as the "successful minority," As the *Newsweek* article tried to emphasize, whites have believed that "if you scratch an Asian, you'll find a WASP." And it's easy to believe this. I'd like to believe it myself: The American Dream is true; if Asians made it, so can every other minority. Hayakawa tends to reinforce this kind of thinking.

The result is a lack of sensitivity and understanding and continuing racial prejudice on the part of whites toward Asian Americans. Charlie Chan is still the Asian prototype, and a growing American minority is unable to penetrate the majority culture. Stereotypes cannot confront the reality of the situation.

Let's deal with facts and not rhetoric. For example, poverty is the rule rather than the exception in the Chinatowns, Little Tokyos, Manilatowns, and other urban Asian American ghettos. In Chinatown, San Francisco, one-third of the families earn less than $4,000 per year. Pilipinos have the lowest annual income of any ethnic group in California. Their average income is $2,925 as compared with $3,553 for blacks and $5,109 for Caucasians. (Figures are from the 1960 census. The 1970 figures are not yet available.)

New Asian immigrants in particular have problems. They are often forced to take positions far below those they were trained for. Pilipino doctors, for example, may be working as lab technicians. Korean teachers with graduate training in this country may find it difficult to break into the public school system.

If the American "success" myth were true for Asian Americans, more would be successful. Hard work and thrifty habits are supposed to breed success, but they don't. If they did, the Chinese laborers who slaved to build the railroad in the West would have risen above the laboring class. But they haven't. Workers who labor for low wages in San Francisco's sweatshops would be able to start up the economic ladder. However, they aren't climbing at all. Some Asian Americans are successful. But Asian Americans are not necessarily the "successful minority." When Hayakawa pushes this image, he is speaking to whites for whites.

Should We Call Our Parents "Bananas"?

So we've heard about Hayakawa. To some Asians it may seem that I'm too critical. Is what Hayakawa saying so different from what we Asian Americans want? After all, I've been reasonably successful. I come from a successful family. My father was an insurance executive, my uncle a successful commercial artist, my brother is a university professor, my cousin a medical doctor. The Parks have made it. We don't seem to have problems. We've never lived in an Asian community. We acculturated, assimilated. I'm a third-generation Korean, I don't speak the language. And I've never been to Korea. Obviously, there are Poles or Italians who can't make these kinds of statements. Why shouldn't I react positively to the kind of statements that Hayakawa has made?

Actually, this is not such a simple question to answer. Part of the complexity is wrapped up in how Asians have had to act in order to live in this country. One thing we have had to do is to push for success. The Parks are successful and somehow it has meant it doesn't matter if we're different. I made it just like my Jewish neighbor and the Italian man across the street. It's like having "Made in America" stamped across your forehead for everyone to see. I'm in the big time, so I can sneer at those kids with whom I got into fights in the schoolyard because they called me a "yellow Jap" or who chased me home with other racial epithets.

Being successful is one way of becoming part of America. And this is how my father and a lot of others in his generation saw it and perhaps still see it. In some sense, however, there is a qualitative difference between what Hayakawa is saying and what our parents did, or even how we have acted until now. For them, economic survival was intrinsically bound up in the process of assimilation. In order to work and to feed families, some method of adapting to American culture was necessary. A methodology had to be developed to meet the circumstances. The only method that seemed to be available was assimilation.

So we assimilated. Each generation got a bit more acculturated until we all became Americans. That is, we talked like Americans, we acted like Americans, but we didn't look like Americans. And somehow that's the real rub. We made it, but we really didn't. In the final analysis, we're still different. Every day we feel some evidence of the fact that America would have been happier if we had all stayed in the old country.

When we tried to assimilate, it was mostly by each one of us trying to carve out their own niche. And success was sometimes the result. But what was the real result? For me, it was being embarrassed that my grandmother who lived with us couldn't speak English. I was relieved when she moved to live with my uncle in California so we could go back to speaking our language. For me, it was a real dislike of Asian food and especially of *kim chee*. I was ashamed of who I was.

And then I woke up. Unfortunately it took a long time. A lot of important questions were rumbling around in my mind. Who am I? Why don't I like to be called a Korean? Some content began to be added to these questions, and it finally dawned on me that maybe something important was missing from my life. I decided that I really didn't know who Phil Park was. What was missing was me—a sense of my own identity.

At the center of the Asian American movement are the same questions. We are beginning to ask what assimilation has entailed. And we are beginning to sense that it has demanded too much. To really assimilate, to truly mix with the majority culture, whites have to be out-whited as well as outwitted. We have to deny who we are. Those childish dislikes were my own way of assimilating, of trying to convince myself that I really wasn't any different from my playmates, But the critical problem was that, in denying my heritage, I really was denying myself, Assimilation has meant this for all Asian Americans. Nothing is worth the denial of one's identity, not even success.

Not everyone has had my awareness experience or has gone the route from denial to acceptance. A number of Asians still see assimilation as the way to relate. For some in the Asian American movement this attitude is tantamount to a kind of Asian "Uncle Tomism," to being a "banana" (yellow on the outside, white on the inside). Personally, I'm a bit reluctant to cast aspersions on my brethren. I've been a "banana"; maybe in the minds of some I still am. But to put all who have assimilated into this category is unfair. The facts are, however, that too many Asian Americans have been brainwashed to believe we can make it in white society and that after we make it, everything will be alright. Labels may or may not be appropriate, but to believe that white society cares for Asians is stupid, irresponsible, and naïve. Vietnam is certainly an example of this. If whites have not gotten beyond stereotypes, how can they possibly become concerned about Asians? Asian Americans have been crunched just like blacks, Chicanos, and Indian Americans.

To go one step farther, there is another failure connected with assimilation. The assimilation route is too individualized. Asian Americans until quite recently have not been involved in trying to solve community problems as a community. When one examines our community's problems—immigrant housing in New York, farm workers in Delano, pensioners at San Francisco's International Hotel—it is evident that individualized effort hasn't touched the basic issue. We have got to solve our own problems but not as individuals. The difficulties of our community have to be dealt with in community and by the people who live there.

Asian Americans cannot ignore the white community. We need, however, a way of relating to the majority community that doesn't deny our identity and that takes our community concerns into consideration.

Yellow Is Beautiful

When the process of awakening occurred in my life, some interesting things happened. Korean culture and language became extremely important for me. *Kim chee* started to taste good. In other words, after a lifetime of denying my identity, I began to affirm it.

A similar process is happening with Asian Americans all over this country. A real pride in national heritage, a new sense of self-esteem, a growing awareness of the need to begin to solve Asian American problems—all of these are increasingly important factors in the Asian American experience. In other words, we are beginning to say, "Yellow is beautiful." This statement is not imitative of any other racial struggle for identity. We might have reached a similar conclusion, but for us this statement comes out of a peculiar kind of struggle with the problem of relations to the majority community—our own struggle.

For an Asian American to say "yellow is beautiful" is a very important step. We have been taught to deny yellow. Our white "friends" had taught us that yellow is cowardly or that the Yellow Peril was evil to the nth degree. And we all reacted as did a friend of mine who said, "I really prefer to think of myself as brown rather than yellow." But yellow is now being seen in very positive terms.

What this means, of course, is that we are not going to allow whites to interfere with anything that is the province of Asians to deal with. White society has never done us any favors. As a small minority group, Asian Americans have been at the mercy of the majority community. But as we develop our identity, we also build a capacity to confront our problems.

In a real sense we are talking about Yellow Power and Asian American militancy. I suppose there have been moments in my life when I've been militant. But here my role was as an advocate for black civil rights. It may seem strange to say so, but I never felt I could be militant about Asian American concerns. The matter was simply a case of "grin and bear it."

But the discovery of the sense of an Asian American community has raised in me both a sense of hope and the capacity for action on behalf of my own community. Hope and action are obviously two major components in any sense of militancy.

A number of things contribute to the Asian American's sense of hope. One, of course, is the increased sense of personal identity and interest in Asian culture. Another extremely important factor is the sense of inclusiveness that is developing in the Asian American movement both in church and community. The Asian American movement is based on the common experience of all Asians in this country, so Koreans and Japanese, Chinese and, Filipinos are learning that we have a common struggle. In this context, the problems of one specific group become the concern of all. This attitude of oneness and concern is the basis for a positive alternative to assimilation.

Hope is the basis of all action. As Asian Americans sense that we can accomplish something by joint concern, then this concern will lead to some positive action. Already, a number of action groups are at work. One is the Yellow Brotherhood in Los Angeles, which among other things is concerned about drug abuse among Asian American youth. A New York City group is called Yellow Pearl. The Van Troi Anti-Imperialist Brigade is a group of Asian Americans concerned about the Vietnam War.

The life of the Asian in America is changing. Pride in our heritage, an affirmation of our identities, and the increasing sense of unity among diverse Asian American groups are components of this new attitude. The new attitude has led to the conviction that we can begin to live in this country as ourselves. We are proud we are Asian Americans. And this pride presages for us a very positive future.

Appendix

Pak Gae Dong is a student at an American university. His family now resides in the Republic of South Korea. Mr. Pak (a pseudonym) is afraid to identify himself further because he is here on a student visa. If he tells how he really feels about political matters, his visa may be withdrawn. He comments on life as a student, on going back to Korea, on the Korean political situation, and on American missionaries.

"My main problem will be language, especially writing papers. Not only is this a problem of language, but also a problem of different thought forms. In Western culture, they live to prove something. Asian thought form is not that kind. From the American perspective it is ambiguous.

"The professor doesn't understand what I'm saying and adjustment is a kind of brainwashing process, I think. I heard a Korean who got a degree at Temple, and he said to go through a PhD program is to be brainwashed. And he said that was one of the reasons he cannot go back home. At first, I didn't agree with that so much, but now it is for me part of the truth too. If I exercise my own logic, I would get a C or D or F.

"One thing I want: I hope I go back. If I decide to stay here, it might be from a couple of reasons. One is political. Here I have experienced an open society where you can say anything you want. You can criticize the president or the government. And political activity doesn't always result in going to jail.

"Other reason for not going back may be economic. This can be applied in general to Korean people here. They have had a better experience than in Korea economically. And once seeing affluency, even though they don't make good money here, it still makes a difference. In this sense, maybe there is discrimination. I heard that even Korean doctors are overtrained; they get inferior jobs here. They are mistreated on the job. They can't use their abilities.

"I feel like I lost my country now. Last October 17th, somebody took my country. [On this date Park Chung Hee, president of South Korea, suspended the constitution and declared martial law.] So far I thought only the power from outside, like imperialism, like Japan, could take over. But now I feel really strange. It's the power from inside that took over the nation. . . . I really want this country to be united. Now I see more difficulty. There should be something of concessions by both sides. Power and reunification are contradictory.

"I didn't have any contact directly with American missionaries. The only thing I remember is when I went to a very famous seashore with my mother. We saw a fence on the best part of the seashore. We found an American missionary family swimming there, but no Koreans allowed. And I remember that really made me mad. We need missionaries in Korea, but good missionaries. I suspect their intentions. They enjoy themselves in their ghetto; they have maids. Then they come back here and say they have personal hardships. But some are very good."

—Philip K. S. Park

Rev. Bing Kong Han is an Indonesian of Chinese descent. He has been in the United States for about five years now and is currently serving as associate pastor at the Church of the Reconciler in Clearwater, Florida. When asked about his experience with discrimination because he is Asian, he had this to say:

"My family and I have had little experience with overt discrimination in this country, but I think that people are often unable to appreciate my Asian point of view. At my last church some members got very upset because I said America had lost the Vietnam War years ago. They did not understand how I could say this and still be fiercely anti-Marxist. I lived under a Communist regime in Indonesia, and I know what it's like. But I also think that the average Asian sees America as a Christian nation. And America is now using very un-Christian tactics in Vietnam and all over the world.

"I feel that the most important fact about Asian ministers is not that they are Asian, but whether they are good ministers. There is an adaptation necessary when an Asian pastor serves a Caucasian congregation. But that adaptation process is strictly a one-way street — the Asian must always adapt himself to the WASP pattern. I refuse to be a part of this process. I have never, for example, considered changing my name or the names of my children. It is already a big concession for me that I now write my family name last instead of first, as is the Chinese custom. To serve the American people I must go by Bing Kong Han instead of Han Bing Kong.

"I hope that as a result of the work of the Asian Presbyterian Caucus, church nominating committees will see an Asian pastor as a human being, a minister, and a Presbyterian, and be aware that he has his own kind of approach because he is Asian. That he can share with them his own specific Asian experience in a way that will enrich both himself and the congregation.

—F. V. B.

This Matter of Integration[*]

ROY I. SANO[†]

> The merger of thirty-one churches of the Pacific Japanese Provisional Conference with annual conferences of the Western Jurisdiction will take place in 1964. This will mark the end of "segregated" churches in the region.
>
> The Japanese churches were organized with provisional conference status twenty-three years ago. This is the extension of a Japanese mission formed sixty-three years ago on the Pacific coast. This year, all the churches of the PJPC are celebrating the eighty-fifth anniversary of Japanese Christian work in America, which began in San Francisco.
>
> More than half of these churches, scattered in Arizona, California, Colorado, Oregon, and Washington, are now fully self-supporting. Membership in the Conference was 6,466 as of June 1962.
>
> Bishop Donald H. Tippett of the San Francisco area says, "It is my considered opinion that our Japanese people are better prepared for integration than any of our other ethnic groups . . . They do not want to be in any way second-rate congregations or members."
>
> During the heart-searching discussions at the last session of the last annual conference, a Japanese Methodist minister made an address on which this article is based, and which we believe has implications for any future de-segregation in Methodism.
> —Ed.

At almost every major church gathering here on the West Coast, churchmen discuss the question of integration and make pronouncements. We are all for it. Lest our adoption of it be only a gullible acceptance, however, we ought to examine this goal with a combination of soft hearts and hard heads.

The Main Question

The main question for us to consider at the moment is not the advantage or disadvantage of integration, nor whether we are ready for it or not. The prior

---

[*] *Methodist Layman*, February, 1963.
[†] Minister, First Methodist Church, Loomis, CA.

question for us to answer is whether the integration we propose is soundly conceived and will be responsibly implemented.

A responsible integration will bear in mind that we are basically disbanding a racial conference and merging the several churches into their respective geographic annual conferences.

When these churches separate themselves from their present association as a provisional conference, a *disbanding* of this conference ought not to mean an *abandoning* of specialized but legitimate responsibilities, concerns, and aspirations.

A responsible integration will bear in mind that union of church bodies brings strength, but they must walk the tightrope by preserving adequate freedom for the specialist without jeopardizing the concrete, organic, and visible unity of the church.

The church must work within communities and to create a new community. One of the reasons we are hampered in our work with racial groups is that our work is not sufficiently within their communities. We are too eager to create new communities and do not want to appear segregated.

We are like a swimmer who complained that he could not swim well in the Dead Sea. His body was not sufficiently immersed in the water.

The Calling of God

There are two questions to answer if we are to work in and create a new community: What is the community to which we are called? And what is the calling of God we must proclaim to this community?

The community to which we are called as a provisional conference is the Japanese community, which is changing but still identifiable. The Japanese are among the most quickly assimilated or Americanized immigrants. They are rapidly losing their distinctive foreign traits. A large number, however, still band themselves together for social, recreational, and religious purposes.

The best example is the Buddhist church. I do not mean to be facetious when I say that the Buddhist church in America is first Japanese, second American, and third Buddhist. She is not trying to be provincial or racially exclusive. She is only following a strong trend of the community to identify themselves racially by associating with their own kind.

A responsible integration will bear this trend in mind and work within this racial community. Through it, they will proclaim the call of God to this community to become the people of God, a colony of heaven.

A Practical Strategy

What are the reasons for this strategy? For one thing, it is practical. This strategy is working in the case of the Buddhist church and among Japanese fundamentalistic groups who ignore the integration question.

Second, a church that would allow racial churches and perhaps even allow them to band together within and across annual conferences could be said to be in harmony with St. Paul's teaching of the body. The unity of the church retains multiplicity and specialization, but it is the multiplicity that does not jeopardize the concrete unity of the church.

Third (and this is still an unexplored reason), we would only be following Christ. St. Paul tells us that although Christ was endowed with regal authority, he laid it aside and assumed the form of the servant and lived within human flesh subject to death.

If we take this passage with radical seriousness, I would take it to mean that the work of the church is to live within the existing racial communities even if these communities are subject to a short life.

Many of us argue that because culture and racial communities are a passing thing, therefore we are not going to get involved. But our Lord Jesus Christ argued quite the opposite. Because these things are subject to sin and its consequence symbolized in death, therefore He decided to live in the flesh.

Although Christ is not a sanctioner of the existing order of things, he is the sanctifier or the transformer. And he did it by living within it—not trying to avoid it or belittle it.

We look on people who do not feel free with the majority of Caucasians and pronounce judgment upon them as "awkward" and "backward" because they impose segregation upon themselves. A responsible integration does not hamper the free choice of human associations nor belittle the many who will work within these communities and associations.

Many of us are afraid to work with a separate Japanese church even in major centers of Japanese population because this would make us vulnerable to criticism of segregation. Many of us feel guilty about the existence of such churches. But if we take the Incarnation of God to heart, we may move forward toward a responsible integration.

Finally, the Incarnation tells us that our Lord lives in and above. He is fully human and fully divine. That would mean that the church can exercise the courage to live within the boundaries of human communities without making barriers to communication.

The church ought to have the audacity to live within the dangerous limitations of human communities, making the distinctions that set us off from one another without being discriminatory. We will be bold to say that we will organize ourselves separately at some points without segregating ourselves.

Isn't this what we mean when we speak of the church in the world but not of the world? Isn't this what Martin Luther meant in part when he said that "A Christian man is a perfectly free lord of all, subject to none. A Christian man is a perfectly dutiful servant of all, subject to all"?

Responsible Integration

And now, let us see how we may implement the responsible integration we have attempted to describe.

In evangelism, occasional specialized campaigns could be conducted cooperatively across ethnic lines within the conference and within ethnic groups across conference lines. But the campaigns could be sustained by an efficient and just distribution and adequate recruitment of specialized ministers in ethnic work. Notice, I did not say "ethnic ministers," but "specialized ministers in ethnic work."

Furthermore, the laymen will very likely want some mutual sharing in developing new leadership.

Stewardship is another topic in churches so easily prey to the "give me" psychology characteristics of some ethnic churches.

And then there are cultural concerns. We are yet to explore the height, breadth, and depth of God's call in the area of intercultural relations here on the West Coast, with its numerous major centers of Asian, Latin, and Negro population.

In addition, there are the migrants of the 1930s, '40s, and '50s. Surveys such as the US Commission on Civil Rights of 1961 bear out the continued need for action on part of the church in promoting fair housing, equal opportunity in employment and education, full participation on all levels of government, and justice before the courts.

Besides the obvious injustices in race relations, we face more subtle problems of prejudice. We need knowledge and respect of each other and ourselves as minorities. We need to know the hurts we harbor, the anxieties that drive us, and the aspirations that arouse us.

We need to feel our full humanity—not only our meanness or majesty alone, but both. Even the Commission on Worship could explore the inclusion of Negro spirituals and Japanese hymns in the new hymnal. But much of this concern will rest on the Board of Christian Social Concerns.

God has a new day to dawn upon us. He is giving us the opportunity for a creative and authentic integration, responsive to the existing situations and the ultimate claims of God.

The Church

One, Holy, Catholic, and Apostolic
*A Position Paper**

ROY I. SANO

Introduction

This is a "position paper" concerning the church's work with Japanese Americans written from a "theological perspective." I offer it for critical analysis. It is not a manuscript to be read for oral presentation. I hope it will foster a consensus about the way the church can proceed in its work with ethnic communities. Two additional features require explanation. Since the position adopted here will appear to depart from the position generally assumed, I will cite analogous moves in other aspects of the church's life and thought. Although this paper deals with the "theological perspectives," it includes sociological considerations. It has become increasingly difficult to "do" theology responsibly without taking account of the social scene.

One and Catholic

Let us turn directly to the church's teaching about its own nature. The 1964 edition of *The Methodist Hymnal* has made the Nicene Creed once again more accessible for public use (no. 739). This creedal formulation, which goes back to AD 325, speaks of the church as "one holy catholic and apostolic." I propose to take these ascriptions in pairs and relate them to our concrete situation. It will involve some extension in the meaning of these terms. However, I do not feel they are misinterpretations. On the one hand, the ascriptions call us to recognize the *unity* and *universality* (catholicity) of the church, and on the other hand, it challenges us to work out the apostolicity and the holiness of the church. I would argue that a wholesome church permits the full expression of both elements of these polarities. That is, a church will drive toward unity *and* universality, apostolicity *and* holiness, at one and the same time. It is important to emphasize the contrary elements in both polarities because it is so easy to narrow our scope and restrict ourselves to one and exclude the other or to emphasize one in our local church or professional career and

---

* The National Consultation of Japanese Work, The United Methodist Church, San Francisco, CA, February 3–4, 1969. [*Ed. note: The original citations in this chapter were presented in the main text. For this edition, they have been converted to footnotes and supplied with some additional bibliographic information.*]

look condescendingly upon those who emphasize the other. The contrary elements can and must complement each other. If we see the contrary element as contradictory, we only have conflict and animosity ahead of us. It will be necessary to deal with the polarities more specifically.

In the face of racial and ethnic divisions, the proponents for unity have contrasted the integration of the movie theatre and sports arena on Saturday nights to the scandalous segregation in our churches on Sunday mornings. We have consequently undertaken many steps toward unity. We have disbanded as many structurally distinct bodies in our church as possible.

However, in the light of the poles of unity and universality, I believe some balancing is in order. To appreciate the contrast between unity and universality, it is important to recognize the diversity implied in the universality of the church. The word "catholic" in the creed means "universal" in outreach. It highlights the inclusiveness of the church, an inclusiveness that bespeaks the diversity it encompasses. For some, the colonnades enclosing (the circular) St. Peter's Square in the Vatican portrayed the wide diversity the Roman Catholic Church encompasses. The encircling colonnades represented the arms of the "mother church" embracing the diverse children; for others, it represented a woman's womb that gave birth to this diversity. Similarly, the word "ecumenical" comes from a word meaning "worldwide" and suggests diversity. Ironically, the proponents of ecumenism on the local level often have in mind the unity of the church which virtually eliminates diversity. Doing things together becomes doing the same thing the same way.

All I wish to point out at this point in the paper is the diversity that the creed confesses. Alongside the unity, there is diversity. The point is obvious and need not be labored. No one actually espouses a unity that inflicts uniformity. But crucial questions remain. What kind of diversity does our ecclesiology permit? On what grounds? What should the specialized structures achieve? A reinterpretation of the second set of poles will provide direction in answering these questions.

Apostolic and Holy

Before we expand the elements of the second polarity, I should clarify how I understand these terms. By "apostolic" I mean that style of life of which we are heir and not so much those to whom we are indebted (the apostles). In other words, I am interpreting "apostolic" in terms of what we stand to benefit more than *who* are our *benefactors*. More specifically, "apostolic" refers to the fact that the church is sent out—into and for the world—just as the apostles were. One might wonder how this interpretation of "apostolic" could stand in contrast to the word "holy." If the word "apostolic" emphasized the involvement and immersion of the church in the world, the word "holy" emphasizes the separateness of the church from the world. The apostles were sent out, into the world; the apostles were also *set apart* from the world.

The polarity between apostolicity and holiness becomes obvious. It provides the foundations for speaking of the *twofold mission of the church to work in the community and to create a new community*. Karl Barth had in mind the same kind of dual emphasis. For Barth, the Christian is one who is always within the history of his own people (and) he will be one of the first to accept these developments, to regard them as right and necessary and there to welcome, affirm and promote them . . . As he holds his near neighbors with the one hand, he reaches out to the distant with the other. And so the concept of his own people is extended and opened out in this respect too. It is true that he belongs wholly and utterly to his own people. But it is equally true that the horizon by which his people is surrounded and within which it exists as his people is humanity. It is equally true that he himself belongs wholly and utterly to humanity.[1]

One cannot help but recall the words of Martin Luther. "A Christian man is perfectly free lord of all, subject to none. A Christian man is perfectly dutiful servant of all, subject to all."

Barth feels his position comes from scripture. His exposition of Genesis 10–11 and Acts 2 clarify the biblical foundations. In Genesis 10, we find the so-called "table of nations." It narrates the proliferation of people under the providence of God. It results in the nations, tongues, and peoples. We have what Barth calls a "differentiated universality," which has been willed by God and, hence, is good![2] However, Genesis 11 follows. It narrates the attempt on man's part to become one people and reach into the heavens. God pronounces judgment upon this enterprise. The punishment? It turns out to be the proliferation of languages and the attending confusion. In this case, the scattering of nations and the diversity of people reads like a punishment for human pretensions. Hence, if Genesis 10 says the diversity of people has come from the providence of God, Genesis 11 says the diversity comes from the punishment of God. Barth feels this ambiguity continues through the Old Testament.

Only when we come to Pentecost, as narrated in Acts 2, do we find any hint of a way through this ambiguity. The coming of the Spirit of God takes the diversity of languages and makes possible the new community. This mighty God dismisses the dangers entailed in the diversity of people. By working in community, we have a new community.[3] This leads Barth to say, "A Christian . . . cannot espouse an abstract internationalism and cosmopolitanism. On the other hand, he cannot espouse abstract nationalism and particularism."[4] By "abstract internationalism and cosmopolitanism" Barth has in mind the ideals of a world community or brotherhood which discounts particularity and nationality; by "abstract nationalism and particularism" Barth has in mind the dangers of chauvinism and jingoism that divorce one from the wider world of which one is a part and for which it is responsible.

The twofold orientation appears in several writers. For example, H. Richard Niebuhr, in *The Purpose of the Church and Its Ministry*, says the "church is never

---

[1] Karl Barth, *Church Dogmatics III/4: The Doctrine of Creation*, ed. G. W. Bromiley and T. F. Torrance, trans. A. T. Mackay, T. H. L. Parker, H. Knight, H. A. Kennedy, and J. Marks (New York: T. & T. Clark, 1961), 303.

[2] Barth, CD III/4, 312.

[3] Barth, CD III/4, 312–323.

[4] Barth, CD III/4, 312.

only a function of a culture nor ever only a supercultural community."[5] The cultural function of the church is twofold: It can transmit an alien culture to the host culture or can acculturate the immigrant to his newly adopted home. Both of these functions can operate in the churches of the ethnic minority as well as the Caucasian churches. We should not fool ourselves by thinking that ethnic minorities in predominantly Caucasian churches have extricated themselves from mixing cultural concerns with religious ones. Another example of the church working in community and creating community appears in Paul Lehman in his article in *Christianity and Crisis*. He says that in "the cultural and social pluralism of our time Protestantism is peculiarly suited to function as a kind of leaven in, with and under the pluralism and the quest for integration that this culture is pursuing under auspices of a secular kind."[6] The same kind of dual emphasis can be inferred from Reinhold Niebuhr's view of man and history. We can see this if we keep in mind how the history of a people embodied in their memories shapes communities. Niebuhr frequently speaks of man as a "creature" of history and a "creator" of history. As a creature, he belongs to a particular community. But his particularity should not be left by itself. We need to remember that man can create new communities because he is a creator of history.

This analysis of several theologians has indicated how the things they have said could permit us to move with a dual emphasis *vis-à-vis* given human community. Most of them admittedly are most reluctant to permit us as a church to move into ethnic communities with specialized structures. The demands, however, for consistency with what they have said on other occasions allows us to keep the question open. As we move along, I want to provide further justifications which will permit us to retain structures in the church which are racially defined. I will do this as I elaborate respectively on the twofold task as well as in the examination of analogous moves made by theologians in other aspects of the church's life and thought.

Working in Communities: The Persistence of the Ethnic Communities.

Granted, for the moment, that we are supposed to work within and through the structures of the ethnic communities, what kind of community do the ethnic minorities form? Are they such as to warrant specialized structures? Milton M. Gordon, in his study *Assimilation in American Life*, provides the much-needed service of conceptual clarification. I will simplify his discussion and unpackage the word "integration" as we use it. In most cases, we have two distinct processes in mind. On the one hand, we have in mind the way the immigrant and his sons adopt the behavior patterns of the host culture. On the other hand, we have in mind the way his intimate associations begin to move beyond the confines of his own kind of people. Gordon suggests that we confine the word "acculturation" to the former

---

[5] H. Richard Niebuhr, *The Purpose of the Church and Its Ministry* (New York: Harper & Brothers, 1956), 57.

[6] Paul Lehman, "Protestantism in a Post-Christian World," *Christianity and Crisis* 22, no. 1 (February 5, 1962): 10.

process and restrict the word "assimilation" to the later. His book establishes very clearly how most immigrant groups have undergone rapid and extensive acculturation but have resisted assimilation. Because of the extensive acculturation, it has become unrealistic to try to preserve sizable portions of alien cultures.[7] In this sense, we cannot expect to implement "cultural democracy" as it has been envisioned by Randolph Bourne and Horace Kallen. However, because immigrant groups have resisted assimilation in any wholesale way, the American ideals of "Anglo-Saxon conformity" or the "melting pot" model have been realized. What we have, according to Gordon, is "structural democracy."

Let us examine the Japanese community to test the validity of his thesis. Gordon's case becomes convincing with little or no alteration. Several students of the Japanese community have observed the rapid and extensive acculturation. At the point of language, diet, attire, residence, vocation, entertainment, artistic appreciation, etc., the Japanese are among the most rapidly acculturated of all immigrants. They are frequently held up as models because they were Asian Americans acculturated into a predominately Occidental culture. However, it should be borne in mind that the acculturation took place on the level of "extrinsic" traits and not "intrinsic" ones (see Appendix A).

Despite the considerable acculturation of the Japanese, there has been a serious lag at the point of assimilation. In the secondary group relations, the Japanese are very cosmopolitan, but his primary group relations are largely confined to his own kind. The "secondary group" includes the "impersonal, formal or casual, non-intimate, and usually face-to-face relations which involves the entire personality, not just a segmented part of it. The family, the child's play group, the social clique are all examples of a primary group."[8] If the church and family are anything, both of them deal with intimate relations. This explains in part the persistence of the ethnic composition of these social units.

If the reader is not convinced, he should come on a tour of metropolitan Los Angeles. What he finds there is only a pronounced example of the pattern found in many other centers of Japanese population. Let us go to a bowling alley. On a given night, we find three hundred young adults. At another alley, we find 150 adults in their fifties! They are all Japanese. Some estimate two hundred Japanese bowling teams. On Saturday and Sunday afternoon, we could visit various playgrounds and find hundreds of players and fans watching children and youth playing baseball. At the end of the summer, we might "crash" a picnic of five thousand people at an awards picnic. Some evening, we might go to a funeral and discover the ties that have continued among these people despite the dispersion of residential patterns. We might look over the clientele of an insurance salesman. We will find how his contacts come from an ethnic community. We could go on. One of these days, someone should. A sociologically trained person should adapt the conceptual tools provided

---

[7] Milton M. Gordon, *Assimilation in American Life* (New York: Oxford University Press, 1964).

[8] Gordon, *Assimilation in American Life*, 31–32.

by such persons as Milton M. Gordon and apply them to the Japanese community. The cohesiveness, the patterns of association, etc. should be documented in a research project.

In these ethnic communities, we do not have a community that is as distinct as the military or the cluster of subgroups associated with institutions of higher learning. But we do have a community, which may be acculturated but is slow in assimilating. If the military and institutions of higher learning require specialized structures to work in them; the church should reconsider its policy of disbanding all specialized structures formed along racial lines.

Why has the church been so insistent upon abandoning specialized structures? Part of the reason lies in the church's preoccupation with the ideal of brotherhood. Every grouping that departs from this ideal has called for moral invectives. The church's practice approaches that illness described by Eric Berne. The capacity on the part of the church's "adult ego" to tabulate fact and calculate probabilities has become clouded by the "parental ego" which engages in moral guidance and judgment. It has come time for the church and its leaders to acknowledge the real world, the world colored or discolored by their rose-tinted glasses. The progress in acculturation and lag in assimilation seems to show that ethnic communities are saying something like this: "We want to be like you, and we want to be liked by you. However, we reserve the right to choose those with whom we associate. We will join you on our time schedule." That troubles many Caucasians as well as the Uncle Tomio's and Auntie Tamiko's in our midst. But the despair on their part should not make them oblivious to the process now taking place. Besides the simple act of acknowledging the persistence of these communities, we should reexamine the low view we take of these communities. According to the low view, the ethnic communities are a concession to human weakness because they only serve the convenience of the backward and insecure. Concerning the leaders who may perpetuate these communities, the prejudiced or the paternalistic use these communities for their own designs or the established leadership among racial minorities attempt to retain their own positions. Although these factors may operate in the preservation of minority groups, there are others that do not deserve the usual censure we inflict upon the persisting groups. The most widespread explanation concerning the perpetuation of these communities has to do with the problem of self-identification. In addition to Milton M. Gordon's explanation in the book already cited, the explanations of J. Milton Yinger and Oscar Handlin place their emphasis upon the problem of self-identification. We identify ourselves to a large extent in accordance with the ethnic group to which we belong. The socio-economic *class* is also important. Thus, Gordon speaks of the "ethclass" as a means of identification. The question of self-identification is a matter of "proximate" concern. However, if Paul Tillich is right, we should turn our attention to these matters because the matters "ultimate" concern appear in them.

It may be helpful to consider a quotation from Milton Gordon concerning the fact of the ethnic communities and their evaluation.

The prognosis for America for a long time to come is that its informal social structure will consist of a series of ethnic subcommunities crisscrossed by social class, within which primary group relations will tend to be confined, that secondary group relationship across ethnic group lines will take place in abundance as a result of the requirements of an urbanized industrial society, and that the intel-lectual subsociety will grow somewhat both in numbers and in institu-tional articulation as a result of the constant increase in the magnitude of higher education.[9]

Ethnic communality will not disappear in the foreseeable future and its legitimacy and rationale should be recognized and respected. By the same token, the bonds that bind human beings together across the lines of ethnicity and pathways on which people of diverse ethnic origin meet and mingle should be cherished and strengthened.[10]

Given the facts and a new evaluation, the church should structure itself so that it can work within these communities. Otherwise, we would be comparable to the farmer who planted the seeds without examining the way the water drains nor the composition of the soil in his field. Our structures should be commensurate with the realities of our situation. The social scientist has called our attention to certain features of the ethnic communities that call our integrationist stance into question. Modifications are in order.

What are the responsible and relevant steps we can take? I will begin from the individual and work toward the larger corporate structures of our church. Speaking of the vocational self-image, we need to take seriously the ethnic ministry as a specialized ministry requiring peculiar training, skill, and orientation, and as such there should also be remuneration commensurate with these special qualifications. Not all of us will expect to undertake this form of ministry as a life-long specialization. Some of us will experiment in numerous fields before we come to an ethnic ministry; others of us will find in the ethnic ministry a place where we are schooled before we undertake other forms of ministry. What applies to the professional minister applies to the laity. A sense of vocation or calling is needed if we are to vitalize the ministry of these churches.

Second, as for the local church, the position stated in this paper will justify the continued use of the ethnic church. However, workshops on the various forms the churches are developing will prove helpful. Population remains the factor to take into account (Appendix B).

Third, something can be said about the conference level. The formation of ethnic committees has proved most encouraging. Given a broader rationale for their existence, they should be given more power to act, especially in cooperation with other conference committees, ethnic groups, and even denominations. Special attention should be given to programs initiated above the conference level by those with special skills and concerns with the ethnic communities.

This brings up the fourth level. I believe that we need an "Ethnic Ministries Committee" on the level of the National Division with specific assignments to

---

[9] Gordon, *Assimilation in American Life*, 264.
[10] Gordon, *Assimilation in American Life*, 265 (italics mine).

churches in the Western Jurisdiction which were members of the Provisional or Mission Conferences. This would include the Latin American, Asian, and Japanese Provisional Conferences. The organization of this committee will include the following. The chairman of this committee will be a full-time staff man with his main office on the Pacific coast. The chairman will be selected in consultation with the former members of the Provisional Conferences. There will be nine members, with three representing each of the former Provisional Conferences. That is, there will be three Latin Americans; three from the Asian (Chinese, Korean, and Filipino) and three from the Japanese.

The organization of this committee will be conducted by the National Division at a gathering of all former ministerial members and lay representatives of each of the churches that were part of these conferences.

The responsibilities of the Ethnic Ministries Committee will include the following:

1. Conduct workshops. The workshops may assume various forms and perform numerous functions. They could be conducted across ethnic and denominational lines. Topics include
   a. Theological foundations for various forms of the church's ministry
   b. Studying the changing patterns and composition of ethnic communities
   c. History and culture of ethnic minorities in their homeland and in the United States
   d. Training in language skills
   e. Train lay leadership for specialized skills
2. Recruit ministerial leadership
3. Consult with the cabinet concerning ministerial appointments
4. Conduct fellowship and evangelism programs

Special attention should be given to the structures that will be required to implement the ideas discussed at the workshops. Persons knowledgeable in Conference organization can help devise the necessary details.

Other than the general theological foundations, there are specific situations to which the Ethnic Ministries Committee will need to address itself. These situations have made it imperative to organize this committee, which had been suggested in a memorandum to the 1964 General Conference. This enumeration will concentrate upon ministerial appointments.

1. When ethnic ministers are appointed outside their ethnic churches, all too often they are appointed to dying situations or situations undesirable to their own ministerial peers.
2. Before a minority is appointed to a predominantly Caucasian church, he is required to be the cream of his kind; a Caucasian who is appointed to an ethnic can be a cull. Up to now, conference leadership could bank on enough of the minorities in these churches to regard the appointment of a Caucasian a favor. Further, the Caucasian is appointed to some of the most desirable and strategic pulpits for evangelization of the Japanese.

3. When two Japanese churches were merged in Northern California, the Japanese ministers understood both of them must move, and they did. When a Japanese and a Caucasian church merged in the same conference, the Caucasian minister stayed and the Japanese was appointed elsewhere. What explains the disparity, especially when the Japanese ministers involved in the mergers were told that it was an unwritten policy to move both ministers in such cases? The explanation ought to be given in public, even in print, since it is a matter that has been discussed in the Japanese community. The explanation will receive careful scrutiny since the explanation offered informally has not proved convincing.

4. A minority appointed to prestigious positions should be given power to participate in the decision-making processes. Otherwise, he only becomes decoration or *kazari-mono*. Certainly, the next district superintendent in Hawaii should be an ethnic minority.

Our cultural heritage has told us that the eyes of the world are upon us and that we should therefore keep our best foot forward. Consequently, these thoughts and feelings listed here were not made public. Those who expressed them to the proper authority were reprimanded by their own kind. It was a kind of vigilante committee that saw to it that shame was not brought upon our name. That kind of stance won acceptance at the expense of integrity. The time has come to deepen the acceptance and to authenticate the depth of our commitment to each other. Before we move on to consider the way to create new communities, I want to describe the kind of program which will heighten the distinctiveness of the ethnic community and thereby make possible a greater participation in the larger community. I have in mind two forms of confrontations. I propose this kind of session because I agree with Martin Buber that "all real living is meeting." What has happened to race relations had degenerated in "race erase-ion." In race erase-ion, we overlook differences and try to disband all groups defined racially. In "race relations" we retain the natural group-ins and work through them. A confrontation brings distinct bodies together and allows them to express their full selfhood, whether it is positive or negative. I have outlined some of the negative situations which we need to talk through. No doubt the Whites will have many things they will want to say.

A Yellow-Black confrontation should also take place. The usual method that attempts to persuade the Yellow to participate in the social revolution has proved woefully ineffective. The few who responded were already morally and socially sensitive, or just gullible enough to do anything the minister told them to do. The vast majority remained unaffected. The alternative is to create a situation wherein the Yellows and Blacks can confront one another. Under the auspices of the church, the leaders of the respective communities can be brought together and engage in open expression of their animosities and anxieties, hopes, and confidences. At one such session, which lasted all too briefly, I heard a Black man say, "Us Blacks have knocked on the door and you Yellows have always walked in!" The *Nisei* who was complaining about the "impatient" African Americans was forced to take a second look at his own advancements. The *Nisei* saw his dependence upon the Black man.

The Black militants called our attention to the inequities in the world of sport this past year. Even *Sports Illustrated* was forced to agree! Similarly, we need to cite those situations within the church where inequities remain. Some of us may not feel these situations are serious. They are serious, and many of them lie suppressed and festering. We have a lot of training in sensitivity to undertake in the church.

But the main point of mentioning the Yellow-White and Yellow-Black confrontation has been to illustrate the basic principle of this paper. By emphasizing distinctive groups, we help some of these groups to begin feeling their real involvement in the wider community. By working in and through the existing communities, we work toward a new community.

Creating New Communities

Our work in communities is essentially a tactic. It fits into the strategy of creating a new community. Speaking in other terms, our work in community is a method in order to fulfill the principle or goal of a new community. The method is pastoral, the goal requires a prophetic orientation. A quotation from Barth will help us move into this emphasis.

> One's own people . . . cannot and must not be a wall but a door. The one who is really in his own people, among those who are near to him, is always on the way to those more distant, to other people.[11]

> The command of God wills that a man should really move out from his beginning and therefore seeks a wider field. He will always be accompanied by some measure of homesickness. He must certainly be true to his beginning. The command of God certainly does not require any man to be a cosmopolitan, quite apart from the fact that none of us can really manage to be so. There is not the slightest doubt, however, that where the command of God is sounded and heard the concepts home, motherland, and people, while they must retain their original sense, will prove capable of extension. If we live in obedience, we can be at home even in other lands without being dis-loyal. Not anywhere we please, but wherever we are called to do good, we can find again our motherland.[12]

Gibson Winters, in his *Suburban Captivity of the Church*, correctly observes the dangers of narrow parochialism in the ethnic churches.[13] Restricted attention to the family which neglects the corporate structures of society has reached epidemic proportions in America. The Japanese community has succumbed to the "privatization" of religion. The sense of responsibility of most adults in these communities is limited to the family. A minister will naturally strengthen the abilities of the Japanese in maintaining strong family structures. However, if it is at the expense of failing to develop an outreach and involvement in the exciting and constructive revolutions, we have failed in our ministry.

---

[11] Barth, CD III/4, 294.

[12] Barth, CD III/4, 293.

[13] Gibson Winters, *Suburban Captivity of the Church: An Analysis of Protestant Responsibility in the Expanding Metropolis* (New York: Doubleday, 1961).

Analogies

Since the task of the church outlined in this paper may appear strange, I wish to cite some analogies from other aspects of Christian theology. These analogies come from eucharistic theology, some aspects of social ethics and Christology. There are three distinct views to consider concerning the Lord's presence in the Eucharist or Holy Communion. The historical order will prove instructive. To begin with, there is the view of Thomas Aquinas. For him, the distinction between a substance and form of a thing is crucial. The substance constituted the very essence of a particular object, such as the bread and wine. The form was accidental and could "attach" itself to various kinds of substances. For example, the color brown could attach itself to wood as well as to leather. As a matter of fact, some dyes come from woods and are transferred to leather. When the priest prays over the elements in the Lord's Supper or Mass, Aquinas thought a change of substance of the body of Christ replaced the substance of the bread. However, the form or accidents of bread remained. Aquinas believed the substance of the object was transferred, and hence his position has been labelled the theory of "transubstantiation."

A comparison with Martin Luther will draw out some interesting implications. For Martin Luther, the presence of Christ in the elements did not depend upon any change in the substance of the bread. The bread remained bread even though Christ's presence had come about. Luther compared it to heat entering iron. The essential nature of iron did not undergo any change when heat entered. Similarly, in his view of salvation, the sinner did not need to undergo any change toward righteousness before God's forgiveness was experienced in his life. If the bread could be bread and the body of Christ at one and the same time, so man could be a sinner and wholly justified before God at one and the same time. By contrast, Aquinas's view led to salvation by works. Man had to move from sin to righteousness before he could be justified. In the case of vocations, for Luther, a man could become religious within the secular vocation. For Aquinas, the distinction of the secular and religious meant a man left the secular to become religious. For Luther, priestliness could be felt by the laity as well as the clergy. For Aquinas, one left the rank of the laity to become a priest. Although both men may not have worked out the full implications of their views, subsequent developments have drawn out the implications. The logic enfolded in history has demonstrated the inferences we can draw from their positions. We can diagram the contrast as follows:

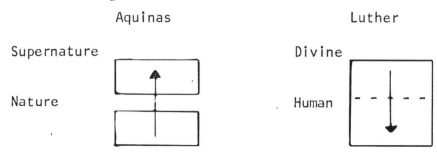

Aquinas	Luther
Supernature	Divine
Nature	Human

The most important feature is the direction of the arrows. In Aquinas, we move from one realm or sphere to another. We move from nature to grace, from reason to faith, from secular to sacred, from human to the divine. In Luther, grace moves into the realm of nature, the divine enters the human, where it is and as it is without changing it. This distinction is crucial for our own strategy. Given the fact that the living Christ comes into the common stuff of life represented in the bread, we now have a model with which to operate. The religious can enter the secular. The church can move out into the world. For social ethics, this means that we can implement God's calling in the structures of creation without altering them. A prime example in modern theology occurs in the writings of Emil Brunner. In his *Divine Imperative*, he speaks of the "orders of creation" within which the Christian fulfills his calling.[14] Although Brunner's approach has received some criticism for his conservatism concerning the existing structures, nevertheless a good part of the orientation that he typified remains in the current social activists.

But the same activists depend upon another figure in Christian history, namely, John Calvin. Calvin's interpretation of the presence of Christ does not fit neatly into our scheme. Calvin was occupied with the impact that the presence of Christ had. An interesting comparison appears in Luther and Calvin's views of salvation. Over against Luther, who emphasized justification of the sinner without merit, Calvin emphasized sanctification that the sinner experienced. A change resulted! We might picture Calvin talking something like this: "Yes, you are right, brother Martin. God's forgiveness enters the life of sinners without the sinner undergoing previous moral improvement. However, once the divine presence comes, we undergo change!" The results for social ethics are clear. Disciples drew a revolutionary theology out of a few passages from Calvin's *Institutes of Christian Religion*. Lutherans were likely to find something good in the evil; Calvinists were more likely to change the evil into something good. As a matter of fact, the social structures did not have a significant position for the rising classes who came to adopt Calvin's theology. They found religious foundations in Calvin to resort to resistance, rebellion, and revolution to make a place for themselves.

If Brunner represented a brand of Lutheran social ethics in modern garb, H. Richard Niebuhr represented some of the chief aspects of Calvin's social theory to twentieth-century man. He gave some hints of this in his *Christ and Culture* when he dealt with "Christ the Transformer of Culture."[15] It also appeared in his earlier study of the concept of *The Kingdom of God in America*. The features relevant for this position paper appear in the dual emphasis upon immanence and transcendence, working within the existing structures and yet effecting improvements. His *Social Sources of Denominationalism* relates how easy it is for the church to remain within structures without altering them. It narrates the sorry story of the fragmentation that the church experienced because it succumbed to the

[14] Emil Brunner, *The Divine Imperative: A Study in Christian Ethics*, trans. Olive Wyon (Philadelphia: Westminster Press, 1947).

[15] H. Richard Niebuhr, *Christ and Culture* (New York: Harper & Brothers, 1956), ch. 6.

divisive forces of sectionalism and social classes.[16] Thomas G. Sanders, in his *Protestant Concepts of Church and State*, applies H. Richard Niebuhr's approach to the relationship between the church and political institutions. One way to see this paper is as an attempt to apply the same dialectical approach to the church's relation to ethnic communities. On a far more abstract level, Paul Tillich has proved most helpful in working through various patterns of dialectical relationships between contrasting poles. Any reader of Tillich comes to recognize a pattern of movement. He posits polarities and then shows how elements of one pole are found in its opposite. Thus, the tension one felt previously is reduced. The analogies with the interpretation of the Christ-event are clear. The divine and human are on opposite poles. However, in the event of the Christ, the divine entered the human sphere and thereby altered it. This did not mean that God sanctioned what he found there; it means he sanctified it by participating in what existed at that time. Most proponents for integration argue thus: since ethnic communities are filled with the evils of racism and represent a passing phase in the acculturation of immigrants, the church should not have anything to do with it. Fashioned after the example of the Christ, I believe we can be led to say something quite different. Since these structures foster evils, and since they participate in the change common to all things human, we should participate in them and direct them. Whether from the viewpoint of eucharistic theology, some forms of contemporary social ethics, or christology, the implications are clear. We are called to work in and through the ethnic communities to create new communities. The church is called to be apostolic and holy. This move can help fulfill the unity and universality of the church.

Appendix A

In his *Culture and Democracy in the United States*, Horace Kallen writes: "In essence, therefore, Democracy involves, not the elimination of differences, but the perfection and conservation of differences. It aims, through Union, not at uniformity, but at variety, at a one out of many, as the dollars say in Latin, and a many in one. It involves a give and take between radically different types, and a mutual respect and mutual cooperation based on mutual understanding."[17]

Several authorities could be cited concerning the rapid acculturation of the Japanese immigrant. A passage from Leonard Broom and John I. Kitsuse in their jointly authored article will suffice: "Considering the *apparent gap* between the American and Japanese culture and the difference between English and Japanese languages, the speed of acculturation is doubly notable. . . . [It is] an achievement perhaps rarely equaled in the history of migrations."[18]

---

[16] H. Richard Niebuhr, *Social Sources of Denominationalism* (New York: Henry Holt and Co., 1929).

[17] Horace Kallen, *Culture and Democracy in the United States* (New York: Boni and Liveright, 1924), 61.

[18] Leonard Broom and John I. Kitsuse, "The Validation of Acculturation: A condition of Ethnic Assimilation," *American Anthropologist* 57, no. 1, pt. 1 (February 1955): 45. I have italicized "apparent gap," because of the nest point.

In the text, I have suggested that the real acculturation took place on the "extrinsic" level and not on the level of "intrinsic" cultural traits. This distinction comes from Milton M. Gordon. "Extrinsic" culture has to do with all those features, which though noticeable, are yet more easily adopted minor oddities in pronouncing and inflecting English. "Intrinsic" cultural traits are more difficult to alter and include such things as "religious beliefs and practices, ethical values, etc.[19] Although there was a "gap" on the level of "intrinsic" cultural traits. The differences that occurred were lists of these traits having been drawn by social psychologists.

William A. Caudill, in his article on the "Japanese American Personality and Acculturation" speaks of their "politeness, respect for authority and parental wishes, duty to community, diligence, cleanliness and neatness, emphasis on personal achievement of long range goals, shame (more than guilt) concerning non-sanctioned behavior, importance of keeping appearance."[20]

Alan Jacobson and Lee Rainwater, in their "Study of Management Representative Evaluation of Nisei Workers," speak of the *Niseis* as "intelligent, diligent, highly skilled, fast workers, ingenious, well groomed, clean, polite, maintain good interpersonal relations, and are oriented up."[21]

The last study cited directs our thoughts to the relationship between the Japanese American and authority figures. In George De Vos's "A Quantitative Rorschach Assessment of Maladjustment and Rigidity in Acculturating Japanese Americans," he speaks of a "dependence on authority for finding situations" on the part of Japanese Americans.[22] In Jacobson's study already cited, he says, "*Niseis* are characterized as 'oriented up' to management for approval rather than horizontally to their associates."[23] In Mamoru Iga's study of "The Japanese Social Structure and the Source of Mental Strains of Japanese Immigrants in the United States," he speaks of "collectively-orientation; authoritarianism; formalism; traditionalism; teachability of flexibility; and external sanction of the extreme importance attached to reputation in the eyes of the world."[24]

The final passage comes from the study by Caudill in the article cited, "The reason for the relatively facile acculturation of the total *Nisei* group (is) due to (a) the nature of the super ego function within the old Japanese culture and (b) certain significant underlying compatibility between value systems of old Japan and those found prevalent in American Middle Class."[25]

---

[19] Gordon, *Assimilation in American Life*, 79.

[20] William A. Caudill, "Japanese American Personality and Acculturation," *Genetic Psychology Monographs* 45, no. 1 (1952), 9.

[21] Alan Jacobson and Lee Rainwater, "Study of Management Representative Evaluation of Nisei Workers," *Social Forces* 32, no. 1 (October 1953), 40.

[22] George De Vos, "A Quantitative Rorschach Assessment of Maladjustment and Rigidity in Acculturating Japanese Americans," *Genetic Psychology Monographs* 52 (1955), 78.

[23] Jacobson and Rainwater, "Study of Management Representative Evaluation," 39.

[24] Mamoru Iga, "The Japanese Social Structure and the Source of Mental Strains of Japanese Immigrants in the United States," *Social Forces*, 35, no. 3 (March 1957), 273.

[25] Caudill, "Japanese American Personality and Acculturation."

Appendix B

JAPANESE POPULATION IN THE UNITED STATES
(1960)

	Population	% of Japanese
United States, Total	464,332	100.0
Hawaii	203,455	43.8
California	157,317	33.9
Washington	16,652	3.6
Illinois	14,074	3.0
New York	8,702	1.9
Colorado	6,846	1.5
Oregon	5,016	1.1
Utah	4,371	0.9
Texas	4,053	0.9
Other States	43,846	9.4

	Population	% of Japanese	% of Area
California, Total	157,317	100.0	1.0
Fresno	6,252	4.0	1.7
Los Angeles-Long Beach	81,204	51.7	1.2
Sacramento	8,124	5.2	1.6
San Diego	4,778	3.0	0.5
San Francisco-Oakland	24,462	15.5	0.9
San Jose	10,432	6.6	1.6
Remainder of State	22,065	14.0	0.6

From the California Department of Industrial Relations, *Californians of Japanese, Chinese, Filipino Ancestry* (San Francisco: State of California, Department of Industrial Relations, Division of Fair Employment Practices, June 1965), 16, 18.

Ministry for a Liberating Ethnicity
The Biblical and Theological Foundations for Ethnic Ministries *

ROY I. SANO

Introduction
Purpose of the Consultation
A few words concerning the purpose of this Consultation on Ethnic Minority Ministries[1] is in order. We are here as ethnic minority ministers to clarify for ourselves and to prepare for the total United Methodist Church a statement concerning the needs we have, the opportunities we seek, and the contributions we intend to make. If we are here representing various boards, agencies, and offices of the church, we are present to sensitize ourselves to the issues in order that we may be among those who will facilitate the appropriate responses of the church to this consultation.

Setting for this Presentation
In order to place this presentation in a wider context of other activities scheduled at this consultation, I recall several levels of questions in planning a military operation. A teacher of missions taught us once to distinguish the three distinct levels of consideration. First, there is the level of rationale and objectives in a military operation or the mission of the church; second, the level of strategies; and third, the level of tactics.

---

* A presentation at the Consultation on Ethnic Minority Ministries, United Methodist Church, September 20, 1973, Claremont, CA.

There are several drafts of the *purpose* for this Consultation. First, based on the discussion of the meeting at Dallas, Texas, October 17, 1972, a statement of purpose was drafted in preparation for the meeting in Kansas City, March 8–9, 1973. It reads: "(a) To explore the needs and opportunities of Minority Ministry, and (b) What distinct contributions which minority ministry can make in the total life of the church."

Second, at the Kansas City meeting the following Statement of Purpose was adopted, as recorded in the minutes of that meeting, page 2, item 10, a. "To share with each other and present to the Board of Higher Education and Ministry the needs and opportunities of minority ministries, as well as the distinct contribution which can be made to the total life of the church."

Third, at the meeting in Dallas, Texas, May 14, 1973, the purpose adopted read: "For ethnic minority ministries and the General Church to examine together the needs and opportunities of the minorities as well as the responsibilities of the church." The minutes of that meeting adds, "The Consultation should provide the General Church with some priorities."

As the church militant on earth seeks to fulfill its mission, it must first ask the basic question of rationale and objective. On this level, we clarify what we seek to accomplish and why. As the title of the presentation indicates, I will concentrate upon the objective of a liberating ethnicity and base it on biblical and theological foundations.

The second task of buck privates, lieutenants, and generals at this consultation of the "army of the faithful" is to specify the strategies. We ask in general terms how we are to accomplish a liberating ethnicity that our biblical heritage and our theological reflection beckon us to facilitate. At this consultation we deal specifically with the contributions of the professionals, namely, the clergy or ordained ministers. The democratization of ministry and the generalization of mission in recent years justifies a session dealing directly with this specialized part of the total ministry of the church. We ask, How do we develop the clergy to accomplish the ends we have outlined? We will discuss a wide range of topics in smaller groups. The topics include

- enlistment of new recruits,
- changing needs in their training,
- deployment (or appointment) of clergy,
- R&R, or rest and recuperation, renewal or recycling (continuing education),
- specialized tasks, and
- development of support systems.

Since the second level of topics will be discussed in smaller groups, I will not deal with them extensively in this presentation. Nor will I deal directly with the third level of topics in the body of this statement. We will explore later in the consultation program what specific steps we can take to develop the ethnic minority minister. We certainly have no illusions that a single statement of requests by us will ensure a significant response from a body so vast and diverse as the United Methodist Church. A follow-through mechanism and procedure will be required.[2] That structure should be answerable to the ethnic minorities we represent. It should also enable ethnic minorities to participate in changes affecting them. Procedures should ensure impacting the total church at the necessary points.

Church consultations often remind me of a childhood pastime. We stand on the edge of a cliff and shout at a distant barrier. When we hear an echo of ourselves, we leave satisfied because we like to hear ourselves talking, perhaps even shouting. But this sport is not the faith that moves mountains; the barrier remains. The childhood game has its place, but we can ill afford the luxury of playing those games at a consultation that deals with our calling and the church we love. Unless we produce

---

[2] Minutes of the planning committee show evidence for concern about the *follow-up mechanism and process*. First, at the Kansas City meeting, March 8–9, 1973, mention was made of a possible "Watch-Dog" Committee to implement the proposals that would grow out of the Consultation. Second, the Dallas, Texas meeting of May 14, 1973 refers to "Channels for Follow-Through." Third, the Program of the Consultation itself set aside time for explorations into implementation of recommendations.

an accountable structure and effective processes to ensure that human needs will be met, legitimate opportunities we seek will be fulfilled, and the contributions we have to make will be facilitated, we have failed. We might as well have spent our days singing, "Little Sir Echo, how do you do? Hello! (hello) Hello! (hello)." Would it help to drive the point home if another figure of speech was employed? Without viable follow-up plans, we will have only come to enjoy the jollies comparable to masturbating instead of planting the seed in the bride of Christ, as we call the church.

I dwell at length on tactics in the introduction because I took several trips over a year and a half for the former Program Council seeking to introduce changes responsive to the recovery of ethnic consciousness. The structure changes adopted at the 1972 General Conference terminated the process, and the agendas have vaporized. I personally am not interested in repeating that exercise in false hopes.

In summary, this presentation will deal with the basic question of rationales and objective of our ministries.[3] Questions concerning strategies and tactics will receive fuller treatments by us at other points on the program.

The Issue of Racism
Why We Avoid the Issue

The central thesis of this presentation is that the primary goal of our ministry is to foster movements which will produce a liberating ethnicity. In other words we seek to mitigate racism in American society, including the church. The validation of these claims and their implications will occupy us for the remainder of the presentation.

Several factors prevent us from appreciating the centrality of the issue of racism and its resolution in a liberating ethnicity. A recognition of these distractions will enable us to see more accurately the terrain we are called to traverse; I will not attempt an exhaustive list of reasons why we place racism on the back burner. One reason is political, the other is theoretical.

First, the issue of racism has been upstaged in recent years and months by the issue of sexism. Observers claim the decade of the '70s is the decade for women. The oppression of women and the movements for their liberation have produced in our church the 1972 report to the General Conference on *The Status and Role of Women in Program and Policy Making Channels of The United Methodist Church.*[4]

The 1972 General Conference mandated we implement the recommendations contained in the report. The prospects are good. The extraordinary financial

---

[3] I have developed a fuller statement on the *biblical and theological foundations for an ethnic minority ministry and church* in a position paper on "The Church: One, Holy, Catholic, and Apostolic," in preparation for the National Consultation of Japanese Work of the United Methodist Church, San Francisco, CA, February 3–4, 1969. [*Ed. note: See pp. 225–239 in this volume*].

[4] [*Ed. note: See* Study Commission on the Participation of Women in the United Methodist Church, *The Status and Role of Women in Program and Policy Making Channels of The United Methodist Church* (Dayton, OH: United Methodist Church, 1972), http://divinityarchive.com/handle/11258/3438].

resources of women, their central power base, and its satellites, and the sheer momentum of their historic involvement in the life of the church, cannot be matched by any single ethnic minority nor even the united efforts of all ethnic minorities if that should ever come about. Even the issue of women in the ordained ministry will very likely produce more results in this decade than the efforts of ethnic minorities in ministry represented by this gathering.

It is not only the nature of racist society that it has the power to determine which issues will be addressed and which will be held in abeyance, but other dynamics are operative. According to Robert Blauner in his *Racial Oppression in America*,[5] the theoretical constructs of the social scientists determine how we order our priorities. The development of American social theory that he outlines is worth reviewing. It explains why the issue of racism has been deferred.

Blauner says American sociologists addressed the issues of racism and ethnic relations between the two world wars. They did their homework and provided significant, albeit not wholly adequate, analyses of American race relations. However, as we began to import the highly imaginative and enormously impressive systems of social thought from Europe, our interests were diverted to issues which were not always as germane to an interpretation of our experiences. American sociologists set aside racial issues and dealt with the implications of urbanization and industrialization. The ethnic groups that were associated with rural and pre-industrial stages of European cultures would, according to Max Weber and company, diminish in their significance in modern society. It was understandable—Europeans were not experiencing the constant enrichment of their societies with immigrants as America had. And besides, the American sociologists themselves were whites whose immigration history has since proved to be quite different from the social history of the colorful non-European ethnic minorities. All of these factors combined to erode quietly and steadily the energies spent previously in understanding and addressing racial differences and conflicts in American society.[6]

---

[5] Robert Blauner, *Racial Oppression in America* (New York: Harper & Row, 1972).

[6] Robert Blauner writes in an important passage worthy of quotation, "For my purpose the most important assumption in this body of social theory is the idea that as industrial societies develop and mature, race and ethnicity becomes increasingly irrelevant as principles of group formation, collective identity, and political action. This assumption, so strikingly at odds with contemporary realities in the modern world as a whole as well as in the United States, can be traced directly to the impact of European social analysts.

"Diverse as were their theories, a concern with interpreting the new bourgeois industrial order which had replaced a more traditional feudal society was a central intellectual priority for each of these scholars. In analyzing the modern world and the social forces that gave rise to it, they devoted relatively scant attention to ethnic and racial division and conflict. They saw such social bonds as essentially parochial survivals from preindustrial societies, and fundamentally opposed to the logic of modernity.

"*Marx* assumed that national differences would dissolve as the world proletariat developed a vision and practice based on class consciousness; he saw the more complex social differentiation of the past giving way to a dynamic of simplification and polarization that was leading to the

Since American theologians were trained in the academic climate influenced by these forces, we can understand why racism has been treated at best with a patronizing air of naive optimism. Whether it was the biblical theologian who espoused the vague universalism of the Old or New Testament and overlooked the powerful emphasis on particularism or the systematic theologian who does not surmise the implications of his major topics for ethnic minorities, they succumbed to the developments Blauner outlines. The same applies to the social ethicists, liturgists, pastoral counselors, church historian or architect, as well as the ecclesiastical hierarchy.

We can speak of the superficial treatment of racial differences and the naive optimism concerning the elimination of racism in American society on the part of American theologians and church persons because of what persons such as Blauner are discovering. He speaks of racism as if it were an independent and powerful demonic entity in American life. For him, racism is less the result of economic inequities, political oppression, or psychological illness and more the autonomous cause which induces these problems![7] Although Blauner does not do so, one feels in reading him that the biblical imagery of satanic powers provides the most adequate explanations. Racism operates in a crafty, sly fashion independent of our conscious

---

predominance of only two classes as significant social forces. *Durkheim* and *Toennies* developed ideal types of traditional and modern social structures: *mechanical solidarity* versus *organic solidarity*, and the *gemeinschaft-gesellschaft* dichotomy, respectively. Ethnic solidarity belonged to the earlier social forms. Their conceptions of modern social arrangements precluded sentimental attachments based on race or ethnicity, or at least the likelihood that men would act on them consistently and frequently. *Simmel* saw the city as a metropolitan way of life in which such primordial bonds (to use Edward Shils's term) must lose their power and persistence. And as for *Max Weber*, perhaps the least disposed among them to an evolutionary perspective and incidentally the theorist whose constructs are potentially the most fruitful for analyzing race and ethnicity, the basic historical dynamic—the movement from tradition to rationality—also appeared to indicate the weakening of these ties. Thus the general conceptual frame of European theory implicitly assumed the decline and disappearance of ethnicity in the modern world; it offered no hint in the other direction. Without significant alteration, American sociology synthesized this framework into its models of social structure and change." Blauner, *Racial Oppression*, 3–4 (emphasis mine).

[7] In a summary of the theses that Blauner opposes, we find hints of racism as an independent force. He writes, "The present work parts company with the leading ideas and implicit assumptions that until recently, at least, have guided most American social scientists in their study of (or reluctance to consider) our racial order:

"First, the view that racial and ethnic groups are neither central nor persistent elements of modern societies.

"Second, the idea that racism and racial oppression are not independent dynamic forces but are ultimately reducible to other causal determinants, usually economic or psychological.

"Third, the position that the most important aspects of racism are the attitudes and prejudices of white Americans.

"And, finally, the so-called *immigrant analogy*, the assumption, critical in contemporary thought, that there are no essential long-term differences—in relation to the larger society—between the third world or racial minorities and the European ethnic groups." Blauner, *Racial Oppression*, 2 (emphasis his).

choices. It grinds out its wreckage without people devising schemes that are formally adopted at a national convention of Birchers or behind closed doors in an ITT Board meeting.

The biblical drama explains the functions of satanic or demonic forces *vis-à-vis* God in heaven and man on earth. At times, the Bible speaks of these forces as gods and lords (I Cor 8:5), at other times as thrones, dominions, principalities, and powers (Col 1:16 and Eph 6:12). These forces can virtually make man into puppets serving their ends. Reconciliation essentially involves liberation from the interferences and domination of our lives by these intermediate levels of beings. But more of this when we discuss liberation and its implication.

Two-Category System of Internal Colonialism

Blauner and the resources he cites explain why we tend to neglect the issue of racism or treat it superficially since we do not know its true nature. His book is an unfinished, though suggestive, description of racial oppression in the United States. Roger Daniels and Harry H. L. Kitano's study of *American Racism: Explorations of the Nature of Prejudice* provides us a framework which can be fruitfully developed to understand racism more fully.[8] They speak of a two-category system operating in American society. The top category is comprised of whites; the lower one is colorful. The colorless dominate; the colorful are oppressed. Some features of the oppression are analyzed by the "internal colonialism" model in Blauner, Carmichael-Hamilton, Cruse, and others.[9] I offer my own development of their insights.

There are three features of the oppression in the two-category system worth mentioning here. First, the top category can maintain the boundaries by distinguishing the two categories. The colorless can mark off a turf they feel belongs to them and they can delineate the "place" the colorless will occupy. The second and third features explain how the boundaries are maintained. The top category has what we might envision to be columns of back-up systems. The second feature of the two-category system will analyze the functions of a single column; the third feature will describe how clusters of columns can act in concert.

I return to the first feature. The overriding fact of American society is the two categories. Attempts to deny the boundaries between them are legion but futile. For example, we might look at a church gathering such as this and say the composition of our group already refutes the boundary maintenance theory. However, to use the experiences of elitists as normative for everyone would be comparable to using the Horatio Alger myth as a model for everyone. It only tyrannizes people and communicates no grace. And then again, individual whites who work in ghettos, barrios, ethnic churches, or Indian reservations might claim they have crossed from the top category to the lower category. However, when the going gets rough, they

---

[8] Roger Daniels and Harry H. L. Kitano, *American Racism: Explorations of the Nature of Prejudice* (Englewood Cliffs, NJ: Prentice Hall, 1970).

[9] Stokeley Carmichael and Charles Hamilton, *Black Power* (New York: Vintage, 1967); Harold Cruse, *The Crisis of the Negro Intellectual* (New York: Morrow, 1967).

can opt out of the difficulty by pushing a panic button. Rescue squads will save them. People with such luxuries simply cannot appreciate how the boundaries in the lower category can restrain the colorful. What is worse, the colorless who function in the category designated by them for the colorful often occupy the best of positions, which should have been reserved for colorful. Finally, there are the colorful who have move in and up the top category. They may feel they have refuted the two-category system. Hardly. Their status in that turf is very precarious.[10] When their kind, the colorful, increase in numbers and threaten to take over that part of the top category, it is the prerogative of the colorless to change that part of their turf into a part of the lower category. Letting neighborhoods opened to minorities deteriorate is an example, as is selling an abandoned church in the inner city to the colorful or, to use another example, it is like my purchase of a sports car. I bought a VW Karmen Ghia that was at one time considered the poor man's Porsche—at least by Ghia owners. Shortly thereafter, not because of my single purchase, to be sure, Porsche introduced their own version of a poor man's Porsche with the 914. The boundaries are maintained one way or another in the two-category system.

Next, consider the way the top category has what we might depict as a column representing segments of that society. Let us take one. We might draw horizontal lines across this column, thus:

Coercive Forces

Federal	National Guards, Armed Services
State	Highway Patrals, Troopers
County	sheriff & deputies
City	Police

Each layer represents a level in that segment of society. For example, we might take this column to represent the system for law enforcement and deployment of coercive measures. Consider a very specific case. In the mid-'60s, when Reies Tijerina stormed the courthouse in Tierra Amarilla or conducted the march from Albuquerque to Santa Fe, the local police force responded. When they could not handle it, the county sheriff offered support. When that proved inadequate, the state troopers, national guards, and Jicarilla Apache police force were called in.[11]

---

[10] Jackie Robinson concludes his autobiography, *I Never Had It Made* (New York: Putnam, 1972), with the following words: "I have always fought for what I believed in. I have had a great deal of support and I have tried to return that support with my best effort. However, there is an irrefutable fact of my life which has determined much of what happened to me. I was a black man in a white world. *I never had it made.*" (Emphasis his.)

[11] Rodolfo Acuña, *Occupied America: The Chicano's Struggle Toward Liberation* (San Francisco: Canfield Press, 1972), 237–241; Richard Gardner, *Grito! Reies Tijerina and the New Mexico Land Grant War of 1967* (New York: Harper & Row, 1970); Ed Ludwig and James Santibanez, *The Chicanos: Mexican American Voices* (Baltimore: Penguin Books, 1971), 16–20.

It is no exaggeration to say that such backup systems exist in the coercive measures of our society. At no level of the system does the colorful control it. The quiescence of ethnic minorities in recent years after the turbulent '60s is in part due to the recognition of this fact. Even when we see outbreaks of protest we find ourselves staging them with the backup system in mind. Otherwise, it would be sheer suicide, as it was in the case of the Black veteran from Vietnam. When he gave vent to his frustration and disillusionment in New Orleans and fired away at whites who were within range, they pinned him down on the roof of a Howard Johnson motel and riddled him with one hundred bullets. Overkill can occur on the lower levels of that hierarchy of the law enforcement backup system.

I have only offered an obvious example in the one segment of law enforcement. One could offer a comparable analysis in other segments, including the banks, education, mass media, entertainment, as well as the church. But we must hasten to the third fascist feature of the upper category. If you think a single segment has sufficient power to scare people back into their place, consider the interlocking system which is operative whenever necessary. One has only to consider the attempt on the part of farm labor to enter the upper category of labor unions dominated by whites. For years, the colorful sought validation of their organization as the legitimate representative of farm workers. Just when they were making an entry, the segment made up of Teamsters joined forces with management and pushed the farm workers back into the lower category. Earlier in their struggles, the farm workers staged a relatively effective boycott of grapes. The growers representing the agribusiness segment of the upper category joined forces with governmental agencies. The federal government stepped in and purchased the grapes that had suffered a loss of markets and sent them overseas to the servicemen and dumped it on the Asian market. The collusion of one segment with another justifies us in diagramming the upper category as a single block despite the additional vertical lines that suggest single segments.

One person in a summer session resisted the implications of the diagram. He insisted that these columns were misleading as well. He accused me of a Joe McCarthy/John Bircher mentality by picturing the opposition in a monolithic picture. He felt no backup system existed in segments in our society, nor could collusions be affected as easily as the diagram suggests. He preferred to diagram circles that had no direct contact with each other, thus:

As a colorless person, however, his position is understandable. He had attempted to move parts of that upper category to treat the lower category more kindly. He experienced frustration. But moving that upper category to treat the lower category humanely is asking it to act alien to its nature. If he tried to move the upper category to maintain the boundaries when the boundaries looked threatened, he could have discovered the support system built into the upper category and the cooperation among the segments.

Cultural Oppression

I have been painting a grim picture of some of the more obvious forms of oppression. Illustrations have been primarily economic and political. An interesting development has been noticed in recent years. We have seen a reduction of attempts on the part of those in the lower category to storm the upper category by force for economic and political gains. More moderate measures have been adopted. Also, they have sought more piecemeal gains rather than the wholesale, systemic ones sought in previous years.

Some of us find ourselves disappointed because we do not see the movements of great numbers of people taking on the giants of industry or the inner sanctum of city halls as they did in the '60s. But perhaps our disappointment comes from criteria that are, inappropriate to tie changing times. We may be asking people to act as if we were in the '60s. It so happens that we are in the '70s. That is no mere fact of the passage of chronological time. We may also be in a different *kairos*, qualitative time.

I became aware of this in looking again at Harold Cruse's book on *The Crisis of the Negro Intellectual* and especially in reading Gayraud Wilmore's *Black Religion and Black Radicalism*.[12] I began to think of the various forms of oppression and which ones we ought to be addressing. We have for a decade or so been preoccupied with political and economic oppression. It may be that we are shifting to an examination of cultural oppression. In fact, Robert Blauner, in another one of his several suggestive comments, speaks as if cultural oppression is the key and most inhumane issue in some ways. He does not elaborate, but it is an enticing idea to test.

Let us say that cultural oppression has to do with the values and basic commitments of people, and let us consider what are the institutions that deal with them in our ethnic minority communities. I believe we will in every case come to the same conclusion as historians of Black communities. The church is perhaps the single most important value-forming community organization. We do not have time to detail the complicated process whereby the church exercises that role. Although the church has played into the hands of those who would subject ethnic minorities to cultural genocide, the cultural function of the church also facilitated the humanizing qualities as well. We may feel that the contemporary ethnic churches cannot exercise that influence because we have been taught that urbanization and modernity in general render the churches powerless. That may be true of the larger white community, but is it true of ethnic minority churches? I believe we have reasons to gamble a bet that the contrary is the case. Ethnic minority churches have an

---

[12] Gayraud Wilmore, *Black Religion and Black Radicalism* (Garden City, NY: Doubleday, 1973).

unrealized potential to contribute toward liberation in the profoundest sense of the word, liberation from cultural oppression.

Cultural Functions of the Church

We have several questions we will need to address. First, concerning our churches, can the church serve a cultural function? But this may be the wrong question since we know that the church has served many cultural functions. To name only two, with reference to the immigrant or alien peoples, the church has acculturated the colorful to the colorless cultural values, and to a lesser extent, the church has helped transmit the colorful culture to the colorless society. Perhaps then the first question is to ask what kinds of cultural functions should the church serve to restore integrity to people rather than subjecting them to cultural genocide? The questions raised abroad by the "younger" churches concerning indigenization will offer us samples of these cultural functions.[13]

Second we need to ask what are the values that will bring liberation? In a recent trip to Santa Fe, Albuquerque, and Gallup, New Mexico, I was inspired with the Chicano community organizations I saw there. The group of mural artists will illustrate my discovery. The artists were trying to identify what they valued. First, they affirmed their mixed background. Despite the frequent practice of communities and cultures that look down on people with mixed background, these artists decided to express pride in their *mestizo* heritage. Second, the evolution of their murals reflected a shift in emphasis from a *mestizo* heritage to an affirmation of their Indian past. They had been ashamed of that ancestry, as if it made them a little closer to the savage or barbarian stages of human evolution. But the paintings of this team of street artists loudly proclaimed the glory of this past. Cultural liberation will come in part through redefinition of our worth, frequently calling for reversals.

One only has to look at our worship services to see how much we have succumbed to cultural genocide in America. To become a mainline Protestant means to become very tame and domesticated to the point of singing controlled music (regular meters), praying de-visceralized supplications and confessions, throwing in pabulum and precooked sermon illustrations into the text, wearing somber, colorless vestments, and minimizing movement. Becoming members of mainline Protestant camps has divisive consequences for our communities. If you think an emphasis on ethnicity induces divisions, think of the divisiveness of the theological camps we are called to select. We are invited to turn religious living into a highly personal form devoid of any relation to societal issues, or if it addresses social issues, it means being forced to neglect the highly personal dimensions of our faith. In plain words, mainline Protestantism offers two tracks, both leading to dehumanizing consequences. Attempts to maintain a foothold in both camps would appear schizoid from the perspective of the two orientations. If you think schizophrenia is bad

---

[13] I explored simplified typologies of the process in "Three Styles and a Sample of Indigenization" (paper, First Conference on East Asian and Amerasian Theology, School of Theology at Claremont, Claremont, CA, August 16–17, 1973).

enough, consider the delusion of treating illness as a sign of health. To become a mainline Protestant often means we will become "color-blind." I know of no other institution in society that treats that illness as a sign of health. People actually become teary-eyed with joy when they can look at the colorful as if they were colorless. You've heard it a thousand times (with arms clutched to breast, head tilted slightly, and eyes heavenward): "For the last six months now, I forgot you were an Indian (Hispanic, Black or Asian)." In that humanizing act of protest, Ralph Ellison depicted the dehumanization involved in being The Invisible Man.

Liberating Ethnicity

Liberation as Normative

If we are following the mainline Protestant theologians, we are frequently browbeaten to engage political and economic issues. We need to address the issue of cultural oppression and foster liberation. When we do so, we see what a difference it would make to the way we do our theology. We will begin to talk about liberation, for one. The word liberation is a scary one for many. Notice how our mission study finally accepted it as a legitimate word. This may in part be due to the critique of "development" as a valid theological concern that Gustavo Gutierrez offered in his book *A Theology of Liberation*.[14] He, along with James Cone in *A Black Theology of Liberation*,[15] has provided for us stimulating reasons to regard liberation as the critical norm which judges what is truly theological.

A recent scanning of theological literature that informed my generation led to a reexamination of Gustaf Aulén's *Christus Victor*.[16] It has been difficult to appreciate this book. Most of us were raised with the moral influence theory or a story about legal transactions. Now, however, since liberation has become the critical norm to determine the primary theological category, we may have grounds to appreciate the work of Christ as an act of redemption. Aulén's historical survey of this interpretation of Christ's redemptive work approximates our view of liberation. In what follows, I will develop a few implications.

Time permits but a brief survey of the implications. First and foremost, the historical and classical view places redemption ahead of reconciliation. Redemption or liberation presupposes oppression by principalities, powers, and rulers of the darkened world, who intervene between God and his people. In the "three storied universe" of the biblical myths, the satanic forces drive a wedge between God and his people, setting them at odds and placing the people out of reach of that which concerns them ultimately. God engages these forces in a warfare or contest to restore the relationship that they have disrupted. The principalities exhaust their armaments in the engagement, and Christ prevails against them. As Paul says, God "disarmed

---

[14] Gustavo Gutierrez, *A Theology of Liberation History, Politics, and Salvation*, ed. and trans., Caridad Inda and John Eagleson (Maryknoll, NY: Orbis Books, 1973).

[15] James H. Cone, *A Black Theology of Liberation* (Philadelphia: J.B. Lippincott, 1970).

[16] Gustaf Aulén, *Christus Victor: An Historical Study of The Three Main Types of the Idea of Atonement*, trans., A. G. Herbert (New York: Macmillan, 1951).

the principalities and powers and made a public example of them, triumphing over them in him [Christ]" (Col 2:15). After the death and resurrection of Christ, these forces are subjected to the one God Almighty and his Lord, Jesus the Christ. Although they may continue to exist in some form, their status is at best ambiguous. (1 Cor 8:5) What is most important is that man is now back in touch with his God, man is reconciled as a consequence of the liberating or redemptive event. Those familiar and reassuring words in Romans 8 convey greater impact if we read them from the perspective of a redemptive act accomplished at least in principle, a defeat in the process of being made effective:

> No, in all things we are more than conquerors through him who loved us. For I am sure that neither death, nor life, nor angels, nor principalities, nor things present, nor things to come, nor powers, nor height, nor depth, nor anything else in all creation is able to separate us from the love of God in Christ Jesus our Lord (Romans 8:37–39, RSV).

We are reconciled because we have been redeemed. Reconciliation thus becomes a derived theological concept; it feeds on redemption. Because of the tension-filled '60s that polarized the citizenry, denominations have adopted various programs of reconciliation. They have rushed to numerous Funds for Reconciliation, the United Methodists included. From the perspective of liberation theology, efforts for the sake of reconciliation seem misdirected. As it turns out, it may be one of the most sanctimonious dodge words in our theological vocabulary, leading to the most subtle snow jobs and inhumane oppressions in our churches and society at large.

Redemption and liberation is the primary work of God and our task as well. Since the mopping-up campaign still exists, the principalities, powers and rulers of the darkened world need to be convinced who indeed is Lord of all petty "lords" and who will be for us our God above all the tin, or gold, "gods." We continue to do battle with these "lords" of racism and "gods" of racists who would oppress and mislead. Since they operate through each of us, at times we must take on that which is oppressing in the other, but in fact, we are not engaged in a warfare with flesh and blood, against human beings, but battling the "spiritual hosts of wickedness in the heavenly places" which operate through us (Ephesians 6:12). Many of the colorful and the colorless do not recognize what constitutes the real issue, the actual battle. Liberation from oppressive racism is the issue and only derivatively reconciliation. The battle does not take place between "flesh and blood," as if we need to create community directly, but takes place between man and those forces that oppress us and divide us. We need not succumb to glib hopes about reconciliation automatically resulting from liberation from racist oppression. We will have to address that issue, but the prior one is liberation.

Further, notice what kind of reconciliation Paul had in mind. His major emphasis in reconciliation dealt with the relation between God and man, and only by consequence did he deal with reconciliation between man and man. Most efforts at reconciliation are therefore two steps removed from the crucial theological issue. They are concerned about bridging the gap between people. Paul was concerned, first, about redemption as a basis for reconciliation; second, about reconciliation between God and his people; and third, about reconciliation between people. Our participation in funds and task forces on reconciliation should therefore bear in mind the prior consideration necessary to affect reconciliation between peoples.[17]

If liberation theology restores the primacy to redemption which Paul and the classical interpretations of Christ's work had seen, we can examine quickly the consequences for other theological categories which have been highlighted in recent years. In the '50s, numerous authors wrote about *renewal* of the church to cope with urbanization; in the '60s we heard much about *relevance* of the church to the growing secularity of our society; and by the '70s, as indicated above, *reconciliation* assumed a position hitherto not assigned to it in church campaigns. From the perspective of liberation theologians, the three R's of renewal, relevance, and reconciliation become subordinate to redemption; they are derivatives of the primary event of redemption. Through redemption, we are reconciled to our God and our neighbor; through redemption, we experience renewal; through redemption, we can become relevant to current issues and contemporary developments.

This shift in emphasis to redemption has far broader historical significance. The current emphasis on liberation may have introduced us to a shift in theological priorities comparable to the transition from ancient to medieval, medieval to reformation, reformation to modern, and modern to the recent existentialist orientation. It was Paul Tillich who outlined those transformations in theological norms. According to him, the ancient church offered man salvation from the problems posed in his finitude, the medieval and reformation man sought in various ways forgiveness for his guilt, and the modern Protestant either turned to the personal and social ideals of human existence or the prophetic message of the kingdom of God. For his day, Tillich offered the New Being to cope with disruption, conflict, self-destruction, meaninglessness, and despair. I suspect a cultural bias in his description of man's ultimate concern. Tillich reflects a European troubled by the loss of initiative and control over world developments. Tillich, for this reason, may be rediscovered as American whites see the passing of their imperial splendor in the years ahead.[18]

One other consequence might be mentioned. While liberation is not only the basis for reconciliation, it may unite diverse movements for liberation. The diverse colorful peoples within the United States and abroad in the Third World can find in the theme a uniting task. Furthermore, other movements for liberation (feminist, gay,

---

[17] Karl Barth's *Church Dogmatics* was projected to move from reconciliation in volume IV to redemption in volume V, the reverse of the order proposed here. Although it is a bit more complicated, one can for the moment say that the theologian of European Protestantism in its autumnal splendor (Reinhold Niebuhr) was doing his theology backwards! J. Deotis Roberts's *Liberation and Reconciliation: A Black Theology* (Philadelphia: Westminster Press, 1973) reads as if it were a black theology of white pacification, in his eagerness to move to reconciliation.

[18] Paul Tillich, *Systematic Theology*, vol. 1 (Chicago: University of Chicago Press, 1951), 47–48.

poor or defrauded whites, etc.) may also find cause to combat oppression as well, in their own special situations.[19]

Cultural Liberation and the Ethnic Churches

Of the various forms of oppression, I have drawn attention to the importance of cultural oppression as the fundamental issue; of the various theological concerns, I have argued for the centrality of liberation. Cultural liberation thus becomes the focal point of issues before us. Further, it has been suggested that the ethnic churches potentially have the most crucial role in fostering cultural liberation since they deal with the ultimate concerns of people. The kind of liberation we are calling for is not a liberation *from* ethnicity but liberation through ethnicity. Just as one would not convert the feminist movement into a massive, transgender operation, we do not propose to convert the movement for liberation of ethnic people into a liberation *from* ethnicity.

I only have time to suggest two important means to promote a ministry for a liberating ethnicity. First, as to the point of training our ministers, we have much more work than we are doing. Theological education is woefully negligent of the ethnic dimensions in Bible study,[20] folk culture in church history, ethnicity in theological positions, racism in ethics, and ethnic possibilities in worship, evangelism, education, architecture, etc. We should demand that all funds from this church should cease from being distributed to seminaries and other centers of training which do not meet criteria of ethnic sensitivity which we feel is authentically Christian. We should call for a decertification of all training centers which do not meet the human standards of taking ethnicity seriously enough to live with it and quit trying to overlook it in us and in themselves or trying to eliminate it. We should mandate our Board of Higher Education and Ministry to take leadership in these issues and to demand affirmative action in staff, faculty, and administration.

Second, if we take this position of the ethnic churches and ethnic ministries, think what we should do about funding criteria. Most church funds are still trying to prove to the world outside that we can be selfless. These funds avoid giving to some desperately poor ethnic churches because we believe, you see, in funding secular organizations who are addressing political and economic oppression. If you accept the reading I am developing about priorities of oppression and liberation, the ethnic church assumes a role hitherto never assigned to it. Even our Commission on Religion and Race, which funds our own ethnic minority community organizations that are addressing political and economic issues, may be misusing funds if they do not deal with cultural liberation. But just any ethnic minority church will not do because it is more often than not staffed and supported by people who became

---

[19] The point made in the above paragraph came as a result of a suggestive remark by Leo Nieto following the presentation of this paper.

[20] My manuscripts for a workshop, Toward a Liberating Ethnicity, at the Earl Lectures and Pastoral Conference, Berkeley, CA, 1973, explored the possible impact ethnic theologies might have upon the contours of the biblical drama as it is usually portrayed. The usual course of events depicted by the "history of salvation school" could undergo considerable change.

Protestants in order to become colorless. We need to support ethnic minority churches that are struggling to define and execute a ministry of a liberating ethnicity.[21]

Conclusion

In this presentation, I have attempted to outline the rationale and objective of ethnic ministries. The central issue we have to address is racism as it expresses itself in cultural oppression and its consequence in cultural genocide. Political and economic oppression, it has been argued, may have become subordinated to the fundamental issue of cultural oppression.

If racial oppression in its cultural form is the key issue, then our ministry should foster movements of liberation from this oppression. The work of Christ as primarily one of liberation or redemption was explored. By implication, our primary task becomes liberation. The liberation from cultural oppression of ethnic minorities might best be affected through that institution which deals with the ultimate concerns of people. The ethnic church could well be that institution, and the ethnic minister could well be the central figure.

The training of those ministers becomes critical and the support of the ethnic churches becomes paramount. Since it is quite obvious that the centers of training which we support are woefully negligent in their training for ethnic ministry and combating racism, and since funding agencies toward which we contribute often direct resources away from ethnic minority churches, it is quite clear we have much work ahead of us. That is why we are here. We have come to clarify what we are trying to do, why and how. "There is nothing quite so practical as good theory and nothing so good for theory-making as direct involvement with practice" (Kurt Lewin). We've probably had enough of theory; let us explore practice and implementation.

---

[21] A resolution addressing these issues was adopted at the Consultation. It called for the organization of a Task Force from the representatives of Asians, Hispanics, and Native Americans attending the Consultation to develop criteria that will determine an adequate education to combat racism and training for effective ethnic minority ministries. The criteria would be used to certify agencies that met these standards and decertify the ones that did not. Further, the criteria would be used to determine what agencies, institutions, center, etc. should be receiving funds and which should be defunded. The resolution also called for staff to be provided by the United Methodist Church to give leadership to the Task Force and implement the decision made by them.

The Bible and Pacific Basin Peoples[*]

Roy I. Sano[†]

During a recent visit to Korea by the Asian American Goodwill Visitation Team, November 23–28, 1974, the team visited with Dr. David Suh of Ewha Women's University.[1] He described for us the heritage of the heroic resistance movement in Korean Christianity. It began from the earliest days of Protestantism in Korea, when the Japanese colonialists occupied the peninsula at the turn of the century. He explained the biblical sources for the resistance movement which has continued to this day against the Park Chung Hee government. He said there are four biblical sources; namely, Moses the Liberator and the books of Esther, Daniel, and Revelation. I was excited. Here I was in Seoul, Korea, and listening to an East Asian theologian speak of the same resources which had come to mean so much to me while working on an Asian American ethnic theology of liberation. The coincidence is worth elaborating. It describes not only the international solidarity one feels with the struggling Christians there but also an emerging orientation of Asian American

---

[*] The following elaborates on several points already explored very briefly in "Problems and Potentialities of Asian American Churches" (lecture, Earl Lectures and Pastoral Conference Monday Workshop, February 8, 1974, Berkeley, CA).

[†] Manuscript of a presentation at the National Inter-Ethnic Convocation, The United Methodist Church, Gunter Hotel, San Antonio, TX, December 11, 1974.

[1] A full report of the Asian American United Methodist Goodwill Visitation Team was published through the Asian Center for Theology and Strategies at Mills College in Oakland, CA. The contents include:

(a) "Statement on the Condition of Human Rights and Christian Struggle in the Republic of Korea" as adopted at the United Methodist Asian American Convocation, Oakland, CA, October 10–12, 1974.

(b) "Resolution" supporting the "Statement" as adopted at the United Methodist Asian American Convocation, Oakland, CA, October 10–12, 1974.

(c) "Statement by the United Methodist Asian-American Goodwill Team to Korea" as released by the team upon its return to the United States.

(d) "Summary Report—South Korean Trip" by The Rev. Juan F. Ancheta.

(e) "South Korea Today" by The Rev. Jonah J. Chang, *Asian-American Newsletter*, December 1974.

(f) "Church Team Goes to Korea," an interview by Brenda Paik Sunoo with Kathleen A. Thomas, *Insight* (December 1974).

(g) News Release on Asian-American United Methodist Goodwill Team to Korea by The Rev. Lloyd K. Wake, December 2, 1974.

(h) "Asian-American United Methodists Visit South Korea" and "Lloyd Wake's Report to Glide from South Korea" by The Rev. Lloyd K. Wake, *In Glide Out*, December, 1974.

and Pacific Island peoples. In this presentation, I will therefore look at Moses the Liberator and then the book of Esther and finally the apocalyptic books of Daniel and Revelation. I hope it will describe who Pacific Basin peoples are and might become.

Moses

First, Moses the Liberator. To appreciate the emphasis, we need to see the alternative to the Liberator among white theologians. One of the fascinating developments among white theologians is the coalescing interest in the covenant and related concepts. In the San Francisco Bay Area alone, for example, there are about five to six theologians explaining the sources and exploring the impact which the concept of the covenant has had on American and European history.

These students see in American Puritan thought the sources of our social and political theories which produced the US Constitution. No small claim. The fuller history of the idea includes the eighteenth-century social contract theorists, the Mayflower Compact, the seventeenth-century English Puritan Revolution, the federal theologians of the Lowlands, and eventually the Swiss Calvinists. From there, the students leap across several centuries to the Bible and find in the concept of the covenant a central motif which unites the Old and New Testaments.

What feeds this widespread interest in the lineage of the covenant? I believe it is a special brand of ethnic theologies for whites who want to find in a central feature of their own culture, in this case the Constitution, its roots in their own faith. It enables them to argue that an underpinning of a crowning achievement of the North Atlantic civilization owes something to their Biblical heritage. It's their way of saying white Anglo-Saxon Protestants can claim a major contribution to their civilization.

Whereas white theologians and all who have bought into their ideas are concerned about a justly ordered society, which the covenant represents, for oppressed peoples such considerations are luxuries. If oppression is the primary reality of a people's situation, such as it is in South Korea today, then liberation is their prior concern. That is, Korean people are interested in Moses the Liberator, not Moses the Covenant Maker. The exodus from Egypt interests oppressed peoples more than the law and covenant at Sinai. The oppressed need redemption before they can talk about reconciliation. Students of the covenant are likely to forget the ethnic movement of liberation from Egypt which helps make sense of the covenant at Sinai. Similarly, the Mayflower Compact makes sense because the Puritans struggled for liberation from the oppressive established church and the king. Finally, the US Constitution must be seen in relation to the Revolutionary War. Antidisestablishmentarians, remember that play-word, have the luxury of talking about reconciliation; the oppressed find it necessary to talk about redemption.

This explains the growing uneasiness liberation theologians have with the emphasis on reconciliation and brotherhood.[2] Concern to unite disparate peoples is a different concern from mobilizing oppressed people for liberation.

To explain why Asian Americans gravitate toward East Asian brothers and sisters resisting oppressive regimes in Korea, Japan, Taiwan, the Philippines, Thailand, and Vietnam, we must explain how Asian Americans feel their oppression. Time for only a brief outline is possible for the moment.

The "two-category system" serves as a convenient analytical model for Asian Americans and Pacific Islanders.[3] Although America was supposed to be "the land of the free and the home of the brave," these peoples experienced imposition of various forms of confinement motivated by cowardice. The confinement, or oppression, they experienced is described in two colorful phrases, namely, the Yellow Peril syndrome and the Red Scare. The Yellow Peril syndrome is the low level of tolerance for Pacific Basin peoples in American society. Whenever we threaten white Americans, we are seen as a peril which must be driven back or at least put in its place. This explains the first century of our sojourn, from 1850 to 1950, as successive waves of Chinese, Japanese, Pilipinos, Koreans, and Pacific Islanders immigrated to the United States. The Yellow Peril syndrome assigned us to the lower of the two categories through restrictive immigration, residential segregation, underemployment, lower income, deprived education, and restricted options for cultural expression.

More recently, the Red Scare has affected our stay here. When the People's Republic of China threatened to invade Quemoy and Matsu in the 1950s, Chinese Americans prepared for a wartime concentration camp because they remembered the imprisonment of 110,000 Japanese in the 1940s without due process of law. In those grim days, Bishop Wilbur W. Y. Choy, then a minister in Sacramento, California, was asked by Chinese American leaders to speak to key white leaders to resist another attempt to evacuate Asian Americans. Later, in the 1950s, Korean

---

[2] Two items in particular by James Cone remain useful illustrations of a critique of reconciliation as a diversion from liberation, viz., *Black Theology and Black Power* (New York: Seabury Press, 1969) and *A Black Theology of Liberation* (Philadelphia: J. B. Lippincott, 1970). J. Deotis Roberts' two books offer examples of an attempt to retain reconciliation as a primary, rather than derived, concept. Roberts has written *Liberation and Reconciliation: A Black Theology* (Philadelphia: Westminster Press, 1971) and *A Black Political Theology* (Philadelphia: Westminster Press, 1974). An argument for the primacy of liberation as the chief theological criterion today appears in Gustavo Gutierrez's *A Theology of Liberation: History, Politics and Salvation*, trans. and ed., Caridad Inda and John Eagleson (Maryknoll, NY: Orbis Books, 1973), 21–42. Liberation and related themes have become prominent among East Asians in their human rights struggles, as evidenced in IDOC, *Mission Through People's Organization: South Korea*, The Future of the Missionary Enterprise, no. 7 (New York: IDOC, 1974), 11, 19; IDOC, *An Asian Theology of Liberation: The Philippines*, The Future of the Missionary Enterprise, no. 5 (New York: IDOC, 1973).

[3] The "two-category" system is outlined in Roger Daniels and Harry H. L. Kitano, *American Racism* (Englewood Cliffs, NJ: Prentice Hall, 1970). *American Racism* offers a history of race relations in California to illustrate the thesis.

American students were threatened with deportation if they spoke against US action in the Korean crisis. Similarly, the Red Scare, which dictates US foreign policies in Southeast Asia, resulted in hundreds of stranded Vietnamese students who opposed the US-supported regime there. A few are now threatened with deportation.

If the Yellow Peril syndrome explains in large measure the century-long exploitation and colonization of East Asians, Pacific Islanders, and Asian Americans; the Red Scare within the last quarter of a century describes the added ingredient which these peoples have experienced at the hand of the upper category. The upper category continues to enjoy greater opportunity, privilege, and security than the lower category. Pacific Basin peoples as a whole spend their lives in that lower category with limited opportunities, fewer privileges, and less security. A few stellar exceptions do not refute the generalizations.

Speaking more broadly, the experiences of Asian Americans and Pacific Islanders in the lower category explains the host of the colorful peoples who are colonized. In the upper category, we have the cluster of colorless colonizers, to use the words of Albert Memmi in his book *The Colonizer and the Colonized*.[4] We can apply the analytical model to the most enlightened, well-meaning segments of American society. I have in mind the church and educational institutions: Ethnic agendas slip and slide down the list of priorities in churches and schools despite all the close friends we have in these institutions. Thus, the two-category system which is operative in the larger society permeates our churches. It has in the past and continues in the present. Oppression is a central aspect of our experiences which in its most insidious form can benumb us to its presence.

The ethnic minority caucus movements in our denominations have acknowledged this reality; their activities proceed on the assumption that the two categories persist. First, we have rejected a wholesale integration of the lower category into the upper category. The rejection of that strategy is axiomatic in caucus circles, I believe. We therefore have limited ourselves to pushing, and at times, even shoving selected persons into the upper category, hoping that they will not forget us when they enter their glory.

Second, besides limiting ourselves to restricted numbers of our people in strategic positions, we do so in hopes to milk the "sacred cows" of American society, including the churches. In our realism, we know our gains never fully obliterate the boundaries between the two categories of people because every move upward on our part often enables the upper category to move upward as well.

We are coming to sense certain limitations in these approaches, just as we came to see the limitations of the assimilationist strategy. We need more than the model of Moses as a Covenant Maker since that model suggests we are making peace or a covenant with the upper category. We may need reconciliation—eventually—but at the moment, redemption is more important. We may need a covenant with the upper

---

[4] Albert Memmi, *Colonizer and the Colonized* (Boston: Beacon, 1967).

category so that a justly ordered society may be created, but in the meantime we need liberation.

Thus, David Suh's reference to Moses the Liberator struck a responsive chord. As an Asian American, I felt an international solidarity with an East Asian. Dr. Suh's remarks illuminated the situation and struggle of Pacific Basin peoples.

Esther

Second, Dr. Suh mentioned Esther. Again, we might compare this to the Biblical model employed by white theologians in the established theological chairs of our seminaries. We have for decades been fed the book of Ruth as our model. You know the story. An alien immigrant makes it into the Land of Promise. The heroine is well chosen. She is a Moabite whom the Israelites found inhospitable during their trek through the wilderness.

No wonder the book has had extensive use in America. It was the secular ideology of the melting pot turned into gospel truth. We are a nation of immigrants whether we have been here three months, three generations, or thirty and three hundred generations, as in the case of American Indians. Being a nation of immigrants, we dream of making it in the Land of Promise.

But Pacific Basin peoples are finding the promises of assimilation have raised false hopes. We may be welcomed as exotic curios but contributions on our terms are less acceptable. Thus, we have been fishing for an alternative to Ruth. We have found it in Esther. The Rev. Lloyd K. Wake started us on this fruitful consideration in his inspiring address at the Second Convocation of the Asian Caucus of The United Methodist Church, July, 1972, Seattle, Washington.

You recall Esther. Talk about making it in an alien society, she was making it with the king. She became the queen. She made it there by denying her Jewishness during a "beauty contest." Her uncle advised her to do so (Esther 2:10–20). But after she was accepted into the inner circles, she discovered she had joined a society where people with power promulgated a decree to exterminate her people. Mordecai, her uncle, reminded her of the realities of her situation. "Think not that in the king's palace you will escape any more than all other Jews . . . Who knows whether you have not come to the kingdom for such a time as this" (Esther 4:13–14). As a person who had obtained an entrance into an alien society, it was time for her to assert her ethnicity and reverse the decree. At the risk of her own life, she broke the law and resisted the king's decree, which was designated to exterminate the "unassimilable" Jews.[5]

---

[5] In the "long chain of abuses" which Asian Americans have suffered, the same reasons were used to terminate an open immigration policy, the first such group to be so treated in US history. The Asian Americans were not "assimilable."

However, with the immigration laws of 1965, the immigration patterns have been reversed. According to the 1970 census, the Asian Americans are the most rapidly growing immigrant group in the US, in terms of percentage. In the decade covering 1960–69, the US population grew by 13.3%. Meanwhile Asians as a group (in this case limited to a tabulation of Chinese, Japanese, and Pilipinos) grew by 55%, the Pilipinos by 95%, the Chinese by 83%, and the Japanese by 27%,

Esther has a peculiar appropriateness for Asian Americans because we are the light skinned who try to pass in American society. We have moved up several ladders. We have penetrated some educational systems and increased our average income above the national average.[6] Of course, this should not be interpreted to mean we do not have the deprived and neglected in our midst. [7] However, by some standards we have become Esthers. We are making it with the king, and like Esther, have denied our ethnicity in order to do so.

---

as cited in US Bureau of the Census, *We, the Asian Americans* (Washington, DC: US Dept. of Commerce, Bureau of the Census, 1973), 6.

The following information has been drawn from the useful report United Presbyterian Church, *A Study of Chinese, Filipino, Japanese and Korean Population in the United States and Projection* (New York: Research Division of the Support Agency, United Presbyterian Church, USA, 1974), made available through The Rev. Philip J. Park, associate for Asian church development.

Population

	1970	1974*	1980**	1985**	1995**
Chinese	431,583	541,457	661,000	843,000	1,368,000
Japanese	588,342	646,635	724,000	821,000	1,054,000
Pilipinos	336,731	474,169	563,000	709,000	1,121,000
Koreans	70,198	182,329	407,000	840,000	1,496,000

(*)   Estimates
(**) Projections

6

Educational and Economic Characteristics

	25 Years or More			16 Years or More	
	Per Cent Completing H.S.	Median Yrs School Completed	Per Cent Completing 4 or more Yrs College*	Male** Median/Mean Income	Female Median/Mean Income
Chinese	57.8	12.4	26	5,223/6,877	2,686/3,512
Japanese	68.8	12.5	16	7,159/8,272	2,785/3,474
Pilipinos	54.7	12.2	22	5,019/5,710	3,513/4,103
Hawaiian	53.2	12.1		6,485/6,682	2,931/3,338

(*) US Bureau of the Census, *We, the Asian Americans*, 14. The US percentage for the same group is 11%. All other data in this chart appears in Bureau of the Census, *Japanese, Chinese, and Filipinos in the United States: Subject Reports, 1970 Census Population*, PC(2) 1-G (Washington, DC: US Dept. of Commerce, Bureau of the Census, 1973). Koreans were not reviewed in this report.

(**) Eleven percent of all American families live below low income or in poverty level, but 9% of Asians fell in this category, including 6% of the Japanese, 10% of the Chinese, and 12% of the Pilipinos.

[7] RJ Associates, *A Study of Selected Socio-Economic Characteristics of Ethnic Minorities Based on the 1970 Census*, vol. 2, *Asian Americans* (Washington, DC: Dept. of Health, Education, and Welfare, 1974), 75–121. This report was not available at the time this manuscript was being prepared. The picture reported in this document challenges the favorable picture reflected in *We, the Asian Americans* cited above.

All the more, then, we should keep Esther in mind. We should not fail to see the covert decrees which call for extermination of our peoplehood and culture.[8] We are expected to become colorless. It has come time to assert our ethnicity. Many people want to penetrate structures of the upper category. They want to flee from their ethnic communities. "*Sal si puedes*" (Get out if you can) is the motto of many Asian Americans outside and inside the churches. Esther calls us to recognize our unique opportunities once we have penetrated the host society.

Thus, when David Suh referred to Esther, it made sense to an Asian American living five thousand miles away. One might add at this point that women in Korean history and contemporary struggles have been conspicuous. The visitation team was privileged to meet several.

I close my reflections on Esther with an observation on the place the book has in white scholarship. In what is probably the most highly regarded and most widely used textbook in Old Testament studies, namely, Otto Elssfeldt's *The Old Testament: An Introduction*,[9] he wonders why Esther has been left in the Christian Bible. He quotes Luther's disgust with this book. Theologians associated with those in power cannot be expected to understand oppressed people with color and their fascination with Esther.

---

[8] Reference to a "covert decree which calls for extermination of our peoplehood and culture" should not be read as an exaggeration. See Samuel F. Yette, *The Choice: The Issue of Black Survival in America* (New York: Berkley Medallion Books, 1971) for a study of black and East Asian experiences.

[9] Otto Eissfeldt, *The Old Testament: An Introduction*, trans. Peter R. Ackroyd (New York: Harper & Row, 1965), 511–512. He writes with a perspective reminiscent of most Euro-Americans who have imperialistically inflicted their cultures upon their respective colonies while being oblivious to their own ethnicity. The cultural genocide practiced by Euro-American Christianity wipes out all other cultures in the name of universalism of the gospel. Eissfeldt writes, "A book [Esther] which is so closely bound up with the national spirit, and which indeed the people itself regarded as a source of its power, could not be excluded by the religion which was bound up with it. This we can understand. But Christianity, extending as it does over all peoples and races, has neither occasion nor justification for holding on to it. For Christianity Luther's remarks should be determinative, a remark made with reference to II Maccabees and Esther in his Table Talk: 'I am so hostile to this book and to Esther that I could wish that they did not exist at all, for they Judaize too greatly and have much pagan impropriety'" (511–512). Luther's offhand table chatter should not be converted into authoritative dogma.

The reader might consult Bernhard W. Anderson, "Introduction and Exegesis," in *The Interpreter's Bible*, vol. 3 (New York: Abingdon Press, 1954). After an unusual appeal to take a positive view of the book of Esther, the melting pot ideology prevails.

He says, "the particularism of the book has been superseded in Christian civilization," and implies that the position he has tried to defend so nobly is after all a sinful position! His magnanimity runs short; it turns out to be nothing but condescension. In his *Understanding the Old Testament*, Dr. Anderson makes allowances for views expressed in the book of Esther, but does not commend it. "In a time of foreign domination and aggressive cultural influence, when the vitality of Israel's tradition was threatened, it seemed that the only course of action was a narrowing of loyalty." Bernhard W. Anderson, *Understanding the Old Testament*, 2nd ed. (Englewood Cliffs, NJ: Prentice-Hall, 1966), 528.

Apocalyptic Writings: Daniel and Revelation

Finally, David Suh referred to Daniel and Revelation. Again, what a coincidence! What a resonance of heart and heart! Asian Americans and Pacific Islanders are finding the same books important as they discover their locus in American society, not to mention world history as well.

Again, I begin with a comparison between white theologians and the reflections of colorful Christians. White theologians gravitate towards the prophets; colorful people who recognize their oppression find the heirs of prophecy, the apocalyptic writers, more helpful. Why do whites and those who have bought into their ideology find the prophets so attractive? The historic origins of the prophets offer an explanation. The prophets became prominent after the Israelites had established their nationhood. By that time the priests had a well-established function to perform, the kings had exercised their power and economic and social leaders had secured their positions. At that point, prophets came as critics to challenge and correct their society. They pleaded with the leaders to mend their ways so that God could again restore wholeness to their nation.

The point to note is the time when prophets rose to prominence. It came at a time when the Israelites had established their nationhood. Whites understandably use the prophets. They are in control of this nation, or supposedly have the ear of its leaders. Thus, religious figures in the history of Israel who addressed their leaders offer a model to whites. Ethnic minorities who style themselves as persons within earshot of leaders also appeal to the model of the prophets.

However, what happens when ethnic minorities find appeals to leaders do not produce appropriate changes? At that point, a continued addiction to the heady wine of power implicit in the prophetic ministry to people in power turns ethnic minorities into impostors. This attraction among ethnic minorities to the prophetic posture is understandable.

Luckily, we can find better reasons to appreciate the prophets. The recovery of the prophetic tradition in the last century represents an enormous gain for Euro-American Christianity. Who had not felt the excitement when an authentic and humanizing quality of our Christian heritage was recovered? But for ethnic minorities, especially for Asian Americans and Pacific Islanders, the posture, though valid for others, will make less sense in days ahead. It has come time to proceed through history with Israel, to move from prophecy to apocalypticism.

This emphasis on the *overthrow of existing social and political systems* reappears in the apocalyptic literature, most prominently in the book of Daniel in the Old Testament and Revelation in the New.[10] They were written for readers who were living under foreign domination. How were they to depict these alien powers in their literature? Isn't it understandable why they depict them in terms of weird and

---

[10] Dr. Won Mo Dong and Dr. Chan Hie Kim have called to my attention that the Japanese colonial rulers first prohibited the use of Daniel and Revelation during the early years of their occupation of Korea. Later, they banned the use of the whole Old Testament.

deplorable creatures fit for imagination mixed with pious hopes and smoldering hatred?

At the time the readers were vassals and colonies, it made little sense to talk about correcting systems. Only overthrowing power structures would meet their needs. Solutions of this sort relied on the *assistance from outside sources*. Nothing within their experiences offered them hope. Hence, they referred to a "Son of Man" who reigned in the distant heavens who would descend on clouds to provide liberation (Daniel 7:13; Revelation 14:14; Matthew 24:30, 25:31; Acts 7:56).

When their redemption came, they would live in a very different world from the one they now faced. How else could they portray these radical departures from one stage of history to another except through schematic periodizations of history? The prophetic orientation led people to see history undergo gradual changes. Any single stage in history was ambiguous, a combination of features from the past mingled with elements from the future. *Radical changes* were left for visionaries such as apocalyptic writers.

Finally, since apocalyptic writers spoke of overthrowing those in power, they presented a threat to rulers. In order to avoid the wrath of governors, the apocalypticists had to work undercover and conceal their identity through false names. Hence the *use of pseudonyms*.

Each of the features of apocalyptic literature which I have cited has at one time or another been regarded as a reason to disqualify it from contemporary Christian use.[11] An illustration of the bad press which apocalypticism suffers in white scholarship appears in *Apocalyptic* by Leon Morris, an English evangelical.[12] He says the apocalyptic writers found it necessary to use pseudonyms because they did not have a direct experience of God. The use of established revealers of God's word was supposed to overcome their second-hand experiences with the divine. Thus, apocalyptic writers used the names of Moses, Solomon, Isaiah, Abraham, or, if any one of these were not enough, they may claim the authority of all of the twelve patriarchs!

Since false names betrayed a lack of direct experience with God, Dr. Morris feels this body of literature is second-rate. He fails to appreciate the connection between the use of pseudonyms and the oppressive situations for which apocalyptic literature is written. They offered oppressed people a religious foundation for resistance movements.

Although I had guessed the usefulness of this body of literature, I was given two vivid confirmations of this within this last year. Through Korean American friends, I was introduced to an international network of those opposed to the dictatorial practices of the South Korean president, Park Chung Hee. A friend showed me a

---

[11] Sometimes the attack on a single feature could occupy a career. Although it may sound scandalously reductionist, one can fruitfully argue that Rudolf Bultmann's preoccupation with "eschatological existence" was an attack on the periodization of history practiced by apocalyptic writers.

[12] Leon Morris, *Apocalyptic* (Grand Rapids, MI: Wm. B. Eerdmans, 1972).

sheet of paper containing two lists of names. In one column I read the names of several acquaintances in the Korean American community; in the second column I saw such words as Panasonic, Hitachi, Mitsubishi, etc., perhaps representing sympathizers to the cause in Japan. I also read names of animals such as antelope, beaver, and lamb and guessed they were American counterparts in the movement. Just as the apocalyptic writers did in the biblical ages, these writers employed false names to conceal their identity whenever they corresponded. None of us who have carried the bits and pieces of papers containing their messages will be the same again. They did not contain second-rate writing! They contained a quality of life no Oxford don, Cambridge scholar, or Tübingen professor could force us to treat lightly!

Similarly, a Pilipino taught me the use of symbolic language. He was enrolled in a course I was teaching at San Francisco Theological Seminary in San Anselmo, California. Before coming to study last summer in the United States, he was detained for two days, ostensibly for "orientation," but more like interrogation and indoctrination on the restrictions of his activities. Before returning to the Philippines to do his dissertation, he worked out with his committee a glossary. When he referred to the "New Society," he said, he meant the martial law of President Marcos, and so forth. Anyone who has read apocalyptic literature knows the use of double talk. The situation requires it.

These experiences have demonstrated to me that false names do not betray low-grade quality of a written document, as Dr. Morris suggests. As in the case of Koreans and Pilipinos struggling for human rights, the apocalyptic writers found it necessary to do their work undercover until that time they could work in the open. What is true in extreme situations illuminates what is true in the subtle and insidious oppressions in American society.

But we must be more precise in relating this comparison between prophetic and apocalyptic literature to our situation here at home. First, there is admittedly a prophetic posture in the biblical tradition. To that degree, the strategy which has characterized the caucus movement up to this point is valid. We have been trying to make our way into positions of power to sensitize the institutions of this society to the needs of deprived peoples. We have, to repeat myself, tried to milk the sacred cows for our people.

However, and this is the second consideration, there may be new options we should keep in mind, and perhaps a few of us had better start exploring another strategy which draws on the insights of apocalyptic literature. The reason is simple. The sacred cows are running out of milk. Or to change the figure of speech, perhaps what we thought were treasure chests are in fact becoming "whited sepulchers," whitewashed containers with the remnants of past greatness. This is an apocalyptic way of periodizing history. At one stage, something is alive; at another point in history, it is dead. We may very well be entering a phase in world history when the domination of this earth by the North Atlantic communities is ending, including the North American part in that power structure. And maybe all the institutions associated with it are exhausted of material and spiritual resources. The imperialistic empires may soon become colonies and vassals.

I had a glimpse of this vision when I read an article in an English language newspaper In Japan while attending the Consultation on Minority Issues and Mission Strategies, May 8–10, 1974, Kyoto, Japan. In an article datelined New York, William L. Ryan wrote about the "Epidemic of Falling Governments: Energy Crisis, Inflation Causes Difficulties Among Advanced Nations." It read, in part:

> The year isn't half over and already it's made its mark in history by producing a startling epidemic of falling governments that presage agonizing uncertainties for the months ahead.
>
> The oriental calendar makes this the year of the tiger, but there are fewer tigers than goats in leadership positions. Throw darts at a map and it would be difficult to hit a spot where leaders aren't having perplexing difficulties as the advanced nations seem to act less advanced all the time.
>
> Canada's Prime Minister Pierre Elliot Trudeau fell last week . . . West Germany is in a dither over Chancellor Willy Brandt's shocking resignation . . . Some of the uncertainty comes from France, Europe's keystone, after President George Pompidou's death . . . Italy's government fell in March and Premier Mariano Rumor formed the nation's 36th Government since World War II . . . Britain's Conservative Cabinet fell in March. A Labor regime succeeded it and is having manifold troubles . . . minority liberal Government teeters on the brink of doom . . . Belgium had general election in March, intended to resolve a crisis.

The article proceeded to report the changes in Portugal, Spain, and Australia. Nixon's resignation still lay in the future, with the soon-to-sour honeymoon between President Ford and Congress yet to come.

A subtler version of this apocalyptic vision of the periods of history appears in one of the high priests of missionary scholarship, namely, Stephen Neill. In a very interesting footnote tucked away in his book *Colonialism and Christian Missions*,[13] Bishop Neill writes about a new era in world history. Previous centers of history were based first in the Near East, then in the Mediterranean Sea, and most recently in the Atlantic Ocean. He says the next center of world history will be found in the Pacific Basin. Now, whether it will be there alone or spread in several directions is beside the point. What is important is that the center will not be in the North Atlantic. Among other things, this means that the flow of human resources will now shift from the tired and frightened centers in Europe and the North Atlantic to other centers. I can only speak from a limited experience of the vitality now emerging in East Asian people who presently number over a half of the world's population. And what I know is but the faintest glimmer of what Mao Zedong had in mind when he announced that "the west winds are blowing!"

Our minds are shifting. Asia is no longer the Far East. It is neither far nor does it lie to our east! We who live on the Pacific coast no longer live on the West Coast, but on the eastern rim of the Pacific Basin. The shifting center gives us a new bearing, a

---

[13] Stephen Neill, *Colonialism and Christian Missions* (London: Lutterworth Press, 1966).

new sense of direction. To name only one change in directions, we now feel we must be the channels to introduce the new vitality to America. No longer should our Board of Global Ministries only think of sending so much as becoming a means of availing themselves of the contributions the emerging forms of faith East Asians have to offer. And no longer only send whites abroad to Africa, Latin America, Asia, and the Pacific Islands to deliver those depleted treasures of the West. Let us help American Christianity experience renewal of faith through our East Asian and Pacific Island brothers and sisters.

Further, to work together we as Asian American and Pacific Islanders plead with all boards and agencies to regionalize their work. In order to appropriate the new thrusts from abroad which we hope will revitalize American Christianity, make the Pacific coast, the Southwest, and Southeast ports of entry. The Northeast is not the fountainhead of all wisdom and riches. To take seriously the apocalyptic vision could usher in a new phase in church history when remnant people will indeed become the creative minority. Just as the religious orders in Roman Catholicism and sectarian movements in Protestantism, the caucuses centered in various regions could provide a new impetus to American Christianity if they are given the channels through which they may convey the gifts God has given them. The Rev. Jonah J. Chang, who suggested this restructuring, should be given an opportunity to elaborate his ideas.

Many more suggestions may be derived from apocalyptic literature, and what is mentioned here could be elaborated. But these inferences should suffice for the moment. I hope they demonstrate what a response David Suh evoked when he spoke of Daniel and Revelation. Our problem is oppression, and the passing of existing power structures should be part of our vision. I do not expect American hegemony will die with a "bang" but something more akin to a "whimper," to borrow T. S. Eliot's familiar phrase. We might keep England in mind. The once proud empire which could claim that the sun (would?) never set on her worldwide expanse has found that within one generation she went from empire to colony. Today, she is for all intents and purposes a colony of the United States. Thus, the sole strategy of penetrating existing systems to introduce alterations here and there is what Martin Luther King Jr. said is comparable to "running into a burning house" for our salvation.

Conclusion

The Bible begins to look very different when we as Asian Americans and Pacific Islanders look to East Asia. We discover we have overlooked historical periods and neglected sizable blocks of literature. The open debate is this: Are we in an analogous historical period which justifies us to draw upon Moses the Liberator, Esther the Queen, and the books of Daniel and Revelation? I believe sufficient analogies exist in our situation and loom on the horizon.

Whether one agrees or not concerning our historical situation, we might at least agree on the usefulness of the Bible in understanding who Pacific Basin people are and might become. In other terms, the Bible is a human document, revealing who people are, and it offers humanizing resources for what they might become. In the case of Pacific Basin peoples, we can say we are concerned about "harmony, peace, and understanding" between people which a covenant maker like Moses offers. But that "We are one," as a bumper sticker reads, is only an aspiration which can be self-deluding if we omit the two-category system which validates the image of Moses the Liberator.

Furthermore, Pacific Basin peoples are not "Ruthless," if the pun be permitted. There are plenty in our midst who still look for ways into the host society. But at the point of a fair share of human rights, we cannot neglect the unintended ways the promises of assimilation have made "jackasses" out of us. We have more often than not obtained at best a precarious acceptance, or acceptance on someone else's terms. Thus, Esther offers more.

Finally, it may be valid to introduce many changes to existing institutions, be they legal systems, welfare organizations, educational programs, and even churches. However, major realignments in the global power centers are in the making, and we cannot neglect these larger budding realities. We may be chipping away for a new entrance into imposing buildings which turn out to be mausoleums. The apocalyptic vision offers integrity.

"So Jesus also suffered outside the gate in order to sanctify the people through his own blood. Therefore let us go forth to him outside the camp, bearing abuse for him. For here we have no lasting city, but we seek the city which is to come" (Hebrews 13:12–14).

The Eccentric Ministry
A Style of Life in the Margin

WILLIAM MAMORU SHINTO

The conception of the "eccentric ministry" began out of my living as a marginal person in United States society. I make no brief that this is a style of life which would be helpful to anyone else or that it emerged only out of "strength" rather than "weakness." That is, "marginality" may be a result of rejection, paranoia, and fear. Nonetheless, I am personally satisfied that the theory of the "eccentric ministry" has been a fruitful and pragmatic one for myself.

However, beyond the personal statement lie other facts. For one, ethnic minorities are "marginal" to our society. The anti-institutional movements, such as the Peace Movement and the counterculture, are also marginal. Moreover, besides my personal pilgrimage, I have vocationally been involved in "specialized ministries"—the ethnic church and the campus ministry, both "peripheral" in the thinking of the denominations. However marginal all of these groups are, in fact, they have all exerted an influence far beyond their numbers and resources. In the aftermath of the anti-war movement, the society conned young people into believing that a "better way" was to work within the system—elections, etc. The truth of the matter is that the most creative change has been effected by the "gadflies" of society: Martin Luther King, Ralph Nader, etc., who used unorthodox methods and bypassed authorized channels in the systems. Marginality may be a more powerful weapon than we have imagined it might be.

Furthermore, the church as a whole needs to struggle with the question of marginality since it is very obvious that the religious establishment has been moved from a central position to the periphery in society itself. At one time, the bishop counseled the king; today, the bishop's younger brother, who went to Harvard Law/Business Schools, shapes the future. Church persons are delegated the task of invocations and benedictions at public gatherings.

It is apparent, then, that marginality is not restricted to the minority experience. However, the concept of the eccentric ministry is principally the result of living in this country as a minority. And it may be precisely because the dominant society oppresses ethnic minorities in such blatant fashion that we become more quickly sensitized to new trends in society. There are some negative things. For instance, it is clear to minorities that when larger numbers of ethnic groups are being admitted to universities that the BA degree is no longer of much value. Subsequent events have proven the point since we now have fifty thousand PhDs without jobs. Not only so, there were drug problems in the ghetto and *barrio* long before the general public became aware of it; our senior citizens' issues were apparent long before gerontology became popular; and the turning of the United States Armed Forces into virtually a non-white group was inevitable when one noted that the anti-draft movement was only the culmination of the white youth's desire to escape the horrors of war.

But there are some positive indicators first made visible among minorities. Some major observations will help set the scene. The best place to note future fashion trends is to visit Harlem or Chicago's South Side. In language, the whole youth generation is almost unintelligible to adults because of their absorbing the language of the ghetto "street people."

For major issues, one only needs to reflect on the powerful impact of Black Power on American society. It has, in spite of the controversy it engendered, been a real cathartic event and a central factor in our day. In the life of the church, the rise of ethnicity and racial awareness really took place with the Black Manifesto, deplored by many white church persons, but in actuality it was the salvation of an inert church.

Finally, there is some truth in the belief that whatever happens to minorities will become the norm for the whole society. That is, the social indicators which would be as accurate, and in my opinion more accurate, is to analyze what is happening to minorities. Being the marginal group, minorities are left without resources and the "normal" support services given to the rest of the society. Thus, emerging social, economic, political, and psychological problems are likely to surface first in the ethnic communities.

My observing public education for several years bears this out. It is only conventional wisdom that tells us that white schools are better. Inner-city schools stripped of all extra services, enrichment programs, and educational hardware reveal the core problems of education. These problems first arise in urban ethnic schools. Basically, it is caused by a wrong-headed educational philosophy—schooling and not learning. In the larger context, one needs to reflect on the excruciatingly painful experience of the American South, which went through a cycle of trauma in the "white-black" confrontation. It is only now becoming apparent that the whole nation is involved in "white racism," not just the South.

For Asians, the emergence of Chinatowns in the late 1800s was a clear indication of the white racism against Chinese, and the evacuation of the Japanese should have been no surprise in 1942. Jacobus ten Broek analyses the evacuation and roots its causes in the century-old patterns of racial prejudice of American life. It is imperative for the whole of America to note that the setting aside of constitutional rights is not a peripheral aberration directed against the Asians, but a pattern of life which will and is now directly affecting the whole of our society. A close reading of what is happening to minorities is a relatively true prediction of what may happen to the whole of society in later decades.

It is also true that marginal persons are much more likely to have broader and varied contacts in the society than the "normal" person.

> The normal person, strongly identified with his group will tend to limit social interaction with other groups. Conversely, the "marginal" person will tend to cross structural lines.

Therefore, the normal person may be much more discriminatory toward other groups than the marginal person.[1]

In essence this is true, but like all generalization it needs corrective. Actually, in large enclaves of Asian concentration, the very tight-knit nature of the community may be a great inhibiting force preventing interaction with others. On balance, however, the marginal person is precisely that because he interfaces with varieties of individuals, groups, and ideas.

There is also something paradoxical about the style and ideas of marginal persons. From one point of view, the marginal person is oppressed and usually in poverty. From a different vantage point however, his/her lifestyle may be a precursor rather than a curse.

> The American black man, with his lack of a nation, is not behind us, but ahead of us. The whites, exulting in the work ethic, always saw the black man as the pre-industrial past; it never occurred to them that he could be the post-industrial future.[2]

Thus, when one looks at the shaping ideas and ideals found among marginal persons, one is at the bedrock of the future. It is in fact in the area of basic styles of life arising out of disparate ideas of living that marginality is most potent. For the church, this means a reconceptualization of theology and ethics, which leads to varieties of lifestyles not presently affirmed among the majority. In truth, the most devastated person, psychologically and socially, in our society is the white American. Whatever roots he/she has have died in the bankruptcy of the nation. The "eccentrics" may have the solution for all of us.

In the life of the church itself, the campus ministry, with which I am presently related, has affirmed the style of marginality as one of its major expressions. However, in the course of the use of the term there have arisen problems for both the campus ministers and the church. The church, already conditioned to thinking of specialized ministries as peripheral, was reinforced in that way of perceiving campus ministry by the term marginality. For the campus ministers themselves there was a sense of actually being insignificant since we are "marginalized." These thoughts also apply to ethnic pastors and ethnic churches. Thus, I have been helped to rethink the idea of marginality in terms of "eccentricity," an idea set forth to me by a denominational executive, Mr. Peter Jensh.

The term "eccentric" is chosen with care. Eccentric is defined as "out of the center; not having the same center, as two circles one inside the other; deviating from the norm, as in conduct, out of the ordinary." It also means "odd," but we'll ignore that. Marginal ministries are eccentric in the sense that they do not have the same center as other ministries of the church, such as the parish ministry. For campus ministry that means a different and double focus: higher education and ecumenism. If you could conceptualize the local congregation as having a central focus in the

---

[1] Roger Daniels and Harry H. L. Kitano, *American Racism: Exploration of the Nature of Prejudice* (Englewood Cliffs, NJ: Prentice-Hall, 1970), 7.

[2] William Irwin Thompson, *At the Edge of History* (New York: Harper Colophon Books, 1971), 26.

worshiping community, its church life is an ellipse which gives its ministry a different shape which takes it outside the boundaries of the parish ministry while maintaining a shared life (see Figure 1).

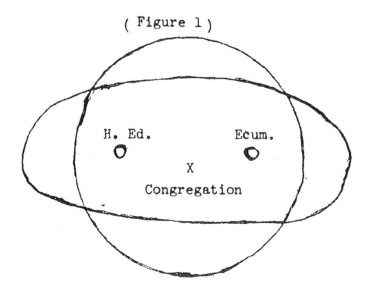

(Figure 1)

So too with the ethnic congregations. Although it is a parish ministry, it too had another focus: ethnicity or cultural difference. This makes it an eccentric ministry, but not out of the church nor peripheral to it (see Figure 2).

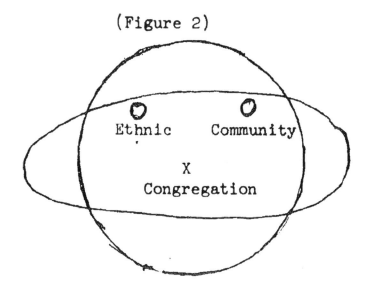

(Figure 2)

All of this points out the fact that eccentric ministries are neither experimental nor peripheral. They are different to be sure, but the longstanding idea that the white dominant parish congregational ministries are the true church while the rest of the ministry is out on the edges of the church must be laid to rest. The most creative and biblical life among Christians may in fact be present in the eccentric ministries.

What can this mean for the Asian American churches? At least it gives us direction in two thrusts. The first is that it frees us from having to emulate the dominant white parishes. The cultural factor gives us a perspective from which to develop a different form of the Christian faith. The underlying cultural forms would be variant, taking into account the fact that life is lived differently among Asians in America. The truth is that ethnic congregations can be more "together"—their forms of worship, choice of music and arts, sermons, style of governance, etc. revolve around a central, culturally identified worldview.

Not only so; in the more important areas of thought and ideas, the Asian Christian can begin to take seriously the differences between Eastern and Western thought. The critical point is that our affinity to Buddhist, Chinese, Japanese, Korean, Samoan, Filipino, etc. thinking is not an unchristian link as we've been previously schooled by white Christians. We reject, in fact, their Hellenistic and Germanic roots by forcefully reminding them of their own departures from the Hebraic beginning of the Judeo-Christian faith. There is no divine mandate that the birth of Christ be celebrated around a probably nonexistent Roman Catholic saint whose clothing and features come from Northern Europe and is called Santa Claus!

Philip Slater points out the basic value problems in the United States. I would like to suggest three human desires that are deeply and uniquely frustrated in American culture:

1. The desire for *community*—the wish to live in trust and fraternal cooperation with one's fellows in a total and visible collective entity.
2. The desire for engagement—the wish to come directly to grips with social and interpersonal problems and to confront on equal terms an environment which is not composed of ego extensions.
3. To desire for dependence—the wish to share responsibility for the control of one's impulses and the direction of one's life.[3]

The primary correlates in American life are competitiveness, uninvolvement, and rugged individualism. It is precisely in community, engagement, and dependence that Asian thought coupled in a creative way with the Hebraic roots in Christianity can lead the way.

For instance, nowhere in Asia is there a value system predominant which does not emphasize community, whether it is the Buddhist *sangha*, the Confucian system, or the extended families. The present understanding of Maoism also demonstrates in a vivid way how an entire nation, the largest in the world, has taken real strides in reducing the very problems which haunt the Western nations. Not only so, but Taoist mysticism, for example, and Zen thought are replete with the fundamental viewpoint which should undergird our ecological concerns—humanity's

[3] Philip Slater, *The Pursuit of Loneliness: American Culture at the Breaking Point* (Boston: Beacon Press, 1970), 5.

relationship with nature as one of harmony rather than antagonism. Indeed, then a real Asian American theology could transform the present apathy and defeatism within the church by giving not only Asians a healthy and more relevant perspective but the entire country.

This leads to the second thrust. Given yin-yang theories and other holistic thought in the East, the Asian theology could be the forerunner of a theology of wholeness—how does the church cope with rising pluralism? Since it is obvious that the church cannot return to the integration ideals of the past, how will it express its oneness in the future? One of these clues is an Asian concept—a move from polarization and opposition to a state of acceptance of difference in a harmonious complementary state, the yin-yang accord. The harshness of either/or is replaced by both/and. This will effect tremendous change in the life and attitude of the church. For instance, it will totally alter our present harsh, demanding evangelistic styles to an acceptance of difference and a harmonizing of variations into a whole. It will in fact drive us to the Christlike stance of acceptance of humans rather than demanding that they change to meet our criteria.

Can the Asian American churches effect such change and in that magnitude? I am reminded that when our Lord set out to spread the gospel, he chose some very unlikely candidates, the twelve disciples. They were neither rich nor powerful; in fact, they operated as eccentrics in the margins of the society—and changed it.

The Ethnic Church on the Edge

The End or the Edge of Life?

William Mamoru Shinto

There is a great battle being waged in the life of the ethnic church. The primary question is whether the church in the minority communities will end or, recovering its sense of mission, become the cutting edge of the Christian faith. The answer is not simple. Some deplore the existence of the ethnic church, citing the fact that the Christian church cannot be a segregated group, that we are the One Body of Christ, and the church cannot tolerate enclaves or provincialism.

On the other hand, there is a growing unease among the mainline church denominations, which are predominantly white both in perspective and power, about the challenges arising from the ethnic congregations. This challenge can be handled with relative ease as long as the demands are couched in wanting to have more of the fiscal and personnel resources of the denominations, the development of ethnically oriented training opportunities, and a voice in decision-making. Money and appointments to boards can solve this. The problem, however, is magnified astronomically for the white church with the rise of ethnic theologies which cannot either be "bought off" by money nor subverted by "tokenism."

The point is that the ethnic church itself is the key to its own future; whether it will survive or end depends upon the priorities which it chooses. Up to this point, the major demands of the ethnic groups have been in terms of shared power and resources. When demands are so made, sooner or later the white dominated denominational leadership begins to understand that it, in fact, is the dominant group. That is, "whitey churchman" soon follows the general racist society in responding with "tokenism" and theories of "brotherhood" and gradualism. Sharing two seats on a sixty-member board is not shared power by any stretch of the imagination. I would also point out that if a major denomination would ever find itself in a position of real shared power with minorities, it would find ways to drain off the resources and hand over an emasculated organization to us.

On the other hand, beginning with the emergence of "black theology" and the inroads of Latin American "theology of liberation," white denominations are really being challenged by another kind of power: the power of new symbols of truth, the power of a variant and innovative "conceptualization" of the Christian faith, and a power to displace white categories of perception of issues. Just as in the wider American society, it is almost impossible to answer the question "Who and what is an American?" So too in the life of the church in the United States, it is becoming increasingly difficult to answer the question "Who and what is an American Christian?"

In one sense, the ethnic caucuses sense that the seat of power in white denominations is in major church governing boards. However, it is my contention that, in a more profound sense, the seat of power is the theological underpinnings which spell out the *raison d'être* of the church itself.

It is this challenge of conceptualization of the faith which cannot be diverted easily by the white church, and I contend that the ethnic churches have not done enough homework nor sorted out priorities to ensure that this kind of challenge of power is not lost. We have majored on what the churches have and can share when we should be majoring on what they do not have and we can share with them. The clues are in the vast breakdown of ethics and moral values among the major denominations and the nation. The nation is in dire straits in searching for an honest person to lead it. The major needs are for *community* to replace the immoral competitiveness of our people, to find ways of overcoming the apathy and individualism by moving in *dialogue and engagement*, and by overcoming the independent pioneer-mindedness by exploring ways of *dependent and interdependent living*. For both social and theological reasons, ethnic churches have community, know the meaning of dependence upon the transcendental and interdependence in life, and provide for the church the pluralism necessary to have a meaningful and productive dialogue.

The Force of Myth and Symbol

Lily Tomlin, the comedienne, has a child character called Edith Ann. You've probably seen her in the oversized rocking chair. Edith is talking with a neighbor, telling her all sorts of things, when the adult finally scolds, "You talk too much and you make up things." Edith Ann then solemnly replies, "Lady, I do not make up things. This is lies. Lies is not true. But the truth could be made up if you know how. . . . and that's the truth."

And I contend that that is "doing theology." The truth can be made up and is no lie *if you know how*. Why would the white church be so devastated if the ethnic churches really came up with theological formulations vastly different from the present theologies in the American churches? Precisely because their "made up truth"—their theology—is now being challenged as a lie. What they believe about humanity, God, nature, and the church is being severely threatened by the inability of it giving any vitality to a morally destitute nation and the challenge of rival faiths, both Christian and non-Christian. The white theology is being questioned as "off the mark"—which is, incidentally, a definition of sin.

Dr. Herbert Jackson, who is now on the graduate faculty of religion at Michigan State, tells of an incident which occurred in Thailand. It was a gathering of missionaries in the home of a lovely Thai Buddhist. There was a long evening of social interaction and serious religious discussion. As Herb went away, he had the gnawing feeling that in that roomful of persons, the most cultured and religiously astute person was the Thai hostess—and the missionaries had come there to save her?

Pearl Buck tells of another incident in China, where her parents were missionaries. The Chinese faithfully attended the church services, suffering politely through the long sermons. One day, one of Pearl Buck's playmates revealed the fact that the Chinese were puzzled why the God of the Christian would make a requirement for salvation to be traveling so far and preaching such long sermons. The Chinese, you see, came to the church services to help Pearl Buck's father receive *his* salvation, not theirs!

Ernst Cassirer once said:

> The philosopher is not permitted to construct an artificial man; he must describe a real one. And the so-called definitions of man are nothing but airy speculation so long as they are not based upon and confirmed by our experience of man. There is no other way to know man than to understand his life and conduct. But what we find here defied every attempt at inclusion within a single and simple formula.[1]

Thus, we had games played on us as Asian Americans and as Asian American Christians. We are told that our cultural roots are in "heathenism."

We are schooled in public education and church schools that there is a simple and single formula which explains human life—and it is essentially Western European in perspective. We are directed to repent of our Buddhist heritage and to accept salvation in a strange "frontier American style"—for me, walking down a "sawdust" trail and humiliating myself before the world. We were taught this; we were led to believe that the false was the truth even when it did not square with our reality.

If we would have depended upon our own intuition rather than being drawn in by the reasoning of white missionaries—they always had a five-point plan of salvation, unassailable rationalism if one accepted their premises (and their premises were bolstered by all that the white society laid on us)—we would have been better human beings with fewer guilty feelings. One of the key points which needs to be challenged by ethnic theologies is the idea of "scientific rationalism" which underlies both fundamentalism and white liberalism. The arrogance and the paternalism of the white society and church is rooted in their mistaken belief in their own superiority because they were the "scientific" and "rational" beings on earth. The rest of us were caught in the abyss of "primitive paganism" and "emotional intuition." That scientific, rationalistic life undergirded by white theologies had led Europe into the excesses of a Hitler and most recently of Vietnam/Cambodia—a war that is still being waged by the United States in 1974 regardless of all of the Nixon rhetoric of "peace with honor."

William Irwin Thompson ends his book, *At the Edge of History*, with these thoughts:

---

[1] Ernst Cassirer, *An Essay on Man* (Garden City, NY: Doubleday Anchor, 1956), 28.

> Western Civilization is drawing to a close in an age of apocalyptic turmoil . . . we are at one of those moments when the whole meaning of nature, self, and civilization is overturned in a revisioning of history as important as any technological innovation. . . .
>
> We will have to come right up to the edge to find out where we are, and who we are. At the edge of history, history itself can no longer help us, only myth remains equal to reality.[2]

I cannot now recount the torturous path by which Thompson comes to this conclusion—nor do I always understand what he is trying to say—but I think that we as an ethnic church need to take seriously the mythic past, both the Judeo-Christian myths and the Asian myths. The purpose would be to pursue the cultural forms which speak to us out of our heritage and to reconceptualize Christian theology out of that perspective in order to have meanings of life which correspond to the truth of our being Asian American Christians.

Not only so, but in our pursuit we must become more prophetic. And that is a task of both reflection and action. The praxis of Asian American theology must be a recognition of both the Word and the Act, and the style must be dialogical.[3]

It is also the symbolic mythic projection into the future. Part of my contention that demanding shared resources is self-defeating in the long run is that it is a prudent thing to be concerned for the survival of the ethnic church by fiscal and personnel help, but survival is not enough. What is needed is a new vision, a symbolic future which draws us into the stream of life with new vitality. This prophetic future is beyond empirical existence and is best seen in the Hebrew prophets. Their future was not a fact but an ethical and religious projection.

> Their ideal future signifies the negation of the empirical world, the "end of all days," but it contains at the same time the hope and the assurance of "a new heaven and a new earth." Here too man's symbolic power ventures beyond all the limits of his finite existence, but this negation implies a new and great act of integration; it marks a decisive phase in man's ethical and religious life.[4]

Thus, the task of theological reformulation is immense, but it is not unattainable. In fact, it is imperative—for if we do not do it, there is no hope for the ethnic church. . . and that's the truth.

The Force of Social, Economic, and Political Analysis

Furthermore, we must root theology in the reality of our ethnic communities. Too often I minister out of a context of "ignorance." For one thing, the kinds of "factual information" we get through the media and the government is inadequate. Every census report has to be reinterpreted by what is going on "in the streets." For example, the high rate of educational attainment among Asian Americans gives the false picture of an intelligent, highly trained, overemployed "model minority." The fact that given the immigration screening, which permits many highly educated

---

[2] William Irwin Thompson, *At the Edge of History* (New York: Harper Colophon Books, 1971), 230.

[3] Paulo Freire, *The Pedagogy of the Oppressed* (New York: Herder and Herder, 1971).

[4] Cassirer, *An Essay on Man*, 28.

immigrants/refugees (highly educated equated with numbers of degrees), the statistics are misleading. The Asian on the streets of Chinatowns, Filipinotowns, Little Tokyos, and in the Korean, Samoan, and Hawaiian communities is underemployed or unemployed, with high rates of disease and higher rates of suicide.

Not only so, but the American church has put a premium on an "educated ministry." This means that, although we take pride in the Asian American churches in the well-trained ministry we have, the majority of Asian American pastors are middle-class, white-oriented seminary trained, and unusually out of touch with the grassroots. For years, I ministered in the Japanese community in Los Angeles, observing with increasing frustration how the clergy and churches almost inevitably sided with the "cover-up" of crime, delinquency, and poverty in the community. Fortunately, I also worked with Asian American radical students and Asian American social workers who knew the other side of the stories. The one glaring and depressing example is the longstanding drug abuse problem among *Sansei*. Whole communities, with the support of their clergy, denied its existence, when on the streets *Sansei* were not only being arrested and harassed but overdosing and dying. Of course, there were sympathetic ministers who worked with the various groups, but by and large the church-as-church turned its eyes away from the needs of drug abusers. The point is that a "street-level" perspective is imperative if the ethnic church is to create a theology relevant to the communities.

The task of theologizing thus must go hand in hand with social analysis. We can find allies in other programs of learning and research, primarily ethnic studies programs in our universities, social services research done through a number of agencies, primarily through mental health sponsorship at this time, and other data which is readily available but unanalyzed in education, old age assistance, city and county statistics, etc. One of the missing perspectives in any analysis of data is the answer to the question "What does it all *mean*?" One of the major inputs (not necessarily *the* answer, however) is a theological analysis. If ethnic studies continues to neglect the religious roots and theological concerns of the Asian American communities, primarily being turned off by years of "Mickey Mouse" Sunday School programs, the primary fault must be squarely upon us who have not participated in the community of learning.

The agenda is large and complex. In years of dabbling on the edges of higher education and public education systems, I have been overwhelmed with both the mass of data available about Asian Americans in education and, paradoxically, with the massive lack of pertinent data on the communities. One of the most damning procedures in research is to analyze by categories and disciplines—"the economic status of senior citizens in San Francisco's Chinatown." In fact, by doing the research in a piecemeal manner and opportunistically, primarily for the needs and status of the researcher rather than the communities, we have no overview of the realities of life in our communities. The truth is that most research is politically manipulated and in fact there is not an "economic" problem; there are simple real problems which are extremely complex and interrelated with a variety of factors. However difficult the task of social analysis seems, the church cannot afford not to begin—at least, learn and listen from others who are at the task.

What Can Be Done?

In an outline from which no effort to flesh out the theological and social analyses is needed, I have set forth the agenda. It is not an impossible one, but it will take at least three things to begin:

The first is raising of the dialogue on theological concerns to a high priority among the churches, and the key persons are the clergy. If we continue to worry and work on survival issues, we shall not.

The second is the pastors' commitment to the theological task. I am fully convinced that most of the pastors have an innate feeling about the communities in which they serve and are doing "theology" daily but not recognizing it as such. That is, theologizing as learned in seminaries is about as irrelevant as it can be. The real theologizing goes on in the daily work of the parish pastor and his congregation— their perspective on life, their understanding of their own cultural roots and practices, and their moves and actions to bring to bear their understanding of the gospel on the life of the real communities in which they function.

The third is to move in an ecumenical and concerted, rather than a denominational and fragmented, effort. The point is that often the very fact of "denominationalism" is theologically based—on the white man's theology. I see no reason why we should perpetuate the quarrels among Calvinists, Lutherans, Baptists, and Methodists—all rooted in Europe—in the Asian American churches. Furthermore, given the history of the American church, which is essentially a "westward" movement, there is only token attention to the "eastward" movement which is more relevant to us. For instance, it is really enlightening to study the life of Paul Tillich, who as an individual embodied the movement of the Western church. His roots and life beginnings are in Germany: middle class and highly intellectual. He moves across the Atlantic and finds a new perspective of life in the freedom afforded him here. Yet his systematic theology is highly instructive only for the Western culture and Western man. In the later years of his life, Tillich "rediscovered" Asia, and if it were not for his untimely death, he would have developed a theology based upon the cultural reality of the East, which he proclaimed to be the real fulfillment of his life quest.

There is also a pragmatic reason for the joint effort. The task as outlined is immense, and for each denominational group to attempt to do it would be self-defeating. For example, an educational analysis is the same whether it is done by a Baptist or an Episcopalian. The duplication of efforts is already a roadblock to clarity.

Vision and Pluralism

The question now raised in major denominational circles is the threatened fragmentation of the church as numbers of "self-interest" groups put forth their varying demands. It too bothers me. However, there are two things to consider. The first is the value of pluralism rooted in the fact of cultural diversity. Ernst Cassirer said that philosophy

> does not overlook the tensions and frictions, the strong contrasts and deep conflicts between the various powers of man. These cannot be reduced to a common denominator. . . . But this multiplicity and desperateness do not denote discord or disharmony. The dissonance is in harmony with itself; the contraries are not mutually exclusive, but interdependent.[5]

Thus, the affirmation of pluralism more nearly parallels nature itself. It is not evil; it is good.

But beyond the pluralism lies the problem of moving in complete separateness, which leads to a kind of cultural superiority, which is precisely what minorities are protesting today. The arrogance which arises out of the emphasis on differences is a trap which the church should be consciously aware of and avoid. The other need, then, is to affirm wholeness—the Christian vision of the future is the oneness of humanity. It is in the mandate to the church to affirm and concretize that unity.

The search for wholeness cannot be a nostalgic return to the "integration concepts" of the past. It is a new unity amidst affirmed and accepted pluralism. How to do this and what basis it has is a task high on the agenda of any Christian theology. The Asian American churches have a unique opportunity to display both the pluralism and the unity which ought to mark human life in the future. Therefore, the theological task is imperative. It is a key to the future of the ethnic church, and I hope we choose to be not on the edge of the abyss but the edge of a new dawn.

---

[5] Cassirer, *An Essay on Man*, 286.

Address to the Methodist Caucus

Oakland, CA
October 11, 1974

William Mamoru Shinto

Introduction

The internal contradictions of Asian American life are captured in a building at MIT—I. M. Pei's Earth Sciences Building. It soars twenty stories high, springing from a narrow foundation standing boldly on two-story high pylons in a tremendous archway. It is a picture of man's conquest over nature, even blocking out natural sunlight with huge bronzed windows.

But, so brilliantly conceived, it yet is dangerous. The stresses have caused the dark windows to crack, and M.I.T. had to rope off the courtyard to protect its students from falling pieces of the window. But even more ironic is that giant archway caught all of the winds coming off that massive building so that the doors could not be opened at all.

William Irwin Thompson observed:

> The building is MIT's symbol. On a personal level it shows what MIT training does to students from foreign cultures. A traditional Chinese, filled with the Tao, would not have forgotten earth, wind and light to design such an embarrassing monument to the study of the earth. In soaring so high, and in straining so hard for Western values, the building renders visible the internal contradictions of Pei's genius.[1]

The internal cultural contradictions, which are present with all Asians in America, and some means toward solutions are the concerns tonight.

And in the explosion of the theme of cultural contradictions, there are two helpful terms from Eric Fromm—*necrophilous* (death-oriented) and *biophilous* (life-oriented)—which will give direction to our quest. A *necrophilous* person loves all that does not grow, approaches life mechanically, and treats all living persons as things. With things of utmost importance, they can relate to objects only if they possess them—so much so that they would rather lose life than possessions. Their life is also egocentric, individualistic. The description almost perfectly fits the analysis of American life set forth by Philip Slater: (1) *competition* with great stress on rugged individualism; (2) *uninvolvement*, the tendency to avoid confrontation of chronic social problems; and (3) *independence*, largely visible in child-rearing

---

[1] William Irwin Thompson, *At the Edge of History* (New York: Harper Colophon Books, 1971), 71.

practices and resulting in a guilt-oriented social context. Necrophilous is death-oriented.

On the other hand, a *biophilous* person sees life in terms of persons and not things, with high premium on the engagement of life both to combat those things which are demonic and dehumanizing and affirm those things which contribute to wholeness. Life is viewed in circles of community and largely recognizes the interdependence of all persons — and groups. Biophilous is life-oriented.

The changes in our span of history are swift and evoke great sadness. As a child, I remember racing to the drugstore to see a strange contraption with a circular face, about four inches in diameter, flashing pictures. The first TV. And just the other day on a color TV, a veritable miracle in electronics but a daily part of our existence, I saw a film of the Monterey Rock Festival of years ago, when the flower children were just blooming. And it was with deep sorrow that I viewed again those rock prophets: Janis Joplin, Mama Cass, Otis Redding, Jimi Hendrix — all gone, all dead.

The lifestyle of the alienated, the hippies, is linked with freedom to challenge all accepted values. At the root is a child-like acceptance of the whole person, the recovery of the sensuous, and the expression of an aesthetic, feeling-filled life of spontaneity, a discovery of joy, a celebration of life. They reversed the normal ordering of life by delineating new priorities: people over things, art over technocracy, idiosyncrasies over homogeneity. But so alienated were the gentle people, whose introverted divergence from straight society was such a reversal of accepted mores, that the majority of Americans literally and figuratively crucified them.

The flower children and their movement died, but it really lives in a life-oriented direction for those who discerned its values. The straight society continues — its Watergates, its double-dipping — but it is really dead: necrophilous, death-oriented.

What has all this to do with the Asian American church caucuses? The convergence of these seemingly wayward thoughts is multiple, but tonight let us at least discern a pattern.

We are, as Asians in America, enmeshed in at least a dual culture, and like Pei need to take care how we find wholeness in the bicultural life and not depart so far from our Chinese, Japanese, Pilipino, Korean, Samoan roots as to create only imitations of the Euro-American culture — resulting in monstrosities.

We also need to examine our life as persons and as a group to see if our direction is necrophilous — death-oriented — or biophilous — life-oriented.

Then we need to understand that if one seeks fervently the underlying foundations of many protest movements in our country, such as that of the alienated, the hippies, one discovers a great affinity to Asian thought. Spontaneity, freedom, joy, and nonrational, intuitive thought spell out Taoist roots. And if the Asian caucuses follow their cultural roots in Asia and their spiritual rebirth in Christ and realistically assess their role in America, we shall have created a critical and daring challenge to the whole of this westernized, individualistic, and technocratic society.

St. Paul said at the end of his life that he had been true to the heavenly vision (Acts 26:19). But it came at great cost. Caucuses can be nice things and good fellowship and live—but in a death-oriented existence. *Or* caucuses can come to terms with the base realities of life and engage in massive struggle, ending in crucifixion, but productive of life-oriented creativity.

Let us now turn to the caucuses specifically. The first agenda is to review the birth of caucuses; the second, to see the caucus as a political act; and the third, to view the caucus as a major activity producing a biophilous, life-oriented community.

I. The Birth of the Caucuses

The role of the minister in the Asian communities is a key to the birth of the caucus. Our communities are still largely interpersonal ones because of the cultural ties and small numbers of persons. One peculiarity of active ministers is that they are acceptable in both the "straight" Asian community and the "activists." Not only so, they remain among the few persons who are able to move across class lines with relative ease and find reasonable access to both Asians and the decision-makers in the larger community. The Asian ministers, therefore, at their best, work at multiple levels of concern: with the congregations, with the surrounding community, with other ethnic groups, and with the larger white community. And, paradoxically, the religious professional seems to have more credibility in the communities at large, both Asian and white, than with his own congregation.

One explanation is that the professional almost reverses exactly the reason for his/her ministry as the churches espouses. The clergy set out to learn about and act out the faith to which they have committed themselves. Their intent is to minister far beyond the bounds of the local congregation so that their real community of work is not that of the gathered, but in coalition with those who work around the same causes and concerns they do. And their analysis of the cultural factor is both the same as other Asians in the need for self-identity but also must go far beyond that by accepting only those cultural modes which fit their ultimate vision of the whole of humanity.

Furthermore, most clergy, at their best, see the archaic moral and social fences erected by the churches as irrelevant and try to persuade the churches to move to more deeply socially based ethics. This simple juxtaposition of clergy and congregation may go a long way to explain the displeasure directed toward the ministers by the ethnic churches and the paradoxical acceptance of the best ministers by the larger Asian communities.

A short review of the way our Asian churches grew may be instructive. I shall speak of the Japanese church, with which I am most familiar, but the pattern is generally applicable to all our groups. The first Japanese Christian group was eight young people who organized a *Fukuin Kai* in San Francisco in 1877. On reviewing the reasons which led these persons to organize, we are struck by the persistence of those same reasons today. The first purpose was the need for companionship and mutual support in the midst of a hostile environment. Thus, a cultural haven still is a prime reason for our congregations.

A second purpose was to find ways to sustain some moral tone to their lives in the midst of a rather primitive society. One twist is that the conservative nature of the church life imposed social restrictions on the embryonic church which continue to be in our tradition. Another reason, unarticulated, was to need to identify as an American and not be considered Japanese. A quick acceptable role for an Americanization process was conversion to Christianity. And of least importance was the desire to learn and perpetuate the Christian faith. One also notes that the group was nondenominational and only later broke up into denominational groupings. Out of this grew a network of various congregations.

What is the future of ethnic churches? Among the older established groups, such as the Japanese, there is some pessimism. Among the groups with stronger ethnic identity, such as the Chinese and Koreans, there is much hope and new activity. Some of the problems of Pilipino Protestants are obviously culturally specific; the large Roman Catholic constituencies, the lack of established congregations, etc., but the spirit is high. The ethnic churches thus persist and shape Asian American life. My own pessimism when I left the local congregation in 1967 is now greatly altered to a firm affirmation that the ethnic churches are vital and potentially positive centers of strength.

Yet this congregational experience is different from that of the clergy.

This conflict has closed the doors of regularized church ministries to many thoughtful clergy and serendipitously opened other avenues of expressing their concern for the humanizing, life giving processes. Among my acquaintances are social workers, educators, businessmen, etc. who are also ministers. Thus, one means of coping with the problem of living out a vision in the regular channels of the church is to shift to a secular position.

But what of those who remain?

The answer for most clergy who remained inside the churches has been a new burst of activity and direction initiated by them. They organized Asian American caucuses inside major denominations.

The "caucus" is a group of like-minded persons who bypass regular channels of authority to goad organizations to accept responsibility for caucus concerns. They claim the support of the churches and the communities, but the critical fact about this is that *the caucus moves without consensus of the congregations*. It is an important breakthrough in liberation when clergy asserted leadership roles on the basis of values rather than consensus, especially in the close-knit, encysted Asian congregations. It is no wonder, therefore, that the initial acts were performed often by clergy who were not attached to congregations, but were in either staff positions or secular positions.

Among the Christian churches, there are now firmly established caucuses in the United Methodist, United Presbyterian, American Baptist, Episcopal, and United Church of Christ. The major impact is in the renewed activity both within congregations and the communities. Church funds and energies have found their way to many of the socially active groups and socially relevant programs in the Asian communities, and the flow of financial aid, new programs for immigrants, and other projects inside the churches is just beginning.

Nonetheless, in the burst of initial euphoria, the thorny questions still remain: Is the "caucus" a move to survive, or is it a revitalized ministry? Will the laypersons in congregations move with enthusiasm following the initiative of the clergy? Will the denominational nature of the caucuses serve to further the gap among the church groups and keep us within our "European" traditions? Will the movement become more establishment and church-oriented rather than continue its outward stance toward the communities? That is, is the caucus moving in a death-oriented or a life-oriented direction?

Whether there is real hope of a rebirth of real ministry depends a good deal on another movement within the church, this also an outgrowth of the caucuses. Like many other ethnic activities, the blacks began a theological renewal by espousing the black theology of liberation. This is paralleled by a revolutionary theology arising out of the church life of Latin America and the Native Americans' renewed championing of their native religions. Among Asian Americans there has been this beginning of such theological/theoretical study, especially on the part of a Methodist, the Rev. Dr. Roy Sano, who organized the ecumenical Asian Center for Theologies and Strategies.

In a capsule, the fact is that although practitioners in any profession may function without philosophical coherence in their working life, eventually under the conditions that arise and the problems faced, they find themselves in deeper and deeper trouble because of the vagueness of the underlying purposes and conceptualization of mission. The existence of ethnic ministries depends, in the long run, on a well-thought-out and solid theological foundation. The pessimism and frustrations of the churches and unease among the clergy are largely attributable to the lack of a real rationale for ministry. For decades, ethnic churches have been viewed as appendages to the "real church" and ethnic ministers as "second rate." No organization or person can long function with creativity under such a cloud. Only as a liberating process.

The vision of the theologically inclined in our midst is for a pan-Asian or Pacific Basin alliance. For all the magnitude of such a venture, it is, finally, the only way to proceed. There is no way for integrity in theological or ecclesiastical activities if we ignore the whole of the Pacific Basin and remain parochialized on the West Coast of the USA. And the emerging theologies of Sano's biblically oriented Amerasian theology of liberation, or my own rudimentary beginnings of a culturally oriented theology of wholeness or harmony, are not restricted to an American perspective. This bridging between Asia and America has only begun but is an exciting prospect for all of the caucuses.

II. The Caucus as a Political Act

How do caucuses operate? It seems that they function on at least two levels. The first is as a political act. This is in response to the death-oriented structures of our society and calls for a style which is often diametrically opposite our Asian cultural roots.

First of all, the situation inside the major denominational structures is little different than that in any major organization in our society. Churches, then, are no better nor worse than police forces, the military, business corporations, or the many arms of the government. A recent Harris poll asked Americans how much confidence they have in our institutions. The highest level of confidence is in medicine: 50%. The second, a tie between the Supreme Court and higher education: 40%. And the confidence in the military is 33%, one point above that of organized religion — which has the trust of 33%. Trust levels are not high when the highest can garner the confidence of only one-half of the population.

My basic wariness of church structures is not to mistrust individuals, such as Bishop Choy, who people the institutions. I also happen to be inside the structures of a denomination and experience the political struggles, the payoffs, the deals, the inordinate pressures of special interest groups, especially the wealthy. I also know that we, as an Asian minority, are well loved because we are well behaved and follow the instructions to go through the regular channels of the church. At the same time, I know that regular channels are bypassed regularly and that following most channels leads to dizziness and running in circles.

During the American Revolution, one of our founding fathers wrote his friends in England. He penned, "My dear friends, we are now enemies." Any caucus which desires to exert political pressure takes this stance — "My dear friends, we are now enemies." Any other stance is deadly. And at this level I perceive that the coming together under the label of Asian American is a political act rather than the community of ethnic groups. In the political sense, there is no *Asian American* — there are very disparate groups — Korean, Pilipino, Samoan, Chinese, Japanese, who merge numbers and influence to create as strong a power bloc as possible.

It also means that since one is struggling within a major American establishment, the major denomination, the rules of the game are culturally conditioned — individualism, pressure, confrontation, demands, threats, competition. It is also true that most Asian Christians discover that their culturally different style of harmony, peace, conciliation, patience work mightily against the caucus. This is the point of great cultural contradiction. The very traits of Asians which elicit the admiration of the white majority are the ones which block any progress in meeting our needs. The white majority inside of the church, in other words, praise us for our patience and low-level approach while at the same time feel relieved that here is a group which presents no crisis and therefore no reason to be taken seriously.

As a political act, the Caucus is faced with a two-pronged problem. The first is how does one preserve one's inner cultural style, basically Asian and harmonious, and still make one's impact on the denomination as a whole? The second is if the use of power is necessary, how does one mobilize and utilize it and still remain Christian?

The choice is for the caucus to make, but it might be useful to state that the use of power is not unchristian and the analysis of the structures and processes of decision-making inside of a denomination is a basic prerequisite to determine how best to use what power you have.

And on the latter, I am not talking about organizational charts or procedural documents which are handed out. Very seldom does decision-making take place according to the "discipline."

If the caucuses, therefore, want to make a political act, the caucus has to become much more hardnosed as realists—and much more astute as politicians.

III. The Caucus as a Life-Oriented Organism

As you heard the preceding analysis of the caucus as a political act, you may have experienced great distaste for that style. It is so because you are in that arena dealing with a death-oriented system and so must resort to death-oriented tactics. I would not leave that alone, however. As little heart as I have for confrontation and threat, often I have engaged in political acts both inside the church and inside education. It is an important activity.

On the other hand, surely there must be a deeper level of caucus activity and engagement. And there is. There has been an inordinate preoccupation inside most caucuses with the garnering of funds and positions. This is viewing the future as future, and is thus self-defeating and rooted in unreality. To live for the future as future is to live in a death-oriented existence. It results in the postponement of life-affirming acts and the paralysis of movement to meet glaring needs now. The upshot of dependence upon the caucus as a political act is that the conversation turns on such sentences as "I will do so-and-so when I get the right position through affirmative action" or "We will do so-and-so when we get money from the denomination." That is viewing the future as future and is necrophilic. Where would we be if Jesus Christ would have said, "I will not go to Jerusalem unless I get funded" or "When I get to be bishop, I will really start creative ministries"? Why not now? The future as now is life-oriented. Time is now, the future is ever evolving out of the present; it is not real in itself, and the promise of the future is only death-oriented if its activity is not rooted in the present.

The Korean who immigrated and is completely perplexed in this strange land—must he wait for some future, or is his future now?

The aged, poverty-stricken *Issei* widow, abandoned and alone—can she wait for the future?

The isolated Chinese child in a classroom, unable to speak English and therefore not learning—must she wait for some future, or is her future now?

Is the Pilipino educator denied teaching credentials because of the inherent racism in the school district willing to wait for the future or is her future determined now?

And what of the churches encysted in denominationalism, captured by Western social norms, parochialized by miniscule cliques of wealth and social class, paralyzed by so-called Christian customs and Western liturgies, in essence enmeshed in sin and death-oriented? Will funding or positions release them from captivity?

It is now time, not in the future, to bring to Christ the real gifts of our various cultures and begin to build bold Asian churches who know how to live in this bicultural environment and remain true both to the heritage of Asia and the rebirth in Christ. In this deeper level, we come together, not as a political base, but first affirming our own culture, be it Korean, Filipino, Samoan, Chinese, or Japanese, and spinning out separately distinct ministries to our specific communities. Caucuses must recognize the pluralism of our group and encourage ethnically specific missions for the separate entities.

But secondly, beyond pluralism, the caucus is engaging the most significant issue in our society: how to live in unity amidst the pluralism. What does the Christian faith and the Christian mission contribute to wholeness, to identifying the commonalities and creating one world community? I have long pointed out to both church officials and government bodies that the Asian caucuses are a true experiment in attempting to find oneness in real diversity.

This summer, during our sessions at Claremont, we explored with our Korean brothers and sister their issues. It is transparently clear that the hundreds of years of conflict between Korea and Japan clearly identify the Japanese as oppressors. Why do we expect the Koreans and the Japanese to act together in mutual trust in the caucus? *Or can we*—because the transformation wrought in Jesus Christ creates a new unity without glossing over the critical concerns and the real human dynamics among variant peoples of the earth?

At this level, the caucus is seeking with a deep sense of mission, a worthy life-death goal, the unity which is promised in Jesus Christ. And although in political acts the caucuses need to act as denominational groups, in this instance the common humanity of our concern means we should seek community in as broad an ecumenical base as possible.

In that sense, may I suggest at least one route worth our mutual consideration? Much of what I have said is theoretical and subject to debate, but in spelling out my concerns I hope that you are beginning to see the dire necessity for our continuing these dialogues and mutual efforts.

The concreteness which we lack in expression is partially a lack of Asian American church institutions. I suspect it is because of our smallness and therefore lack of self-confidence that we have solid church institutions only as local congregations. We do not have many, if any, Asian American institutions for theological education, higher education, medicine, law, social welfare, and public education. Now, many of these institutional forms may not be full-fledged autonomous entities—many should be pursued in coalition with or substructures under established institutions. Some, however, lend themselves to Asian entities—such as the ecumenical ACTS or some preliminary explorations by the United Methodists in Southern California for the beginnings of an Asian higher education institution.

These things can best be done ecumenically. All also will need endowment and funding. The Asian churches need to expand the vision of what can be done and spin out some projects worthy of our mission. If we do this, I am convinced, we shall find in the rank and file of our congregations the funds and other resources to do them. For lack of vision, the churches may vanish. But if we can together project the need for the churches' involvement in value formation and creating unity amidst pluralism, we can recapture our mission, our unique Asian American Christian mission, and become a dynamic force not only in our communities but in the *oikumene*—the whole earth.

Conclusion

And the task is formidable and the prognosis, from the perspective of man, is not good that we will succeed. But the real question is can we be true to our calling if we do not try? And basically, we have no way of really knowing what impact we have. We are like the geese in the poem of an eighth-century Chinese sage who wrote:

> The wild geese fly across the long sky above.
> Their image is reflected upon the chilly waters below.
> The geese do not mean to cast their image on the water;
> Nor does the water mean to hold the image of the geese.[2]

The unintentionality of mutual interaction may be the way God works his mysterious ways. Yes, the flight of the geese and the image cast on the water is an existential moment of beauty and creation, and that moment for the caucus is right now.

---

[2] Chang Chung-yuan, *Creativity and Taoism: A Study of Chinese Philosophy, Art, and Poetry* (New York: Harper Colophon Books, 1963), 57

Alternative Futures for
Asian American Christians

WILLIAM MAMORU SHINTO

Introduction

At the turn of the century, six hundred Chinese miners lived in Eureka, Nevada, tormented and harassed in a strange land. They sought refuge beneath the ground, and the tunnels that underlie this old town are their legacy. One of the remaining structures below is called the "Underground Cathedral," with large rooms of twenty-foot ceilings, archways, and a maze of tunnels. The outward hovels were a facade so that outsiders could not discern the real life of the Chinese. They lived an underground existence.[1] The Asian American movement, both secular and religious, is the emergence of an unwanted peoples from the bowels of the earth to claim their rightful place in the United States.

Having emerged visibly onto the scene, we, as Asian American Christians, have a large agenda—to understand the meaning of the rising militancy of our communities, to think through theologically where we stand, and to act concertedly against the dehumanizing forces about us and in accord with the creative changes ahead of us. It is thus that our dialogue on alternative futures is critical and has to begin and to continue with force.

In addition, Rollo May, as many others, points out that our whole United States society is at the end of an era.

> The age that began with the Renaissance, born out of the twilight of the Middle Ages, is now at a close. The era that emphasized rationalism and individualism is suffering an inner and outer transition and there are only harbingers, only partly conscious, of what the new age will be.[2]

The shape of that new future has much to do with the option of whether the United States will continue on its course of contradiction, a supposed democratic nation acting imperialistically in Asia and the Pacific Basin, so tragically demonstrated in Vietnam, or will find a new close, intimate interrelationship among the many peoples of the Pacific Basin. Not only economically and politically but, for the church, there is an intense need to come to grips with the ideologies, cultural

---

[1] Charles Hillinger, "An Underground Cathedral," *Los Angeles Times*, March 2, 1975.
[2] Rollo May, *Power and Innocence,* (New York: W. W. Norton, 1972), 47.

differences, and ways of life and thinking of the varied groups that compose the Pacific peoples, including the United States.

To begin at that global dimension is proper since the role and situation of the Asian American minorities in the United States, for good or ill, is closely tied to our nation's attitudes and actions in the Pacific. To see ourselves in the total context is vital, for it reminds us to deal with alternative futures in a realistic manner. For instance, an *alternative* is a choice of possibilities and involves a dimension of freedom. However, to say that freedom is, after President Roosevelt's Executive Order 9066, for the Japanese in the West Coast to have the alternative of leaving either by train, automobile, airplane, or on foot is a nonsensical use of the meaning of freedom.

So too with the future. To say that we have a future is also an unreasoned use of the word because whatever we do or do not do, the future inevitably and inexorably breaks in upon us. Hannah Arendt says, "There are a few melancholy side effects in the reassuring idea that we need only march into the future, which we cannot help doing anyhow, in order to find a better world."[3] In the practice of prediction by futurologists, all that they say will come to pass will—only if nothing of any importance or surprise happens. Arendt continues, "It is the function, however, of all action, as distinguished from mere behavior, to interrupt what otherwise would have proceeded automatically and therefore predictably."[4] Thus, what we want to do is to explore the meaning of *true* alternatives, and consequently real freedom, and the creation of the future through an intervention of events, both of our making and of God's grace, through the exercise of power.

Our watchword is Jeremiah 1:10: "See, I have set you this day over nations and over kingdoms, to pluck and break down, to destroy and to overthrow, to build and to plant."

The tearing down and building up are both essential: They both embody the use of power. Alternative futures are creatures of the uses of political power and theological power. It is to that we shall now turn.

I. The Uses of Political Power

In all situations of human life there is present both the creative and the demonic. There is no movement in life unless we confront the demonic and not dismiss it. Therefore, ethnic congregations are neither inherently good nor evil. Nor are ethnic groups.

One truth which is beginning to dawn upon me is that ethnicity in the United States is basically a creature of the white majority. And in the general public, most of us view the Black-White issues as the key paradigm of race relations. Not wanting to minimize the contribution of Blacks, both to our group and to myself, I still believe it is imperative to study the experiences of the Native Americans.

---

[3] Hannah Arendt, *Crises of the Republic* (New York: Harcourt, Brace, Jovanovich, 1969), 129.
[4] Arendt, *Crises in the Republic*, 133.

The accusing cry of genocide which rises from the ghetto is usually met by a condescending smile on the faces of the authorities. However, when one recounts the experience of the Native American Indian, one realizes immediately that genocide, massive violence, and final solutions are a reality.

In a realm of immediate relevance to us, how is it that we are categorized as minorities known as Asian Americans by the government? Now, please be understanding and follow this argument to the end, for in much of our consciousness we are aware that in a sense we ourselves asked for this ranking. However, the term "Asian American" does not refer to any reality. Of course, it can be turned into a positive force by creation of a new entity and identity, as we shall explore later. Yet in the context of general history, it is no more than what the United States has ever done with non-white groups: clearly identifying us and grouping us for ease of manipulation. It also means that we are surfaced and marked as "inferior," as "minorities."

Morton H. Fried, writing in *Natural History* magazine, describes in detail "The Myth of Tribe." He says, "I think there is ample evidence to indicate that states created tribes rather than having evolved them." Anthropologists steadily refuse to use the term "tribe," with the Native Americans embracing the term for political reasons, a means to negotiate further on the treaties, so-called. The general public also believes in the tribes. Fried writes, "But, curiously, it did not become a general term of reference to American Indians until the nineteenth century. Previously, the words commonly used . . . were *nation* and *people*."

I will not review the whole of his argument, but he reasons that because bands and villages of pre-state societies were so formless (or seemed so for the purposes of colonial powers, including the expanding empires of the ancient world), the encroaching states had to transform them. As precondition for their manipulation, exploitation, and, ironically, their expropriation, they had to be pinned down.

Even the names are of suspicious origin: *Parintintin*, which means "the stinking people," Crow, Blackfoot, Digger, and Creek, just to list a few.

In the evolution of the state there is a heterogeneity—"the differential access to basic resources among different members of the same society: the defining condition of social stratification. Stratification means that a society is divided into haves and have-nots, a condition of inherent conflict." When a state then begins to encroach or penetrate upon the territory of a different group it gives birth to tribes. The peoples themselves involved in the process become confused. They think they have always lived in tribes, and the people in states, looking at them, think so too. The myth of tribe, however, is not benign but malignant, and can be, if understood and used in a positive way, creative.

Take for instance the fact that a decade ago there was no category "Asian American." As the pressures grew among ethnics and with rising militancy, especially among the young Asians on campuses and in the streets, the state began to poke around for a convenient way to deal with us. They used the term "Oriental" for a while, and the resulting myth was the creation of the category called "Asian American."

It includes persons who, in some instances, are not Americans. It includes some technically not Asian. And nowhere does it make sense to think that Japanese, Filipino, and Chinese, for example, share much more than deep hostility among themselves. The point is that from the perspective of the government, and I say also the white church denominational leadership, as always they had to pinpoint this racially different group in order to be able to more easily manipulate, exploit, and expropriate it.

Another matter of real concern for us in the church is that the state needed to create chieftains—the agents of the oppressors, some persons to take orders, convey messages, link with them, and even to act as a conduit for siphoning off as much of the surplus as they could drain from these peoples. When one reads Genovese's book *Roll, Jordan Roll*, regarding the world the slaves made, among the many positive things that he says about the black slave church, he notes the demonic dimension of the mediating role of the preachers. Such is the trap set for the clergy and the churches vis-à-vis their ethnic communities.

The demonic character is twofold: Asian Americans categorized as an ethnic "tribe" are easily dealt with by authorities, and secondly, the constant division and hostility inside the so-called Asian American communities helps them postpone decisions until they smugly say, "You all get your thing together."

This analogy has relevance to mainland Asians, although we did not occupy land as a starting point. But it should have deep and significant obvious relevance to the peoples of the Pacific Islands, especially in our day, the peoples of Micronesia. In any event, the discussion of the demonic dimensions of ethnicity cannot be ignored in any dialogue about the future.

In this context I want to state my perception of the Japanese American churches, principally on the mainland. It may have relevance to you—it may be true or false, but is nonetheless my observation. The segregation and self-segregation of the Japanese congregations was viewed as normative, good, of value, by most involved, both the Japanese themselves and the dominant white churches. The result was and continues to be in many instances congregations which are not viewed as "true churches" but as compartmentalized marginal experiments in "missions" or "specialized ministries." Our reaction was

1. to reject our cultural past in order to be accepted: the process of *assimilation* which of course never really happens;
2. to buy the integration pushed by liberals, which only perpetuates the paternalism of the past and denudes us of our culture; or
3. retreat to the sanctuary—to forget the real world in order to find commonality, not communion, to *survive* in a pseudo-atmosphere of acceptance of each other—the warmth of the cradle.

All of these *reactions*, in psychological terms, are a neurotic behavior. And often we cannot break out of the paralysis because we tend to think about Christianity as an ideal faith rather than facing the fact that the churches are human manifestations which are subject to all kinds of frailties. It is our freedom which is at stake—unless we deal with the reality, rather than the idealistic picture, of the church, both the white denominations and the present authorities and ourselves, we are truly lost. This is to say that Christianity as it is taught in our mainline seminaries and practiced in our predominantly white mainline denominations cannot free the Asian American Christian from bondage and servility.

Thus, the plight of the Japanese American Christian and his ethnic congregation is deeper than the fact that we are a small and reacting organization. It is rooted in the nineteenth century in the anti-Chinese movements based upon white supremacy/manifest destiny ideology, most of it justified by American frontier Protestantism. My insistence is that it is rooted even deeper than that. The norm of behavior for the meeting of white American with non-white peoples is the genocide of the Native American Indian.

Persons of the world external to ourselves as Asian Americans determine our lives. Their thrust, whether secular or religious authorities, is conditioned by an inferior-superior class system based upon skin color rather than a yin-yang interrelatedness.

We buy acceptance/we lose our freedom.

We settle for half-life/we cannot know wholeness.

For instance, we turn the positive theory of Asian tranquility/calm/nonaction into a demonic evil of Asian American docility/passivity. The intent of the Asian nonaction is positive and active—it is a sharp and keen instrument of will/love/compassion/power. With the pressures of whites and the white supremacy bearing down upon us, we tend to use the positive concept of nonaction, deeply rooted in our cultures, to assuage the impact of prejudice and paternalism— turning Asian tranquility into a dull, negative and useless factor, a giving in, which leaves us in a powerless and hopeless situation.

Thus, for the first part of this address, I want to deal with the issue of power as it relates to the necessity for performing political acts as Asian American Christians in order to break out of the trap of only reacting to life instead of acting in strength.

Jesus charged his disciples, as he sent them out in mission: "Behold, I send you out as sheep in the midst of wolves; so be wise as serpents and innocent as doves" (Matt. 10:16).

Within each ethnic movement there is a good deal of talk about "power." Rollo May observes, however, that "I cannot recall a time during the last four decades when there was so *much* talk about the individual's capacities and potentialities and so *little* actual confidence on the part of the individual about his power to make a difference psychologically or politically."[5] And for Asian American Christians, power and its uses are problematic. The basic reason is that we have been taught that the state of *powerlessness/nonviolence* is the positive opposite of *power*, which is

---

[5] May, *Power and Innocence*, 21.

supposedly evil. It is rooted in American frontier Protestantism, which declares that we live in a chosen land as people establishing a new Jerusalem—a perfect community evolving in everlasting progress. Inherent in that conception of life are three factors of relevance to us:

1. The *innocence* of the Christian Americans: If we are the new Jerusalem, obviously we are the innocents of God, the possessors of the true blessings of God.

2. Since we are the perfect nation of God, then obviously we are *superior* to the rest of humanity and are commissioned to convert them to our way of life.

3. And the "we" above referring to Americans is not inclusive of all who live here but is meant to be understood as those in the *white Anglo-Saxon majority,* excluding non-whites who are not of the corporate body but inferior to it.

If we are innocent and superior then the words of Benjamin Franklin are characteristic of white American attitudes:

> If it be the design of Providence to extirpate these savages in order to make room for the cultivators of the earth, it seems not improbable that rum may be the appointed means. It has already annihilated all the tribes who formerly inhabited the seacoast.[6]

Those fulfilling God's will are the whites, the cultivators of the earth; those others, the Native Americans, are the evil ones whose genocide is the will of God.

Furthermore, it is this divinely justified merging of innocence and superiority which results in the constant use of violence in United States life, from the genocide of the Native Americans, the hanging of Chinese in the streets of Los Angeles, to the killing of white students on the Kent State campus. The American white churches taught us "innocence," coupled with their "superiority," resulting in our submission to their force in various guises of violence: They were and are a group of snakes in doves' feathers.

Asian Christians need to make a deep analysis of this deadly thrust of white American ideology: an innocence which denies guilt and evil, a racist ideology of white supremacy, and an equation of violence with power.

Innocence denies the demonic, but the whole person cannot live by denying guilt but dealing with it. Rollo May affirms:

> It is a considerable boon for a person to realize that he has his negative, side like everyone else, that the daimonic works in potentiality for both good and evil, and that he can neither disown it nor live without it. It is similarly beneficial when he also comes to see that much of his achievement is bound up with the very conflicts this daimonic impulse engenders. This is the seat of the experience that life is a mixture of good and evil; that there is no such thing as pure good; and that if evil weren't there as a potentiality, the good would not be either. Life consists of achieving good not apart from evil but in spite of it.[7]

---

[6] May, *Power and Innocence*, 51.
[7] May, *Power and Innocence*, 259–260.

One popular and liberal means of avoiding guilt is to plead that we are all guilty. When all are guilty, no one is. Hannah Arendt warns, "Confessions of collective guilt are the best possible safeguard against the discovery of culprits, and the very magnitude of the crime is the best excuse for doing nothing."[8] A very common mistake of ethnic groups is to buy the collective guilt ploy. You hear a bitter lament of the churchpeople who say that of course racism is bad. The whole United Methodist Church is guilty. Sounds good, but when you have a grievance, you cannot talk to the United Methodist Church. Find out the telephone number of the administrator and, whoever answers, hold him/her responsible.

Power is not the same as violence. Power and violence are opposites. Hannah Arendt again states:

> Violence appears where power is in jeopardy, but left to its own course it ends in power's disappearance. This implies that it is not correct to think of the opposite of violence as nonviolence, to speak of nonviolent power is actually redundant. Violence can destroy power; it is utterly incapable of creating it.[9]

In fact, even in world power politics, violence is increasingly becoming problematic as a weapon of superiority. Francis Hsu tells us that the Boxer Rebellion of 1900 involved only twenty thousand soldiers of the allied forces, seven Western nations and Japan, who invaded Peking and the war lasted less than a year. In Vietnam, sixty years later, over half a million American soldiers, with ultramodern weapons and massive air and naval support, failed to crush the Viet Cong's ability and will to fight. Professor Hsu bluntly states that "if [one] has to go around waving a big stick or bundles of money and demanding that [others] recognize his superiority, his prestige is nonexistent."[10]

Ethnic groups need to see that any thrust of imitating the oppressors in our society by using violence, thinking it to be power, will end in failure. For one thing, the overwhelming force of United States police and military weapons of violence is unquestioned. You cannot make a gain by pitting Saturday night specials against the modern weapons of the police or the National Guard. On a more relevant level, one cannot pit our fragile resources as ethnics in a contest of force with the overwhelming strength of the white majority. To a certain minimal point, violence, that is, in our context, marches, protests, disruptions, can dramatize grievances. But if continued in ever escalating force, it may well bring about a full-fledged racist ideology to justify "law and order." "A majority of citizens would be willing to pay the price of the invisible terror of a police state for law and order in the streets."[11]

All of this is to say that there is emerging today a new phenomenon. There have always been minorities in United States society, but what is happening now is that these groups are demanding *power*. Andrew Greeley, a sociologist, believes that the

---

[8] Arendt, *Crises of the Republic*, 162.
[9] Arendt, *Crises of the Republic*, 155.
[10] Francis L. K. Hsu, *Americans and Chinese: Passages to Differences* (Garden City, N.Y.: Doubleday, 1972), 411.
[11] Hannah Arendt, *Crises of the Republic*, 174.

"basic social dynamic at the root of ethnic conflicts is the struggle of immigrant groups for political and social power."[12] It is thus that I want to discuss the use of power in political acts as one ingredient in moving forcefully into the future.

For the Asian American Christian, one important step toward wholehearted engagement in using power is to recognize the untruths which have been taught us — these, I have pointed out: innocence, superiority, and violence under the guise of power. We have been taught to be innocent as doves while our "teachers" have been as wise as serpents. It is that recognition of hypocrisy which turns our *engages* into *enrages*, our encounter into violence.[13] The sense of rage is increased by the bureaucratic nature of both the society and the church in which "no man, neither one nor the best, neither the few nor the many, can be held responsible, and which could be properly called rule by Nobody."[14] But out of this rage we would do well to turn, not to violence, but to using our power in concert.

The rage releases us from the bondage to the innocence of the past. The next step is to become aware of the fact that what makes a person a political being is the ability to act. But in order to act, things must be different. Liberation of the self and the group is thus important: to imagine what could be different about the future and to realize that we are free to change the world and start something different.

> Without the mental freedom to deny or affirm existence, to say "yes" or "no" — not just statements of propositions . . . but to things as they are given. . . . no action would be possible; and action is of course the very stuff politics are made of.[15]

It is thus very important that we break the chain of docility which so often marks the Asian in America. We have to move up to a level of consciousness in which we know if internally that we are actually free to act.

Once having delivered ourselves from bondage, we need to recognize that power is not just the ability to act, *but to act together*. Power is not the property of an individual, it belongs to a group, and in our society and inside the churches, we need to be together, to combine our strength in order to evolve into an organized disciplined instrument called the "Asian Americans."

In summary, there are no "Asian Americans"; this term is a grouping of disparate people in order to "tribalize" us for the purpose of manipulation. As Asian American Christians, taught in the ideology of innocence and conditioned by a survival syndrome through nonaction/passivity, it is imperative to recognize the bondage we have placed ourselves and been put in.

A seminary professor of mine told the story of the use of a well to keep prisoners. The guards lowered a ladder into it in order to put the prisoners down to their watery cell. But a ladder is only an instrument; the guards made people go down, but the reverse is also true: the prisoners can use the ladder to come up and out. So too with

---

[12] Andrew Greeley, *Why Can't They Be Like Us?* (New York: Institute of Human Relations Press, 1969), 3.

[13] Arendt, *Crises of the Republic,* 162.

[14] Arendt, *Crises of the Republic,* 137.

[15] Arendt, *Crises of the Republic,* 5.

us. We have been placed into the "tribe" called Asian American for the manipulation and exploitation of our various peoples. But, by the same token, we need not accept that, but can turn this evil around into a positive good. Having been forced together, we can turn this evil around into a positive good. Having been forced together, we can now unite and form a political bloc both in society and in the church, breaking out of our powerlessness as some small fragmented groups and committing political acts from a base of strength.

Two quotations aptly summarize my feelings. One is from Harold Laski, the political scientist: "When leaders of the people ask their followers to die for a dream, those followers have a right to know on whose behalf the dream is being dreamt." The second is from the country singer Rex Allen: "I don't want to stand behind someone else's dreams; I have some of my own."

It is time to gain strength from each other in a political group and to stop quarreling about whether Chinese and Samoans are both "Asians," whether the hostility among the Koreans and the Japanese can be overcome, and whether we can act in powerful dissent against those who are in authority both in the church and the society. The issues of a common life are important, and I want to deal with them in the latter half of this address, but in the political sphere it is the concert of action, the common front, the power of people together which counts. We need as a political church group to develop sophistication in political activity.

Almost the first thing asked of an ethnic group is for us to prove our point by conducting a survey. Saul Alinsky said, "If the road to hell is paved with good intentions, there must be a thirty-six lane boulevard to hell paved with surveys." But the problem is not resolved by refusing to conduct surveys or provide basic information about the state and condition of our ethnic groups. Asian American Christians need to have a database of dependable knowledge about our communities, our churches, our issues. Our gathering and using of such data may be best done by working cooperatively with governmental agencies, private agencies, and the universities. But for our specific church and religion information, we must mobilize to gather information ourselves.

But now that you have basic data and approach persons in responsible positions, they will surely know that the strategies we propose and the funding we need are rational requests. Not so. I have used the word "political acts" and mean them to be applied to our immediate reality—the political structures and processes of our various ecclesiastical organizations. I am also saying as forcefully as possible that the innocence and concern voiced by those in power is the trap of our general society. Just because an organization is supported by the church doesn't mean it will act in Christian love. Those with power do not share power voluntarily. The fact is that through the years our being harmless as doves has made us welcomed visitors to church administrators. They like to talk to us; we are so kind—they are so forgetful. It is time to become wise as serpents if we want to shape our future.

What are the administrative ploys which divert our Asian Christians from accomplishing what is necessary and obtaining the resources which are rightfully ours? I want to quickly run down a few:

1. Alternative of sub-choices

There was a drug store chain in the '20s which bought eggs for 10 cents a dozen and wanted to sell them for a nickel apiece. They came up with a gimmick. Instead of asking a customer if he wanted an egg in his malted milk drink, the fountain clerk would hold up two eggs and ask, "Two eggs or one?" They sold twenty-nine thousand cases a week. That play is called an alternative of choices.

A variation of this is used with minorities. It is the alternative of sub-choices. The caucus raises a demand for staff positions and adequate program funds. The response is an alternative of sub-choices: Would you accept a temporary half-time staff position or no staff and two thousand dollars a year for a three-year experimental program? Smiling all of the time; and we graciously accept one or the other, both options so inadequate that we will never do what we need to do.

2. Ushered into the presence of power

Doctor, bishop, president, executive secretary, etc. will see you. Our fear of authority immediately paralyzes us—fear/courtesy/muted requests. Never go to an interview alone; in fact, as often as you can, fill the room of the bishop with twenty of your colleagues and raise hell.

3. "Thirty pieces of silver" ploy

All smiles, we would like to help you but there is no budget left; the money has been all allocated. Incidentally, have you ever seen a budget with items not allocated "Slush fund—$50,000.00"? But out of the kindness of my heart, I have squeezed out a few hundred dollars to get you started. The familiar thirty pieces of silver.

4. Divide and conquer play

We have only $10,000 and so many requests from so many minorities. Why don't you Blacks, Chicanos, Asians, Native Americans, and now women go into the next room and divide the money?

5. "Personality before business"

You have had years of fine personal friendship with a person who now is a decision-maker and administrator. You are reluctant to confront such a person and risk breaking a long-term and good friendship. Benjamin Franklin wrote to his friends in England at the beginning of the American Revolution: "Dear friends, we are now enemies." Business before pleasure.

6. Decisions in the halls

Even if you are placed on a board or in a situation where decisions are officially made, don't think you will be making decisions. Almost all major decisions are made in hallways, behind the scenes.

7. "We don't have any problems here."

I have heard that you are a troublemaker, Dr. Sano. You know, I checked with Taro Tsukemono and Johnny Chop Suey, and they refute your contentions. In fact, they say we have no problems here.

Just remember, if you have a grievance and you show up in an office to voice it with the backing of your ad hoc committee, you are the problem. If the "man" says we have no problems, just say, "You have one — me."

8. They

I'm doing the best I can, but *they* or the *Board* or the *churches* won't let me do anything for you. There is no "they." Get names and telephone numbers.

9. Scientific attitude

We need evidence, hard facts. So, instead of giving you funds for ministry, they give you funds to study . . . yourselves.

10. The memo war

Get everything in writing and keep carbon copies of everything you write. Always tape interviews if you can or write a summary and send it to the person. Use carbon copies to send information to a third person; never negotiate when only two persons are present — always have a third person to verify. Always use deadlines for requests, demands, and information. The paper chase — tedious, but necessary.

Up to this point, I have been describing "political acts" in the real world against the various institutions which hem us in, including and specifically the ecclesiastical structures. This is to turn around the "tribalization" of Asian Americans into a weapon for actions of protest. It depends upon a united front, ignoring the deep cleavages inside the Asian American movement itself, for the basis is self-interest of persons and groups. The rationale for our being together is to oppose overwhelming power with power of our own. The issues are grievances which we are protesting.

The point is that if we are to seize the future rather than stumble into it, the display and acting out of political moves is essential, both for building our base in a unified Asian American Christian group and in coming out of the "underground" into the reality of United States life, both in the society and in the church.

But the whole is not done, since protest and self-interests are only half of the total development we need to engage the future. Rollo May says of protest:

> But if will remains, it stays dependent on that which it is protesting. Protest is half-developed will. Dependent, like the child on parents, it borrows its impetus from its

enemy. This gradually empties the will of content; you always are the shadow of your adversary, waiting for him to move so that you can move yourself.[16]

So too with self-interest. Although it is a powerful glue for our life together, there is no reality to the idea of "enlightened self-interest." Enlightened self-interest is a contradiction. Self-interest is concerned with the immediate needs of the self or the sub-group but cannot reckon in terms of long-range interest.[17] Even if self-interest is one of the first steps of bringing us together, it cannot, in the long run, hold us together, for it is a variation of privatism; while what we need as Christians, both white and non-white, is a conviction about the *res publica*, "the public thing."

What I have been describing are "revolutionary acts" which seek external political change. It more than likely will, if successful, only replace white oppressors with non-white oppressors—both of whom love and utilize force in controlling others. In analyzing the various movements in the 1960s, Arendt describes what is necessary. She says that real change could come if there is

> a real analysis of the existing situation such as used to be made in earlier times . . . The theoretical sterility and analytical dullness of this movement are just as striking and depressing as its joys in action is welcome.[18]

However much political acts to alter the external situation are necessary, we, especially as Christians, need to turn to the other more positive side of this process of moving forcefully into the future: We need to become *rebels*, not merely revolutionaries.

A rebel opposes authority, breaking with custom and moving toward an internalized change—changes in attitudes, emotions, and outlooks. While revolutionaries collect and use force, rebels work for the sake of a vision of life and a new society. While the revolutionary slays the master and becomes a master, the rebel saves the master as well as the slave.[19]

It is this task of "building up" after destroying that is the most difficult and most neglected. Inside of the churches, it appears as the theological task of analysis and creation of a new vision of the future. To this I shall turn now in the last part of this address.

II. The Necessity of Theological Formulation

The rebel function is necessary for the renewal of culture expressing itself in the form of dissent, civil disobedience and the freedom of human beings to control their own lives. It is also basically an internal change in attitude and a new understanding of society and theology.

Authorities both in the society and the church easily overlook this aspect of the current ethnic unrest to both our detriments. It is simple for an outsider to mistake what is most conspicuous for what is most important. They see the dust rising from

---

[16] Rollo May, *Love and Will* (New York: W. W. Norton, 1969), 192–3.

[17] Arendt, *Crises of the Republic*, 175.

[18] Arendt, *Crises of the Republic*, 206.

[19] May, *Power and Innocence*, 220.

political activity and never see the fundamental need for change which the theological thrust is pushing.

The urgency of a new theological formulation has not yet dawned upon the church's leadership in theological education. The present dearth of life-producing theology is apparent, and the dialogue is "in the family." It is much like a scene described by Abraham Lincoln. He said,

> I remember being once much amused at seeing two partially intoxicated men engaged in a fight with their great coats on, which fight, after a long and rather harmless contest, ended in each having fought himself out of his own coat and into that of the other.

The neglect of Asians and Asian thought by Christian theologians is not only sad but almost heretical. It is a damning indictment against the Christianity of the West that it has for years neglected, yes, ignored one-half of the world's population and centuries of the most continuous cultures mankind has known. It is to our loss that one of the last of the formidable theological minds of our generation, Paul Tillich, died before realizing his quest to learn about and incorporate Asian thought into his theological thinking.

Asians and Asian thought are culturally most distant from the thinking and being of the West. It would prove to be the most significant encounter in the history of Christianity if it can occur consciously. I say "consciously" because, like it or not, one of the strands of Asian thought—Maoism—has already challenged the West by developing a new society born out of but contiguous with the most ancient culture in our world.

John Baillie talked about reality:

> The test of reality is the resistance it offers to the otherwise uninhibited course of my own thinking, desiring and acting. Reality is what I "come up against," what takes me by surprise, the other-than-myself which pulls me up and obliges me to reckon with it and adjust myself to it because it will not consent simply to adjust itself to me.

For Asian American Christians, then, it has a twofold purpose. The first is to rediscover our heritage and therefore our very being and life. Margaret Mead ruefully notes:

> The loss of a useful art—as with the South Sea Islanders who no longer know how to build canoes and so were forever prisoners on the tiny islands to which they had once come as bold mariners—could give the imagination a horrid chill. If simple men in islands forgot how to build canoes, might not more complex people also forget something equally essential to their lives?[20]

At this level, we are not dealing with politics—we are dealing with our very lives.

The second purpose is what unites us with our white and other non-white Christians. It is to move out of the parochialism and paternalism of a European and Anglo-dominated theology and church life into one which has within it the dynamism of pluralism and the unity of common Christian concern.

---

[20] Margaret Mead, *Male and Female: A Study of the Sexes in a Changing World* (New York: William Morrow, 1949), 11.

Moses said in the speech near the time of his death in Deuteronomy 30:15, "See I have set before you this day, life and good, death and evil. . . . I call heaven and earth to witness against you this day, that I have set before you life and death, blessing and curse; therefore choose life, that you and your descendants may live, loving the Lord your God, obeying his voice and cleaving to him." What are the alternative futures? There is but one choice, the choice between life-affirming and death-embracing; reaction to life is one-half of will; the other half is embracing life.

And in reality, we are Asian American and we are Christian. We are whole human beings and cannot be divided into two parts. But in analyzing our situation and need, we have to separate and deal with the two parts, culturally being Asian American, religiously being Christian.

When a group of Dutch men came to Hendrik Kraemer during the occupation of Holland and asked what they should do—collaborate or resist by subversive activity, his answer was "I will not tell you what you should do, but I will tell you who you are."

When they heard who they were, their resistance movement began to take shape.

A. Our Ethnicity

There are several layers and kinds of culture of which we are a part. The first is the "national culture" which is the product of the technological revolution and massive urban societies. It is both good and evil, and is committed to "progress" in terms of greater wealth and leisure, among many things.

The second is the "common culture." This is the general heritage very largely from Anglo-American traditions and sustained by the English language. It is a very rich inheritance, embodying a good deal of Western Christianity; at the same time, it is demonic in its ideas of white supremacy and vast paternalism, resulting in a very real imperialism both at home and abroad.

Then there are the subcultural neighborhoods, primarily the non-white minorities in the land. These are characterized by a variant rootage in world cultures—African, Latin American, Asian, etc.—and sometimes marked by different languages. These ethnic enclaves are vigorous and real. Often, however, some of us deny that they exist or at least protest that we are not a part of them. Andrew Greeley, the sociologist, bluntly says, "Ethnic groups are something like the Rocky Mountains or the Atlantic Ocean—whether we like them or not really doesn't matter very much; they are concrete realities with which we must cope, and condemning or praising them is a waste of time."21

Gunnar Myrdal then reminds us that

as science is nothing but highly sophisticated common sense, we might most usefully start our inquiry by attempting to characterize the world outlook of ordinary people in our society.22

---

21 Greeley, *Why Can't They Be Like Us?*, 30.
22 Gunnar Myrdal, *Objectivity in Social Science Research* (New York: Random House, 1969), 14.

If there is any future for us as churches ministering with ethnic communities, our relationship and understanding with the grassroots in those communities has to increase and become primary. Mao recalled, "You know, I've proclaimed for a long time: We must teach the masses clearly what we have received from them confusedly."[23] Any Asian American theology and strategy has to do precisely that. We have to listen and understand what each segment of our coalition is thinking, saying, and doing, often in a very confused way. The church thus should take all of this confusion and systematize and clarify it. This is a theological task, in my opinion. Then we have the responsibility to return the thoughts and strategies back to the people in a clear and precise manner. As those working and relating to ethnic groups, let us work out of their reality and not out of our idealism.

In many instances, the Asian American churches have been unmindful of the Asians at the bottom of the social scale and, having bought the integrative tendencies of the white churches, have effectively cut ourselves off from both the actual people who should become part of our congregations and the cultural strength of the ethnic life. Too often, we are only replicas of middle-class America, strangers in our own communities.

If we are to have a future, Asian American Christians need to become responsibly related to the inflow of large numbers of immigrants from both Asia and the Pacific Islands. Their plight is our signal to conduct a meaningful mission. In a more massive sense, the issues about Micronesians and their relationship to the United States, which wants to build a line of military bases across the Pacific, are also ours. And then, internally, it is imperative that we recognize and allow the vast pluralism of our Asian American Christians to be expressed and embraced. The Samoan no less than the Japanese; the Filipino no less than the Chinese. Diversity is to be positively reinforced and encouraged.

One fear for such a pluralism and affirmation of diversity is that we shall end in a "balkanized" state. Ernst Cassirer, the scholar on culture, many years ago noticed the simplistic ideas of the unity of mankind, on the one hand, and the dire predictions of the radical unbridgeable differences among the varied human cultures, on the other hand. After his studies of cultures, he came to believe that humanity requires multiplicity and multiformity—"a dialectic unity; a coexistence of contraries," he called it.[24]

We should further note that not all that we inherit as culture is good. It is mixed with the demonic. For example, Asian male chauvinism is not a positive aspect of our heritage. Yet, cultures are the results of centuries of human groups in common life, and cultures can die even though men survive, and that is what threatens us today. And a basic question which has to bother us as Asian American Christians is whether the practice of Christianity and the underlying theological justification

---

[23] Richard H. Solomon, *Mao's Revolution and the Chinese Political Culture* (Berkeley: University of California Press, 1971), 195.

[24] Ernst Cassirer, *An Essay on Man* (Garden City, NY: Doubleday Anchor Books, 1956), 279.

through the two hundred years of the existence of the United States is destroying rather than creating life. As historian Henry Steele Commager warns,

> It is American standards that must be accepted as the norm everywhere—in Europe, in Latin America, even in Asia. Thus it is normal and right that the United States should be an Asian power, but unthinkable that China should be an American power . . . so the nation is bankrupting itself materially, socially and morally for a security which always eludes it, and which it can never attain because it seeks to win it not by equality and cooperation but by superiority and the imposition of its will on much of mankind.[25]

It is probably true that the so-called norms of our society and the institutions which we have are those which we have become accustomed to. The challenge is for us to affirm our varied cultural heritages, culling out that which inhibits our freedom and responsibility and moving forward on a new and different course from the American norm, in a life embracing direction.

Where will ethnicity lead us and how? They tell of a couple of persons who were discussing a piece of gossip. One person finally said to the other, "I won't go into all the details; in fact, I've already told you more about it than I heard myself." What I do know is that the future is unknowable, but the present is unthinkable. It just may be in the reinterpretation of our roots we may surface the myths which may give meaning to our lives. And a myth is not a rumor. As William Irwin Thompson states, "In a religious society myth tells the people who they are, and where they come from; to change the myth is to run the risk of becoming lost in the most profound ontological sense."[26] For Asian American Christians, the need for ethnic roots is thus doubly important because the Asian has never divided the religious from the cultural.

B. Theological Roots

Just outside of Hong Kong is *Tao Fong Shan*, The Mountain of the Logos Wind. It was created by one of the most imaginative missions led by the Norwegian Lutheran Karl Reichelt. The symbol of the mission is the cross rising out of the lotus. Paul Clasper writes, "The two belong together—neither cancelling the other out, nor ultimately competing with each other in exclusivistic terms. . . . To be sure, this is dangerous. But so is everything about the Gospel."

This is not talking about universalism, a bland "every road leads to the same summit." Of course, it isn't hard for minorities to succumb to skepticism. Professor Hsu tells a story about the Chinese student who applied for financial assistance at Northwestern University, a Methodist-founded institution. In the space for religion, she wrote, "Willing to become a Methodist." Hsu gives another interpretation to this, but I want to say that it only follows our American church propensity to move from the authority of God to the desires of the parishioners to carry out our common life. If there is an alternative for the future of Asian American Christians, it is the basic dealing with the "gospel of Jesus Christ" to find a new root age in our faith.

---

[25] Hsu, *Americans and Chinese*, xxvii.
[26] William I. Thompson, *At the Edge of History* (New York: Harper, 1972), 202.

One disturbing aspect of much of the new social movements, whether they be the anti-war movement of which our ministry in higher education participated or the ethnic movements which are our present concern. That is, the degree of subjectivity and inner search without any transcendental dimension. As Stackhouse reminds us,

> The theologically true for some is heresy for another; one man's god is another's demon; one woman's salvation is another's damnation . . . Is everything a blur, or are there any grounds upon which to stand?[27]

By affirming pluralism, let us not make the mistake of the neglect of Christ's kingship over culture. There is either a common ground, firm and central, or we all sink into the abyss of death.

As Asians, as an immigrant people, as minorities—we find ourselves often on the margin and on the boundary. I affirm, however, that living on the boundaries is a powerful and creative place. One begins by standing on the boundary of the divine-human. One cannot depend upon one's subjective judgment. This was the mistake of the campus ministers who wholeheartedly accepted all that was propounded by the student revolutionaries and the anti-war movement. We almost exclusively engaged in action without reflection, especially without benefit of standing on the divine-human boundary and sorting out what was happening. We generally embraced what affirmed our own activity through God's "yes," but we also ignored the fact of God's "no."

Stackhouse describes this boundary:

> A boundary both divides and relates. It is a place where distinctions are made and where things are looked over. It is also a place where transition and interaction takes place. . . . A boundary is a point of passage and invitation when things are proper and in good order; a point of critical scrutiny and rejection when things are dubious or suspicious.[28]

We are therefore persons who receive "free grace" from the moving of the Spirit of God over the chaos and gripping us with "ontological surprise." The presence of such grace refines and deepens our lives in a manner not available to us when we participate wholly in the secular arena, apart from the inflow of God's presence. It also calls for courage to live on the boundary, on the fringes of human existence, not in despair but in real hope.

And as Asian American Christians, we can stand on the various boundaries which are our lot—between Asia and America, rural and urban, intuitive thought and rational logic, immigrant and citizen, Korean and Japanese, minority and majority, non-white and white—and use this as a point of dialogue and expansion of our lives. It is the audacity of the Asian American Christian, and those others in the Christian community who would join us, to affirm that the happenings at the margin and the boundary are truly the center and the opening into the future of a life-affirming humanity.

---

[27] Max L. Stackhouse, "On the Boundary of Psychology and Theology," *Andover Newton Quarterly* 15, no. 3 (January 1975): 199.

[28] Stackhouse, "On the Boundary," 196.

As one looks at the history of the church from Paul to Kagawa, Luther to Bonhoeffer, none were systematic theologians, but persons who lived out their lives in the context of their societies always on the boundaries and spoke out of that living situation. It is thus that Paulo Freire helps us to see that the "word" has two dimensions of reflection and action. Out of that contextual theology is to speak a true word to transform the world.[29]

And here is the future, life-giving if we can turn the tribalization of the Asian Americans, primarily a negative and death-oriented concept, into a life-affirming community. If, presently, our unity depends more on political expediency, we can covenant together to move out of that iron trap into a freeing experience of life together as Christians, and more importantly as humans. If we can forge a deeper life together as Asian American Christians, then we can include the others who are presently our enemies in a community of humanity. In that way, we turn the whole situation around so that we need not either literally or figuratively "slay" our enemies but can be free to stand by them and together live before God.

Bonhoeffer warns that such a community is not a wish dream about what the Christian community should be.

> By sheer grace, God will not permit us to live even for a brief period in a dream world. He does not abandon us to those rapturous experiences and lofty moods that come over us like dreams. God is not a God of the emotions but the God of truth. Only that which faces such disillusionment, with all its unhappy and ugly aspects, begins to be what it should be in God's sight, begins to grasp in faith the promise that is given to it.[30]

It is this challenge which lies unremovable before us. We have taken the steps of being together in a political sense, and it has been a hard road just to get each of the Asian and Pacific groups into the same room and to dialogue in understanding. But the harder task is ahead if we are to have a future. It is to understand theologically who we are and how we build a lasting, truly human, and humane community not apart from our pluralism but together.

In pursuing the thought of serious persons studying United States chaos, one is struck by the unanimity about the possible solution. Arendt talks about "councils", not communes, which are a renunciation of life, but neighborhood groups of a small number who participate and debate about the public issues. Rollo May is concerned that we lack caring communities of small groups. Professor Hsu talks about facing the dangers of our privatized and individualized existence through creation of the strength of the primary groups. Eric Fromm believes that cultural revolution must be based in groups, which cuts across many different ideologies but share face-to-face and strive to become new persons.

What is remarkable about all of these proposals is that if we can break out of our layers of denominationalism, our edifice complexes, our inane and irrelevant attempts of mere survival, one is immediately aware that potentially the local congregations and other groups of concerned Christians are precisely the kind of

---

[29] Paulo Freire, *Pedagogy of the Oppressed* (New York: Herder and Herder, 1971), 75.
[30] Dietrich Bonhoeffer, *Life Together* (London: SCM Press, 1954), 27.

groups, councils, communities, primary entities which all of these persons are advocating. But it takes a new kind of church life. Not "new" in the sense of novelty, but new in the sense of undergoing a critical analysis and embracing a common life, cutting across race, social class, pietism, dogmatism, but retaining a truly pluralistic and dialogical character.

Hendrik Kraemer, several decades ago, advocated that the church be an *interfering community*. Churches cannot be a "reservation" (as in "Indian reservation") for religious people, split from each other by irrelevant denominational, racist, and social class walls. He insists that the church be

> reconciler in the grievous conflicts that separate men and communities; questioning the world incessantly and inducing it to put the right questions in regard to its problems; letting itself be questioned by the world, contradicting it when necessary, and reminding it of the divine Judgment which hangs over everything and everyone; throughout all this service, reconciliation, contradiction and questioning, sounding the note of the certainty of God's triumphant love.[31]

And we must serve notice on the larger church that we are not engaged in mission only for ourselves. We are an interfering community which calls the whole church to repentance. Ethnic congregations and ethnic theology are not only for the purpose of finding our direction. It is surely not in the general cop-out called "doing your own thing." It is a call for conversion. We are building out of a center of reference in the Christian faith, which becomes the basis for minorities to address the larger society and church to find a truer basis for their lives as well as for ours. This is not sentiment, but truth.

Further, Kraemer called for the involvement of the laity. The movements I am describing, though involving clergy, are too important to leave to them. The laity of the churches are the dispersion of the faithful into the life of the world. The laity is thus the ones who can play a decisive role in positive change in the future. It means we move beyond survival for the sake of religious communities to engagement in the real world where life and death issues are being debated and decided. It must be done cross-culturally, ecumenically, and based on a process of theological reflection.

Conclusion

And where better to begin than Hawaii? A major and key area of the world is the Pacific Basin. There have occurred and will continue to occur acts of violence around the Pacific Rim by the United States. If for no other reason, the sheer physical toll in terms of military casualties and death by starvation should spur us on. We are Americans, and as citizens we are a part of the reason for the racism and militarism of our country as we create chaos and destruction from Korea to Indochina, from the Philippines to Micronesia, from Seattle to the Mexican border — all against peoples of the Pacific Islands and Asia.

---

[31] Hendrik A. Kraemer, *Theology of the Laity* (Philadelphia: Westminster Press, 1958), 186–7.

And in the eye of this hurricane is the state of Hawaii. Hawaii is the center, as the epitome, the magnet which draws from all of these regions. It is the symbol, on the one hand, of concentrated US military force and aggrandizement, and on the other, as the fantasyland of the United States. Neither is completely true, but what can be? It is, in a real sense, exploited in every direction. It is put forth against other minorities as the example that the melting pot really works, an example of what free enterprise can produce, a church community which has assimilated. But its lands are exploited; the people are exploited; and neither the land nor the institutions are really of the people.

You are, in a sense, outsiders—whose good life is manipulated for causes you couldn't affirm; whose bad life is blamed upon Asia. But the truth is that Hawaiian Christians could take the offensive both socially and psychologically. The possibility, the potential, of a real theology of wholeness for empowerment out of diversity exists in Hawaii. My judgment, however, is that we have been riding very high in the euphoria of apparent wholeness and togetherness and also very shallow. To change the situation is to create dimensions of wholeness and ethnic pluralism which has depth and strength to confront the daemonic rather than ignoring it. To create a real unified common community is neither automatic nor easy. Yet Hawaii, set in the very middle of the Pacific Basin, so fully represented by the various and multicolored peoples of the world, is almost predestined to play a critical role in the future of not only Asian American Christians but of humanity.

And, to do so, we must reach back into our culture and avoid the trap of American pragmatism and concern for success or failure. Wang Wei, a Chinese poet of the eighth century, described the Taoist mind:

> The breeze from the pine woods blows my sash;
> The mountain moon shines upon my harp.
> You ask me to explain the reason of failure or success.
> The fisherman's song goes deep into the river.[32]

To debate success or failure is to fall into despair and paralysis. Instead, like the poet who gives an irrelevant answer to the question of success or failure, we too should not be concerned with that. The poet is saying that our lives are lived in deep underlying harmony, and this opens us to the art of living. And it is in the living out of our lives that we fulfill God's purpose. It is being faithful and becoming whole.

---

[32] Chang, *Creativity and Taoism*, 91.

Oppression—White Domination[*]

LLOYD WAKE[†]

The word "evangelism" turns me off because it is related to my experience of oppression. Those of us here and in Third World countries, who have been targets of the Christian missionary thrust, were brought into a church dominated by a Euro-American theology, culture, and value system. Being part of this church made us WASPs (or YASPs—Yellow Anglo Saxon Protestants). It is questionable if it has helped us to be Christian, human, or proud to be who we are as an ethnic people.

Black people and other Third World people became aware that unquestioning participation in this church prevented us from dealing realistically with the prejudice, racism, and subtle and overt Euro-American arrogance that keeps us oppressed. The recent movements toward racial pride and ethnic identity, toward an indigenous mission methodology, toward formulating a theology that grows out of the experiences of oppression, has caused a painful reappraisal on the part of both the white-dominated church and the Third World people of the Church.

Why has it taken so long to realize the necessity of having ethnic minorities in major decision-making bodies of the church? Why must black and ethnic seminarians push so hard and shout so loud for ethnic studies in theological seminaries? Consider these questions and you'll realize that words like "oppression" and "white domination" are more than rhetoric.

I am participating in the "evangelistic" task as I work to eliminate dehumanizing situations that keep people oppressed. Jesus sent me to preach good news to the poor (bread for the hungry, adequate, housing and health care, guaranteed minimum income); to proclaim release to the captives (free Angela and all other political prisoners) and recover the sight of the blind (you can't see San Francisco Chinatown through a gray line bus window); to set at liberty those who are oppressed (Get off our backs! Freedom now!); to proclaim the acceptable year of the Lord (don't talk about the future rewards—today is the day).

---

[*] From *Methodists in Action*, January 28, 1972, published by the California/Nevada UMC Conference.

[†] Pastor, Glide Memorial UMC.

A Revolutionary Message[*]

LLOYD K. WAKE[†]

Once upon a time, many years ago, there was a man named David.

> He was king of a country which became rich and powerful by exploiting the weak and small countries and crushing them in war. The king was both respected and feared by many.

The people sang a song which proclaimed the fame of King David:
> "Saul has slain his thousands,
> But David has slain his ten thousands."

David said, "I am a powerful man. I take what I want when I want it." So, he took to himself a beautiful woman who was wife of a general in the king' s army. The king ordered the general to the front line of the battle where he was sure to be killed, and he was, and then the king had the widow all to himself.

But a strong and free man named Nathan, a prophet, confronted King David with his evil deed. "You have used your personal power and the prestige of your office for cruel and inhuman purposes. Set things right with God and Man."

Because of this confrontation, the king became more human and responsive in the years that followed.

Many centuries later . . . there was another man named Richard, who became king of the richest and most powerful nation on earth.

When little countries far away, like the Philippines, Korea, Cambodia, and Vietnam struggled to make their country a good place, King Richard sent troops to preserve and protect his country's industries that were exploiting and colonizing, and his troops killed many, many people.

When the poor at home complained about their poverty, he said, "You wouldn't be poor if you would get a job. Get out and earn your bread."

So they rioted, looted, and burned in frustration. But the poor got poorer and the rich got richer.

---

[*] Delivered in San Francisco, CA.
[†] Community life minister at Glide Memorial UMC.

Then the people learned that King Richard's palace guards were corrupt—they were selling favors and sent spies among their own people. The people lost faith in King Richard and his men.

King Richard had a friend, a holy man named Rev. Billy. This man was so holy he kept his mouth shut and said nothing to the king about the obscene and immoral acts perpetrated against other countries and the people at home, so King Richard continued to be arrogant, evading the questions and covering up the corruption. But the people themselves got on the king's case . . .

The moral of the story: If you are a dirty old king, it's better to have a man like Nathan around than a house chaplain like Billy.

Theologizing

An Asian American Perspective

WESLEY WOO

This paper represents some personal reflections on current concerns for, and attempts towards, developing an "Asian American theology." These are shared here in this consultation in the belief that out of critical dialogue will emerge theological perspectives not only relevant to Asian American concerns but also meaningful to a more universal understanding of the Christian faith. But let me begin with a proper Asian opening—by apologizing. If much of what I have to say sounds repetitive, it is because my focus is on just a couple of themes, but from several different angles.

"Theology as critical reflection on praxis" is the understanding of theology emphasized by Gustavo Gutierrez in *A Theology of Liberation* and which forms the foundation from which my thoughts spring forth.

> Theological reflection would then necessarily be a criticism of society and the Church insofar as they are called and addressed by the Word of God; it would be a critical theory, worked out in the light of the Word accepted in faith and inspired by a practical purpose—and therefore indissolubly linked to historical praxis.[1]

In this understanding, it is explicit that theology is tied to involvement in history (praxis). The primary concern is not for building an objective system of thought, though this has been the sole concern of too many theologians.[2] We could fall into the same trap in trying to build an "Asian American theology," especially if just for the sake of having such an entity or for the sake of having a flag to wave. Instead, Gutierrez's definition suggests that our concern ought to be for making sense of, and giving direction to, Christian involvement in history. Theology then evolves only at the level of trying to organize and systematize this concern. Whether this theology is labeled "Asian American" or not is ultimately unimportant—as long as it leads to the liberation and humanization of people as understood in the light of the Word of God.

But for our concern here, the point needs to be made that critical reflection on praxis means critical reflection on the Asian American experience, in all its dimensions. It is beyond the scope of this paper to go into the nature and meaning of the Asian American experience. Suffice it to say that a prior condition for theologizing is that we be in touch and involved with that experience. Only then will

---

[1] Gustavo Gutierrez, *A Theology of Liberation: History, Politics, and Salvation*, ed. and trans. Caridad Inda and John Eagleson (New York: Orbis Books, 1973), 11.

[2] Walter Wink, "How I Have Been Snagged by the Seat of My Pants While Reading the Bible," *The Christian Century* 92, no. 30 (September 24, 1975): 817.

we find meaningful ways to share God's freeing Word with Asian Americans. Only then will we be able to contribute to the richness of the Asian American experience towards a deeper understanding of the faith. Without such grounding, there is little validity, and even less use, for an Asian American theology.

Given the above understanding of theology, let me suggest three guidelines for theologizing. What will be said here and in the following section is not new but does seem to deserve renewed emphasis in light of Asian American Christian concerns.

The first guideline for any theologizing is the most obvious, but is also one that is bypassed often enough, albeit usually in subtle ways, to deserve emphasis here. Theology must keep integrity, with faith in a God who calls us to full and authentic humanity. Thus it is that theology must be rooted in Scripture. Anything less and all we end up with is the proof text for an Asian American ideology.

But lest my concern by misconstrued in regards to this point, let me state two distortions to be avoided. First is to assume right off that the understanding of Scripture that has been generally transmitted is in fact scriptural. This is especially true, for our concerns, of the understanding that has been transmitted by White America. Too often, this understanding has been really the co-opting of Scripture to justify White values. Also, too often, this understanding has been used to claim universal truth for those same values. Thus, to be Christian is to be White American, and vice versa. The second distortion is to assume that the meaning of Scripture as given in the English language is self-evident and need not be studied, interpreted, and translated into specific languages and experiences. Not to do these things is de facto to serve the purposes of oppression. Both of these distortions are in fact unbiblical, denying God's love for humanity in all particularity and God's working in and through history.

The second guideline stems from the first. Any theologizing must generate insight-action. That is, it must provide insight that leads to, and manifests itself in, action. "The insight which the Biblical material tries to evoke is characterized not by conclusions, but by decisions."[3] When a lawyer asked Jesus who his neighbor was, he was told the parable of the Good Samaritan and then told, "Go and do likewise." Thus, a question regarding being is answered in terms of doing. So, while it might be significant in the field of comparative religion to study similarities and contrasts between Christian and Buddhist thought, this has no significance for Biblical theology — unless it leads to or facilitates action.

The third guideline is that any theologizing in an Asian American perspective should be done in a corporate context. This means, first of all, as already stated, that it must be rooted in the Asian American experience. But secondly, it means that theology must be nurtured in the midst of an Asian American Christian community. In this way, we maintain consistency with the Biblical understanding of the interdependent nature of humanity. We also maintain consistency with the nature of

---

[3] C. Daniel Batson, J. Christiaan Beker, and W. Malcolm Clark, *Commitment without Ideology* (Philadelphia: United Church Press, 1973), 112.

the Asian American phenomenon to date. Though we are Chinese American, Formosan American, Japanese American, Korean American, and Pilipino American, and though very few in Asia consider themselves "Asian," yet in America these different groups have come together and given flesh to the idea of "Asian American." Thus it is that we have created one tangible expression of corporate identity. But be aware that this does not mean that we reduce pluralistic understandings of the gospel to one format. Rather, it means that we allow the corporate body to criticize, validate, and enrich our theologizing. It is perhaps in this tone that Paul submitted his gospel to the brethren in Jerusalem for their inspection (Gal. 2:2).

So far, what has been said can have relevance for anyone concerned about Biblical theology. Let me now suggest three emphases or characteristics for an Asian American perspective. Again, these are not new, but seem critical in the light of Asian American concerns.

The first characteristic of any Asian American theologizing is that it be prophetic in style. "Now the task of the prophets was to arouse, rebuke, call to repentance, warn, and threaten with the judgment of Yahweh, and to promise a turn of future in a coming age" on condition that there were some who realized the holy will of Yahweh.[4] Thus, a prophet attempts to effect a change in the present situation towards the direction of God's purposes. The process for effectuating this change is important for us to consider. Batson, Beker, and Clark suggest that this has been done traditionally in the Old Testament by pointing out and heightening some conflict latent in a situation or person and thus forcing resolution.[5] The prophet, of course, tries to move this resolution in the direction of God (repentance) but stays true to his task, whether successful or not. Thus, for example, the prophet Nathan, in dealing with David's sin against Uriah, used a story to point out strongly the conflict between this sin and God's blessings to David. As a result, David repented (2 Sam. 12). Or we have the example of Jeremiah, who set himself up against the false prophets around him. While these false prophets were preaching that there would be peace and that the nation would not be destroyed, thus blurring the contradictions and conflicts existent in the nation, Jeremiah preached that there would be no peace and that God would punish His people. In short, the prophetic task then is that of pointing out and heightening contradictions between God's will and humanity's sins and demanding repentance.

The second characteristic is related to the first. The prophetic message involves the debunking of dehumanizing "realities." Berger and Luckmann have shown in *The Social Construction of Reality* how social, cultural, and political forms are humanly produced.[6] But they are perceived as standing over against humanity as independent reality—i.e., they become reified. It was against such reified institutions that the prophets were continually speaking against. So too, theologizing in an Asian

---

[4] Johannes Lindblom, *Prophecy in Ancient Israel* (Philadelphia: Fortress Press, 1967), 217.

[5] Batson, Beker, and Clark, *Commitment without Ideology*, 100.

[6] Peter L. Berger and Thomas Luckmann, *The Social Construction of Reality* (New York: Anchor Books, 1967).

American perspective must include the task of debunking (de-reifying) "realities" that deny authentic humanity to peoples and that instead perpetuate oppression. On a value level, for example, we must challenge the notion of the rugged individual. Though this is a relative value having significance in certain historical situations, yet it has been treated as the prime American value and given Biblical legitimization. In fact, in our day this value has existed to protect racism. For, amongst other things, it prevents us from seeing the institutional roots of racism. Instead, we blame ourselves for not trying hard enough to "make it."[7] On another level, we ought to be debunking institutions—theological, political, or otherwise—that serve also to perpetuate oppression. On a third level, this debunking should help us to see that trying to "make it" itself may be a dehumanizing value. In sum, perhaps it is in this debunking process that we begin to challenge the "principalities and powers" that try to "separate us from the love of God in Christ Jesus our Lord."

Before moving on to the third characteristic, permit me to pause and suggest why Asian Americans are in a position to take on the prophetic and debunking roles mentioned. Berger and Pullman suggest three conditions that allow a debunking orientation to develop.[8] First, there is a breakdown in established systems and a condition of anomie. Secondly, cultural contact and shock exist and provide alternative ways of perceiving reality. Thirdly, there are individuals and groups in positions of social marginality, with de-reifying tendencies. All three conditions were realized at the time of Israel's settlement of Palestine and thus impacted her role in the Ancient Near East. So too, all three conditions seem to be realized today. There is widespread questioning and breakdown of existing institutions. Cultural shock is evident, especially in the lives of Asian immigrants, but has fallout implications for native-born Asian Americans too. And we certainly are in positions of social marginality. All in all, it can be said that the time is ripe for challenging existing values (including theologies) and that we stand far enough outside these and have different enough perspectives to debunk them.

Getting back to the characteristics of Asian American theologizing, the third of these is that we must focus on salvation as a corporate process. That is, we must point out that salvation occurs only in a corporate context. In a sense, our coming together as Asian Americans gives us a taste of what that means. The notion of individual salvation is concomitant with the notion of the rugged individual, especially in the sense that every man must fend for himself. Both of these notions are, in my mind, unbiblical. It is only in the commitment to the salvation (liberation and humanization) of others that we ourselves are saved. When the rich young man came to Jesus seeking salvation, he was turned instead towards the salvation of the poor (Mark 10:17–22). In this story also, it is suggested that salvation ought not to be the goal of Christian faith. It is really the byproduct of active commitment to God's love

---

[7] Wink, "How I Have Been Snagged," 818.
[8] Batson, Beker, and Clark, *Commitment without Ideology*, 129.

for all humanity. One is called not to "save" himself but to "spend" himself for others. Apart from this, Christian discipleship has no meaning.

In summary, I have tried to point out some guidelines and some possible characteristics for theologizing in an Asian American perspective. None of these are new or unique to us. But it does seem that the Asian American experience provides us with some unique resources, and thus perhaps a special mandate, to focus on at least these points.

Appendix

What follows are two attempts to theologize in an Asian American perspective. These thoughts are still in the rough, but are shared here in brief form for purposes of dialogue.

I. Sojourning—A Biblical Lifestyle

Chinese first came to America as sojourners with no plans to remain permanently. In this instance, then, apart from any effects of racism encountered, theirs was a deliberate alienation from American society. Though Chinese today, and other Asian Americans, do not view themselves as sojourners, there is perhaps some value in reappropriating that heritage. This is especially meaningful if we compare the Biblical understandings about "sojourners" with this history.

1. Israel is called to remember that she was once a sojourner in Egypt, and that Yahweh delivered her and established her in a land. This past is to affect her attitude towards other sojourners. "You shall not wrong a stranger or oppress him, for you were strangers in the land of Egypt" (Exod 22:21).

2. Even though settled in the land, Israel is still a sojourner. "The land shall not be sold in perpetuity, for the land is mine; for you are strangers and sojourners with me" (Lev 25:23). Perhaps it is that we are all called to be and remain as sojourners. "Foxes have holes, and birds of the air have nests; but the Son of man has nowhere to lay his head" (Matt 8:20).

3. The sojourner attitude is that of one searching for something better, something in the future. "For people who speak thus make it clear that they are seeking a homeland. If they had been thinking of that land from which they had gone out, they would have had opportunity to return. But as it is, they desire a better country, that is, a heavenly one. Therefore God is not ashamed to be called their God, for he has prepared for them a city" (Heb 11:14–16).

Social marginality, including the hyphenated identity, is something that concerns all of us here. Perhaps that is in fact the role we are called to. Thus, we are called away from attempts to preserve the status quo and to live prophetic lives, debunking always-present "realities."

On a deeper level, perhaps this speaks to the human, tendency to feel anxious about never really being "in" or never really feeling "settled" and "satisfied." Rather than getting anxious, we ought to thrive in this discontent and viewing instead the situation as God's challenge to us to move into the future.

II. The Land and Room to Breathe

A couple of years ago, I was involved in a discussion over needs for improving the community I was then living in. This community was primarily White until the last ten years. Now, it has a significant population to Asian Americans. At any rate, the discussion centered around needs to preserve family housing units—something I agree with. Yet I felt uncomfortable because plans to preserve family housing meant the preservation of one-unit buildings (houses) and the reduction of multi-unit buildings (apartments). But significant numbers of Chinese families live in these latter units.

A second but related concern that came up to me personally was over the Chinese immigrant perception about how much space is necessary for any one family to live in. Immigrant families from Hong Kong tend to have more people in a unit (usually an apartment) than native-born persons. They are less wont to "waste" space. This attitude is of course shaped by the situation from which they came. Space is precious in a dense metropolis like Hong Kong.

In mulling over the above concerns, I found the Biblical understanding of "the Land" helpful. The Land in the Old Testament is God's gift to Israel. But along with this gift is responsibility to till and care for it (Gen. 2:15). Also, they are called to live on it for the purpose of witnessing to God's involvement in history (Gen. 12:2). In other words, the Land becomes a concrete locus of God's activity. But American Christians have tended to pervert this understanding such that the Land now becomes the symbol of one's status and one's right to ownership.

Also helpful is to consider the psalmist's understanding of salvation as having "room to breathe" (Ps. 4). By virtue of environmental influences, the necessary "room to breathe" is perceived differently for Chinese immigrants than for native-born Americans (including most Chinese Americans).

In juxtaposing the above thoughts, one is challenged to rethink the purpose of having land (space) and what is really necessary for survival. One outcome might be that we need to redistribute land such that all have room to breathe and space to witness.

Theological Understanding of Women[*]

Eun Ja Kim Lee

"Cock-a-doodle-doo!" is a proud cock's cry.

How does a female cock, a hen, cry? Well, she does not cry.

There is a very well-known Korean proverb which says, "When the hen talks back, the entire household falls into doom!" Isn't it a nonsense? Yes, it is, in a way. But in fact, it is a serious expression which tells about the traditional image of woman and the consequent social structure in Korea. Here, the hen signifies the wife, the woman, or the female in the family. It connotes that like a female cock, woman is supposed to be silent, mute, submissive, and subservient in order to maintain the peace in her household. Only the cock, in other words, the husband, the man, or the male in the family, is supposed to have the authority to cry out or to say, "Cock-a-doodle-doo!" — whatever that means.

Korea has been influenced for a long time by the ascetic teachings of Confucianism and Buddhism, which take negative views toward women, and it has been a strongly male-dominated nation. The concept of superior-man and inferior-woman is deeply rooted in the minds of most people. Women were considered to be incapable and subordinate beings. Women were denied training and education that would have made them capable. Equal opportunity for women in society and politics was beyond imagination. Therefore, having many sons — not daughters — was regarded as one of the five supreme blessings on earth. Even now, to a great extent a baby girl's birth is a sorrow to her parents, while a baby boy's birth is a joy.

Induk Pahk, a Korean author, gives a vivid description about her first schooling as a child in her autobiographical sketch, *September Monkey*. Induk's widowed mother was a very progressive Christian woman. She felt that her daughter was just as important as somebody else's ten sons, and she was full of yearning heart to educate her young girl, Induk. She had to do something to fulfill her desire. At last, she disguised Induk in a boy's outfit and sent her to school which was supposed to be for boys only at that time. Amazingly, Induk was also courageous enough to pretend to be a boy in order to be educated just like the boys. Nothing was able to quench their burning zeal for education.

---

[*] Delivered February 1974 at the National Asian Women's Seminar of The United Methodist Church.

Some may think it is just an amusing episode, but I think it is a heart-breaking, painful experience that represents our women's long struggle for freedom from sexual discrimination and our continuing strife for equal rights.

Today, as one of the educated Korean women, I feel very much privileged and obliged to the great labors of the Western missionaries in Korea. I believe it was a miracle worked out through the Holy Spirit that just less than a century ago, those pioneer Christian missionaries were able to open the school doors for girls. They educated the girls despite the hardness of the so-called Hermit Kingdom's inhabitants, who firmly believed that it is far better to educate the cows in the field than to educate the girls.

Indeed, Christianity was a revolutionary thing. It has enhanced women's position in Korea. However, Christianity was not the final solution. It did not bring any utopia to women. Women were still second-class citizens. The priority in the job market went to the men, and the lower positions and lower salaries were women's in spite of the same quality and same amount of education. Even in the ways of Christian teaching, there were some weak points that failed to deliver the positive message for human equality. When I look at all the phenomena in the educational, religious, legal, social, economic, and political fields which directly or indirectly suppress the women's potentiality to grow and live as full human beings, I can hardly remain a mere distant observer. The more I look at these phenomena, the more I desire to be a needed woman and a wanted woman for the cause of women's freedom rather than to be a famous lady.

Up to now, I have talked mainly about illustrations of my own country. How about the other Asian countries? In my religious point of view, the particular religion of each country has been a powerful instrument to lay the basis of the social setting on sex roles in its own respective country. I view all the major religions in Asia, such as the Shintoism of Japan, Confucianism of China, Roman Catholicism of Philippines, Buddhism of Thailand, Hinduism of India, and Islam of Pakistan, and note that they all take a negative attitude toward women. They link women with ritual impurity, sex, and sin, and they give little positive regard to women. So, let me say that the religious boom of Asia has naturally and positively aided the building of strongly male-dominated societies in Asia. Consequently, most Asian women have lived in the patriarchal joint family system as mute hens, or as those who are virtually deaf and dumb, secluded from all developing social influences. Without mentioning that abhorrent Indian suttee, the cremation of a widow on her husband's funeral pyre, we can easily witness countless situations which oppress woman, *onna, yoja, nuren, babae, wahine* . . .

Thus, as far as "women's problems" are concerned, let me say that we are identical sisters. That's why we are here today, aren't we? Because we are all aware of it and concerned about it, we have gathered here to share our common difficulties and to search for the way to a better humanity.

Now, let us look at the Western scene. Western culture is predominantly based on Christianity. It is true that Christianity helped to raise the status of woman and promoted monogamy. So, in general, Western women seem to have better privileges of education and enjoy more latitude than their Oriental sisters. However, even within the church, the Christian institution, woman's role is restrained and generally limited in practice. Female elders, female rectors, female ministers, female priests, and female bishops are a rarity within the church. In society, "equal pay for equal work" has been a taboo notion. Western women also see that their society is male dominated, and the world is suffering from an overdose of masculine assertiveness. Why is this so? Let me approach this with my theological viewpoint.

In our church history, the Judeo-Christian tradition established men as the wielders of religious power. When the Roman church became the predominant political institution, it forced its concept of the inferiority of woman upon all other institutions. The Roman Catholic Church, and later the Protestant church, imposed its conviction of male supremacy and superiority on the entire Western world. Where did this conviction come from? It is a fact that early Christian theologians and philosophers were greatly influenced by the thinking of pagan writers, like Plato and Aristotle, with reference to women's inferiority, but the main stream of their male supremacy came from their one-sided theological interpretations of the Bible.

Our first theological concern in relation to women's inferior position is our whole society's misunderstanding of the nature of God. The concept of the masculine, patriarchal image of God, in other words, God the Father—not God the Mother—seems to be the approved concept in our society. People think God is male. He is a masculine God; He is a he-God. However, nowhere in the Bible is a human sex attributed to God. So, it is quite possible to talk about God as the transcendent reality without giving God any sexual characteristics as Paul Tillich and some other theologians did. Nevertheless, the image of God the Father runs very deep in our collective history. With this wrong concept of the image of God the Father, many people support the idea of sexual hierarchy in this society. In other words, they think it is in the nature of things that society should be male dominated. They think only man stands in direct relationship to God because man is made in the image of God and woman is once removed.

However, let us read the Bible carefully. Genesis 1:27–28 in the Old Testament clearly states that "God created man in his own image, in the image of God he created him; male and female he created them. And God blessed them."

Here, we have to know that the word, "man," "Adam" in Hebrew, does not mean that particular male human being only, but it means mankind or humanity, and it is a general term that is never used in the plural form. Therefore, Genesis 5:1–2 says, "Male and female he created them, and he blessed them and named them man (*Adam*) when they were created."

In these verses, again we have to know that the word "image" does not mean the physical likeness, but it means the reflection of God's own nature in both man and woman. That is, divine presence in all human beings. God is neither male nor female, but He possesses the best qualities of both masculine and feminine. God's feminine side is seen in various Biblical descriptions, such as in Deuteronomy 32:11, where God is like a mother eagle spreading her wings to bear her young ones on them, and in Matthew 23:37 where Jesus is like a hen gathering her chickens under her wings. Also, it is of importance to know that the female figure of Wisdom in Proverbs (8:1, 3, 22–23, 30) in the Old Testament is the forerunner of the New Testament figure of *logos*, the Holy Spirit.

However, unfortunately, in Hellenistic times when Judaism came under the influence of Greek rationalism, the feminine qualities of God—such as creativity, subjectivity, relatedness, compassion—were neglected and forgotten. Thus, in our day, God is seen almost exclusively as the all-powerful, rational, and abstract Mind. Today we are in great need of this healing, personal God of nature.

Therefore, our whole society should understand that the image of God the Father is only one image of a reality, the full dimensions of which we can only guess. Thus, according to these Genesis verses, it is clear that woman is precisely equal to man in participation in the image of God. Then why should we think we women are inferior to men? Certainly this wrong concept that the image of God the Father implies a human sexual hierarchy should be changed.

Our second theological concern is the so-called "order of creation." Traditionally, with the two accounts of the creation story in Genesis, women's inferior place was justified, and the role for women was confined as that of subordination to men. Women were to fulfill their roles as wife, mother, subordinate because it was God's eternal plan to create Eve "second" after Adam and let Eve fall into sin "first" before Adam.

However, this view of women as "two-time losers" is not substantiated by a careful reading of Genesis chapters 1–3. We must look at this creation story in the context of the author's point of view. Apparently, Genesis's author's concern for this story is not to blame woman for sin or to picture her as inferior. Rather, the concern is to explain why it is that man and woman have a complementary relationship to each other. When Adam is alone without any partner, he is "lonesome." God created human beings as "twosome." The fact that Eve was created from Adam's rib does not necessarily imply that she is inferior. Can we say that Adam is inferior to dust because he was created from dust? Good heavens, no! The author is concerned with the closeness of man and woman and why they are driven to cleave together. Because woman is formed from man's side, she is always close to man, ready to "help" him, and he is always ready to cherish and defend her as part of himself. In Genesis 2, we are told that Eve is to be a "helper" to Adam. That is, Eve's role is to help Adam. To be someone's helper is not to be inferior. The term "helper" connotes inferiority in English, perhaps like "assistant." At worst, the term suggests that Eve is to be Adam's housekeeper or perhaps his maidservant. But the Hebrew word *ezar*, which is here translated "helper," carries no such connotation of inferiority. In fact, the term *ezar* is used many times in the Old Testament, and it usually refers to God as the helper of all human beings. Thus, in Psalm 33:20, we read, "The Lord, He is our help."

Indeed, it is extremely unlikely that the author of Genesis 2 intended to convey the idea that Eve was Adam's inferior by describing her as Adam's helper. Truly, this cannot be used as evidence for woman's inferior or subordinate place in the order of creation. Therefore, I would say, it is a limited vision of the past that this profound Biblical passage has been interpreted in favor of men only from St. Paul's day to our own day. I believe now is the time to reconsider this old concept of the order of creation.

Our third theological concern is the doctrine of subordination of women to men based on the New Testament, especially on St. Paul's first epistle to the Corinthians. Chapters 11 and 14 of 1 Corinthians have long served as governing the proper role of women in the church, and also as the main theological argument against the priesthood of women. It is true that changing social conventions have opened other areas of the church's life to women, but in the central institution of the priesthood, this doctrine of subordination of women to men still applies. Because of this, the ordination of women to the priesthood is coldly opposed.

When we first look at these Corinthian texts, we are really confused because of the contradiction. In 1 Corinthians 14:34, Paul is urging silence on all women in the churches, yet in 11:4–5, Paul seems to assume women will pray and prophesy in public church gatherings. We see the same Paul, on one hand, instructing women to be subordinate "as the Old Testament law says so," and on the other hand, telling about the necessity of the interdependence of men and women, saying in 1 Corinthians 11:11–12, "In the Lord woman is not independent of man nor man of woman; for as woman was made from man, so man is now born of woman. And all things are from God." Also in Galatians 3:28, Paul asserts, "There is neither Jew nor Greek, there is neither slave nor free, there is neither male nor female; for you are all one in Christ Jesus."

Then the New Testament outlines two types of man-woman relations—those which obtain under the law and those which exist in Christ. Now, we, the contemporary Bible readers, are at the point of deciding which of these two approaches best embodies the central message of the gospel in order to find a guideline for man-woman relations today. In this modern age, we all note that old patterns are changing, and accordingly, sex roles are changing too. In fact, as women are entering every sphere of human endeavors, we can no longer be as clear as we used to be about which sex should do what. Therefore, we are concerned to express the good news of the gospel in ways relevant to this modern world. I believe whoever has a concern would prefer Galatians 3:28 to 1 Corinthians 14:34 as the embodiment of the central message of the gospel. That is, "God so loved the world that He gave his son." God's love affair is with the world—not with the church. He is a humanist—not a Christian. In Christ's death and resurrection, people in the world, both men and women, are freed from bondage to the sinful conditions of existence they obtained under the fall in the Garden of Eden. Therefore, in Christ, we women are no longer subordinates to men.

Finally, let us look at Jesus' view of women. Whatever the doctrine of subordination of women to men asserts, we Christian women, have already had a foretaste of God's saving grace, human liberation, and we are assured of it, just as the Samaritan woman at Jacob's well in the town of Sychar tasted the liberating love of Jesus.

This woman, as stated in the Gospel of John chapter 4, was a Samaritan woman, a Gentile woman, one whom all the Jews despised and had no dealings with, but Jesus initiated the conversation with her. This woman was an adulterous, sinful woman upon whom all the people turned contemptuous, scornful eyes, but Jesus gave her kind words. This woman was a perpetually thirsty woman. No one was able to satisfy her thirst, but Jesus gave her living water. He set her free from her bondage. He satisfied her thirst for love, her thirst for humanity. Indeed, Jesus was the greatest humanist!

We know that in Palestine at the time of Jesus, the male Jews offered their daily prayer of a threefold thanksgiving in this manner: "Praised be God that he has not created me a gentile; praised be God that he has not created me a woman; praised be God that he has not created me an ignorant man. "What a sex-discriminating prayer it was! From the circumcision to the burial rite, only male Jews were considered to be chosen Israelites in a true sense. The status of the Jewish woman was very decidedly that of inferior. Under such a rigid social circumstance, Jesus' favor of women, his promotion of the dignity and equality of women, treating them primarily as human persons certainly indicate that Jesus was a feminist; a radical feminist! His teaching was not merely "Do as I say!" but "Do as I do."

Today, we are his followers. As his followers, can we attempt to be anything less? He really did care for women, and so do we! Didn't the wistful face of the Samaritan woman at Jacob's well at last turn back toward her village with the fullness of joy? Didn't she run into the village even leaving her old precious water pitcher behind her in order to witness about Jesus' liberating love, her restored humanity? Isn't this exactly what we, Christian women, should do?

We have a message to tell! We have a voice to speak out! To those female human beings who are brainwashed into passivity, mental sluggishness, and self-contempt, who but we can say, "We are not at all second-class citizens. It is our right to restore our own God-given human right."

Once, Richard Brainsley Sheridan, an eighteenth-century British author asked a lovely lady, "Won't you come to my garden? I would like my roses to see you." Likewise, today, I would like to ask each of you: "Won't you come and join the journey to a freedom land of human equality? I would like others to see the joy of liberation in you in that fully humanized new world."

Bibliography

Beach, Diana Lee. *Sex Role Stereotyping in Church School Curricula*. Louisville, KY: John Knox Press, 1972.

Daly, Mary. "After the Death of God the Father." *Commonweal*, March 12, 1971.

de Beauvoir, Simone. *The Second Sex*. New York: Knopf, 1953.

Dooly, Sarah Bentley, ed. *Women's Liberation and the Church*. New York: Association Press, 1970.

Hewitt, Emily C. and Suzanne R. Hiatt. *Women Priests: Yes or No?* New York: Seabury Press, 1973.

Millett, Kate. *Sexual Politics*. Garden City, NJ: Doubleday & Company, 1969.

Pahk, lnduk. *September Monkey*. New York: Harper & Brothers, 1954.

Russell, Letty Manderville. *Ferment of Freedom*. New York: National Board, Y.W.C.A., 1972.

Russell, Letty Manderville. "Women's Liberation in a Biblical Perspective." *Concern*, May–June, 1971.

Seward, Georgene H. "Changing Sex Roles in Western Culture." In *Sex and the Social Order*, 125–143. New York: McGraw-Hill, 1946.

Stendall, Kristen. *The Bible and the Role of Women*. Philadelphia: Fortress Press, 1966.

Swindler, Leonard. "Jesus was a Feminist." *Catholic World*, January, 1971.

Theobald, Robert, ed. *Dialogue on Women* (New York: Bobbs-Merrill Company, 1967).

Van Vuuren, Nancy. *The Subversion of Women*. Philadelphia: Westminster Press, 1973.

"Women's Liberation." *Christian Home*, January, 1973, 25–54.

From Silence to Sounds[*]

June I. Kimoto

Our nation has begun the bicentennial celebrations in earnest! The International Women's Year continues to attract attention. Asian Women are awakening from a disturbingly long period of **silence**.

We need to reflect briefly on the past and acknowledge the damages done to us as individuals, as women, as Asians within the framework of this country and with emphasis on American Christianity as found in our churches. We must look back so we can realistically take charge and shape an equitable and just future. I will not give the historical dates of Asian migration to this country since there are a number of documentations available.

There have been several forces which have had dramatic effects on our society. Four very strong influences converged at one point in the '60s. Three of these were triggered by one, but each went spinning spontaneously into a very distinct entity. *The civil rights movement* began in the late '50s and the continued frustration of Black Folk for parity in economic, political, social, and educational life. To this, the writings of Betty Friedan's *The Feminine Mystique* began a renewed thrust for *women's equality*. The third influence was with *youth*—more educated, more affluent, more mature than any generation of the past—discontented with a nation's singular interest in the frenzied concept of **more**, and the deep concern for the moral integrity of a nation. The final influence was the intense and honest search of people for *self-identity*. People were confused because abundance could not add quality to life. The insatiable appetite for luxuries (the Depression years denied), pressed on by the medium of television and the rampant acceleration of technology, all worked toward eroding the traditional values of past generations. The consequences to "immediacy" have taken a toll on human dignity and self-worth. The search, from a non-person status created by the pushbutton craze of machinery and computerization to a more humane existence. A nation moving too fast, and the Earth literally exploding, showing strains of exploitation, as were the occupants on that Earthly globe. Alvin Toffler, author of *Future Shock*, and Vance Packard's *A Nation of Strangers*, are but two books documenting the stresses of our time. From these the civil rights movement, the women's movement, the challenge of youth for authenticity, and the search for one's own personhood converged. And Asian women are awakening from a hypnotic state.

---

[*] An address presented to the Asian Women's Ecumenical Conference (AWE), Sturge Presbyterian Church, San Mateo, CA, November 8, 1975.

From this turbulent period came my own search, not as hectic, leisurely paced, but searching for a past as an Asian woman and somehow to authenticate a right to be whatever it was that I wanted to be. In the mid-1960s, as I had begun my silent inquiries through readings, lectures, and listening, there were two interlocking happenings. One was an interview of my family by some young Asian College students who were writing a term paper and needed to do research. What finally evolved was an inquisition. We were baited, prodded, and provoked—the search for honest answers. The students were articulate, impatient, and mostly just angry. What was to have been a one half-hour interview became a four-hour marathon. From this highly emotional session came the question of "why?" "Why had we been so silent about the WWII experiences?" "Why didn't we tell them who they were?" The "we," the "us," was the older generation who have somehow unwittingly withheld vital information about the pains of those horrid years, the personal stories that went secret, the voices long muted.

Next, was a church conference attended by Whites, a large number of Blacks, and a few Asians. The problem most simply stated was a White-Black issue and neither recognizing any other coloration. I, as an Asian, felt trapped and totally frustrated. Frustrated because I could not state the case for Asians—only a prickle of feelings. Frustrated because we were in a middle sandwich slot—to be used by Whites and Blacks alike. Frustrated because I had not done my homework concerning racism nor had clarified my own thoughts into action words. These then accelerated my search.

The war years have damaged me. I cannot refute that. Although we lived in the safe zone in Utah and were not driven into the concentration camps, we lived in great fear for our lives. As a pre-teenager whose ego state was still very soft, I simply could not toughen in a short period of time and in turn became unmanageable, a misfit, incorrigible. As my husband and I have been comparing childhoods, the other night, he softly said, "I'm glad I didn't start the war." I stared at him. For here, I had assumed responsibility for the war! How tragic, a nation should place the burden of guilt on the shoulders of the very old and the very young of our peoples—that each of us had carried through these thirty years a *personal* responsibility for those grotesque years.

This journey, of sorting out my feelings and anger have taken me into nooks and crannies of my life, and I have finally resolved the past. Once this was accomplished, there seemed to be a new source of fresh energy that came from having struggled so intensely with the soul. Nathanial Branden, author of *Disowned Self* and *The Psychology of Self Esteem*, perceptively states, "Self-esteem is a basic need of man, a cardinal requirement of his health and psychological wellbeing."

There, then, came a realization I had not wanted to face but could no longer be hidden. This was to admit to myself the collusion of the institutional church as an active participant in the *Asian dilemma*. We have held with great sentimentality the sacred ground of the church, but the time for the veils of innocence *had to be lifted* to see the truth. The White missionizing really had left an innocent people disenfranchised, and the Sunday rituals of heaping ashes on our heads was sheer mockery. With the Asian sense of shame and Christianity's guilt we really managed to box ourselves in. But the guilt was not ours. We bore the callous brunt of White America's guilt—for it was she who had not reconciled her racist acts, and American Christianity upheld those acts.

Strange as this may seem, one by one, those individuals, like myself, who were in search of an Asian Christian identity began to find one another! We have finally recognized that we are not the **mad** ones!—like the scenes from the movie *Gaslight*, the practice of madness on us was very real.

Knowing that one is not mad, but sane, then brings forth **sounds**! Great sounds of weeping, rejoicing, hysterical laughter; anger, rage, and the spewing of obscenities. But the sounds, too, have begun to settle, and the harshness and hardness loses the jarring effects as individuals steeped in Christianity get down to working together. A very determined cooperative effort—for the uplifting of Asian peoples and a right to be.

Asians, both men and women, find it difficult to focus on "I," the person, the self, the individual. We find it more comfortable to talk of "you." Christianity's emphasis on "you"—outside of oneself—is comfortable for Asians. But for a race to survive in an alien land, it must know who it is.

There is a game I mentally play when it seems the guilt is building up and must seem to be becoming my own prisoner. I clear off my head screen and flash the word "Christ" across the screen in large, bold letters. Then in equally large letters, I place the word "church" under "Christ," making certain the vowels are in alignment. Then I proceed with the vowels. The *i* in Christ allows me freedom to deal with self and legitimizes internalization. The *u* in Church is my external self at work, and this too is authenticated. To take the game one step further, drop the *i* next to or in between the *u*—continue to deal with pronouns—this can be the *w* of "we"—time for oneself and time for others with the scales in balance and no adverse attachments.

As a race, we have placed so little emphasis on I, the race—it is difficult to find information about Asians. As an oral people, there are few personal stories recorded. The literature or research that has been done—has been *on us* by anthropologists, historians, or sociologists—are abstractions. A positive step we are now witnessing is taking command of our own history. We have too long acquiesced our lives to the White masters, although trying stubbornly to cling to our cultures. The Protestant churches have continually scolded us for usurping the master plan of total assimilation and we have managed to maintain the ethnic churches despite the pressures.

This path of passivity has been interpreted by both society and the institutional church as contentment or satisfaction with the status quo. Ah yes, we-Asians-can-care-for-our-own stereotypes. But this respect for an orderly life has bequeathed us with multiple problems that center around two contradictory ideologies: the Asian orientation of community and the American orientation of I, the rugged individual.

Within this talk, there needs to be special focus on us—Asian women. As we are seeking commonality with other minority races, the "three steps behind" syndrome has also been Third World women's entrapment.

The State of California Advisory Commission on the Status of Women indicates women have a life expectancy of seventy-four years. One fourth of those years (18.5 years) is spent as children and adolescents. The prime childbearing and child-rearing period constitute another quarter of the life cycle. From one-half to three-eighths of our lifetime is unplanned or unaccounted for—that is, if we make the end goal "housewife." We are now seeing the disillusionment and discontentment and its devastating effects on White women, and this surely will seep across all color lines. It is important for us to have strong models beyond mere conformity, lest we lock another generation of girl-women into narrow life roles. We, as Asian women, can then release, give permission to, our girl-woman to explore, to seek, to search, to stretch to her fullest self. What might be achieved should not be hindered or penalized by the long shadows of the "three steps."

Since 1945, more than 150,000 women from Asia have married American citizens. There are enormous and complicated problems arising from these unions: disenchantment, desertion, abandonment, prostitution, and suicides. What then of these women? What then of the children? The social services for Asians cannot help but become increasingly acute.

Using the statistical research done by the Support Agency of the United Presbyterian Church (using the 1970 census figures), we can identify close to a million and one-half Asians. The projections for 1995, some twenty years hence, estimate well over five million Asians. Within the same timeframe, this influx coupled with the aging of Asians will all lead to the Asian dilemma. Those who are now forty years old will fall into a new category. A conservative estimate will be 20% of the 1970 statistics without incorporating any new figures. With the Asian concentration most heavily on the West Coast, the 60% estimate (California Advisory Commission to the US Commission on Civil Rights) will surely be too low. This possibly means compaction of the already congested and crowded communities. It would be well to note at this time, Asians are still in many instances classified as "others." "Others" means we are of such an insignificant number or problems to warrant a separate category—hence no special considerations. The areas of housing, economic security, education, and the mounting psychological problems will be explosive issues. All areas of service, where Asian input is neglected, mean it will be that much more difficult for those new settlers who will be unable to articulate adequately in the host language.

As it now stands, neither the institutional church nor society is willing to acknowledge the Asian dilemma. Therefore, a new approach must be used to call attention to our fragmented, neglected, and decaying communities. This approach is with sounds. It is adopting the concept of the "squeaking wheel" and is possibly the only language and sounds to be understood by today's social systems, including the church. If we are to think beyond today, and that we must, we must know what part *silence* has played in the Asian dilemma.

The change begins with us—as individuals—one by one. Abraham Maslow's ladder or scale of needs can be a very useful tool towards shifting of strategies. The bottom rung is the *basic* survival needs of food, shelter, sex, and clothing. If these needs are NOT met, it is extremely difficult to consider a higher rung or level. Above the base rung is *security*, the feeling of comfort, having a permanent income, home, etc. Advertisements in magazines, radio, television work hard to lock both men and women at the two lowest levels—examples: the life or death decision about what coffee to drink; the abnormal emphasis on the right deodorant, soap, shampoo; the cleanest wash in town. Next, is the *social* level, where you want to belong—to a group, to church, to clubs. Then the *ego* level—wanting to be somebody. The last level is that of *self-fulfillment*—leaving a mark, a worthy life. At this level, one considers not only herself but also the esteem of others. The more upward the drive, the more self-determined one becomes. All levels are continually threatened by fear. This is an adaptation of Maslow's theory used by Thelma Adair, a Black educator.

In this search for self, we can easily adopt the ladder concept or techniques to really begin a caring process for ourselves. There can be a supportive climate affirming our diversities and distinct selves. This can be a strong, enabling factor for timid individuals—and we are that! We are not comfortable with the extremes of consciousness-raising that has commanded much publicity, but we can be compatible with support groups that will respect our more conservative form of life and behavior. Thomas Harris' book, *I'm OK, You're OK*, is a good starter, as is Muriel James' *Born to Win*; O'Neill and O'Neill, the authors of *Open Marriage* and *Shifting Gears* offer insights to self and strengthening partnerships. Continue to remember: books are for gleaning—use whatever you can from them. An interesting book was *Black Rage*, by two psychiatrists, Grier and Cobbs, who expose the problems of Black Folk—there are parallels that can awaken the Asian minds.

There are some books written about Asians that give the needed background to your particular ethnicity. A strong resource book that covers a full range of articles is *Roots: An Asian American Reader* by Amy Tachiki, et al. Vine Deloria Jr. has authored several books about the Native American Indian that combines logic with biting humor. Dee Brown's *Bury My Heart at Wounded Knee* gives exhaustive documentation of the persistent and relentless pursuit of the American Indians and offers Asians an insight to the workings of White thoughts.

If we are to disarm the institutional church from its paternalistic role and to begin a more enabling role, then we ourselves must be willing to work. I do not believe we are on such sacred grounds that Asian women cannot be activists. We must be willing to cross over denominational lines or religious lines where need be so our work can be consolidated and more united. The town meetings need not be an encampment of Buddhists on one side of the aisle and Christians on the other. The specialized skills of the leadership should be identified to avoid haphazard usage. Resources, both human and material, must be considered precious. In the local churches, we tend to misuse and abuse human energies as though expendable, and have not really capitalized on these riches as a building process. Without better management of these talents, we will continue to erode our ministries. We need to set goals, both short term and long term, for the local communities and churches. Distances between communities/churches should be considered for clustering to conserve energies and resources.

Yes, there is much to do.

When our tightness relaxes, we can release energies towards dreams and visions—for they will surely unfold. We have experienced what silence has been for Asians—**nothingness**. Silence is merely acquiescing one's right to be treated as a human being.

Today is our day. It has been designed for Asian women. Let it be resolved this *awesome* day that active sounds will emerge from us!

You Decide!
*The Dilemma of One Asian Woman**

LESLIE LOO†

While sitting here, responding to a request for an article on Asian women, I must confess to a real sense of frustration. What is there that can be said, that needs to be said, regarding Asian women to a non-Asian audience? In the last few years, there has been so much to say from Asian to Asian, from Third World person to Third World person, from sister to sister. And so much lost time to be made up for.

For years, we Asian sisters have been discouraged from "sticking together." Gym teachers used to tell us not to congregate together, for ours was a democratic high school. So, when we saw each other, we would automatically disperse—one Chinese on this team, one Chinese on that team, etc. And if there were more of us, we would divide accordingly—three Asian women in basketball, three Asian women in volleyball.

Those were the years when we were quiet; when, if we spoke up at all, it was within the bounds of understood limits. For example, if we were invited to join high school sororities, we declined. We knew we had been invited mostly because the school system forbade exclusive sororities. Since black sisters were not asked to join, we were to be proof of the clubs' democratic nature.

When we did communicate verbally, it was usually with non-Asians about things that mattered most to non-Asians. Because, you see, to spend too much time with those of one's own skin color was to regress to the "old-fashioned, insecure clannishness of our elders." We were the new generation (third, to be exact). We were the new Americans. We would be American if it meant throwing the whole thing out the window—that is, even if it meant denying our roots, our families, and our very being.

Some of us have decided not to do that anymore! We will not become dehumanized in order to participate. And so today we have so much to say to each other, we Asians, we Third World people in the United States, we Asian sisters. We are discovering marvelous things together—painful things and inspiring things. We are making up for all the things we didn't say to each other in those silent days.

Well, herein lies my dilemma. There is so much lost time to retrieve among our own, so to speak, that I am at a loss for what must be said to others. In fact, how can

---

* March/April 1973.

† Ms. Loo was doing graduate work in sociology and working with Asian women at the University of California at Berkeley and with Third World women in the San Francisco area.

I say *anything* without offending the reader's sense of Christianity? One Caucasian friend said to me recently, "Must you think of yourself in terms of a group?" My answer was that because I had been told all my life that it didn't make any difference what group I came from, I had subtly learned that differences were undesirable. I added that this more recent group consciousness or "consciousness of kind" was a first step away from group self-hatred. It was frustrating to try to explain to this woman the things that now matter to me. Because she lacked my point of view, she could only believe that I had regressed to narrow clannishness—an anti-American pattern.

That brings me right back to the beginning. What to share with the reader? Can I write that this new consciousness among Asian women is a great way to learn about class consciousness in America? How many people in the church would scream about subversion?

Can I say that Asian women, like American women, are tired of the "let-me-show-you-what-I-want-done," "stay-in-one-place," "always-be-available-and-pleasant" syndrome? Can I add that we are also trying to come to terms with the desire of many American men of all colors to think of us as exotic dolls and sources of mystery?

Can I say without hurting feelings that American women (especially in the church) think of us only as "superb" tea pourers or subconsciously as sources of cultural education for their families? How does one explain that, because of an ancient culture, we have absorbed the virtue of "inoffensiveness"—and that this virtue sometimes prevents us from speaking up? One Filipino woman confided to me that sometimes a Caucasian or black person will offend her. Whether the offense is intentional or not, she will accept it, because she doesn't want to embarrass the other person, and also because as an Asian, she has been raised to be diplomatic and to have greater regard for the other person's feelings than for her own. "All the while," she said, "it is hurting me inside."

Perhaps it would be better to say that as minority Americans and as second-class citizens (women) within that minority, we have all maintained an acceptable passivity in order to survive.

Or would it be more nearly correct to say that as minority persons we have been powerless and therefore had situations such as the Japanese concentration camp era forced upon us?

Perhaps it would be necessary to say that American women in their quest for liberation and American women in the church need to face their own racism in regard to Third World women. Do you realize that labor conditions and legislation improved for American women at a point in history when the United States began to use the labor of women and men in Third World countries? Are you aware that Third World women make the lowest wages in American industry? And have you bothered to think that Third World women were forced to clean other people's homes and to serve other people's *hors d'oeuvres* so that American women could do "community work" and become emancipated? Have you heard that the suffragettes, when they won the vote, included literacy tests at a level which, in effect, excluded Third World women? Have you searched out the facts regarding the legislation excluding Asians from citizenship and participation as witnesses in plaintiffs in courts of law? Do you know that American women, as they separate themselves as a distinct class in the United States, are getting the minority quota jobs that Third World people need? And do you still wonder, as I used to, why Third World women are so absent from the movement of white middle-class women in America?

Perhaps, then, it would be best to conclude that American women need to reach beyond sexism, to deal with their own racism, and not even to stop there. They need to go on to discover that sexism and racism have a greater master—to discover that even if the effects of sexism and racism could be erased, there would still be hunger and injustice. Even if we should reach zero population growth and offer abortion on demand, hunger and injustice would remain.

There is a force that we all, men and women of every station, must recognize before the job of eliminating injustice is begun. It is the force that, among other things, places a lower value on Third World lives. As an Asian woman, I wince when US bombs are dropped on Asian kinspeople in Indochina. What a shock it was for me to realize that historically, large American bombs have been, perhaps unwittingly, reserved for use in Asian countries. And what a horror it was to discover that gas pellets containing thalidomide are now dropped by remote control to cover entire Vietnamese villages. All I could think, when I saw pictures of deformed newborn babies, was, "Those could have been my babies!" Just recently I read about a Vietnamese student who hijacked a plane to avoid deportation—and certain death—to Saigon. He was shot five times and kicked out the door of the airplane. What do all these facts say to this Asian mother about American regard for Asian lives?

And it is not just Asian lives that are disregarded. Are you aware that napalm is being used in Angola (in Africa) by US-supported Portugal, or that US monetary aid to Brazil is dependent upon Brazilian population control? It can only be called systematic genocide when women who enter Brazilian hospitals are sterilized without their knowledge or consent. Think of the position of the Brazilian woman when she must face a husband who believes his masculinity (machismo) is dependent upon child-begetting. And was it not systematic genocide when American soldiers in our pioneer history knowingly gave to Native American clothes and army blankets that had been infected with smallpox?

How much more and how much less should this Asian woman be saying? Certainly, we will continue talking, studying, and making plans among ourselves regarding justice and injustice in this society. How much the reader needs and wants to know beyond this is negotiable. In some sense, it depends upon whether there is a greater concern for personal "liberation" or for justice. It is a matter of priorities.

How much needs to be said? You decide.

Biblical and Theological Basis of Korean American Ministry[*]

CHAN HIE KIM

I now realize that it is true that God treats all men on the same basis. Whoever fears him and does what is right is acceptable to him, no matter what race he belongs to.
—Simon Peter (Acts 10:34–35, TEV)

This is a confession made by Peter after he was "converted" from exclusivism to universalism. Like many other Jewish Christians in Jerusalem, Peter could not believe that Gentiles could become Christians. However, when he was confronted with the conversion of Cornelius, a Roman centurion, Peter's eyes were widely opened to see God's plan of salvation for all the people of the earth.

We are familiar with the story of the great Jerusalem conference mentioned in Acts 15 and Gal. 2:1–10. Here again, when the Christians in Jerusalem heard from Paul about the work of the Holy Spirit among the Gentiles, they were also "converted." They then realized that Gentiles as well as Jews could become Christians. In fact, the church at Antioch where the believers of Christ were first called "Christians" was a multiracial congregation. They were simply called "Christians" regardless of their ethnic background.

We call attention to the events that took place at the formation of the early Christian church in order to show that at the beginning of the Christian church, pluralism was one of the matter-of-fact realities. These early stories reveal how the church crossed the cultural frontier of the Hellenistic world, thus incorporating cultural diversities within its structure. From the very beginning, the church was formed by people of various ethnic and cultural backgrounds. The constituency of the primitive Christian church was not homogenous but heterogeneous in terms of race and culture; yet the leadership of the church did not attempt to put all disciples into a melting pot for a certain unified pattern of Christian life. Rather, they affirmed the plurality and different lifestyles of their membership. Unlike the Jerusalem conservatives, James, Peter, and Paul all came to agree that Gentiles did not first need to become Jews (viz., to be circumcised) in order to become members of the Christian

---

[*] A resource paper for the National Consultation on Korean-American Ministries, Chicago, IL, October 9–11, 1975, and three regional hearings.

church. Based on this principle of plurality set by the early church, Koreans in America do not first need to adopt Anglo-American lifestyles in order to become Christians. Prof. Keck of Emory has said, "The fact that faith produces a style of life does not mean that it must produce only one style of life. Hence, Philip saw that a Samaritan could believe in Jesus and still be a Samaritan."1 We Koreans, too, affirm that we can be Christians and yet still be Koreans and enjoy our heritage in this multicultural society of America.

There is no East and West, no white and yellow in Christianity, but there is East and West, white and yellow for Christians. Christianity transcends all the imaginable human elements in our church, but Christians are people of different cultures, races, languages, and traditions. The Christian faith has no boundaries of any kind, yet the expression of this faith takes various forms and styles depending on who the believers are. Therefore, Prof. Keck says, "Every cultural imperialism in the name of the Messiah (every attempt to make Western men out of Asian converts) is a betrayal of the hope for the Messianic Age and an idolization of one's own culture. If the church does not transcend every cultural situation, it will confuse itself with the kingdom of God."2 Thus, it is not enough for the church at large merely to recognize the plurality of its constituency; it must positively and actively engage in proclaiming the gospel to the ethnic minorities, affirming their ethnicity and different Christian lifestyles.

Now, let us take a close look at the Korean community in America. We notice it has a unique phenomenon peculiar to this group as well as problems common to every ethnic minority community and church.

Since 1965, when the Immigration and Nationality Act (Public Law 89-236) eliminated all the previous discriminatory immigration laws, the flow of immigrants to this country from Korea has noticeably increased to the estimated number of three hundred thousand. And at least 30% of them are Christians, products of North American mission work. It should be noted that Korea is the only country in Asia where Protestantism (mainly Presbyterianism and Methodism) was first introduced by US missionaries. Not only this, Korea is the only country in the world where American protestant churches carried out their mission work so successfully as to convert 10% of her population into the Christian faith within the period of less than a century (a surprising statistic in light of Japan's 1% conversion to Christianity).

Despite the close ties and intimate relationship with American Protestantism, Korean American Christians have created their own Christian lifestyle different from other Americans already in their native land, and it is their hope and desire to preserve it in this adopted land. The evangelistic zeal of late nineteenth and early twentieth-century American Methodism is still alive among Korean Methodists. For example, it is no wonder that we find Korean Christians gathered together for worship and fellowship every Sunday in towns and cities wherever a few hundred

---

1 Leander E. Keck, *Mandate to Witness: Studies in the Book of Acts* (Valley Forge, PA: Judson Press, 1964), 90.

2 Keck, *Mandate to Witness*, 101.

Koreans reside. Their commitment to the Lord and devotion to the church are highly commendable attitudes to be appreciated by the whole United Methodist Church.

Like many other ethnic and cultural minorities, Korean Christians have dehumanizing problems and are suffering from pressures of the surrounding Anglo-American culture and value system. As Michael Novak has well pointed out, "All ethnic groups have their own confusion. All acceded for far too long to the pressures of Americanization—which was really WASPification."3 The American society experienced by Korean Americans is not a melting pot but an Anglo pressure cooker in which diverse cultures are boiled together to the point that they lose their individual savors and identities. The measure and extent of loss of identity could be said to be more acute for Asians than for the European minorities. Because of physical appearance, Asians have nothing with which to identify once they lose their own cultural heritage. Unlike European minorities, Asians never become wholly Americanized.

For the Korean community, the church represents more than a religious institution. In Korea, Korean Methodists confess "We believe in the Church as the fellowship for worship and for service of all who are united to the living Lord" (The Korean Creed). According to this creed, the church is not only a worshipping community but also a community that exists to serve. But for Koreans living in America, the important concept in this creed is fellowship, for the church is a genuine fellowship in a strange and occasionally hostile society. Many Koreans, regardless of their religious affiliation, join the church because here they find comforts and consolations. The church for them is a community where they can receive individual recognition that they do not find elsewhere—the place where they are fully accepted and respected as persons. It is the place where they can meaningfully celebrate their life with their own language and express appreciation of their own culture and religious heritage. Beyond even this, the church is the community which provides good recreational programs and community service. Often, it is here that significant social activities take place. The church is, in a sense, the refuge for the tired and oppressed people in this foreign society. Thus, the church is not just a community but the community for the majority of Korean Americans.

The opportunity for mission and evangelism within the Korean community is ripe; the remaining question now is how to nurture and at the same time serve them so that they may have a meaningful and pleasant life in their new country. The church has, therefore, a challenging mission to minister to these people. In order to help meet the need, the Korean church must be strengthened by a strong ministerial and lay leadership, by a greater number of local churches, and by community involvement. Like the sandalwood tree, the Korean congregations must depend on the older tree of the United Methodist churches until they have grown and become strong enough to grow on their own. Once they have grown and become strong, the older trees will appreciate their fragrance and sweet aroma.

---

3 Michael Novak, *The Rise of the Unmeltable Ethnics* (New York: Macmillan, 1971), 114.

An Analytical Study of Recent Korean Immigrant Churches in Southern California

A Psycho-Religious Approach to the Basic Needs of the Korean Congregations*

Steve Sangkwon Shim

Introduction

A. Background

Recently, on both national and regional levels, the American society has been increasingly aware of rapidly emerging Korean immigrant communities in the metropolitan areas throughout the United States. It is in part true that this increasing awareness and interest in minority identity among the American public has resulted from the Black civil rights movement in this country. However, these incredibly fast-growing communities are creating an increasing socio-economic-psycho-religious dynamic in their own right in the pluralistic society of America.

Various resources indicate that the largest concentration of Korean immigrants in the whole North American continent is found in Southern California. Some Korean community leaders in Southern California estimate that seventy thousand Korean immigrants are living in the area. This is considered one-third of the whole Korean population in the United States.

There is a saying prevailing among other Asian American communities: "When Chinese came to America, they open restaurants. But, when Koreans come, they establish churches." The latest study indicates that as of March 1975 there are 293 Korean immigrant churches established and 523 Korean ministers identified in the United States.[1] And the informed leaders of the Korean immigrant community in Southern California estimate in a conservative figure that there are 250 Korean immigrant ministers residing in the Los Angeles metropolitan area.[2] Also, it is

---

* A project presented to the faculty of the School of Theology at Claremont in partial fulfillment of the requirements of the degree Doctor of Ministry, June 1975.

[1] Joseph H. Ryu, *A Study of Korean-American Population, Korean-American Churches and Congregations, and Korean-American Ministers in the U.S.* (New York: United Presbyterian Church, USA, April 1975), 7.

[2] The Rev. Byung Ock Koh of the Korean United Church in San Fernando reported his personal research (as of December 1974) showing 203 Korean ministers residing in the Los Angeles metropolitan area to the Korean Protestant Ministerial Association Annual Meeting on January 20, 1975 at the Bethany Korean Church in LA. The report noted that an estimated fifty

estimated that there are at least eighty to one hundred Christian congregations or gatherings already organized in the form of churches in the area. This is also the largest concentration of Korean immigrant churches in America. Since a similar, although more limited, phenomenon is taking place all over the country, the mainline denominations in this country are now openly expressing sensitivity to the situation of the Korean immigrant churches.[3]

B. Statement

Keeping this background in mind, it is the author's purpose to undertake this project in an attempt to provide American readers with some general information on the recent Korean immigrant churches together with their problems and needs. In a way, it is an attempt to construct a communication bridge between the American majority and the Korean minority.

There is at present no research available to mainline American churches for their understanding of the life of the Korean immigrant churches in America. Thus, it is hoped that this study will be a concrete tool for concerned American readers to better understand the Korean church and community and their contributions and needs in the United States today. At the same time, another purpose of this project is to provide Korean immigrant ministers with a guide for the self-development of their ethnic churches in Southern California. Thus, this project is aimed at conducting research on the rapidly emerging Korean immigrant churches in Southern California in light of their pastoral care of recently arrived Korean immigrants.

The author sees three objectives for this project. The first is to identify the basic needs of the recent Korean immigrants arising from their immigrant life situations. The second is to make an analysis of the roles and functions of the Korean immigrant churches in rendering their need-satisfying ministry to these immigrants. The third is to make theoretical formulations, both theological and functional, of pastoral care for these immigrants.

C. Hypothesis

This project is built on a dual hypothesis: 1) that immigrant life in America creates extraordinary basic needs in Korean immigrants that are entirely different from needs experienced by them in their homeland; 2) that, among all community organizations in the Korean community in America, the Korean immigrant church is placed in a most strategic position to meet these vital needs of Korean immigrants

---

ministers not yet identified also lived in the area. See Byung Ock Koh, *The Joong-ang Ilbo Miju-Pan* (Los Angeles: The Joong-ang Ilbo Los Angeles Bureau, 1975), 1.

[3] The 186th General Assembly of United Presbyterian Church in the United States of America held in Louisville, KY, on June 17–26, 1974, has officially adopted a recommendation that the Program Agency report for action a study of the needs of the Korean (immigrant) churches and ministers in the United States to the following General Assembly in 1975. The Assembly estimated that one hundred Korean Presbyterian ministers scattered in the US have not yet established any denominational affiliation in America.

since the Korean immigrant church functions in the role of the extended family to its community.

Therefore, it is the undertaking of this project first to identify what the basic needs of the Korean immigrants are and then to demonstrate the unique role of the Korean immigrant church to the Korean community in America and to the American society as a whole. Furthermore, the author will endeavor to identify and develop a working theology and methodology to enable the Korean immigrant churches to provide effective pastoral care in meeting these vital needs of their congregations and community in America.

D. Methodology

The method adopted here is a combination of academic and empirical methods. This means that the author is making use of available articles, journals and books for the assessments of the historical backgrounds of the Korean immigrants and churches in the United States. Also, the author is employing some random surveys and personal interviews conducted by himself in an effort to identify the basic needs of Korean congregations and churches in Southern California for effective pastoral care.

However, it must be made emphatically clear that this project by no means pretends to be a direct result of . . .

[Text ends here.]

Chapter V

A Theological Formulation for the Recent Korean Immigrant Churches

It must be asserted that Christianity can never be completely separated from culture. Christ and culture cannot be completely separated because of our human finiteness. Paul Tillich states: "Church and society are one in their essential nature: for the substance of culture is religion and the form of religion is culture."[1] It is thus necessary to talk about a universal church with a kind of plurality that takes into account the integrity of the cultural and racial backgrounds represented in America.

The phenomenon of the awareness of differences among minorities in America seems to characterize our era. Minority groups are increasingly aware of their own responsibility to search for ways to satisfy their most fundamental human aspirations—liberty, dignity, the possibility of personal fulfillment. This is their search for liberation from all that limits them or keeps them from self-fulfillment and from all impediments to the exercise of his freedom to be different.

In this regard, the author shares (despite some ambivalent feelings about its political orientation) with the views of the Latin American "theology of liberation" by Gustavo Gutierrez when he states:

> Modern man's aspirations include not only liberation from exterior pressures which prevent his fulfillment as a member of a certain social class, country, or society. He seeks likewise an interior liberation, in an individual and intimate dimension; he seeks liberation not only on a social plane but also on a psychological plane. Psychological liberation includes dimensions which do not exist in or are not sufficiently integrated with collective liberation. . . . Liberation expresses the aspirations of oppressed peoples and social classes, emphasizing the conflictual aspect of the economic, social, and political process which put them at odds. At a deeper level, liberation can be applied to an understanding that man is seen as assuming conscious responsibility for his own destiny. This understanding provides a dynamic context and broadens the horizons of the desired social changes.[2]

The biblical message, which presents the work of Christ as liberation, provides the framework for this interpretation. "For freedom Christ has set us free" (Gal. 5:1)

---

[1] Paul Tillich, *The Interpretation of History* (New York: Charles Scribner's Sons, 1936), 235. Also H. Richard Niebuhr, *Christ and Culture* (New York: Harper & Brothers, 1951), 29–44.

[2] Gustavo Gutierrez, *A Theology of Liberation History, Politics, and Salvation*, ed. and trans., Caridad Inda and John Eagleson (Maryknoll NY: Orbis Books 1973), 31, 36.

refers to liberation from sin insofar as sin is seen to refuse to love one's neighbors and, therefore, the Lord Himself.[3]

Christ the Savior liberates us from sin, which is the ultimate root of all disruption of friendship and of all injustice and oppression. Christ makes people truly free and enables them to love freely. It is the Biblical message that being free means "being free for the other," and the foundation of this freedom is openness to others.[4] The fullness of liberation—a free gift from Christ—is communion with God and with other people. Bonhoeffer has said that "freedom is not something man has for himself but something he has for others."[5]

Therefore, the goal of the theology of liberation must be seen not only as better living conditions through radical change of social structures but also "the continuous creation of a new way to be human, a permanent cultural revolution."[6]

The theology of liberation for ethnic self-development must not be seen simply as a fad of the time but must be understood to arise out of deep compassion and critical reflection on the situation of the oppressed and the poor. It has become a deep conviction of the author that the theology of liberation for self-development should be a vital concern for the future survival and development of Korean immigrant churches in America. At this point these churches are inseparably sharing their common concerns and destiny with other Asian immigrant churches in America.

Asian Americans have been suffering many facets of oppression. They are economically oppressed when any majority oppresses any Asian minority with economic control. They are also politically oppressed when the majority group uses political power to keep Asian Americans out of the decision-making process, even when those decisions affect the lives and destinies of Asian Americans. Another form of oppression for Asian Americans is social oppression, which alienates and ostracizes them, keeping them from interacting with one another as equals. In fact, all these types of oppression are familiar experiences to other minority groups in America.

There are also psychological and spiritual oppressions which are the most subtle and yet the most devastating—forms of oppression which victimize Asian Americans particularly. It is the psychological aspect of oppression, when they do not have the freedom, the capability, or the opportunity to express or define who they are and to define their relationships with others. Furthermore, there is spiritual oppression when they have lost the will to resist and fight against what they believe to be wrong, when they have become paralyzed by an oppressing dominant system so that they are unable to take any kind of action. For Asians in America, there is a definite need to rethink, to articulate, and to appropriate an interpretation of the Christian faith which combats rather than perpetuates oppressive thought patterns that say dogmatically: "The right and responsibility of Asian Americans to challenge

---

[3] Gutierrez, *A Theology of Liberation*, 35.
[4] Gutierrez, *A Theology of Liberation*, 35.
[5] Gutierrez, *A Theology of Liberation*, 36.
[6] Gutierrez, *A Theology of Liberation*, 32.

present oppressive structures violates the principles of Christian life and reconciliation."[7] Asian American churches need to begin the process of developing an interpretation of Christian faith which encourages self-affirmation and indigenous self-development in Asian churches and communities in America. They must encourage a critical analysis of those ideas, values, customs, and structures in America which oppress not only Asians but other minority groups as well. It must also encourage the development of an Asian frame of reference which can make its own unique contribu-tion to the developing Third World theological dialogue, to the global theological task, and to liberation movements in the United States and in the world.

The necessity for a Korean church's theology of liberation, or self-development, is rooted not only in a growing awareness of oppression among Asians in America. It is also rooted in the growing awareness that the church must be more responsive to often-ignored groups if it is to relate meaningfully and effectively in a fast-changing world. There is a new challenge to the Korean immigrant church's mission to relate meaningfully to its people and to other Third World people.

The question is whether Korean churches will be able to respond adequately to the growing aspirations for self-development and liberation, especially among Koreans in America. New and creative interpretations of the Christian imperative from the perspective of Asian Americans are essential for the future growth of the Korean churches in America. It is the author's belief that the Korean churches in America have but one mission. The ministry of the Korean churches with their people in America must be first the enhancement of their basic humanity. Their ministry should be a process of total humanization and of freeing persons for full human growth. The demands now are for self-determination and empowerment for liberation.

Korean churches must not withdraw from full interaction with contemporary life, or else they risk failing to confront the full range of concerns of the people they address. Paul Tillich is pointedly right when he asserts that "the sociocultural task is a major mission of the church, and it has the function of transformation."[8]

In the opinion of the author, the response of the Korean churches in America to the social challenges of the present time is meager and far from adequate. Their primary concern today is institutional survival. And they have not yet developed any systematic approach to social involvement. Involvement by the churches has been limited by the obvious lack of resources (money and membership) and the lack of expertise. Much of the progress in the area of social involvement depends on the quality and the commitment of ministerial leadership and the presence of concerned laity.

---

[7] Dennis Loo, "Why an Asian American Theology of Liberation?" *Church and Society* 64, no. 3 (January–February 1974): 54.

[8] Tillich, *The Interpretation of History*, 236. Also Niebuhr, *Christ and Culture*, 190–229.

The liberation theology for ethnic identity and consciousness will eventually result in new awareness of the responsibility of Korean immigrant churches to become the advocates of their people and of others who are victims of racism and oppression in the United States. Whether they can meet this challenge in the future remains to be seen.

Chapter VI

Implications for Pastoral Care in the Recent Korean Immigrant Churches in Southern California

The American churches in general are increasingly recognizing their churches to be "centers of healing and growth," where the brokenness of individuals and relationships is healed or where individuals find stimulation for lifelong growth toward their fullest humanity. Likewise, the Korean churches in America are inevitably confronted with their mission of service to meet the needs of the total person in order to foster mental health through the growth and fulfillment of their congregations as individuals. For this mission, they need to involve themselves in changing the social conditions which block human actualization for self-development and liberation. They need to fill the "prophetic function" to help their congregations become involved with their community and society.

Seifert and Clinebell, in *Personal Growth and Social Change*, introduce an important concept of the inseparable relationship in the pastoral and prophetic ministry of the Christian churches in light of individuals' mental health. They say:

Both the focus on helping individuals and the focus on working to change person-damaging social conditions are indispensable aspects of the mission of the church. . . . The church exists to help people grow toward their God-intended wholeness, their full humanity. This includes helping individuals who are blocked in their growth by inner conflicts and by outer injustice.[1]

It is a crucial part of mental health care of Korean immigrant churches to engage in changing the injustice, discrimination, alienation, and exploitation which are part of the present system and which block self-development and self-actualization. The churches can and should enjoy an opportunity to help their congregations cope constructively with crises, and satisfy their interpersonal and spiritual needs. They are most vital social centers in their community for human growth and actualization of their congregations.

In addition to the Korean church's potential contribution to mental health care in inter-group conflicts between majority-minority relationships, they also need to be essentially engaged in mental health care of intra- and interpersonal conflicts in and

---

[1] Harvey Seifert and Howard J. Clinebell Jr., *Personal Growth and Social Change* (Philadelphia: Westminster Press, 1974), 13.

out of their community. They should provide pastoral functions such as counseling and nurturing the growth of individuals and families in church.

Clinebell describes eight unique contributions of churches in mental health care in a very convincing way:

> (1) The need for an opportunity to periodically renew basic trust is satisfied by religious groups through corporate worship, symbolic practices, sacraments, and festivals. (2) The basic need for a sense of belonging is provided by meaningful involvement in religious groups. (3) Religious groups also provide an opportunity and resources for meeting the crucial need for a viable philosophy of life. (4) A related need is for a humanized view of man, a doctrine of man which emphasizes his capacity for decision, inner freedom, creativity, awareness and self-transcendence. (5) Religious groups can help satisfy the universal needs for experiences of transcendence, providing vacations from the burden of finitude (the sense of being caught in nature with. its sickness and death), and the tyranny of time. (6) Support of individuals and families in both the developmental and accidental crises of living is another need-satisfying function of religious groups. (7) Religious groups can meet the need to move from guilt to reconciliation utilizing the time-tested pathway to forgiveness (restoration of the broken relationships). (8) Religious groups can help meet the need of persons to be instruments of personal growth and social change.[2]

Clinebell also speaks of the church's involvement in the areas of prevention and treatment as part of mental health care program. Prevention in mental health care is as important as treatment. Especially in the life of Korean churches in America, the preventive pastoral care is extremely appropriate and important. Clinebell pointedly mentions three levels of prevention for mental health care that churches can actively engage in. They are "primary prevention" to eliminate unhealthy and promote healthy growth conditions, "secondary prevention" in detection of emotional problems for referral, and "tertiary prevention" in rehabilitation.[3]

Therefore, the churches can be major social institute for mental health in the community if formal or informal social gatherings provide a cohesive and coherent sense of healthy human relationships that "guide, sustain, and encourage healthy emotional attitudes" in their congregations.[4] The area of primary prevention is one where the churches must and can take the lead to provide this type of normal everyday nurturance which everyone needs and without which congregations will run into emotional distress.

The most important function of the Korean churches in America is their weekly Sunday worship services. The majority of Korean churches in Southern California, for instance, hold an average of two services per week. The Sunday worship becomes

---

[2] Howard J. Clinebell Jr., "The Local Church's Contributions to Positive Mental Health," in *Community Mental Health: The Role of Church and Temple*, ed. Howard J. Clinebell Jr. (Nashville: Abingdon Press, 1970), 47–53.

[3] E. Mansell Pattison, "An Overview of the Church's Roles in Community Mental Health," in *Community Mental Health: The Role of Church and Temple*, ed. Howard J. Clinebell Jr. (Nashville: Abingdon Press, 1970), 21.

[4] Pattison, "An Overview of the Church's Roles," 21.

the central point of the life of the Korean churches. The services are exclusively conducted in the Korean language. Another important activity of the week is the coffee fellowship right after the main worship service on Sunday. This post-worship fellowship is a universal phenomenon in Korean churches throughout the United States. Through the main worship service and the post-worship fellowship the congregations experience their relatedness with others—cohesiveness, intimacy, acceptance, trust, support, giving-taking, communications, etc. The use of the same worship order from their home country church and the use of the same hymnals and Bible versions are furnishing special meanings, both culturally and psychologically, to their worshippers. In fact, a whole experience of worship should foster a sense of "belonging, personal integrations, diminishing of one's guilt and narcissism, reestablishment of a sense of trust, worthy self-investment, and strength for handling one's problems constructively."[5]

Of increasing importance today in Korean churches and their communities in America is the ministry to families. Individuals live in families, and families possess histories, ideologies, role expectations, and unique communication patterns. Besides the survival issues in the Korean families, marital problems are a forefront concern troubling both the family and the Korean ministers who are in position to assist the troubled family. Without going into detail, a major cause of marital conflict among Korean families in America seems to be a head-on collision in values of role expectations between husband and wife, where husband discovers with a shock that his wife is rebellious against his traditional male superiority.

The churches need to realize their responsibility to undertake more careful pastoral care of the family, for they are ideally situated and possess great potential for an effective family ministry. However, in some sense, the Korean churches are now very ill-equipped for this. Since pastoral care and counseling for family relations and development demands professional skill, it requires training and competency in communication, psycho-social relationships, and group process. The present tragedy is that almost a zero percentage of Korean ministers active in their parishes in America have received or been exposed to any sort of clinical training or seminary courses in these subjects in their professional preparation.

Despite the existing deficiencies in their pastoral care and counseling to the families in their congregations, Korean ministers are hopeful of better equipping themselves in their profession. Most of them readily recognize their strong need for training in family counseling and guidance. It is evident that a majority of them would welcome some form of continuing education in the field. Perhaps such on-the-job training would be a realistic approach to an increasing demand for education in our present time. It can be a pattern most appropriate to the ministry. Through it, the Korean churches can fulfill their leadership requirements for their congregations in a rapidly changing society in America.

---

[5] Howard J, Clinebell Jr., *The Mental Health Ministry of the Local Church* (Nashville: Abingdon Press, 1972), 75.

Now it becomes obvious that the single most crucial factor in mental health care of Korean churches in America is the quality of leadership. Leadership to date has been authority-centered where honesty of communication does not occur, and the congregations tend to hide their real feelings and thoughts and to withhold themselves from whole-hearted participation. Korean congregations are not necessarily satisfied with clergy who demonstrate authoritarian leadership.

There are two reasons which the author has found to support this assertion. One is consensus in the minds of Americans that Koreans (like any other Asians) are inclined to depend on an authoritarian leadership. In terms of the past, prior to the time of World War II, this was true in the minds of the majority of Koreans. However, in terms of the present, the consensus among Americans is a myth and an untenable, sweeping judgment. Without going into detail, Korea is one of the countries which since World War II has been going through a dramatic change on a conscious level in values of individual rights and integrity through their Western-style public education systems. In addition, the Korean public has in recent decades been immensely influenced by the Western world in their attitudes toward human rights as a result of the incredible modern technology, especially by the rapid communications media. The changes in attitudes and values toward individual rights and integrity among Korean people in general are much more drastic than most Westerners are willing to admit. The Westerners should realize that the Asians need not express their individual rights and interests necessarily in their ways. As further evidence against the allegation of dependence of authori-tarian leadership, it is a personal experience and observation of the author that rebellion and dissatisfaction are bound to appear in social gatherings of Koreans where their leader is exhibiting authoritarian leadership.[6]

Furthermore, the dissatisfaction and rebellion against authoritarian leadership is further reinforced in Koreans in America who have been consciously or unconsciously influenced by the individualism prevailing in American society. All these factors seem to be favorable in regard to the future of Korean churches in light of their developing leadership.

In order to maximize the growth-stimulating effects of their congregational life, the clergy of Korean churches in America need to be equipped with democratic leadership, which is "therapeutic or developmental leadership."[7] Here are some functions of a group-centered leader or growth-leader according to Clinebell:

1. The leader assembles and launches the group.
2. By example, he teaches growth-awakening relating.
3. The leader facilitates development of group identity through significant relating and sharing.

---

[6] The author has been very closely involved with a gathering of Korean ministers in Southern California for the last several months. He has frequently witnessed this group openly protesting against their authoritarian leader.

[7] Seifert and Clinebell, *Personal Growth and Social Change*, 151–152.

4. The leader maintains awareness of both the individual and the group organism.
5. The leader focuses on releasing the unused potentialities of individuals and the group, thus encouraging group members to do the same.
6. He encourages the group to employ the growth formula—caring plus confrontation produces growth.
7. The leader offers tools for enhancing communication and practicing deeper relating.
8. The leader helps individuals who need further support or involvement.[8]

Such a leader is a catalyst "to serve as midwife" to facilitate the group process.[9] He actively helps the group to release its own potentialities. His function is "to assist the natural process by which human beings experience the birth of self-other awareness and grow in their ability to cope constructively with their life situation."[10]

Having discussed democratic leadership, engaging in training the clergy (and laity) as growth group facilitators seems a strategic program and a real answer to the present key problem of the Korean churches in Southern California and in other states. Adequate training for a growth group facilitator offers three essential dimensions of experience that Korean ministers are seeking: growth group experience, conceptual understanding, and supervised skill practice.[11] In other words, this type of training would provide for the Korean ministers not only personal growth in pastoral identity through self-awareness and value clarification but also professional growth in pastoral skills through learning various styles of group facilitation.

At this point, it is necessary to mention briefly how the training for Korean ministers can be realistically implemented. Realistic approaches seem to be short-term and long-term implementations. The long-term plan has to do with the mainline denominational seminaries which should widen their doors for training Korean ministers/students, especially in the field of pastoral care and counseling. Up to now, the American seminaries have practically refused to train Korean ministers/students directly from their country like any other Asian students in that field. For instance, the resistance by these seminaries to train them is a direct cause of the present poverty of the trained leaders in Asian countries in that specific field. In the case of Korea, the tragedy is the fact that there is no one yet from Korea who has achieved a doctoral degree in pastoral care and counseling in this country, while many Koreans have earned degrees in all the other disciplines in theological training here. Their alleged contention that it is the cultural/language barriers which have discouraged from their programs people from Asian countries is proved largely due to the fear of risk and to racial prejudice. Among many evidences against this contention is the

---

[8] Howard J. Clinebell Jr., *The People Dynamic* (New York; Harper & Row, 1972), 37–42.
[9] Seifert and Clinebell, *Personal Growth and Social Change*, 144.
[10] Seifert and Clinebell, *Personal Growth and Social Change*, 41.
[11] Seifert and Clinebell, *Personal Growth and Social Change*, 53.

personal experience of the author in his academic and clinical trainings in pastoral care and counseling in the recent years. In the beginning stage of his training, the author experienced a severe under-evaluation for admission to the American seminaries in the field. He was literally treated as non-potential for training in the field, primarily due to his seeming language/cultural barriers and partly due to their alleged theory of "irrelevance" of American pastoral care and counseling to Asian people. Thus, the author has had to take extra effort and time to demonstrate his own potential and ability in the field. The author regards the discussion of the relevance and need of training Asian students in the field as completely another subject. So, at this juncture, he just wants to establish evidence that he, as a student from an Asian country, has satisfactorily completed all his academic and clinical training in this country in spite of all the handicaps and hurdles with which he has had to contend.[12] The point here is this: that despite the language/cultural difficulties which certainly do exist, it is still possible to train Asian students who possess much potential in the field. And the contention of "irrelevance" of American pastoral care and counseling to Asian people is proved to be a myth to a great extent.

Therefore, the mainline denominational seminaries (and clinical centers) need to take more willingness and risk to admit Asian students to the field. In fact, it is a Christian responsibility to American seminaries to train Asian students, especially in helping professions since America is basically a pluralistic society of many cultural polarities, and each ethnic group or community plays a vital part in prevention and treatment of mental health in America.

On the other hand, the short-term approach which is an immediate and more realistic method is to establish a training institute by a mainline denomination for the continuing education of Korean ministers in America. This short-term training will be very effective and appealing to most Korean ministers largely due to the limited economic and logistic conditions they are in. It could be either in-service training or intensive training for a short term. However, it is vitally important to have the short-term institute operated bilingually for its availability to a larger number of candidates. The ethnic staff will be the best facilitators for the short-term institute for training. And the contents of this short-term training must be determined by the immediate needs of the ministries in their ministry.

Lastly, the most effective way that the Korean churches can utilize democratic leadership for the spiritual and mental health is to provide small growth group activities that offer intimacy, and support in relationships. Korean immigrants in church can maintain their integrity as humans through the emotional and spiritual nurture they receive from family, friends, and associates in small groups in church. The Korean churches in their programs can effectively provide opportunities for participation in a number of small spiritual growth groups and task force groups that provide this normal and necessary human nurture. They also can provide group

---

[12] Despite his culturally biased observations on Asian students in his own CPE context, Keith W. Keidel advocates CPE for students in Asian countries in general. Keith W. Keidel, "Adapting CPE to an Asian Life Style," *The Journal of Pastoral Care* 29, no. 1 (March 1975): 35–41.

social relations to persons who are exposed to particular life stresses which make them emotionally vulnerable.

The most neglected age groups in Korean churches presently are youth and older people. Another important small group needed in Korean churches is a growth group for families. In addition, one small growth group applicable to all ages in the Korean congregation is a grief group since all of the Korean immigrants have been to some degree experiencing grief in the loss of their important human ties with their kinfolks and friends in their home country. So, small growth groups in church can provide opportunity for human contact and relationships to people who are relatively isolated and who need structured means of participating in human relationships. In this way, the Korean immigrant churches can be a real laboratory community for humanizing interaction.

In relation to the potential role of the Korean churches in mental health care for their congregations, the democratic leadership and small growth group have been proposed. At once, it may appear to Americans' minds and to some Koreans that the idea of small growth groups is foreign and intolerable to the mindsets of Korean people in general. To the contrary, it is a personal belief that the growth model seems, first of all, a very appealing and appropriate concept to the hearts of Korean immigrants in America. The appeal comes partly from the fact that all Koreans in this country have deeply repressed feelings and have been in touch with inner urges to relate themselves with others. Moreover, the Koreans here are generally more apt to feel free to express their inner feelings as long as they are facilitated by their group leader. In addition, the idea of small group is a very familiar one to the Korean congregations. They have been very much used to various types of small groups in their church life. A problem for these small groups in Korean churches has been the only type of group leadership available to them which is authority-centered. At the present moment, the small growth group seems the best tool the author can find for the present needs of Korean churches in America. In fact, the author feels much indebted to his professor, Dr. Howard J. Clinebell Jr., who has introduced to him the concept of the small growth group as a tool for the needs of the church universal.

The author has been deeply convinced of the effectiveness and usefulness of the tool for the life of Korean churches because his personal life has been already affected by his own experiments of small growth group with other people. Nevertheless, the personal conviction of the author in the effectiveness and usefulness of small growth groups with the Korean churches in America is yet to be tested by author's actual experiments with them in the days ahead.

Chapter VII

Summary and Conclusion

Thus far, the author has developed this project into three parts: Part one makes a study of the Korean immigrants in America in which a brief historical review of the early Korean immigrants (1902–1945) and an analytical review of the modern Korean immigrants in America (1946–1970s) are discussed. Part two deals with a study of the Korean immigrant churches in America in which an analytical review of the history and function of the Korean immigrant churches in America and a study of the basic needs of the Korean immigrant churches in Southern California today are made. Lastly, part three deals with theoretical formulations for effective pastoral care in Korean immigrant churches in Southern California today in which a theological formulation and the implications for pastoral care in Korean immigrant churches in Southern California are treated.

To put it differently, on the basis of one assumption, that every individual, family and race has come from its own history, this project was geared to attempt an assessment of the present life of Korean churches in Southern California in light of the histories of Korean communities and churches in America.

The uniquely non-assimilating character of Korean people was observed from the national background of the history of Korea. This non-assimilative characteristic of Korean immigrants is also reflected in their community life in America over the last seventy years. This characteristic of Korean immigrants seems to be a key factor for understanding the existence and necessity of Korean churches in America. In other words, Korean churches in America have not assimilated into American society but have remained as a bicultural church in the last seventy years on American soil. Political ideology and nationalistic patriotism were the predominant concerns of the Korean churches in their first fifty years in America.

However, the major concern and activity of the recent Korean immigrant churches are more toward econo-social services for their congregations, directing their focus on institutional survival concerns such as building funds, self-support budget, and membership.

On the other hand, a basic need which Korean churches in America have most neglected is the mental health care for the life of the Korean congregations, whose basic needs are not only the socioeconomic survival but also psychological survival in the American society. Every individual and family of Korean immigrants is undergoing a severe self-identity crisis and value crisis. The Korean communities in America are experiencing crises in the individual and family, which are the basic units of human society. In addition to the pressures from under- and unemployment of individuals, the Korean immigrant family is suffering severely from increasing gaps between the parents and their rapidly assimilating children. The immigrant family is suffering from the physical and emotional inability to deal with the welfare of their older folks. Of increasing importance and necessity are the marital problems between husband and wife largely due to the conflicts in difference of male-female role expectations in the American society. At the same time, Korean churches, which are most ideally situated for a family ministry, find themselves helpless in terms of their skills in giving any sort of professional help or effective pastoral care to the suffering family. A key factor for noneffective functions of Korean churches in America seems to lie in the inadequate professional preparation of their clergy. As a matter of fact, the clergy as a key facilitator of the Korean churches are normally unable to perform their maximum function due to the predicaments of their own personal needs and struggles from their distressing life situation.

Therefore, a key answer to the survival and development of Korean churches in America seems to lie in engaging leadership training for their clergy. Training for democratic leadership seems most fitting for the needs of Korean churches in light of facilitation of self-development and self-actualization of the congregational life. To enhance the growth stimulus for the Korean congregations, the idea of the small growth group in the Korean churches seems to be most appropriate and effective in helping the congregations to cope constructively with their conflicted life experiences and to overcome their oppressed life in America. The small growth group along with democratic leadership is found to be the most effective tool in enhancing mental health care primarily in prevention in the life of the church universal and most likely in Korean churches in America, too. Due to deficiencies in leadership, the Korean churches are unable to actively and systematically engage in a treatment program for the mental health of their congregations and communities. In this respect, the Korean churches as a uniquely healing-saving community are not yet able to fulfill their potential contribution in their mission to their congregations and communities.

At present, the Korean churches are contributing more in the area of prevention than treatment for mental health in their mission that their leaders are aware of. However, the concern is that their mental health care in prevention is being carried out off-focusedly and unsystematically, primarily due to the lack of understanding the needs or importance in the field.

In the judgment of the author, the most important contribution that the Korean immigrant churches are making in preventive pastoral care is the effect of corporate worship in reinforcing and undergirding self-esteem for their worshippers. Their worshippers are strengthened to incorporate into their self-identity the awareness of the transitoriness and challenges of their daily existence in America.

The conclusion of this project is that the Korean churches in Southern California and other states have been providing vital contributions to the life of the Korean immigrants in America for the last seventy years. Since the massive increase of Korean population to nearly a quarter million in recent years, the Korean immigrant community now begins to emerge as a visible minority group in the eyes of the

American public. Accordingly, the Korean churches in America are also increasingly visible, with their potential forces and contributions both to their own communities and to the American society. They are beginning to emerge as viable, inseparable, vital, social organs in the American scenes of life. Their missions for the quarter-million Korean population in America cannot be replaced by any other social organs. They possess a unique reason, purpose, and mission in their existences in this country not only for the Korean communities in America but also for America as a whole and for the world. The potentials of Korean churches in their contributions to the community, nation, and world are yet to be seen in the days to come. Therefore, the Korean churches must not be looked at as a church either experimental or peripheral but as a church essential to the pluralism of American society. And they deserve the further attention of the public.

The Korean churches are the only social organs in their community that furnish relatedness with oneself, neighbors, and God to the Korean immigrants in America.

TABLE IV (continued)

9. Basic Needs of Korean Ministers

Basic Needs	% Responses	% Priority
Family Support	50 %	40 %
Language	50 %	60 %
Job Opportunity	20 %	50 %
Child Education	50 %	40 %
Cultural Adjustment	60 %	50 %
Insurance/Pension	80 %	45 %
Continuing Education	50 %	60 %

10. Basic Needs of Korean Congregations

Basic Needs	% Responses	% Priority
Legal Assistance	45 %	40 %
Language/Culture	75 %	60 %
Job Opportunity	65 %	75 %
Child Rearing	65 %	60 %
Social Welfare	55 %	17 %
Immigration/Visa	65 %	60 %
Marital Problems	55 %	50 %
Church Participation	75 %	45 %
Discrimination	40 %	10 %

Problems and Promise of Filipinos in Hawaii*

BEN JUNASA

Introduction

At the outset, may I bring you the greetings of Aloha and Mabuhay from the people of Hawaii. Also, I would like to express our grateful appreciation to the National Committee of the Asian American Conference for bringing us together. I understand this is the first attempt to bring together the Asian minds among the United Church to discuss our problems and possibilities in an American society.

There was a popular anecdote in the early days of the anti-poverty program. A pig and a hen were walking across a former mining village. Touched with kindness upon looking at undernourished children and dejected men living in extreme poverty, the hen suggested that they should do something. But the pig responded: "What can we do; you are only a hen and I am only a pig?"

"Well, at least we can feed them ham and eggs" said the hen.

And the pig answered, "For you it will only be a contribution, but for me it will be a total commitment."

I believe a conference like this will undoubtedly make an impact in the structure and ministry of the United Church. But its burden of consequence and ensuing commitment will rest heavily among all of us here today. Perhaps, as we listen to each other in this conference, we should struggle to find a commonality of our experiences and seek cross-cultural understanding in pursuing our common objectives. Allow me now to present the problems and promise of the Filipinos in Hawaii.

I. The Early Filipino Immigrants to Hawaii
A. Socioeconomic Conditions Which Facilitated Their Coming to Hawaii

It was through some accidental design in historical process that Filipinos came to the islands. At the turn of the century, Hawaii was in critical need of plantation laborers. The Chinese and Japanese laborers were leaving the plantations to seek more promising opportunities outside the plantation industry. No new replacements were coming from these countries because the Chinese Exclusion Act became applicable to the islands when Hawaii became a US territory and also Japan and the United States signed the famous "gentlemen's agreement" to stop Japanese immigration to the United States.

---

* Panel remarks, April 20, 1974.

368 | BEN JUNASA

On the other side of the Pacific Basin, before the turn of the century, the Filipinos finally won the revolution against Spanish rule but only to be conquered by another colonial power under the command of General Arthur MacArthur.

Looking for a labor supply free from external control, the Hawaii Sugar Planters' Association found the Philippines as the answer to their problem. Thus began the importation of Filipino laborers from 1907 to 1946. In this span of forty years, Hawaii recruited some 109,513 Filipino men, most of whom were single or, if married, the majority were not allowed to bring their families.

B. Linguistic Description of the Early Filipinos

1. *Tagalogs*. The Tagalogs were the earliest Filipino immigrants to Hawaii. They were recruited from the vicinity of Manila and neighboring central Luzon provinces. Because of their wider contact with foreigners, they became more diverse in occupational experience. The Spanish culture had been known to have penetrated most extensively in the Tagalog region. Consequently, the Tagalogs who came to Hawaii were more sophisticated than any other Filipino group. Because of their urban background, they were less adaptable to plantation life. A great majority of them are now living in Honolulu and in other urban centers.

2. *Visayans*. The Visayans were the next Filipino group to come to Hawaii. They came from the provinces of the Visayas and Mindanao and were oriented more to farm life. The Spanish customs and ceremonies were extensively incorporated in the Visayan culture. The Visayans were known to be devout Roman Catholics and decidedly rabid in their religious faith. The Filipino fiesta is an important part of Visayan living. They have the reputation of being easygoing and much more hospitable. Consequently, they always created a labor problem the day after payday. They always took off to spend their money more freely.

3. *Ilocanos*. The Ilocanos were the last but the largest *sakada* group to come to Hawaii. They came from the northern provinces of Luzon known as the Ilocos region. Livelihood is much harder in the Ilocos provinces than in the other two regions previously mentioned. This is one of the factors why the Ilocanos are thriftier and harder-working compared to the Tagalogs and the Visayans. Ilocanos are referred to as the "Scots" or "Pakes" of the Philippines.

C. Handicapping Problems of the Early Immigrants.

There are a number of serious handicapping problems that slowed the process of acculturation among early immigrant Filipinos in Hawaii. In fact, the Filipinos are still the most foreign and unassimilated group in the islands.

1. *Limited education*. The Filipinos were primarily recruited for plantation work and therefore recruitment was primarily among the noneducated, the manual workers, and the strong and physically healthy. Because of the plantation's experience with previous imported groups, the plantation

wised up by accepting only those who couldn't read and write and whose potential to conform and not complain was great. In selecting these workers, the plantation officials were unaware of the negative impact they would make in the general community.

2. *Highly imbalanced in terms of sex.* There was a very abnormal distribution of male and female among the early immigrant Filipinos. As a consequence, they were not adequately provided with wives and the conditions of normal family living. According to the US Census of 1950, there were 628 men to every one hundred women among the foreign-born Filipinos. In earlier years, the ratio was unusually high: In 1924 to 1930, the ratio was nineteen men to one woman. In the early 1920s, the ratio was thirty to one. May I cite some resulting health and social problems as a consequence of abnormal population distribution.

   a. Young men devoid of sex and family life resorted to commercial entertainment, including prostitution. Prostitutes appeared more visibly in plantation camps during paydays.

   b. Wife-stealing or constant shifting of husbands were common during the early plantation life. This practice consequently undermined family stability and created low motivation for education among their children.

II. The Local-Born Filipinos

The appearance of local-born Filipinos is very slow. It is only very recently that native-born youngsters have begun to appear in greater numbers. The few who overcame their unfavorable background are now professionals and hold responsible positions in the community. Let me mention three most sensitive problems among the local born.

A. Identity Crisis

The local born Filipinos have the roughest time in making the adjustment. They are torn between two conflicting cultures. At home, they try to observe the culture of their unsophisticated parents and school and community, want to be as Western as anyone else in their peer group. The deviant behavior of the early immigrants and the low social status of their parents has influenced many youngsters to deny their Filipino identity. In fact, police records show that then a Filipino youngster is apprehended, he usually identifies himself as Filipino-Spanish or Filipino-Chinese or Hawaiian-Filipino and never as Filipino. For there is nothing yet in the Filipino image that can help them boil out of trouble or move up in Hawaii's social ladder.

B. Economic Handicap

In the Filipino family, the boys were usually advised to enter the labor market as early as possible to help support the family. The girls were encouraged to finish high school or pursue higher education. The resulting consequence has worked against the group to move up from the bottom of the totem pole. Among the local born, we have more educated women than men. At marriageable age, they became incompatible, and we find more educated Filipinas married to men of other ethnic backgrounds. In this process, Filipinos were good in raising their girls to be highly educated and very good wives but failed to raise their boys above the levels of their fathers, who in our society have the responsibility to perpetuate the family name and to carry the identification and obligation of the Filipino community.

C. Lack of Filipino Community Support and Influence

The absence of a stable Filipino community is only a reflection of the unstable family life. I have heard allegations of mistrust, noncooperation, and even undercutting of each other among the elders of the Filipino community. In fact, it was said that Filipinos need no outside enemies—they fight among themselves. Major emphases in community affairs were always the fiesta, the social, and terno balls. Consequently, the youngsters found only few people to emulate as models and also found less community support in their aspirations for a better tomorrow.

III. The Recent Filipino Immigrants

Allow me to inform you that the state of Hawaii is the only state in the union that has a public agency to facilitate the adjustment of newly arrived immigrants. I brought twenty-five copies of our 1973 report, which identified the problems confronting our newcomers. While the report covers all immigrants, it truly reflects the Filipino immigrant.

Since 1965 to 1973, when the US immigration laws were liberalized to allow reunification of families and to obtain needed skills, approximately 27,300 Filipino immigrants were admitted to Hawaii—over two-thirds of whom came to join their families. Let me discuss this time and some of its problems which I believe can be resolved with the help of the churches.

A. The Problems Related to Cultural Conflict with the Host Society

1. *Interpersonal relation.* Unlike the local residents, Filipino immigrants avoid direct personal confrontation. They regard interpersonal relations as vital and would rather employ a third party to resolve a potentially explosive situation. In an American setting, however, this Filipino trait tends to complicate rather than resolve interpersonal problems.

2. *Parental ties and the extended family system.* Filipinos regard family ties as the most essential of all human relationships. Most often, the social status of a person is derived from family position, family achievement, and family wealth. Success is seen in terms of family enterprise rather than individual efforts. To be a good member, one has to be subservient to the family. In fact, there is a common saying in the Filipino community to this effect: Don't raise your head above the crowd or else someone will chop it off. Oftentimes, children remain submissive even to the point of giving up personal ambition, including marriage, if they run against the wishes of their parents. This peculiar Filipino family characteristic somehow stifles individual initiative and makes the person less responsible for his actions.

3. *Life's dominant philosophy*. As a subject people for more than four hundred years, the Filipinos developed a colonial mentality. They learned to live a life of blind submission to the hands of supernatural power. Generally, they do not regard obstacles to be overcome but rather to be adjusted to. Planning and problem-solving processes are alien to their experience because they believed that problems can be resolved through the passing of time and at the disposition of a power beyond their own. They have yet to develop critical and analytical minds and adopt some systems approach in looking at social problems.

I am reminded of an immigrant who was guest to a football game. At intermission, his host asked him how he liked the game. He replied, "I am enjoying it, only that there are too many committee meetings." Like any less sophisticated people, Filipinos need to huddle more and agree on what game plan to execute if they are to remain in an American ball game.

B. *The Problems Pertaining to Their Entry into the Labor Market*
1. *Civil service positions*. Government is one of the biggest employers in the state. But civil service jobs were not opened to immigrants until recently, when the courts declared that they are as eligible as US citizens. In many instances, however, immigrants passed the written examination but failed in the personal interview because of communication and lack of familiarity of Western rules of keeping a job. If one even passes an interview and becomes certified as one of the top five candidates for appointment, the chances of being chosen by the hiring agency is very nil. There are indications of discrimination in civil service appointments, and the federal government raised this question about one of the state's departments having one predominant ethnic representation.
2. *Licensed occupations*. Besides current civil service restrictions, the other major barriers to appropriate employment is present licensing regulations for professional and skilled occupations. There are ten occupations which require US citizenship and nine which require graduation from an accredited American school before one qualifies to take the licensing examination. Exceptions were granted to some graduates from European and Canadian schools. Many of the regulations are unrelated to ability and qualification in the practice of the profession. It is indeed a waste of trained manpower to continue to deny these immigrants their rights to practice their professions simply because they are not US citizens and are not graduates of American schools.
3. *Labor exploitation in the private industry*. There is evidence to indicate labor exploitation among immigrant workers by some employers in the private industry. This includes: payment of wages less than those specified by the employers in his petition to hire immigrant workers, failure to pay overtime compensation as required by law, and complaints by immigrants

that working conditions and living accommodations were below the standards originally represented by the employers. These violations serve to jeopardize labor standards and will adversely affect not only the immigrants but all other workers in the state as well.

I want to emphasize the fact that there is nothing so essential to immigrant adjustment to American life as a job and a fair deal in the exercise of their occupation.

C. The Problems Generated by Adverse Community Attitudes Toward the Immigrants

Immigrants are faced with problems not only in making a living but also in getting along with people of different backgrounds. The process of acculturation is always a difficult and painful experience. For every new trait gained, a culture is disowned or an identity lost. Such experiences can be minimized or aggravated by the attitudes of the host community.

By and large, the American community has always been kind to immigrants. Indeed, we are grateful to numerous groups who showed deep concern and interest in the foreign born and looked upon them as positive assets to American society. But we cannot deny that there are also other groups who looked down to new arrivals and displayed anti-immigrant attitudes. These attitudes seemed to flourish during hard economic squeeze and its consequence is often blamed to newcomers. Let me point out some areas which give rise to misrepresentation.

1. *The stereotyping of Filipinos as spendthrift, hot-tempered, and over-sexed.* These characteristics may have more truth among early immigrants. But these standardized pictures have taken an enduring and exaggerated quality which is no longer appropriate. This negative judgment about the Filipinos inhibit free and open interaction in the general community. In fact, some non-Filipinos in plantation communities still advise their young girls to keep distance while meeting a Filipino on the road because they can become impregnated by the swift of the breeze. This deviant sexual behavior of Filipinos in the early plantation days should not be wholly blamed upon them. It was largely a result of a bad recruitment policy of bringing in mostly single men and segregating them in isolated plantation camps.

2. *The notion that recent Filipino immigrants are overloading the state's welfare system.* This allegation is unfair and represents a great disservice not only to immigrants but to the total community. Intake information does not support such allegations because it is never identified whether a client is an immigrant or not. The assumption was based on the last address of the clients before coming to Hawaii. The DSSH survey on the impact of in-migration on Hawaii's welfare system as of January 1973 revealed that active cases whose last address was the Philippines constitute only 8.8%. This one category includes clients like returning US citizens and children of US citizens, early immigrants who came since the

US immigration laws were liberalized in 1965. It has to be noted that the senior citizens program, the Model Cities Outreach Services and the grassroots campaign of the welfare rights group have something to do in a large increase of applicants in welfare assistance. Generally, immigrants would rather hold on to two jobs to survive than be put on public assistance. It is not true that new immigrants are coming in droves and overloading our welfare system.

3. *The academic prejudice that Filipinos are not intellectually compatible with other ethnic groups.* The study *The Children of Kauai* by Werner, Bierman, and French reinforced the unwarranted opinion that Filipinos are of an inferior mentality. The Kauai study should be subjected to critical analysis because it was conducted through a biased Western research instrument and led the researchers to prove that some racial groups are superior to others. Social workers, school teachers and counselors, and other professional groups have the influence to correct and minimize this unfair distortion of the Filipino potential. It has come to our attention that some high school teachers deliberately discouraged Filipino students to take up academic courses which would have prepared them for college admission. The Filipino students are as capable as others to achieve greater heights if properly motivated and guided in their critical years of adjustment.

Forty-two years ago, a teacher took a personal concern to assist a nine-year-old immigrant who could hardly speak English. If it were another kind of teacher, the boy could have been easily consigned to special education. The immigrant student made the adjustment and went further to college and professional training. Two weeks ago, this person was appointed associate judge of the state supreme court.

IV. Its Promise in the Near Future

The probability of a better tomorrow for the Filipinos in Hawaii is supported by the following trends:

A. *Growing Number of Filipinos in the United States*

Recent population information reveals that there are approximately 725,000 Filipinos in the United States, of whom 475,000 are in California and 115,000 in Hawaii. The detailed information on Hawaii's Filipinos as of June 30, 1972, is as follows. Distribution of Filipinos by age and birth:

Age	Birth		TOTAL
	Local born	Foreign born	
14 and under	37,841	3,560	41,401
15-24	14,740	3,378	18,118
25-54	20,091	16,092	36,183
55-64	1,239	10,669	11,908
65 and over	761	6,974	7,735
Total	74,672	40,673	115,345
Percent	64.7%	35.3%	100%

The Filipinos in Hawaii constitute about 13.5% of the state population and comprise the third largest ethnic group in the island, next only to the Caucasians and Japanese. It should be noted that two-thirds of the Filipinos are local born and predominantly reflect a young population.

B. *Participation in the Larger Community*

1. *Citizenship.* Becoming an American citizen is significantly important to Filipino immigrants. About one thousand a year, or 50% of those who become naturalized citizens in the state of Hawaii, are Filipinos. As American citizens, they now begin to identify themselves as members of the American community and assume their share of the responsibility in continuing to build a better society.

2. *General motivation.* Generally, the new citizens want to get ahead economically. They want to advance in their jobs, own their own homes, establish their own businesses, and make a decent living. Increasing numbers of them are beginning to be active in community and professional organizations. This exposure is generally beneficial to the Filipinos and the larger community as well. I will not be surprised if they become smart in maximizing their numbers in the game of politics.

3. *New efforts to understand the roles and unique contributions of various ethnic groups in our American society.* The American public is now beginning to be more receptive to the idea of knowing other minority groups in the community. This growing interest finds expression through the establishment of the East-West Center and the creation of ethnic studies at the University of Hawaii. Through these efforts, the community is becoming aware that the immigrants are not only consumers of goods and services of the state but also creators of employment opportunities and positive assets in sustaining a dynamic society. Through these efforts, the Filipino youth are now beginning to reestablish continuity with their own culture, gain status in their own eyes as a distinct people, and evaluate their potentialities. Encouraged by this feeling of sense of worth, they now can objectively choose to assimilate or discard elements of both the Asian and Western cultures struggling to find their proper place in a multiethnic community.

Conclusion

I find it very difficult to relate the experience of the Filipinos in Hawaii with the local Christian churches. May I make it candidly clear that despite the church's shortcomings, we are appreciative of what the Christian faith can offer and sincerely grateful for whatever assistance we received from the church, the conference, and the national instrumentalities of our denomination. However, I would like to mention some disturbing failures in order to bring healing. And reassure us that the church shares our hope for a better tomorrow.

A. Its Failures

1. *The misuse of the Christian religion.* The decision-makers of the Hawaii Board of Mission were identified as sharing the same aspirations with the plantation industry and consequently became captives or willing tools of plantation managers. The church shares the guilt of being used to place the Filipinos in a subservient position and make them content to their oppression. The tales of abuses and exploitation were undecidedly unchristian and yet the church never lifted a finger to rectify the situation. It was not until organized labor came that the laborers were given a break. To the Filipino laborers, then, it is the labor union and not the church who is the bearer of good tidings in stopping the oppressive practices of the plantation industry.

2. *The short-sightedness of the Board to establish the churches in the plantation compound.* By locating the Filipino church within the plantation compound, it limits her perspective and encouraged dependency upon the plantation economy. The church then became almost exclusively for the plantation laborers and has not appealed to the larger community. Its message and ministry were not relevant to the conditions of the larger community. Therefore, at the decline of the plantation economy, the church was the first institution to suffer and die of attrition.

3. *Double standard of ministry.* The history of our churches in Hawaii documents the double standard of ministry reserving of course the best exclusive standards for the Caucasian ministers and recommending submissive virtues for the Asians. I am sure there is this eternal struggle in the hearts of all Christians with regard to this problem, and I hope the Asian ministers would be accorded the same rights and dignities which belong to all men. I would like to see, someday, qualified Asians and Hawaiians become general secretary of the conference or executive director in one of our instrumentalities.

B. Its Possibilities for Tomorrow

I would hope that someday the church will become the center around which the Filipino finds the source of power and inspiration to fully express his humanity—that it will become a shelter and a training center for us who are committed to challenging a hostile and an indifferent world. My hope is that the United Church of Christ, with its vast influence in economics and body politic, will lead us again in the fight for equality and justice for all. My time is up, and I hope I have stimulated you enough to recommend to the United Church of Christ inclusion of the problems and aspirations of the Filipinos in the United States on the Synod agenda. *Mahalo* and *maraming salama.*

A New Wind Is Blowing

FRANK G. MAR

Several years ago, Karl Heim compared the Church to a sinking ship:

> The Church is like a ship on whose deck festivities are still kept up and glorious music is heard, while deep below the waterline a leak has been sprung and masses of water are pouring in, so that the vessel is settling hourly lower though the pumps are manned day and night.[1]

That was Karl Heim's dramatic and subtle way of stating that the Christian church as an institution is indeed going through a gigantic crisis today. Scores of writers have, of course, in recent years expounded on the same theme warning Christians of dangers the church is facing today.

That the crisis our church faces today is extremely real no one doubts. But the question of what Christians should now do to meet this crisis raises many other questions involving the rethinking of the nature and mission of the church and reordering of the church's goal priorities. It is this reordering of priorities which will finally give us the mandate to deploy our forces and to dispose of all our resources for Christ's sake.

Concerning the basic rethinking of the church's nature and mission, many church leaders have again written volumes in the past decade. Yet the local churches in general still seem to be without any far-reaching goal for mission.

I believe that this lack of a sense of direction has caused much of the dissatisfaction and restlessness in the hearts of members and ministers of our churches. As a pastor serving a Chinese church, I have particularly experienced these agonies. Nevertheless, it was out of these trying experiences that I have rediscovered God's peculiar call to the Chinese Christians in America. This rediscovery has been a refreshing strength to me. For a hopeful vision has now replaced the frustrations and discouragements I once had. Consequently, what you are about to read is not an academic paper presenting lofty ideas for intellectual discussions. It is simply an attempt to share one individual's spiritual struggles out of which he has rediscovered the dynamic power and the exciting promises of the gospel of Jesus.

It is hoped that these pages may stimulate many of my kinfolk to effect a unity among the Chinese Christians in North America so that together we might claim God's promise to us as a people and fulfill our common destiny to proclaim the gospel to our people in newness of strength and spirit.

---

[1] [*Ed. note:* Karl Heim, *Christian Faith and Natural Science* (New York: Harper & Brothers, 1953), 24.]

Personal Struggles

After more than a decade of ministry serving three Caucasian churches, I began to find myself questioning the whole meaning of the Christian ministry and the existence of the institutional church. It was not because I had met up with failures. On the contrary, all through those years I enjoyed not a small measure of satisfaction, feeling that I was, indeed, playing an important role in our denomination's concerted effort to bring about integration in the church. My personal vanity had even led me to believe that I was courting with success. However, deep within me, I had become increasingly restless. The things I was doing had seemed to be just a part of a job. There was little compelling purpose in them.

It was under such feeling of futility that I had begun to examine the ministry and the church as an institution. With a mental scalpel, I had dissected them and carefully looked at the parts to see how my life was involved in them. This mental probe revealed two hidden elements causing my spiritual restlessness. One was the fact that in spite of my seemingly successful ministry in the Caucasian churches, there was little depth in the work I was doing, for the racial barrier was often a hindrance to my relationship with people. The other was the subtle discrimination in the Caucasian churches in general, which appeared certain to continue and make opportunities for vertical and lateral professional movements very scarce and difficult.

Once I came to that realization, I began to gravitate toward the idea of serving in the Chinese churches, as I believed that, there, I would have a ministry more involved in the lives and the living of my people with whom I have a natural affinity. But it was in this particular period when our denomination had implicitly embarked upon a policy to phase out the little so-called ethnic churches. The idea of serving in some Chinese church was, therefore, not a very viable avenue to continue my service in the church. So, everything seemed to point to a dead-end road for me as a Chinese minister. The most logical step to take had appeared to be one that would lead me out of the pastoral ministry.

God moves in mysterious ways. He holds many surprises for us. And in His devious ways he deterred me from leaving the pastoral ministry. He opened to me the door to begin a ministry serving the people of the Chinese Presbyterian Church in Oakland.

As I attempted to minister to the Chinese people here, my thinking and outlook toward the ministry began to change. In retrospect, I believe this change came about through the combined influence of many external forces and my internal reevaluation of my own commitment to the gospel of reconciliation.

Three major external forces are worthy of mention here. The first one to confront me was the facts and statistics about the new immigrants from Hong Kong. They opened my eyes to see the appalling needs of these, my people, living as strangers in our midst, and the great opportunities for Christian service.

Since 1967, thousands of these strange neighbors in the San Francisco Bay Area have been living under degrading poverty conditions. Yet there seemed to be no concerted effort, public or private, made to help them gain a sense of dignity in this land of affluence and opportunities. The concrete needs of the Chinese in the areas of employment, housing, the aging, and health care were so apparent that they cried out as prophetic voices summoning God's people to act. I felt they cried out particularly to the Chinese Christians to show their Christian concern because if Chinese Christians would not come to the aid of their soul brothers and sisters, then to whom could they go for help? What right do we have to expect some other people to minister to a people with whom we share a common heritage? Such questions and others brought to focus for me the unique responsibility of the. Chinese Christian churches.

The second external force which influenced my thinking was that of the Asian identity movement. It played a large part in reawakening in me the unique spirit of being Chinese.

When I became aware of my true identity as a Chinese, I realized, for the first time, that I had lost my own identity in the process of assimilation. Looking back, I think it was this loss of my own identity which had essentially caused much of my inner restlessness. How could one lose his own identity? It is quite easy for a minority person living in this predominantly white society. Because everything in America tends to point to some pattern of living or behavior set up by the white majority as the norm, the minority person tends to give up his individual characteristics. He often consciously or unconsciously suppresses his individual characteristics in order to gain acceptance in our society. Since racial traits are the most apparent hindrances to acceptance in this country, the minority person often takes great pains to cover up his racial identity. In my case, the hiding was so gradual and subtle that unconsciously I was led to feel ashamed of being Chinese. It was not what I wanted, but it happened just the same. Thus, helping the Chinese to know their own identity remains a real task for the Chinese churches.

Since I had not been emotionally identified with the Chinese people in some vital relationship in my ministry, for years I had no compulsion to think much about the mission of the Chinese churches or the destiny of the Chinese people. However, my rediscovered identity has changed my thinking and given me visions and challenges which make my present labor in this particular part of God's vineyard exciting and meaningful. No longer do I feel the need to become a quasi-white Christian. And I believe no one should ever be pressured into becoming such.

The third factor responsible for my change of thinking and outlook has to do with my becoming increasingly aware of the Chinese people's vital and crucial role in world peace. More and more, the world realizes that China holds one of the major keys to unlock the door to world peace. Hence, it is paramount that the Christian Church should exert her leadership in bringing about better relations between China and the United States. However, since the Western church is regarded by Asians as an agency of white imperialism, she cannot, at present, play the role of a reconciler effectively. Who is, then, in a better position to undertake this supremely vital role in the cause of world peace? The Chinese Christians in America, I believe, are uniquely equipped and motivated to build bridges of understanding which would span the chasm of misunderstanding between the East and the West. If Chinese churches could help to effect a new rapprochement between the East and the West, it would be our real contribution to world peace.

In a period of these several years in Oakland, I have gained new insights into the Chinese people. I have now been led to a new level of understanding of the destiny of China, the Chinese and the Chinese churches in North America. I no longer feel that the Chinese churches need to continue to exist as little ethnic congregations with insignificant ministries. We are not just some inconsequential specks in some predominantly white denominations. On the contrary, the Chinese churches in North America today have a supremely important ministry to perform locally and in the world. The importance of our ministry is unsurpassed. If we are faithful in discharging our monumental responsibility, our ministry will no doubt have worldwide effects in the future.

The conclusion arrived at above is awesome and exciting. It points to great promises, but it also brings to all Chinese Christians in America a sense of destiny and urgent challenges which may lead them from the lukewarm traditional practices to costly discipleship in ministries of many facets.

Before we look into the possibilities of new ministries, let us briefly review the history of the Chinese churches in America. It will help us to know where we have been, where we are and where we need to go in the light of God's unique call to us and of the world situation today.

Chinese Churches in America

The first Chinese permanent settlement in American soil probably dates back to 1848. These pioneers were essentially pilgrims. For they migrated to this New World only in the hope of doing business and making a bundle of money and returning to their native land to enjoy life thereafter.

Since San Francisco was the major port of entry for practically all the Chinese immigrants, a Chinese community grew up naturally and took roots in that fast-developing city on the Pacific coast. By 1850, there were approximately eight hundred Chinese living in San Francisco.

As the main objective of their pilgrimage in this new world was to find gold, the early Chinese immigrants were not at all bent on having any interest in religion, or any Western culture for that matter. Hence, they were very difficult to reach with the gospel. Dr. David Te-chao Cheng, in his book *Acculturation of the Chinese in the United States*, cited the followings as great hindrances preventing a Chinese from becoming a Christian in the early days:

His worldly economic motives.

His advanced age.

His great mobility in search for wealth.

His seclusive life on the weekdays, which tended to annul any sporadic and fragmentary Christian instruction on Sundays.

The hypocrisy of professing Caucasian Christians they encountered.

Against such odds, the missionary zeal of the Christian church, nevertheless, prompted the Presbyterian Church to begin work among the Chinese in San Francisco quite early. According to William Speer, the first Chinese Mission was started in 1852 with his own effort under the auspices of the Presbyterian Board of Foreign Missions. Let me quote his own words:

> My labors were begun among their sick, of whom there were great numbers on account of their crowded condition during their long passage over upon the old and rotten ship which was engaged in transporting them and the bad insufficient food given to them on ship board. Regular preaching in their own language was commenced during the winter, which was well attended. A church was organized November 6th, 1853, composed of several men who had been members in China. This was the first Chinese church in the New World . . . The next step was the opening of a night school, with which was connected lectures on astronomy, geography, chemistry and other sciences, illustrated by proper apparatus or a magic lantern.[2]

In this same record, we find that many other Chinese missions sponsored by different denominations followed: the Baptist Church of Sacramento in 1854, the Episcopal Church in San Francisco between 1855 and 1856, and the Methodist Episcopal Church in San Francisco in 1868. All these missionary efforts were undertaken by men who had been in China before.

That was the beginning of organized Christian work among the Chinese in America. How far has that work spread in the last 120 years? What shape have the Chinese churches taken in that period?

A recent survey showed that there are now over 150 Chinese churches and scores of Christian groups scattered in twenty-two states in America and in six provinces in Canada. Apparently, the ripples caused by the founding of the first Chinese church in San Francisco, 1853, have become ever widening circles of Christian witness all across this vast land. But in order that you might have a better knowledge and understanding of these Chinese churches, let me here cite some findings of a recent study.

According to the study made by the Bureau of Community Research in Berkeley in 1968, the Chinese churches of the San Francisco Bay Area numbered at least 34, scattered from Vallejo to San Mateo. They represent many denominations. But in San Francisco alone they have a total membership of approximately six thousand and another three thousand non-member constituents. Together they represent about 15% of the total Chinese population in 1968. However, the total membership of these churches accounted for 95% of all Chinese Christians in that city.

This study revealed also that the membership was younger than that of non-Chinese churches, with over 50% being professional, business, and clerical workers. These professional and skilled workers were gaining high occupational status in their communities. And not a few were becoming involved in high-level community affairs.

---

[2] William Speer, *The Oldest and the Newest Empire: Chinese and the United States* (Hartford, CT: S. S. Scranton and Co., 1870).

Most of the Chinese churches in this study had experienced healthy membership increases in the post-World War II era. The average membership was 240 for San Francisco churches, while it was 120 for churches in the East Bay. Approximately 64% of the members were native-born Chinese. And with the exception of five churches in San Francisco, all churches were served by one full- or part-time pastor.

Financially speaking, the average Chinese church was not very strong. The average annual budget was about $15,000. Seven congregations reported having self-supporting status, while several others showed that they were receiving not more than 10–12% of their budgets from their mission boards. But a few showed that they were still receiving 25–40% from their mission boards.

What does this historical picture show us concerning the Chinese churches in America? The one apparent thing it shows is that each congregation has had its beginning in the bosom of its mother denomination. Like a child, each has to go through the stage of *dependency*. For seven of the thirty-four studied, the stage of dependency is past. They are functioning in the stage of *independence*, which entails more responsibility in the process of self-determination. This transition from dependency to independence is as natural for an organization as it is for a child. A child who continues to live in dependency on its mother will grow old without maturing and becoming an independent and a self-determining organism. Hence, every organization has the natural desire to move from the stage of dependency to the stage of independence. Nevertheless, this drive to become independent oftentimes blinds the vision of the people as they look upon the status of independence as their ultimate goal and forget that the true ultimate goal of a people of God is to be faithful in the mission of the gospel of Jesus Christ.

Becoming independent is not unimportant. For without independence, no organization can truly be responsible. But let us be reminded that independence is not an end in itself. Being independent in the biblical sense always means having adequate resources and being more responsible to do more in the gospel ministry. "Unto whom much is given, of him much is required" (Luke 12:48) is the dictum for all Christian living and sharing of responsibility. Thus, the congregation that functions and lives in absolute independence is leading a truncated life. There is little future in that kind of life and ministry.

In order to live the kind of life with a future, each congregation must first wean itself from *dependency* and then grow in *independence* toward the full life of *interdependence*. For only as interdependent institutions are churches able and willing to learn how to participate and interact fully as integral members of the body of Christ, thus effecting the unity so much needed to bring God's redemptive power to our world today.

Recently, a number of Chinese pastors and lay leaders began to ask the question "Where are the Chinese churches heading in the 1970s?" This is a very encouraging sign. Such an inquiry does prompt us to think and plan. More significantly is the use of the broad, all-inclusive term "Chinese churches." It implies that there is some inherent affinity or commonality between Chinese churches regardless of their denominational ties or theological persuasions. If that is true, then a more fundamental question should be asked. Namely, *what is the destiny of the Chinese churches in North America?* It seems that if this question concerning our common destiny could be clearly answered, then we can begin to set tangible and attainable goals by which we all will have the direction toward fulfilling that destiny.

From Abraham down through the centuries, God has always chosen individuals and groups of people to be instruments of his redemptive purpose for the world. The biblical records also reveal to us that God seldom called individuals or peoples to do something in general. He calls specific persons to specific tasks. At this point in history, I believe God is specifically calling Chinese Christians in North America to be his unique ambassadors to Asians in Asia. That is our destiny!

A Strategy for Mission

It is my hope in helping the Chinese Christians to come to grips with God's urgent and unique call to us to be his vehicle to carry the gospel message to Asia that a strategy for world mission is here proposed.

However, before we consider any proposal, we must assume a new attitude toward our ministry. We must have a new consciousness of our unique call from God. Therefore, we have not thought much of our role in God's world mission. We have been functioning as little religious enclaves in the midst of a vast sea of predominantly white churches. That kind of mentality has permeated almost all our religious life and witness. If we are to fulfill our destiny, we must liberate ourselves from thinking of our role as being little ethnic churches indistinguishably enmeshed into the grand plans and patterns of predominantly white denominations. We can begin taking our new stance by not asking what role should we play in the scheme of the white denominations but rather by asking what role must we have within the economy of God's kingdom on earth.

Although it is no longer very fashionable for many American churches to talk about evangelizing to the world, serious Christians cannot honestly turn their deaf ears to their Lord's Great Commission: "Go therefore and make disciples of all nations" (Matt. 28:19).

Chinese Christians in North America, as integral members of the body of Christ, have no reason to excuse themselves from that worldwide mission either. And if we do subscribe to the assumption that the Chinese churches have a common destiny because God has called them to a unique ministry, then the time is long overdue for all Chinese Christians to start thinking of devising a bold strategy and of shaping new organizational forms to fulfill that destiny. There is a new spirit moving amongst us. A new spirit must have new forms for expression. For "No one pours new wine into used wineskins. If he does, the skin will burst, and then the wine pours out and the skins will be ruined. Instead, new wine is poured into fresh wineskins, and both will keep in good condition" (Matt. 9:17).

Consequently, the following proposal is put forth not as a final plan but rather as a point of departure. The reader is encouraged to analyze, criticize, and revise, to the end that we might have a viable strategy to unite the Chinese Christians and to involve a great host of committed disciples for God's world mission.

Briefly, my proposal can be described as a strategy having three stages or three levels of operation. But the best way to visualize it is to put the three stages in the form of three concentric circles, A, B, and C, with A being at the center, C the largest and furthest from the center. Circle A representing the most basic arena of operation is where two to six local churches in one geographical area, such as San Francisco, Oakland, New York, or Vancouver would work together as a cluster having a common ministry.

Apparently, in the beginning it would not be easy. For most Chinese ministers and church members have long been accustomed to thinking and working in their own little religious enclaves. And even in recent years, not much dialogue and sharing have taken place to facilitate the shaping of such cooperative ministries. However, if these Chinese churches are committed to the fulfillment of their common destiny in God's kingdom, then sincere Christians within those churches would surely see God's mandate to them to work for unity and for joint programs of Christian nurture, Christian service, and Christian outreach.

There are a great number of meaningful projects and programs a cluster of churches could initiate to give witness to their living faith. As examples, some of them are here enumerated under four main areas as pertain to the needs and challenges in Oakland:

I.   Christian nurture
    A. Christian education
    B. Leadership training
    C. Inter-church retreats and conferences
    D. Day camp
    E. Religious festivals
    F. Education for special ministry to Chinese

II. Christian service
    A. Ministry to senior citizens
        a. *Doh On Yuen* Home
        b. Senior Citizens Activity Center
        c. Visitations
    B. Ministry to immigrants
        a. General orientation
        b. Language classes
        c. Housing
        d. Employment training and referral service
        e. Health care
        f. Newcomers Association
    C. Counselling service
    D. Day care center
    E. Preparation for marriage classes

III. Community involvement
    A. Chinese Community Council
    B. East Bay Chinese Youth Council
    C. Chinatown Redevelopment Project
    D. Lincoln School Community Council
    E. Cultural education
    F. Role of reconciling third force in the city
IV. Evangelism and outreach
    A. Religious census
    B. Community-wide evangelistic meetings
    C. Development of visitation teams
    D. Support for Christian outreach centers

As the nucleus group of churches in Circle A are organized to function cooperatively, then the cluster will naturally see the opportunities for witness, service, and outreach in cooperation with other clusters or churches within a much larger region. For me as a pastor serving in Oakland, the wider Circle B would quite naturally represent the entire region of the East Bay Area.

Some of the projects and programs churches in East Bay might initiate are as follows:

1. Regional inter-church conferences for youth and adults
2. Campus ministry to Chinese students on seven East Bay college and university campuses
3. Development of evangelism materials relevant to Chinese thinking and style of life
4. Establishing outreach Christian centers
    c. Richmond
    d. San Leandro-Hayward area
    e. Fremont
5. Asian studies programs
6. Live-in facilities for needy youths
7. Additional senior citizens homes
8. Convalescent homes for Chinese
9. Institute for cultural and Christian learning
10. Health center
11. Support for world mission projects

Finally, we come to the outermost, Circle C, which represents North America for our present thinking and planning. However, since the projects and programs to be considered and initiated are all ultimately directed toward ministries in China, we must not limit participation to Chinese. On the contrary, we must actively recruit people and solicit resources from all Christians sympathetic toward our missionary enterprise in China.

Some of the projects and programs churches and Christians all over North America might work together to promote and support are as follows:

1. Promotion of Chinese churches' world mission strategy
2. Dialogue with various denominations for understanding and support
3. Program for training Chinese missionaries to work in China and other parts in Asia
4. Support for higher education in Hong Kong and Taiwan. (Resources are being channeled to Tunghai and Chung Chi through the United Board.)
5. Support for seminaries in Hong Kong and Taiwan. (The Chinese Presbyterian Missionary Society has done a little in recent years.)
6. Scholarships for seminary students. (Quite a few have been provided for students in Hong Kong by the Chinese Presbyterian Missionary Society in the last few years.)
7. Translation of major theological works (English to Chinese and vice versa)
8. Seminary students' and pastors' exchange program
9. Research on ministerial needs and problems in America and China
10. Cooperation with or coordination of missionary work of other agencies of like purpose. Major ones are
    a. Chinese Christian Mission, Michigan
    b. Ambassadors for Christ, Washington, DC
    c. Evangelize China Fellowship, Los Angeles
    d. Chinese For Christ, Los Angeles
    e. Ling Liang World-Wide Evangelistic Mission, LA
    f. Chinese Christian Literature Society, Kowloon
    g. Chinese Presbyterian Missionary Society, San Francisco
    h. China Graduate School of Theology, Inc.
11. Pastoral conferences
12. Support for National Conference of Christian Work Among Chinese
13. Request for resources from major denominations
14. Research and development of radio and TV ministry to Chinese here and in Asia
15. National student conferences
16. Theological study centers for development of new theology from the Chinese perspective. (For over 1,900 years, we have been looking at the gospel almost entirely from the Greco-Roman or Western man's perspective. Time has come for Christians to approach it from the Eastern man's perspective also. The Chinese churches can take the lead in such a development. It will uncover more of the riches of the gospel for all Christians. GTU in Berkeley might be approached to help in its development.)

STRATEGY FOR MISSION
(SEEING IT FROM OAKLAND)

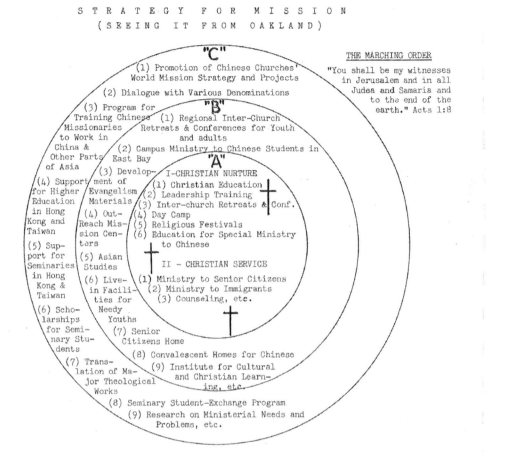

THE MARCHING ORDER
"You shall be my witnesses
in Jerusalem and in all
Judea and Samaria and
to the end of the
earth." Acts 1:8

In Circle A, the responsibility will rest exclusively on the churches in Oakland (Jerusalem).

In Circle B other Chinese churches and religious groups would be included within the East Bay region (all Judea).

In Circle C, all churches are to be included (Samaria). (This would become an important arm for the world mission strategy of the whole Christian church in Asia.)

Conclusion

What is laid out above as a strategy for mission may invoke a variety of responses. Some people may say that it is just a dream we could never realize. Others may think that the plan is simply too ambitious for the Chinese churches, for our churches are having a hard enough time just keeping alive. Nevertheless, I hope some might be challenged by it.

Seriously, I believe that if we're at all concerned about where the Chinese churches are heading, we must realize that changes in our attitudes and approaches to mission are absolutely necessary. The world around us is going through rapid and drastic changes. The changes of the '60s, radical as they were, will be accelerated progressively in every future decade. Even at the present rate of change, this world will soon be out of reach if our churches remain as they are today.

The many feelings, assumptions and convictions which have led me to make the proposal here are more than my subjective pattern of thinking. They are being experienced and held by many others in the Chinese churches. There is now a new awareness of the destiny of the Chinese people. A new wind is blowing. Its currents are moving toward the spirit of self-determination. If our Chinese churches would follow them, we would discover our common destiny in mission. Together we would bring about new forms for exciting cooperative ministries in our communities and in Asia.

Moreover, my hope for that kind of cooperative ministry is reinforced by the conviction that the churches in the future will become less and less parochial. For if there is one sure indication of the futures of the church, it is the dying of narrow dogmatism, the breaking of sectarian barriers, and the enlargement of a common vision for world mission. Thus, there are ample reasons to believe that congregations would very seriously consider effecting new forms of ministry together. The activities and programs suggested for Circle A and Circle B may truly be things our churches must now do to be in touch with the changing world and in tune with the prevailing wind.

Regardless of how any one feels about the mission of the Church, a Christian or a congregation must always return to the Scriptures to check his bearings. Unfortunately, oftentimes such a natural process of reexamination leads many sincere Christians to division instead of cooperation simply because different individuals find different mission emphasis in the Bible. Consequently, I suggest that the combined thrust of Luke 4:18 and Acts 1:8 be our compass for our pilgrimage in mission.

It is my conviction that in Acts 1:8 we have the Lord's strategy and marching orders for mission: "You shall be my witnesses in Jerusalem and in all Judea and in Samaria and to the end of the earth." And I am equally convinced that in Luke 4:18 we have our Lord's general description of the nature of our ministry. To that ministry we all have been called. We as individual Christians and as separate congregations sprinkled across North America must now choose whether or not we shall respond to that call in unity and obedience.

Asian Americans
*A Forgotten Minority Comes of Age**

JOINT STRATEGY AND ACTION COMMITTEE, INC.

From Stereotype to Reality

Americans are fond of pointing to the successful Japanese businessman as an example of the efficacy of the great American melting pot theory or to the ubiquitous Chinese laundryman proving daily that perseverance and hard work are virtues that America rewards.

Occasionally, however, the public is treated to another glimpse of Asian life in America—a view that is incongruent with the cherished image of the Asian American community as a self-sufficient, thrifty, hard-working, contented minority. Two years ago, tourists walking through San Francisco's Chinatown were startled by angry shouts of "Out of the ghetto, honky" followed by a barrage of firecrackers thrown into their midst. This spring, a CBS TV news investigation of the working conditions of Chinese Americans revealed the incredible existence of turn-of-the-century sweatshop conditions in the backrooms of New York's Chinatown.

Such reports only confirm what many Asian Americans have known all along and some are now beginning to articulate: that the melting pot paradigm has been used in America to mask a condition of internal colonialism. Here are some of the startling facts:

- Filipinos in California have an average annual income of $2,925, even though many were trained as professionals in their native country.
- 70% of the housing in San Francisco's Chinatown is substandard.
- 66% of the adults in San Francisco's Chinatown have less than a seventh-grade education.
- The suicide rate in San Francisco's Chinatown is three times the national average.

More subtle than the conditions of physical deprivation which exist behind the bamboo and lacquer facades of Chinatown USA is the internal deprivation suffered by those Asians who have "successfully" assimilated, but at the price of the love of their heritage and identity.

Spurred by the movements for ethnic identity among other groups, by the arrival of new immigrants from the Orient, and incensed by some of the racist aspects of the American presence in Indochina, Japanese, Chinese, Filipinos, and Koreans—each

---

* *JSAC Grapevine* 4, no. 4 (October 1972).

with distinct cultural histories—are discovering a new source of unity in their common experience as Asians in America. During the last two years, Asians have caucused together on college campuses, in their communities, and in the churches to assert their cultural identity and to press for more power and representation in the institutions which affect them.

Asian Americans and the Church

The double standard applied to Asians by American society—on the one hand pointing to them as exemplary assimilationist models, while on the other hand denying them a place of power and mobility in the society—is not without its analogue in the church.

The church has learned from the black experience that unity cannot be achieved between unequals, but it has been unable to see the Asian experience in the same light. As one Asian churchman put it: "Racism is seen only from a 'black-white' perspective. The church is reluctant to recognize that white racism extends in more subtle but just as vicious ways to Asians, American Indians, and Latinos."

Often from the best of intentions (Christian unity), the church has sought to assimilate its Asians into the mainstream without recognizing them as an oppressed minority, the victims of racial discrimination, whose needs for unity among themselves, cultural identity, and a sense of power cannot be met by being swallowed up.

Thus, the integration of the Oriental Provisional Conference (Chinese, Filipino, and Korean churches) and the Japanese Provisional Conference into geographical conferences of the Methodist Church during the 1950s and '60s did not meet the rather naive ideal for unity it had been set up to accomplish. Failure to consider the impact of cultural differences on the human psyche, as well as the failure to recognize its own latent racism, led the church to create more problems than it had hoped to solve with the merger.

As a result, Asian Americans have been deprived of certain structural power bases in the church and of access to leadership and resources which they enjoyed under their own ethnic conferences: Asian clergymen have experienced very limited job opportunities (they are still often subtly excluded from prestige appointments to WASP churches), and there has been a marked decline in enthusiasm and evangelical zeal among both clergy and laity because of the dispersal of ethnic leadership. A similar situation prevails in the United Presbyterian Church, where only 44% of the Asian ministers serve churches at all and where those who do serve are among the most poorly paid.

New Directions for Asian Ministries

As they come together to share experiences and the consciousness of their condition, Asians are exhilarated by the contribution they believe they can make toward a new understanding of the Christian faith and ministry. Perhaps their most important tasks will be to help the rest of the church forge a new concept of Christian unity for a pluralistic world—a unity which does not gloss over or seek to eradicate differences but which appreciates — even celebrates — them. Such unity will be based on an experientially and theologically grounded concept of identity and personhood, without which true communion cannot exist. Traditional theology, made by Western males, has long overlooked this important concept. Moreover, as they reinterpret the gospel in terms of Eastern values and traditions, Asians provide a needed corrective to some of those alienating and destructive cultural influences (such as excessive reliance on individualism and materialism) which have characterized Western Christianity and the Western missionary approach.

The following are some of the actions being taken by Asian Americans in those churches in which they are numerous.

United Methodists

As the urging of an ad hoc group of people connected with the former Japanese Provisional Conference, the Board of National Missions set up the Advisory Committee on Asian American Ministries in 1969. The Committee's task was to serve as a channel between the National Conference Boards of Mission, local pastors and churches, and the College of Bishops to help to create a climate in which the following purposes (outlined in a Committee position paper) could be accomplished:

1. to seek ethnic unity, consciousness, and self-identity
2. to seek fellowship which will uplift morale and renew evangelistic zeal to translate, interpret, and apply the gospel to ethnic peoples in terms of and through methods indigenous to them
3. to communicate the unique ministry and divergent traditions, customs, and cultures of Asian American Methodists
4. to affirm the concept of the inclusive church and the "wrongness" of making integration mere absorption

Since the Committee was set up, it has tackled the job opportunity problem by having bishops consider the appointments of Asian Americans across conference lines and has held training seminars for lay and ministerial leaders of Asian congregations. Along with the Commission on Religion and Race, the Committee has initiated an Office of Research and Development for Asian Ministries, which puts out a monthly newsletter, entitled *Asianews*.

In March 1971, over two hundred Asian American Methodists gathered for a Convocation on Asian American Ministries and formed themselves at that time into a continuing Asian American caucus within United Methodism to work on problems related to their constituency as well as to cooperate with other ethnic groups within the church in order to combat racism and to develop new styles of ministry and theology. Largely because of the efforts of the Asian caucus, an Asian American was recently elected to the episcopacy in the Western jurisdiction.

Contact: Rev. George Nishikawa, Executive Director, Office of Research and Development for Asian Ministries, United Methodist Church, 281 Santa Clara Ave., Oakland, Calif. 94610.

United Presbyterians

An Asian Presbyterian Caucus was officially formed at a meeting in St. Helena, California, in March of this year. The purposes of the caucus, similar to those set down or acted upon by the Methodists, are:

1. to give effective voice and advocacy to the problems, concerns and insights of Asian Americans
2. to facilitate the representation of Asian Americans on boards and agencies of the church
3. to provide mission strategy to Asian American churches and the wider community
4. to combat racism
5. to explore study and appreciate the values of Asian heritage and to develop new ministries to Asians and Asian American movements
6. to maintain communications with Asian caucuses of other denominations
7. to provide training and education for Asian ministers and laymen

The caucus meeting concluded with the statement that "self-development is a response to the effects of racism and is a necessary step to the authentic reconciliation, equality, and justice for all peoples." The caucus was present at the 184th General Assembly and proved its muscle by getting an Asian American on the nominating committee and nine Asians elected to boards and agencies. It will be pushing for serious consideration of Asians for key staff positions in the new structure.

Contact: Rev. Lemuel Ignacio, Chairman Asian Presbyterian Caucus, 5089 Yucatan Way, San Jose, Calif. 95118.

American Baptists

An Asian American Baptist Caucus was formed in August, 1971, at a meeting in Gardena, California. As its chairman, Paul Nagano stated: "The Caucus provides the power leverage for love both for the oppressed and the oppressor." There cannot be love between those who are free and those who are not free.

In seeking to recapture the sense of power and identity lost by Asian Americans, the Baptist Caucus' first order of business was to consider specific project proposals related to Asian American ministries and social action and cultural programs. Some of these projects are

- development of new or struggling Asian ministries in certain locales, especially in California, where there is a tremendous influx of new immigrants
- cooperation across denominational lines to encourage the formation of permanent centers of Asian American church studies in two locations in California
- support of Asian youth programs in communities and on campus
- support of an Asian American social worker to do research in the way Asian Americans in certain localities are faring with regard to housing,

child care needs, drug abuse, mental health, and old age homes. (Because they have been overlooked as a minority, Asian Americans have been singularly missing in research data.)

- the development of lay leadership
- cultural training for Asian American clergy
- proposal of a central file of Asian American Baptist pastors to be kept at Valley Forge
- more church personnel to deal with Asian American ministries
- church internship training programs for Asian American college and seminary students
- the encouragement of Asians to fill missionary positions in Asia

Contact: Rev. Paul Nagano, Japanese Baptist Church, 901 E. Spruce St., Seattle, Washington 98122

Asian American Baptist Convocation[*]

Jitsuo Morikawa

Youth, Blacks, feminists, are not unique in their quest for identity; all peoples are faced with the crisis of identity—"Who are we?" "Where did we come from?" "Where are we going?" "What is our central role and purpose?" I am assuming that Asian Americans, and Asian American Baptists in particular, are also faced with this fundamental question of human existence, compounded in geometric proportions, facing simultaneously what it means to be human, what it means to be a person and people in American culture while our historic roots lie in Japan, China, Philippines, or Korea; and when those ethnic antecedents are divided by hostile boundaries into North and South Korea, People's Republic and Nationalist China; and when the alliances between the US and these nations are in a state of incredible flux; and when we as Asian Americans have lived isolated from each other and we constitute a negligible minority without the strength of numbers Blacks and Hispanics possess; and to further compound our complexity, we are called to engage in the decisive historic identity question of what it means to be the church in this age of secularization!

I. Who Are We?

Who are we? We are a people who by act of providence and historic events are rescued out of a narrow American provincialism and parochiality and thrust into the historic mainstream of living in a multinational and multicultural world. The days of neatly boundaried cultural and political nationalism are over as also the sharp sectarian denominationalism in the church. We are living in an age of universal history, ecumenicity in the church as a sign of the emerging secular *oikumene*, the whole household of the human family. We can no longer live in our particular world, isolated and cleanly identifiable; we are called to live in the bewildering complexity identified with many communities in the world. Citizenship in one nation may no longer be adequate. We may be moving toward a future when we retain citizenship in several nations, and what has been regarded as treason, such as dual or multiple citizenship, may become the mark of a world citizen. We have unfortunately regarded the hyphenated American as a liability in the past and attempted to reduce our ethnic visibility by deliberate or unconscious disregard of our ethnic language, culture, history and tradition to prove that we were Americans. And in so doing, we have impoverished and eroded two generations of Asian Americans of the rich

---

[*] 1971.

cultural legacy of our forefathers. In part, cultural coercion brainwashed us into assuming incongruence of Asian with American culture, but basically we hold ourselves accountable that we failed to value, claim, and turn into currency and use our rich heritage.

Who are we? We are a people who by the pressures of history have learned to endure suffering, internalize the pain, live for long periods of time without exteriorizing and giving vent to our inner fires of resentment and protest. Asian Americans, and I want to speak of Japanese Americans in particular, have been labeled by Bill Hosokawa of the *Denver Post* as "the Quiet Americans." We quietly accepted the Japanese Exclusion Act of 1924 denying immigration into the US and the denial of citizenship to Japanese immigrants and the denial of the right to own land in California and the denial of civil liberties by accepting indiscriminate and mass evacuation and internment without trial and due process of law and lost all our possessions hard earned over a generation of toil—and this with hardly a whimper. And in response to these successive waves of injustice, we volunteered, we begged for the privilege of fighting and dying for our country, and many died while their parents, brothers, and sisters, were still lingering in Poston and Manzanar and Tule Lake.

Professor William Peterson of the University of California, speaking of the Japanese Americans, says that no ethnic minority in American life has suffered the degree of discrimination and injustice. Yet in contrast to other minorities, Asian Americans have engaged in no loud protest, nor engaged in demonstrations, in little corporate political action, and minimal action through the courts. Is this good? Have we achieved comparatively more by our invisible and quiet approach? Is there moral power and judgment in silence and in internalizing the pain and seeking to transform that pain into creative endeavor? One part of me says we were morally irresponsible for quietly accepting the perpetration of injustice, and another part of me says that while the style of life today is uninhibited expression in the name of honesty and integrity, I believe life at its profoundest level is mystery and silence, the secrecy of the human spirit known only to God, so that there are dimensions of human reality not available for the marketplace, but only for the secret chambers of the heart. "Inscrutable Oriental," used as a discrediting label, may in fact be a tribute and a mark of respect. But the other part of me that resents the silent posture we maintained feels that we have confused and equated self-expression with self-assertion and the exercise of power with self-aggrandizement. There is much in our Asian background which looks with suspicion upon anyone who is too forward, aggressive, and particularly one who is self-assertive. He is described in Japanese as being *gehin-na-hito*, meaning an uncouth person. Someone who holds himself in check with modesty and humility as being *enryo-bukai* is lauded as a *Mohan-seinen*—an exemplary person. In my family, my brother Katsumi was a quiet, un-self-assertive, *otonashi-mohan-seinen*—acknowledged in our family and in the community as a model person. I suffered, by contrast, everything he was not—perhaps that's why I learned to need a Savior before all others!

But in our quest for humility, we may have diminished our ability to exercise power. Power is an ingredient without which we cannot achieve legitimate goals and objectives. In fact, a contemporary rediscovery of human reality is that change rarely occurs without the exercise of responsible intellectual, spiritual, political, social, and economic power. Few who possess privileges, preferential status, and power voluntarily surrender these toward an equitable distribution. The Blacks have learned this lesson of history, and the Bible has much to say about the exercise of power: "Ye shall receive power"; "All power is given unto you"; "that I may know Him and the power of His resurrection." We need to take a serious look at the responsible use of power in the moral governance of society.

"Who are we?" We are a people, co-heirs and co-inheritors, entitled by right of birth to all the privileges and rights as citizens of the United States. There are certain inalienable rights which are ours by virtue of being human, by virtue of being born, by virtue of being members of the human family, by the sovereign grace and act of Jesus Christ. These are not negotiated or determined or won or seized or given or mediated. They are ours—already ours—as a gift of God—no one can take them away from us, inseparable ingredients of our personalities—freedoms, liberties, and rights. To become fully human through the exercise of unrestrained responsible freedom is our legacy and our inheritance from the Lord of history. But we—that is, Asian Americans—have acted out of a posture of negotiation and appeal to the white majority, to have them consent and permit and dole out to us with reluctance or generosity what rightfully belongs to us! We have reinforced white arrogance by thanking them for giving us what belongs to us, by being impressed when as Asian American gets elected to the Senate or the presidency of a university. We ourselves need a change in consciousness, a recovery of who we really are—to renounce our psychic servitude to the white majority—denounce the dehumanizing and destructive enterprise of earning and achieving equality rather than to accept, acknowledge, and admit our equality and live it out. For some time to come, we will have to live with the fact of white arrogance, the assumption ingrained even among some of the noblest of the whites that somehow if minorities are to have equality and freedom, they will have to "give" these to us. Perhaps the demands of the Black Economic Development Conference through James Forman were based on the assumption that American economic affluence, which means affluence primarily for the white majority, has been extracted out of the sweat and suffering of twenty million Blacks living in social and economic squalor, and that the demand for a few million dollars is but a small claim on that part of the nation's wealth which is rightfully theirs.

II. What Is Our Calling and Mission?

We began by saying the question of identity is one of the profoundest issues confronting human existence, not only for persons but peoples and institutions and nations. Not only is the perplexing question framed in terms of "Who are we?" but also in terms of "What are we for?" Hendrik Kraemer placed that question at the center of the church's agenda—"What is the church for?"—which anticipated the same question being raised by every human community—education, medicine, business, government, and even the nation-state. Thus, we also face the same serious question: "What are Asian American Baptists for?" Is there a particular calling to which we are called, a vocation to fulfill, a constraining purpose to which the tides of history lure us?

We have a common calling with all Americans. That needs to be nailed down once and for all. Every avenue of human enterprise open to every other American must be open to Asian Americans. The ethnic stereotypes must go, for they are tragic reminders of a period in American history when most occupational and professional doors were closed to Asian Americans so that as recently as the Second World War, Asian American college graduates had little to look forward to beyond pushing lawn mowers, tending fruit stands, running a laundry, fishing, or farming.

While we have a common calling with all Americans, a basic universality, we also represent a certain particularity which provides clues as to certain unique responsibilities and opportunities as Asian Americans. President Nixon's proposed visit to the People's Republic of China opens up the possibility of a whole new era of relationship between the US, the People's Republic, Nationalist China, Japan, South Korea, and the Philippines at least, toward a piercing point of crisis fraught with danger—and hope, judgment, and possibility. What happens among these nations affects the welfare of the whole world.

The church cannot escape responsibility by suggesting hers is a spiritual ministry and not a political mission, that her task is to save souls and not to save the peace, or to barricade ourselves in our little churchly bunkers, convinced of our impotence in the face of awesome international realities.

We have several things going for us. This whole Pacific arena of the world will require recruitment and training of specialists—political, economic, educational, and religious—on an intensive, massive scale, to engage intelligently and creatively in the international enterprise—men trained in the profoundest understanding of these nations, peoples, and regions. How tragic has been our misreading of the Vietnam situation; our involvement has been a series of miscalculations, misreadings, and faulty intelligence. We have operated in the dark in relation to Red China, refused to listen to lonely voices like John Patton Davies, who years ago advocated membership of Red China in the UN; and then the McCarthy purge silenced and destroyed the careers of many of our best Sino scholars. The President's disregard of political protocol with America's strongest ally in the Pacific, sending Kissinger to Peking without advance notice to Prime Minister Sato, may possibly precipitate the beginning of the end of the Mutual Security Pact, for it strengthened dramatically the growing power of the military and those nationalists who continually charge that Japan cannot rely on the integrity of the US, who will follow policies only germane to her national interest. She has the industrial capacity of becoming a nuclear power overnight. The events of the 1930s prove that a small but armed military clique can override a peace-loving majority in the nation, including the emperor, to plunge a nation into the devastation of war. The so-called political coup by President Nixon in relation to the People's Republic of China may bring about a whole new shift in the political alliances, possibly driving Japan toward Russia or at least to a course of dangerous independence.

Again and again our historic human tragedies have arisen out of reliance on outmoded myths and assumptions. America has demonstrated her incredible capacity to operate out of narrow, sectarian, parochial, and fundamentalist views of international reality, particularly in relation to Communist nations of the world. Total human welfare cannot afford not to bring into being the mobilization of a massive missionary movement comparable to the great days of the Student Volunteer Movement, when, from the classrooms of Yale and Harvard and other universities, great missionary recruits arose, like John R. Mott and Sherwood Eddy and Kenneth Latourette, to "proclaim the gospel and evangelize the world in one generation." While the call to evangelize the world in one generation became a slogan impossible to fulfill, and while the theology which drove thousands of volunteers was motivated to rescue millions from a Christless grave of eternal damnation, and while most of them went to the villages and hamlets of undeveloped nations of the world, we are in fact living in apocalyptic times demanding repentance now in this generation or we may perish, and our theology had better have possibilities of damnation and even extinction, and we had better engage in massive recruitment to missionary service, but missionary service in a new sense—evangelizing, bearing witness to the gospel of God's "shalom" in the diplomatic, political, economic, health, and educational arenas of a highly sophisticated urban technological society.

Why shouldn't Asian American Baptists do what a group of deacons did with a young boy, George W. Truett, when they said to him, "We think God is calling you to be a preacher;" and apparently God spoke to that boy through those country deacons. I doubt very much that I would be in the ministry today had not my pastor asked me one day, "Have you ever thought that God might be calling you to enter the Christian ministry?" Your approach would be so different today. To raise this question of vocation is to evangelize; to call a life to a decision is to raise the question of his relationship to Jesus Christ. It may very well be that evangelism and missionary recruitment are simultaneous events or a single event, so that confronting and negotiating the future vocation and plan for a life as co-laborer and co-creator with Jesus Christ in the bewildering complexities of international relations may become the central mission of the Asian American Baptists for some years to come.

"What is our calling?" We are a people who have felt the full force and impact of corporate and institutional decisions of American people. Despite many fine individual Americans whose personal morality we would applaud, the nation's collective morality reflected in institutional decisions—the Immigration Act of 1924, the California land acts, the evacuation order—have inflicted permanent scars on our lives and memories. These institutional decisions have affected the total wellbeing of the total Asian American community, not just economic and political wellbeing, but the spiritual, moral, and psychic as well—the whole range of human life. This is a way of suggesting that an integral part of our Christian ministry is the participation in civic responsibility, to participate in politics or the science of the *polis*, or the city, as coworkers with God in the reshaping of the metropolis.

During my visit in Japan two years ago, the director of the research center for the Tokyo metropolitan government said that Tokyo's most critical need is the development of civic consciousness among its people. Public welfare, he said, looms low in the people's priority. Personal welfare looms high. Public behavior stands in sharp contrast to private behavior. As Asian American Baptists who have learned through their tragic history, ministries can no longer be understood to be simply person to person, or even just to families, although we are responsible to minister to each man, to each individual, and to every family. But we are called to minister to institutions and organizations and collectivities, to the "principalities and powers" of which the Bible speaks, where the awesome decisions are made to affect the welfare and destiny of millions of people. The God revealed to us in Jesus Christ calls and summons not only individual persons like Abraham, Isaac and Jacob, and special peoples like Israel and the church, but He also holds accountable institutions and organizations and structures of men which the Bible describes as "nations." We are called to evangelize to these institutions through a new kind of ministry, the ministry of the laity, to function as creative change agents, leading and directing institutional decisions toward fulfilling the purposes of God and the welfare of all men.

Biblical and Theological Statement for the Asian American Baptist Caucus

Paul M. Nagano

The essential Christian motivation for the Asian American Baptist Caucus or, for that matter, any positive ethnocentrism ("a view of things in which one's group is the center of everything, and all others are scaled and rated with reference to it"[1]) is the necessity for identity, human dignity, and freedom. Theologically, it has to do with the nature of man and the nature of God as love. Biblically, it has to do with God's redemptive act through Jesus Christ. It must be said that from a racial and point, ethnocentrism is not necessary except where some characteristic of the race is the object of discrimination. In case of the Blacks and the Asians, the discriminatory characteristic is color.

Theologically, man's identity is related to his sense of being over against any anxiety that may come about from nonbeing or threats that the ground on which the individual or group stands is being taken away. According to Tillich, "The human experience of having to die anticipate the complete loss of identity with one's self."[2] The threat that confronts the racial minority is that of being treated or becoming a thing rather than one's identity as a person, grounded in his environment. Man is a self and the bearer of subjectivity. The polarity in which man is caught is between the fully developed personality or identity representing one pole and the mechanical manipulated tool on the other. Everything resists the fate of being considered or treated as a mere thing, as an object which has no subjectivity. This is the threat of nonbeing or loss of identity.

The Asian American in American society is losing his sense of identity by being absorbed by the majority, by adopting a subservient and accommodating stance, by developing a poor self-image, and by making decisions according to the expectations of his environment. He has been dehumanized to the point where any attempts to affirm his identity becomes a threat even to himself.

In the biblical creation stories, God produces individual beings and not universals, Adam and Eve rather than the ideas of manhood and womanhood. Added to this, humanity is created in the image of God. Humanity not only is completely self-centered; they are also completely individualized. Christian theology affirms the uniqueness of every person and the creation of each person in the image

---

[1] William Graham Summer, *Folkways* (Boston: Ginn, 1906), 13.

[2] Paul Tillich, *Systematic Theology,* vol. 1 (Chicago: University of Chicago Press, 1966), 197–198.

and likeness of God. Added to this, God is no respecter of persons and loves the world and provides salvation for every human. What does this say regarding human dignity? It means that individualization, God-likeness, and participation in the salvation provided by God reaches the ideal form when one's personhood is recognized. We must ask what strategies in society provide the most conducive environment for authentic personhood?

It is the belief that only by determining one's own strategies and ethnocentric communions can the full experience of human dignity and ego-strength be developed. The Asian Caucus provides such a communion as a prelude to the communion with the larger society. Before genuine communion can be established, authentic personhood is necessary. Once individuals are respected in the fullness of their personhood, communion on the highest level can be experienced.

The danger here is the destruction of personhood within the group when there is the desire to conquer one another. Through a history of oppression, it is very easy for minorities to be jealous or destroy one another due to their poor self-image and their inability to handle power and leadership. The inability to develop cooperation and unity of purpose at the grass roots level is indicative of this. Either a Moses must appear or minorities must turn their attention to a common object of concern. According to Williams, "Social solidarity among individuals or groups is enhanced by recognition of the sharing of a positive and noncompetitive regard for a common object of concern."[3]

The third Christian motivation for the Asian Caucus is that of freedom. Freedom, according to Tillich, is experienced "as deliberation, decision, and responsibility."[4] Freedom is the function of man, that is, of that being who is not a thing but a complete self and a rational person. Man is man because he has freedom. As long as decisions are dictated by the power structure, and not the result of individual deliberation, the essential function of man is destroyed.

In the light of this motivation of freedom, the meaning of destiny becomes meaningful. What has happened in my past determines my freedom, and my freedom participates in shaping my destiny. Without freedom, my destiny is not mine.

In dealing briefly with the theological motivation for the Asian Caucus relating to the nature of God as love, God seeks to deal realistically with the evil and injustices in the world. Love must destroy what is against love. As with Luther, "Sweetness, self-surrender and mercy are the proper work of love; bitterness, killing and condemnation are its strong work, but both are works of love."[5] What Luther means is that it is the stronger work of love to destroy what is against love.

This presupposes the unity of love and power. As with Tillich, in order to destroy what is against love, love must be united with power, and not only with power, but also with compulsory power. "The Criterion is: Everything that makes reunion

---

[3] Robin M. Williams Jr., *Strangers Next Door* (Englewood Cliffs, NJ: Prentice-Hall, 1964), 390.
[4] Paul Tillich, *Systematic Theology*, 184.
[5] Paul Tillich, *Love, Power, and Justice* (Oxford: Oxford University Press, 1954), 49.

impossible is against love."[6] Thus, love tries to save and fulfill the person that destroys by destroying in him what is against love. The theology of love seeks to have all people come together as equal; therefore, refuses to speak of love without justice and mutuality.

The Asian Caucus finds its theological motivation in the nature of God as love as it seeks to speak of love with justice, and this is not possible without a power base. The Caucus provides the power leverage for love both for the oppressed and the oppressor.

Here again, it is the belief that the true product of love is to become unreservedly a person for others, and this is possible only for the one who has become free to be themself. The Caucus attempts to free the Asian American to become a person for others.

Biblically, the motivation for the Asian Caucus is found in the Old Testament, as *Yahweh* (God) identifies with the people of Israel who are oppressed and downtrodden. The Asians Christians take seriously the experience of the oppressed since it is so close to their own experience of prejudice and, for the Japanese Americans, evacuation into the wilderness. In Exodus 3:15–17, God appeared to Moses:

> God said to Moses, "Say this to the people of Israel, 'The LORD, the God of your fathers, the God of Abraham, the God of Isaac, and the God of Jacob, has sent me to you. This is my name for ever, and thus I am to be remembered throughout all generations, Go and gather the elders of Israel together, and say to them, 'The LORD, the God of your fathers, the God of Abraham, of Isaac, and of Jacob, has appeared to me, saying, "I have observed you and what has been done to you in Egypt; and I promise that I will bring you up out of the affliction of Egypt, and to the land of the Canaanites, the Hittites, the Amorites, the Perizzites, the Hivites, and the Jebusites, a land flowing with milk and honey'" (Ex. 3:15–17, RSV).

As God affirmed Israel, the Asian Caucus affirms that God understands and identifies with the Asian's plight and predicament in the United States.

The Caucus believes that in Christ, God enters into human affairs and identifies with those who are hurting. Their suffering becomes His; their despair, divine despair. God's word of identification with the feelings of the Caucus is "I know the meaning of rejection because in Christ I was rejected; I know the meaning of physical pain because I was crucified; I know the meaning of death because I died; I know the meaning of being despised and rejected because I was the 'despised and rejected' of man." But my resurrection in Christ means I am present with you and that alien powers cannot keep you from the full meaning of life. "I am come that you might have life, and that you might have it more abundantly" (John 10:10).

For this reason, in the relation and events in life of his people, God always takes his stand unconditionally on behalf of the oppressed. Barth writes,

---

[6] Paul Tillich, *Love, Power, and Justice*, 50.

God always takes his stand unconditionally and passionately on this side alone: against the lofty and on behalf of the lowly; against those who already enjoy right and privilege and on behalf of those who are denied it and deprived of it.[7]

The Asian Caucus believes that it is biblically motivated as it looks to the ministry of Jesus as it is outlined in Luke 4:18:

The Spirit of the Lord is upon me,
because he has anointed me to preach the good news to the poor.
He has sent me to proclaim release to the captives
and recovering of sight to the blind,
To set at liberty those who are oppressed,
To proclaim the acceptable year of the Lord.

It means that God in Christ seeks not only to preach the good news to the poor but is actively engaged to fulfill the purpose of the gospel in actual existence. Jesus' ministry affirms that his work is essentially one of liberation. Becoming a slave himself, he opens realities of human existence formerly closed to man. Through encounter with Jesus, man knows the full meaning of God's action in history and man's place within it.

The book of Ephesians clearly presents that God wills a community of love constituted by Jesus Christ. The church of Jesus Christ is a microcosm of God's ultimate purpose. The church, though imperfect, is the decisive community in transforming the earth and shaping the destiny of those who inhabit it. The Caucus fulfills its Biblical purpose in its endeavor to establish community as the object lesson or "wisdom of God" (Ephesians 3:10) in history. According to John A. MacKay:

There is no sublimer thought in the Ephesian Letter or in all Scripture than this. The history of the Christian Church becomes a graduate school for angels. . . .

God's will to unity is thus the most central thing in cosmic and human history. This Divine drive none dare ignore, for whatever man attempts that runs counter to it will ultimately be frustrated and shattered by it. As for the Christians it is important that they explore the fullest degree the nature and implications of the unity which God pursues, this order of life which He is establishing.[8]

The Asian Caucus find its motivation for its existence in this biblical injunction for unity. It refuses to embrace any concepts of God which makes the suffering of the oppressed as the will of God and hope in the hereafter as the reward for suffering. The Bible clearly states that God is interested and involved in history. That this unity in history can come about in seriously confronting any system or structure that hinders or destroys this unity. The common concept that only the assurance of heaven (hereafter) is important is not essentially biblical, but rather God calls his people and the church to responsible action and community within history.

---

[7] Karl Barth, *Church Dogmatics II/1: The Doctrine of God*, trans. T. Parker, W. Johnston, H. Knight, and J. Haire (Edinburgh: T. & T. Clark, 1957), 386.

[8] John A. MacKay, *God's Order: The Ephesian Letter and This Present Time* (New York: MacMillan, 1953), 61–62.

In the fulfilling of the Great Commission as found in Matthew 28:19–20 ("Go therefore and make disciples of all nations, baptizing them in the name of the Father and the Son and of the Holy Spirit, teaching them to observe all that I have commanded you; and lo, I am with you always, to the close of the age"), the Caucus feels its special responsibility to fulfill its calling to the Asian community in America as well as participate in the growing Asian missionary arena abroad. As part of the family of God, the Asian Caucus feels it is our responsibility to call into the service of Christ the whole church to participate as true partners in the mission to bring the gospel of Jesus Christ in its power to change individual and nations, and the Asian American community is the unique area of our responsibility.

This has been an attempt in love to present a rationale for the existence of the Asian American Baptist Caucus from a theological and biblical perspective. It does not even begin to deal deeply into many reasons for the Caucus; however, it endeavors to bring together both at the grass roots level and denomination level a greater unity of purpose and cooperation.

At the grassroots level, it is true that the problems of self-determination and self-assertion of the Caucus may be seen as a part of a vicious circle. Asian Americans have developed a subservient posture through discrimination and cultural syndromes and find it difficult and sometimes threatening to begin to assert themselves. It is hoped that the Christian basis presented here will grant us the courage to affirm ourselves and determine our own destiny. It is with the prayer that the Caucus can be a means whereby social solidarity may be enhanced by the sharing together of a positive and Christ-motivated common concern that this paper is prepared.

Asian Presbyterians
*Let's Get Organized!**

LEMUEL IGNACIO†

We didn't get organized for the sake of organizing. Someone may think that we got organized because the Native American Indian Presbyterians, black Presbyterians, Latino Presbyterians, women Presbyterians, and Presbyterian youths got organized. But what really happened was this:

We read about a man who formed and led a movement. We were challenged by the simple idea he taught and simultaneously translated into action—the concept of using power to liberate and gain selfhood by organizing the powerless. The man's name is Jesus.

We, Asian Presbyterians, are the powerless within our denomination. We were motivated to get organized by the gospel of liberation, justice, and equality. The gospel is central and fundamental to the Asian Presbyterian Caucus (APC). The birth of the Asian movement within the United Presbyterian Church in the USA is the gospel of Jesus Christ exemplified once again in modern times.

One hundred twelve lay and clergy Asian Presbyterians living in the United States unanimously affirmed the historic decision to create the Asian Presbyterian Caucus to "assure the full selfhood and cultural integrity of our particular heritage" at St. Helena, California, on March 16–19, 1972. Seventy-nine percent of the conferees were laypersons and youths; 21% were clergymen. The delegates came from the state of Washington, the state of New York, and twenty-three other states in between.

For the first time in the history of the United Presbyterian Church, thirty-two Chinese, twenty-two Filipinos, two Indonesians, thirty-nine Japanese, and seventeen Koreans met under one roof to share common concerns. The multiethnic and multigenerational conferees included recent first-generation immigrants from the Pacific Rim countries, the American-born second-generation bicultural individuals, and the third-generation Americanized persons with faint traces of their Asian heritage.

The five Asian ethnic groups declared as one body their wish to "join all Christians in the total mission of the church recognizing in full the contributions of our Asian brothers and sisters in the total mission of the church of Jesus Christ."

---

* March/April 1973.
† Mr. Ignacio was chairman of the Asian Presbyterian Caucus.

The Statement of Concerns of Asian Presbyterians adopted at the meeting in St. Helena appears in the adjoining box.[1]

In addition, twenty-one resolutions were approved by the initial Annual Assembly of APC. These resolutions were grassroots concerns in the areas of education, health, social action, mission strategy, and development among Asians; adequate pension for Asian ministers who were paid very low salaries during their entire active ministry; formulation of a Southeast Asian Caucus; ministry among Asian senior citizens and youths; recognition of the Asian Women's Caucus; cultural and/or ethnic identity and awareness; and many other concerns equally relevant and significant.

The National Steering Council carries out all the policies and resolutions adopted and mandated by the annual APC Assembly. The steering council is composed of three Chinese, three Japanese, three Koreans, and three Filipinos elected by their respective caucuses. The council has also an Indonesian member, who will develop the Southeast Asian Caucus; a representative from the Asian Women's Caucus; and a youth elected by one of the ethnic caucuses.

It is noteworthy to point out that 50% of the steering council members are laypersons or youth; and 50% are clergymen. Also, half are US born and half are immigrants to the United States. The first Annual APC Assembly elected this writer, a Filipino, as chairman; Carnegie Ouye, a Japanese layman, as vice-chairman; Syngman Rhee, a Korean university pastor, as secretary; and Ira Lee, a Chinese layman, as treasurer. The Asian Presbyterian Caucus is indeed a coalition of ethnic groups in the real sense of the word. The uniqueness of the Asian Presbyterian Caucus is its ability to respect and allow an ethnic group to be different and at the same time to enable the diverse groups to speak and act as one body.

The 184th General Assembly of the United Presbyterian Church USA, which met in Denver in May, 1972, affirmed the organization and continuation of the Asian Presbyterian Caucus as the instrument to express the concerns and perspective of Asians to the wider church and to the larger community. The 184th General Assembly mandated that

1. the Asian Presbyterian Caucus be consulted relative to the significant and real participation of Asians in the decision-making processes of all boards, agencies, and judicatories; that this be done by placing Asians in the membership of those policy-making bodies.
2. the Asian Presbyterian Caucus be consulted in the development and operation of task forces on Asian concerns and issues here in the United States and throughout the world, particularly in Asia.
3. there be serious consideration of Asians for staff positions in all boards, agencies, and judicatories.

---

[1] Presented as an appendix on pp. 411–412.

4. the 184th General Assembly direct the appropriate officers to consult with the General Council for the purpose of finding $120,000 to fund the Asian Presbyterian Caucus for organizational and developmental purposes.

Nothing has been done so far to truly bring to fruition the commitment of the 184th General Assembly relative to the last three mandates. There have been some minor initial gains in relation to the first mandate, but this was solely through the gut efforts of the key leadership in APC. The following were named to national boards through the pressure exerted by APC: Cayetano, Santiago to the Nominations Committee; Carnegie Ouye to the Council on Church and Race; David Nakagawa to the Vocations Agency (also as Vocations Agency representative to the Council on Church and Race); Frank Fung Chow to the Council on Church and Society; Donald K. Toriumi to the Board of Pensions; and this writer to the Program Agency (also as temporary Program Agency representative to the Self-Development National Committee). William Ng and Bert Tom are members of the Self-Development National Committee.

In spite of the lack of funds, operating on an almost zero budget, APC has accomplished some measurable successes. At the writing of this article, only four months since the recognition of APC at the General Assembly in May, 1972, APC believes it has survived the real test of a true caucus.

APC has been involved in a regionalization strategy in the light of the denomination's reorganization. Two strong regional APC's have emerged: the APC in the Synod of Southern California under the leadership of Abe Dohi and the APC in the Synod of the Pacific under the leadership of Frank Mar. There are emerging APC groups in the Chicago area, New York area, Pittsburgh area, and Michigan-Indiana-Kentucky area.

On the local level APC has endorsed a renewal ministry project in the Richmond district of San Francisco to provide a new and needed ministry to a growing Asian population, of which the majority are Chinese. The Synod of California APC took action at its August 10, 1972, meeting that a mission probe be made of the needs of the Filipino community in metropolitan Los Angeles. They also recommended the establishment and development of a Japanese community center in Garden Grove, California. The national APC and the Southern California APC are deeply concerned about the growing Korean population in Los Angeles. A ministry to the Koreans is an APC priority, APC has lent a supporting hand in the organizing efforts of the Filipino community in San Francisco to build a mass people-power base. It is deeply involved in the development of an ecumenical center for Asian theology and ministry.

The internationalization strategy of APC included establishing direct contacts with Asian leaders in Asia. This is being done to eliminate the unnecessary middleman, usually a white churchman. Syngman Rhee was in Japan and Korea last summer on behalf of APC. Another APC member was in Hong Kong establishing contacts with grassroots leaders and churchmen. Fraternal relationship was officially established between APC and ZOTO (Zone One Tondo Organization), a mass people-power organization in the largest slum in the Philippines. APC sponsored the study tour of Mrs. Trinidad Herrera, two-term president of ZOTO, to major cities in the United States with a large Asian population. APC was host to the 1972 Japan social workers' team during their visit in the Bay area. An APC Internationalization Task Force was formed on September 2, 1972, to design and implement a strategy that gets at the core problem of Asians in the United States and throughout the world, particularly Asia.

The Asian Presbyterian Caucus has many grassroots plans. It has a regional program and strategy. It also has a national and international program and strategy. The arena for these plans, programs, and strategies is the church, but more important, it is the wider Asian communities in the United States and in Asia.

Asian Presbyterians sounded the call to organize! Asian Presbyterians are organized!

APC was born out of a belief that Asians can create and live in a new social milieu in which cultural differences are not blotted out and stifled into monotonous conformity. This was the reason why the Filipinos had their own caucus at the St. Helena conference and so did the Chinese, Japanese, Korean, and Southeast Asians (mostly Indonesians) separately. That I continue to be a Filipino in thought, word, and deed as I became a part of the total Asian Presbyterian Caucus. That I can still retain and enrich my Pilipino-ness and my Asian-ness as the Asian Presbyterian Caucus may possibly join a larger minority coalition of blacks, Hispanic Americans, and Indian Americans. That I can still be a Filipino and Asian as I worship with my white Christian brother.

APC was born out of a belief that Asian Americans have a distinct and unique role and contribution in the eradication of racism in this country and around the world, and the building of a just and humane society that fosters cultural and ethnic diversity.

APC was born out of a belief that Asians can contribute their insights and native talents toward the restructuring of the United Presbyterian Church in the USA and the reordering of its priorities in order that Asians can significantly participate in the decision-making processes of the church and receive their just share of the financial and human resources made available to minority groups.

APC was born out of a belief that the concept and practice of liberation, equality, and justice move beyond the sphere of human relationships into all aspects of human life, especially its political power base and its socioeconomic base—the whole works.

APC was born out of a belief that Asians recognize the international dimension of the Asian problem and potential here in the United States. For example, the immigration problem among Filipinos in San Francisco or New York is international in scope. The solutions and strategies relative to that particular problem must involve both countries, the United States and the Republic of the Philippines. The Filipino farm labor problem in the United States has international implications.

APC was born out of a very strong and deep personal conviction that there is a Christ who liberates us all. Asians can find their humanity in Christ and in fellowship with their brothers and sisters of all colors, including our white brothers and sisters. But do not deny our Asian-ness if we are to find our humanity.

Asians came to this country hoping to get a decent job and to provide for their families; but it did not take them long to find out that the American Dream which was publicized so glamorously in their respective home countries turned out to be an American Nightmare.

There is a chance for that Dream to come true via the Asian Presbyterian Caucus. Thank God for its birth!

Appendix: Statement of Concerns

We believe that God has created the people of the earth to be one family of Jesus Christ—one family which includes all races with their unique cultural expression.

The Confession of 1967 affirms that the church is called to bring all men to receive and uphold one another as persons in all relationships of life. The Scriptures state: "The man who does not love is still in the realm of death, for everyone who hates his brother is a murderer, and no murderer, as you know, has eternal life dwelling within him" (John 3:15, NEB).

The Scriptures and the confession of 1967 lead us to an understanding of the power of self-development. To love, receive, and uphold one another as persons means to accept one another's racial background and tradition. It means to allow the power of self-development and self-determination.

For the past hundred years, since the initial and successive migration of Asians to America, this group has been the most silent of minorities. Because of the peculiar history of racism and the popular notion of the "melting pot," Asians have been forced to deny their cultural and historical background to become a part of America. They have suffered the loss of self-hood. Asians have suffered from all forms of racial barriers: prejudices, discrimination, segregation, isolation, rejection, exclusion, and genocide.

There is one other difficulty for Asians in America. It is the fact that Asians are often not recognized as a minority, nor have they been given the "white" status. In fact, Asians have been in limbo up to the present time in spite of the enormous contributions that Asians have made in this country.

Even within the United Presbyterian Church there exists a certain subtle and an even overt discrimination: restrictive economic and vocational mobility, token exposure to certain jobs and positions, and virtually no Asians in decision-making positions. In addition, there is the widespread illusion about Asians that they are the "model minority," with no problems. This has perpetuated the exploitation of all minorities, including Asians.

Self-development is a response to the effects of racism and a necessary step to authentic reconciliation, equality, and justice for all peoples. To deny the right of self-development to any people is to subvert their humanity, destroy their dignity, and create dependency. Self-determination is, then, the necessary condition for the preservation of a people's heritage, development of human potentiality, and the affirmation of humanity.

When Asians are able to achieve self-development significantly, then there is the opportunity to live out the gospel more fully in the particular cultural context. This is the task which must be done in order to be effective in the mission of the church among Asian people.

Therefore, the purposes of the National Asian Presbyterian Caucus are

    a. To coalesce isolated Asian Presbyterians to give effective voice and advocacy to their problems, concerns, and insights;

    b. To facilitate the Asian presence and representation in all judicatory levels and boards and agencies;

    c. To provide mission strategy to Asian American churches and the wider community;

    d. To cooperate and Join in the struggle against racism, repression, and exploitation in the United States of America and throughout the world;

    e. To explore, study, and appreciate the values of our Asian heritage and develop new ministries to Asians and Asian American movements;

    f. To maintain communications with Asian caucuses of other denominations;

    g. To provide in-service training and continuing education for Asian ministers and laymen.

Address Delivered at the Council of Japanese American Churches Annual Meeting[*]

Teruo Kawata[†]

These have been good days. You of the Fresno church have been very, very gracious hosts and hostesses, and I thank you. In a real sense, I feel I have come home. I grew up in Delano. After WWII, I picked peaches, apricots, and grapes in Reedley. I began my ministry at the Hollywood Independent Church twenty-three years ago. It was they who took this very young, green, and inexperienced novice, straight out of school, and with their patience and kindness, helped me learn how to be a minister. I shall forever be grateful to them for the years that I spent, though short they were, at the Hollywood Independent Church.

Well, I am glad to be here, and I'm grateful to you for giving me the high honor of being the speaker for this year's meeting. As I came down the line in preparation for this occasion, I was moved to change the title of my address. I shall call it just simply "A Journey." Really, I was moved to make this change out of a worship experience not long ago where the worship leader (Paul Hammer) reflected on the concluding part of the Easter story as it is recorded in the twenty-fourth chapter of Luke. I liked what he said. And so, I have recast what I had planned to say into the framework that Paul Hammer had laid out.

I should like to read a portion of the story, beginning with verse 13.

It was a journey begun at the River Jordan when Jesus was baptized and commissioned to a ministry. He immediately called together a group of disciples. It was a time of despair and hope, of pain and dreams. As the people gathered around him, they asked, "Could this be who will be the fulfillment of our dreams, our hopes, our aspirations, the one who will deliver us from bondage and lead us to liberation?" And there were a few years of excitement and activity. Then, it seemed as if on the threshold, when their dreams were to be fulfilled, when Jesus would rise up as the new king, they encountered Golgotha.

And *Golgotha* is translated "the place of the skull." It is the place of death. Indeed, for the disciples, it was the place of death. For all the hopes and dreams they had invested in Jesus came to naught. Their dreams were shattered. Their hopes came crumbling down. And, perplexed, hurt, disappointed, defeated and fearful, they left Golgotha.

---

[*] Fresno, CA, May 5, 1975.

[†] Associate secretary, San Francisco, CA.

And they journeyed away from Golgotha, as the story records it, and they were on the road to Emmaus — pondering the painful and tragic things that had happened.

Now, the root word for Emmaus is the same as that for Emmanuel, which means "God with us." And the story has it that as they came to Emmaus their eyes were opened. They came to understand their suffering in a new way — that even in the crumbling of their dreams, God was present; that even in defeat, God was with them. And they said, "Did not our hearts burn within us?"

And, the story continues, they arose that same hour and returned to Jerusalem. Now, Jerusalem is the "city of shalom," and shalom means peace, justice and wholeness. And you know the continuing story of how the followers of Jesus have returned to bring into being the new Jerusalem — the new city of shalom.

There is a haunting, gut-level familiarity to that story, isn't there? For it is the kind of personal journey that we have walked.

But tonight, I want to look at the journey of our people, the Japanese people in the United States, in that context. For it seems to me that the journey of our people is the journey from the Jordan to Golgotha to Emmaus.

America was the land of promise. And so our parents, you *Isseis*, came to this land. You had dreams. It was a struggle. You encountered bigotry and prejudice, ridicule and injustice. But you endured. Do you call it *gaman* or *gabaru*? And, you built. You sacrificed, and sent your daughters and sons to college. And just when it seemed your labors were to bear fruit, just on the threshold of the fruition of your dreams, when your sons and daughters were about ready to take their places and establish themselves in America, we encountered Golgotha, the place of death. For it was in 1942 that the dreams were shattered. The hopes and struggles of a lifetime were crumbled. It was a time of great fear and disappointment and defeat. We were stripped of all that we had and trundled off into the deserts and imprisoned behind barbed wire fences.

I was only a high school boy then. Those of you who are older than I know more of the magnitude of the pain and suffering and despair of those days.

But, my friends, my sisters and brothers, we discovered that Golgotha, that death, could not defeat us. I wonder if this is not what the Emmaus experience is all about. That "God with us" means precisely that God is in the midst of life — not an outsider God but an insider God who is in the places of defeat and pain and suffering. And, in the midst of that, who calls us out and empowers us to live out the ever-new possibilities. God calls courage out of us. God calls new dreams out of us, and thus we can overcome defeat and despair and create new life.

Our eyes have been opened in a number of ways along that journey. For having known imprisonment, we know the preciousness of freedom. For having known the shattering of dreams, we know the stuff out of which new dreams can be created. For having known the experience of being nonpersons — untrustworthy, unworthy scum — we have hammered out a new affirmation of our own dignity and worth as human beings — as Japanese and Japanese American human beings.

We, and all who have been an oppressed people in the United States, owe a great deal to our black brothers and sisters. When they began to get in touch with the beauty of their blackness, they got in touch with the very foundation of the whole liberation struggle—the struggle for dignity, human beings. And since they began to talk about "black is beautiful," the reds, the browns, the yellows, and the women have been helped to understand just what it means to affirm the dignity and worth and beauty of their own beings in a new and fresh and liberating way. Yes. Yellow is beautiful.

Now, when we say that yellow is beautiful, it is not to say that white is not beautiful. It is never to say that yellow is more beautiful than white or black or red or brown. If that is what you say, then you have distorted it tragically. You do not know what the liberation struggle is about. It means that you are not on the side of liberation and human dignity, but you are on the side of arrogance and imperialism—precisely that same arrogance and imperialism of which we ourselves have been the victims.

Rather, to proclaim that "yellow is beautiful" is to affirm that there is a distinctiveness about who we are; That out of our bi-cultural, bi-historical experience, there has come into being a people of distinctiveness, and it is a story of beauty and majesty. It is an Emmaus experience. It is the experience of having our eyes opened to the fullness and the beauty of who we are. It means that we no longer need to deny our Japanese-ness. Rather, it is to be able to hold up our Asian faces with pride; not with arrogance, but with dignity. It is to feel a burning within our breasts of a new kind of affirmation of our own humanity.

Well, for the disciples, the eye-opening experience that made the fire burn within their hearts made them turn resolutely to Jerusalem. And they returned to Jerusalem to tell the story of what they had discovered, to let others know the truths they had found along that road.

Now, when we begin to talk about Jerusalem, the journey to the city of shalom, it is not to speak of that city where everything is hunky-dory, and all is peace and quiet. That is a kind of utopianism that is a stranger to the biblical story. Quite the contrary, the journey to Jerusalem is a call to create a new city of shalom, a new community where justice prevails, where persons are free, and the dignity of each person is uplifted and affirmed. Yes, as the Scripture says it, "Where there is neither Jew nor Greek, nor male nor female," where there is neither black nor white nor brown nor yellow nor young nor old. We are all human beings, and we are one people.

Now, if we can begin to see the new Jerusalem, the city of shalom, in these terms, what is the meaning of the journey for us now? If indeed we have had an Emmaus experience, what does it mean for us to turn our faces now to Jerusalem?

It is commonplace these days to say that the United States is in crisis. Watergate and Vietnam are but signs of Golgotha. Indeed, the United States has been at the place of the skull. For what Watergate and Vietnam, in all of their manifestations, have revealed is the brutal and horrible betrayal of those ideals that called our nation into being and formed it into a nation two hundred years ago.

America is now on the road where we need to reevaluate our commitments, our priorities, our policies, our value systems. The question is: Will it be on the road to Emmaus? Will it be a time when the United States will once again have its eyes opened to the reasons for its being? I submit to you that there is a distinct and unique word that people like you and me can bring to our nation in this time in history. For we are a people who have been pushed to get in touch with the meaning of our own experience and existence, as those in power never quite have to do. We have known the pain of non-freedom, and the privileges and joys of freedom. We know how precious, indeed, are the great ideals of justice and liberty. Might it be, for example, that because of the words that people like you and me bring to the United States in this time in history—when the United States is preparing to celebrate the bicentennial—that the bicentennial celebration shall not be a time of national chauvinism, as it could very easily be. But rather, that it shall be a time of renewal and recommitment to the great ideals of freedom and democracy that called our nation into being at its beginnings. If the bicentennial time can be that kind of time, indeed it would be an Emmaus experience for the United States. And, indeed, it would be on the road to a new Jerusalem, a new city of shalom for ourselves and for the world.

Well, those are great ideals. And the ways in which our experience might enrich the experience of our nation are things that I believe we need to continue to search out. It is my ongoing hope that through organizations such as ours and through PAAM and through ACTS (which is the ecumenical agency which brings all the Asian groups in the denominations together) that somehow we shall become a voice that shall bring the word of renewal and recommitment to our nation.

For these concluding moments now, I should like to reflect for a little while on what it might mean for us who have spent these days together in reflecting upon the life of our Japanese American churches. What might it mean for us to turn our faces to Jerusalem?

I would like to suggest, first of all, that we use what we have learned on our journey as a minority people in America to understand the Christian story with a new kind of freshness. For our story, the struggle for liberation and dignity and fullness as human beings, is precisely the biblical story. That is what the whole story is about, from Moses delivering the people of Israel to Jesus Christ who delivers humanity from enslavement of a whole variety of kinds. As we begin to get in touch with our liberation struggle, perhaps the biblical story can begin to come alive in fresh ways for each one of us. Even as we have learned to get in touch with our identity as Japanese, and as Japanese Americans, and have come to be able to affirm it and celebrate it anew, and there is a new kind of power and joy in that, so might we use that very learning to get in touch with our identity as Christian people. And that even as we are able to affirm that yellow is beautiful, that we shall come to affirm with a new kind of freshness that Christian is beautiful. If we can do that, our churches will come alive with new vitality and power.

But I remind you again that if we believe for a moment that to affirm that Christian is beautiful is also to affirm that Christians are better than Buddhists or Christians are better than any other kind of people, then we shall be guilty of the same kind of distortions that we have been the victims of in a whole variety of ways through our journey. And that we would be taking on the coverings of imperialism, even as we have been the victims of imperialism; that we shall be the arrogant ones, even as we have been the victims of the arrogant ones.

Christianity, as it has essentially been lived out by the white Western world, is essentially an imperialistic religion manifested in many ways all over the world. It may be that out of our experience, we can interpret the Christian faith in a whole new way that will shed it of its imperialism. That is, to affirm that Christian is beautiful is not to say that it is more beautiful than something else, but it is simply to witness from the depths of our being the things that we have discovered — that God is indeed with us, calling us out of pain and suffering and defeat into new life, over and over again. That in every moment of our lives, we are called to a new humanity and to create a new city of shalom.

And so, it may be that our task is to use our learnings as a minority people as the basis upon which we shall come to a new and fresh experience of what it means to be Christian.

Second, I suggest that the larger church needs to learn that too. You see, the Christian church is a minority group. The trouble is it doesn't know what that means because it is essentially controlled by a people who really don't know what it means to be a minority people. The Christian church is controlled by the white Western world. And I submit to you that if people like you and me, the people who have come out of oppression, can begin to help the larger church get in touch with what it means to be minority, then it may be that the church can begin to go on that journey that will lead it to that Emmaus experience where its eyes shall be opened and it shall know in a new and fresh way that to be Christian is beautiful. And if the whole church can get in touch with that, then the church can become a power for renewal and healing in the world that is so broken and bruised.

Well, the journey moved from Jordan to Golgotha to Emmaus to Jerusalem. We began with promise. We have known death. But our eyes have been opened. Will we now move to build the new city of shalom?

I should like to close with the text from Scripture that I was to have used tonight. Kay Sakuguchi illuminated it so well in this morning's worship.

> For this commandment which I give you this day is not too hard for you, neither is it far off. It is not in heaven that you should say, who will go over to heaven for us and bring it to us that we may see it and do it. Neither is it across the sea that you should say, who will go over the sea for us and bring it to us that we may hear it and do it. But the word is very near you. It is in your heart, and in your mouth, so that you can do it . . . I call heaven and earth to witness against you this day, that I have set before you life and death, a

blessing and a curse. Therefore, you choose life that you and your descendants may live (Deut. 30:11).

Well, if it is to happen, it will happen because you make it happen.

National Conference of
Asian Americans and Pacific Islanders
in the United Church of Christ*

Purpose †

- Identify the issues and problems of Asians and Pacific Islanders in the US and the United Church of Christ
- Explore Asian theology
- Identify the contributions the Asian constituency can bring to the United Church of Christ and American society
- Develop necessary strategies for addressing these issues and problems, e.g., should we organize as a recognized caucus group within the United Church of Christ

---

* San Francisco, CA, April 19–21, 1974.

† Formulated at the Steering Committee meeting, October 6, 1973, El Cerrito, CA. Present were Asian American and Pacific Islander representatives from Hawaii, New York, Chicago, and Southern and Northern California.

national conference
on the concerns
of
asian americans
and
pacific islanders

chinese ○ filipino ○ hawaiian
japanese ○ korean ○ samoan
southeast asian
and other ancestries

san francisco
april 19-21, 1974
uicc

In Remembering[*]

Lord, we remember, and we praise you, for

when the waves of blue and white, reflected the beauty of the sky, and when the Diamond Head laid its shadow across the islands, and when up and down the Pacific Coast the tides came in

> To these lands which promised the great hopes and dreams of a new frontier

> Came the peoples, small in stature, but tall with dreams, and vigor to work;

> For their visions they put aside the warmth of mother, father and family, support of society, and exhibition of pride.

> Innumerable was the amount of hurdles to overcome, work designed for large peoples, but food and wages designed for small; hurdles of language, habits, and a hostile culture.

We thank you, O Lord, that we have this heritage of dreamers with indomitable courage.

Lord, we remember, and we praise you, for

when our peoples secured their own livelihood, they relied on their hopes with pictures of a bride and a sweet home, full of cultural heritages.
when the land made them fighters against the demonic laws of Oriental alien's ownership of land, and of immigration.

> They erected their churches, not out of plenty, nor out of sophistication, but out of scarcity, out of simple mind, and out of hope.

We pray, O Lord, grant to us that kind of faith.

Lord, we remember, and we praise you, for

when our peoples felt the sting of injustice and oppression,

---

[*] A poem written by Jonah Chang, revised and edited by Kay Sakaguchi, and read as a prayer during the National Conference of Asian Americans and Pacific Islanders in the United Church of Christ.

when communities were torn asunder, families uprooted, people put
into physical and spiritual desert, their hopes crushed and their
dreams shattered,

Your steadfast love was with them, and your kindness endured,
and they returned unto their places to rework the land, and to
rebuild their communities, and to renew the rightful spirit
within them.

We ask, O Lord, that we, like them, may endure through faithfulness and love.

Lord, we remember, and we praise you, for

when the Lord restored the fortune of Zion, we were like those who
dreamed;
then our mouth was filled with laughter, and our tongue with shouts
of joy.

Then they said among the communities, "The Lord has done great
things for us."
Yes, You have done great things for us: The church became our
homes, our shelters, our arena of celebration. Through the
church you fostered for us the leaders, the educators, our
spirit and pride.

We pray, O Lord, make us remember:

Those who founded the church,
Those who led,
Those who followed,
Those who comforted and were comforted; and
Those who fought for their pride, dignity, faith, and hope.

In remembering, make us worthy of being sons and daughters of
such hardy peoples.
In remembering, make us worthy of being followers of Christ and
peacemakers for days to come;
In remembering, make us worthy of being people who have held
their head up high as we struggle for freedom for us and for
our children; In the name of our Lord and Saviour, Jesus
Christ.

Amen.

Resolution to Organize
Adopted 4/20/74

The delegates assembled for the National Conference on Asian American Concerns, San Francisco, April 19–21, 1974, petition the Executive Council of the United Church of Christ for recognition as a Special Interest Group. The peoples with which the group will be concerned shall include those of Chinese, Filipino, Hawaiian, Japanese, Samoan, Korean, Southeast Asian and other ancestries.

Purpose

I. Development of peoples
- A. To secure funding and initiate programs to develop leadership, lay and professional, within the Asian American and Pacific Islander churches in the UCC
- B. To encourage the nominating committees at all levels of the church to seek persons from the Asian American and Pacific Islander constituency for membership and leadership on boards and committees
- C. To examine the unique situations and meet the needs experienced by Asian American and Pacific Island youth as a result of the multi-cultural situation in which they are set

II. Development of communities
- A. To identify strengths and weaknesses in Asian American and Pacific Islander ministries and formulate and implement remedies
- B. To address the conflicts and problems faced by Asian Americans and Pacific Islanders who experience multi-cultural conflicts and ambiguities
- C. To research Asian theology and the unique insights of the heritage of Asians and Hawaiians, etc., for better understanding of the faith
- D. To encourage cooperation with other Asian American and Pacific Islander congregations and with other denominational Asian caucuses

III. Development within the United Church of Christ
- A. To secure necessary funding for programs to strengthen our churches from our own constituency and churches, and from conferences and national agencies
- B. To formulate and petition the appropriate UCC instrumentalities to adopt policies based on self-determination with reference to Asian American and Pacific Islander needs and concerns:
    1. Ministerial education
    2. Lay leadership development

      3. Christian education programs and publications

      4. Mission

  C. To cooperate where appropriate with other UCC ethnic caucuses: Blacks, Native Americans, etc.

  D. To enable the development of a new and truer image of Asian Americans and Pacific Islanders through the use of the various media within UCC.

  E. To represent the concerns of this Conference to all levels of the United Church of Christ:

      1. To act as liaison between Asian American and Pacific Islander churches and the appropriate agencies of the church

      2. To provide a forum for ministerial concerns and a vehicle for presenting these concerns to the appropriate agencies of the church

      3. To be supportive of appropriate actions or positions initiated by local churches

IV. Development of Christian mission and outreach programs and strategies

Because the following alternative proposal was not adequately discussed, it was agreed by community consensus that the Organizing Committee will consider and incorporate parts of the following resolution into the above resolution which was adopted.

Whereas, there is an absence of leadership development and training programs for lay people and pastors in the Pacific Basin,

Whereas, there is an absence of Pacific Basin people's representation on boards of the UCC,

Whereas, there is an absence of adequate resources for implementing the mission for Pacific Basin peoples,

Therefore, be it resolved that the Pacific Basin people's special interest group of the UCC be organized for the following reasons:

    1. Organize a structure, i.e., Pacific Basin People's Conference of UCC

    2. Call upon the national church, local conferences and associations to elect and select representatives as recommended by Pacific Basin Peoples to the Boards

    3. To call upon the Office for Church Life and Leadership to consider and plan for an adequate program of leadership development and for training Pacific Basin Peoples

Significant Dates in Asian American History[*]

Philip Kyung Sik Park

1610, 1613	Japanese diplomatic missions visited Mexico.
1848	Chinese immigration begins with the California gold rush.
1852	Entry of Chinese contract laborers.
1856	Passage of Foreign Miner's Tax as a means of curtailing Chinese activity in the gold fields.
1859	Exclusion of Chinese from public schools in San Francisco.
1870	Naturalization Act excluded Chinese from citizenship.
1878	One of many anti-Chinese riots in which white mobs burned and looted in San Francisco's Chinese ghetto for several weeks without significant interference from law enforcement agencies. Similar acts were perpetrated against other Asian groups.
1882	Chinese Exclusion Act "suspended" immigration of Chinese laborers for ten years and forbade the entry of wives of Chinese laborers then in the US.
1886	Beginnings of Japanese contract labor in Hawaii.
1892	Geary Act prohibited Chinese immigration for another ten years and denied bail in writs of *habeas corpus*.
1898	Annexation of Hawaii by US; movement of Japanese to mainland begun.
1902	Congress "indefinitely extended the prohibition against Chinese immigration and the denial of naturalization."
1903	Korean contract laborers arrived in Hawaii. In 1904, movement to the mainland began.

---

[*] March/April 1973.

1905	Japanese children in California ordered to attend segregated schools.
1906	Beginnings of Filipino farm labor in Hawaii. California's anti-miscegenation law amended to bar marriages between whites and "Mongolians."
1910	United States Supreme Court upheld the 1870 Naturalization Act being extended to other Asians.
1913, 1920	California Alien Land Act prevented Asians from acquiring land.
1923	Filipinos begin to move to mainland.
1924	Exclusionary Immigration Act completely ended Asian immigration, except for Filipinos who were "subjects" of the US.
1925	Legislative act made Filipinos ineligible for US citizenship unless they served three years in the US Navy.
1934	Tydings-McDuffie Act gave Philippine Islands independence and a US immigration quota of fifty persons per year.
1942	Beginning of Japanese incarceration during World War II.
1943	Repeal of Chinese Exclusion Acts.
1948	California antimiscegenation laws repealed.
1950	McCarren-Walter Act conferred the right of naturalization on Asians not born in the United States and set a quota of one hundred immigrants per year for Asian countries.
1965	National Origins Act raised Asian immigration quota to twenty thousand per year per country — the same as for European countries.
1967	Anti-miscegenation laws ruled unconstitutional by US Supreme Court.

Made in the USA
Coppell, TX
02 September 2023

21137485R00267